MEA
CUBA

MEA CUBA

GUILLERMO

CABRERA

INFANTE

TRANSLATED FROM THE SPANISH

BY KENNETH HALL WITH THE AUTHOR

FARRAR STRAUS GIROUX

NEW YORK

Translation © 1994 by Farrar, Straus and Giroux
Copyright © 1992 by Guillermo Cabrera Infante
All rights reserved
Originally published in Spanish as *Mea Cuba*, © 1992 by
Plaza & Janes Editores
First printing, 1994
Printed in the United States of America
Printed simultaneously in Canada by HarperCollins*CanadaLtd*

LIBRARY OF CONGRESS CATALOGING-IN-PUBLICATION DATA
Cabrera Infante, G. (Guillermo).
[Mea Cuba. English]
Mea Cuba / Guillermo Cabrera Infante ; translated from the Spanish
by Kenneth Hall with the author.
p.   cm.
1. Cuba—Politics and government—1959–   I. Hall, Kenneth.
II. Title.
F1788.C2213   1994   320.97291—dc20   94-30856   CIP

Acknowledgements

The essays and articles that follow (and one or two interviews) were originally published by *Primera Plana*, Agence France Press, *El país*, *ABC*, *Diario 16* and *Cambio 16*, *Quimera*, *Claves*, *Vuelta*, *El nuevo día*, *Die Zeit*, *NZZ Folio (Neuen Zürcher Zeitung)*, the *London Review of Books*, the *Daily* and *Sunday Telegraph*, *The Independent* and the American literary journals *Linden Lane*, *Salmagundi* and *Escandalar*.

To Néstor Almendros, a Spaniard
who learned to be a Cuban

Contents

Cuba unites us all on foreign soil.

José Martí

Notice

I have delayed, perhaps too much, the publication in book form of these essays and articles published everywhere from 1968 until now. I held the opinion that their appearance, together with the disappearance of a regime of opprobrium, would turn out for me to be a kind of political colophon: no more flags. But each day confirms my conviction, expressed in many places before, that the celebration of the half-millennium of the discovery of that island, which could be called La Infortunada, is an occasion as opportune and perhaps more legitimate than the flight or the death of a tyrant. Cuba was not discovered for history five centuries ago but for geography: a fact more decisive than the historical aberration that has afflicted us for thirty-three years. History, that is time, will pass, but always there will remain geography – which is our eternity.

GCI

MEA
CUBA

Genesis

Cuba was discovered by Christopher Columbus and his fellow travellers (the Pinzón brothers, the Rodrigos de Triana and de Jerez, the *converso* Luis de Torres and the diverse but unanimous crew) on 28 October 1492, a Sunday.

'The Admiral says,' being rewritten by Father Las Casas, 'that never saw he such a beautiful thing.' That is, it was a version of Paradise.

On a map of America when it was not yet called America, in 1501, Cuba appears twice. First as an island, then as a continent.

Exodus

I left Cuba on 3 October 1965: I am careful with my dates. For that reason I keep them.

Shipwreck with a Sunrise
in the Background

*M*ea *Cuba* arose from the need to lend coherence (or, if you wish, cohesion) to my political writings. Or to the writing of my political thinking – if it exists. In the book there is much of what I have written up to now about my country and about the politics that have been imposed on it with never deserved cruelty.

My essays and my political articles try to elucidate some of what can be called the problems of Cuba, while I explain myself before the reader as an historical conundrum. What's a man like me doing in a book like this? Nobody considers me a political writer nor do I consider myself a politician. But it happens that there are occasions when politics is intensely transformed into an ethical activity. Or at least into the motive for an ethical vision of the world, a moral motor.

My parents – as my friends know only too well – were founders of the Cuban Communist Party. I grew up with the myths and the hard realities of the thirties and, above all, of the forties and among the contradictions not of capitalism but of Communism. Some samples from a book of examples: Stalin hanging next to Christ in the living room (when we had a living room, most of the time it was only a room for the whole family: the famous scene of Groucho Marx's crowded stateroom in *A Night at the Opera* was enacted a thousand and one nights by us thanks to the other Marx), Batista scorned as a tyrant, my parents imprisoned by Batista, Batista elected with the help of the Communist Party and the enthusiastic collaboration of my parents, especially my mother, the Hitler and Stalin pact, then: 'Cuba out of the imperialist war', Hitler invades Soviet Russia, then: 'Support the USSR in her struggle against the Nazi Beast.' They were contradictory slogans for anyone who was not a Communist. Or for one who lived as I did, in a Communist household with a father responsible for Party propaganda.

Some people will think that the title of my book is irreverent. They are the reverent ones. I do not think I am making an unexpected revelation if I say that the title comes from Cuba and *Mea culpa*. Cuba is, of course, *mea maxima culpa*. But, what guilt? First of all the guilt of having written the essays in my book, of having made them public as articles and finally, of having put them together now. There is no innocent writing, I know. *Mea Cuba* can mean 'My Cuba', but it also suggests the guilt of Cuba. The operative word, of course, is guilt. It is not a feeling foreign to the exile. The guilt is much as such: for having left my land to be an exile and at the same time having left behind those who were going on the same ship, which I helped to throw into the sea of troubles.

The metaphor of the ship that wrecks and a Cuban Lord Jim who cowardly saves himself is completed not with Fidel Castro's favourite phrase ('The rats are leaving the sinking ship!' he shouted in a speech with that zoological obsession of his of calling his enemies, even those who flee, especially those who flee, vermin's names: rats, worms, cockroaches), but with the sinking of the *Titanic*: the ship that could not sink destined, precisely, to sink. A single member of the crew managed to escape with his life, Lieutenant Lightoller. Questioned by a severe English judge (all English judges are severe) as to why he had abandoned ship, Lightoller answered not facetiously: 'I didn't abandon my ship, your lordship. My ship abandoned me.'

Many Cuban exiles can say that they never abandoned Cuba: Cuba abandoned them. She abandoned in passing the best. One was *Comandante* Alberto Mora, a suicide. Another is *Comandante* Plinio Prieto, shot by firing squad. Still another, General Ochoa, scapegoat, shot too. But if something caps the measure of abandonment and loss it is exile. One truly feels that it is a shipwreck ('Every man for himself!') and nothing resembles a ship more than an island. Cuba, besides, appears on the maps dragged by the Gulf Stream, never anchored in the Caribbean Sea and cast aside by the European Atlantic. Decidedly it is a ship adrift. In the fury of the speech Fidel Castro was incapable of controlling the metaphor of the ship that is sinking and the disaffected rats and had to add hurriedly, almost in despair: 'But this ship will *never* sink.' That ancestor of his, Adolf Hitler, repeated *before* those same words in 1944: 'Germany will never sink.' (The absence of exclamations is due to the loss of power.) The shipwreck survivors know more and better: from Germany, from Cuba.

My friends have asked for it, my enemies have forced me to make a book from these obsessive articles and essays that have appeared in the press (to say world press would be pretentious, to say Spanish would be scanty) for the past twenty-five years and almost thirty of exile. They provoke and repel a nostalgia that fits in a single phrase: 'Distant Cuba, how horrible you must be!' The ejaculation mixes two illustrious exiles from one hundred years ago, he Cuban for ever, she become Spanish: *la* Avellaneda and Cirilo Villaverde, with the sentimentality of a tango lyric. After all, the tango was born, like me, in Cuba.

By the Way

Not long ago I turned sixty-three. Some months before, Fidel Castro celebrated (if one can celebrate a burial) thirty-three years in power without opposition. Thirty-three years is more than half my chronological life and in all that time my biography has been written, one way or another, by Fidel Castro with the words of his tribe of scribes, inside and outside the island. To presume that Castro governs only in Cuba is to refuse to admit that a political exile is an enemy: one who flees from those who won't extend to him a silver bridge, but a long hand that can reach him anywhere. To illustrate this paranoid image (which Freud would catalogue as Castration complex) I can tell a story from what is usually called real life.

In 1985, attending the film festival of Barcelona, I received an urgent call from my younger daughter in London. She told me that burglars had broken into our apartment. I shouldn't worry though because strangely enough the thieves had not stolen anything. My astonishment was boundless but I stayed put: I had to remain in the festival until its end. When I returned to London there was scarcely a sign of the robbery. Everything was in its place except for an enormous padlock provided by the police that stood in for my security lock. An ad from the latter's maker assures Londoners that it is a decisive protection against all intruders.

My daughter told me that not only had the local police come to investigate, but a detective from Scotland Yard had become interested in the robbery that was not a robbery. During his visit he had asked my daughter who I was, what I did for a living and whether I had any personal enemies. My daughter told him that my only status, apart from being a writer, was that of an exile from Castro. The agent from Scotland Yard asked her to get me to contact him personally on my return.

On our return Miriam Gómez and I confirmed that in fact the thieves had not stolen anything. Even an envelope that contained a thousand dollars had been exposed, opened and returned to its precarious pigeonhole without its envelope. These unusual looters were not looking for money – or didn't accept dollars.

The detective from Scotland Yard turned out to be much more intelligent than the notorious Inspector Lestrade, whom Sherlock Holmes accused scornfully of having an intelligence made valuable by its scarcity. I invited him to sit down. He did so. I offered him a coffee. Cuban. He didn't accept it. (The agents of Scotland Yard on the job cannot accept the kindness of strangers.) From his seat he swiftly signalled various objects visible in the room (an *art nouveau* statuette, *art deco* vases, books that he called 'rare' and not first editions, two new videocassette recorders) and said: 'All that stuff fits in two large bags. I don't understand why they didn't take anything.' Me neither. 'They must have gone to a lot of trouble to get in,' he admitted. He knew that they had attempted to force my maximum security lock, guaranteed against all rapes. When they couldn't break it they had tried to lift the (new) door from its hinges. But it was big and heavy. Finally, arming themselves with a crowbar, they succeeded in breaking the (old) door frame to dislodge the lock. 'The operation is noisy and must have taken them some time,' said the detective. Then he added: 'They took their risks.' No neighbour had seen or heard anything. I told him so but by his silence I knew that he already knew.

He remained silent and then looked me in the eye – which is an old police technique in search of optical truth. 'Your daughter says,' he told me rather than asked me, 'that you are a writer and a Castroist exile.' That's right. 'Have you received any threat from Castro?' he asked me. No, I told him, but his minions have tried since 1965, when I left his island, to make life as difficult as possible for me. Literally and literarily. I deemed that I should not give him examples. 'Are you an active exile?' Sort of, I told him, but the harassment began before I became active. He seemed to think about his next question. 'Have you found any manuscripts missing or some writing of yours connected with your exile?' It hadn't occurred to me that the robbery might be faked to get hold of my manuscripts, the ones that were not housed in an American university. I had not taken into account my other manuscripts, among which was this book you're reading now, reader, and a work in progress that takes place in the Castroist ruins of Havana. But I told him emphatically I wasn't missing anything. It was at that moment, while saying no, that I saw the main motive of the robbery, failed but faked.

The man from the Yard stood up. He was leaving. But he stopped to say: 'It's strange.' What was? 'The exiled writers from Eastern Europe have had unfinished novels and unpublished pamphlets stolen. You've been luckier.' For a moment it seemed to me that he was in doubt about my luck, but the police never doubt. 'One of them,' he said, 'a Bulgarian writer, was killed not long ago near the BBC.' 'I know,' I told him. He was referring to Georgy Markov, assassinated by the KGB with a pellet of poison – ricin, the most lethal substance known to man. The assassin had hidden the firing arm in an inoffensive umbrella.

The whole story came out in the press (even the BBC dedicated a special programme to Markov), and acquired an aura of a spy novel that in some way accentuated the political character of the assassination. The apparent motive was that Markov, a novelist with a name in his country before being exiled, was putting out on British radio a series of intimate revelations on the life and miseries of the unnameable Bulgarian ruler, a true tyrannic toxin. The difference is that I never talk about the nocturnal adventures of Castro. Only his diurnal misadventures concern me.

Before leaving the Yardman said to me: 'There's a policeman who covers Gloucester Road up to Palace Gate.' That is a span of barely ten blocks. 'I'll tell him to take two turns rather than one along your pavement.' I thanked him. 'But,' he told me finally, 'I want, if you notice any irregularity, no matter how small, for you to call me straightaway at the Yard' – and he gave me his direct number. But the robbers without a motive or an *apparent* motive, never returned. Now I'm waiting for those uninvited guests of mine to find in this book what they were looking for. They don't have anything to lose – except, of course, the price of a copy.

PERVERSIONS OF HISTORY

Answers and Questions

Among the miaows of Offenbach the cat and the incessant crackling of the apple that Miriam Gómez his wife was munching, Guillermo Cabrera Infante jotted down the four questions of an improvised questionnaire and mixed them among the papers and the photographs on his desk. In a month, he returned to *Primera Plana* ten pages of answer, with the requirement that they be transcribed without alterations. Here they are, and – although it may be obvious – they are all his own.

Unsolicited preamble

When I left Cuba in 1965, when I went away from Havana on 3 October 1965, when the plane took off from the airport of Rancho Boyeros at 10:10 p.m. of the third day of October of 1965, when we passed the point of no return after four hours of flight (it was not the first time that I had travelled between Cuba and Europe and I knew that beyond Bermuda the plane can no longer return to Rancho Boyeros, come what may), when finally I got out of my seat-belt and looked at my daughters sleeping beside me and took the case, so ironic, my attaché case, and opened it to cast a tranquillizing glance at the irregular, clandestine sheets dedicated to converting *Vista del amanecer en el trópico* into *Tres tristes tigres*, I knew then what would be my destiny: to travel without returning to Cuba, to care for my daughters and to occupy myself by/in literature. I don't know whether or not I pronounced the magic formula – 'silence, exile, cunning' – but I can say now that it is easier in this time to adopt the literary style than to copy the lifestyle of James Joyce.

For a long time I kept silent. I refused to give interviews, I locked myself up to work and I got as far away from Cuban politics as from Cuban politicians of all colours. I still do not write to anyone in Cuba but my immediate family, sporadic, meaningless letters. To no avail – because Communism does not allow drop-outs.

My name was dragged into a polemic in which the noises of the caucus-race of *Alice* serve as incidental music to the libretto of *Ubu Roi*: there where stage reality transforms Kafka into a socialist realist. Insults, unheard of intrusion into my private life, were made into the eccentric axis of a struggle for cultural power and cursed *genius loci* – all said with the scarlet and purple prose of that Cuban bearded version of the Soviet *Krokodil, El caimán barbudo*. But, of course, the problem was not limited to a literary polemic after a Russian fashion, where the animal farm's dogs bark while the master doesn't even bother to open the gate, as happened with the insults and attacks on Neruda and Carlos Fuentes, and the assault on Asturias when he defeated the local hero Kid Carpentier, the red rose of the ring, in this corner, the eternal Cuban aspirant to the belt of literary heavyweights.

The cayman's mauling was followed and preceded by other more direct attacks: personal and political calumnies, refusal of permission to work at Unesco, confiscation of books sent by post, minute inspection of family correspondence and deliberate literary persecution. For me all this did not have nor does it have much importance, and that *TTT* was converted into underground literature pleases me, seems to me a privilege. (Someone, T.E.M., corrects me in time: 'But your book is in the library of the Casa de las Américas.' Correction of a correction: in East Berlin I saw a library, called ironically Humboldt, where one could obtain '*all* books', a fitting lapse by the interpreter, 'that are enemies of the people', from Adorno to Zinoviev passing through Nietzsche, Heidegger, Kafka, Sartre, Bertrand Russell – who were not yet friends of the people at that time – Koestler and Adolf Hitler. 'Provided that one demonstrates the *necessity of reading them*,' added the interpreter, 'and the person requesting them takes responsibility with his name, address, occupation and reason for reading.')

But there is more. A European novelist is invited to a televised panel on Cuban literature in Havana, with the express agreement that he not mention my name. The guest is well mannered and keeps his word, but with personal loyalty and honesty that are exemplary (or suicidal, in the Communist world) he speaks of *Tres tristes tigres*. Olga Andreu, librarian, places my novel on a list of books recommended by that so democratic library of the Casa de las Américas, in a bulletin that she edits. A few days later she is separated from her job and condemned to a list of temporary lay-offs, which means a terrible future because she won't be able to work in a responsible job any more and her only way out is to ask to go as a 'volunteer' for agricultural labour. Heberto Padilla writes a paean to *Tres tristes tigres* and, with a roll of drums that will not abolish music, starts the aforementioned polemic. Within a week he is fired from that official daily whose name has overtones of *Little Red Riding Hood*: '*Granma*, what great big teeth you have!' Now, after months of prohibition from publishing and with another editorial board (the former one for having publicized the polemic), *El caimán* published Padilla's 'Answer to the Editorial Board', to close the polemic. But, disposed now to travel to Italy, with a ticket bought in Milan, to see his book of poems published by Feltrinelli, Padilla sees his exit visa abruptly withdrawn and his passport taken away and he is fired. Again? The latest news places Padilla in the position of every intelligent and honest person in the Communist world: an interior exile with only three options – *opportunism and demagoguery in the form of acts of political contrition, prison or true exile.*

Why this metaphoric persecution and this trial by proxy, and this verdict after the sentence?

> 'Let the jury consider their verdict,' the King said, for about the twentieth time that day.
> 'No, no!' said the Queen. 'Sentence first – verdict afterwards.'
> 'Stuff and nonsense!' said Alice loudly. 'The idea of having the sentence first!'
> 'Hold your tongue!' said the Queen, turning purple.
> 'I won't!' said Alice.

What crime has the author or the book committed? One only, and both committed it. Being free. (Cf. Wilhelm Friedrich Hegel speaking of his monarch: 'There can be only a *single* free man in Prussia.')

> 'Off with her head!' the Queen shouted at the top of her voice. Nobody moved.
> 'Who cares for *you*?' said Alice (she had grown to her full size by this time). 'You're nothing but a pack of cards!'

Now I can answer all the questions. Cards on the table, please.

Why are you outside Cuba?

If one really believes with Ortega y Gasset that man is nothing more than being and circumstance, the only means of saving the menaced self is to change circumstances, the sooner the better. When unlivable situations must be lived through there is no way out other than schizophrenia or flight. I am going to illustrate this passage.

In the summer of 1965 I returned to Cuba from Belgium, where I was cultural attaché, for the funeral of my mother, who had died in strange circumstances (otitis media; she enters unconscious into the hospital at eleven in the morning and without proper medical attention until well into the night; she dies in the early morning of an illness from which no one has been dying since before the Second World War: but her death is also a pathological accident that can occur anywhere if precautions are not taken in time) while I was flying towards Havana.

I did not make the trip in a plane but, like Brick Bradford, in the spinning top of time. In Belgium I missed Cuba, its landscape, its climate, its people: I felt nostalgia (from which I am not yet free) and I only thought about returning. But a country is not just geography. It is also history. When I came back bodily, in that first week when I still could not comprehend that my mother had disappeared for ever, I knew, at the same time, that the locus from where I had come into the world was as dead as the *locus solus* I came to. Havana was a city that I did not recognize and I was returning not from Paris but from a provincial and dark Brussels, an ugly place. In Cuba, the moon was shining as before the Revolution, the sun was the same sun: nature lent everything its eponymous beauty. Geography was alive, but history had died.

Cuba now was not Cuba. It was another thing – the double in the mirror, its *doppelgänger*, a living robot from which an accident by its maker had provoked a mutation, a genetic change, a switch of chromosomes. Nothing was in its place. The features were recognizable, but even in Havana the buildings showed a new leprosy. The streets were covered with a visible viscose, oil drops dripping from the motors of the scarce vehicles because of an unsurmountable fault in refining Russian petroleum, foul fuel in the tropics. In its blackish stickiness women left their shoes (prehistoric artefacts that some entrepreneurs rented at fifty cents an hour!) in their tracks. It was the metaphor of a moral viscosity.

The Malecón was decayed, ruinous. In the flower beds of El Vedado, before an elegant suburb, bananas were growing instead of roses, in a desperate effort by the residents to supplement their rations with their stunted fruit. The coffee stands that used to make coffee before the customers on every corner, as in Rio de Janeiro, had vanished by the art of Marxist magic. In their place there were two, at most three stands to a district that served coffee to avid clusters of clients, and only at certain hours of the day, when they weren't in long lines to buy the coffee that the ration book promises but never delivers. (These *cafeteras* were called, like everything else, by a new name, pilot-coffeepot, with the same pompous 'technical' terminology that christened factories 'production units', public beaches 'workers' leisure circles', and the popular urban buses known as *guaguas* 'rolling units'. This Utopian jargon competed frankly with the newspeak of the MinRex – Ministry of Foreign Affairs, MinEd – Ministry of Education, MinInt – of the Interior, INIT – Institute of the Tourist Industry (?), ICAIC – Institute of Cinema Art and Industry (!), while the factories were retitled Consolidated, if not with cryptograms such as C518 or C15A.)

The store windows *really* showed off clothes, because no one could buy them, since they were *unique* samples – in the best cases. In others, the shop windows served to enclose Marxian or Leninist allegories, more as decoration than from political fervour. But most of the windows were totally empty, and walking along San Rafael or Neptuno, Obispo or O'Reilly (Cuban versions of Fifth Avenue) was as unreal as walking with John Wayne around the main street of a ghost town. In other parts of the city walking was truly strolling along the island of Trinidad in 1959. Or having returned to one's native town, from which hunger had expelled in the forties 82 per cent of the population.

In an incredible Hegelian capriole, Cuba had taken a great leap *forward* – but had fallen *backward*. Now in the poor clothes of the people, in the bastard automobiles (except, of course, the official limousines or the swift late-model Mercedes in the motorcade of the Premier), in the famished faces, it was seen that we *were* underdevelopment. In theory, socialism nationalizes wealth. In Cuba, by a strange perversion of the practice, they had socialized poverty.

I knew, before returning (and I said so to anyone who would listen), that in Cuba a writer could not write, but I believed then that one could live, vegetate, go along putting off death day in, day out. A week after coming back I knew not only that I could not write in Cuba, but that I would not be able to live either. I told this to a friend, a kind of revolutionary non-person who was at the equipoise in the precarious equilibrium of the a-revolutionary non-persons and the counter-revolutionary non-persons. (Cycle of the non-person: request for exit from the country, automatic loss of job and eventual inventory of house and household goods; without work there is no work card, without a card there is no ration book; the permission for exit can take months, a year, two, following the rules more of political lottery than of socialist chess; meanwhile, the non-person finds himself obliged to live by using the money he has saved in the bank: to leave he must restore even the last cent that he had in the bank at the moment of requesting the exit visa; if the bank account is not in order the exit visa is automatically cancelled: new request for exit visa, etc., etc.)

I spoke with this friend who was decorated with exes – ex rebel *comandante*, ex-minister, ex-diplomat. He had just returned from political prison, where he had spent six months, 'punished' by being forced to work with counter-revolutionaries, and upon refusing, out of principle, to show that he was a revolutionary – he had doubled his initial sentence of three months! I talked with him while we crossed an empty plot, far not only from the mad crowd but from clerical ears as well. 'You can't even talk riding in a car,' he said. 'There are German detection devices that can be installed in any garage.' I told him what I said above. He didn't speak, he just looked at me. He knew. I asked him what he was going to do. He took a while to answer, first placing himself in profile to the parallel streets that bordered the empty plot. I knew why: he knew that there were agents capable of reading lips. 'I'll stay here,' he told me. 'You're walking with a dead man.' He did not give me time to reply because he added: 'I'm a political cadaver.' Then he confessed that he prayed every night (to which god he didn't say) that they let him go to join Che, who he believed was in a guerrilla war in the Congo.

Now I know that this friend has had less luck than Guevara: today he is not an immortal but a political zombie. Cuba is populated with them. Many, and not by accident, are literary zombies.

How do you work outside your country?

You want to know how I fared in fair Spain? You know we Spanish-Americans have everything in common with the Spanish. Except, of course, the language.

Why did you choose London?

I didn't choose London. London chose me. I was in Madrid, too busy transforming my vision of dawn in the tropics, lashed to the galleys, taming three tigers at a time, trying to get the *TTT* to explode and, of course, having forgotten that money, like time, is a fungible. Then they knocked three times on my door. As I know that the landlord knocks more times than the postman, I let my wife open the door. There were three who were knocking: a functionary of the Spanish Government to tell me that they were denying me my resident's visa (my past catching up with me), a man/boy with a telegram and, last but listing, the landlord, also known as the Abominable Rentman. My wife, struggling with this bowlegged *yeti* (as a speed-reader of *Blondie* the landlord had left his foot between leaf and jamb to obstruct the door), managed to toss me the cable, which I barely managed to hold:

GUIERMO INFANTA
NEED WRITE MASTERPIECE
SCREENPLAYS STOP LONDON IS SWINGING
STOP PLANE TICKETS TO FOLLOW STOP LOVE
JOE

How could I doubt it for a moment? I leapt through the window. On my way down (we lived on the third floor) I said to myself: *Anch'io sono Swinging-Londoner!*

Under what conditions would you come back?

If Lezama Lima were named Minister of the Interior.

Not even in that case. I would think twice about it and would try to remember what criticism I wrote (or left off writing) about *Enemigo rumor* or *La fijeza*. Besides which there comes between us the parody of 'The Possessed who has just Been Penetrated Bodily . . . by a Soft Assegai'.[1]

'It is dangerous to leave one's country, but it is more dangerous to return to it, because then your countrymen, if they can, will stick a knife in your heart.' Those sage words are of the Yei-Yei, or JJ, of James Joyce. As on other occasions, I make them mine – only I add a modern piece of wisdom: where JJ puts heart I would be able to say back.

Besides, I am a true exile. The other Latin American writers who live in Europe can return to their countries when they wish. In fact they do it often. I cannot. Apart from the fact that physically I wouldn't last a week in freedom. (Or, in the best or worst of cases, I would be turned into a non-person, into a political pariah, into a historical leper. I have suffered that *mal de Marx* already, when *P.M.* was prohibited and *Lunes* was closed down.) There remains to them, besides, the recourse of sending me to reap the wild cassava. Or to cut cane. Or to pick up butts at a bus stop, a punishment to which not long ago they submitted a well-known playwright, a militant (of the Revolution, but also, alas, of homosexuality) reluctant to accept agriculture as a destiny. But although I could come back (supposing I overcame that hurdle unique in America, a privilege that we Cubans enjoy with other Communist countries: the application for a permit for a citizen to return to his own country!) without reprisals, there still remains the problem of a vehicle and where to land. More than a top I need the trope of time. Cuba no longer exists for me other than in memory

---

1 *Enemigo rumor* and *La fijeza* are books of poems by *Lezama Lima*. The parody is included in the novel *Tres tristes tigres*.

or in dreams – and nightmares. The other Cuba (even the one of the future, whatever this may be)[2] is, in truth, 'a dream that turned out badly'.

A colophon never desired

I know the intellectual risk that I run with these inopportune declarations, now that the (lay) patron saint of Cuba is neither Marx nor Mao but Marcuse. I am not forgetting the theory of illustrious laboratory workers of socialism (of the logically senile logician Norman the Mailer, without tarnishing Jean-Paul the Apostle – of the next Millennium – and his carnal Simone), who strive to make guinea pigs of those Cubans who are not already guinea worms. I know about the migratory risk of remaining without a passport. Severo Sarduy, by being infinitely less explicit, spent two years without any documents, until he had no other way out than to become a French citizen.

I know of other risks. I know that I pushed the button that starts up the Extraordinary and Efficient Machine for Fabricating Calumnies. I know some of those who suffered its Left-side effects in the past: Trotsky, Gide, Koestler, Orwell, Silone, Richard Wright, Milosz and an enormous list of names that, if they are steadily becoming less important, can end in one Valeri Tarsis: some so different from others, but all marked by the same iron. I know that leaving your Party is not the same as abandoning your country – although your country now *is* a party. I know the answer to the motto 'My country, right or wrong' – which is the same thing Chesterton said: 'That is like saying, "My mother, drunk or sober." ' But I know also that the argument that was not good enough to exculpate the Nazi war criminals serves to excuse the Soviet peace criminals: they were loyal to their cause.

No consequence of that unhealthy knowledge worries me. My only worry is the fate of my family left behind, exposed to any or to all reprisals, from being fired to being sent to a forced labour camp – camouflaged, of course, with initials: UMAP, UVAP. But I had to begin to tell these things some day although it may cloud my friends' vision. Some of them, from chasing so many rainbows on the political horizon, have been incurably

---

2 Even if this pandemic were shown one day to be only an epidemic (I almost wrote epizootia: the resemblance of Cuba to *Animal Farm* is so real that one thinks of its sequel, *Return to the Isle of the Parrots*), not an endemic but a controllable outbreak, after this continued attack of Castroenteritis the country would be so extenuated morally, so exhausted in its spiritual resources that returning to it would be like spending the rest of one's life at the bedside of a sick person who will perhaps never come out of his coma.

blinded by the red spectrum. I regret, truly, to have to disturb their dreams. I cannot do otherwise. I would tell these truths even if all my friends were called Plato.

(30 July 1986)

Expulsion

T he pianist Ivette Hernández and
the writer Guillermo Cabrera Infante have been expelled
from the Union of Writers and Artists of Cuba, as traitors to
the revolutionary cause.

This decision was adopted unanimously by the Directing
Committee of the UNEAC, in a session held the 15th day of
August, 1968.

Havana, August 16, 1968
UNION OF WRITERS AND ARTISTS OF CUBA

Polemic with a Dead Man

Rodolfo Walsh was one of the *desaparecidos* of Argentina – which is a pity. He should have lived to see his paradise far from paradise, Cuba, complete its vocation of hell, while the Communist world, which he believed eternal, was falling apart, like the Berlin Wall, each day. Now even the Soviet Union has attained it Utopian destiny: she is, like every Utopia, to be found nowhere.

Walsh reproached me for saying that history had died in Cuba because it is falsehood. Quite the contrary: it not only has died but it did not die a natural death, like ancient history. The history of Cuba died because Fidel Castro killed it with his own pistol tucked in his army fatigues of perennial olive drab. There was in 1959 a song of brief fashion but lasting receipts. 'The fun is over,' it said with exact precision and continued: 'The *Comandante* arrived and commanded it to stop.' But here the composer made a mistake with his verbs. He should have said: 'The *Comandante* arrived and commanded it to be killed.' Few times in the tradition of military tyrants in the Americas, which goes from Rosas in Argentina to Trujillo in the Dominican Republic, has there been a man more of a wolf to man – and to woman.

My letter to Walsh was never published in *Primera Plana* owing, allegedly, to scarcity of space. I reproduce it now because my response shows not how accurate I was but how mistaken were these amateur revolutionaries who dug, as Saint-Just would have it, their own grave – and, in passing, the graves of others by releasing from their cages the beast of the Right but also of the Left. Walsh killed himself with his political act, but if suicide is, when all is said and done, a private matter, inciting to massacre is not.

Another patriot of those times who now are not the same was David Viñas, who did not dig his grave, like Walsh, but that of his daughter, to take refuge later – who would have thought! – in the capitalist paradise. Or at least in one of its gardens of academic delight as a guest professor in an American university. The delicate insults that Viñas dedicated to me for saying that Fidel Castro was an emperor with no clothes, written together with his brother and other colleagues from the journal *Problemas del Tercer Mundo* (which was an Argentine fiction, something like the 'Tlön, Uqbar, Orbis Tertius' of Borges reduced to 'Orbis Tertius'), formed part of a fierce campaign with its seat in Buenos Aires, that demonstrated that a Communist is an animal that after reading Marx attacks man. But where have all of them gone? I have to confess that they were, in 1968, for me, a form of fun.

INVITATION TO WALSH

It is well known that Communism does not allow drop-outs. Not in Eastern Europe, not in Cuba, not in Argentina either – as one can see from the personal attacks made upon me by Rodolfo Walsh in his letter to *Primera Plana*.

It seems that my description, euphemistic as it was, of 'the way it was' in Cuba in the summer of 1965 is going to be transformed into what I feared: a polemic somewhat longer than the number of days (and nights) of the one-person one-vote Government of Fidel (Fido to the Soviets).

I never cast Rodolfo Walsh as Plato. Just as I never imagined that the Extraordinary and Efficacious Machine for Fabricating Calumnies would start running in Buenos Aires with a mere turn of the screw. That R. Walsh (not to be confused with the director of the film *High Sierra*, R. Walsh) would contrive such claptrap, with so few elements, to fulfil his quota, demonstrates that he is a grateful fellow-traveller – and a far-seeing one. A kind of super grasshopper who is at the same time his own ant hoarding *merits*. Not only is he paying now with an issue of lies the invitation that they made to him in the sweet January of the Caribbean (a suddenly last summer of fallaciousness) as a tourist of socialism (passages paid with scarce funds, free stay in the Havana Libre *ci-devant* Hilton, excursions to Varadero, named Playa del Pueblo – don't forget that Volkswagen was Hitler's People's Car – always warm and blue and tropically fetching, and the enjoyment of the coffee and milk, the steak and the fruit forbidden to the majority of the adults who live in that (theoretical) paradise. Those men and women who aren't lucky enough to come back later as guests of honour (the Chosen Ones or the Happy Phew), to visit the land they left when 'things get very tough, *che*!' How this same Walsh wailed, meek and shrinking in his last refuge of an office at Prensa Latina, a Government news agency, justly frightened by the increasing buffeting from the extremists of that period when he lived in Cuba – when Fidel Castro in fact ruled with the pseudonym of Aníbal Escalante. Those human beings, condemned to be just Cubans, patient guinea pigs for Dr Cyclops, cannot enjoy this garden of the lights with the felicity shown awhile by the inconclusive statistics compiled by Walsh – at the same time that he is assured of another invitation to the waltz of the future. So he won't have to pay fourteen pesos (fourteen equivalent dollars) for a steak and two pesos (two dollars) for a beer, if he wants to see from his sunny *barrera* how the experiments *in anima vilis* are going and how the experimental subjects are behaving – how cheerful or melodious is their grace under pressure.

Although I detest any political diversion, even polemics, I am going to try to clear up (for Walsh) and to eliminate (for the Argentine reader) some confusions – more in a spirit of geometry than of contradiction.

I don't have on hand the issue of *Lunes* to which Walsh alludes because it stayed, along with my library – patiently, painfully formed over the years, in that past of mine which now belongs to Brick Bradford. But I am sure that the phrase of Saint-Just (hyphenated, s.v.p.) if it appeared in *Lunes*, was never in that context in which I am described as an agitator behind the curtain, suggesting pogroms in whispers into the hairy opportunistic ear of Osvaldo Dorticós. As far as the safeness of Saint-Just (hyphenated, s.v.p.) is concerned, I can say that today I know more than Saint-Just. A revolutionary always digs graves. In fact, he does nothing but dig graves – most of the time other people's graves, as has been amply proved by Stalin, Mao and Fidel Castro.

The conjectures about my trip to Brussels in October 1962 dissipate as soon as one knows (as Walsh does or should) that the 'beautiful weekly that was called *Lunes*' was suppressed exactly one year before, in 1961, when its editor and contributors and scores of Cuban intellectuals signed a letter protesting against the kidnapping of *P.M.* by the ICAIC (Film Institute).

The letter was never published because the Government (with the skill that shows that Fidel Castro's bedside book is not by Marx or Marcuse but by Machiavelli) postponed the First Congress of Cuban Writers and in its place convened three meetings (one every Friday), consecutive but secret, though Alfredo Guevara, director of the ICAIC, made sure that each contribution was taped, to play them back later for Aníbal Escalante in the *sancta sanctorum* of the seat of the ORI (Integrated Revolutionary Organizations) and for *Comandante* Ramiro Valdés in his *penetralia* of the MinInt (Ministry of the Interior). While we the guileless spoke of literature and liberty and liberty in literature, our respective police files grew, enriched by the diverse coloraturas singing an opera buffa in the National Library. During which *Lunes*, its editor and its staff were accused of all crimes possible: against nature and even against typography. To Fidel Castro then, as to Walsh now, our inverted Rs were a nuisance.

When *Lunes* disappeared, this Havana-raised cosmopolite was eight months without a job (just like Padilla now), living off his wife who was a stage and television actress. The Revolutionary Government literally didn't know what to do with my case, among other things because my apartment in the Retiro Médico was a meeting site for intellectuals who were every day more numerous, every day more discontented, every day more daring. It was for this reason that they offered me that obscure post as second secretary in a second-rate embassy which no one wanted – not even I. It was for this same reason that they stretched out to me an aerial bridge too near to leave Cuba the second and definitive time, now that my father's house was filling up every night with intellectuals and artists, then no longer discontented or discouraged but truly hunted, some for being homosexual, others for being heterodox, all for being disobedient, since disobedience is the only crime that the New Orthodox Church does not pardon. Some of these friends, in their desperation and dragged along by the militant wake left by Allen Ginsberg before they deported him from Cuba, wanted to put out manifestos (now pederasty and lesbianism were *political* crimes identical to abstractionism: the inverts as culpable as the Rs) and filing in front of the Palace with placards:

Homosexuals of the world, unite! You have nothing to lose but your sex!

In my first exile with an official blessing, it was the formerly all-powerful Furtseva of Cuba, Edith García Buchaca (head of the National Council for Culture at that time, now under house arrest, accused of being an 'agent of Imperialism') who revealed the true intentions behind diplomatic appointment. In my second and final exile, it was *Comandante* Manuel Piñeiro (better known by his pirate nickname, 'Redbeard'), chief of Intelligence and Counter-Intelligence, who uncorked the hidden bottle. Both pronounced the same sentence: 'Let him leave, to see if he seeks asylum!'

I want to believe that Walsh knows nothing of all this. Although I know that he knows what he's saying. He is less ignorant than he pretends. I don't even want to have to read again some of the idiocies that he adds on to give local colour to his arguments, much less argue with him. Calling me Sacred Writer, in capitals, is another attempt at an insult and is nothing more than *milonga* lyrics. If it were true, I wouldn't be in exile, but aspiring to the Nobel Prize from Havana, supported by a Government and a State. Sacred writers would thus be Nicolás Guillén or Alejo Carpentier. Declaring that I came to Europe because I liked 'French wines' is not even clever. Anyone who, like Walsh, has lived in Cuba knows that we Cubans don't drink wine, not from temperance but because of the temperature. The few (or the many: I don't even know the quantity) wines that remained in Cuba used to be drunk by foreign visitors. All those writers who timidly sidled up to the Cuban Revolution one day from moral motives and who have ended up in a militancy to the death (of others) that justifies everything with the expediency of statists, with political opportunism and with arguments worthy of a gang boss, all of them – strange coincidence – are foreigners who became Cuban experts (from the black night of reaction to the radiant morning of progress) in one or two visits as avid tourists to the Cuban spa: being baptised as converts to Marx in the lukewarm waters of altruistic calculations. Full of sun, of rum, of music on Cuban beaches, some (overly timid) bring their wives, others (nepotists) get all their family invited – and have a double social and sensual enchantment. And if the coasts of Sicily, Corsica or Sardinia make up the Club Med for summer capitalism, now on the soft sands of Varadero, in the lucid waters that surround the Isle of Pines and on the florid keys of the Jardines and Jardinillos, summer socialism has its Caribbean Club!

When I left Cuba for Belgium (if Walsh knew how to tell the truth he would have said, instead of 'the Europe that he loves', the New York that I loved) I abandoned my apartment in a luxury highrise facing the ocean as well as my convertible (which Walsh knew well and I bought in the summer of 1958, when I was a journalist with too much success, in the press and on television) that I left running around with thousands of similar, better, automobiles, for a Belgian streetcar and a room on the inhospitable Avenue Brugmann, since the salary I was earning (in dollars, yes: like that of all Cuban diplomats, paid by the Narodny Bank of Moscow: the same bank that pays the Casa de las Américas prizes to foreigners) did not stretch far enough to support my wife, my daughter and myself in Brussels, a city more expensive than Paris. For two years I had no clothes other than the two suits of Chinese wool made in Havana and an old English overcoat, loaned by a friend whose rich father bought it for him in London. (I don't want to seem like a model of virtues when I'm rather a design of defects, but if someone like Walsh purports to write my biography, I would prefer it to be made with facts.)

Curiousmore and morecurious, Alice would say: going to perfect one's English in *Brussels*! In case Walsh forgot living geography while he was trying to resuscitate the cadaver of socialist history, I can give him the up-to-the-minute news that English is spoken, in Europe, *only* in the British Isles. Did he mean to say to perfect my *French*? Or was he perhaps referring to Flemish, which is not only, of course, a school of painting but the language of the Belgians of Flanders?

Concerning the veiled references to my not having been in the Sierra (I could have, in my turn, following Walsh's method, asked him why he didn't die with his old chief, Masetti, in an Argentine guerrilla war), this is an antecedent with little importance now in Cuba. There are diplomats who are old Batista supporters, such as the present Cuban Ambassador in Bulgaria, who was still a cadet in Batista's Naval Academy on 1 January 1959, and there are former prisoners of Batista and revolutionary diplomats in prison, as is the case of Gustavo Arcos, who was wounded in the assault on the Moncada, imprisoned and exiled by Batista, his brothers killed in the wreck of the *Granma*, his family exiled from their native town, and was Ambassador of the Revolution in Brussels when I was there from 1962 to 1965; since January 1966 he has been rotting, literally (he has a lame leg resulting from the bullet in his spinal cord at Moncada), in Castroist prisons (first La Cabaña, then Isla de Pinos, until that was disguised as an artificial paradise while the neighbouring big island became an enormous Cayenne, and now a concentration camp in Guanacahabibes, on the westernmost extreme of Cuba), without ever being sentenced, without even being charged, because his crime is nowhere to be seen.

I can continue the argument by reminding Walsh that that Incomplete Past (which he calls 'the wound'), as Arturo de Cordova the film actor used to say, 'doesn't have the *slightest* importance!' I was with President Dorticós, appointed for life by the Unique Elector of Prussia on the Caribbean, when he went up to the Sierra Maestra for the first time: in the presidential plane *Guaimaro* in May 1959, to sign the Agrarian Reform Law, of which he was a simple compiler as Minister of Revolutionary Laws. It is true that he had more than enough practice for being now president, acquired in the days when he was *Comodoro*, with a sailor's cap and everything, of the exclusive and racist (for rich whites only) Yacht Club of Cienfuegos.

I wish to complete Walsh's statistics for him, as he forgot these numbers:

> 55,000 political prisoners;
> 950,000 passports applied for to flee from such an amiable labyrinth (without counting the 600,000 persons who are now exiled, which makes a conservative census:
> 1,500,000 have abandoned or are trying to abandon a country with only

7,000,000 inhabitants: not even the Germany of the Wall can improve on this ratio!;

of each: twenty-seven (27) Cubans, one (1) is an agent paid by the State as security police (September 1965);

2,000,000 (the number was thrown out with his usual Mussolinian mixture of jutting and strutting indiscretion and boasting terrorism by the Prime Minister himself, nicknamed by his pals *El Caballo*, in a recent speech: straight from the Horse's mouth) *two million* Cubans belong to that sedulous service of house to house espionage that is the Committees for the Defence of the Revolution (initials please: CDR), without the permission of which *no one* – believe it or not, a political Ripley would say – can even take a *radio set* to be repaired! An onerous antecedent is Hitler's *Blockwarts*.

Between them the Ministries of the Armed Forces and of the Interior spend more money than the *total* budget of the nation in 1951, the last year Cuba enjoyed a Government elected *by* its people.

Speaking of 1951, corrupted and exploiting capitalism managed that year to produce seven million (7,000,000) tons of sugar. Seventeen years later, with the whole people mobilized in slave labour, the Government of Fidel Castro is incapable of reaching that figure. Not due to a blaming blockade, so many times invoked as the Big Brother's Big Excuse, but because the Government has irretrievably destroyed the sugar industry. It is thus not astonishing that these are the sad numbers of the present reality of Cuba that many wish to make the future not only of Latin America but of the world. ('Not one Vietnam but many' was the slogan of an ex-Minister of Industries, the idolized Che Guevara, who once said: 'We must put an end to sugar' – and he put an end to the Cuban economy.)

Monthly living allowances per individual
3 pounds of rice
6 *ounces* of coffee
2 pounds of beef
4 pounds of other meats and fish
2 pounds of fats (vegetable and animal)
Some vegetables (if there are any)
1 pint of milk (only for people older than 70 and younger than 7)
Only sugar, bread and eggs are not rationed
(These figures, given by the Castro Government this year, 1968, and published in *The Times* of 16 July, are *ideal*, not real.)

Finally I wish to speak of the pathetic politics that floods the shallow arguments of Walsh like a tearful miasma. It is a surfacing of the old Russian *poshlost* to which Nabokov gave a new and definitive meaning: not only tacky but also ridiculous, opportunist and demagogic. The whole

Argentine Fidelista Left is a flooded pampa of *poshlost*. The letter from Walsh is not its only sample and example. It is everywhere. What else but *porteño poshlost* is the literary act of an august and celebrated writer who writes a serious novel around the thesis that for the Argentine intellectual 'only two options are open', to imitate Che Guevara or to copy Cortázar? As Borges would say: *'Pero che!'* (This phrase you can't just hear, you have to read it.) Apart from the fact that options are not oysters and are therefore not *opened*, one must imagine that in 1935 this dual dilemma would have become triple by the possible addition of the name of singer Carlos Gardel. Then for the Argentine writer there would be three doors opened on to promissory *paysages* as in Flemish triptychs: to die in Bolivia, to write in Paris or to sing tangos on Broadway!

Walsh sticks to fallacies in which the *petitio principii* follows appeals to authority or *ad hominem*. If he says that my *Tres tristes tigres* is not underground reading in Cuba it is to back himself up with avowals by readers. As if he did not know that clandestine literature has more readers than official literature precisely where literature is most official.

If I said that one could not write in Cuba I was referring, as almost always, to myself. But now that he speaks of Lezama, of Carpentier and of Guillén, I want to say to Walsh that Lezama could always, and always will be able to, write in Cuba, whatever may happen. His motto declares that he always can 'find virtues and expressions on other preserves of greater dignity'. It was thus that he could survive the years as a criminal lawyer and as a functionary of the Institute of Culture of Batista. (Yes, he too.) Carpentier wrote all his best books in Venezuela, some under the triumvirate of the Three Little Pigs, and he even managed to organize an international music festival for the dictator Big Bad Pig Pérez. (Yes, *him* too.) Nicolás Guillén is an old nightingale of emperors. He started out as a press censor for Machado in 1932 and since then he has not ceased to serve all the tyrants with his cheerful pen: he commended Stalin to the protection of his Afro-Cuban gods, he regaled Batista with off-colour stories narrated in his Congolese voice in the forties, he wrote for Aníbal Escalante and he still composes *guaracha* lyrics in praise of Fidel Castro. This last matter, nevertheless, didn't prevent him from speaking his mind to me on the patio of the Writers' Union, under a mango tree, reacting to the denunciation that Fidel Castro had made recently in the university. In front of the students Castro called him a lazybones, well-off poet and addicted to *la dolce vita*. Guillén told me then *sotto voce*: 'Kid, this guy is worse than Stalin! Stalin died and they buried him but this one is going to bury us all!'

In my answers to *Primera Plana* I said that for the unlivable Cuban situation there were only two solutions: schizophrenia or flight. The admirable *morceau* of Reinaldo Arenas's novel *Celestino antes del alba* published in *Primera Plana* shows to what extent I was right: it is Cuban literature itself that is becoming schizophrenic. One doesn't have to be a great reader to see in those hallucinatory pages a metaphor of Cuba, where reality is a menacing forest of axes that form roofs, walls and floor. A cruel land ruled by a tyrant who chops down with blows of an axe the trees on which verses are carved. The ultimate terror of the narrator is justified: he knows that in that nightmare the executioner is capable of decapitating anyone who dares to write poetry about himself: i.e. to conceive his life as one who composes a poem.

Neither of the two Fernández poets is a friend of mine – he of that name who was one was in another city and he is dead. A friend of mine is Heberto Padilla who did not manage to get my book published in Cuba, but was instead thrown out of all his jobs and now, in the latest number (Epoca II, No. 21, June 1968) of the *Kyman*, he succeeds in provoking Lisandro Otero, a new boss of Kulture (Khrushchev on the outside, Furtseva on the inside), to flatten him with an official terrorist prose that I had not read since Zhdanov made shreds of Zoshschenko in Leningrad. Another friend of mine is Luis Agüero, a talented young novelist who tried to leave Cuba amicably and did not get to, but upon asking to leave the country as an exile, on the very day after he had presented his papers, was sent to work in agriculture for a year, as punishment, in that green belt around Havana that so thrills the Walshlost. (How many writers on the Left, Right or Centre, Argentine, Bolivian, Uruguayan or Chilean, have drawn this lot when they have wished, they too, why not, to come to drink *French* wine in the 'Europe that they love so much'?)

Walterio Carbonell is a friend of mine, one of the few black intellectuals that there are in Cuba and an old Marxist, expelled, first, from the UNEAC (Writers' Union) for saying in a colloquium given – my God! – to French *tourists* in the Casa de las Américas, for *daring* to say that in Cuba there was no freedom of speech, and for talking about the *P.M.* case, about *Lunes*, about the play *Los mangos de Caín*, then, as he could talk now about *María Antonia* and the *Cuadratura del círculo*, and upon making this criticism (insignificant if it is compared with the protests and the meetings, and the books that are published daily, anywhere, that make severe criticisms of their respective regimes, without a single, simple reprisal, upon saying to some *French* tourists that in Cuba there was no freedom of speech he fell struck by the lightning from Roberto Retamar, MC of the debate, and of Haydée Santamaría, director, as an 'agent provocateur', he earned a mark of ash on his forehead. Now Carbonell has been condemned to two years of forced labour. An interesting point is that he always maintained the thesis that in Revolutionary Cuba there was a frank majority of whites in power, when one observes a distinct majority of blacks in the Cuban population. Then he was accused of being an agent of Black Power and sent to a labour camp.

Those are my friends inside Cuba because I want to claim that they are. My Cuban friends outside, all in exile, include Calvert Casey, one of the truly great short-story writers of America, gone fleeing from Cuba because of his homosexuality (what a crime, eh, Walsh?) and pursued all the way to Rome – where Castro's Ambassador prevented him from working in the FAO. My friends include Severo Sarduy of whom I spoke. My friends include Juan Arcocha, possibly the bravest of Cuban writers, living in Paris, also denied permission to work at Unesco. My friends include Néstor Almendros, the extraordinary cinematographer of *La Collection-neuse* now, but for years living in extreme poverty in Paris, chased by Cuban calumny since he abandoned Havana in 1962.

My friends are those anonymous Cubans who for nine months I saw arrive in Madrid with only the clothes they had on because they had to leave everything in Cuba to pay the price of being free. Cubans of all classes and of all the races (and if he doubts it, let Walsh come to Madrid to see for himself: I will not be able to pay his plane trip, nor put him up in the Castellana Hilton, but I can take him where he will see them: eating together in depressing dining rooms of international aid, wearing old mission clothes, but happy in their diaspora, these Jews of Spanish America). They really are blockaded, persecuted and defamed! For months, years, they must wait to be expelled from paradise without committing an original sin apart from the indestructible human need (for some only the stubbornness) of liberty. When they succeed in leaving Cuba, they find no door open other than those of Spain, USA, France or Mexico, because they can't come to England unless they have a visa for re-entry into Cuba, because they can't enter the Netherlands or Germany or Austria – and *all* South America is forbidden to them.

I am a wandering Jew who has spent three years in England renewing my ninety-day *permis de séjour* every three months without knowing what will happen in the coming trimester, while many declared mouthpieces of Communism travel all over the world without any bother other than jet-lag. Concerning the writers – officials all – of Cuba it is true that many are not zombies, they are something worse: *Sholokhovs* of the Caribbean, *Ehrenburgs* of the tropics, coloured *Yevtushenkos*.

I don't believe that Walsh could say with bad intent that I am against my country ('the goodies') and in favour of the 'Nazism of today' ('the baddies'). I don't believe that it is bad faith but *poshlost* of the pampas. Although I know (like everyone who reads the newspapers this morning) that the road to Prague is paved with Russian tanks armed with the best intentions.

This last – really, the last – ghost of Walsh has been unmasked before you can say *poshlost*, unveiled by the stubbornness of history, a concentric chaos, and by the refusal of the truth to sink into any opportunist Lethe. It is what a liberal out of fashion with the New Left, Thomas Masaryk, founder of the Czech nation, called 'Pravda vitezi'. *Truth will win.* It has just won in his defeated country, in the aborted foetal democracy of Czechoslovakia. As in Cuba Fidel Castro finally proved right the Cuban bourgeoisie who discovered early on his tyrant's biology, so in Czechoslovakia the Russians have proven right the senile Eisenhower who said that the Communist ideology is shown everywhere to be dangerous still: aggressive, implacable and cunning.

I don't believe that the naked truth of the Czechs can vanquish the cosmetic *poshlost* of the Walshes of this world: those who say or repeat that the US is the Third Reich of this time; those who always find excuses to cover up the crimes 'of the Left' with the tag of 'errors inevitable in the process of construction of the new blablabla and bla'; those pilgrims to *Poshlostia* who, with the Soviet myth over and done, invented a Chinese paradise where a thousand flowers soon withered, sought their last refuge under the paranoid beard of Fidel Castro – all of them followers of the simurgh, who flee from the truth. That truth that demonstrates every once in a while – stubborn, palpable but uselessly for them – that Communism is the poor man's Fascism.

(22 August 1968)

Letter to Tomás Eloy Martínez
of *Primera Plana*

London, 23 September 1968

My dear Tomás E. Loy – Now the second postman has gone, after the first one rang three times to contradict my near namesake and old artificer, James M. It happens that one must knock more than three times to awaken me at 8:15 Greenwich Mean Time. Another one came (or the same one returned) at eleven o'clock with your letter all stuffed and loaded with mystery – which was no more than the mystery of when information returns transformed by the medium: the galleys are the message, McMamalujo would say.

I have read your letters, I have reread them, I have re-reread myself (that odious 'writer's reading', as Faulkner said, that you should know quite well with its whiff of tar in the glottis) and, my dear Tomás, I have arrived at the rapid, but not for all that less mediated, decision that it is better *not* to publish my answer to the letters in answer to my answers to your questionnaire. As you well know (or should have known, after interviewing me) I had no way out other than to answer your questions as I did. That is, I have voluntarily renounced any political blueprint for living my life. What I opine in private I am disposed to maintain in public, anywhere – the reverse of many of my South American colleagues. I suffered for too long that condition to which all (and I say, *all*) Cuban writers are subject, even many of those who reside abroad, who speak filth about the Revolution and Fidel Castro in private (believe me and I can swear to you on my mother's grave or if you believe that is too melodramatic, Argentine, I can swear on the safety of my daughters and if you believe that oath is too easy, I can give you my word of honour that those lines that I put in Nicolás Guillén's mouth are a verbatim quote of what Nicolás said to me one day in August or September on the patio of the UNEAC, along with other more intimate things that I do not wish to repeat) and who show up in public supporting the Revolution, without apparent benefit but knowing that the consequences of being consequent are always onerous. Not everyone writes *Mein Kampf* and follows it afterwards *ad pedem litterae*. (If this, by leaps of memory, seems like Nazism to you, I ask you to look at my colour photos to see the colour of my skin and then I inform you that my maternal grandfather was named Infante Espinosa while my maternal great-grandmother was named Caridad Espinosa and her husband was a Spanish military man named Sebastián Castro Sidonia native of Almería: it is *impossible* with these mixtures of *huanche* – my father, Cabrera, was born in the Canaries – black, Indian and Sephardic, to want to make an apology for the Aryan ideologies!)

Your pruning has been masterful, but I appear as a simple refuter of Walsh – a victory that even Pyrrhus would have considered onerous. Who wants to flatten a journalist so well-informed that he believes they speak English in Belgium? (For sure, there is a fact I'd forgotten, but of which I was reminded by the journalists Juan Arcocha, by telephone, from Paris: as early as the first half of 1959, at a party that Pablo Armando Fernández gave in his apartment in the Retiro Médico, ten floors above mine, Rodolfo Walsh had a heated argument with Juan over Walsh's claim that what there was in Cuba was Fascism! Look where the new political winds have led this weathercock – which is only another word for weathervane in the metaphoric way the English have.)

But, frankly, I cannot accept your offer. What are these refutations worth if all their humour has been lost? Thus the quotation from Carroll, to which I gave a cachet of maximum actuality after having used it in my response as an apparently decorative element, has disappeared in your galleys and with it almost all the swing and soul of an argument in which, right off, I saw myself dragged along by the vulgarity of my contenders. Something rather as if Jigoro Kano, the legendary founder of the Kodokan school of Judo, were to condescend to fight with Willie Pep, one of the dirtiest boxers in the annals of the ring. Let me tell you that from the moment I sent the first cable – the one that said VIÑAS ATE BAIT etc. – until I came back from the post office, after sending you the cable authorizing your changes, my decision only became steadily more negative. Why should I combat such vigorous agents of Good? Why waste my time when I, like Marcel Duchamp, was also born for leisure? What do they matter to me, all these people who, if they are honourable, will one day be horrified at having endorsed such an old rottenness that is presented as the Only New Order now. If they are not, they simply aren't worth the trouble. Let me tell you that one of the reasons for my autumn discontent with those lines written in high summer is that you pruned every initial reference to the *poshlost* and to its pampa variety that gave my response a certain aloofness that I would like to believe elegant. Another is to appear in October answering insults of August, as if I had dedicated myself all this time to thinking about how to confront such formidable opponents, when you and *Primera Plana* know that my response was immediate to reading the letter by Walsh published by you. For another thing, many of my arguments rested on the notes, in which I presented testimonies of people alluded to as affidavits of my assertions, e.g. the poem by Padilla, the references, acrid acronyms! And so on, and so on.

I didn't know that you had sent the *Primera Plana* to Havana. I did know that they had received it, because I have letters from people who read it (among them two from functionaries of Culture whose names I keep to myself) in one of which they accuse me of having lied and in the other – received by the intermediary of travellers to Madrid – they reproach me for not having said even a hundredth of what really happens in Cuba: 'You also, Caín, have lost perspective and you comment on frivolous things when there is so much tragedy still to know about.' Now, as well, the reprisals have begun, indirect and direct. They are making life impossible for Marta Calvo, mother of my daughters, a functionary in the Casa de las Américas. My father will have to return to his home town on account of the comments that pursue him day and night. I have here a communication from UNEAC, published in the newspaper *Granma*, in which I am declared (along with the pianist Ivette Hernández, who found asylum in Spain: a typical trite twinning in which I am yoked with an apolitical musician *ex profeso*) 'expelled from the Writers' Union as a traitor to the revolutionary cause'.

A thing that, after all, does not fail to be comic – if it were not that it is a tragedy for my family. I say comic because in UNEAC all sorts of filthy things have been said about me and after the official all-out manhunt I should have been expelled from it a long time ago – or so I thought.

I deduced that you wanted to balance my statement with certain concessions to Cuba and her Argentine pals when I saw the immediate and successive publication of texts, canonical or approved or awarded by Kuban Kultur – e.g. Cisneros, Barnet, Reinaldo Arenas's *Celestino Before Dawn*. I understand. I have worked on magazines and newspapers in Cuba, under capitalism and in socialism too, long enough to understand the reasons of state of the Fourth Estate. I know that to publish is always to do politics by other means. None of this impedes me, nor will it impede me, from continuing to be your friend, in the first place, and a friend of *Primera Plana* and even its collaborator (ugly French word). I understand the reasons that induce you to sympathize with Cuban reality, to be in agreement with it, but I can understand them less after Czechoslovakia. I do not believe that life in Cuba is better than in Poland or in Russia. But I know that the USSR is, like England, like the United States, like Japan, like Germany under Hitler, fulfilling, with all reservations and possible differences taken into account, carrying out its destiny as a great power. As China and India and Australia will do in the near future and perhaps one day, Brazil, Mexico and Argentina, or South Africa and France now. Great nations will always be great on account not only of history, but much more so of geography. In Poland, despite the sleazy efforts of Gomulka, there is no Stalin. In all the socialist countries (including Albania) there is a legality that exists at least on paper. You don't know, Tomás, what it is to live in a country without a constitution, without individual rights, where the enormous repressive apparatus (my statistics, also suppressed, are not, believe me, invented), is at the service not of an idea or of a regime but of the biology of a *single* individual. This is, the more I think about it and in spite of the leftist fashion, in spite of the fact that the anarchists wear Mao buttons on their lapels, in spite of the fact that the flower children have become poisonous buds, this Cuban situation, this *Cuban Thing* so cheerfully sung by Gelber,[1] is a historical monstrosity. Think – I'm not talking to you about Tropicana or the Capri, places that, indeed, never figured on my habitual map, but of places of music where I could inhabit the art, habitat of the monsters of popular creation, that were also hovels like Chori or lowlife dens like the docks or a poor street musician singing a serenade. I didn't go to Tropicana (and I'm not excusing myself, simply explaining) until 1955, the Capri was put up in 1958 – and I lived in Havana from 1941.

I could well have spoken (and I will speak in *Cuerpos divinos*) of the Shanghai Theatre, of the Zombie Club, the *Ñáñigo* parties, of the Havana carnival and its masquerades, of the life that Prussianism has eradicated from Cuba. I don't see why one has to sing to the Spartan life, when one knows that sybaritism is a life no more decadent than the Hellenistic or the Victorian lives, when one knows, with scientific certainty, that all ideology is, in the last analysis, reactionary.

1. Jack Gelber, beatnik playwright. *The Cuban Thing* is a play, a mediocre one, from 1968.

The Twisted Tongue of the Poet

Rather than in those 'worst and best of times' with which Dickens represented the French Revolution we are living the moment when Macbeth, addicted now to power and history, assassinated the noble good king Duncan in his sleep – and spread equally guilt and terror.

> Things fall apart; the centre cannot hold;
> Mere anarchy is loosed upon the world . . .

Thus Yeats described the Russian Revolution in his 'Second Coming', in 1921. But in 1968 still

> The blood-dimmed tide is loosed, and everywhere
> The ceremony of innocence is drowned . . .

Three weeks ago, in these same pages [*Primera Plana*], not only did confusion create another masterpiece, but a ceremonial of innocents was drowned in vituperations. The Cuban Heberto Padilla, perhaps the only revolutionary poet of his country and for that very reason a hunted man – among many other things for defending a book of mine in public but also because 'a government does not want writers, it only wants scribblers', as Solzhenitsyn says – attacked me bestially, maybe after reading Marx. My crime: having revealed abroad that they were chasing him, breaking thus the silence barrier. I thought I was returning to Padilla a literary and human favour and here you see I have committed a nameless crime, an abjection (cf. Yevtushenko vs. Sinyavski and Daniel: 'I agree with what was done with them . . . Are we going to let our dirty laundry hang *outside* the house?').

In Cuba, by putting Marx on his feet they have stood Martí on his head. It was José Martí who said about another tyranny: 'To witness a crime in silence, is to commit it.' Now to say that one has witnessed a crime (in Cuba) is to commit one. This tropical confusion is the dreams of the reason that eats the lotus leaves of History. Evil are the times when the nightmare is presented to us as the only dream possible, when they impose chaos on us as a New Order. Then politics is a branch of metaphysics, religion by other means – and Communism turns out to be one of the avatars of evil.

No scholium is left, only eschatology. Or perhaps to read it all as a play better fit for the theatre of political cruelty. Nevertheless, despite myself, I have to take Padilla's written word literally, because – he knows it better than anyone – *quod scripsi, scripsi.*

'I think it unnecessary to make it clear that I write these lines in total freedom,' said Padilla in Havana one September morn. But I received this letter from Cuba dated the 27th of that month: 'I have learned that the UNEAC [the Writers' Union], after having expelled you as a traitor, "invited" Padilla to "respond" to you, and that he is going to do it in a form quite hazardous to his health.' Not so, not so much, correspondent – unless the front page of *Primera Plana* be not the Western front where all used to be quiet.

Someone called 'E. R. G.', hardly a name, writes in *Triunfo* of Madrid, in November: 'It is true that Padilla defended himself in a direct letter to Cabrera, impugning those declarations, a letter that was not published.' Where 'was it not published'? (The initialled Spaniard is careful to clarify but not to lie when he says that I 'deserted from the Cuban diplomatic corps'.) 'A new letter – which has not appeared, but which *Indice* will no doubt insert – reiterates his theoretical opposition to Cabrera, although it does not renounce his friendship.' Perhaps another *index librorum* may reveal this Medieval mystery. If Padilla doesn't confess before then to being a saboteur of buses or an incendiary of canefields. Why not? After all, Bukharin was a philosopher and in the Moscow trials 'in total freedom' he confessed to 'having poisoned all the wheat in the *Ukraine*'.

For those who may doubt the possibility of an incarnation of the Slav(e) soul in the tropics, I can cite a tirade by Haydée Santamaría de Hart, head of the Casa de las Américas and heroine of the Revolution, who revealed this secret of a totalitarian state to the poet Pablo A. Fernández and to me, not long after she arrived from Russia: 'In the USSR there was not a single artist in jail. Never! No creator was ever put in prison. But not *one*! Comrade Furtseva explained to me that the abstract artists and the decadent bourgeois writers who were imprisoned, were put there for being agents of Nazism.' Pardon me if I laugh while transcribing it. It isn't so much that Yeyé Santamaría pronounced *Ur* instead of USSR nor that in the same conversation she confessed that she believed that Marx and Engels were a *single* person ('You know, like Ortega y Gasset'), but that I recall the glance of glee that PAF and I exchanged. Imagine the Two

Thieves hearing JC say: 'Lord, a few more thorns, spears and nails, s.v.p.' Then you will have a remote idea of the discomfort it produces in two sinners to be obliged to escort for ever a saint with a mission on earth.

But I know that I can make jokes, jibes and parodies from the pleasure of playing with words, while Padilla uses words because it is his life that is in play. Sure. No less sure that I chose this state of free will, while Padilla chooses History and slavery. Although I can assure the readers (not Padilla; he knows it too well: 'Socialism is sadness,' he used to say, 'but it gives you shelter') that freedom brings more risks than slavery. One of its perils is knowing that freedom of speech can mean slavery of the press. I don't say it on account of the travails and toils of a free man, who moves away from his literary destiny as inertia brings the point of arrival nearer in inverse ratio. I say the absence of a *free* press. What Alejo Carpentier expressed with the *esprit* (and accent) of a Frenchman: '*Zeek asylum* in France? Idiots! As if I didn't *know* that any writer who leaves the Left is lost!'

The Theorem of Alejo was solved a few days ago by my Catalonian publisher. After reading my interview Carlos Barral wrote me a letter that tried to be insulting and succeeded only in being stupid. More than stupid, drunken with revolutionary zeal. This literary boss who has decided to defend Communism in the Very Faithful Isle of Cuba to his last foreign peseta and to the last Cuban, criticized my English as that of an 'immigrant' (it won't be once five years have passed: then it will be 'naturalized' English) in the same paragraph that he wrote *Topica* instead of Topeka! This is of course the last letter that Barral will write me, as *Tres tristes tigres* was my first and last book for (Seix-) Barral. The sentiment of disgust is mutual. But I want to dabble into that viscosity now only to cite the ending that is a coda: 'I am sending this letter ... to the Casa de las Américas, who would surely *wonder* at my silence.' Once more Orwell is right: 'To be corrupted by totalitarianism one does not have to live in a totalitarian country.'

Padilla says about me: 'Assuming the role of every counter-revolutionary who tries to create a difficult situation for anyone who has not taken his same road ...' Not only the 'role of every counter-revolutionary', but also of *every* 'revolutionary' on *another* route, since it was literary commissar Lisandro Otero who accused Padilla of being a *disguised counter-revolutionary* (*Le Monde*, 5 November), who is trying to 'awaken in our fatherland *Czechoslovak problems* ... (and) who wants to place the writer and revolutionary power in contradiction'. Otero, a possible version now of Andrei Zhdanov in Cuba, talks next with the voice of a prosecutor: 'Action must be taken against these elements.' Can it not be that the word counter-revolution is used in Cuba as Jarry used to say that philosophers used metaphysics: to make *invincible* the *invisible*? (Or maybe it's to make *vincible* the *visible*?) But who was the 'counter-revolutionary' (according to Padilla) who made it difficult for a 'counter-revolutionary' (according to Otero) by creating for him a 'difficult situation'?

The 'difficulties of Padilla' did not start with my interview (*'Answers and Questions'*, above). Not in the least. To think that this is so would be to admit the vanity of believing that a 'cumulus of falsehoods' (as the Left has decided to call my declarations, demonstrating that the Right is the only political faction capable of telling the truth today) has been able alone to push an 'outpost of progress' into what the calumnist of *Triunfo* calls 'a grave crisis'. Nor did these difficulties begin with the polemic about the entry of my novel *TTT* into the Castroist Index, settled by Padilla a year before with Risandro Otelo, who with his rampant orthodoxy tries futilely to erase today his past association with the Cuban *haute bourgeoisie*. They did not even begin to persecute Padilla when he published a poem in the same anthology of *Ruedo Ibérico* in which Roberto Retamar declares himself 'a man of transition' to shrill thrills from 'E.R.G.' and the Communist *poshlost* and laughter from everyone who knows Retamar, a man of *transaction* if there ever was one. This poem by Padilla is called 'En tiempos difíciles' ('In Hard Times') and there someone (the voice of revolutionary conscience, the Party, Fidel Castro, whatever) asks him to give all of himself and when the poet has given all, but all, *anatomically* speaking ALL: '*They explained to him later that all this donation would be useless without giving his tongue*' too.

This temerity (which in a *non*-totalitarian country would be poetic licence but is close to suicide in Cuba) was committed by Padilla in a Rubén Darío commemorative issue of *Revista Casa* (May 1967), for which poems were requested. As with the critiques commissioned by *El caimán* concerning the novel by Commissar Otero, Padilla 'did not adjust himself to what was requested' with his poem, and although Retamar attempted to *pers(uad/ecut)e him*, he insisted on its publication. But the perils of Padilla did not begin even then. Like a chronic illness, they only became worse.

It was the same illness that he contracted (Padilla and every true intellectual) when a private judgement was made (first the verdict, then the sentence, next the view of the trial: in the National Library, in 1961, with Castro as judge/prosecutor/jury) of the short film *P.M.*, an innocent essay in free cinema shot in a country that was beginning to show that the mere adjective free induces in all totalitarians the biological necessity of committing crimes against its name in its name: *Liberté, combien de crimes* . . . From that moment on, from the slimy 'Words to the Intellectuals' (pronounced after Castro had thrown his perennial pistol on the table, in a gesture of a gangster in *pourparler*: obscene but obsolete) as a colophon, *P.M.* was prohibited, the atrocious Writers' Union was created, *Lunes de Revolución* was shut down, the persecutions of writers and artists for supposed moral perversions were made systematic (e.g. for pederasty: Virgilio Piñera, José Triana, José Mario arrested, the *El Puente* group destroyed, Raúl Martínez tossed out of the art school along with scores of exemplary students – there and in the universities – Arrufat made destitute after being fired as editor-in-chief of *Casa*, etc., etc.) when in reality they were castigated for aesthetic deviations (i.e., Sabá Cabrera, Hugo Consuegra, Calvert Casey, GCI, exiled; Walterio Carbonell, a black sociologist and old Marxist, first expelled from the Writers' Union for saying in public that in Cuba there was no freedom of speech and now condemned to two years of forced labour – for organizing a Cuban branch of *Black Power*! – Luis Agüero, one of the island's best young writers, condemned along with thousands of anonymous Cubans to work in that vegetable belt of Havana – which so moves the fellow-traveller poets and the tourists of socialism – for the nameless crime of applying for an exit from the workers' paradise etc.) and the Cuban Revolution, like all betrayed revolutions, converted hope into hype and physics into metaphysics and ideology into eschatology. Or just into scatology?

It is curious that Padilla does not admit in his letter what even an old professional Communist proclaims. Saverio Tutino, previously correspondent for *L'Unitá*, writes in *Le Monde* of Paris of the anguish of Padilla (and of Antón Arrufat, who was not even mentioned in my interview) excommunicated by the Cuban orthodox church: 'the *revelation* of (these) divergences marks the end of *ten years' truce* between the *Revolution* and the *artistic world* . . .' Curiouser and curiouser this alibi by the criminal Padilla offered to his inquisitors ('I [would be] on the side . . . of the stupidest trials' against GCI), when even *L'Express* in France (24 November 1968) calls this phenomenon that makes the *poshlost* and the Walshlost cry, moved, 'a Stalinism with sun'.

'The revolution is not a bed of roses,' declaims the poet. Of course not. It is a bed of Procrustes, capable of cutting off even the tongue given in offering if 'it does not adjust itself to what is requested'. After writing in September the letter by assignment from the Writers' Union, after being attacked by the political maroon, obviously frightened by the barking of the pack, for *my* having said that *he* was persecuted, after making confession (written) and contrition (published), the sinner Padilla is further than ever from the heaven's gate of the believer. *Verde Olivo*, the weekly arm of the Cuban army, accuses him of 'multiple crimes' – among which is having misappropriated foreign funds of the Socialist State!

But there is still more. Not long ago Padilla won a Writers' Union poetry competition – which included a trip abroad. This state office attempted to reject (and thus to influence) the verdict of the international jury. When they finally accepted it, it was by publishing this prior repudiation: 'to let it be known that ideologically he (the poet) manifests himself outside the principles of the Cuban Revolution, it was agreed ... to express its absolute disagreement with this work'. Adding as a Party shot: '*This accord is extended to "Seven against Thebes", by Antón Arrufat.*' Now, after Padilla has given over not only the tongue but also the dignity and the virtue of the poet, the UNEAC (why does this name sound like a magpie's caw?) publishes his book of poems, *Fuera de juego* ('Out of the Game') – conveniently giving it a prologue. Here I have some of those pearls not for but *from* swine:

> Padilla has the old bourgeois conception of a Communist society (and) tries to justify – (with) fiction and masking – his notorious absenteeism from his fatherland in the difficult moments in which it has confronted imperialism, and his non-existent personal militancy; he converts the dialectic of the class struggle into the struggle of sexes [sic]; he hints at persecutions and repressive climates, he identifies the revolutionary with inefficiency and stupidity; he is moved about the counter-revolutionaries and about those who are shot for their crimes against the people and he hints at complicated ambushes against him that can only be an index of an arrogant delirium of grandeur or of a profound resentment ...

And they don't call him paranoiac (and put him in a madhouse, after the Russian fashion) because a police state is the best cure against paranoia: no mania of persecution is possible where persecution is a mania.

In those blows (on the breast) that did not abolish the official lash, Heberto Padilla, on making a donation of his tongue, suggests that in another burning September ('in 1965, when he returned to Cuba') I also surrendered what Quevedo used to call 'that boneless thing' to the Creator. There is no need to insinuate it when I admit it. Yes, I donated my tongue in Cuba then and I would have given other soft parts of my body (a reluctantly Vangoghian ear, for example, or my ear for music), I would have given all – even my life – provided I escaped from that paradise with an inborn sin (cf. Che Guevara quoted by *Verde Olivo*, or the monster praising Frankenstein: 'the guilt of ... our intellectuals and artists resides in their *original sin*: they are not authentically revolutionary . . . The new generations will come free from original sin . . .' – or else) and freed myself from that Ordeal by Fidel or Judgement of Marx. Then I advised all my friends in Havana to camouflage their historical pockmarks with cosmetic excuses and contrition makeup – but to follow as soon as possible the sage advice of Francesco Guicciardini, a friend of Machiavelli, given 500 years ago: 'No rule is useful to live under a bloodthirsty tyranny, except perhaps one, the same as in times of plague: *flee as far away as you can.*'

My crime, incautious reader, was not to create or to *support* or to *cover up* but to *denounce* infamy, to reveal who ate the lotus of the intellectuals, to warn that the red apple has been poisoned, to lift my eyes and to see disrobed the despot they describe to us as the good king dressed in promises. Whether this unveiling amounts to a counter-revolutionary action, to heresy, to treason or whatever is all the same to me. It was some time ago that I assumed that blame. I want, yes, to say that I consider Heberto Padilla infinitely less an accomplice than all those political guests with their baggage of excuses, who spend their vacations in the *triste tropique* and when they are not describing a society of miseries like the Land of Cockaigne (of sugar), they return imitating the simian trinity: they saw *nothing*, they heard *nothing*, they say *nothing*. Because

> Great is truth, but still greater, from a practical point of view, is silence about truth. (Aldous Huxley, *Brave New World*.)

(1968)

Throwing a Cable

NR 198 23 / 12
LONDON. JDE. (AMSUDET REDCHEF VOTRE 6–1357).
CABRERA INFANTE, UN.

'I detest any compromise, whether it be political or "human".' It is because of this totalitarian politicization of life, because of this "*engagement a la rigueur*" that I have left Cuba.'

Speaking is Guillermo Cabrera Infante, the most well-known Cuban novelist of his generation (he is 39 years old). His latest book, *Tres Tristes Tigres*, winner of an award in Spain, is soon to be published in France: he has books translated into French, English, Italian, Swedish, Hungarian, Czech, Polish and even Chinese and lives in London in a modest ground floor flat, with his wife Miriam, two daughters from a former marriage, 14 and 10 years (both very tall, pretty and, as he says, 'painfully shy') and a fantastic lilac-coloured Siamese cat called Offenbach.

Any question which is put to him, Cabrera Infante transcribes on his portable machine, in front of which he remains seated. Then he writes what can be read below:

'You can say that I am a "drop out". But Communism, like the Mafia, does not allow resignations. It was Brezhnev who said: "When one chooses Communism, it is for always." I spurn this eternalizing of public attitudes. I know that leaving your country is not leaving your Party – although your country has been converted into a party and into a single party at that: *The* Party. In Cuba writers have to adjust their points of view to the political needs of the Government and the Party. Down there writers share the same opinion as their Government only afterward.'

SUIVRA EG 20.00

NR 199 23 / 12
AMSUD
LONDON, JDE. CABRERA INFANTE, DEUX.

Guillermo Cabrera Infante, native of the province of Oriente, like Fidel Castro – and like Batista – was a diplomat of the Cuban Regime from 1962 to 1965, in the capacity of cultural attaché and later chargé d'affaires in Brussels (Belgium). He returned to Cuba for the funeral of his mother, whose death had been caused as much by neglect in the hospital as by illness, although he is the first to say that these are accidents that can happen anywhere in the world. But there he saw and judged what had happened to his country – and when he succeeded in leaving to join the wife he left in Brussels, it was with the intention of never coming back.

'But hasn't it been like that since the beginning of Castroism?' we asked him.

'As in Soviet Russia in the Twenties, there were times – that lasted more than ten days but less than ten months – that moved Cuba,' he answers. 'A glorious time. Unfortunately that golden age ended some time ago – the rest is propaganda.'

Q. 'It couldn't last?'

A. 'I don't know. I only know that they did not do the impossible, not even what was necessary for it to last. There is a popular Cuban joke that is perhaps a form of folk wisdom. You know that Fidel Castro said: "History will absolve me."

'In this story the people say to him: "Yes but geography condemns you."'

Q. 'Is your attitude shared by the young intellectuals and writers?'

SUIVRA EG 20.07

NR 200 23 / 12
AMSUD
LONDON, JDE. CABRERA INFANTE. TROIS.

A. 'My information is fragmentary and therefore incomplete. But if we attend to the words of Lisandro Otero, Vice-President of the National Council for Culture, there are "counter-revolutionary intellectuals who act underhandedly" and must be replaced by new intellectual cadres who are totally partisan. Where Otero, a tropical version of Zhdanov, says "counter-revolutionaries", I would say "intellectuals with critical spirit – and moral valour". The word "counter-revolutionary" is a useful weapon of terror. The Czech intellectuals are counter-revolutionary for Brezhnev and for Gomulka – but also for Fidel Castro. Not long ago, they arrested in one night 500 youths accused of being "hippies" – that is "counter-revolutionary". But none of this affects the regime since in Cuba of every 27 persons one is an agent of State Security.

'The recent accusations against the poet Heberto Padilla and the playwright Antón Arrufat show to what point the latitude of the word "counter-revolutionary" reaches. Padilla is accused of having defended me publicly in Cuba, but also of crimes against ideology. Arrufat is condemned for his plays but also for his homosexuality. Nevertheless, the two have only one feature in common: disobedience. This is the capital sin for the Communist religion.'

Q. 'Is it true that there is a campaign of condemnation against you in Cuba, conducted on a national scale?'

SUIVRA EG 20.16

NR 201 23 / 12
AMSUD
LONDON, JDE. CABRERA INFANTE, QUATRE DERNIER.

A. 'In effect it is a campaign of defamation, but one that follows a pattern.

'My only crime has been to break the barrier of silence, to terminate that agreement of red and pink gentlemen regarding the injustice created (in Cuba) in the name of justice. This conspiracy does not surprise me. It was Orwell who said that "To be corrupted by totalitarianism one does not have to live in a totalitarian country".'

The interview was over. While getting up to go, it occurs to us to think about the portraits of 'Che' Guevara that adorn the shops and flats of the nearby King's Road, about the cult that so many young English people dedicate to him, about the fervour that the Castroist regime has aroused among European students.

And we ask the writer, when he is already closing the door on his modest home cheered by a small lighted Christmas tree: 'But? How about this nostalgia that has been spilled around the figure of the *Caudillo* Fidel Castro?'

He has this definitive answer: 'This is an up-to-date *Caudillo* – as Perón was for Argentina and Trujillo for Santo Domingo.'

FIN EG 20.25

(23 December 1968)

Letter to a Chain Gang

Mr F. F.
Revista *Indice*
Madrid

London, 15 January 1969

Sir – I have just read in Number 258 of your journal about a supposed polemic sustained between Heberto Padilla and me. As you well know, the said polemic never took place and has been entirely fabricated in *Indice* – or, worse, somewhere else. By choosing a text mutilated, arranged and published by the newspaper *Granma*, organ of the Government and the Communist Party of Cuba and not my interview just as its originators published it in *Primera Plana*, you have not only opted gratuitously for a historical and literary falsification, but have been converted in passing into publishers of the Cuban ideological and political line – in a word, into Castroist (press) agents. It does not amaze me that you can change so cheerfully in *Indice* from the bleak black swastika on the brown shirt to the red carnation in the lapel; what amazes me is that you still have energy down there to be an apologist for rigidity in opinions and political militancies. Or perhaps you are right and your current Fidelism is nothing more than *falangismo* by other means: to take a leap forward from a dying totalitarian state towards a thriving totalitarian island. If this is so, I salute in *Indice* the signs of the effective continuity of a certain Spanish political thought. You are the worthy inheritors of those who pronounced one of the vilest celebrations of slavery – I refer, of course, to that royalist slogan, '*Vivan las Caenas!*'[1]

---

1. *Translator's Note*. This refers to the cries of 'Long live the chains' with which King Ferdinand VII (a most reactionary monarch in a dynasty of truly backward kings) was received when Napoleon kidnapped him and he was restored after a series of popular (and loyalist) revolts. After his restoration in 1814 he repudiated the Spanish Parliament, reimposed the Inquisition and ruthlessly repressed the Liberal uprising of Rafael del Riego, that was in effect a first Spanish Republic.

The polemic about Padilla is, in truth, a crisis of growing up.

Julio Cortázar in *Primera Plana*, 20 May 1969

BACKGROUND TO EXILE

The Turk's Head

Nazim Hikhmet, the Turkish poet, spent seventeen years of his life in a Turkish prison. What is rare, truly extraordinary, and significant is that when he came to Cuba in 1961, recently freed from jail, he never spoke of the Turkish prison. Perhaps he thought that his prison was a form of freedom. He spoke of Russia: of the Russia of Stalin, of the purges of Stalin, of all possible forms of Stalin.

During an interview with the board of *Lunes*, he turned to one of the interviewers – José Hernández, he who will never write *Martín Fierro*, the *exaltado* – and said to him: 'Don't kill yourself please. Don't imitate Mayakovsky. Above all, one must not commit suicide as one must not let oneself be killed. Look, I was in Moscow, I lived in Moscow, when Vladimir killed himself.'

'He was going to try on a new suit that morning.'

'Then, once he was dead, everyone threw themselves on his corpse like political jackals. Even his most intimate friends (you know them by name, I knew them personally) spoke ill of his last gesture. One must let oneself be killed by his enemy, not by his friends.'

Then, more in private, he spoke with the editor of the revolutionary magazine. In parables and Oriental anecdotes he made him see that he was in danger, that another Stalinism was in*cuba*ting, that the purges would not be long in coming.

'Leave,' he said, finally. 'Travel, manage to travel, invent trips. Make yourself seen outside, be a presence with your absence. And, above all, start to choose your lucky star!'

After many a moon José Hernández, also known as Pepe el Loco – Mad Pepe – killed himself by bullfighting with a bus on Linea Street. The bullbus was actually a mad cow.

P.M. Means Post Mortem

This is the biography of a little night movie found guilty before it opened.

P.M. is a brief essay in free cinema, following rather than the English school of film making the films of the Maisles brothers and in particular *Primary*, shown by one of the Maisles in Cuba with the aim of making a movie on a day in the life of Fidel Castro. *P.M.* lasts barely twenty-five minutes without an apparent plot line and it depicts the ways and joy of a few *habaneros* one day at the end of 1960. It is therefore some sort of moving mural about the end of an era. One sees Cubans dancing, drinking and, in one moment of the camera's travels through bars and seedy cabarets, a fistfight. The movie starts early at night in downtown Havana and ends early in the morning on the other side of the bay.

P.M. is visually centred in the place of the action. But at the end pop singer Vicentico Valdés is heard singing his hit, the *bolero* 'A Song in the Morning'. The images and this sweet song create in the spectator a sensation of solitude and instant nostalgia. That this little movie has achieved such a feeling among Cuban spectators is perhaps its greatest achievement. Formally, as the American critic and novelist, Irving Rosenthal, then a visitor to revolutionary Cuba, pointed out – it is a study in film textures.

Made with the most primitive means (an old wire recorder to which a long cable was added to make it portable, a 16mm hand camera, mistreated by daily newsreel use, roll-ends for film) and its cost barely $500, *P.M.* had an appreciable critical success in Cuba and abroad. This is not gratuitous because the film was ahead of its time and someone as demanding as Jonas Mekas, the apostle of American underground cinema, praised it as 'formally interesting', at the Festival of Experimental Cinema at Knokke le Zoute in 1963.

What indeed turned out really extraordinary is that this brief documentary was converted into a document. Not in itself, certainly, but as the lever of a whole upheaval in the annals of culture under Castro. It was the first work of art submitted in Communist Cuba to accusations of a political stripe, brought to historical judgement and condemned as counter-revolutionary. That there has been no criminal more innocent in the history of relations between the Cuban Government and the culture of the country, only emphasizes if not its nature at least its destiny: chosen as unique by a historical process that started out being a-totalitarian. The political trial to which *P.M.*, its makers and the defenders of both were submitted has not ended. Ten years later many of those who participated in that process are still being persecuted for crimes as diverse as 'left-wing infantilism', 'homosexuality' or 'application for counter-revolutionary emigration'. It is an indication that the accusations against *P.M.* were labels to cover up a design which was not merely political but made in a police state.

THE PROTAGONISTS

Sabá Cabrera was born in Gibara, Oriente province in 1933. In his adolescence he was one of the most interesting painters to be found in Cuba in the forties. Praised by the masters of the time – Víctor Manuel, Wifredo Lam, René Portocarrero – he gave up painting when he found himself impeded by the tuberculosis that he suffered between the ages of fourteen and twenty-one. After being completely cured, he abhorred painting, perhaps from associating it with his illness. He studied journalism, which he had to abandon when the school was shut down in the last years of the Batista dictatorship. Connected in the school with students like Guillermo Jiménez, Santiago Frayle and Ricardo Alarcón, he found himself involved in more or less clandestine activities from 1956 on. In 1957 he was invited to the World Youth Festival in Moscow. In 1958 he started work as a newsreel editor at Channel 12, which was beginning the transmission of colour images on television in Cuba. With the triumph of the Revolution and with Channel 12 shut down, he moved over to work for Channel 2, also as editor of its newsreel and later as curator of its film library. He met Orlando Jiménez-Leal at this time. After the *P.M.* affair, he was sent to Madrid as commercial attaché. When his mother died in 1965 he came to Havana, where he was sacked without explanation. Sent to Madrid to 'collect his things' – a diplomatic-revolutionary euphemism for being dismissed from one's post – because of the Minister of Foreign Trade's desire to show a degree of independence from the security services, he decided not to return to Cuba and flew to Rome where he made counter-revolutionary statements. Later he travelled to New York, where he now lives, working at a clinic for 'restoring films'. He has made no more movies since then.

Orlando Jiménez-Leal is a boy wonder of the cinema. Barely nineteen years old when he filmed *P.M.*, he already had more than five years' experience of 'shooting film'. But nothing in his childhood presaged such an aptitude. Son of a baker from the suburb of Regla, his association with the cinema is the history of an obsession. At thirteen he left home. Not to join the navy or to travel with a circus, but to live in a film-studio – literally, since there he slept and ate. It was the nearest thing in Cuba at the time: the headquarters of a national newsreel.

After the *P.M.* case he was accused of an even greater crime while filming inside the Presidential Palace for the Channel 2 newsreel. The security service caught him in the act of committing what was called a counter-revolutionary crime: showing in close-up the nervous hands of President Dorticós as he made a speech. Expelled from the Palace first and then from his job, Jiménez abandoned Cuba. Currently he lives and works in New York, as co-owner of an advertising agency. He also co-directed *El super*, a full-length film of great success, and made, with Néstor Almendros, *Improper Conduct*, a short documentary denouncing Castro's treatment of homosexuals.

Bites from the Bearded Crocodile

The decline of the so-called Cuban cultural renaissance started when Virgilio Piñera came down the ladder of the Czech aeroplane that brought him back from Brussels via Prague. He disembarked with mincing steps and, fluttering like a tropical butterfly suddenly sprung alive from a collector's case, stopped briefly and then kneeled and leaned forward to kiss the red Cuban soil – only to smack the tarmac instead. (This gesture proved to be some sort of near-miss-cum-hubris for, you see, the runway had recently been covered with a Russian blacktop.) Though it didn't really all begin then, but a few months earlier when *Lunes*, the literary supplement of the newspaper *Revolución*, on which Virgilio Piñera was one of the principal collaborators (the word was usually meant in its second sense), was banned and closed down for good. Only it didn't begin then either, but when they censored and sequestered *P.M.*, a documentary that didn't have any political content to warrant the seizure. That was really the beginning of the end. But let's start at the beginning – which was when dictator Batista decided to flee instead of fighting and the 26th July Movement took over the Government in the name of the Revolution, its martyrs and the poor people of Cuba.

Let's face it once and for all: it is true that there were more houses of ill repute than publishing houses in Havana before the Revolution – or more properly, Fidel Castro – seized power in 1959. But you can say the same of New York now, where, on a stroll down Broadway, you'll be able to meet more whores than writers and see more pimps than literary agents – no equation intended. If this happens in the metropolis, imagine the colonies. Havana was then the nearest Latin city to urban America – unless you want to insult Tijuana and call it a city. Before 1960 there were a few private houses but these mostly published textbooks. Other adventurous printers, whom you could equate with gigolos, were engaged in some kind of vanity publishing. Even José Lezama Lima, one of the true great poets in the twentieth-century Spanish-speaking world, submitted to the extortion willingly, even gladly. It was his rich friends who paid for the publication of such masterpieces as *Enemigo rumor* ('Alien Rumour', 1941), *Aventuras sigilosas* ('Adventures in Stealth', 1945) and *La fijeza* ('Transfixed Beauty', 1949). It didn't matter that Juan Ramón Jiménez, the fastidious Spanish poet, a Republican refugee and future Nobel winner, had made seemingly extravagant claims about young Lezama's poetry. If he wanted to see his poems published, Lezama (or his patrons) had to pay for it. It was a flagrant literary mugging: your money or your silence. For Lexama, as for most Cuban writers then, it was a question of perish to publish.

Of course there were real publishing houses then, not just one, as they have in Cuba now, run by the State at the service of Party propaganda. The one they have now is the National Printing Press where, under the rule of Alejo Carpentier (more later), 100,000 copies of *Moby Dick* were published – slightly abridged. The Cuban publishers had cleverly rewritten Melville. You had Ishmael, you had Queequeg, you had Captain Ahab, of course, you even had Father Mapple: but you couldn't find God in the labyrinth of the sea. Before the Revolution, some *ci-devant* publishing houses worked for the government in power, any government, even foreign ones. They would print Venezuelan authors in costly and garish editions, paid for not by the writers but by Venezuela herself, a country always rich in oil but poor in ink.

But there were other cultural achievements beyond printing deluxe editions of Cuban classics in the very young Caribbean republic. One must not forget that Cuba was the last colony in America to become independent from Spain. This happened only in 1902, and after that the small island was submitted to some sort of dependence on the United States until 1958. The strong links were only economic and political, though, and the American influence never really amounted to much in Cuban cultural life, which was oriented towards Europe, especially to France and Spain. Most Cuban writers could read and write French fluently, but very few had any English. The only thing American that was truly influential – and this only at a popular level – were Hollywood movies, as pervasive in Cuba then as they are everywhere now. Those remarkable achievements I mentioned before were in painting, architecture, the theatre and, of course, Cuban popular music: though actually extinct on the island, like the Cuban manatee, its irresistible siren song can be heard from Paris to Paraná.

Believe it or not, the history of Cuban literature is one of the longest in America. It is not as long as the history of literature in England, naturally, but there were poets writing and being published in Cuba before they named the American colonies New England. According to lore, the first Cuban poet was a Canarian settled on the island who had the appropriate name of Silvestre de Balboa – his last name was fit for a conquistador, his first for silvan poetry. But Balboa wrote an epic instead. Published in 1605, *Espejo de paciencia* ('The Looking Glass of Patience') is a long poem that lay forgotten for more than two centuries, until it was rediscovered in 1834. It was about that time that José María de Heredia (cousin to the French Heredia, famous for *Les Trophées*) wrote what is considered the first Romantic poem ever written in Spanish, 'The Ode to Niagara', conceived under the influence of Chateaubriand's prose and composed in exile in the USA. The nineteenth century gave us José Martí's powerful prose, written in exile in Spain and New York. Martí is perhaps the greatest prose-writer in all of the Spanish nineteenth century. A spellbinding novel, *Cecilia Valdés*, was written by Cirilo Villaverde in his exile in the 1880s in New York. Besides many minor poets, the Cuban nineteenth century produced a great poet, the subtle Symbolist Julián del Casal, after Rubén Darío the greatest *modernista* poet ever. One should never confuse *modernismo*, with a small m, with Modernism in English, a quite different, later literary mood. The *modernista* was a strictly poetic movement, initiated in Latin America but taking off from the French Symbolists: ten poems that shook the Spanish-speaking world, mainly through the genius of Rubén Darío, the Indian poet from Nicaragua who sang of swans in Spain. Martí, himself a poet, was a precursor of *modernismo* without actually having to do with Symbolism, French or otherwise. Martí was a true original. Unfortunately, he is known today only as the man who provided Pete Seeger with the lyrics for his apocryphal song 'Guantanamera'. The gospel according to Vanessa Redgrave is that José Martí, who died on a Cuban battlefield in 1895, is a close friend of *Comandante* Fidel Castro's! Of course anachronism is Miss Redgrave's forte – but this time she was dead right to show us how anachronistic it would be for a poet to be friends with *Comandante* Castro.

During the infamous Cuban Cultural Congress in 1971 (much more later), Fidel Castro said in his closing speech that before the Revolution there was only one theatre in Havana. He was lying, of course. But then the British reader might say that at least the man cared about culture. It would have been better if he didn't. One bit of learned advice to the British reader: if you hear Margaret Thatcher or her successor speaking in the Commons on the state of the box-office in the West End, you'd better brace yourself because an English version of Dr Goebbels is surely limping his way down Whitehall – to take care of the Ministry for Public Enlightenment and Propaganda. The truth is that Fidel Castro never cared about the theatre or literature, or even mural painting, for that matter. He only cares about power and its total tool, propaganda. He is known even to have used Beckett's plays, to have said that *Waiting for Godot* showed the kind of capitalist-induced misery you'll never find in Cuba now. Godot forbids.

With all its political infirmities, and there were many, travellers to Cuba were surprised at what they saw. Even in 1958 somebody as alien as Sacheverell Sitwell enthused over a song about Havana nightlife. As late as 1959, the British historian Hugh Thomas recognized that Cuba was one of the few tropical countries to have created a modern culture of its own. He also noticed that Fidel Castro owed his power not to guerrilla warfare, as Thomas had believed before visiting Cuba, but to television. The way Castro used the television screen for his seizure of power was very similar to the use Adolf Hitler made of PA systems in Germany in the thirties. At the time, 1960, Cuba had more TV sets than Italy, statistics that come as a surprise to too many. In 1969 I was at a party in Hollywood at the house of a famous and wealthy film-maker, when he began asking me about life in Cuba. Those were the days of the war in Vietnam and Americans were regressing to the late thirties, the decade when they suffered the vision of the blind in seeing Stalin as a saviour of civilization as they knew it. Among the guests of this liberal director there was a well-known Austrian philosopher, now deceased. He had been a refugee from Nazi Germany since 1937. Both he and the movie director were Jewish. So was the director's beautiful wife. After hearing my story of dire needs and disasters the popular philosopher asked me in his still thick German accent: 'But isn't it true zat unter Doktor Castro de island has made a great progress in public health and education?' I'd heard the question before in many languages, with different accents, and I had a bitter double analogy on the tip of my logical, not ideological tongue: 'Mussolini made the Italian trains arrive on time for the first since they were invented. Hitler, on the other hand, not only laid out the autobahns' – he grimaced at my plural – 'but lifted Germany out of its economic and moral morass. At least, that's what my favourite great-uncle used to say over and over in my home town in Eastern Cuba. This happened before World War Two. Funnily enough, my great-uncle, a sweet soul, was a Nazi who became a vegetarian when he knew Hitler was one. Even funnier, Fidel Castro was born barely thirty miles away from us about the same time I was born. He could have been indoctrinated by my great-uncle. After the war, my great-uncle used to say over and over that Hitler was not dead. That was American propaganda. Hitler was alive and biding his own time to come back to power. One day he stopped believing Hitler was alive. I knew it because he dropped the Führer's name for good. When Fidel Castro came to power my great-uncle became a *Fidelista*, but only after he saw that Castro was the typical tough tyrant. You see, my favourite great-uncle was a diehard totalitarian. He was also the town's savant.' The professor, a survivor of the concentration camps and then a teacher of Marxian dialectics in Hollywood, saw I had a point when I hinted at a Hegelian *bon mot*: 'Even if the education programme was a success, which it wasn't,' I said, 'what good is teaching millions to read when only one man decides what you read, in Prussia as in Russia? Or in Cuba.'

In Britain, there is an ignorance of Cuba which is of the Right ('Please tell me,' I have been asked by Sir Keith Joseph, a Conservative intellectual of sorts, 'is there any freedom of speech in Cuba?'): but British gentlemen of the Left, believe me, also ask stupid questions, full of political naïvety signifying furious ideological ignorance. They often ask me eagerly about *samizdat* in Havana and how Cuban dissidents are faring. They, of all people, should know very well that *samizdat* (for a Cuban the very word is alien and it only makes sense in Spanish as an anagram to ask for my cup of coffee *dame mi taza*) is a typically Soviet phenomenon of the sixties. It exists now only because the present Soviet Government permits it. The same applies to Soviet dissidents, grandchildren of Khrushchev or sons of Brezhnev, who are expediently allowed to emigrate to Europe and America. Stalin, quite simply, would have sent them straight to Siberia. Who are the dissidents in East Germany or Bulgaria? Nobody, merely because the Communist Governments in those countries cannot afford their existence. Writers in Czechoslovakia comply with Communist dicta or go to gaol directly. Where are the dissidents in Albania? Nowhere, of course. Cuba, sad to say, has become a Latin American Albania, a deadly oxymoron. But few foreigners know this. Political hell is paved with the ignorance of strangers. The Holocaust was fully known only after the war. The gulags were publicized only after the death of Stalin. The atrocities of Castro, not all of them literary, will be known in full only after his demise, whenever that may be. Then people not only in England but everywhere, those of the Right as well as those of the Left, will know the true nature of the regime led by a man of infinite cunning and deceit, a beastly power-hungry egomaniac who is the bearded white double of Amin. It's not for nothing that he is Cuba's Commander-in-Chief, Secretary-General of the Party and President for Life. He also likes to be called a doctor, when what he really is, again like Amin, is a crude actor playing his version of *Macbeth* to the largest captive audience in the Americas.

But when Fidel Castro entered Havana in January 1959 like a larger Christ (as Severo Sarduy wrote from Paris with love), some of us saw him as some kind of younger, bearded version of Magwitch: a tall outlaw emerging from the fog of history to make political Pips of us all. However, the outlaw never became an in-law, only a law unto himself: the Redeemer was always wearing a gun on his hip. When Castro took Batista's place there were three great older writers in Cuba: two powerful poets and a maverick belletrist. They were all strongly influenced by French literature. This holy, unholy trio were José Lezama Lima (1910–1976), Nicolás Guillén (1902-) and Virgilio Piñera (1912–1979). The first two were the poets – one popular, populist even, the other unpopular and hermetic. Later Lezama surprised everybody with the publication, in 1966, of his dense, impenetrable masterpiece *Paradiso*, a novel that is a confession and a memory and had a *succès de scandale* in Cuba for its intoxicating scenes of pederasty mixed with poetry in a prose that made Hermann Broch's look easy in comparison. Virgilio Piñera was a short-story writer, a novelist and a playwright – and also a sometime poet. Nicolás Guillén, a mulatto who in the twenties had written *poesía negra* (which had to do with Negro poetry what Shirley Bassey has to do with black music), fell under the spell of Lorca when he visited Havana in 1930 and shortly afterwards his Negro poetry was transformed into some kind of tropical flamenco. Later on, in the thirties, he was writing so-called social poetry and became a member of the Cuban Communist Party – to his undoing. Guillén had a truly poetic gift, though in a minor key. In fact, he is, together with César Vallejo and Pablo Neruda, the most widely translated Latin American poet of the century and has been nominated several times for the Nobel Prize. The musical connection is an apt one, for Guillén was a writer of pop poetry *avant la lettre*, the composer of soft song lyrics rather than of a powerful verse. His words cried for music and they got it. But it is really a pity that Pete Seeger was not around when Guillén wrote his early *sones* (a kind of rumba), to compose another 'Guantanamera' with Guillén's lyrics instead of Martí's verse. For Guillén was the true contemporary of these Cuban folk tunes that don't have to pay royalties to their real composers.

The fourth horseman of Cuban literature had not even been living in Cuba for many years, if he ever lived there at all. Earlier, when he was young, he left Havana for Paris and didn't come back until the Nazis chased him out of France. His name was Alejo Carpentier (1904–1980). Born in Havana of a French father and a Russian mother, Carpentier was a failed architect, a dabbler in *poesía negra* (he even wrote a Negro novel dealing aptly with black magic, meaning Afro-Cuban *santería*), a fine musicologist and finally a serious writer. But it was only when he moved to Venezuela in 1946 that he started writing his truly important novels, from *The Kingdom of this World* to *The Chase* and, perhaps his masterpiece after *Explosion in a Cathedral*, *The Lost Steps*, extravagantly praised by Dame Edith Sitwell (ah, those Sitwell siblings, meddling in things Cuban!) and Graham Greene and Tyrone Power. (Power wanted to write, produce and star in successive film versions of Carpentier's *Kingdom* and *Lost Steps* but he lost the crown to a coronary.) Something peculiar happened with Carpentier and Cuba: he loved the island but the island didn't love him. In Havana, he was just a journalist, almost a hack in posh magazines. Abroad, he became an all-round author and a true novelist. He even wrote in Paris the libretto for an opera composed by Edgar Varèse. (This filled him with Parisian pride in a Varèse vein.) Back in Cuba in 1940 meant for Carpentier, a vain man, back to journalism and the radio. But once established in Venezuela in the late forties and fifties, he wrote his best books. At the same time he was the holder of a Venezuelan passport and was a cultural force to reckon with in Caracas. But to his everlasting guilt, he even organized an international music festival sponsored by the Venezuelan version of Batista, Pérez (the Pig) Jiménez. When he finally came back to Cuba for good – after the Revolution was safely in power – he became a bureaucrat (as manager of the only printing house in town) and though he was later promoted to France, for services rendered, as a deluxe diplomat living in the Seizième, he never wrote another novel there – though he published at least five books with such a label on the cover.

Carpentier suffered from two lifelong obsessions, somehow interconnected: the art of the novel and the Nobel Prize for Literature. Chasing after the latter, he lost his writing steps and the kingdom of this world became a lethal tyranny that has finally done him in. As the Frenchman says: 'Nothing kills a man more quickly than to be forced to represent a country.' Carpentier, the poor son of a bitch, represented for twenty years a cause that he never believed in. In the end, ill with terminal cancer, Paris became a painful feat. He had to write in the early morning and later have breakfast and lunch and sometimes dinner with important French writers, with the exception of Sartre who despised him for being a civil servant with two masters. His output became meagre and his books grew poorer in style but richer in political content to please Havana and thus stay in Paris. He never got the Nobel Prize, by the way. Death got him first.

Those were the most representative names in Cuban literature when

Fidel Castro came down from the mountains armed to his rotten teeth. (Then he wore tattered olive-green fatigues, now he wears a general's uniform and his teeth have been beautifully capped.) There were other writers, of course. Lino Novás Calvo, for example, one of the best short-story writers in Latin America, Hemingway's favourite translator and the man who first translated Faulkner and Huxley and Lawrence into Spanish when he was living in Madrid and collaborating with Ortega y Gasset on his *Revista de Occidente*, a review that changed a culture. There was Fernando Ortiz, the anthropologist and the man who coined, among others, the word transculturation, a cultural concept more than a word. And Lydia Cabrera, a white girl from a former rich family, the first woman to penetrate the sacred *santería* cult and the *abakuá*, originally a secret society for men only, with blood initiation rites which excluded, under threat of death, women and pederasts. Her work in what could be called anthropoetry was pioneering in America, where black cults of the occult, from Haiti to Brazil, are sometimes stronger than in Africa. The black continent didn't create voodoo: America did.

Other relevant artists of some international standing who were born in Cuba and remained are Alicia Alonso, the dancer, Wifredo Lam, the painter, and two great musicians, Amadeo Roldán and Alejandro García Caturla, probably better composers than Brazil's Villa-Lobos and the Mexican Carlos Chávez. Both died too young to be known abroad, except in such recherché musical circles as the coterie around Nadia Boulanger in Paris or by John Cage's epigoni everywhere. Roldán, also a remarkable conductor, died of a skin cancer in the face in his early thirties. Cruelly deformed, in his last performances he had to climb the podium wearing a silk mask. Caturla, a country judge who used to compose even on the Bench, was killed by a thief on bail: he had refused to acquit him the day before. Ironically, this petty criminal was never pardoned and died in gaol – not because he had killed a judge but because he had assassinated the Great Caturla.

Mme Alonso had been a prima ballerina with the American Ballet Theatre since its inception in the early forties. When she decided to come back to Cuba and form a ballet company she was sponsored by a local brewery and later by the Batista Government, who thought her international star status was good propaganda for Batista, who hated the ballet. Later she was adopted by the Revolution as our dancing daughter. She has indeed been around a lot and is still shuffling along at seventy. Of all the artists mentioned above, she is the only one who was trained in the United

States and belonged to the American school of dancing. Today her *corps de ballet* dances *à la Russe* – in opposite steps to their *prima ballerina assoluta*.

You cannot call Francis Picabia or Anaïs Nin Cuban. They merely happened to have been born on the island, but were later formed in France, where they made their reputation – whatever that is. They were as Cuban as José María de Heredia, who at the turn of the century dreamt of the coral reefs and azure seas and verdant hills he saw in his native Santiago de Cuba – but wrote of them in French alexandrines in Paris. Or Italo Calvino, born in a village near Havana but raised in Rome. But there have been some important artists born in Cuba who stayed in the country, like those painters who belonged to the Cuban school of painting of the forties and whose works can be seen in museums all over the world. One of these painters was Fidelio Ponce de León. He claimed to have been a descendant of the Spanish conquistador who discovered Florida by chance when he was looking for the Fountain of Youth. He died an old man at the age of fifty – the painter not the discoverer, dreamers both. One of his best paintings hangs for ever on a wall of a smart, make-believe New York apartment, where it dominates the single set of Hitchcock's thriller *Rope*. Ponce, who was constantly asking friends and foes alike, 'Do they really know me in Paris?' never saw the film. He died, destitute and tubercular, before *Rope* opened in Havana in 1948.

The most famous Cuban artist ever was, of course, José Raúl Capablanca, also known as the Chess Machine, considered by many to be the greatest chess-player who ever lived. Born in Havana in the late nineteenth century he has been buried in Cuba since 1942. Can anybody imagine how the Castro regime would have capitalized on the living legend Capablanca was? Fêted and filmed everywhere, the immortal story of his short, successful life is the stuff of which propaganda is made. Even Che Guevara mourned his death – twenty years later. Twelve facsimiles of Alicia Alonso dancing dozens of demented Coppelias wouldn't have meant so much to Communist Cuba.

I am not forgetting – how could I? – countless minor poets, bad poets, terrible poets and short-story writers by the dozen who thrived in the tropics with their small talents and enormous egos, opportunists all. It was in 1959, when editing *Revolución* (which he founded clandestinely in 1956) that Carlos Franqui, then a revolutionary Cabinet-maker (four or five new ministers owed their jobs to him and not to Fidel Castro), decided that the paper needed a literary supplement. That's how *Lunes* was born – a goat-child, a devil-goat, a scapegoat finally. A journalist since 1949, a movie critic from 1954 onwards and managing editor of *Carteles*, the second most popular weekly in Cuba and the Caribbean, I was appointed editor of *Lunes*. It would prove an almost fatal mistake for everyone involved.

Revolución had been the voice from the underground of the 26th of July Movement, the organization which did more to put Fidel Castro in power than the puny guerrilla he has made everybody believe did the job. Above ground now, *Revolución* became a very powerful newspaper indeed, the first in Cuba and the only one that had access to the innermost recesses of power in the Government and in Cuban political life in general. Moreover, it had, for Cuba – at the time a country of some seven million people – an enormous circulation. *Lunes* profited from all this and became the first literary magazine in Latin America or Spain to boast of a circulation of almost 200,000 copies. *Lunes* had a lot of pull – and not merely literary push.

My first mistake as an editor was to try and clean out the Cuban literary stables by sweeping the house of words with a political broom. That's called an inquisition, and it can induce writer's block by terror. The magazine, with the heavy weight of the Revolution and the Government behind it plus the 26th of July Movement's political prestige, literally blasted many writers into submission – or oblivion. We had the Surrealist credo as our catechism and Trotskyite politics as our aesthetics, mixed like bad metaphors – or heady drinks. From this position of maximum strength, we proceeded to annihilate respected writers of the past, like Lezama Lima, simply because he dared to combine in his poems the anachronistic ideologies of Góngora and Mallarmé, now joined in Havana to produce disjointed verse of a magnificently obscure Catholicism. We actually tried to assassinate Lezama's character. There were other, older casualties, like the Spanish dentist who wanted to be a Dantist and whose recently published novel was pulled from its Asturian roots with laughing-gas. At the same time, the magazine exalted Virgilio Piñera, a man of Lezama's generation, to the position of a Virgil out of double hell. He who had always been a pariah in his own country, a novelist who was terribly poor, almost destitute, became our favourite father-figure, the house-writer. Another mistake. Besides being an excellent short-story writer anthologized by Borges, a playwright of genius (he penned a play after the fashion of the theatre of the absurd when Ionesco hadn't yet staged *The Bald Prima Donna* and long before Beckett wrote *Waiting for Godot*) and a pleasant poet, Virgilio had a particular fault. As with San Andreas, it was a very visible one. Virgilio, like his Roman counterpart, was a pederast. Perhaps the epitome of the literary queen, a Cuban Cocteau known not for his plays but for his playmates. That was food for gossip in Paris, but this was revolutionary Havana and there was no room left for queens shouting 'Off with his head!' in a revolution: all Cuban queens ended up with no head, not even their own, especially not their own.

Third original sin in a row: there were too many talented people grouped around *Lunes*, each one supporting the Revolution in their fashion. José Baragaño, the Surrealist poet who came back from his exile in Paris where he was befriended by André Breton himself, who hated Sunday painters and minor poets, was pet poet and pet pest on the magazine. Heberto Padilla, born in the same town as Baragaño (the funnily named Puerta de Golpe in Cuban tobacco country: Puerta de Golpe literally means, as if Larry Grayson had named it, 'Shut the Door'), came from exile in the Berlitz Academy in New York, and cultivated an easygoing but mordant style of verse. Padilla was a powerful poet in *Lunes*. Both Baragaño and Padilla, pugnacious poets, were out to get the older generation, many of them civil servants from Batista times and even before, as was the case with Lezama. Calvert Casey, who, in spite of his name and having been born in Baltimore, was not only a Cuban but a true *habanero*, delicate and precise in the exquisite concealments of his homosexual prose, though he had a mulatto lover, openly a couple. Antón Arrufat was a disciple of Piñera – and not only in playwriting. Pablo Armando Fernández, a minor poet but an accomplished diplomat capable of extricating the magazine from any critical jam, was our pint-size Sebastian, a moving target. He is still in Cuba, still a diplomat but no longer a poet, minor or otherwise. He is professionally dedicated to being host to political tourists from the United States, where he lived in a closet in Queens, before returning to Cuba, already married, in 1959. Like Padilla and Hurtado, I persuaded Pablo to come back to Cuba from the States. Oscar Hurtado, also an economic exile in New York, was a dear giant of a man, like the family elephant, but an incredible shrinking poet, inimical to Lezama and his *Orígenes* group, and died not only unrecognized but unrecognizing in an asylum, suffering silently and alone from a varicose brain. And, never allowed to leave the boat when it was listing (*Lunes* was on all the lists of the security service, the counter-espionage service and the police), there was I, who, though an inveterate smoker, couldn't share the peace pipe because I smoked only cigars then. The magazine, as you can see, was manned by a manic crew of pederasts (wait and you'll see why this fact of life became crucial to our demise), the happy few, as Che Guevara labelled us, who were not real revolutionaries, with a skipper who, no doubt due to myopia, saw the danger signals very, very late. Too late, in fact. I discovered that we had no true power when we hit what seemed a mere sectarian wave but was the tip of the totalitarian iceberg. *Lunes* should have been called the *Titanic*, for very soon we were in deep, cold waters. Before sinking, I saw clearly that we had tried to make the Revolution readable, therefore livable. Both tasks proved utterly imposs- ible.

In its heyday, however, *Lunes* expanded quickly. Soon we had branched out into a publishing house (*Ediciones R*), whose first published book was *Poesía, revolución del ser* ('Poetry, Being's Revolution', though, only a few months earlier, its author, José Baragaño, still the Paris Surrealist, had titled it *Being is Nothingness*). This collection of poems was, in 1960, a rehashing of all the Surreal formulas of the preceding twenty years, but now sang a song to the Revolution and to the Heideggerian being for death. Though now, instead of nothingness, it offered everythingness. Opportunism, thy name is poetry. Then we had an hour, at peak time, on television, second channel to the left. We formed a record company, called Sonido Erre, or Sound R, R for Revolution. Our publishing venture – quite successful, by the way – was at the time the only independent publishing house left in Cuba. All the rest had already been nationalized. But it was no privilege, this solitary printing-press under private owner- ship. It was, in fact, as ominous as a smoke signal in Apache territory. It was then that I committed a mistake which proved to be a blessing in disguise. I helped Sabá, my brother, with the completion of a documentary he was making with the cinematographer Orlando Jiménez-Leal – at the time the youngest photographer in Cuba, capable of handling a Cinema- scope camera when he was fifteen, quite a film feat. As its title suggests, *P.M.* would be a view of Havana after dark, the camera peeping into the small cafés and bars and dives patronized by the common Cuban having a last time before the political night closed in. I liked the idea. I gave them the money to edit the documentary, print two or three copies and design the titles. All this was done outside the Film Institute – that is, officialdom – in our TV channel labs but quite openly. *Lunes* got the exclusive rights to show the picture on its programme and we showed it. There was no censorship for us on television. As in my magazine, we were our own boss. After all, we were the offspring of *Revolución*, the newspaper of the Revolution, the voice of the people. We were omnipotent – sort of.

But a spectacle needs spectators, and the film-makers wanted to show their little night film of music to a live audience. There were still two or three cinemas not yet nationalized in Old Havana. One of them special- ized in documentaries. The owner agreed to run the film: the next step was to obtain permission from the *Comisión Revisora* to show the picture in public. The *Comisión Revisora* was the same censorship office as in Batista's time and further back: at headquarters you could see *The Great Train Robbery* and even Edison's *The Kiss*. In the past, what the censorship office did was to cut a bit of bare ass here or a tit there, in French films mostly, which were not even soft porn but were treated then as the hardest core. But, now, the *Comisión Revisora* was under the control of the Film Institute, which is nothing like the British Film Institute but a state monopoly which controls everything that has to do with films – from making pictures to importing, distributing and exhibiting them. The Cuban Film Institute owns all the cinemas, drive-ins and movie-houses in Cuba – and you must go to them even to get a roll of film for a snapshot camera. On top of that, they had a long-standing feud with *Lunes*, which they labelled as decadent, bourgeois, avant-gardist and, the worst epithet in the Communist name-calling catalogue, cosmopolitist. In turn, we saw them as despicable bureaucrats, a bunch of ignoramuses with artistically reactionary ideas and no taste at all. The director of the Film Institute, Alfredo Guevara (no relation to Che Guevara), was the worst Communist commissar to deal with films this side of Stalin's Shumyavsky. To take *P.M.* to the Film Institute for approval was a naïve and daring thing to do – like Little Red Riding Hood drilling the wolf's teeth. But, you see, it simply had to be done. Some time later, *Revolución* was going to be killed and reborn under the name of *Granma* – and it has indeed shown big bad teeth ever since. Nevertheless, we didn't expect such a brutal bite. The *Comisión Revisora* not only refused to give any seal of approval to *P.M.*, but banned the film, which was accused of being counter-revolutionary and dangerous rubbish and licentious and lewd. Furthermore, they seized the copy sent for approval.

This was more than we could stomach – even if there was to be a purge at the end of it. We had been expecting a showdown with the Film Institute. But it was to become a shoot-out. The banning of *P.M.* occurred in June 1961, in what could be termed a period between two wars. In April that year the Bay of Pigs invasion took place. All the invaders had been impressively routed in less than forty-eight hours and, rather hastily, Fidel Castro had declared Cuba a socialist republic, though the country would be neither. The times were auspicious for the Communist Party (now merged with the remnants of the 26th of July Movement and the ghost of the Revolutionary Directory into one single party called ORI), so much so that its Council for Culture had decided to stage a writers' congress in Havana and to invite a few foreign novelists of note, such as Nathalie

Sarraute, who were sympathizers of the Revolution but not necessarily Communists. In the meantime, in some kind of political montage (hooves of Klansmen's horses galloping, then cut to damsel in distress, then cut to threatening blackamoor), *Lunes* was seen busily collecting signatures to protest about the sequestering of *P.M.*, the little night film. This was going to have wider implications, with the Communist congress about to take place.

When they saw us coming and knew we meant business the Council for Culture panicked. They asked us please not to turn the letter against the Film Institute into a manifesto by making the statement public. In turn, they promised to postpone their congress and wash our dirty linen indoors by orchestrating a meeting (of all the factions concerned) with Fidel Castro and almost the entire Government. It was a sneaky ambush, the varmints. They invited all the intellectuals involved – and then some. The meetings took place every Friday for three consecutive weeks and were held in the spacious hall of the National Library, built by Batista but claimed by Castro.

The day of the first meeting came like doom. On the rostrum were Fidel Castro, President Dorticós (since deposed), the Minister of Education Armando Hart (now Minister for Culture), his wife Haydée Santamaría, head of the Casa de las Américas (later a suicide), Carlos Rafael Rodríguez, then an influential Communist leader, now the third man from Moscow in Havana, his former wife Edith García Buchaca (then the head of the Communist cultural apparat, who later lived under house arrest for fifteen years), Vicentina Antuna, boss of the Council for Culture (under the political spell of Buchaca), Alfredo Guevara, no Che at all but a tropical Machiavelli giving advice not only to the Prince but also to the King. Then bringing up the rear came the scapegoats, lambs feeding with lions: Carlos Franqui, editor of *Revolución*, and I, as editor of *Lunes*.

President Dorticós, who thought then he was the president, declared open the meetings that were to become a trial. He announced, with the nasal voice of the commodore of a yacht club, which he had been, that everybody could speak his mind freely. Anybody could have their say now. Speak up comrades. Nobody did. We were all paralysed and gagged by such a panoply of political power. Suddenly, out of the blue alert: a timid man with mousy hair, frightened voice and shy manners, slightly suspect because he looked frankly queer in spite of his efforts to appear manly, said that he wanted to speak. It was Virgilio Piñera. He confessed to being terribly frightened. He didn't know of what, but he was really frightened, almost on the verge of panic. Then he added: 'I think it has to do with all this.' It seemed that he included the Revolution in his fear, though apparently he meant only the crowd of so many so-called intellectuals. But perhaps he was alluding to the life of a writer in a Communist country: a fear called Stalin, a fear called Castro. We'll never know. Virgilio didn't say any more and meekly went back to his seat. Nobody was allowed to speak from his own seat: to have your say, as President Dorticós boomed his order, you had to stand in front of a microphone on a proscenium, facing the audience but taking good care that you didn't turn your back on Castro. Political distortions meant physical contortions. Eventually everybody talked, even those who didn't know how, like Calvert Casey, a compulsive stammerer.

It became evident to everyone (defendants, prosecutor, jury, judge and witnesses) that this was a show trial held in private: it was not only *P.M.* but *Lunes* (and everything it stood for in Cuban culture) that was in the dock. Kafka in Cuba, Prague in Havana. Most of the people who took the stand were sworn enemies of the magazine – and some had reason to be. Like the fat woman who sent in some sonnets that were published in the magazine with the title: 'From the Fat Lady of the Sonnets'. The pained dentist who thought he was Dante *al dente* complained bitterly. He not only complained but cried and prayed (he was a Catholic convert) and called us chartered murderers who assassinated writers as if they were so many characters. We were the hit-and-run men of culture. The Marxian Mafia perhaps? It was an impassioned though toothless speech – and he got what he wanted all along: a job as Ambassador to the Vatican as a consolation prize.

There were other witnesses, all for the prosecution, and a masked witness took off his mask for everyone to see his face: Baragaño, the Surrealist poet who instigated all the attacks against Lezama and his disciples, had turned on us! There was an expected enemy, though: Guevara, by now a guerrilla speaker who couldn't say his r's, delivered a blow below the belt at both *Revolución* and *Lunes*. Before I was an *Infante terrible*, now I was a babe in the wood. Fidel Castro himself talked to us. Characteristically, he had the last word. Getting rid first of the ever-present Browning 9mm fastened to his belt – making true a metaphor by Goebbels: 'Every time I hear the word culture, I reach for my pistol' – Castro delivered one of his most famous speeches, famous not for being eight hours long, but for being brief and to the point for the first time since he became Cuba's Prime Minister. His deposition is now called 'Words to the Intellectuals', and it ends with a résumé which Castroites everywhere claim to be a model of revolutionary rhetoric but which is really a Stalinist credo: 'Within the Revolution, everything,' he thundered like a thousand Zeuses. 'Against the Revolution, nothing!' Everybody applauded, some in good faith. Though not I. I *had* to applaud even when I knew full well what he meant by his slogan. It had been the case of a sentence without a verdict: through-the-looking-glass justice.

The outcome of the trial was that the Film Institute gave back the seized copy of *P.M.* to its makers, but the film remained censored. *Lunes* was banned, too, and barely three months later ceased appearing. There was an official explanation for the stay of execution: an acute shortage of newsprint. A likely story. Three more literary publications saw daylight after the meetings: *Union*, a monthly from the Writers' Union, dedicated to Communist culture, *Gaceta de Cuba*, a weekly published by the Writers' Union that resembled *Lunes* like Cain resembled Abel, and an illustrated magazine issued by the Council for Culture that looked like a tattered *Tatler*. Three red reviews all in a row. The Communists had their congress (why do they need congresses so much? – is it a fixation or a fix?) with foreign writers as guests. In a typical gambit I was made one of the seven vice-presidents of the newly formed Writers' Union, so I wouldn't complain. I didn't. I never intended to. You see, I had been in the Soviet Union the year before and found out what happened to all the writers who dared displease Stalin, even *sotto voce*. A tropical version of Stalin, even behind beards, could be tropically lethal.

It was then that Virgilio Piñera came back from Brussels via Prague and missed kissing Cuban soil by about three feet. Some hubris. Early one morning, on militia duty at the gates of *Revolución*, I had a phone call from him. I was surprised at first, then I was astounded. Virgilio was calling me from the local gaol at the beach where he lived. He told me he had been arrested on charges of being a passive P. Virgilio meant P not for Piñera or for poet but for Pederast. The night before there had been some sort of carnal *Kristallnacht* in Havana. A special branch of the police called the Social Scum Squad arrested on sight everybody walking the streets at night who looked to the naked eye like a prostitute, a pimp or a pederast. (This police operation was called the Night of the Three Ps.) But at the time Virgilio was miles away, in bed (he believed it was healthy to go early to bed and to rise early), in the shack he christened his big bungalow on the beach. How in hell was Virgilio in gaol?

The explanation lies in an infamous collective illness. The Government had and still has an obsession with queers, queens and kinks – in a word, all kinds of pederast. Five years later, they were even to build concentration camps for homosexuals, especially those with a cultural bent. In the

Congress for Culture and Education of 1971 one of the main resolutions, which sounded more like a resolve, was not to allow homosexuals (now called 'infected with a social pathology') to occupy positions from which they could pervert Cuban youth. (What about Cuban children?) They should have no prominent place in cultural circles or artistic activities, nor represent the Revolution abroad. (That was when Alicia Alonso's male *corps de ballet* took a step, a grand jeté from Prague to Paris.) It was Fidel Castro himself who closed the Congress with those words.

Why this 'pathological' aberration? Fidel Castro is, as gays in the United States like to say with terrible Spanish grammar, *mucho macho*. On the other hand, Che Guevara considered homosexuals to be sick people who must give way to the politically healthy 'new man' made by Communist Cuba. There are multiple levels of irony here. The other Guevara, Alfredo, was a notorious fag, protected by Fidel's own brother, Raúl Castro. Che Guevara ended up as the name of a boutique in Kensington that folded years later. New Man is a brand of jeans made for boys and girls alike, while narrow trousers were prohibited wear in public in Cuba. A Castro convertible in New York is not a sofa-bed as advertised, but a man who goes either way – what Gore Vidal now calls a bisexual. A final irony is that the heart of the homosexual world is in San Francisco and is called Castro Street. Gay, yes, but with a vengeance.

Piñera the Pederast got out of gaol, thanks to the intervention of Edith Buchaca, not out of pity but from political considerations. She knew the trouble a homosexual writer in gaol can make. She had read Oscar Wilde and she remembered the lines:

> In Reading gaol by Reading town
> There is a pit of shame.

She mispronounced 'Reading', but knew the ballad by heart. After the closure of *Lunes*, 'that pit of shame', most of the homosexuals on its payroll (Calvert Casey, Antón Arrufat and Pablo Armando Fernández, my managing editor) went to work for Casa de las Américas under Haydée Santamaría. This curiously contrary woman (whose personal and political contradictions led her to commit suicide last year) was a true Fidelista. She was one of only two women to take part in the attack on the Moncada barracks in 1953, where both her brother and his fiancée died after being tortured. (She was forced to witness the torture.) She had been with Castro's guerrillas in the mountains since 1956. But she had a 'weakness for culture', as she explained, while admitting that she was just an ignorant peasant woman. The first claim, being ignorant, was true, but not the second. She was the dutiful daughter of a well-to-do family of the provincial bourgeoisie, which was not richer but more influential locally than its Havana counterpart. The rich in Cuban provinces elected mayors, selected high-society members and ran the local high schools. In tobacco country they were even more powerful – but they could all be illiterate. Once she told us and not in the strictest confidence: 'What a coarse peasant ignorant woman I am! I always thought that Marx and Engels were a single philosopher. You know, like Ortega y Gasset.' More relevant, however, were Haydée Santamaría's revelations when she came back from her first trip to Russia and confided radiantly: 'I met Ekaterina Furtseva in Moscow. You know, the Minister for Culture. A beautiful woman!' – which she was – 'and so kind', which she wasn't, Old Steelsmile. 'You know what she did? Minister Furtseva explained to me, woman to woman or, rather, comrade to comrade, what happened to those writers and artists who died under Stalin – and why they simply had to die. They were not killed because they were hermetic poets, bourgeois novelists and abstract painters. Actually, they had to be shot because they were Nazi spies, not artists. Would you believe it? Hitler's agents all of them! They had to be exterminated. Do you understand?' I understood. Ah, what a naïve and dangerous revolutionary woman she was! A gust of old Russian cold crept up my spine.

Nevertheless, she allowed Arrufat to transform the *Revista Casa* into the best literary review in Latin America since *Sur*, edited by Victoria Ocampo and Borges. Until Antón ran into trouble for publishing a pederast poem by José Triana, a young playwright who has recently taken up exile in France incognito. The poem spoke obscurely of some innocent, not indecent, homosexual practices – like daubing themselves with KY jelly, an emollient used for love-making – and asked naïvely how many flavours you could get abroad, which is now the Flavour of the Month? Haydée Santamaría didn't know a thing about homosexual love – for her, heterosexuality and the missionary position were what the Revolution ordered. But she had to dismiss Arrufat on the spot because an envious poetaster, Roberto Retamar, formerly cultural attaché in Paris, personally informed President Dorticós of Arrufat's heinous crime against nature and the revolutionary people of Cuba. Arrufat was sacked and Retamar rewarded, as in any Soviet socialist realist novel, with the editorship of the coveted *Revista Casa*. Arrufat was even accused of the grave mistake of inviting Allen Ginsberg to Cuba. Ginsberg was a Communist from New York, but, being an ur-gay, he was seen as less than pink in Havana. Furthermore, while in Cuba, he made some scandalous statements in public. Enough is more than enough in Castro's Cuba, and Ginsberg was held incommunicado in his hotel. The next morning he was put on a plane and sent packing to Prague, where he could have a Czech mate.

Meanwhile, in another consolation prize-giving (the closure of *Lunes* had left me without a job, vice-president of the Writers' Union or not), I was appointed cultural attaché in Brussels (just on the other side of the moon as seen from Havana), that dark secluded place Virgilio had come from. It was there that I found out all about the shenanigans of Retamar and the expelling of Arrufat from his haven by Haydée. I knew of the existence of UMAP, concentration camps behind their camouflaging acronyms: Units for Military Help to Agricultural Production. Apparently, the final solution for the homosexual population explosion was the sugar-cane plantation. As Joseph Tura would have put it: 'Concentration camps for queers: we do the concentrating and they do the camping.'

Even poor passive peaceful Calvert Casey got into trouble when he dared tell a Mexican writer of the Left, just one more political tourist, that there were camps for homosexuals all over Cuba – and they were not exactly summer camps. This was a carefully guarded secret which Calvert knew about through the gay grapevine. Next morning, as in a guilty hangover, the Mexican tipped off Haydée Santamaría that she had counterrevolutionaries in her house, who told tales, very dangerous lies for Casa de las Américas. He whispered a gringo name, Casey. Calvert was severely reprimanded and demoted, but never sacked.

When in 1965 I came back to Cuba for my mother's funeral, Havana seemed like the wrong side of hell. Virgilio, more than a guide to Avernus, looked as if he were playing the shivering old maid in one of his plays of the absurd: a queen playing canasta all the time. Lezama was secretly embroidering his *Paradiso* in the dark every night, telling nobody, not even his wife, in the morning: always cunning, being both Ulysses and Penelope. Huge Hurtado was now more shrunk than small Virgilio with his fear of breathing. Only Arrufat, impelled to follow in the wake of an alien (an Allen Ginsberg he never really met) wanted to take a band of gay desperadoes to shout out slogans before the place where Dorticós lived. This was as suicidal as the kamikaze attack on the Palace, where Batista hid in 1957.

To dissuade him from such follies, Virgilio had to tell him stories about what it was like to be a pederast writer, formerly from *Revolución*, now in gaol: 'Counter-revolutionary thugs would simply tear you apart, child. They'll have you drawn and quartered for a cause that has ceased to exist years ago.' Arrufat finally saw the light (Virgilio was his master) and shut himself up in his room to write a play. It was based on *The Seven against Thebes*, with a Zeus who wore a black beard and thundered from Mount Olympus for hours on end. Still eager to provoke, he wanted to call the play 'Death to the Infidel'. Virgilio then quoted the other Virgil: *'Facilis descensus Averno.'* With crocodile tears, I decided to leave Cuba. I had seen and been heard long enough and had made my mind up. I didn't tell anybody I was leaving for good, but I did.

Enter Padilla laughing. My unpublished novel *Three Trapped Tigers* had won Spain's most prestigious literary prize, the Biblioteca Breve Award, in 1965, the year I left. The runner-up was *The Passion of Urbino*, by Lisandro Otero, who had been my classmate at the School of Journalism from 1950 to 1954: he was a staunch anti-Communist but he had become a paunchy bureaucrat at the Ministry of Foreign Affairs.

Otero was a sometime friend of Padilla's, who used to call him *La Bella Otero* and other names and was always pretending that he lusted after Otero's wife, a Cuban ivory beauty, who had belonged to Havana high society and was now Haydée Santamaría's right arm at the Casa – but still a beauty. She knew how to spell Engels and could tell Karl from Groucho, gesturing amiably with her long white hands and even longer nails. She had exquisite manners too. We could all see what Lisandro saw in her: but what could she see in Ugly Otero? asked Padilla.

Pasión de Urbino was published in Havana in 1967, and as Otero was such a big shot now at *El caimán barbudo*, Cuba's echo to the Russian *Krokodil*, they asked for reviews, or rather favourable opinions, from all and sundry. Padilla sent his – which was a vicious panning of Otero's novel and a paean to mine, just published in Spain after having a spot of bother with the Spanish censors. 'Scandal!' 'Slander!' they cried at *El caimán barbudo*, which literally but not literarily means 'The Bearded Crocodile'. Daggers flew from the bushy beard of the Communist cayman. Padilla had dared to praise a bad book by a counter-revolutionary living in exile in London, while failing to see the enormous merits of the excellent novel by Comrade Otero, a revolutionary living in Cuba – as he did when Batista was in power. (My comment.) The Padilla Affair had its roots in Communist dialectics: he who does not praise a Party member is an enemy of the Party. But Padilla, though not a Surrealist, sees the poet as a literary *agent provocateur*, his words a concealed weapon, wearing cloak and dagger. He never recanted about the review. His enemies never relented, and in a Communist country, which lives and dies by the book, a war of words is considered warfare by other means. Silence is the last refuge of the class enemy and scepticism a dangerous deviation to the Right. Silence, rather than acquiescence, was what saved Boris Pasternak. Being outspoken or indiscreet, more than being relevant, was what lost Osip Mandelstam. Padilla, who had lived in Moscow, chose to be both poets at the same time. He could write a poem deriding Fidel Castro and keep it quiet, playing a safe Mandelstam, and, like Pasternak with Stalin, he would talk with Fidel Castro on the phone as *l'enfant prodigue* of Cuban letters, a wayward child of the Revolution who could always be chastised and mend his ways – the Prime Minister playing the role of a Cuban sugar daddy. But Padilla's heart belongs to dallying.

Padilla was not Pasternak and Fidel Castro was not Stalin: the poet became a case – known in Cuba and all over the Spanish-speaking world and beyond as the 'Padilla Case'. But Padilla was not going to be arrested by Scotland Yard and tried at the Old Bailey. Totalitarians never bother with what they call bourgeois justice: Fidel Castro was a lawyer by training and so was Dr Goebbels. In 1968 Padilla won a prize for poetry in a contest sponsored by the Writers' Union in Havana and awarded by an international jury. Among the jurors was J. M. Cohen, a British critic, translator and anthologist of Spanish literature, then vaguely connected with the Cuban cultural milieu. The title of Padilla's book was *Out of the Game* and this very name was anathema to some members of the Writers' Union, especially its president, the old Communist poet Nicolás Guillén, who tried to put pressure on the jury to reverse their judgement. According to the dicta of the Writers' Union, Padilla's poems were flagrantly counter-revolutionary. But were they? The poem that gave the collection its title was dedicated to Yannis Ritsos, a Greek Communist poet, and began like this:

> Dismiss the poet!
> He has nothing to do.
> He doesn't play the game.
> He isn't enthusiastic.
> His message is muddled.
> Doesn't even think about miracles,
> He meditates all day.
> He always finds something to complain about.

Innocent enough lyrics and the music was always by Theodorakis. On top of that, Ritsos had been imprisoned in 1967 by the Greek military junta. Obviously, this couldn't happen here. Other poems were even less critical (if you can call the preceding lines critical). Perhaps the most daring poem was 'To Write in the Scrapbook of a Tyrant':

Protect yourself from those who vacillate,
because one day they will know what they don't want.
Protect yourself from those who mumble,
Juan-the-stutterer, Pedro-the-dumb,
because one day they shall find their strong voice.
Protect yourself from the timid and the frightened,
because one day they will not rise when you enter.

Is this the poetry that will launch an American invasion? Not bloody likely. At the time, in the frightful Spanish-speaking world of juntas and generals, in Franco's Spain, Blas de Otero was writing and publishing openly Communist poetry and getting away with it. He died in Spain. Nicanor Parra, in Pinochet's Chile, was cryptically critical and nothing ever happened to him. He still lives in Chile. In Mexico, Octavio Paz, a strong voice for strong words, resigned as Ambassador to India as a gesture against the Tlatelolco Square Massacre ordered by his president, but it was his own conscience that forced him to quit. He has always lived in Mexico. This was the international climate when, in Communist Cuba in April 1971, Heberto Padilla was arrested *à la Russe*: in his house, early in the morning, stealthily but, a Cuban touch, having been given a quiet alarum by members of his block's Committee for the Defence of the Revolution.[1] Padilla remained barely a month in gaol, but this time, as didn't happen with the closure of *Lunes*, which was very cleverly staged, there was an international uproar. The mail carried private communiqués for discreet official eyes only and an open letter was sent to Fidel Castro himself. The missive from former friends was considered by the Cuban PM as an enemy missile. It was signed, surprisingly enough, by such leftist writers and sponsors of the Revolution as Jean-Paul Sartre and Simone de Beauvoir, Italo Calvino, Marguerite Duras, Hans-Magnus Enzensberger, Juan Goytisolo, André Pierre de Mandiargues, Alain Jouffroy, Joyce Mansour, Alberto Moravia, Octavio Paz and some others who couldn't even pronounce the name of Padilla correctly – much less read his poems. It was a case of tit for tat. The European and Latin American intellectuals had been disillusioned with the Cuban Revolution for quite a while, and Fidel Castro was fed up with what he considered trespassing into his

---

1. These Committees are para-police groups that operate in every large building, in every town or city, supposedly to protect the Revolution from its enemy within – the most powerful army in Latin America will take care of the enemy without. The members of Committees for the Defence of the Revolution are some two million Cubans, who engage in these activities willingly or not – though the Committees, like the People's Militia, are supposed to be strictly voluntary.

personal domain. The truth is that the foreign writers and the Cuban dictator were no longer useful to each other.

For a moment, though, it looked as if the poet's head were about to roll. But Fidel Castro is a cunning version of Stalin, and Padilla, who wrote a poem about the tongue of the poet being requisitioned by the state, recanted and was released – though not before he had made a *viva voce* confession at the Writers' Union main lecture hall. The trial of *Lunes* had been *in camera* and its verdict private. Now we had not a quiet show trial but a public confession that was quite a show. Padilla, not reading from any script but obviously following a scenario, in a very Orthodox Russian and un-Cuban Catholic way, confessed to all kinds of literary and political crimes – and even crimes against the state and the people of Cuba. He also named a few accomplices, among them the august, orotund figure of Lezama Lima, conspicuous that evening not only because he was publicly called a subversive poet but also because he was the second Cuban literary figure to be absent from such a nice cultural soirée – obviously staged by State Security. The other absentee was also significant. It was the President of the Writers' Union, Nicolás Guillén, who conveniently pleaded being ill with the catarrh.

After the Soviet-style confession – 'I know that my experience, comrades, is going to be an example. It must serve as an example for others' – there was an even more vehement and indignant letter to Castro, signed by yet more writers on the Left, like Nathalie Sarraute and Susan Sontag. The undersigned were ashamed (and angry) at the outrage of a poet confessing to imaginary political crimes. They talked of the despicable indignity meted out to Padilla. They didn't, of course, say how many unknown workers and anonymous peasants had been forced to do the same all over Cuba in the past (since the inception of the Revolution in fact) and how many more will one day find, *in corpore*, that Padilla's public recanting was no cruel and unusual punishment but a confession devoutly to be wished.

In Communist countries you have, as Milosz once said, the captive mind. But what about the captive body? Let me speak now of sadder, wiser men, like Valladares and Cuadra, poets in prison, captive minds in captive bodies. Armando Valladares, the poet in a wheelchair as he has been called in France, was condemned to thirty years in gaol in the early sixties, when he was barely twenty. In prison, as a result of ill-treatment and his various hunger strikes in protest against ill-treatment, he became an invalid. (By the way, many political prisoners have died in prison in Cuba, after suicidal hunger strikes directed at atrocious prison conditions. Not a single one of those who have died is known to the outside world, not even José Luis Boitel, the former Castroite student leader. International press agencies and the big newspapers of the Western world have not printed a single news item about those men: it is a lot easier to write interminably about Bobby Sands.) Angel Cuadra was sent to prison in 1960 as a convicted counter-revolutionary. He was released in 1976 and arrested again in 1977, without ever being allowed to leave the country. The second time round his crime was to have written poems about his miserable life and sent them abroad to be published. In England, nobody, except those with Amnesty, knows about these exotic people and their pathetic rather than poetic plight. They have suffered in Cuban gaols and in the process have learnt how to write poetry in silence. Their minds are not captive any more, only their voices.

After Padilla confessed crimes that were as ludicrous as confessing to setting the Reichstag on fire, blowing up the battleship *Maine* in Havana harbour and masterminding the Gunpowder Plot, a season of calm came over the island. All was quiet on the Cuban cultural front – for a while. Lezama Lima, who couldn't publish anything after being implicated by Padilla, died. Death came to him as a Catholic. He died in obscurity, unrecognized in a public ward at the old hospital which before the Revolution was only for the destitute. (The ward was curiously named Sala Borges.) After Lezama's death, nothing was said about him for a while. Later, the state-owned National Printing Press published a prose poem by him about a dead poet called Licario, l'Icare, Icarus, the enraptured flyer who is killed by his own poetic flight. It was full circle for José Lezama Lima: from vanity publishing to vanishing print.

Then came Reinaldo Arenas, who looked a little bit like Lezama and a little bit like Padilla with a red head. He has read enough books to be able to spell trouble. Arenas (whose name means sands) was the only Cuban novelist who could be called a child of the Revolution: a poor peasant from Oriente Province, living in Havana. It was there that he published his first novel, *Celestino antes del alba*, with too much Faulkner in it but a truly remarkable book. Being a peasant (remember, this was supposed to be a peasant guerrilla revolution), he was adopted by the Writers' Union as the great red hope of the revolutionary novel. Not for him the Catholic erudition of Lezama or the degenerate decadence of Piñera's cadences or the cosmopolitan vices of a novelist exiled in Paris like Severo Sarduy, also young, also brilliant.

But Arenas had, as they say in Cuba, *un defecto*, which sounds almost exactly like 'disaffected' in Spanish. He was a homosexual – and a very obvious one: now a Havana *loca*, a mad girl. He didn't do anything to suppress or even to hide it. He belonged to the younger generation of homosexuals which produced the gay movement elsewhere. Not that the Writers' Union didn't try to *reform* Arenas. They even proposed to him that he should marry, settle down into a revolutionary household – and he would be left alone. They had successfully experimented with several actors who only liked to play the queen. This was a form of therapy closer to Pavlov than to Freud, more Russian than Viennese: a cure by marriage. But Arenas was a peasant and, like peasants everywhere, a stubborn man. He refused to comply and went on with his gay ways. But then he wrote a second novel, the brilliant, original and successful *Hallucinations*.

Suddenly, Arenas was gay but hot. Not in a donkey's year had a young Cuban novelist still living on the island had such an international success – for him a *succès de folle*. It was, of course, the golden ass again. After his novel had been rejected by the Writers' Union, incompetent literarily but very competent politically, Arenas sent the manuscript abroad – without consulting the Writers' Union, a publisher who, even when rejecting a book for ever, wants to know what happens with it. Above all, *after* rejecting a book. Especially a book about a priest persecuted by tyranny. The priest was Mexican, tyranny universal. What came next to Arenas was not success but sudden recognition, disguised as a hideous nightmare. He lost his job at the National Library (a very minor post), he could no longer receive guests from abroad and he was carefully surveyed by State Security – a very literary bunch of cops. Finally, he was thrown in gaol, accused of corrupting a minor. At his trial, the *corpus delicti* was a hefty man of twenty-five with a fully grown beard and much taller than Arenas. (Arenas insists to this day that his partner was a Castro lookalike.) Be that as it may, Arenas was found guilty and sentenced to four years in gaol, for crimes against nature – and against man. He served only one year, but in the Morro dungeons, a fortress that had not been in use as a prison since the English seized Havana in 1762! He survived his imprisonment for the same reason that he was in prison: he was a stubborn peasant.

When he was finally freed, forty pounds thinner, he tried to leave Cuba come hell and high water. A pen pal from Paris sent him a rubber boat in the diplomatic pouch of a daring diplomat. They all belonged to the gay network – except the rubber boat. The inflated raft worked perfectly on the beach when Arenas tried it one night – but once in the ocean its Mediterranean manufacture couldn't cope with the pull of the Gulf Stream and split open. Arenas had to swim all the way back from the Stream through the shark-infested sea. Then he tried to swim (I could never find out how a peasant boy from the sticks became such an excellent swimmer in high water) across the Guantánamo Bay to reach the American Naval base at Caimanera, two miles away – a sanctuary for many lucky Cubans. Death or cruel punishment met those who couldn't make it: the whole no man's land, like the border between East Germany and West Germany, is jammed with self-manned machine-guns, touch-mines and electric traps; all triggered by electronic devices. Luckily, his escape attempt was a non-event. Arenas was able to leave the lethal zone and steal himself back to Cuban soil – and the prospect of gaol again.

Being fearful of coming back to Havana, he hid in Lenin Park, which is a wooded area outside the city limits. He stayed there for months, hidden in the heavily guarded woods, Lenin a lenitive and a threat at the same time. Fortunately, he had a couple of faithful friends: twins so queenly and gentle that he called them the Brontë Sisters – Brontë with an *accent aigu* over the e. It was thanks to them that he was able to survive at all and, a greater feat, to return to his flat undetected. His flat was actually a small room in an ancient and crumbling colonial hotel in Old Havana. He was there writing (and hiding what he wrote from the State Security's avid readers) when the assault on the Peruvian Embassy began. Some desperate Cubans took refuge there one day, including Arena's missing lover. Three days later there were 11,000 people seeking asylum in the embassy compound, a feat without precedent in the history of diplomacy – not even the 55 days in Peking during the Boxer Rebellion could be compared with this. Arenas thought of seeking sanctuary too, but he told himself that his streak of bad luck would abort his mission before he attempted it.

Then came the boats from Miami, the Freedom Flotilla, to the rescue in the last reel, and with them the boat people trying to leave Cuba on anything that floated. Is this the island that Columbus once called Paradise Green? The Government, to justify their contention that only 'social scum' had sought asylum at the Peruvian Embassy, forcibly filled the privately hired boats from Florida with all kinds of criminals, taken out of gaol, picked up on the streets of Havana and released from insane asylums. One day a delegate from the Committee for the Defence of the Revolution on the street where Arenas lived came to knock on his door – which was open anyway to exorcize the heat and snoopers alike. He was officially informed that he had to leave the country immediately, for he had been skimmed as scum. As it were, *la crème de la crème* of socialist degeneracy. For Arenas, it was a heaven-sent insult. He got dressed in a jiffy, ready to leave his room and ride down to Mariel, the port of departure for decadence – a Dunkirk for Cubans. Arenas had to wait for forty-eight long hours at the beach, come shine or come more shine. When his boat finally left, they were lost for two days on the dangerous Gulf Stream waters before they reached Key West, where he was locked in an American internment camp for undesirable aliens. But all this was paradise found for Arenas. Hell was left behind in Mariel, while he waited for his boat to come, fearing the Writers' Union Reading Committee might know he was leaving, for the vigilante Defence Committee had taken a decision at local level. On the beach, bleached white by the scorching white heat from a torrid sun, there were olive specks. This was not vegetation, but men: out of Doré or Dante, army personnel carrying enormous books in which every man or woman or child about to leave the island was carefully annotated – name, occupation, former address sounding like name, rank and serial number. To Arenas, this monstrous red ledger became a nightmare version of the Doomsday Book.

Is this the reward for a writer? It seems to me like the wages of an unnameable sin. But I saw Reinaldo Arenas in New York in January, and he seemed the happiest man alive. A Happy Ending. Arenas reunited with his lover in Miami, both rescued by Arenas's uncle, a mean menace in mien but a lovable man in spite of being a city policeman. In New York, it was freezing outdoors. Not the kind of weather for a boy from the sticks in Cuba, but Arenas took his shoes off and danced barefoot down those mean night streets. 'Look at me!' he shouted. 'Like Geene Kellee.' He was humming 'Singin' in the Rain'.

At the same time, almost to the day, Heberto Padilla left Cuba for good. American admirers had approached Senator Edward Kennedy to intercede in his favour with Fidel Castro. Senator Kennedy called Castro collect and twenty-four hours later Padilla had an exit permit, two plane tickets and a lukewarm farewell from Fidel himself – as Padilla told everybody later. The story belongs in the universal history of infamous fathers. Padilla was summoned to one of Castro's many palaces hidden in Havana. After shaking hands, Castro told Padilla that he had heard the rumour that he, Padilla, wanted to leave Cuba. A sly look in his eyes, he asked: 'Is this true?' Then added: 'You know that this is your country and it will be yours until the day you die. The Cuban people is your people. You can go now and you can come back whenever you want. Your house will remain intact. Neither a brick nor a book will be touched. I want you to know that.' Then the dictator dismissed the poet and sent him out of the game.

The Viennese philosopher and the Conservative thinker and the Hollywood director I'm sure will sing in a chorus: 'Ah but you see, the man really cares about poets.' So did Augustus with Ovid – and Stalin with too many poets to put in a ledger. Padilla did the right thing: he left the house and the city quickly and silently. In 1933, Joseph Goebbels saw a film by Fritz Lang. He thought it was Wagner in pictures. Knowing that Lang was one of the few great German directors still living in Germany who was not a Jew, he summoned him. In his enormous office, Goebbels told Lang that he wanted him to assume immediate care of the German film industry in the name of the Führer. Fritz Lang screwed his monocle, said that he wanted to think about it overnight, if Herr Doktor didn't mind. He begged to leave – not forgetting to click his heels before exiting. Next morning, Lang left secretly on the first train to Paris. Like Lang, Padilla had learned the axiom of the plague years.

An American editor wanted to publish an anthology of Cuban writing and he came to me for advice. I mentioned several names in secret and added that he should include the writers left in Cuba. There were about five, I believe I told him. That was last year [1979]. Early this year [1980] he came back to me again: 'How many writers for my review are there left?' I felt like a bookie. 'Well, Virgilio Piñera and Alejo Carpentier died.' Edmundo Desnoes, Reinaldo Arenas and Benítez Rojo (who was Haydée Santamaría's answer to Carpentier) exiled themselves to the United States. José Triana, in some kind of *larvatus prodeo*, did the same in France. 'I reckon there's only one writer of international standing left in Cuba, Nicolás Guillén, and about five minor poets with unpronounceable names.' 'Not much, eh?' he said grimacing or perhaps grinning. I had to agree. No, not much, really. Not bloody much.

Alejo Carpentier died, as he wanted, in Paris, but not the way he wanted. Instead of the merciful heart attack in his sleep, he had a throat cancer and awoke in the dead of night. He had suffered a haemorrhage. Then he choked in his own unwise blood. Embalmed, he was sent back to Cuba to have a state funeral and a personal wreath from Fidel Castro: 'To the great writer of the people,' said the funeral inscription – and it lied. The only true writer of the people left in Cuba, Virgilio Piñera, died a different death.

The death of Virgilio didn't come swiftly or easily either. He was in his small flat in Havana and he felt ill. Somehow he managed to phone for an ambulance, but it took three hours for the ambulance to come. Paperwork. A police state is primarily made of forms to be filled in and out. When the ambulance arrived, they found him downstairs, lying in the street, already dead. Alejo Carpentier, who wanted a heart attack, was almost eighty when he died. Virgilio Piñera, who didn't want any heart attacks, was sixty-eight. Carpentier's funeral was stately, pompous. Virgilio's funeral was another play of the absurd by himself. Rumour spread (in socialist countries, rumour runs, Party news crawls – and a running rumour is always trust-worthy) that Virgilio had died. He was to lie in state in a humble *funeraria*. There was a small group of writers, his old friends and a bevy of young writers who looked queer – and queer they were. Virgilio had been their only true teacher, their mentor, their master in the *gai savoir*. There were fast-fading flowers and there was even a wreath from the Writers' Union, with no inscription.

There was everything you need for a funeral – except the body. Some people remembered having seen it very late the previous night. It had disappeared, though, taken away in the early morning. The explanation for sneaking Virgilio's body out was that he needed a second autopsy. Virgilio needed a second autopsy like he needed a hole in the head. He had died of cardiac arrest, everybody knew that. The real reason why the body disappeared as in a cheap thriller by Agatha Christie was that the Govern-ment (or the Writers' Union) feared a crowded funeral parlour, followed by a wake, finished with a riotous funeral procession. The body was brought back from the cold half an hour before the time the funeral procession was to take place – though the funeral procession never took place.

Instead of driving the hearse at a walking pace (the custom in Havana, where funeral homes are never very far from the cemetery), as befits a decent funeral procession, the driver, following orders from the Writers' Union (or from the Government), sped away, as if he were racing in Le Mans, to elude any camp-followers. But the disciples, a new school of Cuban queers, even newer than the school of Arenas, chased the hearse in cars, on bicycles and even on foot, running and grieving: '*Ay, Maestro*, alas! You are being spirited away now but your spirit will remain with us! *Virgilio vive!*'

But Virgilio Piñera was dead as a doornail and his body is still in his tomb (or must be) at the Colón Cemetery, one of the most sumptuous graveyards in the Americas. (Even bigger than the famous Recoleta in Buenos Aires, where Borges longs to be buried to dream that he is dead.) Knowing the regime, I'm sure that Virgilio has been buried not in the Patriots' Pantheon but in what you could call a pauper's grave – though there are not supposed to be any pauper's graves in the land of socialism. All socialist dead are buried equally but some are buried deeper. This doesn't pain me at all, because it wouldn't have bothered Virgilio in the least where his body lay to rest.

It is Piñera's writings that will live, twist and giggle for ever. I am truly worried about what happens to his body of work. I know that he will soon be out of print in Cuba and never be printed again. What was left unpublished remained for a while in his furnished flat, its door sealed by State Security, illiterate agents so strangely concerned with writers and their writings. His old flat will have new, anxious tenants ready to move in, eager to clean out. All the papers found there – Virgilio's last literary will and theatrical testament – will be put in a cardboard box and buried in one of the secret sections in the basement of the State Security building. That place, where Reinaldo Arenas's unpublished novels ended up, is known by the State Security men who deal with Cubans of a literary leaning and a subversive bent (political, aesthetical, sexual) as Siberia. This long, rambling article is an effort to show it all – the cellar, the State Security building, Havana and the island – as Siberia-in-the-tropics.

But I often wonder. Why was Virgilio so eager to kiss Cuban soil that he missed?

(1981)

HAVE A HAVANA

Lorca the Rainmaker Visits Havana

Address to the Ibero-American Institute in Madrid on the fiftieth anniversary of the poet's murder, 20 May 1986

In the spring of 1930 (which was summer in Cuba as usual: a 'violent season', as the poet Paz warns), Federico García Lorca, the Spanish poet, travelled to Havana by sea, the only way to get to the island then. At the same time Hart Crane, the American poet, homosexual and alcoholic, travelled from Havana to New York – and never arrived. He jumped overboard to disappear for ever, leaving behind as cargo a long poem and various virulent verses as testimony to his mincing steps on earth. Lorca, on the other hand, was in his prime. He had just finished *Poet in New York* with its splendid 'Ode to Walt Whitman'. I am not going to comment on this book, that long lucid lament, except to touch on its musical, merry coda, that '*Son*[1] of Blacks in Cuba' which transformed Cuban popular poetry and the American vision of Lorca.

Around that time, apart from the more lamentable than lamented Crane, writers and artists who would later have as much of a name as Lorca visited Cuba. Some lived in Havana 'for free'. Never, by grace or disgrace, did they meet Lorca. Not in Old Havana nor in El Vedado nor in La Vibora nor Jesús del Monte, not in Cayo Hueso nor in San Isidro nor in Nicanor del Campo, which was not called Nicanor del Campo then.

Hemingway for instance was living in Old Havana, in a hotel whose name would have pleased Lorca, *Ambos Mundos*. There, in the best of both worlds, Hemingway wrote a novel of love and death (of little love and dour death) whose first chapter offers a view of a city of dreams and nightmares.

The novel, *To Have and Have Not*, deals in a violence that Lorca never knew. In any case not before his end in Granada. But it is possible that in 1930 he would have known by sight one of those three men who now

---

1. Cuban dance rhythm.

started for the door, and I watched them go. They were good-looking young fellows, wore good clothes; none of them wore hats, and they looked like they had plenty of money. They talked plenty of money, anyway, and they spoke the kind of English Cubans with money speak.

At that time, in that country, Lorca must have dressed like them and worn pomaded, plastered down hair. Dark as he was, for Hemingway he could have been a rich Cuban boy, and he would know what happened to a rich Cuban boy when he played games of death.

As they turned out of the door to the right, I saw a closed car come across the square toward them. The first thing a pane of glass went and the bullet smashed into the row of bottles on the show-case wall to the right. I heard the gun going and, bop, bop, bop, there were bottles smashing all along the wall.

I jumped behind the bar on the left side and could see looking over the edge. The car was stopped and there were two fellows crouched down by it. One had a Thompson gun and the other had a sawed-off automatic shotgun. The one with the Thompson gun was a nigger. The other had a chauffeur's white duster on . . .

Old Pancho . . . hit a tire on the car . . . and at ten feet the nigger shot him in the belly . . . He was trying to come up, still holding onto the Luger, only he couldn't get his head up, when the nigger took the shotgun that was lying against the wheel of the car by the chauffeur and blew the side of his head off. Some nigger.

Lorca never knew that terrible Cuban violence nor those Havana blacks, *sbirri eccellenti*. His blacks were sons of the *son*, *reyes* of the rumba. Lorca had this habit of doing the rounds of the popular districts of Havana, like Jesús Maria, Paula and San Isidro and sometimes reached the Plaza de Luz, the Caballería dock there beside it and even La Machina dock, where the opening action of *To Have and Have Not* takes place. But he never knew the obscene night that ended with sleeping beggars and dead rich kids. Although at the end, like Hemingway, he found out what a violent death at dawn was.

Another American who came to Havana in those first years of the thirties to leave in the bay a wake of art was the photographer Walker Evans. Evans recalls: 'I did land in Havana in the midst of the revolution.' I don't know how these Americans always manage to fall right into the middle of a revolution in Cuba! As Evans was in Havana in 1932 and the dictator Machado did not fall until 1933 to be replaced by Batista months later, Evans could not have fallen into the middle of any revolution, except the revolting solutions that a feisty rum gives you. But Evans insists:

'Batista was taking over' and Evans was drinking Bacardi. 'I had a few letters to newspapermen, which turned out to be lucky because it brought me to Hemingway. So I met him. I had a wonderful time with Hemingway. Drinking every night.' What did I tell you? It's the revolution called Cuba-libre. One part rum to one part Coke. Stir. Serves two. According to Evans, Hemingway 'was at loose ends'. Easily explained. Those are the uncertain years of *To Have and Have Not*, his first Cuban novel. But Evans did know where he was going and his photos of Havana are like 'Son de negros en Cuba', a graphic romance in which the blacks of Havana are revealed as dapper dandies in white.

I can't even attempt to describe these masterful photos that now belong in the museums. But there is a black dressed in pure white linen, with a straw hat and shoes just shined by the shoeshine boy seen in the background. Well dressed with a brown tie and matching handkerchief, a dandy detained for ever on a corner of Old Havana, next to a magazine stand, his sharp stare directed towards an object hidden by the frame of the photo that we now know is time: this makes the photograph a portrait, a work of art, a thing that *To Have and Have Not* never was, never will be and that Lorca's sinuous *son* is.

But Havana was not so violent or so violet a city.

The writer Joseph Hergesheimer, as American as Hemingway and Evans, says of Havana in his *San Cristóbal de La Habana*, one of the most beautiful travel books that I have read:

> watching the silver greenness of Cuba rising from the blue sea, I had a premonition that what I saw was of peculiar importance to me . . . Undoubtedly their effect belonged to the sea, the sky, and the hour in which they were set . . . The Cuban shore was now so close, Havana so imminent, that I lost my story in a new interest. I could see low against the water a line of white buildings, at that distance purely classic implication.

These are poetic not historical visions of the city. But, one moment, there is a second – or maybe a third – opinion about this *ancien régime* Havana. I found this description in the *Encyclopedia Britannica*, at times our contemporary:

> Capital and commercial metropolis and the largest port of Cuba. The city, which is the largest in the Antilles and one of the first tropical cities of the New World, lies on the north coast of the island, towards its western extreme. Its location on one of the best bays of the hemisphere made it commercially and militarily important from colonial times and is the greatest factor responsible for its constant growth from the 235,000 inhabitants that it had in 1899 to the 978,000 of 1959. Other factors that contributed to its

growth are its healthful climate and its picturesque setting and those cheerful entertainments that once made it a Mecca of tourism. The average annual temperature varies by only ten degrees Celsius with a mean of 24 degrees. Although many mansions of the residential districts have been expropriated, from a physical point of view the view is no less impressive. *The appearance of Havana from the sea is splendid.*

That was the Havana that Lorca saw. There he composed one of his freest, most spontaneous pieces. It is a letter to his parents in Granada published in Madrid not long ago. Lorca speaks of his successes as a lecturer, quite real, and of his imaginary risk when witnessing a crocodile hunt and taking part in it in cold (and sometimes burning) blood. Fortunately Lorca was not a hunter and exempts us from the corpse count of wild animals that Hemingway would have made. Maybe it would sadden Lorca to know that in that region of Cuba, the Zapata swamp, where he saw uncountable crocodiles, there was *circa* 1960, scarcely thirty years after his tale, a pen that was only a low wood fence, where a single immobile crocodile dozed in the sun, as if he were already stuffed.

A sign at the side begged the visitor: 'Please do not throw rocks at the gator.'

Lorca sees in Havana (how could he not see them?) what he calls 'the most beautiful women in the world'. Then he makes the local Cuban woman into a whole world and says: 'This island has more feminine beauties of an original type' and immediately the celebration becomes an explanation: 'owing to the drops of black blood that all Cubans carry.' Lorca reaches a conclusion: 'The blacker, the better.' (Which is also the opinion of Walker Evans, photographer, for whom an elegant black is the acme of the dandy.) Finally Lorca praises the land ('this island is a paradise') to warn his parents in Granada: 'If I get lost look for me . . . in Cuba.' The letter ends with an extraordinary hyperbole: 'Don't forget that in America being a poet is something more than being a prince.' Unfortunately it is not true now – nor was it true then. Not in Cuba at least. I have known poor poets, sick poets, persecuted poets, imprisoned poets, moribund and finally dead poets. They were all treated not like princes but like pariahs, like the plague: suffering the leprosy of letters. But for Lorca Havana was a party and so it should have been. There is no need to contaminate his poetry with my reality.

On Lorca's visit to Buenos Aires Borges accused him of a crime of *lèse legerté*. Lorca told the young Borges that he had discovered a crucial character. In him was hidden the destiny of all humanity, a saviour. His name? Mickey Mouse! It's strange that Borges, with his sense of humour, did not find that behind the statement by Lorca there was nothing but a joke: silly sallies by a poet with a comic sense of life. To Borges the joke was a yoke. Lorca wanted to amaze: *pour épater le Borges*. In Havana, on the contrary, he delighted his Havanan friends, fans of the silent cinema, with his piece 'El paseo de Buster Keaton', composed only two years before. Buster Keaton is not here a redeemer who tries to return to Bethlehem on his second coming. But neither is he the sobbing Mickey Messiah, with his always open eyes, his four-fingered gloves and his shoes of a mouse with hundred league boots. Mickey is insufferable, Keaton is insuperable. The motto of this last little piece is 'In America there are nightingales', which is another way of saying that poets can be princes. Lorca in Havana, by not wanting to amaze anyone, amazed everyone.

An anonymous author at the time describes Lorca's stay in Havana as 'the agitated rhythm of his Havana existence, full of gifts, of chats and of homages and burdened with the sweet and social tyranny of friendship'. But Lorca did not go only to Havana. So much did Lorca declare in Havana that he would go to Santiago that he almost didn't make it. Many people still doubt whether Lorca really went to Santiago de Cuba. They are the people who think of poetry as a metaphor in action. Indeed, after several failed attempts, Lorca finally went to Santiago. Not in a 'coach made of black water' and with the blond head of Fonseca, but in Santiago de Cuba he really stayed in the Venus Hotel. Lorca truly was the poet of love. Those who doubt it, should read his 'Romance de la casada infiel', or the unfaithful Andalusian bride. Few poems written in Spanish are as erotic.

As a poet Lorca was a definitive influence for Cuban poetry. This, after the Modernist lay-back, was beginning a phase of a populism called in the Caribbean *negrismo*. It was a vision of the poetic possibilities of the black and his dialects that was then more alien than alienating. The word might be exotic but exotic in Cuba is a Scandinavian seaman not a black steve-dore. The best poets of that generation, who would have been Lorca's age, cultivated *negrismo* as an amenable fashion. Others were like Al Jolsons of poetry: whites in black faces. The poem was thus becoming some kind of greasepaint.

Lorca's brief visit was a hurricane that came not from the Caribbean but from Granada. His influence extended throughout Cuban literature. That kind of poetry was made to be recited: the mouth chanting couplets. That is the sorcery of poetry (and that other form of poetry, song lyrics): it demands at the same time silent reading and reading aloud and will even stand reciting. Poetry, then, is another form of music, as Verlaine wanted:

'*De la musique avant toute chose.*' Lorca, in his 'Son de negros en Cuba', murmurs an exotic song that becomes instantly familiar. 'I will go to Santiago' is in effect the refrain of a *son*. As in the *Cuban Overture* by Gershwin, the melody is familiar and the harmony lingers on.

Lorca arrived in Havana at the Machina dock. The trip he made was the reverse of Crane's. Although *La zapatera prodigiosa*, a piece full of Andalusian sun, dates from the time he lived in New York, he also wrote there his dark in mood *Poeta en Nueva York*, that opens like a premonition, 'Asesinado por el cielo' ('Murdered by the Sky'), and ends with his 'Huida de Nueva York' ('Flight from New York'). Almost immediately, in the book and in life, the poet composes his 'Son de negros en Cuba', where he invokes a sortilege to the moon:

> When the full moon rises
> I will go to Santiago de Cuba.

His poem, which has the poetic form of a *son*, a Cuban love song to dance to, blooms here like a tropical flower: spontaneous, exceptionally beautiful. The poet flees from civilization to native life, exotic nature. Almost like Gauguin did. Although I seem to be hearing the Shakespeare of *The Tempest*:

> the isle is full of noises,
> Sounds and sweet airs, that give delight, and hurt not.

After the discovery Lorca now wants to sail around the isle where

> The roofs of palm will sing.
> I will go to Santiago . . .
> I will go to Santiago . . .
> With the blond head of Fonseca
> I will go to Santiago
> And with the rosebush of Romeo y Julieta . . .
> Oh Cuba! Oh rhythm of dry seeds!
> Oh warm waist and drop of wood!
> Harp of live trunks, crocodile, tobacco flower!

There is a traditional *son* that sings:

> Mamma I want to know
> where the singers come from . . .

Lorca knew: those singers, like the *son*, came from Santiago de Cuba. Deciphering poems is the work of academicians, but I want to show how Lorca made a poem from the obvious, for Cubans, that turned into poetry for all. The 'palm roofs' are the roofs of the *bohíos*, traditional peasant dwellings, built with leaves, trunks and fibres from the royal palm tree. No one in Cuba would call the *palma*, *palmera* as Lorca does. Not even in a poem. 'The blond head of Fonseca', which intrigued so many, doesn't belong to any of his Cuban friends but to the cigar maker of that name, whose red head appears as a chromo on the boxes of his brand. 'The rosebush of Romeo y Julieta' is not that thicket where Romeo gives Juliet what she gave him the other day, but another brand of Havana cigars. The rosebush is a lithograph. 'The dry seeds' are of course inside the maracas and the 'drop of wood' is the musical instrument called *claves*, a couple of percussion sticks. I hope not to have to explain what a 'warm waist' is.

This poem written in Cuba wears a luminous aura such as one only sees in Havana. This is attested to by the fragment of Hergesheimer, that is a frieze from a tropical edifice and, especially, the photographs by Walker Evans with the fruit stands in the sun, the women who adorn a patio and the motley façades of the numerous, numinous movie-houses with their open invitation to the grand tour.

In that laughing and confident era, gone with the wind of history, Lorca was blinded by Havana, but managed to open the eyes of Havanans who were indifferent to the brilliance of their city, as capital as a sin. There are still some who remember Lorca as if they were seeing him alive and kicking the flamenco floor. One of those Havana dwellers is Lydia Cabrera. Lydia recalls Lorca from the beginning. She met him in the house of another Cuban in Madrid, José María Chacón y Calvo, who was later instrumental in Lorca's trip to Havana. 'What charm he had!' says Lydia. 'What a vital child he was!' Until she went back to Havana she used to see Lorca every day in that Madrid, the reverse of Havana, that has not been lost but won. Celebrating the occasion, Lorca dedicated to Lydia the poem she would like most. The poem (and maybe the dedication) scandalized one of Lydia's brothers, alarmed perhaps by all the erotic imagery that Lorca displays from the first line until the revelation of this virgin with a husband. She, Lydia, was not in the least put off and it is still her favourite poem by Lorca. She recalls that after five minutes of conversation with Lorca she was bewitched. (The word is hers, she who knows so much about bewitching.) She always called him Federico.

Lydia Cabrera says about Lorca's end: 'When I learned about the tragic details of his death, I thought with consternation of the horror that Federico must have felt. He was so delicate! So horrible a death must have caused him unimaginable horror. It was an unforgivable death. I thought a lot, a great deal about him.' Everyone who knew Lorca in Havana, and even those who didn't know him, lamented his death. About his assassination Lezama Lima had a curious opinion. It is not a political but a poetic version of the death of the poet: 'What killed Lorca was vulgarity.' Cryptic rather than a critic, Lezama adds: 'Not politics.'

That was the end. At the beginning Lorca arrived in Havana and surprised everyone when he introduced himself: 'I'm Federico García.' Choosing to use his common middle name excited speculation. Someone asked: 'Are you gentlemen really sure that this García man is Lorca?' As there were so many Garcías in Cuba, from the general of the wars of independence, Calixto García, to the most vulgar politicians, many Cubans felt related to Lorca.

At that time the Colombian poet Porfirio Barba Jacob, a man of successive and sonorous pseudonyms, lived in Havana. Formerly he had been called by his proper name, an obscure Osorio, then he had been Ricardo Arenales and Maín Ximénez, until finally he hit upon that twice queer pseudonym with porphyria. All these names and that man make up a considerable Modernist poet, an endangered species. Barba Jacob was famous in Havana for a verse and its obverse. The writer declared in a poem: 'In nothing I believe, in nothing.' The man was a pederast poet. Very ugly, he was called 'the man who looked like a horse'.

Barba Jacob added to those hurdles of love a new one. He was missing a front tooth which he always insisted on replacing with a false one made not of chalk, as some historians have it, but of cotton or paper. His conversation began in the evening on the Acera del Louvre, in the vespers Hergesheimer talked about. As the night progressed that tooth whiter than the other teeth would disappear only to reappear towed by his tongue not to its goal but to another part of his mouth. Barba Jacob's tooth shone white now in the forest of his mouth, now on his livid lip, or it just flew to alight on the beard of Barba. The poet believed that his conversation was truly fascinating, to judge by the faces of his listeners. But the fascination actually came from that ambulatory mock tooth. Or better, shipwrecked tooth: a sailor in white who sailed on the raft of his tongue, between dental Charybdis and the Scylla of his gums.

The mention of a mariner, even a metaphorical one, leads us to the great amorous transport of Barba. It is said that the poet of Modernist decadence found his sinning sailor when he, literally, 'covered the waterfront'. Littorally they found each other on the docks. The sailor became the lover of the pederast and pessimist rhymester (remember, please, his motto: 'In nothing I believe, in nothing') and, beneath it all, a poor poet. It was 1930 when the bard Barba was showing off his freshly caught mariner. It was Barba's bad luck (or poetic injustice) that the sodomite sailor and he crossed Federico García's path. He who was the opposite of the Colombian: graciously gypsy-like and, to top it all, a famous poet. Lorca proceeded, with all his charm and all his teeth shining bright in his dark face, to rescue the Scandinavian sailor stranded in the tropics. Barba lost his soft tooth for ever.

Around 1948, almost twenty years after the amorous *double entente*, it was still possible to see that pseudo-Swedish sailor walking the night (up Prado, down Prado) like a shipwreck from another age. His clothes were, yes, navy blue: he wore a windbreaker to make hallucinatory the tropical night. A dirty blond, an anchorite with the anchor still around his neck, perhaps Norwegian, perhaps Galician, he wandered like the shade of a wandering sailor, without seeing anyone. For, you see, no one saw him. But invariably pedestrians and poets that gathered on the corner of Prado and Virtudes, where the least virtuous neighbourhood of Havana by night began, looked towards the odd parapet of the central promenade hoping to catch sight of this mariner shipwrecked in Havana, to whom Barba the bard sang: 'There are days when we are so lubricious, so lubricious' (a sigh), 'And there are days when we are so lugubrious, so lugubrious.' Now an irreverent index appeared to finger him and a vile voice came to reveal: 'That one too!' The laugh was like the draught that moved the cotton tooth of Porfirio Barba Jacob, who believed in no one, in no one.

The culmination of Lorca's visit to Havana occurred when he was offered a farewell meal, a banquet, a lunch was launched in the dining room of the Hotel Inglaterra at the end of the Acera del Louvre, at times called del *Livre*. Lorca and his future disciples were there. Literary Havana was also there, the one that did not write poems but was disposed to write prose as Lorca wrote verse. Through the open doors of the hotel (the air was not conditioned yet) could be seen the numerous columns, all white in the sun, the pavement of the Louvre and the park in the background, with the sunny solid statue of another poet, José Martí, who was killed, like Lorca, by that bullet with a name that always comes to kill poets when they are most needed.

Suddenly, as happens in the tropics, it started to rain. To rain for real, without warning, without anyone expecting it and without a break. The water was falling everywhere from everywhere. It was raining behind the undaunted columns, it was raining on the pavement, it was raining on the asphalt and on the paving of the park and its trees that could no longer be seen from the hotel. It was raining on the statue of Martí and its livid marble arm and the accusing hand and the pointing finger were all liquid now. It was raining on the Centro Gallego, on the Centro Asturiano and on the Manzana de Gómez and even further, on the little Plaza de Alvear, on the fountain of the beggars and on the façade of the Floridita where Hemingway used to come to drink. It was raining on the Cytherea of Hergesheimer and on the black and white landscape of Walker Evans. It was raining all over Havana.

In the dining room where the diners were devouring the hot meal indifferent to the rain that was melted crystal, humid mirror, liquid curtain, Lorca, only Lorca, saw the rain. He stopped eating to watch it and on an impulse he leapt to his feet and went to the open door of the hotel to see how it rained. Never had he seen it rain so for real. The rain of Granada sprinkled the villas, the rain of Madrid converted the never distant dust into mud, the rain of New York was an alien enemy – frozen like death. Other rains were not rain: they were drizzle, they were dew compared with this rain. 'And the windows of heaven were opened,' says Genesis – and the Hotel Inglaterra became an ark and Lorca was Noah. There were giants in poetry back then! Lorca continued his vigil, on his watch (there would be no siesta that afternoon), looking at the rain alone, seeing the deluge organize itself before his very eyes.

But soon they noted his absence from the banquet and they came, sole and solicitous, then two by two to make a rude circle around him, as happened to Noah with his zoo. Lorca had already written that the Cubans talk loud and louder talk the Havanans, the *hablaneros*. Lorca lifted a finger to his lips as a sign of respectful silence before the rain.

The racket of the banquet had ended in the roaring of the torrent. For the first time for the journalists, writers and musicians who met in that simple symposium, Federico García Lorca, poet (poet as we know means *maker* in Greek), had made rain in Havana as no one had seen it rain before, as no one saw it again afterwards.

Walker Evans: Eye Witness

Perhaps the most durable of the American photographers of the thirties, Walker Evans (1903–75), was in fact the first photographer who had – instantaneous posterity – a one-man show at the Museum of Modern Art of New York in 1934. In 1941 his most celebrated book appeared, *Let Us Now Praise Famous Men*, done together with the film critic James Agee, who wrote the literary portraits of 'the famous men' (the title and the phrase come from the *Apocrypha*) who, ironically, were the poorest sharecroppers in the United States – the ignored of the earth. The enduring beauty of the book is given it by the miserable farm workers whom Evans portrayed: the innocent faces, without malice, of the so-called 'white trash'. The book was actually ruled by the aesthetics of poverty that the unfortunate sociologist Oscar Lewis would celebrate in the future. Later Evans had the good fortune to work for *Fortune* and to be in *Vogue*.

There have been other books by Evans (*Walker Evans at Work* and *Walker Evans First and Last*) where there appears the photographer's particular obsession with Havana. In only three weeks in another town Evans saw (and photographed) the splendour and the misery of the city.

'It was a job,' he explained. 'It was commissioned. You must remember that this was a time when anyone would do anything for work.' (Evans was referring to the Depression.) He continued: 'This was a job of a publishing house publishing a book about Cuba.' Some job. The book in question was a pamphlet written by a Stalinist journalist named Carleton Beals. The book and its author have been long forgotten, but the photos by Evans, timeless, have survived.

There were many visitors to Havana in the early thirties. One was García Lorca who came from dark New York to Cuba and the sun. Another visitor was Ernest Hemingway, who came to stay. Once during a day of fishing in 1956 he told me that all he wanted in life was 'to stay here' for ever. History of course interfered with his wishes. The third man in Havana was Walker Evans, the photographer with a mission: to find *The*

Crime of Cuba (the title of the book) in order to illustrate it. Now the illustrations also want to find its Cuban crime.

Evans said (all photographers, when they talk, are liars) that he had arrived in Cuba 'in the midst of the revolution'. But there is no revolution nor even a minor revolt in his photos of Havana. It is not even known whether he was in Cuba in 1932, as he says, or in 1933 as his biographers say. Evans also said that 'Batista was taking over'. That first cousin of nostalgia, the rearview mirror, is talking now. Batista was a doubly dark sergeant when Evans took his photos and left running. Evans was talking of Havana in an interview in 1971 – forty years *after* going to Cuba.

There is no revolution visible in the photos that Evans said he had taken by storm. At times the city looks as splendid as another American visitor around that period, Joseph Hergesheimer, recalled it: 'Havana was artificial, exotic: built into a semblance of the Baroque.' In other photos Evans portrays poor people, wretches and beggars and urban groups and solitary women bathed in the melancholy aura of the tropics. The city that never sleeps, according to Hergesheimer, is full, according to Evans, of banished families who sleep in the sun on any bench of any park. The *guajiros* (landless peasants) look lost in the streets of Havana. Evans found what he was looking for: *The Crime of Cuba*. But somehow these disinherited people seem less poor than the white sharecroppers whom Evans portrayed in Alabama years later. Although it is obvious that Cuba, as much as the United States, is a victim of the same depression. But the blacks of Havana are seen much better off (see below) than the white trash of Alabama and their equivalent, the hopeless blacks of the Deep South, who at that time are never seen.

Evans returned to New York bringing back alive all the women he winked at with his camera, stopped in time but still moving: the beauty that *nada* can shroud. He also takes down the solid and gracious colonial architecture of the city – visions of the Cuban Baroque and the façades of the cinemas that always attracted Evans are his version of Arcadia every night.

Around this time Hemingway was living in the Hotel Ambos Mundos in Old Havana. There he met, drank and got drunk with Evans and his revolution: ten days that shook Bacardi. Or at least their rum bottles. As was his custom Hemingway paid for the drinks – and the dregs. Around that time he started his novel *To Have and Have Not* like this: 'You know how it is there early in the morning in Havana with the bums still asleep against the walls of the buildings . . .' Often Evans seems an illustrator of Hemingway rather than of Beals.

Havana 1933* carries (or better drags) a very long French introduction so inexact that it seems to have been written by a scholar in gossip. It talks about the photos as if, for example, they were illustrating *The Chase*, the novel by Alejo Carpentier, and almost makes them both contemporary. In fact the Carpentier novel, published in 1956, is set in the constitutional period of Batista in the forties, not under the Machado dictatorship. It even speaks of a poster of the Havana Philharmonic, photographed by Evans, as a felicitous visual coincidence with Carpentier because one can read on the poster the title of Beethoven's Ninth Symphony. Just by opening *The Pursuit* you see that the score of musical allusions refers to the *Eroica* Symphony. Everywhere the prologue does with the photos what *Le Monde* does with the news: the commentary is anything but impartial. Which would explain the absence of the happiest photos that are Evans's still lifes, with the tropical fruits made copy and cornucopia. Besides, the graffito that says 'Down with the Imperialist War – PC' with which the book ends is an anachronism. The slogan of 'imperialist war' is an invention by Stalin from 1939. If it were genuine the Cuban Communists would have a potent prescient vision of history: they were not rewriting the past but already writing the future!

In all those books where Walker Evans returns and makes us return to Havana in the dream (and in the nightmares) of his portraits there is always a disturbing presence – a constant ghost. It is the image of a black dressed implacably from head to foot in white. He is standing on a downtown corner watching half the world go by. Evans calls him 'the citizen of Havana'. He is wearing a spotless linen suit and an immaculate collar shirt and a black tie with white polka-dots and a handkerchief in his pocket and a straw hat that was then very much in vogue. This man in a white suit may be a *sbirro* – whom Machado invented and Batista inherited. (He looks so dangerous perhaps because he is so well dressed.) However that may be, the man is there stopped in time and only his eyes appear to be moving. But of course his eyes cannot move either. Now he is frozen by the photograph and that moment has been made to last forever. The *dandy dangeroso*, as Walker Evans would say, will keep his eyes peeled while he watches the invisible witness who has made him immortal with a wink, black on white, like the photograph.

(November 1989)

---

* *Walker Evans – Havana 1933*, Thames and Hudson, 1989.

Havana Lost and Found
A Dead City – or the City of the Dead?

To Professor Levi Marrero, a Cuban
who knows Havana

A saying says: 'Only those who don't know Havana don't love her.' Now a book entitled *La Habana* makes the reader doubt. This reader is a citizen of Havana who has made the city into his *genius loci* and the stuff his dreams are made of – and his nightmares too.

But what would happen if some photographer came and aimed at Madrid or Barcelona or Seville, and portrayed the *ramblas* and Paseo de Gracia or the Gran Vía or even La Giralda's towering beauty, with no one in the streets: no one in the corners, no one in front of a door or a gate or behind a grille, no hand on a knocker. No one to be seen – *no one.* These cities would have to have been abandoned because there is not a single urban vision that wouldn't include their inhabitants. Such photographs would make one think of a cataclysm, of the aftermath consequence of biological warfare or bombing with clean bombs. Or perhaps of a medieval city decimated by the plague. No one would believe, of course, that that city has been converted into a museum. Havana, according to *La Habana*, photographed by Manuel Méndez, is a collection of palaces, buildings, houses and streets where one sees no one (except for a modest model who accentuates the lonesome road), because, simply, no one lives there.

The explanation is more sinister than the guessing game that the book, beautifully printed, proposes to the reader. At least it poses it to this reader, witness of the apotheosis of a city and a resident of the real Havana, which these photos (for the first time the negative is not retouched, but the subject is photographed with heavy makeup) and this book, try to eliminate. A testimony is always a truth with documents – and always dangerous.

In *To Have and Have Not* Havana is the *genius loci* of the early thirties, and already Hemingway knows how to evoke the city as a luminescence:

I dropped the Morro out of sight after a while and then the National Hotel and finally I could just see the dome of the Capitol . . . standing up white out of the edge of the sea . . . I could see the Morro light way down to the westward and the glow of Havana.

A near contemporary of Hemingway, Joseph Hergesheimer, writes in the first pages of *San Cristóbal de La Habana*:

There are certain cities, strange to the first view, nearer the heart than home . . . approaching Havana in the early morning . . . I had a premonition that what I saw was of peculiar importance to me . . .

Then the premonition is a dream that is a vision. Later for Hergesheimer more than for Hemingway the vision becomes a dream and the dream is made of the hard facts of stone:

Then it was that I had my first premonition about the city toward which I was smoothly progressing – I was to find in it the classic spirit not of Greece but of a late period; it was the replica of those imagined cities painted and engraved in a wealth of marble cornices and set directly against the tranquil sea. There was already perceptible about it the air of unreality that marked the strand which saw the Embarkation for Cytherea.

Nothing could have made me happier than this realization; an extension of the impression of a haunting dream turned into solid fact . . . I heard, then, the voice of Havana, a remarkably active staccato voice, never, I was to learn, sinking to quiet, but changing at night into a different yet no less disturbing clamour . . .

That clamour was perceptible, as Hergesheimer hears it, in Old Havana, where everything was bustle, a human throng, a racket of people. Virgilio Piñera, one of the great Cuban writers, concerns himself with that Havana with a fidelity that is very far from the panegyrists of silence that announce this book, these photos. Says Virgil, guiding us through what Lezama Lima called Paradiso:

Havana seems to be stimulating. At least in this the travellers who have come successively since the seventeenth century are in agreement. And stimulating in what sense? Well in the sense of the senses: the five joined in a frenetic night watch. Havana is highly apt for being tasted, seen, heard, touched and smelled.

These pertinent pages were written at the end of 1959. Any reader would be capable of reading the ludic lines of Piñera and finding an art for premonition in phrases like 'slave market' or 'the plaza . . . goes on breathing the past'. But, in its present, the tumult is a throng of *habaneros*, men and women, who were going to Muralla to buy fabrics in its many garment stores.

We could go back in time to the sixteenth century, when Havana was already the capital of the island. But the judgement of foreigners is preferable. This third, accurate opinion is from Richard Henry Dana, the famous author of *Two Years Before the Mast*, who visited Havana in 1859. This is what he wrote in his book *To Cuba and Back* published in 1860:

> As you go up the hill a glorious view lies upon the left. Havana, both city and suburbs, the Morro with its batteries and lighthouse, the ridge of fortifications called the Cabaña and Casa Blanca, the Castle of Atarés, near at hand, a perfect truncated cone, fortified at the top – the higher and most distant Castle of El Príncipe . . . Young Ocean, the Ocean of today! The blue, bright, healthful, glittering, gladdening, inspiring Ocean! Have I ever seen a city view so grand?

One of the prolix prologuers of this book (of a beauty at once exotic and Spanish, thanks solely to the extraordinary photographer Manuel Méndez Guerrero, who knows and shows how much Havana has of Seville, of Cádiz and of all Andalusía), speaking of Old Havana like an antique, wrote: 'But it was a forgotten sector, hidden behind the noisy traffic of the perimetre avenues.' Which were they? Which are they? The prologuer does not say, affirming instead that 'the luxury commerce was abandoning its streets . . . The most important task of preserving it was an attitude of intellectual minorities.' And we already know what happens to those minorities (among whom I once counted myself) in a totalitarian regime.

But in the last reel this appears: 'The triumph of the Revolution opened up promising perspectives for the conservation of the old city.'

The prologuist lies by proxy. Old Havana was crisscrossed by bus routes and before that by trams, on four narrow but crucial streets. It opened at the bottom on the Malecón, on the Alameda de Paula and on Havana Bay. Above, where it began or ended, was Bélgica Avenue, also called Egido or Monserrate Street. Parallel to Monserrate, immediately behind the Prado and the Capitol, was Zulueta Street, where, in number 408, an old hotel now a tenement, I lived from July 1941 until April 1951. I knew these streets and this Havana well. Much better, in any case, than those who now try to preserve what they have earlier destroyed.

Between 1941 and 1951 there was a single radical modification, signalled by the Capitol dome (of which Hemingway speaks), and its esplanade of granite and asphalt, and the new Paseo del Prado, which is one of the most beautiful groves of America. The Zanja de Albañal was converted into Zanja Street, heart of Chinatown (another of the great racial contingents that gave Havana its metropolitan accent: like the Jews, the Chinese emigrated *en masse* after the Revolution), and in front of the Capitol, in its *al fresco* cafés, female bands played boleros until the end of the night. Early in the morning, the lights of the *paseo* were another dawn.

Che Guevara, who did not see Havana until 3 January 1959, when he came from the Sierra like a bearded and bereted Argentine, stuffed into olive fatigues too large for his asthmatic body (one of the jokes of the time was that they were Fidel Castro's discarded fatigues), hated the city from the first night – and declared Havana a loathsome collaborationist. But Fidel Castro, old-time nighthawk when he was an anonymous pistol, was seen everywhere in the Havana night now that he was celebrated as Caesar coming back from Gaul: in all the night-spots and in restaurants like the one on the corner of Twelfth and Twenty-Third, where it was possible to have supper and breakfast at the same time. In spite of the gang wars before Batista and of the Batistan repression, Havana had always been a peaceable city. It was not usual to see an assault, a robbery or a purse-snatching. Crooks, as in all places, were friends and fiends of the dark, but they made themselves scarce in what Lezama Lima called the poetic apotheosis: 'Insular night, invisible gardens.'

Alejo Carpentier, acquainted with different and successive Havanas, has a story entitled 'Back to the Source' (the source is another time, other ages), in which an old black restores, by means of magic, some ruins from the debris of a colonial mansion being torn down. The plot of 'Back to the Source', the only masterwork by Carpentier written in Cuba, is in part a demolition job.

Carpentier is also the writer of the sentence, 'Havana is a city sick with columns.' The city never dreamt that a fifth column was being prepared for its obliteration.

The destruction of Havana during the thirty years of the Castrato has been sloppy. Castro may not hate Havana as Guevara did, but the needs created by his Government and the opportunism with which these problems were barely resolved have been more visible in Havana than in any other city in Cuba. The excuse is that the Revolution (if you wish, in capitals) took care of the whole country to compensate for the predominance of Havana.

Let us see what the man who was Mayor of Havana in the last ten years has to say about it. A recent report by Efe, the Spanish agency, says: 'The Mayor of Havana himself admits that the Revolution has been hard on the city.' That ex-Mayor, now Ambassador to the United Kingdom, *Coman-*

dante Oscar Fernández Mell, a member of the Armed Forces like almost all the old Cuban bureaucrats, declared that the city received 'the blows of revolutionary justice'. That is, the Castro regime condemned the capital to death. The Spanish reporter says: 'A walk through many of the streets and plazas of Havana shows that revolutionary justice was implacable with one of the most beautiful cities in the world.' Of course, Fidel Castro was unmoved by these ruins, while his lieutenant Fernández Mell mentions that Havana's crime was that of being 'a developed [sic] city. In '59, probably one of the most developed cities of Latin America, its standard of living was in opposition to the standard of living of the rest of the country.'

Which can be said for certain of London, Paris, Rome, New York and Madrid. Cuba was 'an underdeveloped country with a supposedly developed capital'. According to Mell, 'the plans' of Batista's Government were supposedly 'to convert it into the Las Vegas of the Caribbean'. This is a deduction that will take by surprise most of the Cubans who once lived in the splendour of Havana.

'The Malecón,' Mell, a medical man and not an architect, informs us, 'was going to be full of hotels and casinos, and Old Havana was going to disappear.' Mell, lousy liar, cannot say that it was precisely under the Government of Fidel Castro that Old Havana disappeared. Mell does not say how the most elegant streets of Old Havana – Obispo and O'Reilly – were delivered over to something worse than demolition and time. Obispo was the street of the bookshops of Havana, O'Reilly was the street of banks and commerce. The bookshops were censored first and then suppressed when the Government took control of the book (published, imported, sold), and their buildings were made into hovels for humble Havanans to hide in. Somewhere there is still a BBC documentary in which they show the old bookshops with their windows boarded up, their metallic curtains drawn and, in the middle, an obscure hollow that is the door of this 'popular dwelling'.

Concerning the peeling buildings and the façades unpainted for decades, Mell the Mayor has a well-considered explanation. 'Paint,' he reveals to us, 'comes in general from the capitalist area.' It is obvious that the moral of this feeble fable is that the preservation of Havana is pell-Mell. It may be for that reason that Castro has rewarded Mell with the post of Ambassador to Britain. In London, a city barely older than Havana (it was destroyed by fire in 1666), he will find that the walls, in dubious battle with mild mildew, humidity and cold, are nevertheless always freshly painted, repaired and sustained more by scaffolds than by tradition. Obviously, capitalism not only builds cities like Havana, it also preserves them.

Havana was a poetic reduction of Cuba, a metaphor. Nero made Rome burn to rebuild it. Castro, quasi-Caesar, made Havana into a ruin that he now restores. The project of Nero was grandiose, the proposals of Castro contemptible.

Centuries ago, speaking of Rome, Horace wrote: 'Ruins will find me unmoved.' Now, the restoration of ruins does not move me. It has, like everything in Cuba, a propaganda goal. The Havana of the book entitled *La Habana* is not my Havana. Instead of a wonderful city it is its double through the looking glass, a restored ruin, nightmare city. Old Havana, in full-colour slides, is a garish whore. There can be no end sadder, in its laconicism, of a city that was loquacious, chatty, the fatherland of the *Habla Neros*. The laconic aliens inhabit it now and Havana has become a ghost city for torpid tourists. Its enchantment is not live, but the gaudy colours of stuffed birds: a painted parrot.

The restoration, the people in the prologue inform us, is completed with gaslight. 'Exactly like 150 years ago,' reveal the restorers, speaking of gas like a contemporary invention. I regret that the restoration of 'Havana', from now on in inverted commas, will not really be complete until we see a Spanish military authority in the Second Lieutenant's Palace and the Lieutenant General living once again in the Government Palace, facing the Plaza de Armas, and, while the Spanish ecclesiastic hierarchy blesses the Cuban faithful from the cathedral, on the Plaza Vieja, renamed the Plaza of San Juan de Dios, there is a lucrative slave market once more.

The slavers would not have to brave an uncomfortable passage to Africa, like Pedro Blanco, and would be able to find sufficient blacks here in this 'Havana', ruled by an irreversible time-machine: stud slaves, childbearing black women and mulatto girls, as not long ago a Spanish journalist saw them: complacent, numerous and all of them possessing steadfast steatopygia. This 'Havana' would not be a bustling brothel or a casino de luxe, but a vast slave market. It is a trip back to the bad seed.

(18 January 1988)

FELOS DE SE

The Martyrdom of Martí

To say it from the beginning, the martyrdom of Martí was his exile and exile was his success. It was a form of failure, but at the same time it was a triumph. Never did any exile in America lose so much when he lost his land and gain more in that he was converted from an obscure apprentice pamphleteer (when they deported him from Cuba, without having reached the age of twenty) into one of the greatest writers in the Spanish language and without any doubt into our prime prosist. Martí learned to write that dense prose in his academic exile in Spain, and in his professional stay in the United States. Martí's entire life consisted of trying to remember his lost land: to end his exile and at the same time to create a free Cuba because, you see, it was impossible for him to live under a regime that was doubly onerous: totalitarian and foreign.

Martí dies when he recovers Cuba. Not when he obtains his freedom but when he ends his *destierro* to gain his land. He was all that a professional writer can be and more: a South American correspondent in the USA and an American columnist, writing his splendid Spanish and his poor English, and even when he wrote in Spanish, he had, at times, from economic pressure, to become a hack and even to commit that sin that is the virtue of the journalist: to speak about what he doesn't know.

Martí, even, came to write reviews of novels that he had obviously not read. And at times it was not a matter of a cheap novel, but of books like *Bouvard and Pécuchet*.

But I don't have the slightest doubt that the writing of Martí – with all its excesses, because of all its excesses – is the most powerful baroque, *conceptista* and eloquent apparatus that literature in Spanish has produced since Quevedo. A piece of Martían prose is not only recognizable at first sight and on a single hearing, but it has the measurable density of certain solid metals like platinum, for example, and liquids like mercury, quicksilver that is lacking in his Argentine contemporary Sarmiento. This prose has been labelled as belonging to the orator who has no time. It's possible. I am not an orator: you will have already noticed that. I don't know how orators write – if they write. But the apparent simplicity of his diary as a guerrilla in the bush with no time at all is equally dense and vibrant. In Martí the evident complexity as well as the apparent simplicity are deliberate. They are, besides, the product of a creative will. All his prose has a contagious urgency, even when it reviews an exhibition of Impressionist paintings. But his campaign diary ends not with the abrupt note of one who is about to die, but in a calm description of life in the *Mambí* camp:

> They cook plantains and mash slices of jerked meat with a stone on the mortar, for those recently arrived. Very turbid is the risen water of the Contramaestre – and Valentin brings me a jar with fig leaves boiled in sweets.

It must be pointed out that the Contramaestre is the river near which Martí fell at Dos Ríos, Twin Rivers. This final paragraph of the *Diary* does not, I believe, add much to the investigation of writing in exile. Martí becomes a writer out of his land, but produces his absolute masterwork upon returning and recovering his island. I needed to note it down before forgetting it. Martí, then and now, is the personification of the writer in exile, become a writer while in exile, become a great writer in exile. Nevertheless, his best book, as one can see, his most perfect prose, his most apt expression is written in Cuba. Is it that exile is not a geographical or historical event but a land that the writer carries with him always? For Martí, Cuba must have been a floating island, because the *Diary* begins in Montecristi, in Santo Domingo, and it is on Dominican land that Martí produces one of the most beautiful sentences of Spanish literature in America.

It is a sample of the art of the writer formed on foreign land, who comes back to his country with the exoticist ardour of the Romantics made immediate reality. The sudden Antillean presence, so near to Cuba and an almost mystical, memorable name of a woman, made him jot down rapidly and voluptuously: 'April 9 – Lola, *jolongo*, weeping on her balcony. We embark.'

Between the Dominican beginning and his end at Dos Ríos, when Martí at last completes his martyrdom, the writer produces pages of his *Diary* that are, actually, bits of memorable, masterful literature. Martí does not set out to write great writing, it is evident, but he cannot avoid it. Going to his death, the expedition is his literary road to perfection: what he wrote about the guerrilla camp, its tribulations and the *Mambís* who march with him on the way to death or victory – to one of those two possible liberties.

Martí comes to a better geography in his writing: the artifice of literature more credible than nature. You will be able to appreciate his writing: it has crossed time and fashions and styles to be eternally up to date. Many Spanish-speaking writers write like Martí without knowing it, others try to copy him without succeeding. Still worse, his work has been used as a political flag everywhere, in Cuba, the two of them, before and now, and although Martí was often a writer of a political bent, time has shown that he was first a writer, then a politician and even when his writing is obviously political, it vibrates with a transcendence that makes us believe that its author, José Martí, was aiming higher. At us, in fact, who are living almost a century after his death, at those who, like me, believe that politics is more often than not the last refuge of the scoundrel and the first vocation of the smarties. We all today, here, know that if there is not a history of politics (the politicians trying to hide in history), there will always be a history of literature. There the prose of Martí is secured, imperishable as this campaign text in his *Diario*:

> Form up when the sun comes up. Mount sleepy. The men have not recovered their strength and they wobble. They barely ate last night. I rested until ten on one side of the road, then the other. From the hovel they send us a gift: a chicken for 'General Matías' and honey. At noon and in the afternoon I write to New York, to General Maceo, who is near by and doesn't know of our arrival; not to mention the letter to Manuel Fuentes, at the *World*, that I finished at daybreak, with a pencil and leaning on my hand. Yesterday, and from time to time, I inspected the field, at ease, satisfied: bugle calls; the men carry on their backs bunches of bananas; the captured cow moos and they cut its throat; Victoriano Garzón, the shrewd black who wears an imperial and a moustache, humble and fervent, tells me from his hammock about his victorious attack on Ramón de las Yaguas; his speech is disordered and intense, his soul good and his authority natural; he mimics with much truth his white lieutenants, Mariano Sánchez and Rafael Portuondo; and if they are mistaken about a point of discipline, he mends their errors. His body is thin, sweet his smile; he wears a blue shirt and black and white pants; he takes care of every one of his soldiers.

I have called this brief appraisal 'The Martyrdom of Martí' and by trying to flee from the cliché I fell deeply into it. All those who, for political reasons, refuse to recognize that Martí committed suicide on the battlefield use the word martyr and are not in error. There was in Martí an eagerness for immolation that was actually a will to martyrdom. This death wish was not new, or unique. Several Romantic poets chose death, like Martí, while they were fighting for life – that is, for freedom.

The Magyar poet Sandor Petöfi died in the Battle of Segesvan, fighting next to the general-in-chief of the Hungarian Army, who was shielding him. Curiously his corpse never appeared and the Hungarians still believe that Petöfi lives and will return a redeemer to Hungary one day. Lord Byron, a poet in search of a cause to fight and die for, found it in the Greek independence from the Turks. But he never came to see combat, since he died of typhus in Missolonghi. Martí was not a poet as cosmopolitan as Byron nor did he have then the importance as a national poet of Petöfi, but he was a better writer than the two put together. Like Byron, Martí died before entering into combat in an obscure skirmish. Like Petöfi, Martí was protected by the chief of the Cuban revolutionary forces, General Máximo Gómez.

His death was less painful and dirty than Byron's and did not have the deceptive dénouement of a disappearance like Petöfi's, but it was no less mysterious. The troop of General Gómez, an important contingent, exchanged some shots with a minuscule Spanish column at Dos Ríos. General Gómez gave the command to halt and advised Martí (or rather, with his dominant Dominican character, he ordered him) to place himself behind him, as if to protect him with his slight body. At the same time he posted Martí's bodyguard (strangely called Angel de la Guardia) so that he would not lose sight of the President. Martí, nevertheless, invited his guard to go forward towards the enemy. At that moment Martí's horse took off in the direction of the Spanish column. Angel de la Guardia could do nothing more than follow it at a gallop – only to see Martí receive a shot in the neck, lose his balance and fall from the horse. Still on the ground, wounded, Martí wanted to get nearer to the enemy, barely visible at some one hundred yards. When Angel de la Guardia is also wounded, a truly improbable incident occurs. A scout of the Spaniards, who was a Cuban mulatto, came up close enough to see the fallen men and upon recognizing Martí he exclaimed: 'You around here, Don Martí?' As if he were on a stroll and had seen an old friend! Then he lifted his revolver to finish off Martí. His corpse fell into enemy hands: it was searched, despoiled and finally stolen away to the Santiago de Cuba cemetery by the Spaniards. There are too many strange elements to believe in the extraordinary. The ordinary is that Martí, like Byron and like Petöfi, even more than both, was seeking romantic death on the battlefield and hurried to meet it. He had been waiting for it for some time. The Hungarians waited many years for the return of Petöfi. The Cubans lamented for decades the disappearance of Martí. There is even a song of 1900 that is sung still. It says in part:

> Here's missing, sirs, a voice
> Oh what a voice!

Of that Cuban nightingale,
Of that brother and martyr
Who was named Martí.

Martí died a martyr. But if he should not have died he should indeed have lived longer. He does live still. His immortal soul is like a genius out of the bottle: his powerful prose, his essays ahead of their time and those articles of his are made of imperishable fabric. It is they that must be remembered, because whenever human eyes that can read Spanish come close to him they will always have to admit, 'But why complain that Martí should not have died? Martí has not died. He is alive in his living prose.' That pure prose is actually the man himself. José Martí is a man made of prose – and of poetry too.

(Miami, 19 April 1980)

Who Killed Calvert Casey?

He was gentle.
He was weak.
He was destroyed.

GORE VIDAL

*(Inscription seen on the tomb of Calvert Casey
in Rome in 1972. Now the tomb, like Calvert,
has disappeared.)*

I met Calvert Casey almost too late. That is, almost too late
for me. Everyone who met Calvert believed they too had met him too late.
Like that privilege that one always believes one has not had in time, that
one hasn't enjoyed properly or has received late, Calvert seemed not to last
us at all. I don't know of anyone who knew Calvert who didn't consider
him to be a gift. One of those precious presents that gift-giving gods
concede to humans because they know that they will have it (or will enjoy
it: the terms are interchangeable) much, much less than an eternity. It was
the shortness of Calvert's life in my life that made this gift unappreciable
for me and at the same time let me see the brief time that the gift would
last. It is true that Calvert Casey lasted us all a short time. But we must not
lament the brevity of his life but celebrate that there existed someone
called Calvert Casey who was unique and extraordinary and that we are
able to say with Hamlet: 'I knew him well.' Without having to lament to
Horatio: 'Alas, poor Yorick.' Not poor Calvert. Poor those who did not
know him.

But I met him late, it's true. In 1960, in fact, when Virgilio Piñera was
insisting that I had to meet Calvert Casey by whatever means and I was
afraid that he would be one of those sterile hybrids, a Cuban-American. I
had already personally endured one of those mules in the abyss who had
tried to insert himself into American literature – 'to which I belong' – and
had got no further than writing trite stories in New York, where they were
never published. He ended up writing for one of those 'Latin American

magazines', published in the United States to be sold in South America. They seem to be written neither in Spanish nor in English and are always accused of being financed by the CIA and never even achieve that official status. Just justice that such mediocrity should have such a destiny. But with the triumph of the Revolution, some sure months later ('Batista strikes back,' I thought: one of the risks of the tyrant in flight is that he can always come back, like Napoleon or Mussolini: Italian bully-boys all) he appeared in Havana disposed to 'integrate himself into the struggle' by writing social novels in an indescribable Volapük that poor Virgilio, ever the guide of the lettered Havana inferno, had to put into Spanish to be able to publish them in *Ediciones R*, the publishing house founded by *Lunes* but funded by *Revolución* the newspaper.

But Calvert Casey was brought to the desk of *Lunes* by Antón Arrufat, as sharp as he was slender and as intelligent as disrespectful: a spindle weaving irreverences.

'Here's the Calvita,' meaning the bald lady and smiling his crooked smile.

I owe many things to the talent of Arrufat, to his capacity for judging a book, to his literary culture that tended towards a certain metaphysical search, but nothing do I owe him so much as that hardly respectful introduction. Calvert Casey, caught between the dilemma of this advertisement for his homosexuality (which I knew about already from Virgilio, from Natalio Galán and from Humberto Arenal, his old heterosexual friend from New York) made in a salacious tone by his very introducer, and the seriousness that he thought appropriate for this appointment, caught the horns of his other social disease (he considered it a true condemnation of the word and not a salvation by the flesh) and tried to tame that bully.

'Mu, mu, mu—' was all that Calvert Casey said.

But Antón intervened, intromitter to the core: 'Well endowed, la Calvita is a garrulous stutterer.'

Now that it became evident that Calvert Casey was stammering, trying to say what he said later, right away, like any stutterer in public, he became suddenly coherent.

'*Mucho gusto,*' Calvert finished saying. Then he added: 'I've wanted to meet you for some time.'

Arrufat, diverted and direct, showing now the red ball on the tip of his tongue (where everyone said that he accumulated his venom, a cobra woman till the end of the word), said smiling: 'Calvert, you're not at the United Nations, dear. Here we all use *tú*. Even Franqui who's a *comandante* and all.'

'Yes,' I assured Calvert. 'As well as along with all of us having also-known-as-names. Here Antón is really called by his pen-name, Antón Arrufátich Chekhov.'

It wasn't true but Calvert, amused, took part in the game: 'The name fits him very well. He could even write *The Avocado Orchard*, now that so many *gente bien* are leaving.'

He hadn't stammered at all. I looked at Arrufat who thought he should intervene in support.

'It suits me fine, as Virgilio would say,' said Arrufat, making fun of the use of catch-phrases, constant in his teacher, playwright Piñera.

Lunes de Revolución was, curiously, a place where one worked with the greatest of ease, Russian style. On top of everything else I, its editor-in-chief, was still cinema critic of *Carteles*, weekly, and in the newspaper *Revolución* every other day. Our literary supplement was made up with very few personnel, but the daily weekday aboulia produced in turn a fantastic frenzy at the end of the week when closing time in the gardens of Gutenberg was approaching and nobody had written anything, not a thing had been translated, and no outside contribution had been received. The magazine was only saved from the wreck, always a menace like a weekend hurricane, by the providence of improvization, the unrestrained last-minute work and the organizing talent of its diverse art directors – who were much more than typographers glorified by their title: artists of the deadline.

Calvert was delighted with this maelstrom every week and with the ship that does not finally founder, so different from the UN, where the duty of each employee was to be seen to be moving the greatest quantity of paperwork with much ease going nowhere: the paradise of all bureaucrats of the world united. He left – thrilled by our creative inefficiency. We agreed beforehand that he would write something for us. 'Something' was of course whatever he wanted. So began his collaboration and, more decisively, our friendship.

Afterwards Calvert would aver that if it had not been for *Lunes* he would not have published anything, choosing to forget what he had written in English in New York and in Spanish in Cuba before the Revolution. But certainly Calvert saved, with one of his rare articles or penetrating essays, more than one issue of the magazine, retrieved now from oblivion because Calvert Casey appeared in them. This massive weekly publication (the literary magazine with the greatest circulation ever published in Cuba and very possibly in all Spanish-speaking America) had put many Cubans in contact for the first time with diverse foreign authors of renown, even classics. Among the Cuban writers that we were able to publicize and open up to a readership of more than the half-dozen they would have had before, was Calvert Casey. Behind his doubly exotic name was hidden a profoundly Cuban writer. Even more, that rarity: a Havana author who wrote an exquisite and at the same time readable prose, who spoke of themes that were taboo, like the suicide of José Martí, or simply exotic, like his discovery of the Isle of Pines, for Calvert a true Treasure Island which he explored with the creative spirit of another Stevenson: a magic island the former, an invented island the latter. Calvert was the ideal writer for an ideal time – while both lasted. He was one of the few who learned early that we were in imminent risk of being expelled from Paradise. Or better, that we were running the risk that they would pull the Garden of Eden, like an inverted magic carpet, from under our feet: dropping some of us into purgatory, others into limbo, others into a hell rarely deserved.

But they were still times of tolerance. Sometimes the *Lunes* team and I would eat in the home of Virgilio Piñera, then a kind of literary star, whose apogee and perigee would be like a warning sign of our political fortune. Virgilio, no doubt in heaven now, would get uncomfortable if he saw himself converted into a tropical version of the pole star. But is is better than to picture Virgilio in hell, for his house was an oasis, a kind of forgotten station in paradise. I have to say that his house on Guanabo beach, his only house, was little more than a bungalow, almost a cabin and we always ate *spaghetti alla Pignera* there, as he called it. We sat at a long table under an avocado tree (providential then, when it fruited – *le mot juste* for Virgilio – in the middle of the Havana hunger) on his front patio because there was no room inside nor a back patio. Later we would have to eat not spaghetti but humble pie.

Miriam Gómez went there with me one Sunday. She had not met Calvert and the introduction was the usual social murmur. Virgilio seated them together. 'Married women on one side,' he said. No sooner had we started to eat that exotic dish (spaghetti in the tropics) than Calvert initiated a conversation with Virgilio, *magister litterae*, at the other end of the table and the literary subject soon became an argument and then a heated debate, almost a row.

Suddenly, in front of a shocked Miriam Gómez, Calvert got a knot of spaghetti in his throat. But it was not in his physical pharynx that the choking was located but in that glottis of the mind that is the vocal cords of the utter stutterer. All the cords are tied into a knot and as he tries to untie the knot with physical force visible in the face and neck, he creates a larger knot and this in turn is converted into a Gordian knot whose only cutting sword is the will – a weapon already blunted by effort.

Calvert was opening his mouth wider and wider and making guttural and gross sounds, ominous now. Miriam went from concern to terror and then started to ask for help. (Virgilio had got up and gone to the kitchen for more pasta.) Miriam cried out for help, shouting: 'Calvert's choking! He's choking!' – exclamations that made Calvert's mouth open even more, his eyes pools of paroxysm. But no one was paying attention to the cries for help (not even me) and everyone kept eating and talking animatedly while, for Miriam, Calvert was being choked to death: drowned on dry land. Miriam Gómez got up decisively, went over to Calvert and started to try to make him let go of the mouthful that was choking him, giving him repeated slaps on the back.

It was then that Arrufat indolently entered the scene (which he later described as one of absolute Grand Guignol) and, without moving from his place or even from in front of his plate (never that) inquired non-chalantly of Miriam Gómez: 'What's up with you two?' Miriam, almost scandalized, not by the phrase but by the tone of Arrufat's sneer, spat out: 'This man is choking on spaghetti.' Arrufat looked disdainfully at Calvert Casey (his head thrown back, his mouth all the way open, his eyes popping) and said: 'La Calvita? Come on, la Calvita won't ever choke on spaghetti! On another *boccato* maybe, but never on spaghetti,' and added in the same tone: 'You didn't know that la Calvita is tongue-tied?' '*What?*', Miriam Gómez managed to ask. 'Stammerer,' said Arrufat with the same parsimony, as if he were repeating an already learned lesson. 'Stutterer. He stutters and sometimes, like now, he chokes on the words that he can't swallow.'

Miriam Gómez didn't want to believe what she was hearing, but as a reaction to this perfidious phrase, Calvert Casey let go of his own half-Nelson, his eyes went back in their sockets, he shut his mouth and said, almost whistling, without a trace of spaghetti or of choking, to the double amazement of Miriam Gómez: 'Thanks love,' to Miriam, and to Arrufat: 'Antón you're a vi-vi-vvv—'

'Vivisectionist?' said Arrufat, pretending to help Calvert in his choice of vocabulary.

'*Viper!*' wailed Calvert finally. We all turned around to laugh at Calvert's shout.

Viper was an ambivalent word in the Havana homosexual vocabulary, uttered as much in rebuke as in approbation, in reproach or admiration or, finally, as an absolutely adulatory term – said perhaps from fear, perhaps from love. It is probable that the ambiguous viper came not from a country where there aren't even any snakes but from a city where one of its socially high-toned and at the same time ruined districts is called La Vibora. Literally the Viper.

That's how Miriam Gómez met Calvert Casey: almost choking to death. Not drowned in the nearby sea of Guanabo beach, the ocean in fact, but in the shallow waters of conversation, in the not very profound puddle of stuttering where he fell unexpectedly after tripping over the least prominent word, like a rock on his oral road even if it were only an oral cobblestone. But Calvert, unlike the rest of us, had a rare fluency for writing in a Spanish that must have been, for more than one reason, his second language. Later I found out that it was actually his mother tongue.

Calvert Casey was born in Baltimore and grew up in Havana. Calvert Casey was born in Havana and grew up in Baltimore. American, Cuban – who cares? It cannot be said with precision what Calvert was since he always evaded classifications and dates. Was he really born in the USA in 1924? No one knows. What is irrefutable is that he was a writer. Above all and above everyone, almost in spite of himself, Calvert wrote or thought about writing or dreamed he was writing. The biographical uncertainty (when did he really return to Cuba?) permits nevertheless some certainties.

In the mid-fifties Calvert Casey was working in the offices of the United Nations in New York (where Natalio Galán, musician and typist, got to know him), translating documents from one side to the other that would be printed with invisible ink or in its most uncertain approximation become red tape. Before the triumph of the Revolution he was already 'back home' (a phrase that fascinated him) in Havana, working in that most Cuban of businesses, a *quincalla*. It becomes incongruous (and funny) to try to remember a Calvert whom I never knew selling combs, pins, clothes pegs, safety pins, pomade (and even maybe KY jelly, a sexual emollient that attracted him like a new sin), toothpicks, cigarettes: golden Cuban Royales, oval Regalías el Cuño, round Partagás, black Trinidad y Hermanos (would he have sold old Susinis and Aguilitas, as Arrufat would wickedly claim, in which the name became the smoke of memories, ardent nostalgia of an extinguished world?), Mazda bulbs of various wattages, plugs, hair rollers and that panoply of the Havana that smokes Havanas: panatellas and even cheroots, brown and obscene like dildos for the mouth, public and evident, exhibitionist almost. Have a Havana! Before becoming a *quincallero*, a popular job then, Calvert, who spoke Havanese without the slightest accent, with his brown hair and his long, languid, penetrating brown eyes, had a Cuban lover who was a mulatto from Santiago. He was Emilio to everyone, one of the most consistently good men that I have known: quiet, almost invisible and at peace with all.

The literary biography of Calvert Casey begins in English and is crowned by a story published in the little review the *New Mexico Quarterly*, which wins him a prize from the publisher Doubleday: from New Mexico to New York. The literary return to Cuba is not even a voyage in the verbal time of language: his Spanish is English by other means and both are nothing more than an end to Calvert Casey. More significant than literature is a voyage in space that is converted into temporal vertigo. One day in the forties (a decisive decade), in Rome, still a translator for the United Nations, Calvert recognizes the Roman landscape as a mirror image of Old Havana – his eternal city. He decides to return straight away to Havana because it looks too much like Rome, in a game of errors and of identities and shifts. Years later he will return to Rome trying to find his lost Havana: it is the trick of *déjà vu* that will be transformed into a recovered never-never land. But it's nothing more than one of the legerdemains of Death: the appointment in Samarra of the Persian short story that had been appropriated by Somerset Maugham and Cocteau and John O'Hara, writers meeting senile death: *all writers die but some writers would rather die sooner than later.*

Another version of the end date with Death is the Cuban story of the hairy man who meets Death in the park and hears her say that she's looking for a hairy man to take with her. The man shaves his head to elude La Pelona, the hairless one, who, failing to find the furtive hirsute man, impatiently decides to carry away in his place the shaven one.

Calvert, La Calvita, Calvito, does not flee from death on leaving Cuba: on the contrary he goes to meet her willingly, smiling, almost cheerful because it is an old promise: Calvert Casey goes on foot to meet his death. Perhaps he saw in Rome the marble Neptune, by an Italian sculptor, which appeared for the first time in a Cuban novel that he had enjoyed in Havana – or was it in Rome? – *My Uncle the Clerk* by Ramón Meza. (Perhaps his name was Raimondo Mezza.) Maybe he never envisaged those furtive, fleeting Roman semblances that became for ever so Havanan to him. But certainly he did not suffer the panic of the elephants, that he declared his own: when nearing death they feel fear far from the place where they were born. Death had no sting for Calvert Casey that day when he decided to choose her as the ultimate freedom because he knew – he had written it – that she was an old fellow-traveller. He simply allowed himself to be carried off by her as by the guide in a maze in a dream: 'between mute columns that remained/a very white, spacious path'.

The mortal body of Calvert Casey had an end in Rome but in Havana began his vital life. Calvert published in the little review *Ciclón* (financed by José Rodríguez Feo, the Maecenas of *Origenes*, but actually controlled by Virgilio Piñera as before Lezama Lima reigned at *Origenes*) what someone, perhaps he himself, called 'existential experiences' – those were still new Sartrean times – but which are also samples of a mastery that grew more evident the less visible the threads of the literary fabric became.

It was soon after I met Calvert that he began to publish his articles that were essays, while in secret he was writing the short stories again and again, until they were exact, that he later collected in *El regreso*, 'The Return'. One of those stories, 'El amorcito' ('The Little Love'), made famous a favourite phrase of Calvert's and one used affectionately in Havana to name the object of a love that does not dare speak its name, homosexual or heterosexual.

From these dates come many of the secret and joyous adventures that Calvert would reserve to reveal to some few intimates. At times, knowing that the anecdote was in reality a story that he would not be able to write in Cuba, Calvert gave them titles. There was one called 'Toque final' ('Finishing Touch') that Calvert must have told more than once, so perfect was his telling. Its protagonist, perhaps Calvert himself, has met a possible little love on the Malecón – a wall and a promenade – where he used frequently to go and sit, to catch fresh air and at times fresh meat. They set up a date, maybe for a *posada*. The hero, more and more like Calvert, shaves, bathes, puts on deodorant, called Finishing Touch, registered trade mark. As a finishing touch to his toilette, Calvert puts the deodorant on all his private parts, gets dressed and goes to the Malecón to sit on the wall to wait for his sure little love. The minutes pass: twenty, thirty, forty and the little love does not come. In his place arrives an unexpected visitor: our hero – or heroine – has started to feel some time ago a strange twinge that is becoming precise now as a prickling rear. Gradually the prickle is changing to burning, then to a kind of medieval torment: a firebrand that is introduced into the rectum and burns like a poker. Calvert is definitely being tortured by that burning sword that penetrates him like a Cuban Edward II, king and queen for a day. Or for half a night. He cannot stay seated any more because the whole wall is impaling him, impelling him. He gets up from his seat as the burning increases. At that moment he remembers a mark of fire and hits on the cause of the malaise: the finishing touch of 'Toque Final', deodorant *in extremis*, has been a mortal blow for romance. The amorous ardour has been replaced by a burning brand. Scorched, almost propelled by his own ignition, Calvert returns to his house, undresses not with loving haste but desperately and sits down in a basin of not cold enough water – to calm his ardent anus that is his onus. Memories of fire that last longer than the love that never was.

On another occasion Calvert Casey, Miriam Gómez and I were strolling along the short street that joins the Parque Central to the Plaza de Alvear, walking along the pavement of the Asturian Centre, lined with laurels, the old blue burnished paving stones reflecting profuse public lights. Now the great iron grilles appear and through the filigree we see the interior of the baroque palace. Calvert stops a moment. The Asturian Centre appears empty but its interior is brightly lit up as on a holiday. 'Do you see that magnificent staircase?' asks Calvert, obliging us to look and see once more the familiar steps of the palace, all marble, wide above and opening out even wider below, with balustrades that become stony volutes at its end, coruscating conches. We tell him yes, of course: not only did I grow up only two blocks from here but Miriam has come with me to this part of Havana many times.

But Calvert had practically forced us not merely to look at these stairs now but to memorize them for ever. Can he be a specialist in staircases, an architect perhaps? 'OK, I have to make a confession to you. More a confidence, really.' 'A confidence to a priest is a confession,' I tell him. 'All right,' he says, 'consider yourselves priests then. You're not going to believe what I'm going to tell you anyway. But it's the naked truth. Please, don't say anything to anyone, but *anyone*.' We swear eternal silence while I imagine the ardent amorous anecdote that once happened to Calvert on that staircase. Maybe he masturbated a masked *amorcito*, hidden beneath it, while around him, louder than love, bustled the lustiest carnival. But I notice that the *perron* is massive, impossible for trysts, masked or not. What could have happened to Calvert there? But now he is telling us.

A present hush but not a future silence after breaking the seal of the eternal oath. A secret is almost like a little love: it only takes on meaning when it is revealed. But it is not a tale that Calvert is telling: 'The desire, the dream of my life is to go down that staircase.' Nothing easier, any day or night that they open the gate, in an Asturian feast. 'But I want to go down it wearing a flowing crinoline, laced and low-cut, my shoulders bare, my breasts bursting out all over. The sleeves will have to be short to show off my perfect arms. On my long beautiful neck a pearl necklace catches the lights, and I wear ruby ear-studs like a drop of blood on my lobe. Also perhaps a diadem, if it is not very burdensome, of precious stones. My sleek blond hair will fall in romantic locks on my naked shoulders. Have I already told you that my shoulders are naked? You'll see my round shoulders and my splendid back. I would be made up to perfection: arched brows, violet eyes, red garnet lips and touches of rouge, very light, a highlight and nothing more, since my complexion will be translucid. Then, decked out like that, I will go down the staircase, step by step, slowly, like a queen, all the lights on my descent.'

'What do you think?' Calvert insisted on an opinion. 'Well, Calvert, forgive me,' I told him, 'but, considering,' I didn't want to utter fatal words like Revolution, Ministry of the Interior, police, 'it doesn't seem very possible to me.' I didn't want to say impossible. Miriam Gómez, more understanding or perhaps more humane, said: 'Who knows, Calvert? Maybe one day.' Calvert looked at the two of us but didn't seem either disillusioned or discouraged. 'It's a dream, of course,' he concluded, 'but dreams have a curious way of coming true.'

It was a dream, yes, and sometimes when I remember Calvert alive and I recall that he is nothing more, now, than a few bones, a skull and dust in the dust, I remember him like a dream I once had: the grand door of the Asturian Centre, that portentous portal, opens wide and before the open-sesame of memory the grandiose staircase is revealed in luminous splendour: all the lights glisten on the marble and, halfway down the mid stairs sharing the luminosity of the moment, there appears, yes! Calvert dressed in antebellum crinoline and silk, his hair long and really blond, cascading over his naked shoulders as he begins to descend the steps slowly, like a true queen. His dream has become reality in another dream: this page and the Asturian Centre belong to the dream.

The dream is of crinoline and silk and jewels but the reality was of lead and gunpowder. Calvert came to tell me one day that they were shooting again, not *Batistianos* this time but innocent people: not the usual lethal spectre but their extremes – Trotskyites and Catholics. I knew of the fate of the militant Catholics who would die shouting 'Long live Christ the King!' but not that of the Trotskyites, those followers without a leader. Calvert knew it from the Horse's mouth: he had clandestine connections other than sexual ones. He was a friend of many Cuban anarchists, some Spanish ones, remnants of the Republicans in exile, some escaped from the old Stalinist terror in Barcelona only to see themselves trapped in socialist Cuba. He also knew Cuban Trotskyites, those Utopians who refused to recognize the open Stalinist character of the Fidelist Government, who were now repeating the ideological destiny of Trotsky – socialism in one island as orthodox as socialism in one country.

It was around that time that the notorious meetings in the National Library took place and Fidel Castro made his reactionary summary: 'Within the Revolution, everything. Against the Revolution, nothing.' The corollary of this aesthetic axiom was the banning of *Lunes* and my firing – without a firing squad. Pablo Armando Fernández, Antón Arrufat and Calvert Casey went on to work at the Casa de las Américas, whose head, Haydée Santamaria, sustained the curious thesis that the *Lunes* group (all of us) were valuable individually but you couldn't let them form a group. Then they could be dangerous. So we turned out to be some kind of political bacteria capable of being dangerous if multiplied. Therefore, what is worse, we were contagious. Calvert had a junior post at the Casa de las Américas, but Arrufat got as far as directing the magazine *Casa*. He converted it from a poor pamphlet to a publication of extraordinary dynamism and considerable literary importance in Cuba and Latin America – the infection of a single microbe.

After a time without work, which I spent writing, subsidized by Miriam Gómez, an active actress, I left for Belgium as cultural attaché, in a kind of official exile. Pablo Armando Fernández would follow me for a similar post in London. For the molesting microbe, a remote isolation. Before my departure Calvert had published in *Ediciones R* – that wastrel of *Lunes* was still functioning, its virulence attenuated – his volume of stories *El regreso*, which seemed excellent to all of us at *Lunes* although it scarcely had critical repercussions in Cuba. But Antón Arrufat had praise that meant instant glory for Calvert and literary just justice: 'What do you mean, Salinger? Salinger, Schmalinger! Your stories are much better than his.' One must remember that when Calvert Casey was living obscurely in New York J. D. Salinger was celebrated and praised as the most sensitive American writer alive. I said something that proved to be a gaffe: 'He is really Pavese.'

In 1964 Antón Arrufat (to whom *El regreso* is dedicated) came to visit us in Brussels, our guest in the elephantine house of the embassy, where by absurd diplomatic chance Miriam Gómez and I were living alone. If Calvert was a wanderer and a man of many cities, Antón, so audacious of tongue, was a timid urban Turk who was afraid of any city that wasn't Havana. I had to go to meet him at the Midi station (he detested flying) and Miriam and I had to be constant company for him at the embassy, from which he only went out twice – to the movies, escorted by the chauffeur. He was moved only by lunch and supper and his favourite phrase was '*¡Qué buena comidita!*' (What a good little meal!), before beginning or finishing. But, as always, nothing else moved him. Antón was a pure intellectual and – such a useful skill in times of tempest – a born survivor. Even today, after innumerable shipwrecks, he survives everything and everybody, including Virgilio Piñera and Calvert Casey, his literary father and his big brother.

One day, after a week of being our guest, Antón received a call from Havana which he listened to almost laughing. After hanging up he said smiling: 'It was la Calvita telling me to come back straight away because things are happening. But he didn't say what things. They must be serious because he didn't repeat a single syllable. Bad sign.'

Antón returned smiling to Havana to meet an accusation of homosexual horrors: the invitation to Cuba of Allen Ginsberg, poet and pederast, was his fault – allegedly. During his visit Ginsberg said things in public that were a crime in Cuba even in private. He said that Fidel Castro must also have had homosexual experiences as a boy. 'We all have them,' Ginsberg clarified, 'why not him?' To top it all off, Ginsberg then confessed his love for Che Guevara – but it was not a proletarian love. 'I would like very much to go to bed with him,' he declared.

A now snowed-under Antón was also blamed for the homosexualization of *Casa* and having published a patently pederast poem by the playwright José Triana. There, perverse verse, stains of ochre love on the sheets, intimate Vaseline and sweat and shit on porous bodies were spoken of. There was no sentence, there was not even a trial: Antón was dismissed *ipso facto* from *Casa* and the directorship of the review was granted as a prize for militant modesty to Roberto Retamar. Before in latent disgrace but now a protegé of President Dorticós, whom he had convinced of his gifts as a Marxist role model (the *données* of Dorticós, although they could just as well have been of the two), Retamar was the apparent instigator of the accusations against Antón – and against nature. Not in vain had Calvert not stuttered on the phone.

When I returned to Havana for my mother's funeral and was forcibly detained there for four months, I saw Calvert many times in my renewed disgrace: a born-again dissident. One time was his visit to thank me for having sent, a year before, rare medicines to cure one of his secret periodic pains. He told me, on the subject of illnesses, that he now thought, like Keyserling, that only pain permits us really to know each other: sickness is the normal state of man. 'Even more so of woman,' I told him, but he did not laugh, or even smile. All in all he was at times content, especially now that he had discovered heterosexual love with a female friend. 'I am charmed by her,' he confessed to me. 'Besides, I believe I'm going to be a father. Isn't it marvellous?' Which, according to Virgilio Piñera, an unrepentant homosexual, turned out to be a false alarm. 'Double default,' said Virgilio finally with mundane malice.

On a Sunday I visited Calvert in his apartment near the Muelle de Luz, along with Rine Leal. Lazy Lotharios, Don Juans on holiday, we had picked up on the street two girls of the new class (read old prejudices) and on a whim we took them to visit Calvert Casey. 'Why is he still called that?' said one of them. 'It sounds Yankee.' 'It's Irish,' I explained. 'He fought against English imperialism then?' 'He didn't but his father did.' 'Oh, fine,' she said, satisfied. 'This, his house, is yours too.' 'Thanks.' They became a decorous duo when I made the introductions. I told them that they had before them the best living Cuban writer. Calvert smiled radiantly and at the same time tried quickly to hide his pride of a writer recognized in his land. But he stuttered enough in front of those frivolous, foolish girls for them to die laughing.

He had been even worse with a serious, sage woman: his admired Nathalie Sarraute, with whom he could not speak at all at our *Lunes* round table. Pathetically, he formulated his questions in writing, so Arrufat could ask them for him. Antón told me, in private, showing the tip on the tip of his tongue: 'La Gaguita must be fearful in French!' Now, three years later, in Calvert's apartment, where he was still stuttering but his friend Emilio stood silent as a bronze statue, I admired the collection of Afro-Cuban idols that Calvert had obtained thanks to Emilio, an old practitioner, a forefather (although he was barely thirty) of *santería*, into which he initiated Calvert, Irish Protestant as he looked, Catholic that he was, American that he did not want to be.

But Calvert had succumbed to another sickness. He had fallen into political disgrace and his situation at the Casa de las Américas was more than precarious. The guilt was not his but the punishment was. It happened that a Mexican writer named Emanuel Carballo visited Cuba on the invitation of the Casa. I never met him but I have not forgotten his name, not for what he wrote but for what he told. Calvert went out several times with Carballo (perhaps more than was his duty as a cultural host) and one night, seated on the peaceful but perilous Malecón, Calvert confided his fears to Carballo, which were sexual, homosexual, but not his own. The confession was a confidence. Naïve but grave error, for Calvert knew that he had to be careful with foreigners who came seeking gifts, Greeks in reverse. Calvert told Carballo that they were removing homosexuals to work farms that were in fact concentration camps, with guards and German police dogs and electric fences.

At the time that hunting down and veiled but systematic sexual pogrom was not known at all. Only a few people in the Government knew about it. It was a secret of the Ministry of the Interior and one always had to be careful with the secrets of the Ministry of the Interior. But Calvert was up on everything, especially the secrets of the devouring sphinx. Besides, he had a black friend who had fallen into one of those silent hauls, true holes. Though captured he had been able to communicate with Calvert. Carballo showed a limitless amazement and even indignation. Also an encouraging interest in the revelation. Calvert gave him facts, names, places but asked that he please not give them out on his return to Mexico. Not yet. Carballo swore eternal secrecy – which lasted one night.

The next day Yeyé Santamaría called Calvert to her office. 'She undressed me,' Calvert confessed to me. At times, especially when he was nervous, it was his Anglicisms and not the stuttering that let him down. Carballo had gone to see Haydée Santamaría and revealed the morning after everything Calvert had told him the night before. He advised her besides that it was very dangerous for the Revolution to have 'such people' in high places. 'I didn't know what to say to Yeyé,' Calvert told me, 'except maybe to remind her that my place was not that terribly high.' Of course from that moment on Calvert's situation at the Casa de las Américas became untenable, surrounded by vigilant eyes and regulated by new prohibitions – among them those against fraternizing with foreigners. Perhaps, with this experience, it was salvation for Calvert.

Not long after beginning my true exile, living in Madrid, I received a pleasant, unexpected visit from Calvert. Fraternizing now with Communist visitors, he managed to get himself invited to Hungary by their Writers' Union. From Budapest, masterful manoeuvre, he flew alone to Geneva, where he had reclaimed his old post of translator at the United Nations. He had not committed a single error: his escape was so perfect that his lover, smiling, had been able to keep his apartment on the Plaza de Luz. We talked, we strolled along the Prado, we went to the movies, I visited his boarding house on the Gran Vía, we chatted, but always his repeated topic, his borer, his obsession was rescuing Emilio for whom he was afraid, imagining reprisals while he was arranging for him another similar flight. But, what union of which socialist country was going to invite poor Emilio to travel to another possible paradise? On one occasion Calvert told me mysteriously, almost in a whisper: 'Don't tell anyone where I am.'

Then we went together to Barcelona where they were going to publish his stories and perhaps a future novel. He asked me not to reveal to his publisher, who was at that time mine, that he had gone into exile. He was afraid that his books would not be published if it were known that he was now a counter-revolutionary – or in Neo-Nazi jargon, a *gusano*. (This fear was not unjustified, as became clear later.) In Barcelona Calvert showed an alternative fear. What if, by their coming out, the books harmed Emilio? But Calvert's new obsession was an old paranoia: he feared being kidnapped and sent back to Cuba. He confessed to me that he had made his trip to Madrid absolutely incognito, only to see me, and he had not visited anyone else – he had not even called mutual friends in exile. Madrid, he reminded me, had a direct air link to Havana and it would not be difficult to load one more piece of cargo on to a Cubana plane.

At this moment we were in the waste ground around the Sagrada Familia Cathedral and Calvert was looking surreptitiously in all directions – as if from behind Gaudí's mute spires enemy eyes and ears were stalking us. I assured him that the fear of kidnapping was unfounded, unreal, that not even I, who had held official positions in Cuba and abroad, entertained such fears. He revealed to me: 'But I know a secret or two.' (Which I never doubted: I knew that Calvert knew not only about imprisoned pederasts or betrayed Trotskyites.) He lasted two days in Barcelona. He left to go back to Geneva and I found myself forced to move to London, not hunted by agents of Fidel Castro but pursued by agents of Franco. Not kidnapped to Cuba as a counter-revolutionary extraordinary but expelled from Spain as a contumacious Communist. History, which repeats even its dramas, sometimes does it in the form of a farce. Karl Marx *dixit*!

In December 1966, now exiled in England, living in London, recently moved to a sordid basement on Trebovir Road next to Earl's Court Station, a terrible terminal – we had a visit from a lively and cheerful Calvert Casey. But his joy did not last long. As soon as he saw our apartment he shook his head and said, 'I don't like it. At all.' But he was not referring to the ethics or the aesthetics of the place. It was not the architecture of the building or the decoration of the flat or the dim light that filtered through the narrow windows, making the basement look even more poorly, like something out of Dickens. None of that worried him. It was the spiritual discharges that were emanating from the flat. What's more, he declared the site *salado* (literally 'salty'), which in Havana means the worst of lucks. 'It's not only the black linoleum floor that is suspect,' he assured us, 'but the whole house. It's *charged*! I'm going to do a cleaning of it right now.'

By cleaning he didn't mean running the feather duster over the furniture and sweeping the floor but was referring rather to an act of Cuban black and white magic in which a bewitched, or about to be bewitched place or person, is freed from possession. Now it was some sort of exorcism before the possession. He proceeded to go out to the dark back yard where there were some trees growing stubbornly on the brink of the tube station brick wall. He tore off two or three stunted shoots that he found miraculously green in the English winter and returned to the living room – where he began an Apache African dance. In fact he was sweeping the floor with the branches, actually passing these ad hoc dusters over the furniture, running them around the walls of the whole living room – but he never went to the kitchen or entered the only bedroom. (Apparently the evil spirits sit only in the sitting room.) Finally Calvert ran to the back yard and threw the 'charged' branches as far as he could, over the station wall, where they landed perhaps on a moving train – on which fell all that malignant miasma.

When he came back from the back yard he exclaimed: 'I can't do any more! I'm sorry because you're running too big a risk here. This place is really charged!' He collapsed into a chair. Calvert, so white, such a born American, now almost European, was incongruous not only in his war dance against all evil but in his vocabulary. 'This place is jinxed, folks!' was his last forecast. The remedy: 'You have to move!'

We didn't move, of course. We couldn't. We tried to forget his warning and even his visit. But then, curiouser, we found out that one of the tenants had fallen from the top floor of the building to his death. It had happened years before but a neighbour, Pop Leibel, remembered it well. The dead man was an Andalusian boy who offered to climb into a room through the window to help two foolish French girls who had left their key inside. The boy went out to a ledge and passed along, but on trying to open the window he fell to the street, four floors down – to end up impaled on the lances of the basement railings. He took hours to die while the firemen freed his body. The lady owner of the building, for reasons other than sentimental, had not told us anything about this Spanish tragedy. It was a sheer coincidence that the Andalusian killed by his gallantry and the fatal French girls were occasional visitors to London, to Earl's Court and to the building on Trebovir Road. But was it a coincidence too that Calvert had been right – that something wicked was marauding in the basement?

Calvert came back to visit us in the summer, after having made a trip to India and acquired a brand-new Italian lover – Gianni was his name with no surname – who immediately struck Miriam and me as the image of the gigolo, of females or fags: Mediterranean and memorable. They are the same who appear in so many poems by Cavafy, where they turn up like lucky, unlucky days. He was, besides, too young for Calvert. They stayed in the marked building where we were living. This time, summer, Calvert didn't see the ghosts of winter. Not only because the days are long and the light brightens every dark corner, but because he was in love and, as we already know, love is blind – it even blinds the third eye.

We went out together often, especially with Miriam Gómez, who was now acquainted with London, its shops and its prices. She told me that Gianni was costly, demanding the best over the good, and was, besides a flirt, a *sato* – which in Cuba is the last step before flirting becomes whoring. 'I caught him winking at other men in the street,' she said. Calvert, of course, didn't see anything – love blinds the physical eye too. On the contrary, he was anxious to know our opinion about Gianni. Of course it was not prudent to tell him – among other reasons because he looked happy. Also because we were learning with the English that the truth is not to be told to everyone. In a moment of mad mirth Calvert came to disguise himself with Miriam's makeup. But it was not the dream of the transvestite going down the steps. We were not living in Havana in a palace and there was no luminous grand staircase. Calvert used lipstick to make a dot of carmine on his forehead. Then he put a handkerchief on his head and without his shirt and barefoot he started to dance a Hindu dance, so grotesque that from then on he made Indian dances impossible for Miriam and me. But Anita and Carolita, my daughters, were delighted to see how that almost bald gentleman became a lady to dance while he chanted very melismatic melodies. Pure parody.

This time there were no exorcisms but, yes, gifts. With his customary generosity Calvert helped to make possible our stay in England. I had to demonstrate to the iniquitous Immigration then that I was receiving money from abroad, since I was forbidden (a condition for entrance into the country) to work anywhere. Or as the totalizing stamp on the totalitarian passport said: 'paid or unpaid'. Thus the professional and the amateur in me were abolished at a single stroke. Calvert, a sweet saviour, lent me enough money to keep myself in London under Home Office eyes and at the mercy of the milkman. It was thanks to this friend, made so few years before, that I could not only survive but live among real Anglos and Saxons and an occasional mythic Celt. Calvert let me know, when making the loan, that I should not worry about paying him until we saw each other again. I did not see him again.

Soon after his visit we moved to South Kensington to this Gloucester Road that Calvert would have liked so much, finding the apartment clean, the building clear, the street broad: a via in no way *smarrita*. He never got to see it but we used to write to each other often and we knew what the other was doing. Of course I keep his letters, some of them full of expressions that I don't call surprising because they came from Calvert. More than a writer he was an extraordinary human being: even in his most trivial letters it was possible to find the gift of genius.

Around that time before we moved a naïve English translator was preparing an anthology of Cuban stories (Cuba was then in fashion in England) to be published by Penguin Books. Wishing to show himself a partisan of the new, already old, regime the anthologist proposed to call the book *Writers from Fidel's Cuba*. Consulted by a then editor of Penguin Books I told him that if the book was going to be titled in such a sycophantic manner I would withdraw my story from the anthology. I informed Calvert of this opportunistic bug of the compiler and he immediately wrote to the publisher saying that he seconded my action and that he too would prohibit the publication of his story in an anthology with such a title. Calvert's letter was courageous because he was still in the hands of his Catalonian publisher and he was afraid to offend his crypto-Castroist sensibility, as susceptible as a political pachyderm that suns himself from the East.[1] 'The East is red,' said Mao, inhibitor.

On another occasion he wrote to ask me to guide Emilio (who had at last succeeded in getting out of Cuba thanks to the exertions of Calvert, who had friends everywhere) who was going to the United States by way of London. His loan of the day before yesterday, curiously, served to aid the transit of Emilio through Europe yesterday. I found Emilio sure of himself, at peace not only with Calvert but with himself: that is, Emilio was identical to himself. He was carrying inside his Afro-Cuban universe converted into a propitious world of his own. In another letter Calvert recounted how he had mentioned me in the blurb of his novel of imminent release and how the Catalonian publisher, like a Fidelista functionary, had suggested that he leave out my name for literary convenience. 'It is evident,' Calvert wrote to me, 'that every day you're becoming more of a writer *maudit*. It won't be good for publishing but it is for writing.' Calvert Casey knew as much about literature as about politics, although many thought the contrary. Like a bewitched prince, Calvert was a sage who simulated being a delicate monster to distance critics and commissars. His wisdom was his labyrinth.

But our letters were not peaceful at times although they were always

1. Calvert learned *in corpore* in Cuba the lesson of dangerous visitors. Now abroad he already knew that one met members of State Security not only on the island. In Cuba they were paid by the Government. Outside they were volunteers. This was the only difference.

friendly. He had told me of constant fights with Gianni, separations from Gianni, returns to Gianni and every time his lover was becoming for me more a hater. Then Calvert sent me a fragment from his next book, novel or collection of stories, which was set in India. He began by saying that the Taj Mahal was so dirty that it was begging for a good wash with the best detergent. It seemed to me that before Calvert would never have said such a frivolity – or worse, such a silly thing. I chalked it up to the influence of Gianni. There is nothing more vulgar than a vulgar Italian and love is catching. Calvert was offended when I wrote him to tell him this and he assured me that Gianni was not only his reason for being but for existing, for being alive and for writing: were it not for Gianni he would never have written another line. I answered him: 'Is Gianni *Lunes* by other means, an erotic Friday?' He didn't answer me. But not long afterwards he wrote to assure me that he had finished with Gianni for ever. He also told me that he had to go to Switzerland but on his return trip from Geneva to Rome he would pass through London. The news of his visit delighted me: it had been some time since we had seen each other. Almost exactly two years.

I vividly remember the last time I spoke with Calvert Casey. He was on the phone. I don't know why the telephone repels me. There is nothing more disquieting than the bell of an unexpected telephone. Late at night, for example. Or early in the morning. It's almost like a spoken telegram. More bad news comes by letter than by telegram or by telephone and nevertheless in exile one waits for letters with illusion, even unexpected letters. That pleasant spring evening we were being visited by an American woman that I like a lot and an Englishman that I detest. He is a film director who was once a photographer and has become inexplicably famous with his scarce talent, making movies as literary as they are pretentious, with his fanatic images that he believes fantastic and his quotations from Borges, who is now the cult author of those who have no culture: the blind man's Homer. That ill-fated night, a blind photographer this man who fell to earth and into the conversation was unfathomable in his superficial profundity and I was struggling at the edge of the abyss of a yawn when the phone rang.

It was Calvert telling me that he could not come to London after all, that he would fly to Spain and from there return to Rome and (which he omitted) to the eternity whence he came at birth. Calvert always returning. We could hardly talk that time that I never knew would be the last: I didn't even notice his anxious or urgent voice, no warning, while at my back my assailant was visualizing with words in front of our mutual female friend labyrinths of water, canals that were Mediterranean seas he wanted to discover for the cinema: to see Venice and die. (Drowned or from arthritis?) Calvert hung up. A few days later, in another telephone call, a traumatic one, Juan Arcocha, a friend who loved Calvert – it was no big deal: all his friends loved Calvert – asked me if I already knew the news. No, I didn't. What was the news? This is a century of acrid acronyms and of late news. 'Calvert just committed suicide in Rome,' said the telephone, absurd as death – or life.

It was hard to accept Calvert's death and I trusted that someone would call and say that everything had been a mistake: Juan Arcocha, an interpreter, had misunderstood. It was not Calvert who had committed suicide in Rome but Calvino, born in Santiago de las Vegas, a district of Havana, a writer who lives in the Trastevere, on the other side of the Almendares River. Why not Calvados instead of Calvert? But Calvados is a spirituous liquor and spirits never die. (You must consider that there was another postal strike in Rome: normal, total, inhibiting communications, that began about that time.) It could easily have been another misunderstanding, confusing Calvert Casey with O'Casey. But O'Casey had died in Dublin, aged eighty, five years before and Calvino was as rampant as a baron. Or maybe it was some other mistake. An everyday confusion, as Kafka proposes. Death happens and there are many kinds of death. What if Arcocha had heard suicide for homicide? Calvert, in a fit of jealousy had killed Gianni, becoming a Moor to Gianni's Desdemona. No Moor descends a staircase fully clothed as Desdemona. Poor Calvert was made of the stuff of victims, not of executioners. Otherwise he would have remained in Cuba to become another vile Retamar fêting other Carballos in the Casa.

I made dozens of person-to-person calls with that invention as malevolent as useful, a double-edged knife. All erroneously confirmed the news badly given at night by Arcocha, an interpreter through the earpiece of Unesco: Calvert Casey had killed himself in Rome in simultaneous translation. But I kept waiting for his letter that would contradict or explain the unexplainable. It never came. (It must have been in those hundreds of thousands, millions of letters thrown into the Roman fire or into the Tiber.) Finally, crushed by the evidence, I did not believe that Calvert was dead but I accepted his suicide with respect: after all that act had been his last will. I sent a telegram to his former lady lover from Havana, the false or true one, more than anything with the intention of propagating disaster or its echo. A telegram took to Cuba the mortal remains of Calvert Casey that I heard over the phone. To Graham Bell's bell pealing were now joined Morse and Marconi, accomplices, transmitting traitors. But I never had even an acknowledgement of receipt from this mysterious notorious woman. It was evident that she did not deserve one night of love with Calvert, whatever the possible positions or combinations may have been, she a Gianni of the other sex.

But the lasting silence was indeed a confirmation. Calvert Casey was dead, somewhere in Rome. Besides, easy as it is to kick a cadaver – they're always fallen bodies – I learned that Calvert dead had been vilified by the whore Roman press (it is no accident that it would create the *paparazzi*, from *papare*, to stuff oneself, to eat carrion almost) when a reporter from an evening daily discovered in Calvert's modest apartment – before thoroughly cleaned, now charged with the emanations of suicide – a piece of evidence and leapt on it. Indian idols fornicating furiously, porno post-cards for pederasts. The deceased had queer acquired tastes. Calvert became, in the press's prose, what he never was in his life: a sodomite, an *evirado*, a *scelerato* – hideous, obscene words. Unkind hands sent me the press clippings. I did not want that filth to be the posthumous judgement for Calvert and I refused the latrine literature.

Later I talked with many people who invariably claimed to be the last person to see Calvert alive and I almost came to the conclusion that Calvert had seen in his last hours more people than ever before in his life. Perhaps he was too alive before killing himself, and he died from an excess of life. Or perhaps all those people were lying almost in unison. But why? Was it because of Calvert or because of his death? Or is it the fascination for whoever voluntarily opens the door to the unknown? I know nothing. But one of those intimate table companions, a faraway and lonely woman, who seems to remove herself the nearer she is, as if always seen through some opera glasses in reverse, told me with a twice remote voice that during his last supper Calvert did not stop saying that he was guilty, the most guilty person in the world, with all the guilt on top of him like an Atlas with a captive globe. I believed all about the last supper of this informant with Calvert because she related it to me *after* I had passed through a depression myself. I only came out of it by playing a continuing game of chess with Carolita, my younger daughter. The two of us playing game after game: pawn four queen, check, rejected queen's gambit, check, castle, check, exchange of bishop for knight, check, king's gambit, check-mate. For the king, the most important piece, is the most vulnerable of the game. Chess is such a monstrous metaphor! At endgame death is always waiting, inexorable, without reprieve on the last square by the governor. There is no chance to abolish with a chessman. Saved from madness by the logic of the game I learned that Calvert committed suicide because he was suffering in solitary the punishment of an intractable depression. This was the murder weapon. But who killed Calvert Casey?

Here I have the clues to follow for those who may wish to solve the self-murder mystery. Calvert's situation within the United Nations had deteriorated to become precarious. He got a position as vice-editor of the *Correo* of Unesco (or of the Bulletin of the FAO or one of those interchangeable international publications for internal consumption), but it didn't appear probable that he would occupy the post. As they did to me before, in 1967, the Cuban Embassy in Paris had vetoed his appointment for reasons of (a totalitarian) state that pure reason does not know about – but practical reason does. His passport had expired and no Cuban Embassy in Europe would renew it. The Cuban Ambassador in England, known in the London press as 'the sweet señorita from Havana', had catalogued Calvert as a morally sick person, undesirable in socialist Cuba. Some sweetness. He could not get a resident's permit in Italy either. What's more, the Roman police had indicated a date for his exit from Italy: *mafioso mentale* his visitor permit in Rome had expired. At the American Embassy they answered his petition to recover his birth citizenship by saying that he could never have it back as an adult for reasons more bureaucratic than political: he had renounced it in Cuba. When Calvert retorted that his sister nevertheless had now got hers again, to feed his guilt he received only a grimace of puzzlement from the consul and in his answer a disturbing revelation: in that case his sister's American citizenship was fraudulent and therefore subject to legal inspection and a possible immediate loss of her civil rights in the USA. Caught in the most perfect bureaucratic trap of the century – a man alive in a catch of consuls – desperate, Calvert sent a personal telegram to Haydée Santamaría at the Casa de las Américas. She never answered. (I wonder, as I write this, in which circle of hell the two suicides will meet now.) Gianni threatened to come back to him – if Calvert got hold of enough money. His books never got the attention they deserved either in Spain or in South America, the critical echo he was waiting for, the public that had been denied him by decree in Cuba – a negation that exile ratified out of ignorance. But Calvert was inured to failure as much as to illness. Success, like health, would have annihilated him.

Then, with all the chessmen on the chessboard now, who killed Calvert Casey? The political guillotine in a hunt for exemplary heads that would roll? The intimate friends that he had, the closer the further away, like me? Gianni, the rented Romeo? *Amor a Roma*? Or Cuba, that island that is a mirage in the Caribbean Sea, land of cannibals? The verdict is the reader's, judge and jury. He has all the time in the world and even all of eternity to deliberate. But, the reverse of an English trial, the defence and the prosecution will never rest.

Now at the end, after years remembering Calvert Casey alive, dreaming at times of a Calvert Casey in the shadows, thinking for months how to write this hollow homage to a writer of so much tact, I believe that Calvert Casey had a destiny that transcends the guilt of his killers as much as a death that is only apparent. That destiny is in that lasting last text, written in Rome in the implacable English in which he recovers his paternal tongue, the authority, after his mother died. She was the transmitter of the voices of the tribe and signals with unusual signs that for him to live meant to die, that he could only be alive as an erotic homunculus, incredibly reduced to his least, lowest potency, who now does not believe in the god of love except inside his lover, venereal virus, that lives in the beloved body as much as in his mind itself, that his death has been a resuscitation in his own writing? Never was Calvert Casey the short-story writer (he was not a novelist) more alive than when he gambles the immortality of his body (and of his amorous soul) in the body of the other. Although the game is, in the last extreme, literary and words are what live and the body penetrated without limits is the Rome of love eternal. Wouldn't it be a final perversion if this beloved host of his ghost as guest were Gianni, condemned to live with Calvert in his own body?

Calvert had thus erected his monument inside the tomb where he lies hidden among words that do not die. But now his perishable epitaph is a captive quotation engraved on granite simulacrum: the pallid stone visible in that faraway cemetery on the outskirts of the real Rome. I visited it in a last station before going through the looking glass, without quicksilver, to madness. (This time chess, a game of logic, became a demented delirium in which all the pieces were spies of the black enemy and there were no white pieces.) That apostatic allusion apparently definitive to his vulnerable body is a false, facile image. Calvert Casey was not weak. He was, on the contrary, strong like the death that he went to meet in the middle of the road to Rome on an unwary appointment. Calvert was the most daring of us all, the men who were *Lunes*, the one who travelled the furthest, an audacious adventurer. Timid and stuttering, Calvert was eloquent till the end, after the end. His literary testament shows that he was resistant enough to be able to die by words to begin to live in language – or is it in the tongue?

A decade after his death Calvert resuscitates, rises from the dead and from underneath the bookish stone stretches out his bony hand that holds up a few pages to let us know what true literature is, visible in that writing that is his winning pawn: his prose is a communicating vessel: on the reverse is life, on the obverse death. Calvert Casey lives and dies in each reading and his text is a Moebius strip of reading: finite, infinite. This image of course is another name for immortality. But who made Calvert Casey immortal?

(October 1980)

Between History and Nothingness
Notes on an Ideology of Suicide

To die for the fatherland
is to live.

From the national anthem of Cuba

I t is evident (if not it will be before I finish this essay with a
shot in another Esenin's temple) that I suffer from a morbid curiosity, a
foetal attraction, a kind of fascination with suicide – not only that of others.
I see suicide not as an escape route but as a bastion of a rampart leading to
an unbreachable wall: the first and last recourse. It could also be an
exploration of the possible extremes of being. But suddenly, one day, after
learning the news of the dramatic suicide (suicide is always a theatrical
outburst, as Hedda Gabler shows: *exit, then sudden last curtain*) of Haydée
Santamaría, heroine of the Cuban Revolution who chose not to be a
martyr, like her brother Abel and her boyfriend Boris Santa Coloma (both
killed after the assault on the Moncada barracks in 1953), but a suicide
instead. It was then that I thought that the familiar Yeyé whom I knew was
not a victim: her suicide was a declaration of principles – as an end.
Suicide was her only ideology, despite the Fidelism that made her a
politician and the Marxism to which she seemed to be converted later.
Haydée Santamaría had not been born for death, like everyone else, but
for suicide. This revealed notion now was the faith of a few fanatics and
the only Cuban ideology possible for the Revolution, for the Republic
before, for Cuba since the last century. All the other suicides, of which I
am going to talk in a minute or two, appear to be voluntarily tragic.

A shorter version of this essay appeared in number 17/18 of Escandalar, *January 1982. Then
it was taken by* Vuelta. *Both versions have been much enlarged: suicides keep on coming in Cuba like
a gross domestic product.*

Actually the Great God that Herodotus invented threatens: 'History or life.' The Cuban Revolution is that promised life.

One cannot understand the Cuban Revolution if one does not consider suicide as one of its integral, almost essential, elements. The term revolution is here, of course, a mere political convention, like the National-Socialism of Hitler. In Cuba they have always talked about revolution and often of Revolution: during the Spanish Colony, in the wars of independence and, supposedly, in the republic, from 1902 to 1958. The party of independence, founded in American exile by José Martí, was called the Cuban Revolutionary Party. It did not seem dangerous then. But from then on every rebellion, revolt or local uprising, more or less confused, against the republican order, more or less democratic, was a revolution. The anti-Machado maximum leader was the university professor and physician Doctor Ramón Grau San Martín – a character truly *sui generis* in Cuban politics. Doctor Grau called the party that he founded Cuban Revolutionary (Authentic), but Grau could be called revolutionary only by the maniacal singlemindedness of Antonio Guiteras Holmes. That Tony Guiteras, son of an Englishwoman and a Cuban, whom Hollywood converted into an American hero (in the movie *We Were Strangers*), because until the sixties it was very difficult for the American cinema to conceive of a Cuban hero – even in *Che*, that epic epitaph, the hero was barely Argentine. Guiteras, who had fought against Machado, combated Batista (who almost inaugurated then his erratic and opportunistic military might with stupidity at times implacable) and lost. He was the hero as loser. A defeated Guiteras tried to flee Cuba, but he chose his exit from the island in conditions of such risk that the enterprise was destined to failure. This chosen destiny made him a martyr. Guiteras faced his sudden death as if he were condemned to the firing squad. That choice was truly a suicide.

But Grau San Martín was anything but a suicide. He seized the confused ideas of Guiteras and made them even more confused. His Cuban Revolutionary Party (Authentic) brought him not to a failed revolution but to the presidency in democratic elections – to hand a defeat for the first time to Batista or to his candidate by proxy. Curious thing: Batista, mulatto, cane-cutter and soldier, chose as his successor an eminent member of the *criollo* upper bourgeoisie. Even more curious, he was supported as well by the Communists and their black leader. The revolution of Grau San Martín, once stable in the presidency, became noted for its absolute absence in a Government more corrupt than those that preceded it – including that of Batista himself in his different political avatars. During the rule of Doctor Grau and of his successor Carlos Prío

(1944–52), gangs of mobsters marauded through the dark streets and the musty ministries of Old Havana, to kill each other for ideologies more obscure than the streets and the pathetic political posts in the aged ministries. Their official names (no one was clandestine then) were Social Revolutionary Movement and Insurrectional Revolutionary Union. This latter had the doubtful honour of counting the beardless Fidel Castro – quite far then from the bearded Marx – among its most audacious *pistoleros*. Such gangs had risen from the violent distintegration under the continuing regime of Batista (1933–44) of a clandestine political association: Guiteras Revolutionary Action, at once a homage and a political pretext to avenge the death of Tony Guiteras. It is not strange that the typical action of this gang was evident kamikaze. Only suicide avenges the suicide.

As we see (see above) the adjective revolutionary is not new in Cuba. Not new either is the use of this word elsewhere, from Thomas Paine in the independence war of the United States, to Joseph Goebbels, who called the irresistible malignant growth of Adolf Hitler, emphatically, 'our revolution'. But you have to have some name for the resistible seizure of power by Fidel Castro. When a political institution that has changed in ideology insists on naming itself in a certain way (the Soviets, the United States) one must accept this imposition as a usage. It is the logical, verbal or historical solution to the problem of state identity. Otherwise one would have to debate eternally obsolete or absurd nomenclatures.

The Cuban Revolution – there it is, the revolutionary name in all its capitals – did not come to power as is believed thanks to the fact that Fulgencio Batista (once again cultivating his military plot twenty years after having learned the technique of the *coup d'état* without having read Malaparte: Bonaparte was enough for him), a general in name only, raised Cain with his third early morning coup on 10 March 1952 – only three months before the democratic elections that he never won and we all lost. He actually gave Fidel Castro – then a student leader with no name, a politician of little electoral future and always a gangster – the opportunity to agglutinate the armed resistance against Batista and cause the eventual fall and flight of this strongman who was actually a weak man ambitious for popularity, power and pesos. But it all began on 5 August 1951, almost a year before.

That sweet summer Sunday Eduardo Chibás, better known as Eddy Chibás or even more intimately as *El Loco* (the Madman), committed suicide in a Havana radio station. Chibás was until that moment the most popular politician ever in Cuba, including Doctor Grau and General

Menocal, both presidents, both untarnished, both become venal men in the presidency. Eddy Chibás, the reverse of the leaders who preceded him, as an honourable man, a rich heir whom money did not interest at all, an honest politician moved by a dominant obsession: absolute public honesty. He knew that he had to clean our Augean stables and he presented himself as the only possible Heracles. That was his error: nominating for a Herculean task a man who was actually incapable of it. Chibás was not very stable emotionally and his nickname *El Loco* seemed at times to be more than a motto or a monicker.

Eddy Chibás had been a vehement supporter of Doctor Grau since he had replaced General Machado in 1933 and had been toppled in his turn by Batista. Disillusioned with Grau as a venal president, Chibás soon went over to the opposition, creating in passing a party he called Orthodox, in counterpoise to Grau's Authentic Party. Both said they were direct heirs to Martí's Cuban Revolutionary Party. Although not in name the Orthodox Party was revolutionary in implication and Chibás had never ceased to consider himself revolutionary. (You see, no one had been able to do it in Cuba.) Now Chibás used the word, his voice strident, his daring oral, in the radio tribunal to make even more vehement his revolution of cleaning out dishonest moneychangers one more time from the temple of the Republic. But in order to cast out the moneylenders from the temple one needs a Jesus and even Jesus himself was crucified soon afterwards.

Chibás conceived his own crucifixion not as the Passion but as a radio version of hara-kiri. The former ally of Grau dedicated himself to lashing out verbally against the still President Grau, stood for the presidency and when the Grau candidate (his old companion from student battles Carlos Prío) won, Chibás became even more virulent in his attacks on the Government and its new chief. He was a maniacal martinet attacking President Prío, his brothers, his ministers, his entire politics. All Prío will perish. He did it by means of an hour of radio rented on Sunday afternoons by the Orthodox Party, but paid for in part by Chibás himself. His shrill voice with lambent r's in funny lambdacism was however an effective instrument through the microphone, that at the same time hid the short stature of the orator, his stubby figure, his sparse blond hair and his weak eyes behind perennially thick glasses. Every Sunday Chibás was more effective in his solitary crusade, almost a personal vendetta against the Government and against Prío. Every day the Orthodox Party was becoming more popular and the Authentic Party in power more unpopular. In successive surveys made throughout 1950 and 1951 Eddy Chibás seemed a decisive winner as a would-be president. There followed him, very far behind, the Prío man, the decorous and gray Carlos Hevia, and still further behind, Fulgencio Batista, almost painfully bringing up the rear guard.

It was then, in 1951, that Chibás committed one of those errors that become fatal in the long run, like a bad chess play – the one that many moves later will result in your own checkmate. Chibás accused the Education Minister in the Prío Government, Aureliano Sánchez Arango, of having lands and some sawmills in the forests of Guatemala. At that time the Government of Prío and that of Arévalo in Guatemala were maintaining very close ties indeed. Prío had even sent effective Cuban fighter planes to protect Arévalo from a *coup d'état* attempt that was supposed to be backed by the CIA, suspicious of his Communist connections. In Arévalo's clique there was a prominent military man, Colonel Jacobo Arbenz, who would be his successor and later protected in his disgrace as a toppled president (by another Guatemalan military man) by Fidel Castro, himself now in power. To complete the simile between politics and the most clumsy game of chess, the verbally poisonous pawn of Sánchez Arango in the Ministry of Education then was Doctor Raúl Roa, who from 1959 would be a vociferous chancellor of the Castro Government. Now it is obvious that rather than with chess one is dealing with a game of grotesque gambits, as in the *commedia dell'arte* or in a complicated coitus. Of history considered as an oral orgy.

But Chibás continued now without pain or pause attacking Sánchez Arango, who was no pushover. Like President Prío, Sánchez Arango had fought physically against Machado from the ranks of the Student Directorate, the one that later, under Batista, would be an urban terrorist organization of mauling manners. Arango was a tough, rough and expert politician, of formidable demeanour who, the reverse of Prío, was always spoiling for a fight. Of course, even if playing with the black pieces, he did not delay the counter-attack. He accused Chibás of being a subversive agent (which he was not), of being a liar (which is a moot point) and he challenged him to present publicly the proof of his accusation. Chibás assured him (and us) that he had those proofs and promised that he would present them only 'before the tribunal of the people'. For two weeks the radio suspense became as unbearable as a political melodrama – or a soap – while Chibás was looking for the incriminating documents that he had said he had, and for a moment it looked as if he had them all and would be able to present them to the press as evidence.

But it all turned out a monumental fiasco – and a tragic one at that. The documents did not turn up anywhere. They never did. Apparently Chibás had been tricked and certainly not by Sánchez Arango or by Prío and his agents, as was said at the time. Simply the orator with a tongue of fire had been a victim of his own character, in which there was a particular flaw peculiar to the politician: demagoguery. Chibás, like the proverbial fish, had been caught by the mouth – and by the mouth he would die. The press, official or impartial, Pilates all, practically crucified him: no one falls lower than an accuser who ends up being accused (see Wilde, a reluctant suicide). On the following Sunday Chibás was punctual for his programme to pronounce one of his emptiest political harangues but also one of his greatest in emotional content. He finished with an enigmatic remark to which he would give meaning immediately. It was to become famous all over Cuba: 'This is my last call!' (Cryptic for the first and last time in his life as a political orator, one supposes that he was addressing himself to the Cuban conscience or consciousness.) His next act was to take from his hip a .32 calibre revolver and shoot himself in the stomach – the place appointed by the ethos of Japanese suicide as chosen for hara-kiri.

Ironically neither the metaphorical call to the Cuban consciousness or conscience nor the real shot nor his fall before the microphone went out over the air. Two or three minutes before, the station had cut off the programme to make way for the *de rigueur* commercials. (One of them, with unintended irony, advertised Café Pilón, 'the coffee tasty to the last drop'.) In his final excitement Chibás had forgotten that his transmission contract was for only twenty-five minutes. In spite of his suicidal mission, he could not avoid being a true Cuban politician – and he spoke for a full half-hour!

The stomach wound turned out to be fatal and he died a few days later. His funeral was an impressive demonstration of spontaneous popular grief but his call barely had an echo. The entire Prío Government trembled for a moment (except Sánchez Arango who was still claiming victory in their polemic, so sensitive in his affront that he didn't notice his insensitivity about the death of his opponent, like an habitual duellist who kills without regret – chess was not his game: he never played.) If they had wanted to the Orthodox Party could have taken power that day: Prío himself already had his bags ready. But, like Chibás, the Orthodoxians were all legalistic men who believed in the value of the vote and in the electoral decision as decisive. Arms were for the military – and, occasionally, for the exemplary suicide. With his death Chibás had deprived the political opposition of their natural leader and had left his party in a chaos greater than the one the Republic was in then. So, some months later, Batista carried out his infamous, fateful *coup d'état* that was both bloodless and easy because

President Prío chose not to resist, his bags always at hand. But among his followers who most resisted later, clandestine, was Sánchez Arango, as audacious as ever. Heading for the underground, all he did was to grow a moustache. He looked, in fact, like a Guatemalan bandit.

The epilogue of this tragedy is equally sudden. Twenty years later, in order to resolve apparently insoluble personal problems, Prío, the president as an exile, opened the door of suicide – with a .32 calibre revolver. But he did break the dread suicidal symmetry: he shot himself in the chest. Prío, like his opponent Chibás, perhaps saw it the only viable exit from history and the entrance to eternity – which is greater than history because it contains it. Eternity *indeed* will absolve us. It has the time to do it.

It is evident (then and now) that if Chibás had not committed suicide it would have been impossible for Batista (or anyone else) to carry out a military coup against President Prío, unless Chibás and Prío had been eliminated beforehand. Batista never would have dared. His early morning coup converted the precarious legality of the Prío Government into an absolute illegality under Batista. As if in a chain reaction, a few months after the Batistan *coup d'état* on 10 March 1952, Fidel Castro attacked the Moncada barracks in Santiago de Cuba in an act of calculated suicide. I say calculated because nothing that Fidel Castro has carried out is free from calculation, no matter what the risk. All the leaders died during the Moncada assault, except Fidel Castro. The dead ones, naturally, were the suicides. The attack on the Moncada (like the assault on the Presidential Palace in Havana on 13 March 1957) was a military failure but, unlike the assault on the Palace, a political triumph. After 26 July 1953 everything would be history in Cuba – brutal, bloody, inevitable history.

Max Weber once said that 'the decisive means of politics is violence'. Almost a derivation Marx's old apothegm that violence is the midwife of history. But there is a slight variant in Weber who speaks of politics and not of history. Never do ends justify historical means, and particularly not when political violence is directed not towards the other, its usual target, but at oneself and an assault becomes then a suicidal attack. A harangue is the hurried testament of a suicide and the militants choose to face any political action other than their own destruction. That is, suicide. In his essay 'Politics as a Vocation' Weber illuminates with a blinding bright bolt the political shadows: 'the world is governed by demons and whoever lets himself be carried away by power and force as means makes a contract with the diabolic powers and from his action it does not follow that it is true that good can come only from good and evil only from evil – but that the opposite is more often true.'

Wifredo Lam, a Cuban surrealist painter who changed his political position several times, but not his palette, a moral but not an artistic illiterate, told me in 1958, when he returned to Cuba from France: 'Here they have let loose the demons!' showing that he knew as much about demonology as about painting. Then, looking at the city with his Chinese eyes that had seen Picasso and Breton alive and the black landscape of Haiti, he added: 'Escaped demons are more difficult to whip back to their cage than when they were first let loose.' He made a remark that seemed to come from Guicciardini himself – or perhaps from his Chinese ancestors: 'One must flee from the Devil. The further away the better.' He went back to Paris. Now, partially paralysed and senile and not able to paint, he keeps his demons within.

The attack on the Moncada barracks was conceived by Abel Santamaría, Boris Santa Coloma and Fidel Castro. Apparently it was led by the latter but the fact that he was riding in the second car and that he did not manage to go into the barracks indicates another possibility. Many military experts (among them an English former chief of commandos) are of the opinion that the assault was a suicidal operation. The relation between attackers and attacked was one to ten (134 rebels against more than a thousand garrisoned soldiers) and the disproportion of armament was so unequal as to be ridiculous: shotguns against rifles, pistols against M–1 carbines, Thompson sub-machine-guns (those preferred by Al Capone) against .50 calibre machine-guns, Springfields against cannons, cars against covered trucks and tanks – combined with the attackers' abysmal inexperience in combat against well-trained professionals in their barracks, most of them living with their families in the neighbourhood. The attackers had in their favour only surprise and disguise. But the Japanese attack on Pearl Harbor shows that military surprise does not always operate in favour of the attacker and his apparently friendly mask, like camouflage, has a limited use in combat. The surprise attack can in the long run be like a weapon that uses up its powder to become useless. The professional American soldiers based on Hawaii took barely minutes to recover from the surprise attack. It is not gratuitous, I think, to take into account the Japanese psychology as the driving force of the in the end suicidal action in Hawaii.

Several survivors of the Moncada assault recounted later that the night before the attack they created among them an almost sexual atmosphere among the men and on the road to Santiago they were singing a *son* by Lorca: 'I will go to Santiago in a coach of black waters.' One of them,

Gustavo Arcos,[1] confessed to me many years later: 'We were really going to meet our destiny and we felt like true Carib kamikazes.'

Appearing in the Japanese Middle Ages as a strictly military ethic and philosophy of war, ritual suicide was an honourable conduct. As much as victory, defeat was converted by death into moral triumph – that is an eternal victory for this ethic. Hara-kiri, whose technique it is not necessary to explain, is known to be one of the most painful forms of suicide known, even more atrocious than setting fire to one's own body. In Japanese *seppuku* (the word and the concept are Chinese) is no more than a direct consequence of self-criticism, which is joined to an indubitable masochistic will of self-destruction.

'Making a living flame of yourself' (the spectacular suicide in public and in photographs that the *bonzes* of Vietnam made fashionable) is one of the favourite forms of suicide of Cubans since time immemorial. But it was only practised, curiously, by women. Men chose the rope around the neck and a beam above. Many girls in Havana and in the provincial towns, for example, set fire to themselves when Carlos Gardel, the Argentine singer, died carbonized – out of mere sympathetic mourning. But one does not need to go as far as the *shogunate* of Kamakura and loyalty to death to follow in the steps of this ideology of immolation.

In 1895 José Martí, indefatigable freedom fighter, apostle of independence, national poet, hero and saint – practically the man who had everything, except death – met his unexpected end on the battlefield, in an inexplicable manner. The occasion was a skirmish of no importance at the beginning of the second war of independence (1895–8), when a reduced Spanish force ran into a Cuban column. Martí, a civilian among soldiers, was sent courteously by *Generalíssimo* Máximo Gómez, commander-in-chief of the *mambí* forces, become expert in the two wars of independence, to retire to a safe spot, barely a few yards in the rear. Martí, who had never been in the Cuban countryside, much less in a guerrilla war, a man of the city always, a bad horseman and a worse shot, straight away invited his escort to go to where the enemy was seen and, despite the protests of his

---

1. Arcos, an invalid veteran of the Moncada assault and later Ambassador in Belgium (1960–5), was a prisoner without a crime, without process, summons or trial for three years (1966–9) in a Cuban concentration camp. In April 1982, when trying to escape from Cuba in a boat along the coast near Havana, he was arrested, judged and condemned to fourteen years in prison. He was accompanied by his brother Sebastián, for a time second-in-command of the Revolutionary Navy. Sebastián Arcos was sentenced for the same crimes to eleven years in prison in the same trial. (See 'Lives of a Hero' in this book.)

custodian, he took off down the riverbank, up to the Spanish lines, where he fell from his horse – wounded without even drawing his gun.

This undoubted suicide, political or personal, was always spirited away by Cuban historians – as the Spaniards did with his body – and all the history books present Martí as a patriot who died heroically fighting the enemy on the field of battle. Martí only fought that day against his own enemy. The death of Martí, soul of the war and creator of the Republic in arms, was an almost fatal disaster for the campaign that was just beginning. This useless, unasked-for sacrifice, and this awful loss were lamented always by all Cubans, even by the people, especially by the people, in the Cuban popular soul.

'Martí should never have died,' said the lyrics. 'Oh, never have died!' The distant song is plaintive, its lament rhetorical, the expression confused. But indeed Martí should not have died – and dying was what he most wanted in life. Like other Romantic poets before him, Martí, retarded Romantic, chose one of the deaths possible for the poets of the nineteenth century. Reader, take your cure for sinners: tuberculosis, laudanum, syphilis, absinthe or the bullet as a heathen in the temple. (A positional game allows one to propose the names of Keats, Coleridge, Baudelaire, Verlaine, Pushkin, Kleist, Larra, Laforgue, Lautréamont – not to take up more than one page of the bio-dictionary – and with Nerval to add the intimate but public gallows of a lamp-post as assistant to his own hangman. Each poet has the right to no more than one death.) But the reverse of those private deaths, Martí brought the Republic of Cuba to birth carrying a great cadaver around its neck. A dead weight who was, moreover, a hidden suicide, like a blot on the family: that one of which one must not speak. Poetic or political, the suicide of Martí was momentous. That is, disastrous.

Other republican Cubans would choose suicide as a political act to give a full stop to a particularly onerous public polemic: Wilfredo Fernández was Mayor of Havana and director of the daily *La Discusión*, the most important Cuban newspaper of its time. One of Cuba's most culted journalists, Fernández backed the dictator Gerardo Machado to the bitter end and was among the few Machadista civilians arrested by the Revolutionary Government in 1933. (This would in turn become the dictatorship of Batista – which lasted longer than Machado's.) Imprisoned in La Cabaña fortress, after a few days he shot himself in the head. It was never discovered how he managed to get hold of the weapon as he committed suicide in his cell. Another notable suicide before Chibás was the then Mayor of Havana (a public position second in importance only to the Presidency of the Republic), Manuel Fernández Supervielle. Mayor Supervielle committed suicide in 1947, after being elected by popular acclamation. He had been accused of prevarication by the Havana press when he could not fulfil his electoral promise to give water to the city. Like Chibás, Supervielle was an honest man, wealthy, coming from the old Cuban bourgeoisie, but a political populist. His suicide, like that of Chibás, was an expression of personal failure and a last affirmative speech by negation: the hole in the head as an ideological testament written in lead. Ironically, the new Mayor – venal, vote-chasing and without class or notion of classes – promptly proposed a monument to Supervielle, now a model Mayor at last: of suicide considered as a fitting flight. *Habaneros* applauded the idea and contributed generously to the collection to erect his statue – which somehow shrank until it became only a bust. The cunning Mayor proceeded to place the head (of hollow bronze) in a tiny little square, barely half a block from the Plaza de Alvear, named in honour of the lofty engineer who was the builder of the first Havana waterworks, immortalized in an eponymous statue and in anonymous books. Humour, purposeful or unintended, is in politics the means of scorn. *De mortuis omni* . . .

Later times saw other forms of political suicide, this time collective, in the very centre of Havana. The most memorable was the *banzai* raid on the Presidential Palace on the afternoon of 13 March 1957. (Dates can be incantatory ephemera.) The assault was condemned to failure beforehand and even the English commandos who attempted to kidnap Marshal Rommel and his staff in their redoubt in Normandy, all voluntary assault troops, would have considered the attack on the Presidential Palace in Havana, a true urban fortress, to be a suicidal operation which could be refused without dishonour according to the English military code of conduct.

It becomes even more incomprehensible if one considers that in this formidable fiasco 90 per cent of the attackers died, three-quarters of them making up the national executive of the group that planned, directed and carried out the assault, the *Directorio*. This was then the only rival to the 26th of July Movement, which Fidel Castro commanded by remote control from the Sierra – and in fact the largest organization of urban guerrillas in Havana. The object of the assault, attempted in full daylight, the strongly-guarded Presidential Palace (whose occupant was a dictator who was not implacable but was indeed cruel), was located in the centre of the city, with serious traffic problems and difficulties of movement. Other direct causes of the mortal fiasco the assault became were the grenades that never exploded, the arms that jammed and the possession of a plan of the building which was five years out of date! Among the renovations to the palace, predictable but unknown to the storm group, was a covered elevator that led from the presidential office to the *azotea*, the flat roof permanently watched by members of the praetorian guard.

It is evident that there was among the attackers – young or old, inexpert or veterans of the Spanish Civil War and the Second World War, all volunteers, all brave – more than a will to win, a decided vocation for failure that meant a sure death: it was an urgency for martyrdom that they did not hesitate to acknowledge by calling themselves, correctly, 'Martían'. Before the attack one of the youngest attackers wrote a manifesto that ended in a phrase like a sentence: 'Either we'll be free or we'll fall with our breast starred with bullets!' Harangue or promise? Or perhaps a programme for political action? In spite of the romantic and rhetorical style – or because of it – one could hear the echo of Martí. The author of the proclamation, Joe Westbrook, died as he promised, not in the assault but soon afterwards in an ambush: riddled with bullets by the police when he was not yet twenty-one. Joe and all the other dead men were not, as *Comandante* Alberto Mora liked to repeat, *d'après Lenine*, corpses with a licence, but candidates elected to the common grave.

The assault on the Palace was, along with the attack on the Moncada barracks, the most spectacular of the actions of suicidal violence carried out under the Batista regime, which lasted seven years. None of them made the dictator abdicate. He fled, as all men flee, out of fear of the unknown: that Roman *annus ignotus*. The Man escaped at the last hour of the last day of the year 1958. But there were many other acts of useless immolation before Batista realized that the god of Anthony was also abandoning him.

The mere fact of remaining an active militant in Havana or Santiago doing terrorism and not seeking asylum in the mountains – which were considered by the terrorists as resorts or watering holes, places for political summer holidays when they were burnt out in the cities – this samurai stubbornness was suicidal. In such solitary sorties well-known revolutionary leaders died quickly. Among them fell Frank País who, in the hierarchy of the 26th of July Movement, was second only to Fidel Castro in the Sierra and the leader of all urban guerrillas. País was finally killed in Santiago de Cuba as he wished – an active terrorist in an occupied city till the end. Like that of Martí, his loss was fatal for Cuba at the time. His altruism became a form of ultimate egoism.

In Havana meanwhile, the terrorists were dying like obstinate political flies. As for the few survivors of the presidential assault (a suicidal gesture is not necessarily deadly: the world is full of failed suicides), not long after their absurd deed they were strolling through the city centre streets with a defiant style that contrasted with their status as outlaws with a price on their head. Meanwhile in the suburbs other terrorists, anonymous actors all, clashed often with the Batista police in a carefree fashion – frequently deadly. They reminded one of certain movie gangsters, immolated simulating, emulating Dillinger or Bonnie and Clyde on the screen. But though one may shout 'Action!' in both, politics is not a moving picture.

At the beginning of Fidel Castro's seizure of power a prominent member of the 26th of July Movement, together with an important if not decisive brother minister, was accused – falsely, as was seen later, but too late – of prevarication, like Supervielle but of a lesser rank. After only seeing his name in the newspapers, without even waiting for the trial or the deposition of the favourable witnesses, this young functionary fired a shot into his temple – the favourite method of Cuban *bushido* to expiate guilt by means of a swift hara-kiri. Even the strange disappearance of *Comandante* Camilio Cienfuegos – chief of the rebel army and right hand of Fidel Castro – was a form of self-extermination. In the search for his lost plane, a little Cessna, the obligatory stop was the Camagüey military airport, from where the plane had originally taken off. Fidel Castro in person investigated, hurried and harsh. He questioned the flight controller who told him that he had given the green light to the plane under protest. 'Fidel,' he said, 'on the radar you could clearly see a storm coming. I told the pilot and all he did was look at the *Comandante*.' The *Comandante* was Camilo Cienfuegos, who turned to the pilot and told him: '*Palante y palante!*' which was then a kind of password of the revolutionary vanguard: 'Go!' The flight controller ended with a remark that was a verdict: 'Flying in those conditions was suicide.' And suicide was the cause of the disappearance of Camilo Cienfuegos. More astonishing than this revelation was the realization that during all the time that the search for the lost aircraft and its eminent passenger lasted, Fidel Castro showed a disinterest that was almost indifference towards the death of his friend and comrade in arms.

In October 1959, on the occasion of his resignation as military chief of the province of Camagüey, *Comandante* Huber Matos was taken prisoner by Fidel Castro himself, who advanced on foot from the airport to the army barracks, followed by a crowd inflamed by his speech in which minutes before he branded Matos as a traitor. *Comandante* Matos waited for his fate in his headquarters. But one of the series of extraordinary incidents that signalled this unheard-of moment occurred when one of his staff officers, Captain Manuel Fernández, seemed to come out on to the balcony to receive the mob, regulation revolver in hand. But immediately he turned the revolver to his head instead and fired a shot, killing himself.

One of the most strange and inexplicable suicides to take place in Cuba after the Revolution and not at all known about outside the country was that of Raúl Chirino, a revolutionary turned counter-revolutionary on account of the Revolution, who committed suicide in 1959 inside a first aid hospital in Havana – while he was being questioned personally by Fidel Castro! No one ever doubted that it was suicide.

Augusto Martínez Sánchez was one of those backward, unreal *comandantes* cloned by Raúl Castro on the Second Eastern Front: the looking-glass guerrilla. His operations lasted only months but his military command became lasting – as lasting as any historical moment can be. Martínez Sánchez clambered to the Sierras in mid-1958. An obscure beardless lawyer in Havana, he went along with another hairless man, the redheaded Manuel Piñeiro, who had lived some years in New York as a professional anti-American in frustration and resentment. His impotence did not extend to sex. At least he married a ravishing American dancer, who loved dance as much as she detested ballet and Alicia Alonso – in that order. Both, Piñeiro and Sánchez, came down from the Sierras like men who had crossed the magic wall: now they were bearded *comandantes*, prepotent in their Communism, rural *à la* Raúl. They had not fired a single shot but they were unerring in their red aims that always hit the political bullseye.

Piñeiro was named by Raúl Castro head of the Intelligence and Counter-Intelligence Service, expert in spying on friends and in the informing now called revolutionary zeal. Nicknamed 'Redbeard', his true handle (with care) was James Bongo – the counter-spy who came in from the cold New York. He still continues in espionage without intelligence, counter or otherwise, and he has not committed suicide because the word failure does not exist in his vocabulary. So short is it.

Augusto Martinez Sánchez passed some time ago not into history but into ridicule and from there to totalitarian oblivion, which is the limbo of the Marxist. In 1960 he had been appointed Labour Minister under obscure conditions, the same conditions under which Raúl Castro always operated in power. His effectiveness in the post, like Piñeiro's, was characteristic of this out-of-tune band within the military mob of Fidel Castro. If Fidel is the Führer then Raúl is Röhm, even in the halo of cruelty and pederasty that has always surrounded him, perhaps on account of his men, atrocious incompetents beyond recognition. But soon, in spite of his intrigues and his unpopular support, Martínez Sánchez was seen running intrepidly to a cul-de-sac. Everyone recognized it: the common dead end that is the way of all shit. The Communists not only let him fall like a warm turd but requested his resignation, effective yesterday. When Sánchez found out that they would force him to step down in spite of the Brother, who now was no longer backing him, and of his militant manoeuvres, the minister, suddenly dignified, locked himself in his office, took out his regulation revolver and shot himself in the chest. With his habitual lack of skill *Comandante* Augusto, to his disgust, had saved his life but not his honour. François I could slip out of his historical situation but a failed Cuban suicide was like a samurai with a wooden sword. The mixed metaphors attest to the fact that it is easier to make them with Vico and the vacuousness of history, than with the viscosity of this criminal class who, like Hitler and his gang, are presented as heroes.

The political (and especially military) career of Che Guevara was a true displacement into the wrong chessboard as a black knight after leaving Cuba and embarking upon the dubious adventures of a political white hunter in the Congo and his later South American disaster. But before dying he made his infamous statement of intent on the subject, when he got as far as saying: 'How near we would be to a radiant future if in the world there were to be launched two, three or many Vietnams with their payload of deaths and their intense tragedies!' These would seem to be the words of an anarchist *in extremis* and not of the orthodox socialist or even Marxist that Guevara professed to be. The man who had indoctrinated Fidel Castro, a political savage, reading to him, to tame him, passages from the *Communist Manifesto*. But it was his political testament.

Such demented hecatombism, true apocalyptic literature, came from beyond, but in the recognizable voice of a world leader, an ideologue of the Third World, a Marxist martyr – and still a pop icon. In reality it was the voice of a man dead before dying. The death of Che Guevara occurred when he let himself be trapped in a Bolivian valley into an asinine ambush. When his exact geographical location was learned in 1967, Mario Vargas Llosa who had lived in Bolivia and was now living in London, commenting on Che's possible fate, said: 'He has no way out. What he has done is suicide' – and suicide it was. Guevara in Bolivia, as before in Cuba, had behaved like a suicide and between a fatigued guerrilla and a political hero or a saint of a new religion, he chose martyrology. Apocalypse later, immolation now.[2]

Javier de Varona belonged to the Havana upper middle class, the one that *was* decisive for Fidel Castro's rise to power. His family, whom he abhorred, had money and they all lived in a grand house in a rich part of Havana. Javier was cheerful, carefree, conspiratorial and given to the most innocent delinquency, like insulting an occasional pedestrian from a moving car: 'What a cute little ass you have, boy!' Or calling Lezama Lima on the phone at three in the morning to wake him up with a coarse phrase – 'Lezama old bugger, I'm going to castrate you!' – to the never-ending alarm of the asthmatic poet. On those occasions Javier would laugh with true gusto in the face of his neighbour's *disgusto*.

With the Revolution Javier de Varona turned to the extreme Left and at some stage he collaborated with State Security as an informer. Which he would have done with the same moral ease with which he earlier used to steal books from public libraries – and the private ones of his friends. He got married and went to work with a financial firm. One day in 1970 (after the fiasco of the fabled harvest of ten million tons of sugar dreamed as an impossible possible by the absolute Prime Minister) he wrote a document in which he analysed minutely the causes that produced that economic, agricultural and human flop. He arrived at the conclusion, already known by everyone without any analysis, that the maximum one responsible for the maximum failure was the Maximum Leader – that is, Fidel Castro himself. He sent out his statement to the Minister for Economy and the analysis followed the predicted course: from the hands of the Minister of those of the Prime Minister.

Javier ended up in goal, incommunicado. After a week they returned him quietly to his house. Without saying anything to anyone Javier de Varona wrote all night long and the next morning committed suicide. What he wrote was his political testament. Naïve, as always, he thought that someone would publish it one day. When his wife discovered her husband's dead body, what was once the jovial Javier, and picked up his written pages and read what he had written, she decided to call the police straight away. In place of the police State Security came. They saw the

2 *Footnote to history*: on 17 April 1961 there was a strange occurrence in Pinar del Rio that only a few people knew about. During the Bay of Pigs invasion Che, who commanded the Cuban Army on the Western Front, shot himself under the chin but the bullet came out through his left cheek. The scar is still visible in his latest photographs. The official explanation was that Che, an expert in handguns, was cleaning his pistol when it fired – accidentally.

dead body which did not interest them much, but they read the document, demented to them, and advised the widow to declare, for the good of all, that her husband had committed suicide because he knew that he was impotent. They implied sexually impotent. They did not say politically impotent. They took away the unpublished document. The body stayed behind like a dead man already buried in failure. The political or economic testament must still be at the Ministry of the Interior, in some dusty drawer. Or, like Javier de Varona himself, it may be only ashes.

Guevara's epitaph is the film *Che*, the pink Argentine incarnated by the dark Egyptian Omar Sharif, all full of face powder, in an impersonation so atrocious that it deserves derision. (Or is it political justice?) The obituary of poor Javier, given to boisterous mirth and to the criticism of pure unreason, is in a newsreel moment of *Topaz*[3] where Alfred Hitchcock makes his shadow coincide for some historical seconds with an excessive and gesticulating Fidel Castro on the people's platform, Revolution Square, Havana, Cuba. It would be a sinister symmetry to know that as the two coincided in film space, spirited Javier de Varona and garrulous Fidel Castro, at that exact moment, the Maximum Leader was announcing to the people that he had reluctantly accepted the popular suggestion to gather a harvest of ten million tons of sugar – to save the people and the Government of Cuba! (Alarming alarum.)

A case even more strange and symptomatic than that of Javier de Varona was the suicide of Nilsa Espín, a double suicide case. Nilsa was the sister of Vilma Espín who is now a revolutionary, with all her titles and privileges, wife of Raúl Castro, member of the Central Committee of the Communist Party, President of the Federation of Cuban Women, etc. The Espíns, like the Castros, belonged to the upper middle class from Oriente Province, the women to the urban upper middle class, the men to the rural upper middle class. Vilma, peak of the educated upper middle class, was educated in an exclusive American private college, Bryn Mawr or Vassar. But she became famous only after the triumph of the Revolution as the apotheosis of the rebel heroine by marrying Raúl Castro – in a stroke of Castroite propaganda and revolutionary social climbing. (The reluctant bourgeoise's progress.) Her photograph as a pretty Cuban with a gardenia in her black hair was published on the cover of *Life* and ran around the world then: the image of the guerrilla beauty at her wedding with a groom in olive-drab, beret and pony-tail. But Vilma was a latecomer who by a

---

3 A film forever banned in Cuba on orders of *Comandante* Piñeiro, alias *Barbarroja* – depicted by Hitchcock red beard and all.

stroke of chance had served as a messenger between Frank País in Santiago and Raúl Castro in his mountain retreat: a pony express that for a pretty rich girl with a good name known to everyone in the region was a walk in the shade.

The one who really had a long rebel history in Santiago was her sister Nilsa, more modest, less photogenic, incapable of sticking flowers in her hair. When the Revolution triumphed Nilsa also got married, but chose as her companion an obscure rebel with no name. No *comandante* or charismatic leader or guerrilla chief for her. Her name never came out in the newspapers, national or international, much less did her photograph appear in any part of *Life* – not even *Life en español*. She and he worked intensely but anonymously wherever the leadership sent them. He seemed vaguely like a Russian revolutionary with his profuse beard and hirsute hair in disorder. He was some sort of Cuban Trotsky – perilous portrait resemblance – and worked in the agrarian reform in Pinar del Rio. There, always the critic, he encountered unexpected opposition – though he might have expected it if he had been less of an idealist. One day in 1969 he shot himself in the temple, to the astonishment of everyone except Raúl Castro. When Nilsa found out she was in Raúl Castro's office in Havana. She shut herself in the bathroom, took out her pistol and shot herself. Raúl Castro was not astonished this time either. It was learned later that the couple had made a secret suicide pact. The Revolutionary Government, now in total control of the press, radio and television, and the news agencies under censorship did not publish the news. *Life* was not going to print the photo of the other Espín: ugly, a failure with a clot of blood in her hair like an atrocious red gardenia. Privately it was commented that it had been known for some time that the deceased couple were disillusioned with the regime and the Revolution. Vilma Espín never explained anything to anyone.

Alberto Mora was the son of one of the leaders of the raid on the Presidential Palace, Menelao Mora, who was killed there. The two were top guns of the Revolutionary Directorate and Alberto, by what he believed was historic chance, would have been among the first to go into the palace but was arrested by the Batista police days before, while struggling to get his father to escape and to be able to head the attack. Alberto was safe in prison when the assault took place and his father and not he died. Now free (Batista was a kind killer who permitted his judges to grant *habeas corpus* while his henchmen released *habeas corpses*) but still clandestine, he risked his life just to eat with friends like me in a fashionable restaurant, in full view, dressed to be killed.

When the Revolution won he shared the initial political disgrace of the *Directorio* – a group that Castro had to annihilate if he wished to rule: he who assaults one palace, assaults two. Then Alberto Mora drifted towards the curious quarters of Che Guevara, united by disgrace – and was protected by the Argentine without a country. Nominally *comandante* of the rebel army, Alberto was named Minister of Foreign Trade, got married and was happy for a time.

Then Che Guevara fell into his penultimate disgrace and Mora was dismissed to be converted into a bashful bureaucrat, a humiliation that he appeared to accept as a deserved punishment: the political penalty for the original sin of being a rebel. Alberto went smiling to his destiny with his twisted smile of always: the bitter Alberto, the friendly, loyal Alberto. At the time of the infamous 'Padilla Case', Alberto Mora, his friend, was among his few defenders, to his derision. Finally, in dour disgrace, he was sent as a sentence to work on a farm 'as a volunteer'. He could not stand this last outrage and shot himself in the mouth with his old army pistol. There was only a brief obituary in *Granma*, the official sheet, which did not even say that he had committed suicide. That last privilege was denied him.

Miguel Angel Quevedo inherited from his father a literary magazine of scarce circulation called *Bohemia*, but not his intellectual inclinations or his elitist taste. When very young the heir converted his magazine into a popular weekly, crude and sensationalist and at the same time profoundly democratic but sentimental. *Bohemia* was in a way one of the creators of the Cuban character of the time and it is no accident that it arose in Cuba along with the apogee of the *bolero*. The rare journalistic talent of Quevedo ran in step with a sound political instinct and so he opposed Batista in 1940, although he had been elected democratically (with help from his friends, the Cuban Communist Party). He then backed Grau San Martín as a presidential candidate – to attack him once in the presidency. As he attacked his successor Carlos Prio – only to defend him once he was toppled by Batista. He again attacked Batista as a dictator with a cunning mixture of audacity and restraint. Quevedo was always ahead of the game in interpreting popular sentiments in politics and making them public in his next issue. Before Fidel Castro came to power (with his backing, among others), Quevedo's favourite politician was Chibás – who never came to power. But Quevedo was anything but a lover of failure. On the contrary, he sought after and shared success (his generosity and the sumptuous weekends spent with friends and collaborators on his farm were famous), but he felt a particular affection for the sanctification of his heroes and so it was not surprising that he had the daring to print a drawing (full page, full colour, detachable) of Fidel Castro, already Prime Minister, early in 1959. The bearded Castro resembled not a possible Marx but another impossible Jew – Jesus!

Years before, at the time of Chibás's suicide, he had converted the photo of a common colonial door and knocker, by adding mourning crêpe and a black title with Chibás's final phrase as an epitaph: 'The last call!' on a *Bohemia* cover that made history. This masterpiece of propaganda (a mixture of allegory and bad taste) was the kitsch of death.

Years later, uniting his heroes of the past, in a final failure, Miguel Angel Quevedo, in a ruinous exile in Venezuela (which is like finding out one is broke in Las Vegas), killed himself with a pistol shot. He left as a testament a letter that ended, 'I am killing myself because Fidel deceived me.' His complex life made his death complicated. A closet homosexual and a very powerful man in Havana (on one occasion Batista offered him a ministry and he declined the offer saying: 'Why do I want to be a minister? I'm more than a minister! I make a lot of ministers sit and wait to see *me*'), Quevedo lost in Caracas his *Bohemia* but he could at last show himself off in public with his young lovers – to the private scandal of his friends and printed rejoicing of his enemies. It is obvious that Miguel Angel Quevedo was not killed by the deceit of Fidel Castro but by having taken part in that deceit – and his own disillusion of grandeur.

This suicidal solitude – that would be praised by the old Catalonian anarchists, the ETA and even Franco's Falangists: 'Long live death!' – was catching. Foreigners like Che Guevara and even those who had come late for the Revolution but early for disenchantment – although they served the Government. One of those was the Argentine Jorge Ricardo Masetti, who came to Cuba as a protégé of Che and thanks to him founded the official news agency Prensa Latina. Masetti had Che's petulance but not his intelligence. Finally he too made, as the Argentines say, his *viaje al muere*: a trip to death in a suicidal mission disguised as a guerrilla war – which he undertook in tardy imitation and early warning.

But not only Argentines were converted into suicides by Cuban contagion. There were Chileans too. Beatriz Allende, daughter and confidante of the late President of Chile of the same name was married to a loose attaché twice darkly in the Cuban Embassy in Santiago. She met the good-looking and modest Cuban before the elections that Allende won to his ultimate regret. Not long after the wedding Blackbeard's wife learned her husband's secret: he was a captain of State Security in Cuba sent by Redbeard (of Party pirates and their nicknames) to Chile with the mission of protecting the President-elect – so that they would not kill him before he took office. They killed him afterwards, of course, and his Cuban guard could not, or did not try to, protect him.

When Allende fell the President's daughter and the bodyguard, shielded in diplomatic immunity, returned to Cuba as a couple. Not long afterwards they separated: mission accomplished for the skilled Cuban agent, who could not impede either, as with her father, the suicide of Allende's favourite daughter. Now Beatriz was living alone behind the sinister but in appearance peaceful headquarters of G2, housed in the formerly elegant district of Miramar. (G2 is the State Security alias: the nomenclature has been inherited without disgust from the Bastista army: the viscosity is mutual.) The neighbours saw her go out sometimes, shy, grey: a shadow of the arrogant woman that Allende's friends knew in Chile. In no time at all Beatriz Allende shot herself, a custom learned in Cuba.

The official communiqué spoke this time of depressions and neurosis. Not so after Beatriz's aunt, Laura, Allende's sister, who was also living in Havana, threw herself from a sixteenth floor to the street. This time *Granma* explained that the other Allende suicide was sick with an incurable illness – which was not the tyranny of Castro, of course. No one said that Laura Allende had been trying for months to leave Cuba to cure the incurability of the illness that killed her.

The unprecedented diplomatic scandal of the mass asylum in the Peruvian Embassy in Havana provoked unexpected nervous breakdowns in previously firm and combative functionaries and the sudden exile of writers on opportune official *tournées* abroad. Some of them worked in the Casa de las Américas under Haydée Santamaría. One of the most solid and firm women in supporting Fidel Castro anywhere, a heroine of the Revolution several times over, Haydée, nicknamed Yeyé, suddenly took her pistol (to every Cuban Communist a Colt .45) and ritually brought it to her mouth, just like a cup of tea. She literally blew off the top of her head. To protect this well-known secret at the wake they had put a covering turban on her, but the real mystery was why she had been given a wake in a public funeral parlour and not in the mortuary of the martyrs on the Plaza de la Revolución. As was learned later Haydée had committed suicide in her own office. Larval neurosis that blooms brutally? Irresistible depression? Why not speak of despair, of total disillusionment or the simple expedient of suicide as the only answer to the defeat that does not see a way out? After all Haydée Santamaría was one of the only two female suicide raiders of the Moncada barracks, as a nurse disposed to die rather than to save lives.

But one must also remember that she knew how to resist then, with enormous courage, the most terrible torture: a Batista soldier presented to her on a tray the eyes of her brother and the testicles of her boyfriend. After the triumph of the Revolution, however, she used to brandish the memory of this atrocious exhibition as a macabre metaphor of her firm revolutionary character and her capacity for mental endurance. She would use this narrative of political Grand Guignol to win ideological arguments – and even cultural ones.

A woman whose lack of intelligence ran parallel with an enormous ignorance, Santamaría was able to found, direct and control for twenty years an official cultural organization, the Casa de las Américas, which was certainly not the Bauhaus but was not far from the Soviet Ministry of Culture under Ekaterina Furtseva. The Casa de las Américas also subtly infiltrated agents into assorted countries of South and North America and offered refuge to many 'friends' of Cuba now in flight from their aboriginal seats. Besides the personal and political confidence of Castro (although the latter may not have understood as much about a house of culture, or even of any culture that did not serve his ends, as did the then President Osvaldo Dorticós), Haydée now enjoyed the protection of her sometime husband Armando Hart, Minister for Culture and a man with whom she could reach a perfect understanding across the abyss of their respective ignorances. Even the notorious opportunism of Hart could counterpoise the lack of ductility of Yeyé.

It appeared then that there was no motive for the suicide of that Yeyé who did not know the meaning of the word boredom: impossible for her to be attacked by a *tedium vitae*. But – is it not possible that she suffered from power tedium? Absolute power disillusions absolutely. After all an opponent is like some sort of cure for paranoia. Also there was talk of a so-called will that Haydée Santamaría served to Fidel Castro on a tray of revolutionary memories. The Cuban press, it goes without saying, said nothing of metaphorical or real testaments and tried to hide the date of her death. According to *Granma* it happened on 28 July. Some in the know in exile maintain that the suicide took place on 27 July, a private date for her mourning for the death of her brother and her boyfriend. You won't have to cheat to wager and win that Haydée Santamaría committed suicide on the 26 July 1980.

There are other less well-known suicides, like *Comandante* Peña, who also chose the last recourse of the pistol, the trigger and the bullet in the temple. Or *Comandante* Eddy Suñol, hero of the guerrilla war in the Sierra, who became Vice-Minister of the Interior in peacetime – or what passes for a time of peace in Cuba. Those deaths are not only possible, but inevitable in a Revolution whose only convincing contribution to revolutionary literature is the *consigna* of '*Patria o Muerte*'. If one compares this mortal motto with the favourite phrase of the French revolutionaries, '*Liberté, Egalité, Fraternité*,' one will see not only the mental poverty but also the moral misery of Fidel Castro's favourite phrase. The motto '*Patria o Muerte*' (the Maximum Leader's maxim, probably conceived by the hero of the urban guerrilla war in Santiago de Cuba, Frank País, who really died and became the martyr he wished to be) is a crude derivation from old Cuban mottoes, like '*Independencia o Muerte*', cooked up in the nineteenth century during the second war of independence, and the slogan, still visible in 1959 on the silver coins of '*Patria y Libertad*'.

But all this must hark back to Martí if one speaks of Cuba and death. It was Martí who ended his famous call to arms in the *Manifesto of Montecristi* with a phantasmal phrase, '*La Victoria o el Sepulcro*'. Martí of his own volition fulfilled a part of the motto and converted it into a morbid prophecy. He had written words no less dark to declare that death is the ineffable breast where all sublime dreams are forged. It is not possible to accumulate a greater quantity of *thanatos* in less creative space. His *Versos sencillos*, so popular, so simple, so full of light, abound in invocations to death. An offering to his cult of death is that verse cited and recited by so many schoolchildren, in which Martí confesses the desire to die with his face to the sun. In spite of the context the expression is frankly political. Curious – or not so curiously – the final phrase was adopted and adapted well into the twentieth century by a Spanish poet who was also a convert to the religion of death. I am referring to the *Falangista* poet Dionisio Ridruejo. The end of that verse was made a motto to give a name to the anthem of the Spanish *Falange*. It is called 'Cara al sol'. Face to the sun. A mere Martían metamorphosis.

Now in Cuba in the motto of '*Patria o Muerte*' the idea of Patria barely makes sense in the context much less in its maximum expression by the Maximum Leader. No one, except his brother Raúl, seems to have the right to say it in public. Or is it that no one else has a full voice in Cuba? In any case Fidel Castro always accentuates the negative at the end of every speech. If not the idea at least the fatal fury that goes with the sound of death looms like the voice of doom.

The three great religions born in the Middle East, that do not reject death but rather seize it like the day, all condemn suicide without dodges. Of the three, the oldest, the original, the one that seems to have invented this proscription, Judaism, declares in the Talmud that given that life is sacred suicide is therefore a sinful act. Christianity is opposed to suicide with extreme emphasis, reasoning more with theology than logic. (Aristotle, for example, would not understand this proposition.) If all human life is the work of God, who gives it and takes it away, the suicide always makes an attempt against the divine will and man tries to raise himself as God by killing himself. Saint Augustine does not excuse suicide either as a flight from pain or from sickness. Not even to escape imminent rape: better the most uncomfortable fornication. All the Fathers of the Church do not hesitate in condemning suicide. In the Middle Ages some Christian legislations prescribed the mutilation of the body of the suicide and ordered the immediate confiscation of all his goods. Of course both punishments were onerous only to the family of the *felo de se*. (This was the technical name of the suicide in medieval England.) Until not long ago (1961) suicide was a crime punished severely by the courts of the Crown. Of course only the failed suicide was punished. The state was encouraging thus the efficacy of suicide rather than succeeding in decreasing the number of deaths by suicide. The sole survivor of a suicide pact, for example, was automatically presumed guilty of murder, according to an English law abolished in 1957. More modern now, they judge him guilty only of homicide. Until the last century the English treated the body of a suicide just as the Hungarians used to exorcize the vampire: they buried the corpse at a crossroads with a sharp stake sunk in its chest.

It would seem that Islam must have been more indulgent with the Muslim suicide than was the Judaeo-Christian world. Quite the contrary. Muhammad himself considered suicide a crime worse than homicide and sent the Saudi suicide to the most feared hell: the eternal desert without the water of Allah. The soul of the suicide was condemned to wander for ever among sands in the sun.

Another prophet, Marx, is no less implacable with the suicide than his Jewish ancestors or the Lutheran Church in whose realm he grew up or Victorian England where he lived and wrote and conceived Marxism as an exact science – although it is actually another Hebraic heresy. His followers decreed that suicide was contrary to Communism. Anti-Marxist and therefore counter-revolutionary. But they had no sooner formulated this law against escape to hell when they encountered heretics, now not among the Disciples but even in the Holy Home itself. (The First Law of the Heresiarch is that all heresies produce heretics.) The first and greatest consternation occurred within the Family with the suicide pact of Paul Lafargue and his wife Laura. When engraving the red tablets of the Materialist Law the bearded god Karl himself had prohibited suicide with the threat of eternal expulsion from the Party and thereby from history. It was only admitted, reluctantly, as a last resort not of the individual but of the revolutionary.

The pistol in the temple must serve to fire for the last time against the bourgeois bastion from the revolutionary barricades. But, ironies of history (and even of the petite Marxist history), Laura Lafargue's maiden name was Laura Marx and she was the favourite daughter of old Karl, whom she used to call the Moor on account of his dark look. Even more interesting is that behind the mask of that Frenchified Paul Lafargue a poor Pablo was hidden. Lafargue was a mulatto from Santiago de Cuba who by the fate – or perhaps wanderings – of the rebel exiled from Cuba came to join the Prussian red progeny of Marx in their London lair. The Marxes used to call Lafargue *el negrito* – always behind Laura's back. In the posthumous Party process that followed the Lafargues' double suicide, the after-the-fact prosecutor of the deceased was a German apostle of Marxism, one August Bebel, an old Communist, friend of Marx and author of a Victorian bestseller that women back then read avidly. It was not a romantic novel but a totally German tract titled *Woman and Socialism*. It would ruin my theory of a Cuban ideology of suicide if I said that Herr Professor ended his days throwing himself from his tower of Bebel. He never did: he died of old age.

Nevertheless, in spite of the Marxist trial, there was another heretic among the Marxes. The third daughter of Karl who lived to be an adult, the most unhappy of them all, married to another Marxist (the young Communists of the age treated the Marx family like pretenders to a European royal house – but isn't that what it was?), the abused Irishman Edward Aveling. She also committed the nefarious sin of ending her ides of Marx.

This old dirty laundry of the Marx family was washed in the light of the white Russian nights. It was on the occasion of the pathetic suicide of Adolf Yoffe, who shot himself in a corridor of the Kremlin. Yoffe, ill and ruined by Stalin, saw no other exit from the Kremlin but suicide. Stalin had forbidden him to leave Russia despite the fact that his life depended on it: he had to go abroad to be cured of an illness incurable by Soviet science. (But not, it appears, by bourgeois medicine.) The death that he chose made one forget the life that he had lived: in illness, in the iniquity of being subservient to Stalin, incipient tsar, and serving under the worst tyrant, pain.

One only saw the dilemma of a revolutionary who commits suicide: a Utopian who rejects the future life to choose death and a materialist who becomes *felo de se*. Stalin solved the problem with a solution spoken with the scorn that already was beginning to be his best political weapon. (Scorn is the only sense of humour permitted the tyrant: Stalin had plenty of it.) 'Marxists don't commit suicide,' stated Comrade Stalin, to whom cantoed General Neruda. 'A Marxist has not committed suicide,' was Stalin's verdict. 'It's a Trotskyite who has committed suicide.' That's what poor Yoffe was: a Jew, an intellectual and the first victim of Stalin as political judge and hangman. But Yoffe's was not the only suicide whose last shot echoed in the halls of the Kremlin. Nadia Alliluyeva, not Jewish and not a Trotskyite but the second wife of Stalin, also committed suicide there. Later this suicide, so private that it could be kept from Western ears for thirty years, would become a world-wide scandal in the memoirs of her daughter, Svetlana Stalin.

According to Freud, who explains as dogmatically as Marx condemns, suicide is always linked to depression – clinical or otherwise. It is the depressed who most often kill themselves and some Freudians diagnose that *only* the depressed commit suicide. A suicide in exaltation, *à la* Dostoevsky, is virtually impossible. Although, as Borges said, Dostoevsky always follows his theory: nobody is impossible. But the Freudians do not stop here: Freud rushed in where Engels feared to tread. To the climatic perturbation of those Marxists who may cherish the idea of suicide in the tropics, there is a sequitur that seems to be none. Depression and suicide can only be understood in terms of an impulse against the other (Hell is other people, according to Sartre), a compelling force that is always turned against being. Or against man. Or better still, against the proletarian hero made a martyr by his own hand. There follows then a battle between the ego and the superego, with the final victory (or defeat) of the superego. Suicide is a continuum of forces of aggression and aggression against the self. Pavese, writer and suicide, who should have known what he was talking about, claimed that the suicide is a shy murderer. According to a follower of Freud, suicide has three elements (a kind of infernal trinity), which are: (1) the wish to kill, (2) the wish to be killed, (3) the wish to die. (All forms of a death wish.) It is evident that the realization of the second wish carries with it the fulfilment of the third – but Freudians like to explain the obvious. A typical not Oedipal complex.

(My digressions, do not, I hope, hide the fact that this theory of suicide has borrowed without attribution from the fable of the hideous monkey's paw, always lethal.)

Another Viennese, Louis Dublin, proposed that the causes of suicide are feelings of fear, of inferiority and the death wish against that other with whom the individual identifies. Dublin, after a paternoster (for Freud) fingered his rosary like an analyst's worry beads, a prayer that it is unnecessary to copy or repeat – it seems to me.

Curious that all these Freudians and Freud himself have never explained why so many analysts commit suicide, among them eminent Freudians like Wilhelm Stekl and Anna Freud. Even the grand old man, Freud not Marx, committed a slow suicide upon learning that he had an incipient cancer of the mouth by never giving up, to the end, the habit of smoking cigar after cigar, Havanas capable of giving you cancer in a closed mouth – so was Freud's before the couch. (A pity that they don't make Freudian cigars in Havana capable of giving cancer to so many open mouths that shout.) One last Freudian note. Freud's own doctor claims that he gave his patient a lethal dose of a painkiller that in fact killed him – with Freud's final blessing.

> As I see it, only the monotheistic, that is Jewish, religions, see self-destruction as a crime. It is still more notable that neither in the Old nor in the New Testament can one find any prohibition or disapproval. Thus the teachers of faith base their prohibition of suicide upon philosophical terrain of their invention. They appear so poor that their arguments lack force. So much so that they try to infuse vigour into the terms with which they express their abhorrence. That is, they recur to the insult.

The above belongs to Schopenhauer and his target is Judaism and Christianity, but they could well be applied to Marxism – of yesterday and today. Marx has become a prophet and, at times, a god. His Jewish schism has been transformed into heresy.

Schopenhauer ends his disquisition with a note at once physical and spiritual: 'What makes suicide easier is that the physical pain associated with it loses all meaning in the eyes of someone affected by an excessive spiritual suffering.' Such suffering, applied to politics and combined with the idea of nation, is, of course, patriotism. The last refuge of the scoundrel is converted thus into the nearest exit from historical life. Says Schopenhauer a little earlier: 'Generally one finds that when the terrors of life surpass the terror of death man puts an end to his days.' The terrors of the political life are, simply, in our days, sheer terror.

Émile Durkheim. contemporary of Freud, in his *opus magnum* on suicide, called, naturally, *Suicide* (1897), classifies suicides into two groups: egoists and those with anomie, the first characteristic of our society, while the altruistic suicide (to the surprise of the Marxists) is proper to primitive societies. This is almost like saying that egoism is the last phase of socialism. As we know Marx castigated egoism with a phrase worthy of Dante the theologian and called its natural element, contrary to militant fire, 'the frozen waters of egoist calculation'. The suicide without a doubt dives into these icy waters on making his last figuring out. Why then does the Communist, an animal who after reading Marx not only attacks man but also wounds himself mortally, commit suicide? There must be a Marxist, that is a philosophic, explanation. There isn't.

The familiar opinion of Albert Camus when he waxes existential to declare that there is only one philosophical problem, that of suicide, is nothing more than a phrase that has become a catch-phrase always taken out of context. But even in its context it is no more than a French phrase, which are often like Christmas baubles: brilliant but empty. Camus was an essayist who wanted to be taken for a philosopher, a novelist who passed as a grave thinker (Dostoevsky who sinks in his Seine) and a playwright for whom all his dialogues were turned into an exchange of French phrases, a league of notions that are no more than *bons mots*, as felicitous or facile as the epigrams of Oscar Wilde – a playwright who was always blamed for his *coups de théâtre*. Camus offers instead fatalist *coups de philosophe* that will never abolish Wilde. According to Camus *le fataliste*, to judge whether life is worth or not the pain of being lived is to respond to *the* fundamental question of philosophy.[4] There are so many fundamental questions in philosophy that finding just one is to exclude as impertinent the most pertinent ones. To Plato, for example, the suicide of Socrates does not answer a philosophical question but rather originates them all. There are more things in philosophy than in heaven and earth, as was well known by Horatio, a good student who did not want to be rudely precise to the vague Hamlet – among other reasons, because the latter was a crown prince who threatened to be a king one day.

Nevertheless the way out of suicide is indeed the fundamental problem

---

4 In passing, Camus, in a footnote to *l'histoire*, speaks of an 'honourable suicide'. He mentions as an example the political suicides, 'cries of protest', in the Chinese revolution – which is surely the permanent revolution of Mao. He wished it so much that he paralysed it. Furthermore, in *From Death Camp to Existentialism*, Viktor Frankl says: 'Not a few cases of suicide could be traced to an existential vacuum – this lack of goal'. Sartre, on the other hand, thinks that existential vacuum is a *maladie bourgeoise*. So much for all Cuban revolutionary suicides!

of politics – even in times not of famine but of hunger strikes: dying as a political weapon. Is the continuous struggle worth the trouble or is it better to exit on time through the narrow door of suicide towards the endless prairies of history, that every ideology promises to its faithful like the paradise of the believer? Even for the fanatics of permanent revolution, the sons of Trotsky, there is a single question, the one that has a sole decisive answer: that of choosing between eternal history or nothingness. A recent collective response came from the Baader-Meinhof gang, which astonished everyone because the astonished aficionados did not have a Cuban notion of history. In Cuba for some time many revolutionaries have been living on the edge of being permanently clandestine. Hamlet might have been a bad philosopher and a worse politician but his 'To be or not to be' is still the Cuban question.

If the theory of suicide is an easy study for Camus, as it is hard practice for Hamlet, the aetiology of suicide is difficult of definition for psychiatrists, psychologists and psychoanalysts – pragmatists as theoreticians, empiricists as doctors.

Inadmissible for religious and materialists alike, suicide ceases to be an undefinable problem when it is observed as an absolute ideology to be in the historical domain. In Cuba, at the beginning of Fidel Castro's seizure, they tried to substitute ideology for practice. It was, simply, the ignorance that does not dare to speak its name – because, among other things, it doesn't know how to pronounce it. From this primitive ignorance (praised by that cockeyed seer that was Sartre) they proceeded to uncertain ideological babblings (sayings and deeds of Che), to learn by heart the *Communist Manifesto* like a primer and to mouth some apothegms of Marx as passwords. (It must be said that none of them knew what an apothegm was and very few succeeded in pronouncing this foreign word without falling into comic caricatures: apathem, arpotheme – this last version doubtless contaminated by another Marx, Harpo. It was decided then that apothegm was a bourgeois utensil. (Like the fish knife.)

Next came the servile times of squeezing oneself into the narrow Russian ideological corset, an artefact conceived, designed and manufactured by a certain Zozo Dzhugashvili, alias Stalin, Marxist dress designer. Of course Fidel Castro never had even to fit into a Muscovite model because the Maximum Leader is beyond theory: he is made of pure practice. That is a place in the geometry of the Hegelian spirit where even the impractical becomes theory and is *fons et origo* of all correct thinking.

Of course it goes along correcting its correction, like a political compass, according to circumstances. This fount of all wisdom keeps changing its source but it is nothing more than the old bathing in the historical Jordan, a purifying immersion capable of baptisms or of dippings.

With Fidel Castro, besides the pure practice, there sufficed one declaration as a degree thesis to reach his graduation *summa cum laude*: 'I am and always have been a Marxist-Leninist!' This outburst is like an announcement from the tribune to the marketplace (*agora*): 'I have always been a Neoplatonist.' Without ever having heard Plotinus speak or read a single dialogue of Plato or even a title for that matter. Of course without learning Greek either: for Fidel Castro all philosophy is Greek. Underdevelopment or ignorance? Simply theory and practice of political opportunism. In 1939 Castro would have spoken of Goebbels and of Rosenberg as ideologues of the new theory.

Later on there was an ideological backsliding – *corso ricorso* in a St Vico's dance, a hysterical or historical malaise. Or an attempt at an ideology departing from Soviet statism, in which any praxis is seen as a revision of Marxist theory. This revisionism was committed in front of someone like Fidel Castro whose only contribution to the theory of Marx as according to Stalin is not a novel interpretation but a new pronunciation of Marx's philosophy, known now as *Marxim-Leninim*. The s's were slid out sloppily but the criticism and even the occasional commentary were really heard as a menace to the total leader in totalitarian Cuba.

To insist on criticism, *any* criticism, is always a suicidal act, as has been seen in cases as diverse as that of Che Guevara, Alberto Mora and Javier de Varona, all different *felos de se* but the same suicide. Or that *suicida magna* that was Haydée Santamaría, whose suicide shook the regime for ten days. Not out of sentiment for the fallen comrade but from her political significance: an idol that is shattered. There are, besides, the many minor deaths, ghosts of Communism that haunt the island with a motto: 'Communists of Cuba, commit suicide. You have nothing to lose but your life.'

The practice of suicide is the only and, of course, definitive Cuban ideology. A rebel ideology – permanent rebellion by perennial suicide. Martí would thus be our early Trotsky: ideologue, politician, failed guerrilla but successful suicide, the *felo de se* with faith in the open grave. To victory by the sepulchre! Death or death! We will perish! (We hear the strains of the National Anthem, sung by a distant chorus of voices from beyond the grave: '*Cuban, die by your own hand / For to die for the fatherland is to die.*')

(January 1983)

POST MORTEM

As the first but not the last link of this theorem to theory (visibly interminable) there must be added the name of Dr Osvaldo Dorticós Torrado.
Dorticós, as everyone called him, was a public personage with a private life
that justifies the adjective checkered. His career was a game of checkers
although he always wanted to believe he was playing chess. His doctorate
was only in law and he had been born in Cienfuegos in the Province of Las
Villas. 'Cienfuegos is the city / that most pleases me,' sang Beny Moré, but
it was really the third city of Cuba, constantly aspiring to the condition of
first. This illusion of grandeur was catching to its citizens: Carlos Rafael
Rodríguez, perennial third man in the regime, Edith García Buchaca,
cultural boss of the Communist Party and, for a time, of the regime of
Fidel Castro (to earn herself a fifteen-year house arrest) and Doctor
Dorticós, who thought himself President for Life – and it was only for
death. Dorticós was the second president elected by a show of one hand by
Fidel Castro to replace Dr Manuel Urrutia, who had been named before
by Castro (in the very January of 1959), who back then was already making
kings – and unmaking them. Dorticós, like Urrutia, was dismissed by Fidel
Castro, this time to occupy his post himself but without a First Lady. He
could be not only Macbeth but Mrs Macbeth as well.

Since then the brilliant star of the *ancien régime* society lawyer, who had
even been Commodore of the very exclusive (give me neither the poor nor
the blacks was its motto) Yacht Club of Cienfuegos, the sun of yore went
down fast – from the ideological zenith to the political nadir – to die out,
extinguished in the nothingness to which it never aspired. Dorticós followed the way of all political flash in Cuba and shot himself with a pistol of
the same calibre as Haydée Santamaría's: it couldn't be smaller. The
Cuban authorities did not hold back the news this time. It was the suicide
of an ex-President, but they did edit it after their Manichaean manner:
they said that Dr Osvaldo Dorticós Torrado suffered from unendurable
physical and mental pains. The physical pains were produced in him by a
simple lesion of a lumbar disc, which is operable even in people given to
curvature of the spine. The mental pains originated in the death of his wife
– which had occurred two years earlier and for whom he never showed a
particular affection. She weighed three hundred pounds at her death and
in life was known as *La Caguama*, the giant leather-backed turtle that
comes to Cuba every year to lay an egg. The truth that the mouthpiece of
the Government did not say was that Dorticós, become a political pariah

(from President to mere minister and from there straight down on the narrow Cuban way), decided to opt for the final solution.

(Some have alleged that it was the reading of the first version of this essay that moved the ex-President and ex-minister to join his Cienfuegos ancestors. This would of course, be to take the effect for the cause.)

APPENDIX I

Rafael del Pino was, like Guiteras, Cuban-American and an eternal law student, like Fidel Castro, whose friend and companion he was in the University Student Federation as in the Insurrectional Revolutionary Union. This UIR and that FEU were the two pistols of a politician: they served for ballots and bullets. Del Pino, an older leader, brought Fidel Castro to Bogotá to a spurious student event, an apparent meeting of *scholars* that would be held to boycott the meeting of the Pan-American Conference that originated the OAS in 1948. As a symptom of what Machiavelli called *la grande confuzione*, Castro's and del Pino's air tickets were paid by Juan Perón, the man who was Evita. Nineteen forty-eight is the year when *1984* was written in London, but in Bogotá it was when they killed Jorge Eliecer Gaytán, the demagogue that all the Colombians called, imitating his lisp, Thorthe Eliether.

Castro and Rafael del Pino took part in the disturbances that followed the assassination of Gaitán and the lynching of his assassin, a madman curiously named Sierra. It is not known what del Pino and Castro did (or did not do) among the killing mobs, but it was not exactly to have a demi-tasse of Colombian coffee. Both had to seek refuge suddenly in the generous Cuban Embassy in Bogotá and were put on a cargo plane headed for Havana. From then on Rafael del Pino was one of the most faithful faithfuls of Castro. This fidelity to Fidel, as happened to many others, would cost him his life one day.

But for a time Felo and Fidel were trigger-happy-go-lucky and together they plotted against Prío. Because of those plots, they had to plot against Batista: that's called swimming in troubled waters. It was in Mexico that the boon brothers were converted into Cain and Abel. Or into Christ and Judas, according to Castro who accused del Pino of treason. Rafael del Pino had to abandon successively the 26th of July Movement, the city and the country. But he returned to Cuba, now free from Batista, in January 1959. A man of 'successive and opposite loyalties', later that year del Pino was accused, precisely, of 'aiding Batistan henchmen to leave the island'.

He was tried for 'conspiring against the powers of the State' – and sentenced to thirty years in prison. As at other times, Rafael del Pino escaped with life by a miracle – or, as Fidel Castro put it, 'thanks to the generosity of the Revolution'. (It makes you shudder to think what a *mean* Revolution would do to its victims!) Finally, Rafael del Pino became a pertinacious suicide when, after innumerable attempts, his guards permitted him to hang himself – in his solitary confinement cell. It happened in the Combined Prison of the East, the most modern and cruel of Castro's prisons. No one ever explained what a rope was doing in the cell of the hanged man.

The suicide of Rafael del Pino, eternal student, occurred in 1980, which was, as are all, a good year to commit suicide in Cuba. Sceptical? I have here some numbers that show that mathematics are crueller (or truer) than the most daring fiction. If anyone still doubts my thesis or does not believe in my words, I donate to them these painstaking, obscene and perfectly incredible figures. The current suicide rate in Cuba is 21.6 for each 100,000 Cubans. It is the greatest cause of death in Revolutionary Cuba between the ages of fifteen and forty-five. This is certainly the highest suicide rate in the Americas. It doubles that of the United States, a cruel and capitalist country, while insurgent Mexico, incidentally, only has an average of 1.8 suicides per 100,000 Mexicans. This morbid statistic appeared in a report from the Ministry of Health – of Cuba. As always they omitted the explanations, even the most obvious ones. For those who believe in chance I can add that these facts were published in 1980. Any doubt? All the figures were compiled by the *Bureau of Suicides* of the Ministry of the Interior.

APPENDIX 2

There is another horseman on the battlefield of death. It was Onelio Pino, ex-captain of the Cuban Navy and skipper of the *Granma*, the yacht on which Castro came to Cuba with his men in the expedition of 1956. Onelio Pino was the brother of the Cuban actress with a Havana name, Orquídea Pino, then married to a Mexican oil engineer. Both aided Castro in his persuasion. In their house in the Pedregal (a wealthy neighbourhood of Mexico City), Castro used to get together with his followers. In Cuba the mental health of Onelio Pino deteriorated as much as his relationship with Castro. One night he shut himself up in his garage, started his car engine and breathed all the exhaust fumes that one's lungs can take in to lose consciousness. The rest was done by the carbon monoxide – or was it too much Castro?

There are suicides by political contamination. In Chile, so far and so near to Cuba, Salvador Allende also committed suicide. A note from *El País* of December 1990 says:

> 'Allende committed suicide,' affirms [Juan] Seoane. According to him and [David] Garrido, 'the versions about how he died in combat and was finished off are pure lies. The fact that he has committed suicide does not take away courage in any way from him.'

APPENDIX 3

It is painful when one's friends are converted into statistics. Pedro Luis Boitel was a revolutionary student and student leader when he crashed on to Castro's power machine. From the university he went on to that other university, gaol. I have related (in the voice of his mother in *View of Dawn in the Tropics*) how Boitel died. But neither his mother nor I said that it had been a suicide: Boitel died on a hunger strike in Castillo del Príncipe – such an elegant name but a sordid prison in the middle of Havana. Boitel, with no weapon other than his voice, died by his own hand.

Olga Andreu appears in *Infante's Inferno* as she was: the muse of all of us far away and long ago. Her strange fascination went beyond her beauty and she was a mentor of writers and poets and film-makers for more than a generation. Her acute critical sense and her insights were hidden behind an amiable accent, but Olga never accepted mediocrity even at the cost of her loneliness. When everything became, more than mediocre, anodyne, she decided to put an end to what remained of her life. She threw herself from the balcony of the sixth floor where she lived most of her life. (Curiously that building carried the name of another suicide, Chibás.) Olga, it must be said, was charm herself: I have known few women so enchanting and at the same time less conscious of their seductiveness. Few recent deaths have been so painful.

Reinaldo Arenas committed suicide in New York, the city that from being irresistible came to be impossible. He was the total exile: from his country, from a cause, from his sex, and he died fighting against the Devil that exiled him. There has not been an anti-Castroist as tenacious and as effective. When AIDS did not allow him to live, he died as he had lived: at war with Castro. But his political activity did not prevent him from know-ing that his Cuban destiny was literature and he has left behind at least two novels that are two masterpieces. He rests not in peace but in war.

A shorter version of this essay appeared in number 17/18 of Escalandar, January 1982. Then it was taken by Vuelta. Both versions have been much enlarged: suicides keep on coming in Cuba like a gross domestic product.

MEN IN IRON MASKS

Asterism

asterism *n.*, three asterisks arranged in a triangle
to draw attention to the text that follows.

Collins Dictionary

The InterAmerican Bank invited me to give a talk, in
Spanish, in its home office in Washington and a Cuban film-maker in
exile, who now lives in Hollywood, came to visit me in London at the time.
We were talking movies in my study in London when the telephone rang.
When I picked it up a woman told me that the Ambassador of Venezuela in
Washington wanted to speak to me. Immediately afterwards, I heard a
Venezuelan voice that asked me if I could postpone my talk. I believed that
he was asking me to choose another date. Maybe, I thought, it is an official
date: birth or death of Bolívar. (I'm not well versed on South American
patriotic ephemera.) But the ambassador told me bluntly that it would be
better if I postponed my event.

I didn't understand because I was still thinking about a collision of
dates. 'I mean to say,' said the voice, 'that it is best if you do not give your
talk.' What did that mean? I still didn't understand: I am rather torpid on
the phone. Without more delay the ambassador proposed that I postpone
my talk *sine die*. I still did not understand: my earwax was becoming as
thick as Bakelite. 'Look,' he said, 'let me be frank with you.' Which was
surprising in an ambassador: diplomats cannot afford to be frank. 'My
Cuban friends have asked me to ask you not to speak in Washington. Not
to come.' It seemed to me that he was totally out of step diplomatically –
and I told him so. How was it that an ambassador of a democratic country
was lending himself as a mouthpiece for a group of Castroite foreign
agents, on American territory? I lost the diplomatic calm that I once had
and informed the plenipotentiary that he, the ambassador of a democracy,
had been put to the service of a mob of gangsters. Did you know that the
Cuban Embassy is not an embassy at all but an interest section? He knew

it. Of course he knew it. Stuttering, the descendant of Bolívar excused himself and hung up. The nerve!

My film-maker friend had not said a word but he had his mouth open. I returned to the phone to call Caracas immediately: an old friend, Sofía Imber de Rangel, knew the political and cultural world in Venezuela inside out. I told her what had happened. When I finished her mouth was as wide open as my visitor's. But she closed it to open it more and to leave me with the most open mouth of the evening. The ambassador was no ambassador at all but a mere cultural attaché. Surely he constantly aspired to the condition of ambassador – perhaps with a little help from his friends. I didn't doubt it. The meanderings of Venezuelan politics take their design from the Orinoco River: all end up in the sea where Bolívar once ploughed. A bitter harvest in the city that was once called Angostura and is now called Ciudad Bolívar.

I gave the talk, of course I gave it. But the Bank, cautious as all banks are, stationed security agents through all the aisles and aislets that were going to flow into my river of parody.

Nota bene. The Castroist emissary at the moment was called Sánchez Parodi, today Castro's Vice-Minister of Foreign Affairs. He might have been Parodi but he was not the target of my parodies. Parody is an act of love and those men are hideous.

Lives of a Hero

THE RELUCTANT HERO

I met Gustavo Arcos, when he was Ambassador of Cuba in Belgium, where I arrived as cultural attaché in October 1962. He then resided in Brussels, on Avenue Brugmann, near the old headquarters of the Embassy on Avenue Molière. There, in the building of the Avenue Brugmann where I would also live, he had his ambassador's residence: a modest studio with a single bedroom, bath and kitchenette. Gustavo, a religious and quiet man, was the living image of the revolutionary in exile that he had been. He was at that time placing those virtues entirely at the service of the Revolution, but he seemed to be an envoy of Loyola rather than of Castro. Nevertheless there was nothing Jesuitical in Arcos, and nothing Communist either. Gustavo was a frank man, incapable of intrigues because he didn't need them or perhaps because he didn't know how. Arcos was a genuine hero of the Revolution. Those virtues were the cause of his demise and final fall.

I had seen Gustavo Arcos in Havana before, when I visited him in the old Orthopaedic Hospital. I went with Carlos Franqui, who had already begun to soldier in the 26th of July Movement. That was, of course, clandestine then. Gustavo was convalescing in the hospital and the visit had a furtive character allowed by the political police of Batista as precarious charity. After a few days Gustavo, semi-invalid, escaped from the hospital. (Franqui, I believe, was no stranger to his flight.) Captured again he was sent this time to the *presidio* on Isla de Pinos. Already a prisoner there was Fidel Castro, one of the leaders of the assault on the Moncada barracks in Santiago de Cuba. It was in that attack that Gustavo ended up gravely wounded. That he was saved from his wound in the combat as much as from the reprisal by the Batista army is a parry that owes more to chance than to history. It was also an astonishing dénouement and, like every crucial historical incident, it is tinged with a savage and at the same time refined irony. One of the agents of that ironic game is General Ramiro Valdés, now Minister of the Interior in Cuba. Then General

Valdés was nicknamed Ramirito, he didn't wear a beard and he was what was called in Cuba a *Russian* mulatto. The correct adjective is of course rufous, but the popular vocabulary has its presciences. Valdés was, is, Russian.

In Brussels I became close to Gustavo. Among other things because we all had to live in the new embassy, a mansion of some ten bedrooms that was, as if by chance, in front of the Russian Embassy. The building and grounds of the Soviet mission were sited, as if by chance, where the general headquarters of the Gestapo in Belgium had been. Chesterton was right after all: there are buildings whose sole architecture is evil. (Or which attract evil.) At times, in that Cuban Embassy which had been a bourgeois hotel, during the short summer nights, Gustavo and I talked until dawn. Gustavo told me then the story of his life. Starting, of course, with where he began his political life and his death almost occurred: the assault on the Moncada barracks and the miracle that saved his life. But one must begin with its antecedents.

In March 1952, when that ambitious and cowardly general, Fulgencio Batista, whose rank and even name were false (he was really called Rubén Zaldívar and, like Fidel Castro, was a bastard) masterminded his *coup d'état*, Gustavo felt what all of us in Cuba who were over twenty felt. Batista had carried out a coup not against President Prío but against the elections that were to have been held barely three months later. He was not only the sudden creator of all our political frustrations, but also a traitor to the same constitution that he had helped to enact twelve years before. Gustavo decided to do something drastic, though he did not know what. It was a response to an imprecise and vague civic pain but one that had to be remedied even if it might deepen the wound. These are almost Gustavo's own words on one of those white nights when he told me of his political life and I composed his biography in my mind.

Gustavo Arcos was a poor student enrolled in the Faculty of Social Sciences of the University of Havana for the year 1951–2. Barely three months before the academic year ended Batista launched his *coup d'état*. 'Bloodless', the dictator and his press called it: bloodless it was but Batista would cause more blood to be spilled in Cuba than any other Cuban dictator, with the exception, of course, of Fidel Castro. The *coup d'état* occurred on 10 March 1952. From that very moment Gustavo devoted all his time and energies to combating the illegal regime. He associated with other students like Faustino Pérez (an intern who later, as a doctor, would be a minister several times in the Castro Government) and with Léster

Rodriguez, through whom he would meet Raúl Castro, a friendship that, with time, would turn out terribly wrong.

Gustavo Arcos participated in several public demonstrations and every Sunday ritually attended the *University on the Air*, to form a claque for the more or less anti-Batista radio interventions – all tolerated by the dictator. Finally the *University on the Air* was raided by Batista's mobsters and the programme was shut down. It was virtually impossible to stage a public political demonstration then. Batista's police were not effective in suppressing the opposition, but they could indeed make it go into hiding. Even the dispersed hosts of the deposed President Carlos Prío were moving on that subterranean ground that undermines the apparently solid edifice of all dictatorships. So when Léster Rodríguez invited him to a demonstration in Santiago de Cuba, Gustavo Arcos decided to move to Oriente Province for a reduced mobilization in Santiago, almost a thousand miles from the capital. The pretext for the displacement of this group of young *habaneros* (Gustavo was then twenty-five years old) was the Carnival of Santiago, to be celebrated, the reverse of Havana, in high summer. None of the demonstrators knew how to dance.

Fidel Castro, along with Abel Santamaría, Raúl Castro, Ramiro Valdés and others, had secretly planned not a civil demonstration but an attack on the Moncada barracks, the second in importance on the island. But the assault was not yet an assault. Few of the supposed demonstrators knew that they were going to a warlike operation: an action of an urban guerrilla that was never defined as the embryo of a rural guerrilla war. Fidel Castro, who had lived for years in Santiago, wanted to seize the barracks and to distribute arms to his partisans to take the city by storm. Others wanted to flee armed to the hills that surround Santiago (knowing that they are part of the bigger formation of the Sierra Maestra). But the majority did not know where they were or what they were there for.

Among them was Gustavo Arcos. When Fidel Castro harangued all those gathered together the night before the assault, before distributing the uniforms with which they would disguise themselves (it was carnival time, remember?) Gustavo Arcos was horrified. He had come from so far for a public meeting that was now being converted into an act of war, surely fatal for many innocents, who would include not only the soldiers who lived in the barracks, but the inhabitants of the city and, no less innocent, those who had come to Santiago, like him, under false pretences. Gustavo refused to participate in the assault.

For Fidel Castro this refusal was inadmissible. What Castro did not know then was that Arcos, already a practising Catholic with a very defined character, was a dangerously honest man. Gustavo explained his reasons. He had come, he said, for a deed of a political nature, not for blood. He paid for this by being branded a coward and shut up with nine other objectors in one of the rooms – the door secured from outside with a bolt. Nevertheless Gustavo Arcos would be the first to shoot – and the first to be wounded in the raid.

Shut up in the room that became his jail, late at night, Gustavo heard his friend Léster Rodríguez joking and jesting in that Cuban manner that makes it seem that nothing should be taken terribly seriously. Neither life nor death. Then Raúl Castro and Léster hummed old Cuban songs. From his room Gustavo heard them singing all night. He made a decision. He knocked on the door and when they opened it asked to be one more raider. Léster and Raúl accepted him with alacrity. Gustavo Arcos was going if not to kill at least to die together with his friends. Without knowing it he had just completed the first part of 'The Short Happy Life of Francis Macomber', the Hemingway story of a man who goes to hunt in Africa and conducts himself like a coward before his first lion – to show immediately after that he is truly courageous. Only his wife made him a coward to destroy him at the end for his courage. For Gustavo Arcos that killing wife would be the Revolution. Then, of course, it was not yet written with a capital R.

Gustavo Arcos marched, like the others, towards the attack and a possible death. He was not going in the third car, next to Raúl Castro and Léster Rodríguez singing *sones* then in fashion. Instead, he rode in the second automobile, now an assault car, beside Fidel Castro, who was the driver and the leader of the operation. Castro was not carrying Arcos at his side from love or from group sense. Why then? Gustavo could never explain it to himself. In any case he was going along trapped between the nervous tension and the speed and the night that was rapidly becoming day. Too soon they would be in front of the barracks. It was then that Gustavo noticed that Fidel was wearing glasses. Fidel Castro detested being seen in public with glasses and when they entered the city he took off that sign of weakness and kept it in a pocket of his uniform. The raiders were dressed like soldiers – but Fidel Castro's uniform was of a sergeant-major.

On arriving at the gate of the barracks, still between night and dawn, the driver of the first car stopped, got out and shouted at the two sentries: 'Let the general pass!' The guards, confused, opened the gate and snapped to attention. Two of the raiders ran towards the guards and disarmed them easily. When the first car entered the barracks Fidel Castro moved forward. But because of the scarce light or because he wasn't wearing glasses, his car mounted the pavement and struck one of the boundary stones at the entrance with force and greater noise. The failure of the assault had just begun but neither Fidel Castro nor the other raiders knew it yet.

Castro looked slowly through the rearview mirror, not knowing that his car was immobilized. Now he turned to Arcos and said: 'There comes a soldier alone. Take him prisoner.' Without asking more Gustavo got out of the car and walked towards the pavement, but as he stepped on the curb he tripped and fell. The two men were so close that Gustavo saw that the other was carrying a paper bag, one side stained with grease. Gustavo thought that the soldier was returning to the barracks with a fried chicken or a steak in a doggy bag. The soldier (up close he turned out to be a lieutenant) looked at Gustavo in uniform fallen on the ground. Somehow he knew that he was an impostor and took out his pistol. Gustavo, still stretched out on the ground, drew his gun and fired, killing the lieutenant with a single shot. It was the first and last man that Gustavo Arcos would ever kill. The early report alerted the garrison. The fiasco of the assault on the Moncada barracks had just been completed.

Gustavo Arcos did not know when he lost consciousness, only that he woke up to find himself wounded. Blood was spurting from his belly: not too much but steadily. Consequently he did not become alarmed. But he noticed that he could not get on his feet – he could not even move his legs. Then somebody called his name. It was Ramiro Valdés who was getting out of a car riddled with bullets. He came to help Gustavo get up from the gutter into which he'd fallen. Ramiro wasn't wounded. Inside the car there were two men he didn't know. They were not hurt either. The car rolled down the street as if pulled by gravity. Ramiro said its tyres were full of holes. Later he claimed that he was sorry but he would have to leave Gustavo on the next corner, then he helped him to the entrance of a nearby house. It was not much help but Ramiro Valdés had saved Gustavo Arcos's life – for the moment. All those who remained alive after the raid anywhere were shot – or finished off if they were wounded. The rescue of Arcos by Valdés was the third twist in this story. But there would be others. History revels in irony and cruel jokes. But she can also be coarse.

Now Gustavo Arcos was paralysed from the waist down outside a nondescript house. Nevertheless he managed to get to the bell and ring. In a while a woman opened the door and no sooner had she opened it and seen Gustavo covered with blood, his legs inert, sprawled on the ground, than she tried to shut it. Gustavo had a saving reflex response and placed his arm between the door and the jamb, preventing it from being closed.

'Please, *señora*,' said Gustavo. 'Pardon me,' said the woman, 'but I am not the *señora*, I'm the maid.' 'But – you believe in God?' 'I'm Catholic, *señor*.' 'I am too,' said Gustavo. 'So, for the love of God, don't leave me here outside. They're going to kill me!' Few people knew then that there had been an armed assault on the barracks, but in the neighbourhood they must have witnessed the din that lasted more than an hour. Distant shots could still be heard.

The woman opened the door and Gustavo dragged himself inside. Now he met a man standing up in the living room. It was the butler. He had asked for sanctuary in a rich house. The butler offered Arcos a change of clothes. The maid explained that the *señores* were on vacation in Galicia: July in Santiago de Cuba is the burning season. Gustavo's wound had stopped bleeding and the clean clothes gave him a more urbane appearance than the stained uniform and the desperado's mien and the alarming fixed stare. (I never saw Gustavo move his eyes, not even in the peaceful Belgian mornings. This cunning concentration, curious thing, he shared with Fidel Castro.)

Gustavo asked for a local phone book. When he got it he dragged himself to a nearby phone table. He had just remembered that the doctor who helped bring him into the world, a friend of the family, had moved not long ago to Santiago. Gustavo tried to reach the phone but he did not make it. He thought a moment about asking for help from the man or the woman. But he had already created enough troubles for them by even calling at the door, much more by going into the house and asking for asylum. That they had helped him to rid himself of the uniform and to get dressed in mufti was more than aiding and abetting – it was itself a crime that could cost them their lives. But the butler came over to dial the number for him. The doctor was not at home, he had already left for his clinic. There they found him finally. Gustavo identified himself. Of course the doctor remembered him! He half explained his situation, the doctor told him not to move, he would come to pick him up in his car – and so he did.

It was at the clinic that Gustavo lost consciousness again. The doctor discovered that the stomach wound, messy, was only the exit of the bullet and was nothing compared to a wound in the back that Gustavo didn't even know he had sustained. The high-calibre projectile had pierced the spinal column: thus the paralysis of the extremities. The doctor decided to operate. It was a difficult double surgery: on the back and on the stomach.

When Gustavo regained consciousness again, the doctor informed him of his condition: he was paralysed, perhaps for life. There was nothing he could do for him now. But there was. The Military Intelligence Service (SIM), the local police and the Cuban Bureau of Investigations were now looking for the survivors of the raid, everywhere, especially in private hospitals and private clinics. The doctor shut himself up with Gustavo in his room. When they came to look for him (it was never known how they found him) the doctor, through the closed door, declared his wish to remain with his patient. 'This man is dying,' he said. Finally the police, convinced, gave up Gustavo Arcos for dead and so he appeared in the casualty lists.

Later Gustavo, an invalid in his wheelchair, was tried and sentenced along with Fidel and Raúl Castro and the other survivors of the assault. Before going to prison, Arcos was admitted to the Havana Orthopaedic Hospital – from where he escaped.

THE REWARDED HERO

In prison Gustavo Arcos was harassed by a Fidel Castro still not resigned to the political wreck of the assault. Its success, he believed, would have carried him to the Presidential Palace in next to no time. Not being in power now was the fault of the failure or fiasco. The person directly responsible for that catastrophe (Castro should have said, on remembering the dead, if he remembered them, hecatomb) was Arcos for having fired that first fatal shot that alerted the garrison. Castro believed, and swore by his belief, that the shot had been intentional, an agreed-upon signal. Or, what was worse, cowardly. Even when the likes of Raúl Castro and Léster Rodríguez and even Ramiro Valdés told Castro of his crass error. At times, when they met in the exercise yard, Castro would berate Gustavo, who did not stay silent, as usual. On one occasion Gustavo responded to Castro that the one guilty for the failure of the assault was his vanity in not wanting to wear glasses in public. Castro did not speak to him again in prison.

When the raiders were all pardoned by Batista, the General also called The Man, he made a mistake (he made many mistakes in fact: no enemy was enough for Batista) and they went to Mexico City: to plot and to conspire and to set up an expedition to invade Cuba. There Fidel Castro seemed to forget his rancid rancour against Arcos. One day, however, Raúl Castro told Gustavo that they had unmasked a spy among them. Without telling him how, whom and when, he invited Gustavo to form part of the Cuban bunch that was at the same time a military tribunal and a firing squad. The 'court martial' had been held in another part of the city and now everyone headed for the outskirts – where the execution would take place. For the first (but not the only) time Raúl Castro would head a firing squad. The shooting squad was a single man and instead of rifles only one small-calibre pistol would be employed. All the time they were positioning themselves to execute the presumed guilty comrade Castro was watching, gun in hand, from the thicket. What first astonished Arcos and then alarmed him most was that while the so-called execution lasted, Fidel Castro insisted on having Gustavo near him. Always, as if carelessly, his gun pointed at Arcos until it was all over. Then they had to bury the presumed traitor. It took more time than killing him. Gustavo Arcos never understood this scene. Until he remembered that of all the plotters only he protested over the obvious murder.

When the hour arrived for the embarkation to Cuba, they all met in Veracruz. Before they left Arcos was attacked by a virulent outbreak of chickenpox. If this had appeared on the high seas Gustavo would have had to throw himself off the boat or be thrown overboard by his companions – for fear of contagion. In his place came his brother Luis. Luis was caught during the landing (or shipwreck rather) and shot by Batista's soldiers. To Gustavo's grief his only epitaph was the name of a freighter. In spite of having being lame, Gustavo showed an extreme mobility: he travelled from Mexico to Central America and Venezuela, stocking up arms everywhere and sending them to the Sierra. When the Revolution came to power, he returned to Havana like the hero he was – to suffer complete ostracism. Several months later he found himself in Havana without a job, without being settled down, without any direction. Evidently Fidel Castro did not forget – nor did he pardon.

But in September 1959 he was called to the Palace by President Dorticós, the same man who later, after being deposed by Fidel Castro, would commit suicide. Dorticós asked Arcos if he would like to go as Ambassador to Belgium. At that time Belgium was, seen from Havana, the other side of the moon. Gustavo said yes immediately.

In Brussels Gustavo Arcos was an exceptional ambassador among the diplomatic corps of the Communist countries. He was not a cultured or too bright man but he was something better: he was discreet. He had learned quickly the graces of diplomacy and managed the protocol and even the etiquette with ease. He represented Cuba with dignity in Belgium, Denmark and Luxembourg. He had made ties with the diplomatic elite and he had close friendships with prominent people in the Belgian socialist party. He even got on reasonably well with the Communist corps, old Stalinists all. Above all he was not an intriguer. In Havana the Minister of Foreign Affairs, Raúl Roa, the man who wanted to be a hero and never could, respected Arcos from a distance.

Gustavo Arcos was Ambassador of Cuba in the Low Countries from the winter of 1959 until the autumn of 1964. He could have been ambassador for many years, but on this consultation trip he was going to remain in Havana for ever. An equal fate befell Enrique Rodríguez Loeche, an old agitator of the *Directorio* and Ambassador in Morocco for a time. Once, *circa* 1952, Loeche, in the middle of Cadenas Square at the University of Havana, had stuck up Fidel Castro with a .45-calibre pistol. It was only a politically public gesture, but Castro never forgave him for it and what is worse, never forgot it. Gustavo Arcos was, in 1965, the man who on 26 July back in 1953 had made the raid on the Moncada barracks fail. Or so believed Castro – still.

Arcos had earlier made another consultation trip to Havana in 1962 and returned in 1963 with two new collaborators. One was Héctor Carbonell,[1] young son (seventeen years old) of a prominent labour leader, a friend of Arcos. The other was Juan José Díaz del Real, whom one always had to call J.J. and never Díaz. Gustavo had met him in his days as arms dealer for the 26th of July Movement in Caracas. Díaz del Real had been Ambassador in the Dominican Republic early in 1959. One day, in the then Ciudad Trujillo, he met an old *Batistiano* acquaintance who from far away lifted a hand to greet him. Without another word, Díaz del Real took out his pistol, fired and killed that cordial Cuban. (To my astonishment and ulterior horror I realized one day that the Cubans were the only diplomats who went everywhere in Brussels with a pistol under their belt.)

Díaz del Real claimed then that he believed his friend was now an enemy and his hand a raised menace. Running, he took refuge in his embassy. An irate local mob chased him and, seeing him shut behind him the door of the Cuban mission, they set fire to the building. Now the entire house was burning but the firemen did not come. Out of pique with Castro (from the days in 1947 when an expedition of Cuban students threatened his stability), Trujillo had ordered that no one move a finger to bail out the Cubans trapped in their burning embassy. Finally the dean of the diplomatic corps, the nuncio, had to intercede and his mediation moved the firemen to save the Cubans in a last-minute rescue. Díaz del Real was

---

1 In 1989 Carbonell was implicated in the General Ochoa-De La Guardia Twins Affair and condemned to fourteen years in prison. He was luckier than General Ochoa and one of the twins – who were shot.

never the same again and if he was, he was the same in another way. Now that terribly sick man, pure paranoia, was coming to help Gustavo Arcos in his embassy.

But, a curious turn, his verbal resentment that he soon poured over 'my friend Gustavo', was directed at first not towards Trujillo but, amazingly, towards Salvador Allende in Chile, whom he blamed for his diplomatic disgrace. It came to pass that after the Dominican duel he was brought back to Cuba to be named Ambassador in Santiago de Chile before President Jorge Alessandri. Díaz del Real preened himself everywhere for his public and private relations with Allende, eternal opposition candidate. Allende, amiable and grateful, even presented a German shepherd dog to Díaz del Real, to 'guard the House of Cuba'. Soon J.J. committed a glorious gaffe. Allende came on an announced visit to the embassy one night and Díaz, a Cuban comrade, received him – in pyjamas! He evidently didn't know Salvador Allende. The virtuous visitor not only turned round and left the embassy, but he wrote a personal letter to Fidel Castro complaining about the offence to his honour. Castro's envious envoy, a fresh Fidelista, was *ipso facto* ordered back to Havana. This time he didn't return a conqueror with the aureole of a Dominican fire but was sent to the ice of the island. From that last disgrace, a purgatory and a purge, he was rescued by 'my friend Gustavo Arcos'. To his own disgrace in turn.

Arcos had to travel to Prague to cure or at least to relieve his crippled leg and Díaz del Real took charge of the embassy as chargé d'affaires. An indefatigable man but suffering from a strange hermit's mania, Díaz del Real shut himself up to work (he never went to one single reception) to 'put the embassy in order'. According to him, the disorder of the filing system, dossiers and documents that he found was enough to make him distrust the ability of Arcos as Ambassador and to discredit him. He was forgetting that an embassy is not only letters that come and go. In spite of his Cuban chaos Gustavo Arcos was an excellent Ambassador. Now it appeared that Díaz del Real was having doubts about his duty. 'I can't saw the floor from under Gustavo,' he said time and time again. 'He's my friend but I am a revolutionary.' Hamlet's mother says of Ophelia: 'The lady doth protest too much, methinks.' There was a moment when the protests of J.J. seemed not to encounter an echo but rather to create their own *raison d'être*. Every day Díaz del Real in fact sawed the floor from under Arcos. He was now a reluctant usurper.

When Arcos returned from Prague it did not take him long to notice the secret sawing system: it was visible in every corner of the chancellery. There began then a fierce fight that was a battle for power so audible that the noise reached Havana. From there came one of the most incredible mediators. (Next to him Dag Hammarskjöld was a traffic cop.) He was called Agustín Aldama. Actually his name was Pablo but he changed it to Agustín because he considered Pablo an effeminate name! Whether called Agustín or Pablo Aldama he was truly impressive – a thin black man who measured six feet four, with long bony hands and blind in one eye, the right one. He wore, to hide his glass eye, enormous dark glasses that made him a Cuban Tonton Macoute. He had lost his eye in one of the gangster gun battles that took place in Havana in the forties and fifties. Aldama militated in the UIR, the same gang to which Fidel Castro belonged before the assault on Moncada. This immoderate moderator was proud to be one of the few human beings to survive a .45-calibre pistol shot in the head. He said it constantly, he repeated it. Bored, one day I asked him how he knew he was a human being. He took it as a joke. It's good, once in a while, to have a reputation as a joker.

Aldama was, besides, the younger brother of the current chief of the DTI, Technical Department of Investigations in Havana, which replaced the old *Batistiano* Bureau of Investigations. The other Aldama was known as the Beast. In exile in Mexico both had been movie stuntmen, specialists in falling from a fast horse. Aldama used to say with pride that he had been the stand-in for Robert Mitchum riding his horse in *The Wonderful Country*. He stopped saying it when I reminded him that that Western had been prohibited in Cuba because its villains were called the Castro Brothers.

His credentials mysteriously accredited him as a fourth secretary but in the embassy there was no third secretary. He was, theoretically, a G2 (or agent of State Security) and although it was alleged that he came as a spy or a counter-spy (or both) no one in the embassy doubted that the enemy he was watching was every one of the Cuban diplomats in Belgium. That is, us. Aldama, everyone's friend, was not long in making an alliance with Díaz del Real, while watching (a spy's job) him work in the embassy basement, his long legs that ended in enormous shoes resting on top of his desk like an atheist mantis. Then occurred what in a demented chess game would be called a double gambit. Díaz del Real was sent as Ambassador to Finland ('I've always liked the cold more', said the firefighter) and Gustavo Arcos would return to Havana among unfriendly and friendly rumours: 'Gustavo is going as Ambassador to Italy', 'Arcos is dead.' But it was neither one thing nor the other.

Agustín, *ci-devant* Pablo, Aldama was finally recalled to Havana as well. Vice-Minister Arnol Rodríguez told me this in Paris. 'We don't want him to seek asylum in Belgium.' 'I don't believe,' I answered Arnol, 'that anyone would want him in Belgium.' Aldama, the false Watusi, the pseudo-agent, the deadly mantis went off to Cuba. Before leaving he insisted on sending by ship an enormous Buick – vintage 1957! – that he had had brought over from Havana with him. Aldama was not a car collector, quite the contrary: the Buick disintegrated under his very eyes. But it was evident that he felt an attachment to this sombre sedan that was the favourite weapon of the gangsters of yesteryear – and the conspicuous secret agent carried the mortal remains of his Buick back to Havana.

But he left behind a memory as long-lasting as his outstanding bill in a Cuban bar (in every port in the world there is a Cuban bar and grill to serve you) in the Midi station area, an outsize Browning pistol with which he didn't want to travel and a mousy Belgian girl, a temporary secretary at the embassy – who became pregnant in Brussels with his Cuban sprout. Her state did not last long, thanks to the efficacy of a Belgian abortionist. But after a few weeks she was calling the former Agustín by the name of Aldamá, which almost rhymes with *jamás*. Aldama went off listing to Cuba but he didn't sink there. In the stirred-up totalitarian sea the Aldamas of this world never sink. But Pablo, or Agustín, had been, for a few months it is true, our coloured James Bond. His *savoir faire* in the hate's labours lost of intelligence and international intrigue made me, nevertheless, call him Hambone. His famous phrase, 'Listen to me, little friend', that was intimidating for a while, became laughable. At least Arcos was laughing at it. He shouldn't have done.

THE PUNISHED HERO

Early in the morning of 2 June 1965 I received a call in Brussels from Carlos Franqui in Havana telling me that my mother was very gravely ill and at the same time giving me to understand that her grave illness was fatal. I quickly called Minister Roa, requesting permission from him to return to Cuba immediately. Permission would always have been necessary, it was indispensable then. I was the chargé d'affaires now and there was absolutely no one else in the embassy – if one excepted Miriam Gómez, my wife. Roa heard my reasons and gave me his personal permission to return to Havana. My mother died while I was on my way to Cuba and I travelled from the airport to the funeral home where the wake was being held. There were familiar people everywhere. Franqui, among others, had gone to wait for me at the airport. Now on the high *perron* of the funeral home I bumped into Gustavo Arcos. He had met my mother in Brussels, where she went on a brief visit. He had invited her to the cinema and to dinner and the two were charmed. My mother found Gustavo as good-looking as a movie redskin (Gustavo looked more Basque than Indian) and Gustavo was surprised at my mother's knowledge (she was an absolute fanatic of the movies) of the stars and both were happy in their double error, for a time.

Now, outside the funeral home, after the condolences, Franqui came up, conversed and continued then towards the wake. Gustavo assured me that Franqui was crazy. I didn't know what he meant. 'Imagine! He's saying that Aldama (you remember "Hambone"?) is going around following me in a car disguised as a taxi driver. Do you want greater craziness?' I didn't say anything. I was still stricken by the sudden death of my mother. 'Look,' Gustavo said to me, 'can you believe that's a taxi, over there, with Aldama inside?' I looked and saw a car that might or might not be a taxi. (Back then taxis were not marked in Cuba.) And a black driver who might or might not be Aldama. Who cares? He was of no consequence now. Nothing was of any consequence now. Not Aldama nor his brother the Beast nor his double mission. Not Franqui's conspiracy theory, nor Gustavo's disbelief. Nothing. Not now.

Inside, after a while, Franqui came up to me and took me to an empty chapel. Franqui has always been a cautious country man. He swore to me that he had seen Aldama casing the funeral home – behind Gustavo evidently. I didn't believe that Franqui was lying or seeing visions. 'You know,' Franqui confided to me, 'or you must know already that imagination is not Gustavo's forte. That is what makes him such a courageous man. He can't imagine death. But neither is he capable of believing that tomorrow the sun will come up. Our friend is lacking in imagination. Sooner or later this is going to bring him problems. With Aldama, with his brother, with Ramirito and even with Fidel.' I told Franqui that at least Arcos was not paranoid. 'He never suffered from persecution mania.' Franqui smiled. 'And do you think that Fidel doesn't know it?' he said to me and we two returned to my mother's chapel.

The next day I went to the ministry for consultations with Minister Roa. Roa said to me, after polishing his shoes on his trouser legs several times: '*Chico*, what's your opinion of Arcos? Is he or isn't he a drunk?' I told him the only thing I could tell him: the truth. No, Arcos wasn't a drunk. I had never seen him drunk. He drank, yes, once in a while some wine with his meals, which is a European custom. 'But you've *lived* in the embassy,' insisted Roa. I never saw him drunk. Not one time, not once. Not even tipsy. 'Well,' said Roa, 'I was misinformed.' Then he went on to give me a surprising bit of news. Arcos would *not* return to Brussels and I must take firm charge of the embassy. 'You're going back as a chargé d'affaires proper,' Roa told me. 'As a minister. You have to go back straight away.' I told him that I was ready.

From the ministry I went to Arcos's apartment, which was on the way from the ministry to my father's house, where I was living now. I didn't tell Arcos about Roa's insistence on seeking evidence of his alleged alcoholism. I told him, yes, that Roa had promoted me to diplomatic minister and had asked me to return to Belgium as soon as possible, as chargé d'affaires proper. Gustavo received the news with pleasure but I don't believe with too much pleasure. At least he rubbed his left leg, the crippled one, which in him was a habit and a signal. Arcos told me that he would have wanted me to go with him to Rome as cultural attaché. He was already sure, he confided in me, that he would be named Ambassador to Italy. Raúl, Raúl Castro, had confirmed it to him. He offered to go with me to the airport for my return to Belgium. That return, of course, never took place.

I never left Cuba that Sunday 13 June. Exactly fifteen minutes before catching the Cubana plane (destination: Madrid) with my two daughters, I received a call from Arnol Rodríguez, an old friend, Vice-Minister of Foreign Affairs. 'Listen,' he said in my ear, 'what a bombshell! You can't board tonight. You have to see Minister Roa, who wants to talk to you.' But I had already seen Roa. 'He wants to see you again,' he assured me. 'But my luggage is already inside the plane,' I argued. 'Get it back, pick it up and come back to Havana. Come to the ministry tomorrow.' At the airport I found that my luggage never got on the plane.

The next day I went early to the ministry and I didn't see Roa. In fact I never saw him again. Like a Kafka character they had summoned me to the Castle, for an interview with the Count, who could not see me. Correction: I saw Roa twice. Once I was on my way to his office when Roa came out and started to walk towards me. When he realized that I was coming towards him along the narrow passage, he opened the nearest door – and brooms, a mop and buckets began to rain on him. He had tried to escape into the broom cupboard. On another occasion I was in Arnol's waiting room, chatting with his secretaries when Roa entered. Roa saw me seated behind the door only when he had closed it. When he saw me, Roa lurched toward the nearest door – and went into the ambassadors' reception room. The two secretaries burst out laughing. What happened? 'Arnol's in there with the Swiss Ambassador,' said a secretary. Arnol had said to the ambassador, on orders from the minister, that Dr Roa was away in Las

Villas Province and could not possibly receive him. I never saw Roa again. I found out later, in a kind of twisted message, that he had said that after what happened at the airport he would never be able to face me: a man whom he had just promoted and sent to his mission. Besides, that man had returned to Cuba for the funeral of his mother. He had even, said Roa, sent his son to the wake with a wreath and his condolences.

No one ever found out why they took me off the plane, why I never saw Minister Roa again, why they held me four months in Havana. *Comandante* Alberto Mora, my friend and the man to whom I still owe my exit from Cuba, told me one day: 'Do you know I ran into El Gallego Piñeiro in a reception at the Chinese Embassy?' I didn't know it but I did know who El Gallego Piñeiro was, a man of many aliases. He was known as Redbeard, he was named Manuel Piñeiro and he was Vice-Minister of the Interior in charge of Counter-Intelligence. He had lived in New York for years and curiously I met him there in 1957 at the home of the painter Julio Zapata, who had a flat in Greenwich Village. Zapata maintained an open-door policy for all Cubans. I recall that El Gallego Piñeiro spent all his time stretched out on a couch, shoes and all, but he kept mum all the time – as befits a future master spy: my lips are sealed.

Alberto Mora interrupted me: 'That guy's not a spymaster or anything! He is only one of Raúl's *comandantes*. He never fired a shot in the Sierra. But how he fires off eulogies to the Maximum Leader now! He never misses.' Alberto often used those warlike images. But what *Comandante* Peñeiro then, today a general without an army, said to Alberto in that Chinese reception was: 'That one,' meaning me, 'is leaving Cuba only over my dead body.' Alberto, who was truly a brave man, said to him: 'We'll see.' Then he told me: 'Do you know that Spymaster is going everywhere with an attaché case handcuffed to his arm?' One day, after a Council of Ministers where he came to inform on God knows what enemy plot, he left without his case. When he had already left his case was found – handcuffed to the arm of his chair! No doubt this was an anecdote to animate me, but Alberto added: 'Now I'll see Carlos Rafael, and with his help, that is worth more than a minister's, I'll go to see Dorticós, who is worth more than a minister and a vice-minister. We'll see who'll step on whose dead body.' Alberto Mora, a true revolutionary, would commit suicide a few years later, in moral revulsion.

On my long visit to Havana, that became too long, I saw Gustavo many times at his home. One day he told me that he had been summoned by Ramirito to his office at the Ministry of the Interior. He asked me to come to see him later, after the interview. I did so. He seemed thrilled. 'I was talking with Ramirito and I came to the conclusion that Aldama is bleeding, wrapped in flames and falling fast!' Gustavo too liked to affect this Rebel Army jargon. 'How do you know?' I asked him. 'Ramirito has this theory,' recounted Gustavo. 'He says it happens when he has a conversation with someone.' 'What do you mean has a conversation?' 'When he interrogates, OK? When Ramirito interrogates a guy he knows straight away if he's guilty or innocent, just by the movement of his hands. Aldama is going down fast now. You'll see.' 'Gustavo,' I asked him, 'and how do *you* know that Ramiro Valdés was talking about Aldama?' 'Because it was Aldama we were talking about.' 'But wasn't it you he was talking about? Wasn't it you who was questioned? Aren't your hands the guilty hands he talked about?' Gustavo gave a start: 'You're like Franqui, who sees ghosts in every dark corner! Ramirito was talking about Aldama. No doubt about that!'

Gustavo was more than excited, he was agitated by something else. Soon he said: 'Do you know what Faustino told me this morning?' Faustino was Dr Faustino Pérez, the old *compadre* of Gustavo from the first days of the agitprop against Batista. Even before Moncada, which he had also survived. 'Faustino said, when I told him I was going off to see friend Ramirito, these odd words: "Gustavo, there aren't friends in Cuba any more. There aren't any left," he said. "You're going to see *Comandante* Ramiro Valdés, Minister of the Interior." That's what Faustino told me.' I left Gustavo preoccupied. I don't know whether from what he told me or from what I told him or from what Ramiro Valdés told him – or from what Faustino Pérez, Minister of Hydraulic Works, told him. Or from all those things.

When I was leaving Cuba for ever Gustavo was still waiting for his Roman retribution. Or was it for a miracle? The last time I saw him I told him to get out of the country, on any pretext. It was obvious that his Rome would never take place. Already he was never summoned to the ministry and not even Raúl Castro answered his calls. But finally he seemed more beaten than resigned, more indecisive than when I had seen him again in Havana – a hero not tired but defeated.

It was only after being in Europe for a while, when I was still living in Madrid, that I learned that Gustavo had been arrested. They say that while he was in prison Ramiro Valdés, the one who had once come to save him, came to see him in his cell. 'Gustavo,' he said to him, 'why don't you confess?' Ramiro Valdés repeated his question on every visit. 'Because I don't have anything to confess, Ramiro. That's why,' Gustavo exclaimed one day. 'It doesn't matter, Gustavo,' insisted *Comandante* Ramiro. 'Confess. Nothing's going to happen to you. It's only a *legal* formality. If you confess you'll even feel good. Afterwards, we make out a confession, you sign it and that's it – and you leave prison,' vouchsafed Valdés. Arcos was in an untenable position: he was a criminal without a cause. In a little while there would come the sentence before the verdict. Only his stubbornness and his inability to establish a relationship of cause and effect kept him firm. Also, it must be said, his mother sustained him. The feeble but formidable Doña Rosina Bergnes, who would say to her son every time she managed to visit him: 'Gustavo, don't you confess. Don't say anything to these Communists, you hear? Not a word.' Gustavo never confessed the crime that he had not committed.

But confession or not Gustavo Arcos was sentenced, without a verdict, and of course, without a trial. The totalitarian world is an orb all of effects: Marx does not need causes. He was in prison for three years. The other five years of the sentence he spent in his parents' apartment, under house arrest – without receiving visits or answering phone calls. Finally, he became free but converted into an outcast: the hero as pariah.

One day he asked permission to leave Cuba, legally, which was refused. Earlier he had been divorced from his wife Fabiola, an Ecuadoran beauty whom he met in Mexico, where they married in 1958. Fabiola left Cuba with their sons Gustavito and David. In Ecuador, Fabiola found out that she had cancer and travelled with their two sons to Miami, seeking a cure. Here Gustavito, twenty-one years old, was run over by the car of a drunk American woman when he was riding his errand bike. The injuries were so grave that he stayed in a permanent state of coma. Desperate, Gustavo Arcos tried by every means to leave Cuba. With his brother Sebastián, who had been second-in-command of the Revolutionary Navy, they got hold of a boat and managed to leave the beach and the coast. On the high seas they were intercepted by the Cuban Coast Guard. Brought back to the beach, Gustavo learned that he had always been watched, even before getting the boat. (It had been, simply, the old cat and mouse game.) The two Arcos brothers were tried at the beginning of 1982 and sentenced – Gustavo to fourteen years in prison, Sebastián to eleven years.

Now the Gustavo Arcos case acquires soap opera overtones. With Gustavito still in a coma, Fabiola Arcos was invited by Fidel Castro himself to come to Cuba, so her son could be treated by Cuban science (sic). Fabiola, desperate, accepted Castro's proposition and was then installed in a room in the Havana Libre Hotel, the former Havana Hilton. Gustavito was admitted to the best hospital in Cuba, Hermanos Amejeiras, in Havana. There Fabiola learned that Castro had given precise orders to cure Gustavito by whatever means. What mercenary capitalist medicine had not managed to do, altruistic socialist medicine would accomplish. On one occasion they permitted Gustavo to visit Gustavito. Then David, the other brother, came from Miami to see his brother, his mother, and (the Revolution is always generous) his father Gustavo in prison: virtually a totalitarian miracle. The interview happened (I don't know if I can use here this hazardous verb) at Villa Marista – an old Catholic school now converted into the headquarters of State Security.

The reunion of the father and the son who barely knew each other took place in a cell in the lower depths of Villa Marista. Gustavo arrived accompanied not by a gaoler but by a Security investigator, who identified himself to David. The inquisitor remained standing up facing them for the exact hour that the interview lasted. David did not even see him blink, much less move. Gustavo was dressed in cheap but new clothes and new shoes. He explained to David that they had been lent to him for the interview. Lent? He would have to return them to State Security later. They talked freely about Gustavito, about David's life in Miami, about the state of Fabiola's health. Finally Gustavo made an extraordinary revelation to David. Fidel Castro had come to see him in prison and told him that he could be free that very moment, provided that he promised him, swore to him by his God, that he would not try again to leave Cuba. Gustavo promised nothing. Fidel Castro left and Gustavo was confined to solitary until that day, the day of the interview with David. When he went back to prison he would go back to his cell in solitary. But he would not be alone. Gustavo, ever more religious, spoke to David about God almost obsessively the whole time that the visit lasted.

This story has been put together from my recollections of Gustavo, from his Belgian conversations, with stories from Carlos Franqui, with facts obtained here and there, and, finally, with a long telephone conversation with David Arcos, his son, from Miami, paid for by the publisher Arturo Villar Bergnes, a cousin. I don't know if the publication of these notes will do Gustavo harm. I truly believe that Gustavo can't be any worse off. Although in a totalitarian country worse is barely worst badly spelt. I don't know if it will do him good either. But I make public his Via Dolorosa because while it was private no one paid any attention: everyone listened but no one heard.

I have tried to help Gustavo Arcos since his first imprisonment. Now I have renewed those attempts. I have seen Belgian politicians, from the socialist party, and influential Spanish socialists and English MPs – and even a member of the House of Lords. I also wrote and spoke to Amnesty International.

I spoke too, not long ago, to Jeane Kirkpatrick, Ambassador of the United States at the United Nations. All has been futile. More futile was speaking with a powerful magazine publisher, an American, who said to me, 'What is Arcos?' I didn't understand. 'Is he a writer or a painter or an intellectual?' I told him the only thing I could tell him: Gustavo Arcos is a human being. I don't think he understood. Nor do they understand in England. Not long ago there was a writers' conference in London with the facetious title of 'They kill writers, don't they?' They invited me to speak. I said thanks but no thanks. I told them that the title was not true. I told them that in totalitarian countries like Cuba, the last thing they kill is writers. They kill workers, peasants, leaders of the clandestine movement, Jehovah's Witnesses, whites and blacks. Everyone. But what they least kill is writers. Those shut up or get scared or their silence is bought with a house and a car and several trips to Europe. Or they leave the country as exiles. They don't kill writers. They kill, precisely, men without imagination like Gustavo Arcos. They kill their heroes.

(October 1984)

The Unknown Political Prisoner

Since 3 October 1965, when I left Cuba for ever, until today, I have not ceased to interest myself in the fate of many Cuban political prisoners. I never forget that I could have been one of them. I have had interviews with people from Amnesty International, with Belgian socialist leaders, then in power, with Spanish socialists now in power. One of them, Fernando Claudín, referred me to a Spanish institution that he called the Fundación Iglesias. 'The Julio Iglesias Foundation?' I asked, and Claudín, offended by my mistake that he believed to be a joke, thundered: 'The *Pablo* Iglesias Foundation!' He never accepted that my error was nothing more than proof of my infantile paralysis in the presence of power: you see, I had met Claudín in Paris, when he was an anonymous exile. In the archives of Amnesty International in London could be found my numerous, different and successive letters, some dating from 1969. I have written, besides, to more than one English politician and the American Ambassador to the United Nations received me to take my petition – this time about a single political prisoner.

But it was a well-known American publisher, a man of irreproachable left-wing credentials, with whom I had lunch in Manhattan, who enlightened me in an unexpected way: my task was futile and not because I was talking about several political prisoners in Cuba. On that occasion it was a particular political prisoner in whom I had tried to interest him. My host was a man who had brought off the deed of extraditing, literally, from the island a poet in peril. Listening to me with deep interest, my host (whom we can classify as a man of letters although he has never written a single line) told me in his languid but preoccupied manner, indifferent to his lunch: 'And this Cuban, what is he? A poet? A writer? A musician? Or is he a scientist?' I knew that there were candidates in Cuba to fill all these vocations. I even knew a Cuban philosopher who was fighting to get out of prison and leave the island. 'No,' I had to answer him. 'He's none of those. He's only a human being.' My host, who was Jewish and should have known about pogroms and prisons and concentration camps, said to me in a low lament: 'In that case I'm afraid that not much can be done for him.'

The political prisoner for whom I was serving as God's advocate with this particular publisher (I had lunch with him only to launch my request), had been in reality crucial in my life. To him I owe not only my being free in the world but even these pages that I write now. But that is another story. Now he was for me an instrument of knowledge.

I came to write several articles making known his life, his inhuman and above all unjust imprisonment, trying to get people to ask for his excarceration when one should have demanded his freedom, which is a right. My articles were serialized in the Spanish press, in Mexico, in Venezuela and in Colombia and were translated into English and published in the United States. In Washington a human rights institution reproduced them in an illustrated pamphlet with a photo of the prisoner taken in his happy days as a diplomat: there is no greater Dantesque pain for him. But nothing happened. The publisher was right: nothing could be done for this eminent political prisoner who was a nobody because he was nothing.

It was then that I asked myself, what happens with a political prisoner who doesn't even have someone to write to the press in his name, to make his case known, to bother friends and foes and indifferent people, all terribly occupied with daily life in freedom – to disrupt their leisure or their business with the tale of woe of an ordeal? What happens with the prisoner who doesn't know anyone, who has always been a nobody and is now only a number and cell in a prison or an anonymous inmate in a concentration camp? What to do for the prisoner no one knows? How to free the unknown political prisoner?

One historical case shows that figure loaded down with political blame whom we know to be innocent because his crime, in a democracy, is nothing more than just part and parcel of the game of politics. In war there are always soldiers whom no one recognizes, disfigured beyond all recognition, without medals or identification tags. He is the so-called unknown soldier who is exalted on cenotaphs on Remembrance Days. Politics, as we already know, is war by other means and totalitarian politics is the total war that makes prisoners. There must be in that constant state of war an unknown man whom no one recognizes, whom no lawyer defends, to whom no mother, girlfriend or kid sister writes. That is the unknown political prisoner. I do not propose a monument for him because now literature has done it: other writers have exalted his life in perpetual prison.

One of those historians, Sidney Dark, an author who must remain in the mystery of his name (dark here means the shadow of a doubt), wrote, 'There is no doubt about the actual existence of the Man in the Iron Mask, whose identity has been discussed for two centuries.' (This text was written more than a quarter of a century ago.)

> In the year 1698, M. de Saint Mars, governor of the prison of the Îles Sainte Marguerite, was appointed governor of the Bastille. He took with him from gaol to gaol a mysterious prisoner who was seen by many peasants during the journey, and who was described as a tall, white-haired man whose features were concealed behind a black mask. In a register kept by the King's Lieutenant at the Bastille occurs the following entry: –

> On this 19th day of November, 1703, the unknown prisoner who has always worn a mask of black velvet, and who was brought by M. Saint Mars, the governor, from the Îles Sainte Marguerite, where he had long been a prisoner, being somewhat ailing after Mass yesterday, died about ten o'clock at night, without having suffered from any serious illness. And this unknown prisoner, who had been so long in custody, was interred on Tuesday, 20th November, in the burial-ground of the church of St. Paul in this parish. In the register of deaths an unknown name was also inscribed.

The registry of the Bastille church offers, all of a sudden, the name of a certain Marchioly, that everyone takes as a *nom de prison*, so common then, and declares that the age of the prisoner is 'forty-five or thereabouts', which is an impossibility or a joke. As always in documents that are meant to be truthful signatures are stamped – this time those of the chief surgeon and the commandant of the Bastille.

Says Dark:

> These documents supply practically all our actual knowledge concerning one of the greatest of historical mysteries. One more thing, however, is known. So great was the desire to hide the dead prisoner's identity for ever, that on the day of his death his linen, clothes, mattress, bed, and chairs were burned. The walls and ceiling of his cell were carefully scraped and the tiles were removed from the floor.

According to Alexander Dumas there was the express prohibition, under pain of death, that the prisoner raise the 'iron visor that covered his face for life'. (Dark actually quotes the Dumas novel: 'He will cover his face with an iron visor which the prisoner cannot raise without peril to his life.') The period when the Man in the Iron Mask lived was the apogee of Louis XIV. The man in the iron mask (to whom history would concede capitals) died exactly twelve years before the king. Versailles, where once perhaps they lived together, outlived the two of them. *Homo fugit, domus manent.*

The *Encyclopaedia Britannica*, not as obscure as Dark and less dramatic than Dumas, proposes other mysteries – or the same mystery under another mask. The iron mask was in reality a veil of black cloth. The prisoner arrived at the Bastille, already veiled, on 18 September 1698 and died there on 19 November 1703. Everything about his life in prison is known – except, of course, his identity. He was registered at the fortress under the false name of Marchioly and it was Voltaire who proposed the theory that he was a bastard brother of Louis XIV. Voltaire described the veil as 'a mask with springs of steel'. The description is not exact, claims the *Encyclopaedia*, but it captured the imagination of many writers, among them Alexander Dumas, in *Twenty Years Later*, translated to English as *The Man in the Iron Mask*. Dumas accepted as well the theory of the royal half-brother. Not without reason, Dumas saw history as just one more work of fiction.

Among other solutions to the mystery of the veiled political prisoner there appears the name of Louis of Bourbon, Count of Vermandois, son of Louis XIV and Louise de la Vallière – the name of Ercole Matthioli – the name of Nicolas Fouquet, Minister of Finance of Louis XIV and, most astonishing, the name of Molière – put in prison by the Jesuits in revenge for his *Tartuffe*. In a *pendant* with Matthioli, moves in Eustache Dauger, valet of Fouquet, placed in custody after the death of his master.

Matthioli is a candidate of impossible choice due to his having died on the St Marguerite Islands in 1694, nine years *before* the demise of the masked prisoner. Dauger was nothing more than the valet (and perhaps the confidant) of Fouquet. The *Britannica* accepts the hypothesis about Dauger but prints a final paragraph that makes us reflect: 'If it be granted that Matthioli died in 1694, the enigma can be regarded as insofar as the identity of the prisoner is concerned. The reason for his arrest and imprisonment for 34 years remains a mystery.'

The only proposition that gathers together all the hypotheses is that the Man in the Iron Mask was a political prisoner and the order for his arrest without a cause and his imprisonment without a trial are typical recourses of the totalitarian state. Our mysterious martyr and his terrible sentence (the mask, the Bastille for ever) are, truly, the monument to the unknown political prisoner.

(August 1986)

Prisoners of Devil's Island

There is a place on Earth whose very name means Hell. It is Devil's Island, the obsolete French penal colony facing the coast of Guyana. The island was notorious as a prison for common prisoners condemned to oblivion. But soon it was also a political prison. One of its prisoners made it famous, Captain Dreyfus, an innocent man sentenced for treason. His best defence was made not by a lawyer but by a writer, Émile Zola. Zola was tried for writing his civil rights tract *J'Accuse* and to avoid being sent to prison he fled to England – not without first creating the League for the Rights of Man. Soon after his return to France Zola was found dead in his study, apparently murdered.

I wrote exposing the Arcos Case in a series of articles published in Spain and in Mexico and reproduced everywhere. Now Arcos has just been set free. Free? Read further please.

The verdict that sent Gustavo Arcos to prison is not a verdict of twelve but of one: a single judge condemns and absolves in Cuba. His name is Fidel Castro. This Maximum Magistrate now reveals the causes for which Arcos was twice imprisoned. 'Arcos,' Castro let it be known, 'has racist, Fascist ideas. That is his philosophy.' One must ask why, if Arcos had these incriminating ideas, did Castro take him to the raid on the Moncada barracks in the car that the Maximum Leader himself was driving? Arcos has never suffered from a philosophy just as Castro has never had a defined ideology. Actually Castro has exploited Marxist theory not for the use of the dauphin (who would be Raúl Castro?) but *ad usum Fideli*. How can Castro talk of racism? One has only to see a photo of the Cuban Communist Party leadership and contrast it with a chance vision of the people in the streets to learn that the great majority is black while the minority that governs Cuba now is all white.

The reason for the unjust imprisonment of Arcos is totalitarian unreason. For those who believe in History as Arcos believes in God, it is a matter, once more, of an *accident de parcours*, as Julio Cortázar said, speaking French with a Castroist accent. Or was it an accident on the highway to the future? A U-topia turn perhaps?

Arcos was imprisoned (without a sentence but without a trial) in 1966. He spent three years as a prisoner until he left gaol to be subjected to house arrest. Prevented from leaving Cuba by legal means, he tried to escape in an open boat. But his plan for escape was designed by Despair. Trapped on the high seas, he was returned to the island, tried and sentenced to fourteen years in prison. It was not taken into account that he was one of the raiders of the Moncada barracks in 1953, that, wounded, he became a cripple for ever, that he shared a gaol with Castro, that he was the leader of the 26th of July Movement in exile, that he had provisioned the guerrillas in the Sierra from Mexico, that he had been Ambassador in Belgium from 1959 to 1965. It can be said though that, like a Greek hero, his virtues not history condemned him. For Castro and his minions Arcos became the enemy who comes back and they had to keep him in check after he fell into the trap of believing in honour among opportunists.

Arcos has left gaol but he is in no way free. He has simply been transferred from Cayenne to Devil's Island. The treatment may be different but the regime is the same. Something more than an open boat in the night, as Zola proposed for Devil's Island, will be necessary to take him off Cuba. Meanwhile, like Dreyfus, Arcos waits.

Carlos Franqui left Cuba for ever in 1968 simply because he could not leave before with his family: Franqui is a family man. I was witness to his attempts in Paris in 1965 to look for a safe passage. He had to go back to Cuba. Finally, fed up to the point of nausea, he managed to leave with his wife and a younger son, leaving behind his mother and his older son – who left just days before his fourteenth birthday. (The Cuban military age extends from fourteen to twenty-eight years: there is not a military service in the world that lasts as long as a sentence.) In Cuba Franqui's mother stayed in the care of other relatives in their old house. There she died.

Now Castro in an interview as garrulous (even his pals say that he talks too much) as it was mendacious has accused Franqui, among other crimes against man, of the crime against woman of having abandoned his mother – obviously to the fate of his regime.

Castro additionally accused Franqui in his interview (published in Spain and in Cuba but without its prudent preface) of having taken his father-in-law away with him. Why his father-in-law and not his true mother? The totalitarian mind begets unreasons that democratic reason never fathoms. What is certain is that Franqui's father-in-law (a musical little old man who after eighty passed his days and nights perfecting the art of the mandoline) died in the Havana district of Santos Suárez three years ago. Why then these lies like raised fists?

Franqui, as is known, has had a militant exile since 1971, the year that Heberto Padilla became a prisoner first and had his confession later. (Remember the Red Queen in *Alice*?) All these years Castro has kept silent about the crimes that he now imputes to Franqui. It is not, as we see, a political allegation but mere gossip. But there is, of course, an extra motive. Every calumny has a paralysing effect. One must waste time denying it and there is always the feeling that to refute is useless. The Spanish saw, 'A calumny gives truth a lie' is the Devil's counsel. But, why besmirch Franqui now and not before? The answer is simple. Franqui has just painted a portrait of Fidel Castro with all his wrinkles. Franqui knows his model very well, he knows many intimate stories about a sitting and lying Castro. There is no other reason for the current mendacity. If there is something Castro has always had it is a sixth sense of expediency and his arm is longer than his tongue. Franqui living in freedom in Europe is still imprisoned in the Fidelista political mesh.

I met Natividad González Freire, then and now Nati, in 1948 at a ballet performance at the Havana University Stadium. Paid for by *Tropical* beer, Alicia Alonso (eternal Alice, always dancing, always sponsored: for Batista then, for Fidel Castro now) would dance – what else? – *Swan Lake*, in the open air, in the tropical heat. Of time and tutus! Nati was one of the cultural organizers from the university and seemed to be everywhere at the same time. She was then very young, pretty and vivacious and besides, I recall, got for my mother, for Franqui and for me the best seats in the front row. One did not have to stretch his short neck to see the pointed toes of the *prima ballerina assoluta*.

Spanish but very Cuban, that is of Havana, Nati was all kindness and charm and was always laughing, showing her perfect teeth. We were all in love with Nati or rather with her enthusiasm – as contagious as a benign virus. She was like a Chekhov character but without the melancholy. She wasn't wearing mourning for life then. She was what the Stalinist aesthetes would call a positive heroine. We pessimists didn't deserve her and she married César Leante, who came from a family of radical optimists and believed in social realism. César's friends back then were progressive people and, like them, with the triumph of the Revolution he became important not only as a writer but as a civil servant of culture. He even ended up being *attaché culturel* in Paris. So when he asked for asylum in Spain in 1981 my surprise was as great as the strangeness of our encounter days later in Madrid in the Wellington Hotel, late at night in the now dark empty lobby: more unusual than the stuffed bull that rules over the lobbyists.

But one must render to César Leante what is César Leante's. That a high Cuban civil servant should seek asylum in the next port of call, Madrid, from a Cubana aeroplane that flies from Havana to East Berlin is an act of courage – moral and physical. Everything was like a John Le Carré yarn and I hope that Leante writes it to weave it like it was some day. But Leante bides his time now: since 1981, when seven years seem like ten – seem like twenty. He waits in Madrid for the reunion with his family lagging behind in Havana, retained by official revenge. (Surely Fidel Castro will accuse him one day of having abandoned his family.) Leante must pay for his deed. I have seen him since and I have become familiar with his rage that does not stop like the lobby bull, for it is the impotence of a man standing virtually alone against an implacable state waving a red flag.

Now a letter, painstaking and brave (in a totalitarian state there can always be *one more* time), from Havana bring me back to the Nati who was a bulwark of Philosophy and Letters. Her favourite philosophical school was the Stoic's. Little did she know how much she would have to put it into practice one day to survive. She knew, she knows, that a discipline of benevolence and justice exists in which the correct conduct always produces happiness, no matter how unhappy the times may be. She was, and is, a happy person whom political vengeance, not justice, has treated, and treats, by the most miserable means of making her unhappy. I have nothing to add to her letter published in *El País* – one of a calm despair. But I can indeed hope that this prisoner of Castro, sentenced without a verdict, may see the fulfilment of Fidel Castro's favourite motto around the time when we were watching Alicia Alonso dance: 'Justice might be slow but it will arrive – eventually.'

The failed meeting for human rights in Cuba held in Geneva, that Castro didn't lose but neither did he win, has meant that almost all the Cuban political prisoners (some 490 are still in prison – according to Castro) have left prison without becoming free: they have only changed islands. They're on the street but without a single civil right: they have left purgatory only to end up in limbo. The Cuban prisons, recently painted, bars and grilles cleaned of rust, floors mopped, make up part of the obligatory route of all political tourists. It is as if Adolf Eichmann organized tours through his camps.

During the hideous Nazi regime the Red Cross, so solicitous, used to visit the camps where not only Jews, but also gypsies, assorted Slavs, religious sectarians, Spaniards and homosexuals were exterminated: all heaped together in the most cruel cages. Before the visitors from outer space arrived, the guards would distribute new blankets. The intimate inspectors came, saw and approved: all in order. As soon as they turned their back, the guards would run round the barracks demanding the blankets back. The intimate inmates called these blankets 'flying carpets'.

At the end of August a Human Rights commission will visit the Cuban prisons, after receiving a long list of endless violations and illegal acts. The prisons are now ready to receive the inspectors of blankets, who will doubtless report afterwards: all in order. A plus for the Castro regime is that in the tropics you don't need blankets.

(August 1988)

Postscript 1994. Gustavo Arcos, now out of gaol, has become an activist for human rights. His house has been repeatedly assaulted by fascist mobs that are actually paramilitary factions called Rapid Action Brigades. As a British journalist was interviewing Arcos a mob staged an 'act of repudiation' and stoned his house. (This could be seen on London television at the time.) Gustavo's brother, Sebastián, has fared worse. He is now in gaol serving a sentence of four years for 'counterrevolutionary activities', i.e. passive resistance to Castro. Gustavo and his friends in Cuba and abroad fear for Sebastián's health. There are places in Hell more hellish than Hell.

PATRIOTS GALORE

An Old Engraving

When I looked for the first time at the engraving with the title 'The Cuban Patriotic Junta of New York in 1896' I saw an assembly of old gentlemen, seated in Victorian chairs with curved backs, around an enormous table, all attentive to a central document. But what I saw, I swear, was a group of gourmets around an ample menu and on one side I saw two violinists who were getting their bowed instruments ready to brighten up the occasion. (The menu was revealed as a map with a caption, 'Cuba'.) As if in a dream the violinists suddenly brandished, instead of a Guarneri or a Stradivarius, obsolete Remington rifles that they were painstakingly greasing: instead of making music they were ready to make war. The engraver, one Theodore R. (his half-signature appears at the bottom), had depicted with his burin an undoubtedly noble gathering. Faced with this sudden scene I recalled a Fascist axiom (did Queipo de Llano say it, did Goebbels say it, did the young Castro say it – or repeat it in his day as a young man with a gun?) that I transformed one day between inverted commas: 'Every time I see a gun I reach for my book.' Where I said gun I say rifle, where I said book I now say this book.

Notable Men in Havana

I am not used to sending letters opposing already published views. I have spent half my adult life at city desks and I know that all letters to the editor are sent post facto. They are actually like echoes that will turn out dumb. But with the article by the Colombian writer Gabriel García Márquez published in *El País* on 19 January I don't want, *I cannot*, as a Cuban, throw it where it deserves and forget about it. This is not my letter but it is my answer.

I know that there are South American (and Spanish) readers (and writers) who read the weekly García Márquez column to laugh out loud, and consider his statements with superior disdain as when observing the chattering of a churl or the flourishes of a *mètèque*: the arriviste who rubs elbows with highest society. Some, benevolently, take it as an extreme form of autobiographical fiction.

These recent readers can discard his obsessive exaltation of infamy every Wednesday, while they gluttonously await his tale of more intimate dinners with chiefs or chefs of State from both worlds (and even from the third), who hear attentively his sage counsels whispered into the ear at midnight. Or the announced chronicle of new plane treks around America, as decisive for humanity or for history (or for both) as Columbus and his trio of caravels. Or the revels with his choirs and dances from Colombia, that with *rastaquoeure* sense of rhythm he teaches all the crowned heads of Europe how to dance. Is this the ultimate peak of the ridiculous or merely a corny copy?

For readers in the know, García Márquez's article in *El País* every week is the sure promise of a *frisson nouveau*. But not for me. I take the novelist very seriously. This writing is the proof. Although there may be some who counter my opinion by fabricating exclusive excuses: man, it's hardly worth it, don't bother, nobody pays any attention. But I do. I believe, with Goldoni, that with the servant one can beat the master.

In his article entitled 'The Twenty Hours of Graham Greene in Havana', García Márquez rejoices at how General Torrijos got Graham

Greene and himself into the United States as official contraband. (Which is not odd, coming from South America.) The content, also general, increases when the author of *Autumn of the Patriarch* recalls how Torrijos even wanted to disguise Greene (or the two) as a Panamanian colonel. (Which is not rare, coming from a Latin American general.) Without even being a general, Fidel Castro had disguised many writers if not as military men at least as militants. Only Greene's English phlegm or rigour (mortis) prevented him from completing this masquerade, more akin to Groucho than to Karl Marx. But it so charmed García Márquez. It still does. It is not strange that Graham Greene would refuse to play such an indecorous role. Greene was the only Englishman in the group and in the United Kingdom they know the difference between decorum, decoration and décor.

This part of García Márquez's article is, of course, silent comedy – mere slapstick. What in the shorts of Laurel and Hardy was called the time for aiming (or everyone with egg on his face) and in Spain was known, I believe, by an appropriate Russian name, *astrakán*. Now it is a matter of revving up the reader on the way in with a perilous buffoonery *à la Tancredo*: the one who baits the bull.[1] The drama comes later, when García Márquez catches the bully by the horns to gripe that those lifelong villains called the Americans don't let him even visit the United States. He only could enter once, to his chagrin – on that occasion of jest and joke under the protective camouflage of the apocryphal presidential committee of General Torrijos. But it is only the *chibcha* churl become a chum.

It is not true that García Márquez could enter the United States *only* by wearing Panamanian disguise, civilian or military. The writer of *Leaf Storm*, who now has generals to write about, abandoned New York in April 1961 in more of a hurry than he left Bogotá the last time and, on the way, deserted the offices of the Prensa Latina agency – which he directed. He did it the reverse of his admired Hemingway: without grace and without pressure. No sooner had he learned of the counter-revolutionary landing in the Bay of Pigs, in Cuba, than he fled right away in the right direction – Mexico. Is it necessary to recall that Havana is thousands of miles from New York? His heart may have had its reasons, but those of us who are familiar with his true biography know that this news (a revelation for many) is *facta non verba*.

García Márquez returned to the United States (in fact, to the same New

---

1 Tancredo's *suerte* is a moment of mirth within a tragedy: the bullfighter becomes a buffoon and the bull a figure of fun. It originated, believe it or not, in Havana!

York that he had left behind in a bad hour), exactly ten years later, in 1971, to receive the degree of Doctor *honoris causa* from a very American (and capitalist) Columbia University. For those who love analogies, I can say that this homage is as if Kiev University had conferred an equal honour on Jorge Luis Borges. (The analogy is political, of course, not literary.) There, in the Plaza Hotel (our modest author, always housed, as Fidel Castro and Martí have it, 'with the poor people of the earth'), the Argentine journalist Rita Guibert interviewed him for her book *Seven Voices*, published in the United States. It was in that interview that García Márquez made his most truthful statement: 'I read practically nothing. It doesn't interest me any more. I read reportages and memoirs, the life of men who have held power; memoirs and confidences of secretaries, even if they are false.' For the public ceremony at the New York university, the author of *Chronicle of a Death Foretold* did not arrive wearing a khaki tunic or olive fatigues or a white Colombian *liqui-liqui* but in a black gown – and he didn't dance the *cumbia*.

It is true, despite him, that many foreign writers cannot enter the United States legally, like other hundreds of thousands and even millions of presumed foreign visitors who are not exactly Colombian writers. Or better, *the* Colombian writer. They are Muslims, Balinese ballerinas, Russian spies, Paraguayan professors, Jamaican jazzmen, Australian actors, Russian spies, English engineers, models, modelettes, male models, Russian spies, pilots and publicity men and poets and, of course, workers of the world, united or segregated. (Otherwise, the illegal Mexican *braceros* would not be known as *wetbacks*.) But among the writers who cannot enter the United States without a waiver visa there is more than one exiled Cuban (a waiver visa is a special permit that requires, invariably and for each application, the direct formal approval of the State Department, and cannot be obtained from an ordinary consulate). At times, the blessing is a curse. But among the writers with the waiver are Carlos Fuentes, who has lived for years in Princeton, Carlos Franqui, who is now visiting New York, and – why not say it? – *moi-même*. I have taught two six-month courses in American universities, given numerous talks all over the United States and visited the country several times since 1970, but always, as if I were an enemy agent (which obviously I am not), with a waiver visa – without the need to disguise myself as anything civil or military. At the same time, there are many writers who act like real anti-American agents and live in the United States and earn a very good living there, without ever being bothered in the least. Contradictions of capitalism? It's possible. But I don't complain nor do I classify this American action as just justice or cruel injustice.

Every country, like every house, receives its visitors as it wishes: at the door or in the living room, or it takes them in as guests, invited or not. Franco's police, for example, did not let me live in Madrid, while García Márquez lived for years in Barcelona, almost until the Caudillo died – studying, as he later declared, the agony of a patriarch: yes, sir, why not, Franco himself.

But Soviet Russia goes further than anyone, and not only does not admit the foreign visitors that it does not desire, but deports by force the nationals that bother it too much. Poland, Bulgaria, Czechoslovakia, etcetera, do the same. It does not seem to me good or bad. What's more, it doesn't bother me. It doesn't even interest me. I don't want those countries, where democracy always needs a modifier (popular, proletarian) to catch up with me. What's more, no one would catch me dead on the other side of the Yugoslav frontier, comparatively Western but always behind the Iron Curtain. The vision of a gondola that may lose its way, go out of the Grand Canal and the lagoon into the gulf and get lost in the Adriatic, and I a passenger on it, to land in a Communist country, is the scenario of a nightmare that takes away from me the desire to see Venice while there is light. Every totalitarian country repels me. But never has it occurred to me to swear in vain (and in a risible ridicule) that while General Jaruzelski is in power I will not write *again*!

What indeed seems lamentable to me and concerns me is that hundreds of thousands of Cubans cannot *return* to their country. (While the exiled author of *One Hundred Years of Solitude* surely does.) Not next month or ever while Castro lives can they go back. They know that they will not be received in exclusive black limousines or housed in mansions reserved 'for Chiefs of State of friendly countries'. They might be, if they are wayward writers, kicked inside one of the many Castroist protocol prisons (crammed in not with Communist writers or guest fellow-travellers who drink 'good Spanish red wine', but, internationalists that they are, capable still of 'consuming six bottles of whisky' – in half a day!), but by human beings, writers or not, who have scarcely anything to eat or to wear. They will be among those same Havana neighbours who use the *same* sewing needle, as García Márquez revealed some time ago with a candour that can be confused with cynicism. There he called this humble handout the 'culture of poverty'. The concept comes from the American left-wing sociologist Oscar Lewis, who taped interviews in Cuba as in Mexico. Later, Lewis was 'invited to leave the country' by the Ministry of the Interior and accused publicly by Raúl Castro of being an agent of imperialism. García Márquez appropriates it now, using sleight of hand like a parlour magician, to show what Castro has succeeded in fomenting in Cuba: creative poverty. Philosophy of misery or misery of Marxism?

The true writers in exile, not in flights as safe as their landing in Havana, nor as sonorous, are called Heberto Padilla, Reinaldo Arenas, Carlos Franqui, Juan Arcocha, Carlos Alberto Montaner, Antonio Benítez Rojo, Lydia Cabrera, Labrador Ruiz, Carlos Ripoll, José Triana, César Leante, Eduardo Manet, Severo Sarduy – but why keep making lists? It is already well known that Cuba by herself has produced more exiles in the last quarter century than all the other American countries put together – and, being writers, without the possibility of ever going back to their native country – as García Márquez will do whenever he wishes. Is March a propitious month for a tiny trip?

Some Spanish readers are able perhaps to remember a totalitarian dictatorship and poets shot at dawn or killed in prison and gaoled writers all over and total censorship and an entire generation condemned to exile and annihilated by time and oblivion. Those would read García Márquez's article with genuine revulsion before the grossest political *arrivisme* and utter sycophancy before the powerful. All full, nevertheless, of an irresistible local colour, as attractive and exotic as the colouring of the *peje piloto*, that fish of the Caribbean that is all grace among sharks: he serves as a guide and as a deceitful decoy.

This display by the writer among Philistines and Fidelines embarrasses his friends and makes his rivals rejoice, as they envy his prize and his sales. But if it didn't concern Cuba, I would see it as a too frequent phenomenon that is believed to be unique. I would read it then with the recurrent amusement with which I see in movies of the circus the eternal triangle of the clown who always falls in love with the lady horse-rider but the lady horse-rider is mad about the strong man with the beard. Meanwhile, from the bleachers, the public, ignorant of the backstage drama of love, applauds the trained dogs and the mad monkeys doing tumbles on the track or the (faked) death-defying leap of the trapeze artist with a net.

For those curious about life among notable men in Cuba, that circus without bread, I reserve some final – or initial – questions. It is a message to García Márquez – if he wants to answer them from his humble mansion in Mexico City. Here goes: why was Fidel Castro so interested, late at night and after an exhausting day for this other patriarch who tries to put off his autumn with gym practice, when he heard this worn-out *petite histoire* by Graham Greene? As he recounts how he was playing Russian roulette at nineteen years old, an age when most English adolescents, of upper class or lower depths, are used to playing more vital games. Did the suicide that never happened perhaps move Fidel Castro – with so many dead people who owe their real suicide to him? Or was it the discreet charm of the failed suicide? Or that the roulette that the author of *This Gun for Hire* used to play was casually called *Russian*?

(May 1983)

Portrait of the Artist
as a Commissar

No one remembers the guillotine any more. Not even when reading Dickens, whose *Tale of Two Cities* is the story of a hoped-for vengeance and of an unexpected abnegation: the guillotine is the leaf that cuts the novel in two. The *Encyclopaedia Britannica* offers a description of the guillotine closer to French history than that of Dickens. It was

> the instrument to inflict capital punishment by decapitation, introduced into France at the period of the Revolution. It consists of two upright posts surmounted by a cross beam, and grooved so as to guide an oblique-edged knife, the back of which is heavily weighted to make it fall swiftly and with force when the cord by which it is held aloft is let go.

The purpose of the guillotine was 'that in cases of capital punishment the privilege of execution by decapitation should no longer be confined to the nobles'.

But the guillotine served at first more to decapitate the citizens than the nobles, whose number was always limited. The most eminent names, besides the king and queen, were Danton, Desmoulins, Robespierre and Saint-Just. The first died protesting against the Terror, the last exalted it until the bloody end. But their heads rolled in sight of chaos into the basket none the less.

Not all the eminent citizens were beheaded by the machine. There were then, as now, opportunists who instigated the Terror and never suffered from it. One of them was the painter Louis David. His biography is an example of an early commissar and a demagogue *in extremis* – in three regimes. He is nonpareil in painting. Now the BBC has made him into an unworthy paradigm.

The programme in the series *Artists and Models* is called 'The Show Goes By' and was written and directed by Leslie Megahey, whom some will recall for an exemplary profile of Orson Welles. Megahey put together now a biography in images that is the portrait of the artist as a commissar.

Jacques Louis David was both things to excess: one of the greatest artists that France has given us and a perfect (or imperfect) scoundrel. When one has seen the portrait of Madame Récamier and *The Death of Marat* one knows the value that the last words of Nero have, '*Qualis artifex pereo*' – or what an artist dies with me. When one sees this brief biography one knows that the great artist was, like Nero, a murderer that the times made possible.

David was the court painter for Louis XVI, the decapitated, and the head of frivolous France: Marie Antoinette exalted him. He had inherited from Boucher the clientele but not the erotic talent. Boucher is the culmination of the venereal rococo, David would be the neoclassical painter *par excellence*; a lover of the togas that barely cover the naked heroes, and he would find in the Revolution many of his themes. Given the speed with which he painted he must have been the first graphic journalist of France – and of history. After his *Death of Marat*, begun a few hours *après l'assassinat*, as he claimed in an aside, and after the public exhibition of the dead body of the revolutionary flopped, David would become something more sinister and more sordid – and more contemporary. He would be a secret agent for Robespierre.

A painter by day, by night David would sign death warrants, sentencing many of the now *ci-devant* aristocrats (his former clients) to the guillotine. David ever after denied his nocturnal activity, but recently discovered documents show him often occupied in his twisted task. We know, too, that he condemned the King to death in the Assembly and some of his famous sitters, like the eminent scientist Laurent de Lavoisier, became famous dead subjects later. David, the portrait artist of the court and the aristocracy (only the nobles had their portraits made then), chose to be a member of the national convention and a master of the Jacobin arts. The journalist of the Revolution had gone on to become a president of the *Convention*.

His famous sketch *The Oath of the Tennis Court*, a report on a truly revolutionary occurrence, gave way to his portraits of the martyrs of the Revolution. Imprisoned soon afterwards he would paint in prison his celebrated self-portrait – in which the brush undressed him as he dressed himself up.

David had (and it is still visible in his portrait) a hardened phlegmon, a cyst that swelled on his left cheek and twisted his face grotesquely. Less visible (at least in the picture) was his stammering that could pass from stuttering to silence in seconds and his last name became Dada. David shared with other revolutionary leaders a visible physical deformation.

Marat suffered from a cruel form of psoriasis, which formed buboes on his body that burst under his clothes. The extreme prurigo forced him to spend hours in a tub of warm water: from there he attended to his work. It was here that the warm weapon (brought from between her breasts) of Charlotte Corday surprised him. The dead Marat became, thanks to David, the first revolutionary icon and is in a certain way a dummy for Lenin in his mausoleum. When one sees the picture in Brussels (I was its obliging spectator for three years) it becomes an absolute persona. Over a box of documents next to the dead man can be read: 'To Marat David'. It is almost, such sad sorrow, a parting message from the painter.

Robespierre, another deformed malcontent, was a dwarf and had a tiny voice that barely reached the Assembly. The nickname of Robespierre the Incorruptible was actually the Inaudible. '*A bas le Maximum!*' shouted the people of Paris when he was about to die on the Place de la Concorde – of discord rather. Danton was the only French revolutionary leader with physical, although not moral, integrity. Despite having pronounced one of the few felicitous phrases of the hour: '*De l'audace, encore de l'audace, et toujours de l'audace!*' he was accused of malfeasance – a political pretext to behead him. In front of the guillotine, Danton said to the executioner, 'Thou wilt show my head to the people: it is worth showing.' But the crowd asked for more. The tenebrous tribe of the *tricoteuses*, weaving and unweaving at the foot of *la machine*, almost got hold of David's head, torn off by an evil Goliath that was still growing. (During the Terror in France – from September 1793 to July 1794 – 20,000 people were decapitated by *La Louisette*.)

When it was not yet known that the only possible destiny for Robespierre was the guillotine, David cried out to the Incorruptible in the midst of the Assembly, 'You and I will take hemlock.' The metaphor was mixed and dangerous. David was alluding to the forced suicide of Socrates that had been the theme of one of his masterpieces. A connoisseur, as few in France were, of the ancient world, David tried to compare the bloodthirsty Robespierre with the sage Socrates – without any doubt a wretched excess.

The next day, with his protector guillotined, the Security Police came after David to oblige him to present himself before the Assembly: to account for his outburst with hemlocks of the day before. David was to all appearances lost. Although in the Assembly his stammering as much as his fear (and of course his opportune condemnation of the late Robespierre) saved his life. But David had to stay in prison for six months in an early sample of inverted house arrest: this time his cell became his house and he was even permitted to paint his self-portrait.

When the Terror turned into bloody French frenzy (Jacobins decapitate Girondists, Girondists guillotine Jacobins) Napoleon showed up on a white horse, the hero (or the villain: history, like Janus, always has two faces) of Thermidor come to put an end to the chaos, David, returned to his studio, was a neoclassicist again, an organizer of parties, a creator of fashion (the Empire vogue was introduced by this man of so many talents) and just as before he had been Madame Pompadour's favourite friend so now he is the *mulata* Josephine's confidant. The cruel republican is the Imperial court painter and as much a favourite of Bonaparte the consul as of the young Emperor. Napoleon admired, and was admired in, the versions of his life according to David. In one of them, the Consul daringly crosses the Alps on a spirited charger – what was actually a short crossing by mule. But David was never more flattering. On the canvas and in life and although he may have missed the days of wrath of the Terror, he was changing into the grand master of the young artists, Realist and Romantic alike, and at the same time the mirror image of the worst academic painters in France. His days as a perennial opportunist landed his old bones in Belgium, exiled in what was then known as the 'dry guillotine': banishment. The penalty, after Waterloo, for his Napoleonic whims. In a future Brussels would be his *Death of Marat*, the posthumous portrait of that man already corrupt in life who said: 'Five or six well cut-off heads would assure the people of calm, liberty and happiness.' Words that David approved of in their time. Although perhaps his classical sense and his concern with fashion and dress would have made the painter think that the phrase 'Five or six well cut-off heads' had more to do with the barber than with the barbarians.

Delacroix, ever so generous, called Jacques Louis David 'the first of the modern painters' and was on the mark in more than one sense. David is the first artist as commissar. Later there would be artist commissars and mere commissars. David was a great painter carried along by an extreme resentment, who found in the Revolution and later in Napoleon a cause (and an effect) that had nothing to do with painting but with the versions and perversions of history incarnated in heroes as doubtful as Louis XVI, Robespierre and Napoleon.

Ironically David would have his perfect present-day equivalent not in an artist like Picasso the neoclassicist, but in Dr Goebbels, whom Hitler warned: 'We must by whatever means keep Bruno Walter from conducting Beethoven.' To say to himself: 'In these things the Führer is never wrong.' Goebbels' *Tagebuch* could be David's *aide-mémoire*. Goebbels ends with a graphic obsession that is also of the century: the cinema. 'I am working at night on the documentary,' writes Goebbels. 'It contains atrocious shots of the Bolshevik horrors in Lvov. Frightful! The Führer calls to tell me that it is the best documentary we have done. I am very happy.' David would have said much the same to praise from Robespierre.

(January 1988)

AS THE MEDIA SEE HER

Quiet Days in Cliché

*Address on 'Cultural Diversity in the North-South Dialogue' at the
Symposium on Diffusion of Catalonian Culture, May 1989*

Not only notorious journalists but famous writers like to
spend their vacations (that is, every day) in a watering hole that I know very
well. Cliché! I'm used to molesting their leisure but I realize that he who
sleeps one siesta will sleep through a fiesta – to dream of clichés in the sun.

Already in the winter of my discontent in 1980 I gave a talk at Montclair
College, New Jersey, USA, to repudiate a too frequent cliché. It's the one
that proclaims 'Latin America' and is already beginning to smell as if it
said '*Latrine* America'. On that occasion I had to call it La Tin America
but I accepted the adjective Hispanic without panic.

The tag of Latin America was first proposed to its clients in the last
century and not in the United States as is thought – if one *does* think about
it. It is curious that this continent of such different countries carries a
name as if it were a single *país*. In union there might be strength but in
reunion I see confusion instead of fusion. What does Cuba have to do with
Mexico? One is a country of blacks and few whites and the other is a
country almost all Indian. In Cuba a Mexican was more foreign than a
Spaniard and Panama was a hat. What does Argentina have in common
with Brazil? Only waterfalls. Paraguay is not even the parody of Uruguay.
Afterthoughts – is Chile like Peru at all? Not at all. These nations have
borders south of the border. I even met a Venezuelan border patrol able to
separate what he believed to be the Colombian dross from the Acapulco
gold of other passengers – who also came by air from Bogotá. When I
asked him how he performed this operation without the help of a passport,
he gave me an answer worthy of a police dog who sniffs out eventual
exploding cigars: 'The Colombians,' he explained to me, 'I can smell
them out.' This happened in 1980, long before the Colombians reeked of
cocaine and let it be sniffed by foreigners.

There is in South America an enormous country almost the size of the continent. It is Brazil – which has nothing to do with its contiguous neighbours. Here the theory of language as an umbilical cord is ruptured: there is not an ordinary Brazilian who understands Spanish. From São Paulo to Bahia (I was there not long ago) the lingua franca is English. Latin is a dead language but in Brazil Spanish is a useless language – when it doesn't give rise to dangerous liaisons. *Cachasa* is a cane liquor, as in Cuba, but never as in Cuba is the best *cachasa* called *pinga*. It happens that with the same spelling and the same pronunciation *pinga* is in Cuba the popular name for the penis. My surprise became glee when, getting off the plane in Rio, I came face to face with an enormous billboard that promised ambiguously but forcefully: PINGA IS A MAN'S PLEASURE!

Returning from the major motto to the topic in the tropics, it was the French who dreamed of a retrograde destiny for South America and conceived the idea that it should be called Latin. It doesn't matter that no one spoke Latin south of the Río Grande. Nor did they speak it north of the Río Grande – come to think of it. (Curiously the Quartier Latin in Paris was once called *Pays Latin*.) Not a single South American region was ever called Latium and Paris not Rome is where South American writers go to die. No one was concerned there with conjugating the verb *amar* properly and the dictators to come did not have to cross the Rubicon: they lived near the Palace. Adding to the confusion, the only American republic where French was spoken was not in South America but in the Caribbean – and Haiti was more African than French. Then – why the *soubriquet?* No one knows. Or at least no one knew then.

I was the third speaker. The other two speakers, Uruguayans both, both critics, both now dead – were Angel Rama and Emir Rodríguez Monegal. They were in fact Settembrini and Naphta but in Spanish. They hated each other to the death in life and I suppose they must be still hating each other beyond death. Unless one has gone to hell and the other is in the heaven of the believers. Now, when getting down from the podium and leaving the hall, I left Emir improvising his talk in English. He knew his subject well (the Boom and who made it) and it was he who gave it a name. But Emir did not master English as he mastered his subject made topic. He could have spoken in Spanish, but he did not do so because Rama didn't speak a word of English and Emir didn't want Rama to understand a word of what he said. The result was that Emir was too concerned with improvising in English and his improvisation was a meandering of stock phrases that flowed into a sea of clichés. Rama, for his part, swung from his name – *rama* means branch – and hung on to a tree that was not the tree of wisdom but the bush of the commonplace. It was a *mano a mano* of one hand. Rather as if Belmonte talked about bullfighters and forgot to mention the bull. As God knows only too well, there is no hate worse than that of the fallen angel – and here there were two angels diving.

When I went out to the courtyard, after speaking of my favourite topic that morning (which was to un-Latin Latin America), Rama was sitting waiting for me on a hard bench in the cold of March in the north (more later) to tell me: 'You should have said that the United States became the United States of America in 1882.' I had spoken of that (stymie) bold moment when the American Congress decided that only the United States deserved to be America and borrowed the French tag to name a continent and a half: what José Martí called not without accuracy 'Our America'. But *all* America had already been the appropriation of a continent by an anonymous Italian who thus became eponymous. (They talk about the rape of Europe but they never talk about the robbery of America.) I didn't believe, I never believed, that the empire would be on the defensive then. The empire always strikes back.

Rama, the guest of the Americans, knew like no other critic the art of biting the hand that feeds you. He told me: 'You should say that the United States has stolen America.' Wrong! Amerigo Vespucci was the one who did it. But it was a powerful cliché. Rama, as a critic, was the cliché without a respite. Of course I didn't say so to him. Instead I decided from then on to demonstrate, or at least to show, that Latin America does not exist – its L is for limbo. The rest is nonsense.

Curiously Rama is in the other limbo now: the one that is south of hell. He died the victim of a cliché. He was flying from Paris to Bogotá on a cultural mission, when the plane was about to make a stopover in Madrid. But the pilot committed three fatal errors. The first was to go down too fast too soon. The second was not to hear (or perhaps to hear badly) the warning of the automatic pilot that was saying in robotic English: 'Danger! Danger! Lift up! Lift up now!' The third (and decisive) cliché happened when the Colombian pilot answered the automatic pilot: 'Shut up gringo!' That was also his epitaph: the plane crashed seconds later. Rama, who did not know English, as Monegal had wanted found out nothing.

(This is an example of how speaking different languages confuses the soul, but always speaking the same language kills the body.)

The Arabs were the south and they still are, but in England being the south does not mean being a southpaw but being able to buy Harrods, which is as if a sheikh were to buy not only Güell Park but also the Sagrada Familia. Of time, of temples! One must remember that in the Middle Ages the Moors tried to take Poitiers but it proved tougher than buying Harrods. It was the Turks from the south who conquered the east of Europe up to Vienna, where they still drink the abominable Turkish coffee. In a café, a venerable Viennese was playing on the zither thither the 'Rondo alla Turca' to make a monkey dance. The monkey was from Zimbabwe, a country that lies to the north of South Africa. In this part of the world not only history discriminates. Geography too. Mark Twain, who wrote pretending that he was going around the world, 'Yesterday we crossed the equator. Mary took photos', could also write: 'Don't talk to me of blacks or of whites. Talk to me about man. There can be nothing worse.' Twain also visited Australia when it had scarcely stopped being an English penal colony. Today it is one of the richest and most civilized countries in the world – there can be no country further south. But in the south of Australia live the Aborigines. That race is the Aboriginal sin of Australia.

Back to America, where Cubans sang a song called 'Immortal America'. (Nothing is immortal but almost everything can be immoral.) There is Mexico to the south of the United States. Poor Mexico! So far from God and so near to its presidents! The United States, where the buffalo went from roaming the prairie to being stamped on the coins, is south of Canada and north of Canada there lies nothing – except for those who believe the Pole comes from Poland. South of Mexico is Central America, a region with central heating, while in the south of South America is Pinochet's Chile, a country uninhabitable to me. But Peru, north of Chile, is more uninhabitable than Chile. (I know that with this statement I have just lost a few friends, but, as they are all writers, I want to believe that they prefer gaffes to *gafe*.) The most interesting country in South America is doubtless Argentina. It is also the most liveable, although it swings always between Patagonia and an agony to dance the tango. There is no song that expresses better the struggle between the *machismo* of its men and the troilism of its women. Two to tango, three to triangle.

It is well to end by saying that the north is an invention of the south. Boreas is a Greek god who represents the north wind, which the Venetians, following the Latins and not the Greeks, now call *bora*. When the north wind rocks the waves (and the gondolas) the Venetians say, as if they were on the South Seas and not on the Adriatic, 'Bora, bora!'

The French diplomats of the last century invented Latin America. De Gaulle, more ambitious, created the Third World. That also seems a bad translation of 'Tlön, Uqbar, Orbis Tertius'. It is literature that is guilty of the confusion. I was born in the south and I live in the north and for me the rose of the winds is a fetid flower. The rest is a tag from a fag.

A phrase from *Hamlet*, when he knows himself to be mad, is *North by northwest.* It was, as you already know, made in Hollywood – which lies to the south. There a celebrated mogul, fed up with so much hackneyed argument, exclaimed: 'I'm about to throw up with all those old clichés! What we need now are *new* clichés!'

I believe that with a little effort we will achieve this goal in gaol.

Guerrillas in Captivity Alas!

In the ideology jungle a Communist writer is that political animal who, after reading Marx, attacks man. (Some actually attack man even without ever having read Marx.) Such beasts are dangerous! In Latin America we used to have plenty of those on the loose. The former were called leftist intellectuals. The latter, guerrilla penmen – though they were armed with a machine-gun staccato style possible only on an electric typewriter. During the past decade South America had been a vast hunting ground for white hunters. (How many writers from *Ebony Magazine* dared to venture south?) The Latin reserves were open to foreign correspondents who didn't have to buy season tickets. You see, the guerrilla writer had decided to go ape for all seasons, making a monkey out of the man who invented Utopia in play and picture. But it was all a game, really. At least some were just game. Though for others it became a deadly game in the end. Nowadays if you search for the Marxmoset disguised as a guerrilla at large anywhere in the Green Continent, you'll find them absent or absent-minded or tried *in absentia*. Gone with the hot wind of their writings. However, you'll be able to locate that motley guerrilla (who once castigated America as a hell made in USA) now thriving in captivity in the land of the Marines: from the halls of Harvard U. to the streets of UCLA!

True-blue guerrillas in green-olive fatigues used to brandish a mortal motto: 'Have gun, will kill' – and they were killed instantly instead. Not so much by erratic enemy bullets (they usually hit only bystanders from the forest) but by friendly revolutionary rhetoric – always deadly. With the guerrillas being verbally forced by the elders further and further into the lunatic Left, Latin America became a minefield of literary minds and littering bodies.

Then the guerrillas were herded politically as well as geographically even further into hotter climates. Old writers did the shoving, new writers did the shovelling. But the guerrillas, all young, did the dying – and not only in fiction. The writers on the Left always managed to give the guerrillas the definite impression that they were ideologically placed left of the Left. The Young Turks should therefore do the fighting and leave the thinking to *homo sapiens*. Your average guerrilla fighter became some sort of primate with a Che beret on his thick head and a Beretta in his hand, playing a historical role not far from the gorilla thugs in *Planet of the Apes*. The intellectual guerrillas were in turn sedulously aping Fidel Castro, actually a poor Marxman posing as a sniper.

Today the native Latin American guerrillas with guns – ignorant, violent and ruthless but also brutally honest and therefore expendable – are an extinct political species in all of South America. The guerrillas with pens pushed their junior partners without brains into an early grave: they didn't need them any more. Now they use a brand-new motto of their own: 'Have grant, will travel' – and then they leave the motto running as they stampede bravely into exile. They were all fake guerrillas, naturally, but most of them were not even true writers.

Soon they were flying off from Rio with Fred and Ginger or having pillow talks with Bob and Carol and Ted and Alice and being bedfellows together or with Melvin and Howard in the Hughes Cadillac. The vehicle depended on how fast they were catching up with American mores in movies (back home, patrons of European films, they always made a point of patronizing Hollywood as a cream and crime factory) seen in those late shows on a television they totally despised before as an opiate of the watcher.

In fact the guerrilla writers had landed on their two hairy feet – which they immediately shaved together with their beards. No more monkey business! Now they were in America (Puerto Rico *is* in America), after negotiating a few immigration hurdles with ease and tease. The imperialist country that committed every murder most foul in their book, the home-base of free enterprise (and of that Friedman fellow to boot), the world Vigilante's Inferno had abruptly become the promise(d) land for every guerrilla writer who could read WELCOME TO THE USA. As Marx said, losers of the Third World unite! After all, you have nothing to lose. But they did the uniting in the United States. The unhappy feudists of lore were now just the happy few. Theirs was in fact an American success story. Marx was right once more. But which Marx was that – Karl or Groucho?

Grants, scholarships, bursaries, lectures, tenures – you name it they got it. (Or will get it soon.) Before, they loved their fellow man. Now they still loved their fellow man but loved their fellowships more. But even back in the fold of the capitalist church they wanted some monumental changes to be made in America. For instance, they would like to see the name of Grant's Tomb changed to just Grants. Pursuing purses like bursaries by rubbing elbows with those that count, they often got bursitis. More like tennis elbow than an occupational hazard, really. Just a Southern discomfort, honest. Nothing that money can't cure these days. The silver dollar is the aspirin of the socialist soul in a capitalist body – the Tom Paine killer.

Latin writers today feel more at ease with Mellon than with Marx. After all, Mellon has a comfortable university chair to offer, while Marx can only give you boils from sitting on a hard library bench. Americans used to be called ugly pigs as seen from the rancorous River Plate banks or from sored Chilean shores. But at a closer range they resemble, well – piggy banks. At least the Fords (especially with a Ford grant in your future) look rather like solid chrome piggy banks to me. It's a thrill seeing them in the flesh, all chrome and glass. Just imagine – any old Ford can give you a piggyback ride to the nearest campus, where the grass looks as green as dollar bills!

Americans don't go about chewing our heads off these days but they really know how to mow a campus loan and keep it green. Now that we are true-blood believers again, why don't we sing just one chorus from 'God Bless America', with a salsa beat? In the meantime the socialist revolutionary down the Argentine way can wait. (That's what Utopias are for, aren't they?) Their true place is in the future. Fellers, let's then carpe here a little bit of a diem – or a per diem. Whichever comes first. After all Rome wasn't built in a day, you know. Come to think of it, neither was Moscow.

(November 1985)

J'accuse at the Woodrow Wilson Center

This is not the first time that I've been invited to eat and had to pay for the meal – either with my money or with indigestion. Of course, I don't remember all those dyspeptic occasions, for nostalgia is the opposite of neuralgia: the pain has been left behind. But there is a particular South American collation that became a recollection. Some time ago Carlos Fuentes phoned me from Paris to say that he wanted to have lunch in London with Mario Vargas Llosa and me. Important news, he added: a literary magazine was about to be born in Paris, we should both be in the masthead, which was so wide that it could accommodate writers from two continents and three cultures, bilingual all. I'm on my way, he said and hung up.

Carlos came, we lunched and he launched the magazine. But the moment of truth (I know, I know: that's a cliché, but remember that some writers spend their quiet days in Clichy and their busy nights in cliché), the truth came in the form of a monstrous bill that looked more like the beak of a toucan recently arrived from South America. Toucan but one couldn't. Carlos leaned over to whisper in my ear: 'Can you take care of the check?' He meant the toucan's bill. He added: 'I haven't been able to change any French money yet.' Then he regained his upright position. I footed the bill. I *had* to: honour among writers, you know. Just as I do now. To foot the food bill. Sometimes this means putting the foot where the food was.

During this London luncheon I overheard that the magazine was to be financed by a trilingual and beautiful Parisienne, a French noblewoman who was, believe it or not, Antenor Patiño's *sole* heiress – to boot. To boot the foot to foot the bill for the food, by a fool. (That's me.) There I was, as poor as ever, funding the Antenor Patiño Foundation. Actually I was working in a tin mine! And all because Carlos Fuentes invited me to lunch in London. Indigestions I've had elsewhere.

But today I'll be giving *you* indigestion as I speak of more serious matters than a literary review, a stunning French beauty from South America and Patiño's tin money. I'm going to talk politics or rather about politics and that thing they call hate. Because of haste, a word cousin to hate, I've just discovered that I won't have time to cash my cheque. So you'll have, for once, to pay for this. I said haste and then said hate. For a comedic writer hate is a hateful word. Hate is one of the weapons of evil, but sometimes, to kill evil, you have to fight hate with hate. Make hate!

It was Mark Twain, one of the greatest humourists ever, who said that the problem with humour is that nobody takes it seriously. For instance, he predicted that he could die with the second coming of Halley's Comet but nobody paid any attention. The comet, the moment of truth for Twain, came and he obliged by dying on cue. A lesser humourist, I won't make any personal predictions today other than that I will finish this speech – even if dyspepsia sets in. After all that's what after-lunch speeches are for: to promote dyspepsia among nations and make ordinary heartburn look alarmingly like a cardiac arrest. After arrest you have the right to remain silent – and everybody will be most grateful if you do. But I'm not promising anything.

A humorist always runs two opposite risks. One is that he might not be taken seriously, the other is that he could be taken seriously. I'm running both risks today. Once I wrote a book which is the tragic story of my country, from island to garrison, from brothel to barracks, from tropical paradise to hell on earth. It was in fact a sad book, but everywhere readers complimented me on how funny it all was. One reviewer even called it a comic masterpiece! My book, called *View of Dawn in the Tropics* became *Review of Clowns in the Topic*. It was Mark Twain again who advised, 'When in doubt, tell the truth.' But he also said, 'Tell the truth or trump – but get the trick.' I got the trick.

I was supposed to talk today about Latin America and the press but I'm sorry I won't be able to comply. I simply cannot do it. You see, I know what the press is all about, but I don't know what Latin America is. Is it a country? Or is it a continent? If so please tell me where I can find it. I don't see it on my map. I know South America and I can certainly tell it from South Africa: there are no elephants in South America. I cannot tell Latin America from any other continent though. Is this land with a Roman profile as near as the Middle Ages are from us? I know the Americas, with a capital A but no capital. But where is *Latin* America? Is this a continent or a container?

To see a continent and a half as one country is like treating a man and his wife as just a couple. Nothing plural, even if singular, can be seen as single. Not long ago, when I was lecturing in Granada, Spain, a young woman asked me about Nicaragua. I told her, and it's true, that I didn't know that country. I had been familiar with only two Nicaraguans in my broad life: Rubén Darío and Bianca Jagger – whom I met when she was called otherwise. I knew Mrs Jagger in Swinging London once, long before she went public. I take it that she is a mouthpiece for the Nicaraguans now. As mouthpieces go I should say that her lips look truthful but with too much lipstick. Her face is still beautiful – if you like Oil of Ulay faces. I do. In fact, all my erotic dreams are cooked in Oil of Ulay. But I must confess that I was more intimate with Darío, with his poems, than with Bianca. Consolation by poetry, if you see what I mean.

In a word, I can only talk about Cuba now. Perhaps through her and her adventures and misadventures in the slave trade, which didn't finish with the Abolition, you'll be able to discern what the problems are when a country is seen mainly through the media – that awesome word that in Spanish only means half of it.

So, I will talk of the press and an American country I can locate on a map. I'll tell you two or three things I know about her and which the press probably don't know – or care to. But first I'll tell you what I know about the press, mainly American – and what it did for Cuba.

The first contact between the Cuban Revolution or, better still, between Fidel Castro and the American press was an act of deception on the part of Castro. At Castro's request, one of his followers (who quickly became a counter-revolutionary), together with the correspondent in Havana for the *New York Times*, 'arranged that Herbert Matthews, a senior editor on the *New York Times* experienced in Latin American affairs, should come from New York to try to see Castro'. This is what British historian Hugh Thomas wrote about the momentous visit – or rather visitation. Matthews met Castro and he (Matthews) was much impressed. 'The personality of the man was overpowering' – this is Matthews writing in his book *The Cuban Story*. 'It was easy to see that his men adored him.' (Now, about how many were those adoring him?) 'The interview,' says Thomas, 'exaggerated the number of men under Castro's leadership.' The deception was much more cruel than that. Hemingway had called Matthews 'brave as a badger', but he didn't mention anything about him being as gullible as a gull.

Here's Lord Thomas about Castro and his actual wild bunch: 'In fact, Raúl Castro kept passing in front of Matthews with the same men and the impression was left that Castro himself was "in another camp" for much of the time' the interview lasted. At the time Fidel Castro had with him only eighteen followers. But Matthews saw eighty indistinguishable Cubans (they all looked alike to him, all beards and fatigues), possibly eight hundred of them, perhaps – why not? – eight thousand! The trick is as old as history and in fact Herodotus, at the dawn of history, describes a similar deception accomplished by the Persians. But Matthews swallowed it hook, line and sinker.

He went back to New York and to his office in the *New York Times* to give Fidel Castro the biggest write-up so far: they gave him the front page and photographs. 'One got a feeling,' wrote Matthews, 'that he is now invincible' – and that was in early 1957! 'Castro so influenced Matthews,' writes Lord Thomas, 'both by his character and his energy that Matthews asked him then "about the report that he was going to declare a revolutionary government in the Sierra." ' (This, you must remember, with Castro having only eighteen men with him, some of them armed solely with home-made shotguns and machetes.) 'Not yet,' Castro replied. 'The time is not ripe. I will make myself known at the opportune moment.' Indeed he did!

The whole story was so crudely laughable that I remember Raúl Castro, in Carlos Franqui's office at the newspaper *Revolución* in 1959, laughing like a young hyena as he told how he and his brother had duped the American journalist with their phoney parade. It became a cruel joke. But the cruelty was not only on Matthews: the joke was on us Cubans too.

What is incredible is that, long after we knew he had been duped, Matthews was still a Fidel fan. In 1961 he wrote his *Cuban Story*. (Of which I've quoted some samples of Matthews selling hard some soft ware – or selling softly some hard ware.) But in 1969, already very long in the tooth, Matthews wrote a book called *Castro* and subtitled it 'A Political Biography'. Here he tells again the story of his tryst with Castro: 'In the Sierra Maestra on the morning of 17 February 1957, as he [Fidel] crouched next to me whispering (we were surrounded by Batista's troops) the hopes, the dreams, the convictions that were, in time, to become realities'. In the first rendering of this encounter Fidel Castro paraded his men up and down the Sierra or, most probably, a hill, shouting orders and behaving like a winning general. In Matthews' last book on the same subject, Castro whispers because he, and Matthews, are *surrounded* by the enemy.

I suggest that this is as big a lie as the first account. It was Matthews who had been deceived, now and before, but it's the same Fidel Castro who is accomplishing the deception with the tricks and treats of his trade. Had Matthews been with Castro not on 17 February but on 1 April, this would have been the perfect day for a Banana Fool. There is however something terribly familiar in this last account. Let's hear it again.

Fidel whispers while giving the impression that he and Matthews are surrounded. (In neither accounts does Matthews talk of seeing the enemy.) The whole phrase, 'we were surrounded by Batista's troops', is kept by Matthews within parenthesis. The whispering suggests intimacy and trust, while the parenthesis reveals that Castro can be trusted but Batista, that hideous form of threat, is a hidden menace. Batista's troops are depicted as a menace and at the same time the word troops gives the reader the impression that the enemy at the gates are many, even formidable.

As you can see, everything that will be here is already there. Fidel, never called Castro, is a good guy always surrounded by bad guys – and even the green fatigues suggest a Robin Hood, with the Sierra as the Forest of Sherwood. There is more than one vicious Sheriff though. Sometimes the baddies are Batista's henchmen, some other times Castro's foes will be labelled *Batistianos*, counter-revolutionaries, and, best of all, *gusanos*, which must be translated not as caterpillars but as worms – viscous and treacherous maggots. But the biggest enemy of all, always surrounding Castro like Matthews' brackets, is of course the United States. Many times, as Shakespeare says, 'With witchcraft of his wit, with traitorous gifts . . . that have the power so to seduce', Castro has won over not only his friends but his natural enemies as well. Is it surprising then that the best editor (and writer on Spanish matters) of the most powerful newspaper in America and perhaps the world, was as a matter of fact, bowled over by this man 'with traitorous gifts'? I should say not. What is surprising is that Matthews' newspaper (and many others) have consistently fallen into a trap that was once brilliant but is repeated over and over and over – *ad nauseam*. Castro, an honest leader, surrounded by the most powerful army Cuba has ever seen, whispers to a foreign correspondent called Matthews, Taber, Walters, Szulc, Lockwood – you name it, you got it – the same sweet something he has been muttering over and over since that fateful morning of 17 February 1957, when he claimed to be surrounded but could count with enough *bravos* (here dey come agin) to die fighting for freedom to the last man. Can't you see that the man is simply lying? The trap is crap. The lie can also be called theology for liberators.

Le Monde is another powerful newspaper, or a once powerful newspaper (please take note), that has been a propaganda broadside for Fidel Castro for at least a quarter of a century. *Le Monde* too sent to Havana one of its best men. But he was not solicited by Castro. His name is Claude Julien.

(Ironically this present writer was Julien's political guide on that visit.) He didn't go as far as the Sierra but went far enough. Later, in 1959 through the newspaper *Revolución*, he met Fidel Castro and fell under his spell. You might say: 'That man must be fascinating!' And I can answer, so was Hitler. Or Stalin, if you prefer a bigger moustache. All dictators are alike, even if they don't look alike. Castro with his bushy, busy beard seems indeed to be a powerful concoction of Charisma Number Two to wet behind the ears. Some of those who drink his words become drunk on him for life. That is the case of Julien and that is the case too of *Le Monde*. If newspapers could fall in love, you might say that *Le Monde* fell in love with Castro. At first sight. (Or rather sight unseen.)

Le Monde is a curious newspaper. It is on the left of the Seine but it behaves like an extremely reactionary sheet. It is a tabloid, but it has no photographs on the front page. Nor on the third. Nor on the back. In fact, *Le Monde* prints no photos whatever. In the world according to *Le Monde* not only can you tell who's who but who looks like what! It could very well be printed in Braille. No pictures, no beards. No beards, no Castro. This love affair then was as with Abélard and Héloïse: all letters – and that's what a correspondent is: a man who writes letters. Some correspondents are as brave as Héloïse, some behave more like Abélard after the fact. As Belmonte said, 'Bullfighting is like billiards, a game of balls.' *Le Monde* is billiards in Braille.

The Times is not in love with Castro. *The Times* is only in love with the cuckoo. But *The Times* has the hideous habit of addressing Fidel Castro as Dr Castro. (By the way, why is it that Stroessner is a dictator but Castro is Cuba's President: who voted for him? Certainly not the Cubans.) This doctoring of Castro induces in the English reader some sort of academic respect, as if Castro were an eminent physician or a genius in physics, rubbing elbows with Dr Fleming and Dr Einstein, as it were. Nobody at *The Times* had paid any attention to the news as old hat that Castro is only a lawyer and it was customary in Cuba to call lawyers, even if they were shysters, doctors. You could also call Goebbels a doctor too.

What irks me is not the hunt for the cuckoo every spring but an apparent new Cuban policy of *The Times* that goes beyond calling Fidel Dr Castro. Recently there was a dispatch by Reuters conveniently displayed on the front page. It was a story on Castro's Cuba – as they so aptly call the island. The Havana Report proved to be very favourable to Dr Castro. Later I found out that this was originally part of a series of four dispatches by a man from Reuters in Havana. He had given the good news first, as usual. But the other cables were a very thorough appraisal of the dire political and economic straits Cuba has been going through for the past twenty-five years. They were never printed. This is not a coincidence, this is *poshlost* by a newspaper that's lost.

What is *poshlost*? It's a Russian word that has no equivalent in English or Spanish. Says my favourite translator from the Russian, Dr V. Nabokov, *poshlost* is 'corny trash, vulgar clichés . . . bogus profundities.' *Poshlost* is also 'social comment, humanistic messages, political allegories, over concern with class and race and the journalistic generalities we all know.' Such as 'America is no better than Russia' or even better than that: 'We all share in Germany's guilt.' Here is one last sample by Nabokov – the naturalist who used to hunt *poshlost* in Darkest Trivia: 'Listing in one breath Auschwitz, Hiroshima and Vietnam is seditious poshlost.' I cannot resist adding one more item to the list of seditious *poshlost*: 'How can a tiny island like Cuba,' asks your naïve Eastern liberal, 'do harm to such a big country as the United States?' That's the equivalent of the *poshlost* of the midget with a Magnum (and I don't mean a big champagne bottle), whom bystanders insist on calling 'that cute small dwarf with a pop gun'. That's *poshlost* beyond all sense of proportions!

Cuba is no dwarf. It is in fact the biggest and most influential island in the whole Caribbean Basin – which it dominates culturally and politically. It has been like that for at least two centuries. It is also the most important island in the Americas. Journalists, ignorant of both fact and fiction, don't know that an old law of geopolitics establishes that all islands have an almost irresistible tendency to dominate the nearest continent. (Britain and Japan are very neat examples.) But not only geopolitics, plain politics and ancient history show that Sparta and Carthage were less than small islands: they were in fact merely cities. You don't have to repeat with me *Delenda est Cuba*, but one *Cave Castro* is enough for you to beware Fidel. It's all I ask. And you can call Castro whatever you want – even a convertible. (More later.)

There is no more powerful blacklisting than to label a writer, a journalist, *any* public man as not being far enough to the Left – or worse still, of being on the Right. Recently a television interviewer asked me in San Juan if I considered myself a man of the Left or of the Right. Instead of answering that this was a *poshlost* category originated in the French Assembly of 1789 under, of all people, Louis XVI, I replied instantly: 'I am a reactionary on the Left'. I could see the young lady blinking fast, thinking fast, sinking even faster and I swear I saw smoke coming out of her eyes and ears – and she didn't have a lighted cigarette in her hand as is customary for smart women now. The girl must have been fuming.

A humorist must make people laugh even when he is writing his own obituary. Does it hurt? Only when they *don't* laugh. A Cuban exile joke declares Cubans to be a confused race. Why are they confused? 'Well, the island is in the Caribbean, the Government is in Moscow and the people in Miami.' What the joker didn't know was that the destiny of all Cubans is in the press. If *only* Herbert Matthews – well, anyway, that's in the past. The future could be truly being wary of Castro and not playing power politics with the souls on board that *Titanic* of the Americas, an island made to float for ever and sinking on her maiden trip.

Be that as it may (it is May, isn't it?), I am glad to be here invited to talk about politics and the press and not about literature. As we all know it is easier to talk politics than to talk literature. Politics is to history what journalism is to literature: everyday life trying to become eternal. It goes without saying that history is a lesser kind of eternity than literature. We know all about Troy thanks to Homer. Who can tell what was the politics behind the Greek expedition? A war did destroy Troy but a poem reconstructed it for the Greeks and for mankind. Politics obliterated Troy, poetry made it eternal.

'Never annoy the Press,' advises William Powell in *The Great Ziegfeld*. Ziegfeld was a man busy with his girls, but he had time for a saw or two after what he saw. 'Men who keep books are never happy,' he expostulates to a girl. Girls gave Ziegfeld expostulations. Instead of men who keep books he should have said men who *write* books. I write books, I travel – and I am not very happy at the moment, making a nuisance of myself here. Even to the point of spoiling your lunch. But you know what? We should have had instead of our gourmet meal some spaghetti with bicarbonate of soda. You see, they cure the indigestion they cause. That's a recipe of my favourite Marx, the man who was Groucho but not an Argentine. Now, give me an exploding cigar. I know I deserve it.

(May 1985)

Cubans Ahoy!

Cubans[1] is – what else? – a bookful of Cubans. But now instead of foreign visitors talking about the natives is *una quinta-calumni-ada*: a fifth-calumnist, an islander who slanders. They might have been the sailors on the *Bounty* denouncing Captain Bligh and his cruel crew. Miami is now a closer version of Tahiti and mutiny is in the air. There are castaways though: from seven to ten thousand so far. One of them, doing the crossing of the dangerous Gulf Stream, was fished from the sea by the Royal Yacht *Britannia*. His raft was made of inner tubes and plywood. Before fainting, the Cuban youth managed to ask, 'Miami yes?' One of the things this book may have achieved is to explain why so many Cubans (almost two million of them from a population of barely ten million: a decimation devoutly to be doubted) risk their lives to escape from Para-dise.

In the beginning there were illustrious visitors to the alluring island. Sartre, Pablo Neruda, Nathalie Sarraute, Hans-Magnus Enzensberger, Susan Sontag, Simone de Beauvoir, Juan Goytisolo, Mario Vargas Llosa. But not García Márquez. At the time he was sent to Coventry after deserting his post as the man from Prensa Latina (the official Cuban news agency) in New York during the Bay of Pigs invasion. Now only the dregs are left. What does attract them? Hemingway was undecided. Is it the sight or the smell?

Cubans begins with a Cuban chronology (starting in 1868 – why?) that is a typically Irish yarn. This chronology does to facts what a juggler does to oranges. It states for instance that Batista was in power from 1934 to 1944. (Ten years that compared with Castro's thirty-two make the former into a dwarf dictator.) At the same time the author forgets to tell British readers that Batista (she doesn't even mention he was black!) was legally elected in 1940 – mainly thanks to the Communist vote. As a reward the Com-munists were promised (and got) full control of the CTC, the Cuban

1. By Lynn Geldof (Bloomsbury, 1991).

Confederation of Workers. Two Communist leaders served in Batista's Cabinet. One of them was Carlos Rafael Rodriguez, the third man in power now. Explanation? He was a hard-core Stalinist then, now Castro is Cuba's Stalin.

The chronology is composed following the well-known principle that if you cannot write history, just rewrite it. The author mentions in passing that in 1980 'twelve people asking asylum crashed through Peruvian Embassy gates'. In fact eleven *thousand* Cubans sought asylum in the embassy in seventy-two hours! It was one of the most notorious scandals in the history of political asylum. Will Rogers said, 'All I know is what I read in the papers.' Obviously Lynn Geldof has not even read the newspapers. Even the *Irish Times* published the news! She should have tried writing about Belfast instead.

The author does not acknowledge that now famished Cuba (Radio Three announced this morning that they have finally rationed bread: 3 ounces daily per person) was more prosperous in the fifties than her native island. A visitor coming from Dublin then would have been surprised how prosperous Havana was. This is not arcana, it had been published everywhere. Even in the Guinness Book of Records.

All this question-and-answer exercise has been done before: same method, same results. The *enquête* book was perhaps invented by Oscar Lewis, the famed American author of *The Sons of Sánchez*. Lewis originated the concept he named the 'culture of poverty' and was also attracted by what was then called the 'Cuban experiment' – as if Cubans were mice in a laboratory. But Lewis was an honest man and he finally fell foul of the Castro brothers and was expelled from Cuba – but not before he suffered a heart attack. He died shortly after. His posthumous *Four Men, Living the Revolution* (1977) is an exact forerunner of *Cubans*.

Yeats, an Irishman of vision, wrote about fanatics, 'the worst are full of passionate intensity'. There is no intensity in *Cubans*, passionate or otherwise. It is, on the contrary, boring, biased and bad.

(May 1991)

Afterthought. With Oscar Lewis the *enquête* method appears to be objective but it is not. At least not in a police state. Even if the tapes are not tampered with, the informants are always doubtful – even the *apparatchik*, above all the *apparatchik*. They all live in a totalitarian country subject to the leaden pressure of state terror. (After all, this could be another way of making them talk.) Even if people agree to be interviewed they don't have the means to know if what they said (and has been taken down) will be used as evidence against them tomorrow. A man interviewed by Oscar Lewis was thrown in gaol *before* he left Cuba: Lewis had a Security mole in his staff. On top of that the sincerity of the informants is always questionable. Witness the unanimous support for the regime we saw in the movies made in Romania before Ceausescu was toppled and the total public repulsion of his regime that followed his downfall. The method seems to derive its strength from being objective but, as Lenin said, imitating Joe E. Brown's famous last words: 'Nobody's neutral.'

Cain's Cuba

Sir – Who is Pedro Perez, and why is he saying these ludicrous things about me? He claims he knew me as Cain but I swear I don't know him from Adam. His letter (*London Review of Books*, Vol. 4, No 24) I do recognize, though. It's the typical production of the *apparatchik*: a massive missive made in Moscow, that Mecca of the political Meccano. This letter is, in fact, a lie a line. I don't have the time, nor *LRB* the space, to answer it now. Pity. You see, I enjoy detecting the hidden Goebbels in every party political broadcast. However, I can't help wondering what Señor Perez is doing so far from the socialist sun, living in this conservative, capitalist cesspool, this septic isle, this England?

I never 'attacked' Graham Greene as he claims (Vol. 5, No 1). I merely quoted from his paean to Fidel Castro (which still remains without disavowal from the novelist) to illustrate how some British writers, whatever their reasons or motives, have consistently misinformed the British public on the Cuban issue – and have never recanted. I also commented on Greene's baffling (at least to me) admiration for a cruel and ruthless tyrant. He's right, though, about who introduced whom at Plaza de la Catedral that Havana night in 1959 when they were shooting Greene's screenplay. I introduced Fidel Castro to Carol Reed. I also introduced him to Alec Guinness, and even to Noël Coward. I had to. I was the only Cuban official there who had any English. I must have confused them with each other and all of them with Graham Greene. But I have an excuse for that embarrassing gaffe: for me, then, all Englishmen looked alike.

I never kept tabs on Greene's trips to Panama or on his flight routes. True, Torrijos was not my cup of tea when he was alive and playing host to writers who love strongmen. General Torrijos is dead now, so I'll leave him to heaven. Cuba is more than somebody else's facts. She is my constant concern. But Greene, like many modern writers, confuses facts with truth. He of all people should know that the Gospels are revealed truth – but are they fact? Moreover, he seems to believe that dates are facts. Is the year Jesus was born faith or fact? For a doubting Catholic, Greene reveals himself to be as factual as a materialist.

In fact (I beg your pardon), Mr Greene really objects only to two dates of mine, but it makes it seem as if my article, like an oasis palm-tree, were full of dates. As a matter of fact (*bis*), he takes exception to one single date: when he last visited Cuba and met Fidel Castro. Immediately after, he wrote his lyrical account of his visit with the Elusive Leader. Greene has never, not even now, had trouble with Castro's cant – or with his own conscience. At that time, 1966, this dissembling dictator had remained in office for seven long years – without ever being elected, not even in a Mexican-fashion election. The aftermath of Castro's seizure of power was thousands of 'enemies of the Revolution' shot by firing-squad and tens of thousands running for cover into exile. Censorship was not selective: it was rampant, blind and total. There were only two newspapers left then from the ten or twelve being published in Havana in 1959. One of those newspapers was the Cuban *Pravda*, called *Granma* (the one Greene mentions cutely in his story as 'the daily paper with what seems to be an odd nursery title'), and large labour camps for homosexuals only (Castro's convertibles) were already blooming like flowers all over that island Greene crisscrossed from west to east on a bus. But I suspect that Mr Greene would call all this a fairy-tale.

A writer of fiction asks me, who was writing about politics and poetry, to have my facts right. Curiouser still, Greene does not mention my quotes from his fictive piece in which he calls Cuba a pleasure-capital (*sic*) under Batista. But it is true that Mr Greene never said that Haydée Santamaría died in the assault on Moncada Barracks. Instead the man who gave us *Our Man in Havana* (set, I suppose, in a pleasure-*country*) concocts yet another 'Cuban' fiction about some mean and evil (but bungling) 'assassins', who tail Heroine Haydée's car to kill her – what else? Their ploy was that once she was dead and about to be buried, foreign agents (who else?) could kill Castro, a revolutionary Romeo, come to kneel at the martyr's tomb in grief.

The above looks as if lifted from a Costa-Gavras Greek tract: *Z* or *Oedipus Tyrannus*. It is – in fact – the plot of a John Huston melodrama: the oldie *We were Strangers*, set in Havana during the Machado dictatorship of the Thirties. The bloody truth is that Haydée Santamaría (I know this *for a fact*), disillusioned with Castro and the nasty regime she helped to establish in Cuba, shot herself through the mouth with a .45 Colt pistol. Fictional counter-revolutionary assassins didn't kill her. Castro did. That's a fact.

(February 1983)

BIRTH OF A NOTION

Hey Cuba, Hecuba?

Address given at the José Martí – YMCA of Miami, Florida,
September 1991

Hecuba, says Lemprière,
proved the chastest of women –
and the most unfortunate of mothers.

An exiled writer, Vintila Horia, a Romanian who died in Madrid, when reclaiming Ovid in vain for the Christian faith, wrote (or rather conceived) that God was born in exile, implying that Ovid, in his exile in Thomis, sentenced by the Emperor Augustus to a death in life, dreamed God. God was not born in exile of course, but literature sometimes desperately seems to have been. It could have been born with Ovid in his *Epistles from Pontus*, that are as abject as any Stalinist poem. Or been stewed over the slow fire of hell that Dante stirred up against his political enemies. But it is the literature of the twentieth century that can recover as its own a certain lot in the destiny of exile. *Exit*, so close to exile, has the same origin as our exalted *éxito* – meaning success. Words are always a metaphysical proposition.

Joyce, Nabokov, Broch, Elias Canetti, Koestler, Solzhenitsyn, Ionesco, Cernuda, Cioran, Reinaldo Arenas: they all wrote in a manifest form of exile. Our literary century cannot be understood without exile. But there is a literature I know that was born and died in exile. It happened in the nineteenth century but those writers are our contemporaries. To read them is to picture them standing in a dark room in front of a window that is opened to watch us. They are watching us. Many of us do not see them. They are in front of the open window but we never see them. They are the ghost writers of America. They were, no more and no less, what we are now.

I am speaking, of course, of Cuban writers in exile. That window that opens is our window now. We live in that house, today, as projects of ghosts. We are the zombies of the future. Like the vampire's victims we are the undead: we dead who are not dead. Before leaving I want to render homage to those about whom Constantine Cavafy sang, a poet in a carbuncle of history that was also an exile: Greece far from Greece. Cavafy called them our dear departed:

> Voices ideal and beloved
> of those who have died or of those who are
> for us
> lost like the dead.
> At times,
> at times [*the repetition is mine*]
> they speak to us in our dreams.

Cuba is the country that has produced the most exiles during more than a century and a half of American history. (That history is the chronicle of a Cuban battle against the Devil.) Cuban literature – what doubt is there? – was born in exile. It was in fact at the origin of the birth of a nation. But it was really the birth of a notion: nothing succeeds like exile. I'm talking now not about Miami but about our literature.

In exile, today as yesterday, there have been not a few writers. But not one, not even José Martí, showed an exceptional talent in Cuba before taking ship 'to sail across other seas of madness' – to leave and at the same time to arrive at our particular Cytherea. Cytherea was an island on the coast of Laconia from where the Laconics came. Curious metaphor for a country that has produced the talkative *hablaneros*! But Cytherea was consecrated to Venus, who was the goddess of beauty, the mother of love, the queen of laughter and the mistress of grace and pleasure and the patroness of free women. If all of that is not Cuba it was at least Havana: Cytherea vade-mecum, that goes with me, that I carry like a voice within.

Almost all those future masters were merely the Sorceress's apprentices. The extraordinary thing is that so many exiles from that century became notable writers. Even, like Martí, great writers. Everything changed abroad, at once cosy and hostile. Or at least more cosy than the island, less hostile for those Cubans who practised writing in the time and space of exile. Curiouser still is that the Cubans who stayed behind, within (on the island that should have seen Venus born but saw instead the invasion of Mars) those stragglers seem to learn badly the art of writing, perhaps because they spend their time in simulating a more demanding adherence. Literature, a jealous goddess, admits no other loyalty than extreme devotion. Those writers *all* come from the same country. They are sometimes from the same generation of islanders left behind by the history that they claim to invoke. Nevertheless the ones gone – the absent ones – as Mallarmé proposed for Poe, distance, a form of eternity, changes them into themselves – into something better than themselves.

It all began in the last century and almost always, as in this century, out of political motives. But for us Cubans this is the century of exile. The Roman zero hour that sounded for Ovid sounded for us some time ago, exiled by a false emperor. A million and a half Cubans have already taken the landless road. It is more than decimated, since that figure represents 15 per cent of the present population of Cuba: it is in fact a tenth and a half. This century could almost be marked down in Cuban history, as was done in the Bible, with the book of *Exodus*. Or, as Calvert Casey, that writer made and destroyed by exile, said, 'Our Diaspora'. Exile is in itself a form of martyrdom. But it is also a rare privilege.

Now to the sad business of the roll call. I will begin by speaking of the poets because they were the first exiles. Cuba has seemed at times an island surrounded by poets. There poets flew high in the tropical sky and the blue waters were open inkwells. In fact the great Cuban literary expression has emerged from the poet's pen. In the last century it was Julián de Casal, in this century it is Lezama Lima: both internal exiles, both longing to leave the island and both dead from fear of abroad. Casal was at the same time the precursor and master of Modernism and there is no doubt that if there are five poets writing in Spanish in this century in whose work talent becomes genius, among them, counted on the fingers of one's hand, central, there will be José Lezama Lima.

Perhaps the real reason why there have been so many writers in exile, *gone* from Cuba, is the historical fact that the island began early the struggle for its independence (before 1830) and the task has become long, almost interminable. For some writers, like José María Heredia (1803–39), exile was a death sentence, with a remission of three months in 1836 when the authorities allowed him to return to Cuba. It is true that his foreign fame was large and that the suffering of exile and the apprenticeship of his *metier* transformed him into the first Romantic poet who wrote in Spanish. But exile finished him off at thirty-six and so he was the first Cuban writer to die in exile. He would not be the last.

In one of his most famous texts, 'Letter from the Niagara' (Heredia was obsessed with the American waterfall), the poet says in an exclamatory tone: 'Oh, when will the novel of my life end for reality to begin?' This kind of punishment is new – of the twentieth century in fact and Sartre probably calls it *authenticité*. Inverting the anguish a century and a half later, Severo Sarduy, another exiled writer, says: 'I want to convert the unreality of my life into an unreal novel.' The times have changed but not the strangeness. That queer notion is called exile.

In the midst of his grandiose poem to the Niagara, Heredia exclaims like a good Romantic – and like an exiled Cuban:

> Why do I not admire
> Around your immense cavern,
> The palms, oh!, the delicious palms
> That on the plains of my ardent land
> Are born from the sun to the smile

The royal palm, a tree particular to Cuba, served in the last century as a rhetorical reference and as an arboreal ideal for the nostalgia for one's own country. Many Cuban poets, Martí among them, made use of this vegetable metaphor. But Heredia was more explicit and in his 'Hymn of the Exile' he composed a poem that is the expression of a lament that we can still exclaim:

> Sweet Cuba! In you there see each other,
> in the highest and deepest degree,
> the beauty of the physical world,
> the horrors of the moral order.

Still more. In the same poem there are some lines that Calvert Casey could have made his own in Rome, in 1969, the year of his suicide:

> There still may be hearts in Cuba
> that envy me my martyr's luck
> and prefer the splendid death
> to their bitter, miserable life.

For poor Calvert, so Cuban, the end in a modest apartment in Rome, a city that so resembled Havana, his death was not splendid but lousy and lonely. The Italian newspapers did not pick up the death of an exile but the suicide of a sodomite, judging by the appearance of two or three Indian statuettes on a console and the consolation of several photos of his lover. Heredia was right when he scorned 'the horrors of the moral world'. Calvert Casey also scorned them.

With Juan Clemente Zenea (1832–71), a poet who belongs in his own right to the *Lute of the Exile*, history and men dealt him a heinous hand. I have briefly recounted his fate in *View of Dawn in the Tropics* where he appears anonymously. During the first independence war, exiled and exalted by the mission of making peace in Cuba, Zenea returned to the island with a Spanish safe conduct to meet in the rebel camp Carlos Manuel de Céspedes. But once facing the haughty President of the Republic in Arms, Zenea did not dare to say anything about his pacifist plan to Céspedes, who would surely have shot him as a traitor. 'He didn't take a single step,' wrote Céspedes later, 'nor did he betray the least intention of being a docile tool of Azcarate.' That is of Spain.

When he was back in Havana on his way to the United States the Spanish authorities revoked Zenea's safe conduct, accused him of high treason and threw him into the old La Cabaña fortress – which still exists, still a political prison. Waiting for his death sentence to be carried out (during the trial his hair had turned white, he had become an old man although he had not yet reached forty), Zenea composed an ode to a swallow that he saw fly beyond the bars:

> How I would like to watch
> what you tried to leave behind:
> I would like to be at sea,
> to see again the sad North,
> to be a swallow and fly!

This is the Zenea familiar from primary school and whose poem is made truly painful by an unjust death. But Zenea wrote another poem, less familiar but that still has urgency. Its subject, very modern, is the hard exile and the opportunism of the *intrigantes* left behind:

> What forces us to emigrate? If I wished
> to live from dishonour and perfidy
> I could return to Cuba and awaken
> in vile people their rabid envy.
> There, to dwell like brutes,
> it is enough to be indifferent to scorn,
> to Claudius Caesar bring tributes,
> to prostrate oneself humbly and one's head to bow.

Zenea was shot in La Cabaña, on the execution wall known later as the Moat of the Laurels, where, already during the Republic, they planted willows and cypresses to honour the memory of the poet who was the victim of a tragic misunderstanding: the Cubans thought he was a Spanish spy, the Spanish believed him a Cuban spy – the theme of the traitor who was never a hero. No one thought then that he was only a running poet.

Of his literary memory there remains that pathetic but poor poem, about swallows and willows and, on the Paseo del Prado of Havana, a remarkable sculpture group that becomes grotesque at times. The statue is a bronze man (bronze for so vulnerable a poet) accompanied by his white marble muse, lying nude at his feet like a venerating Venus. In a typical turn this monument was changed later into an obscure object of jest by the Havana ne'er-do-wells, who made the white mound of Venus of the marble muse into a charcoal pubis, shockingly black. This is the continuing Cuban comedy. The sad short tragedy is that the novelist Reinaldo Arenas, an exile and a suicide, was a prisoner in La Cabaña in 1977 – exactly 106 years after Zenea. There are no laurels for Arenas now. To all poets, the poet's grave.

Heredia and Zenea (the latter to a lesser degree since he was a minor poet) were destroyed by exile. One can argue that exile distinguished Heredia as a major poet, but Zenea was erased by a fusillade of ten guns. Even if exile destroyed the best men that were born in Cuba then, the nineteenth century was able to perfect in exile the art of a truly extraordinary novelist. His name was Cirilo Villaverde. That man with a memorable name was the best novelist that Iberoamerica had in the nineteenth century – if one excludes the major author in Brazil who was Machado de Assís. His only possible rival (I'm referring to Villaverde: Machado had no rival) was the Colombian Jorge Isaacs with *María*. But *María* is a late Romantic novel from 1867. The first part of *Cecilia Valdés* was published much earlier, in 1839. Villaverde was also a Romantic but an odd Romantic – that is, an exceptional writer.

Don Cirilo was already a well-known writer when he had to flee from Cuba in 1849 because of his political associations, not his *actions*. Like Heredia and Zenea and like Martí, he could not resist the lure of the island (that would be fatal to Zenea and to Martí) and he returned to Havana in 1858.

But he had to exile himself again, this time for ever. That was the man of whom Galdós, with the arrogance of a new big city writer (Benito Pérez Galdós was born in the Canary Islands but for a time he hesitated between emigrating to Havana or to Madrid: Madrid won out), had said that 'I never would have thought that a *Cuban* could write *so* well.' So much condescension towards a land that produced José Martí, the greatest writer in Spanish of the nineteenth century, is insulting. Not only does Villaverde write well but he is a refined Cuban and has the courtesy, that I don't have, not to say of Galdós: 'I never thought that a canary, besides singing, could write too.' But literary revenge can be poetic justice and Villaverde brings off, in a single one of his novels, what Galdós could not do in all of his. Villaverde created a type, or rather a prototype, Cecilia *la Mulata Nacional*. A myth as powerful as Carmen was years before. The feisty gypsy leapt out of a story to be sung in *habaneras* and in arias and to bewitch the air of her century (and by the way of ours) with her perfume of crime. Cecilia is Carmen by other means, but her odour is a penetrating scent of sin, incest. The novel *Cecilia Valdés* is excellent, but that excellence was only possible in exile. I don't know what the book would have been like (it began as a story about a little girl who was a Lolita from Havana), *that* book in that Cuba. I only know what it was – what it is.

Cirilo Villaverde dedicates his masterpiece in this nostalgic manner: 'TO CUBAN WOMEN: Far from Cuba and without hope of seeing her sun, her flowers nor her *palms* again, to whom but to you, dear compatriots, reflection of the most beautiful side of the fatherland, could I dedicate, with more justice, these sad pages?' Villaverde wrote this dedication in New York in 1882, when *Cecilia Valdés* was published there. It was the rewriting of the first part printed in Havana forty years before. In between there was a whole life of political conspiracy, even of renunciation of literature and above all, always, of exile. Cirilo Villaverde, who was born in a town in Pinar del Rio, died in New York in 1894, aged eighty-two and barely four historic years from the independence of Cuba. Nevertheless in all that time he only visited the island once and under peril of death. He was lucky. Zenea and Martí were not: they did not hear the fatal counsel of Pythagoras: 'Never return.'

One must speak now of the Great Lady of Exile, Gertrudis Gómez de Avellaneda, better known as La Avellaneda. There is no other woman like her in the American letters of her time. She was a promiscuous and sensual Romantic who devoured men in the tropics as if they were bananas and in Spain, like nuts. The virago wrote verse with the same ease. Among them (among her verses, not her men) there is a sonnet entitled 'Al partir' (Upon leaving), that is in all the anthologies of the best Spanish poems of all time. It may be apposite to know that this sonnet says in part and in art:

> I am about to leave! The diligent rabble,
> to wrench me from my native soil
> hoists the sails and before unfurling them
> the breeze comes from their ardent toil.

Then suddenly:

> Farewell happy country, beloved Eden!
> Farewell! Already the swollen sail slides . . .
> the anchor is raised . . . the trembling boat
> cuts the waves and silently flies!

It goes without saying (it seems to me) from where the poetess was leaving who says farewell to her land and at the same time to the 'diligent rabble' in a neat sonnet. (If the sonnet seems short I can say here in confidence that I swallowed a line or two, besides countless exclamations.) Doña Gertrudis was a vehement woman whom exile made not only important, imposing – and also foreign. Gertrudis Gómez de Avellaneda died Spanish – and is classified as such by the history of literature. It is evident that the literary salons of Madrid turned out to be more attractive to her than the gatherings of Havana, more political than poetic under the Spanish dominion. The metropolis was what the light of a lamp was for the tropical butterfly become a Madrid moth.

Another exiled Cuban poet, in the last century is Julián del Casal, but his exile, like Lezama Lima's in the twentieth century, is an internal exile. But he dwelt in vileness as in a prison. A precursor of Modernism, a Francophile who was on friendly terms with Baudelaire, living in the stultified and stupid colonial Havana among Japanese screens, Hokusai engravings and verses by Verlaine, that man was like daylight in the dark night. Casal was anxious to leave Cuba, to abandon Havana, asphyxiating for him (he was the eternal invalid) and to live in Paris, also called the City of Light, to stroll along its boulevards, to drink absinthe and then *flâner*.

There is a poem in which the poor poet declares his desire to:

> see another sky, another mountain,
> another beach, other horizon, another sea,
> other towns, other people
> with different ways of thinking.

To contradict himself right away:

> But I don't depart. If I departed
> in an instant I would want to come back

In fact, the poor poet (his family had been ruined by the independence wars and now was living within the walls of Havana, dreaming of France while he negotiated the muddy streets between the miserable houses and suffered the epidemic yellow fever along with the endemic idiocy), the patient poet managed to get together enough money to set sail for Spain. Destination: Paris. He got no further than Madrid. On the way back to Havana he declared: 'I didn't want to know Paris. To see it in reality would have been to destroy a dream.' Casal was an avatar of the poet shut up not in his marble tower but in his horrid house.

Another avatar, in the twentieth century now, was Lezama Lima who lived always in the same house where he died – on premonitory Trocadero Street. Another Cuban poet, now exiled in Madrid, Gastón Baquero, invited Lezama to go to Mexico once. But Lezama, poetically, never got to Mexico City. From that three-day trek there remains a poem, 'To Reach Montego Bay'. Montego Bay is not in Mexico. It was a stopover in Jamaica by the Havana–Mexico City flight on the ancient aeroplanes of two propellers and no seat-belts – the passengers killed by either boredom or fear.

But Julián del Casal was a poet who lived in his dreams – and on his nightmares. Always ahead of the game, even at the cost of his health and his sanity, he wrote a revealing verse: 'Artificial bliss / that is the real life' in a poem entitled 'The Song of Morphine'. Julián del Casal died in Havana in 1893, before his thirtieth birthday.

A terribly unlucky man, besides suffering from perennial tuberculosis from adolescence, he was the platonic lover of one or two real women and a journalist haunted by political censorship, until finding himself obliged to follow one of the most unusual but most jejune jobs: to braid a bull-fighter's *coleta*. (To buy Susini cigarettes whose stamps he collected.) He lived and died in a shabby single room embellished by his unerring good taste: surrounded by exotic *bibelots*, by *japoneries*, by rare books. Besides much morphine, he smoked opium and hashish – and perhaps marijuana – to make his paradise artificial and his hell tropical. Like all men, said Borges, he lived in bad times – fortunately for him it was not for long. During a dinner with some friends, someone told a riotous joke. (We Cubans are wild jokers.) Casal liked it so much that he burst out laughing. The laughter produced in him a haemoptysis: the unstoppable enemy blood. An incoercible scarlet vomit killed him, as he would have liked to have said, Frenchified to the death, *sur place*.

Lezama Lima, as you might have expected, dedicated a whole ode to him:

> Let him, greening, turn around;
> permit him to go out from the party
> to the terrace where they are asleep . . .
> Let them accompany him without speaking . . .
> . . . His cheerful cough
> powders the mask of Japanese warriors.
> No stanza by Baudelaire
> can equal the sound of your cheerful cough.
> Permit him to turn around, now he's looking at us.
> The death of Baudelaire babbling

insistent . . .
has the same quality as your death,
since having lived like a dauphin dead from sleep
you managed to die dead from laughter.
Your death could have influenced Baudelaire.

Yes, indeed it could – as a disciple influences his master. As it could move General Antonio Maceo, his hero, whom Casal asked for an autograph the night they met on the Acera del Louvre in Havana between the wars of independence.

But Casal's death would not have influenced Martí at all. Martí died his own death. José Martí (1853–95) lived, like many Romantic poets then (one only has to mention two, the Hungarian Sandor Petöfi and Lord Byron), next to literature, among ideals of freedom that somehow created confusion around these men become heroes. As if they had wanted it more than anything in life, they became martyrs when they died: rebels in search of a death. Martí was a small man, shorter than Petöfi and Byron. Early prison had left an incurable wound that was also imprecise. What was it? Was it on the thigh or on the ankle? Shackle scars or just a hernia? When he died he was missing a front tooth and prematurely bald. He did not look at all like an actor.

Martí learned everything, even his *ars poetica*, in exile. First briefly in Spain and, especially, here in the United States, in that New York where he wrote like a forerunner his American *crónicas*, written like poems in prose of a rare beauty. His mastery of written English was astonishing and he could, if he had wanted, have been an American writer as Conrad was an English writer. But Martí was a Cuban even before Cuba existed as a nation. That nineteenth century job he learned, paradoxically, in exile.

One of the facets of Martí's character that made him, like Heredia, a Romantic are his American love affairs (in Guatemala, in Mexico, in New York), some idealized, others real, but all have the aura of erotic myth. It was common knowledge in Cuba that Cesar Romero, that gay blade of yesterday in Hollywood, is his grandson. In fact, in that tall, smiling American there is always a diminutive Martí fighting to get out: his grandfather. I don't believe that Martí, always taciturn, would like to be incarnated in a movie star who is all teeth. (Apart from the fact that women never interested Cesar Romero other than as dancing partners.) But render unto Cesar (Romero) what is Martí's and unto Martí what is Cesar's (Romero's). The poet would have been pleased, I think, that his grandson, the son of his daughter, illegitimate but his favourite, would

parade through Fifth Avenue with some of his Latin looks and his defini-
tively Martían moustache among cute chorus-girls.

Be that as it may, right now a Peruvian writer, by writing a monograph
on the woman he calls 'the New York girl', committed a crime of *lèse
majesté* and has been attacked equally in Cuba and in exile. It's a case of a
dedicated Martían treated like a Martian. There's more. Instead of exalting Martí's life, even Cuban folklore mourns his death.

> Here's missing, sirs, a voice,
> Oh what a voice!
> Of that Cuban nightingale,
> of that brother and martyr
> who was named Martí.
> If Martí had not died,
> another bird would sing,
> the country would have been saved
> – and Cuba would be happy.
> Martí should never have died,
> Oh, never have died!

The naïveté of this brief Afro-Cuban lament (originally it was a *clave*,
which served as a pavan for a dead *mulata*), its lyrics reveal, better than
anything, the sentiment of irreparable loss expressed by a popular poet.
Martí, it must be said, died on the battlefield – but not fighting. His death
was really a calculated suicide. When did he decide on it? After the
disastrous reunion with Gómez and Maceo in La Mejorana? On that
parting for Cuba that is his return? No one knows, we will never know.
The pages in question from Martí's diary, that would have let us know an
uncertain or certain inference, disappeared after his death – torn out, it is
said, by merciful hands. In any case Martí took his secret to the grave. But
his last letter contains a confession *in extremis*. 'My only wish would be to
stay there', *there* is what is not *here*, in exile, nor *over there*, in Cuba: *there* is
the alien territory of death, 'to stay there by the last tree, to the last fighter:
to die quietly'. A final felicitous phrase is infelicitous in the extreme: 'For
me the time has come!' It is a prologue to the epilogue: his death was
without doubt premeditated.

An impartial investigator, the Argentine writer Ezequiel Martínez
Estrada, was needed so that we could learn from his prologue to the latest
edition of the *Diary*, that a Cuban mulatto (who was serving as a guide to
the Spanish column that intercepted General Máximo Gómez's troops)
was the one who last saw Martí alive. Apparently Martí had not been
wounded fatally. This other Cuban, vaguely identified as the Spanish

General Valmaseda's scout, saw Martí on the ground, badly wounded, recognized him (there is always someone around to recognize a writer) and said to him: 'You around here, don Martí?' The *guerrillero* (in the Cuban independence wars the Cubans who served in the Spanish Army were called *guerrilleros*) smiled hospitably and then emptied his percussion revolver (of enormous repercussion) into the poet's head.

Strange, isn't it? More extraordinary still is that Martí's bodyguard, who died trying to rescue his precious charge, was named Angel de la Guardia. Even more odd is how moments before dying Martí ran towards the enemy bullets, disobeying General Gómez's order that he get under cover. There are explanations that try to make sense in the chaos. Martí got confused in his first battle (actually a skirmish) – but he was the only one who got confused. Another explanation claims that Martí's horse got spooked towards the Spanish lines. All the versions try to explain the inexplicable by the unusual way. The only possible explanation is that Martí, by his motives, without motives, committed suicide. They say that Rubén Darío, the great Darío, said upon learning the news, 'What have you done, Maestro?'

The Campaign Diary (never given such a title by Martí, of course), that masterpiece of Spanish literature written in exile and on the remote return, ends not on an abrupt or fateful note but in a calm description of life in the rebel camp. On returning to Cuba (to what is known as the *manigua*, the backwoods) his *Travel Notes* became the diary of a guerrilla, not a diary of war. The only warlike action that Martí saw was the first and the last – that he could not describe. On beginning his return ('Don't ever return,' once again insisted the Pythagorean master, now Pythaugurean), José Martí writes what is a masterpiece of literature. He presents us with one of the most beautiful farewells in that language of farewells that is in Cuba the Spanish of the nineteenth century.

This note gathers together in a single phrase, brief and cryptic, the exoticist ardour of the Romantics, the American presence and a woman's name that becomes memorable in the mouth of this man who is going, in the Argentine's phrase, 'to meet his South American destiny'. Martí writes in the last entry in his *Diary*, a poetic rather than a political binnacle: 'April 9' (we must remember that Martí would die 19 May next) 'April 9 – Lola, *jolongo*, weeping on her balcony. We embark.' The concluding verb points out, it seems to me, the only act that makes equal all the poets who like Martí are born in exile. *We embark.*

It was outside Cuba that José Martí wrote his most popular verse:

> I want when I die,
> without a homeland but without a master,
> to have on my grave a bunch
> of flowers and a flag.

This is his epitaph but it is also the epitaph of all of us.

And of My Cuba, What?

In the historical limbo that was created on the island in the interregnum (a no man's land that lay between the defeat of Spain in 1898 and the creation of independent Cuba in 1902) there were many auguries and a single certainty: at the end of the cruel and anachronic Spanish dominance that had lasted more than three centuries. Cuba, by Spain's design, was not present (the patient to be operated on not to be found on the operating table) at the signing of the Treaty of Paris (1898), that conceded Spanish defeat, American victory and Cuban independence. This situation of presence by absence generated a motto, a song and a greeting that I used to hear when I was a boy, in Gibara, my native town in Oriente Province. By an occurrence of geography, Gibara is twenty-five miles from Banes, where Fulgencio Batista was born, and twenty miles from Birán, where Fidel Castro was born. History, a mediocre writer, proposed the young but poor Batista cut cane on the sugar plantation of Castro's father – a rich Spanish landholder. The history of Cuba, it is evident, learned to write by watching the films of D. W. Griffith, full of sentimental violence and opportune coincidences – as can still be seen in that movie called not by chance *The Birth of a Nation*.

Before the birth of my nation Cubans used to repeat that catch-phrase that became a slightly ironic *saludo*: 'And of my Cuba, what?' As a boy I heard it said, repeated and turned into a musical moment. As it always contained a certain nostalgia I imagined Cuba, a child's choice, as some sort of melancholy rainbow that was splendid but shone beyond the blue horizon. The phrase, the greeting, the sentimental password, whatever, referred without a doubt to the whole island – floating in the deep sea of history as in suspension.

To understand not only the political past of Cuba but her terrible or fortunate future and her vile present, which has lasted more than three decades, one must comprehend first the geography of Cuba. It has now been five hundred years since Cuba entered history and, more important, showed up on the maps. The geography of Cuba has determined her past history and, of course, will determine her future – which is more decisive than past and present history and the new limbo that some propose for us as a terrible purgatory. Cuba is (see the map, please) a long and narrow island. But there is more (see the seas). Cuba is the largest island in America, located at the entrance to the Gulf of Mexico. It is, more decisively, an island bathed in the north by the Atlantic Ocean and caressed in the south by the Caribbean Sea. This position creates a dichotomy and forms and conforms the Cuban character. There is no other country in America split between civilization, the Atlantic, and the barbarians, the Caribbean. Cuba is divided between an indigenous sea and a European ocean – and it will be thus for many years to come. That is, from here to eternity – which lasts, I should think, more than history. Cuba is also, forever, ninety miles from American shores. Geopolitics is, what doubt is there, more decisive than politics. (Think about it.)

Those Cubans from my childhood, picturesque patriots, who said, repeated and sang, 'And of my Cuba, what?' at times, to vary their way of thinking or to do a musical variation, counterpointed, in an everyday art of the fugue, 'And of *what* Cuba, what?'

When I returned to Havana in 1965, after my official exile as a diplomat in Belgium, for my mother's funeral, I could say that I had just gone back to the future – and nothing worked. This depressing description was the reverse of the exaltation of the easy-says-it Steffens, who explained that he had visited the future, a Soviet Union that worked. (The laugh you heard is mine now.) It contributed to my immediate removal as chargé d'affaires in Brussels and, what is closer to grave, to a retention (a kind of city arrest) for four months by order of the Counter-Intelligence Service, which, as its name indicates, always works counter to intelligence. My stay among the zombies, in the ruins of Havana, in a quite *triste tropique*, made me write not long after, in 1968, during my flight back from the dead, a depreciation rather than an appreciation of the Castro régime. 'The country,' I said, 'in a frank Hegelian gambol has taken a leap forward – to fall backward.' Friendly echoes immediately became enemy voices without having noticed my rigorous mortis to condemn me, inside and outside Cuba. I heard words that were not in the Bible: counter-revolutionary, CIA agent, *gusano*. My condemnation was not so much for seeing the truth (many others had done as much before) as for kissing Circe and living to tell it. Now, because of the deterioration of the economy, of capital and of the capital, of the whole country that has ceased to be Cuba to become the Albania of the Caribbean (a phrase with which I portrayed the whole island then), the nation has been demolished, ruined and brought finally to a fate worse than death: to take corruption in life. Havana is as destroyed physically as Beirut, in a civil war made by one man. Fidel Castro lives out his last days in his Palace (read bunker) surrounded by physical and moral ruins. The odious present is the last caper by a man who, through lust for power, has been a South American *caudillo* but also a tropical version of Hitler, Stalin without Stalingrad. He has just declared an option zero that is, in fact, zero option.

I am often asked what Castro's future will be. I always answer that he has none: he spent it all on his urge to keep himself in power. He may die (all men die) like Hitler, committing suicide under the ruins. He may die like Stalin from a stroke that his minions, frozen Russians from fear of awakening the sleeping tyrant, turned his nightmare into a never-ending rosy dream. He may like Mussolini try to escape to the mountains – but the Duce ended up hung by his feet by his pursuers. He may (and it is his most frequent threat: when the bully dies) destroy Cuba with the Russian weapons that he still possesses. This final solution is called in Spanish a Numantian destiny.

Numantia was a city of Iberian Spain. After an effective Roman siege that lasted eight months, its inhabitants were reduced by hunger. The survivors (only 133) surrendered. Spanish legend has it that the entire city was blown up by the besieged before they surrendered. Of course the Numantians never invented powder. What they invented was collective immolation as an act of political propaganda. Many still remember the destruction of Numantia, but nobody says that Augustus, emperor of the Romans, rebuilt it immediately.

It is not by accident that the hunted Honecker has asked Castro for asylum now. All Cuba, as Berlin once was, is surrounded by a wall guarded by a *Todesstreifen* more effective than the one that Ulbricht created and his successor in flight continued with such success. Fidel Castro, more fortunate or more atrocious, has been helped not only by history but also by geography: Cuba is an island. But it is also a clear dystopia: there one sees quite clearly the failure of the Communist Utopia. Curiously, the only place where Utopia has been finally established, since its invention by Thomas More in the sixteenth century, is in the Soviet Union. Utopia, as everyone knows, means the place that is nowhere. (Laughter.)

A Havana radio comic *circa* 1940 used to ask his invisible audience, 'And of my Cuba, what?' To add in answer to himself: '*Chévere*', which could have meant very well instead of thanks. That comedian was a *novus homo*. Not the New Man that Che Guevara asked for, a special elite within the Revolution that ended up wearing *New Man* pants. The humourist was really a *parvenu*. The republic, in fact, had made *parvenus* of us all by premièring that year a new constitution, created – ta-da! – by Fulgencio Batista, the dictator who wanted to legitimize the power he already had. That same Batista, who offered (in his words) to the crippled republic the crutches of his constitution, with a pass of the red flag gave it a fatal sword thrust which was his *coup d'état* of 1952. Fidel Castro, a true matador, would in 1959 give it the finishing stroke so that we would all grant him not only tail and ears but the whole bull. (The taurine metaphors, mixed but not stirred, are as alien to Cuba as Communism is: bullfights have been prohibited on the island since 1902.)

Cynically (or more aptly, with sarcasm) Castro inaugurated his seizure of power with a speech that began with what would be a refrain of false pacifism, 'Arms, what for?' Said as an interdiction by a leader, maximum on a minimal island, who exported expeditions, from as early as 1959, to the Dominican Republic and then successive guerrilla wars to Venezuela, Colombia, Bolivia, Argentina, Uruguay, Nicaragua and El Salvador and sent whole armies to Angola and Ethiopia, where from the 1970s he stationed more than 300,000 troops armed to kill Africans. (Arms for everyone, obviously.)

And of my island of Cuba, what? The Cuba of Cubans I mean. Without Cuba, a Père Ubu of the twenty-first century would say, there are no Cubans. But, I add, tell me who those Cubans will be and I will tell you what Cuba will become. To start with there will be no Communists.

A billboard seen in Havana last year proclaimed, 'Communism or Death!' Suddenly beside its side appeared a graffito. It was a logical proposition: 'Where is the contradiction?' With the contradiction eliminated Communism in Cuba is eliminated. With Communism eliminated it will be replaced, as everywhere, by democracy. Unlike Russia, one will not have to play back seventy years of errors, full speed reverse in a political time-machine. It will not be an experiment *in anima vilis* because there was already successful capitalism in Cuba before Castro. (The Cuban economy was more favourable to the Cuban than almost everyone else's in Spanish America was to them and even than Spain's itself – and in passing, Ireland's.)

The Cuban economy continued to flourish under Batista, who was an intermittent tyrant who came to steal and, like some thieves, was forced to kill: there is no perfect coup. He also created an intolerable climate of rupture (of the constitutional order that he himself had created) as a political vacuum. It was into that vacuum that Fidel Castro knew how to insert himself with violence. We all asked him to free us from Batista however he might, but nobody asked him to stay in his place for thirty-three years with the help of state violence and in passing to create the economic and human chaos that made life regress to infrahuman levels only known in America by Haiti. Doctor Castro (as *The Times* calls him) was converted for us first into Doctor Jekyll with his Hyde (at times played by Raúl Castro) riding piggyback and then later into an impossible version of the Haitian Papa Doc – Papa Doc Fidel. (It's not an invention of mine. During the trial of General Ochoa none other than Raúl Castro declared, 'Fidel is our papa' and 'Fidel is the papa of all the Cubans.' Almost, 'Our Papa who art in the Palace.' But Castro is closer to little father Stalin than to Papa Doc. With a Galician father and a Lebanese mother, he is as Cuban as Stalin was Russian.

Castro (sometimes called in Cuba the most expensive expert on agronomy in the world) painstakingly destroyed not only Cuban agriculture but the whole Cuban economy. When he seized power in the name of a strange ideology this never was, not in its best times, as effective as the previous system – a national product not only of Cuban history but of geopolitics. (The Cuban economy has flourished now in Miami by other means but with an identical system.) Castro, master of propaganda, has created two perverse myths: Havana, that is Cuba, was in the past only a brothel and a casino for Americans. Miami is, on American territory, Havana by other means (part of it is even called Little Havana), but there are neither casinos nor brothels in Miami and the Cuban population itself voted massively against the establishment of gambling in Florida. Meanwhile every tourist in Havana knows that the Castroist Government permits prostitution, masculine and feminine, which is more and more extensive in the city. Castro has created besides a new form of racism all over Cuba. The refusal of entrance to Cubans to hotels, restaurants, beaches, resorts and night-clubs – unless they are accompanied by foreigners – is an indecent *apartheid*. In a catch-22 inhuman in its perfection Cubans can visit all the tourist establishments if they, like the visitors, have dollars – but no Cuban can have dollars because their possession is a serious crime. What we have here are followers not of Karl Marx but of his brother Chico, an expert in legerdemains.

Never have there been, let it be said in passing, as many Cuban millionaires in the history of Cuba as there are now in Miami. (The statistic not only includes the republican era but the colonial Cuba of the nineteenth century.) There are besides, among the million and a half Cuban exiles in the USA, more university graduates than there ever were in Cuba. Castro, for his part, spreads the Goebbelsian lie that before his personal power there was in Cuba 95 per cent illiteracy. Why not, so that it would be believed better, 99.99? Before the seizure of power by Fidel Castro there were more women graduated from universities in Cuba than, in comparison, in the USA. Now the number of women with a career in exile exceeds all the old statistics. If Fidel Castro vituperated the past to present his regime as a model of virtues (and he has had not a few gratuitous collaborators in the democratic world, more than in Communist Europe), to praise himself as the promoter of free education and public health, his fall, whether *à la* Ceausescu or Honecker-like, will reveal that this line is as great a lie as the one that declared that the Italian trains arrived on time for the first time with Mussolini or that Hitler was the last-minute rescuer of Germany from the swamp of Weimar. Castro unites, to the harm of Cuba, the infinite capacity for infamy of Dr Goebbels with the oratorical histrionics of Hitler – or better still of Mussolini. The destiny of those ancestors was to serve as models for lie and fear as a projection of the state. One of the young Castro's favourite readings was *The Technique of the Coup d'État* by the Mussolinesque Curzio Malaparte. His favourite phrase, pronounced before a tribunal in 1953, was said before by Hitler in 1923, when his *putsch* in Munich failed and he was gaoled. Penal antecedents obviously.

The old chestnut of a racist Cuba from which Fidel Castro saved us, does not stand up to the most cursory historical analysis. Batista was a mulatto and the chief of his army was mulatto as were several prominent generals and politicians. The composition of his troops was about 75 per cent blacks and mulattos. His last mercenary levy to complete a professional army, realized in 1958, cast a percentage of ninety black soldiers for each one hundred troops. The best defence, as we know, is attack and Castro has practised it in a masterful manner.

Now in Cuba the racial composition of the population is 70 per cent blacks and mulattos. Nevertheless in the Government of Castro, whose regime functions like a dynasty (there are four Castros at the summit of power), there is a single token black, an old *comandante* promoted to general without winning a battle. The Army General Staff, with his brother Raúl at its head, and the Presidium of the Party are characterized visibly by the absence of blacks. A white man is the Minister of Foreign Affairs, so is the Ambassador to the United Nations. A white man is the Minister of Culture, a white man is the equivalent of the Minister of Propaganda, the head of the Film Institute.

Who is the racist then – the black Batista or the white Castro, who boasts of his Galician origin? A measure of monstrous racism implanted from the beginning of the regime was to deny the blacks exit from the island. A black asking for a passport was a heretic, a black requesting an exit visa was a traitor. Several beautiful *mulatas* left Cuba but only by marrying Europeans and only during the Mariel exodus in 1980 could blacks leave Cuba *en masse*. But the physical ordeal to which they were submitted (which included the use of guard dogs to chase the fugitives on the beaches) is a shameful chapter from the history of the regime. Only when these decades of hate end will Cubans, white and black, live in the harmony in which they lived before Castro.

One of the first tasks of the next attorney-general of the republic (which will without doubt be called the Second Cuban Republic) will be to put on trial – with the moral weight of a nation that will be small but restored to democracy – several institutions and foreign organizations that collaborated and are still collaborating in spreading the mephitic emanations from Castro with which he attempted to injure, insult and defame a whole nation. One case of political halitosis is the aforementioned description of Havana as a brothel and a casino. Another is the indecent libel that all Cuban women were, before their purification by Castro with red-hot irons, 'whores for Americans'. Another, that Batista delivered Cuba over to the Mafia.

There were not, I can swear it, more casinos in Havana than there are today in London. Just where I live, South Kensington, there are *five* casinos. There are nations, like Monaco, and an American state, Nevada, where gambling is legal and serves as public support. It does not occur to anyone to occupy Las Vegas militarily or to launch a *coup d'état* against Ranier because they permit the roulette to spin. Berlin was a city of notorious decadence (whorehouses, transvestites, drugs) in the twenties, but no one can believe, after 1945, that Hitler was the only remedy.

How to bring back the country to paradise after thirty-three seasons in hell? How many have died on the long crossing of the Florida Strait? (No one knows, no one will ever know.) How many have died trying to escape from the island? A hundred times more, for certain, than those who died trying to escape from Communist Germany. Many in flight have been murdered by the shoot-to-kill policy. Others have drowned in the Gulf Stream. Others have made a feast for sharks. Many more have died lost in the ocean. They have died of thirst, they have died of fear, they committed suicide. But all were killed by the Maximum Leader. He is the *maxima culpa*.

How many have been shot? How many have died in prison and in the concentration camps created especially for homosexuals, recognizable by the sign over the gate: '*Work Will Make Men Out of You*', in maximum *machismo*? No one knows but he will know eventually. Thirty-three years of tyranny is a lot of time, too much. In this period of mourning that has been the worst of times Castro has obliged the Cuban people to be informants, his *semblables*, his accomplices. He has created a Cuban version of the Nazi *Blockwarts* in the Committees for the Defence of the Revolution, on which every Cuban is forced to spy on his neighbour, children on their parents and every person on each other. Compelled to hold partisan parties in lieu of the traditional ones: as a peak of historical dementia Castro moved Christmas Eve to 26 July and instead of the New Year, he changed 1 January into the celebration of his accession to power. After such injury, what forgiveness?

Leví Marrero, a Cuban economist and geographer exiled in Puerto Rico, still very much alive at his eighty years, told in a speech that I had the privilege of hearing in Miami (given with a generosity that is no less noble for being very much like the man) how Cuba recovered in less than ten years from the Ten Years' War (against the Spanish yoke) that ended in 1878 with the island ruined. Also how after the end of the Three Years' War, still against Spain, from 1895 to 1898, with the American intervention, in which the ruin was still greater, to the foundation of independence in 1902, Cuba was a nation recovered with American assistance. At the end of the onerous dictatorship of General Machado in 1933 (with ruin and famine although Machado only governed for nine years) the republic had already recovered by 1940. 'It happened three times,' concluded Professor Marrero, 'and it will happen again!'

Now, went Leví Marrero's final assertion, with the capital accumulated in Miami and other parts of the USA, Cuba will be prosperous again in less time than it takes to say her name. The best, without doubt, will return to the island – once the worst have fled.

Or as soon as Castro falls (the law of gravity, even graver in Cuba than in Eastern Europe, will make him fall as Dantesque bodies fall), when there will be completed the flight of those whom Castro himself, in a speech, called the rats that are leaving the ship before it sinks, castigating his accomplices in flight. Where will they go after the shipwreck? To China, to Vietnam, to North Korea? No, they will go, they are already going, to the United States, to South America, to Europe. (As is well known, tyrannies, when they fall, lean towards democracy.)

To paraphrase Laplace's well-known Law, if only one knew the state of Cuba after Castro in all its details at every given instant (or the infinite in the present), one, you, all of us, would be able to decipher the future of the island however impenetrably arcane it may seem now. As this knowledge is virtually – that is, physically – impossible my predictions must be read as a scenario of possibilities.

I must remind the reader that Pierre Simon, Marquis de Laplace, was the son of peasants and survived the bloody years of the Revolution because this was not a system but a chaos with a single centre, the guillotine. Laplace, who had a great sense of humour, was the man who under Napoleon Imperator could dislodge an arbitrary remnant from the Jacobin era, their comic calendar: brummagened by Brumaire he terminated with Thermidor. Laplace also completed his theory of the continuous becoming of life with a phrase that is Nietzsche's theory of the eternal return *avant la lettre* – and reversed in the mirror: 'and the future, like the past, will always be present before your eyes'.

After scientific analysis only prophecy, it seems to me, is left. When tyrannies succumb they leave behind the enormous weight of the past and no visible, foreseeable future – only the present can be creative. Thus one will have to extend the present of all Cubans to the immediate future, tomorrow, to wonder, and of my Cuba, what? To hear the echo that answers as if a sonorous mirror, *'What Cuba?'*

(January 1992)

Has Socialism Died?

The German weekly *Die Zeit* organized a poll among scientists, intellectuals and writers from all over the world. The lead question was: 'Is this the end of socialism?' The specific questions were:

1 In 1990 McDonalds will open the first fast food restaurant in Moscow. Has capitalism finally defeated socialism?
2 What price will the world have to pay for such a victory?
3 What will it sell?

This is my answer.

Once Aldous Huxley, one of the most intelligent novelists in an era of intelligent writers (Thomas Mann is another of them and this is perhaps the reason why both seem like antiques today: the present-day reader does not want intelligence, he wants entertainment), this man, Huxley, demanded in anguish: 'Time must stop!' Of course, by time Huxley meant death. But death, which will always stop us, never stops. Why not stop history instead? History is not life. Life is another thing – while history is nothing more than a book called history.

Herodotus, the first historian, an Athenian born in Asia Minor, was a professional storyteller who called his books *istoriai* – which does not mean history (history was not yet called history) in Greek but inquisition. What today we call survey. The English scholar M. I. Finley reveals that much time passed before the word history was given 'the specific, narrower use the word now has'. Herodotus was depending, like Plutarch, on second-hand reports, on legends, on myths, and – why not? – on gossip. In his First Book Herodotus was already balancing himself on a Greek tightrope between mythology and rumour. It is no wonder that the ancients, who knew about these things, called him the Father of Lies.

So began history. Now a Japanese historian who lives in the United States holds that history has died or has already ended. But history has not died: we have only arrived at the end of the first book. Surely there will be more books called history. Nietzsche said: 'God is dead.' (Others cut him off saying that it was Nietzsche who was dead.) It's curious that nobody wonders if the Devil is also dead. God may be dead but the Devil is alive and kicking everywhere. If not, who invented the concentration camps? I'll tell you who. It was Valeriano Weyler, Governor-General for Spain of the Always Faithful Island of Cuba – in 1896 to be exact. It appears quite clearly in the *Encyclopaedia Britannica*, the layman's Bible. Later the English would perfect this Devil's invention during the war against the Boers in South Africa. The barbed wire and the electric cable did the rest – with the help of Adolf Eichmann.

It is socialism that has defeated socialism. One could see on the six o'clock news that the socialist superpower that has missiles by the thousand, rockets that go to the moon, satellites to explore space, nuclear submarines in all the oceans and tanks that would make General Guderian, commander of the *Panzerdivissionen*, envious, then they, the Russians, did not have even one miserable *brass* bulldozer to clear away the rubble after an earthquake. It had to be a second-rate capitalist country, England, that would give the Russians not only a hand but also all the equipment necessary for the rescue operation. (Weren't Marx and Engels two vaudeville comedians from the Victorian era?)

I am sure that the people of Moscow would be delighted to find hamburgers on Red Square and hot (not police) dogs opposite the Lubyanka. Eating plastic food is better than having nothing to eat. The man in the street in Havana prefers McDonalds to *Comandante* Castro – not to mention the colonel with the fried chickens: two legs good. Chickens of the world, be fried. You have nothing to lose but your feathers!

Since Adam and Eve the price of victuals has never been in proportion to their cost. Of course now we're paying for those past delights. Nevertheless even Adam and Eve had to be expelled from paradise. In our days of change for man (and for woman too) a possessive God prevents them from leaving paradise. You see them every night and sometimes at high noon. Those Germans who flee, why do they run? They do it to save themselves from someone else's Utopia and, as many declared to the press, they fled for their *future*: a private Utopia becoming public. So we see that obvious workers leave in flight from the workers' paradise. Adamant Eves and Mad Adam too.

They can be seen now in East Germany but I have seen them closer. In 1980 eleven thousand Cubans requested a sudden exile in the Peruvian Embassy in Havana. It was, as in East Germany, a well-named safety valve to prevent an explosion. As occurred in Hungary in 1956. Or in

Czechoslovakia in 1968. Or in China this summer of the students' discontent.

A felicitous phrase has it that exiles are people who vote with their feet. In this case it is better to say that they vote not only with their feet but also with their hands, with their whole body. Or with their dead bodies: more than eight thousand Cubans have died, in the sea or on the coast, trying to escape from the island conceived as an enormous Stalinist prison.

For us Cubans socialism was a ponderous joke that killed us laughing. It is still wearing us out – a joke on us.

The price of socialism (we have already seen it many times in the century) is slavery, brutality and death – all in the name of man. (And of woman too.) Wasn't it Stalin who proclaimed that one had to take care of man as one takes care of a tree and then armed himself with chainsaws for his massacres? It must not be forgotten that the Nazi Party was also called, as Goebbels proclaimed more than once, socialist, and Hitler filled his mouth under the minute moustache to howl *Sozialismus*.

Socialism is nothing more than a Utopia destined always to become a dystopia: the Devil's paradise. Now we have seen those Utopian paradises like Hungary and Poland, Catholic countries all, decide that the kingdom of this world cannot be a Utopia.

Anxious to see what is on page one of the twenty-first century one must turn the last page of the twentieth century and close the book of history – to open a new book. Perhaps it will not promise us earthly paradise or the millennium, but at least we will leave behind the night and the nightmare: the incumbent incubus called Lenin, Stalin, Hitler, Franco, Mao and, of course, in its ultimate avatar, Fidel Castro. We will leave behind the heralds of a future felicity awhile that only produces instant poverty, humiliation and death. The worst death: the death that spares life for us to make us into lifers. Those Messiahs of misery must stop and have an end. But – will they stop?

(November 1989)

What is History, *pues?*

The slight Caracan idiom, *pues,* then at the end and not at the beginning, is not a homage to Bolívar ploughing a *mare nostrum* – but a necessary interjection. Well yes, what is history after all? Or, more metaphysical, why history and not nothingness instead? In the famous phrase 'history is written at night', alluding to the bed but also to strange bedfellows, history is impersonal but at the same time, curiouser, its own author: history writes itself. History is a book without an author. In the infamous phrase, said by Hitler first and Fidel Castro much later, 'History will absolve me', history, like justice, is a goddess but is not blind. This pathetic fallacy is very much in the line of German totalitarian philosophy from Hegel to Marx. It is astonishing, certainly, to find Nietzsche (called Niche in Cuba) in such company. But the fact is that geography amazes more than history.

Another assertion, true or false, proclaims that history is always written by those who win. But the first history book was written by Herodotus, who never took part. Herodotus (born in Halicarnassus, Asia Minor, in 483 BC) saw himself more as an investigator than as a participant. 'I give you,' he writes in the preface, 'the results of my investigations.'* That is, not history but survey. Herodotus is actually the first organizer of records whom history (what else?) records.

It is a kind of (poetic?) justice that nothing is known about him. It is known, for sure, what his detractors, who were not a few, said about him. The Greeks called him the father of all lies and his daughter, history, was known as the mother of infamy. Or as a whore who slept on Procrustes' bed. She settled not the accounts but the members of those she invited to sleep: long legs bad, short legs worse. None other than Plutarch, who conceived of history as a gallery of portraits to be read, wrote an essay entitled 'On the Malice of Herodotus'. The single task of Thucydides, his successor, was to rewrite the history that Herodotus wrote.

*According to Professor M. I. Finley's translation.

But Herodotus, writer of the most massive bestseller after the Bible (the latter a book written by authors who wrote crooked to be read straight) explains his method thus: he writes 'so that the memory of what men have done will not perish from the earth. Nor that their achievements, be they Greeks or barbarians, lack anyone to sing of them: they and the cause for which they went to war are my theme.' (Pardon the translation but I have no Greek.) When that war took place (to which he gave its name for ever) Herodotus had not yet been born. His history is some sort of hagiography. 'Homer and Hesiod have attributed to the gods all that is disgraceful and culpable among men: robbery, adultery and deceit,' wrote, as a colophon, Xenophanes of Colophon. For Xenophanes, as for many ancients, including of course Herodotus, history and mythology were the same source of infamies.

Herodotus, like his critic (to each author his review) Plutarch, was depending on secondhand reports, on legends, on myths, and – why not? – on village gossip. (Villages are what the greater part of the cities in antiquity were.) Thucydides, who comes after Herodotus but who was second to no one, believed that knowing about past events *per se* was futile or sterile. For Thucydides the task was to write (or rather to rewrite) the present. This was a step ahead of Herodotus but Thucydides nevertheless came behind. Xenophon, the third man always, who forms the trio of eponymous Greek historians, believed in history as action and in his *Anabasis*, the famous retreat to the sea by the ten thousand Greek mercenaries in the service of Cyrus, after his failed *coup d'état*. (Perhaps the first but of course not the last in the barracks, the royal courts and even in the palace of the Kremlin.) The *Anabasis* was his epic chronicle and one of the most widely read Greek books. Even a French poet from the Caribbean, Saint-John Perse, borrowed its title. Xenophon was, like T. E. Lawrence, an adventurer who wrote well. There is no ancient history better written nor more thrilling than his *Anabasis*. But Xenophon also had in the Greek world (including his lover Socrates) a reputation as an audacious boaster. No more nor less than Lawrence, that El Orans of the Arabs.

It intrigues present-day readers that Athens, which had invented history, would ignore Alexander, the Macedonian who conquered Greece and all the known world at the time. The Greek historians also fell silent faced with a historical event more worthy of attention than the Greek conquests: the birth of the Roman Empire. When Plutarch, another Greek who was bearing the gift of history (Trojan horses all), writes about the Romans, he does it in the decadence of the Empire. To reveal (or rather to expose) his sitting subjects, Plutarch chooses in his portraits 'a light occasion, a word, a hobby'. But his biographies seem to exist to give plots to Shakespeare and Shaw and even the movies. It must not be forgotten that Plutarch, besides being a famous biographer, was an obscure priest in Delphi and perhaps an arbiter of auguries. As a historian he proved unable to report the birth, life and death of Jesus. As an augur he never even dreamed in Delphi of the creation of a religion that was going to be more powerful than all the ancient empires – and the modern ones too.

Tacitus, the Roman Plutarch, is a man without a name or date of birth. He was an un-person and on account of this he was the historian in a pure state. His *Annals* appear tacitly interested in the moral, that is immoral but entertaining, flaws of his biographic subjects. His portrait of Tiberius (to whom a pre-Christian stentorian voice announced, 'The great god Pan is dead!' – to warn that Christ had been born) can be read as a history (or a story) more pornographic than graphic, while his *pièce de résistance* is the death of Nero. It is the cult of the depraved personality.

Suetonius, famous for his *Twelve Caesars*, was the reluctant historian. An exemplary writer, he wrote much but published little. Nevertheless, in his time he was considered anecdotal, facile and given to gossip. (It may be for that reason that he is so entertaining.) In any case some day justice will be done to gossiping and the historical necessity of knowing that Napoleon suffered from a small penis or that Hitler bathed little and smelled bad.

Gossip, of course, is essential to literature, where it is called anecdote, occurrence or fact for fiction. It must be central to that other literary genre, history. But gossip is also revelation. Through Suetonius we know that Julius Caesar had a penetrating stare and his haircut (copies by all the Caesars and even by Mark Anthony: see *Julius Caesar*, the movie, as a fashion show) was the only way he had to hide his baldness, Caesarean vanity. In passing, Suetonius, to the benefit of Shakespeare, makes a detailed narration of the assassination of Caesar and offers a phrase for a particular history of infamy – '*Et tu, Brute?*' In *The Twelve Caesars* Suetonius recounts as well that Augustus was short in stature, with an aquiline nose and wore not always august togas. If he recounts the bisexual escapades of Tiberius in Capri, he has also left a description of the ultimate moral depravation of Caligula that has been copied by the historical novel, the movies and Albert Camus – in that order. Robert Graves, historian of fictions, owes him fame and fortune for his *I, Claudius*. (That is, Suetonius brought up to today and tonight for television.) The fact is that a historian, then and now, is nothing more than a writer with his eyes in a rearview mirror. That slow glance at the past is what we could call Proust's sight.

A return to Herodotus (one always must return to him: it is a return to the sources) who was actually a travel writer. He was, no more and no less, a traveller who tells stories: some kind of Jan Morris before her change of sex. But Herodotus was a Greek traveller and believed in the gods. His narrative of the Persian Wars was organized, after his death, into nine books, each called by the name of one of the nine muses – like so many other Hellenic fictions. We must not forget that during his stay in Athens they built the Parthenon, that devout homage by Pericles to his gods. One of the Athenian histories of Herodotus concludes with the account of the vengeance of the Athenian gods against the heralds of Sparta.

Says Peter Levi, the classical scholar: 'almost all his information appears to come from personal questioning of witnesses'. Herodotus is, then, the first journalist. But, concludes Levi, 'there was no Herodotus before Herodotus.' Before Herodotus, simply, history did not exist. The Greek historian could have said then, 'L'histoire, c'est moi' – if he spoke French.

But Herodotus thought that Homer was an exceptional witness to pre-history (of course he never called it that) although he believed, firmly, that the past is always mythological. His history is, in the pagan manner, a sacred history. 'Everyone,' he declared, 'knows the same about divine matters.' On another occasion he wrote that 'the Thessalians themselves say Poseidon created the channel where the Penetos runs'. Only to add – 'which is quite probable.'

Plutarch, who much later believed in the Greek (and Roman) gods, published a 'perverse pamphlet' against Herodotus. But to write *Parallel Lives* (Plutarch sees history as a mother with twins) one would have to have believed beforehand in the history Herodotus told. Historians, all of them, depend like Plutarch more on the extolling and the calumny, appreciation and depreciation of the past, than on the truth of the facts. Every history is a doubtful tale because none of it is provable. History as scientific matter, historical materialism, has had as defenders the biggest manipulators of history – the Marxists. Those who most respect history are not the historians but the novelists. Dumas wrote a declaration of independence for every historical novelist: 'If I rape history,' he proclaimed, 'it is to make handsome sons for her'. For another thing Henry James said: 'Essentially, the historian wants more documents than he can really use.' While Friedrich Schlegel wrote that 'the historian is a prophet in reverse'.

History, with Thucydides, seems to have been born in exile. Or, better, it was produced by some sort of spontaneous regeneration. The true goal of Thucydides was not to do history but to secure a monumental and at the same time truthful compilation. The inventor of chronologies, Thucydides does not believe that history is written by those who won but rather by the victor's historians. But it is irrefutable that, despite tyrants and totalitarians, then and now, history was born from the democracy that the Greeks invented. The Age of Pericles is what permits Herodotus to tell his history.

Herodotus was one of the first, if not the first, to write in prose in Greece. He originated as well the scholarly talk and the public reading by the author – a performance that Mark Twain and Charles Dickens seemed to have invented in the last century. One Hellenist has said that Herodotus 'did not write history' but that 'he wrote religion'. On the contrary, Herodotus invented history as a literary genre. It was Herodotus who taught Thucydides and the other Greeks the trade of historian. But Thucydides is a writer conscious that history is style. In his narrative of the plague in Athens, Thucydides in passing invented reporting. Which confirms the opinion that newspapers did not invent journalism.

An English novelist of this century, Ford Madox Ford, treats Herodotus as a colleague in fictions. 'He knew,' he writes, 'what really happened to Helen after she fled, one supposes, with Paris.' To start the Trojan War with Homer as a correspondent. For Ford, Herodotus 'was related to the most notable of all the detective histories'. But instead of history, a suspicious word, Ford says stories. Ford, finally, describes Herodotus the man as 'at once credulous and cynical'. Where Ford says cynical one must say sceptical: Herodotus was *at once* credulous and sceptical. It was this unstable balance that forced him to invent for himself a trade, historian, and create a new vocation.

But in Herodotus history really supersedes the story that comes from the poetry of Homer and of Hesiod. That is of mythology: both were on familiar terms with the gods. More than twenty centuries later with Hegel (who died on a date as recent as 1831 and was a contemporary of Goethe and of Beethoven) history is written with a capital H and is converted into a form of religion but with a plot. Although it carries out (one supposes, by itself) the divine purposes. History has ceased being a goddess to be God. In a life parallel with Herodotus, Hegel was an avid collector of clippings from English newspapers – a chronicle of the century that fed the dreams and the nightmares of Karl Marx.

Nations (that one supposes are made by history and not the reverse) for Hegel are founded not by God but by heroes, who take them out of savagery thanks to religion – and of course, thanks also to that other form of religion, philosophy. Hegel, who wanted to explain history not as sacred but as divine, would have found it difficult to exonerate his successors in the company not of God but of the Devil, Marx and Nietzsche.

Both served, without knowing it, to justify in history the return of savagery with their followers, Hitler and Stalin. Hegel would have said, if he had said anything, that both tyrants were only pretending to be followers of a philosophy they could not understand. Or perhaps, as their critics had it, history ended with Hegel's philosophy of history and the future barbarism was ahistorical – it stayed voluntarily outside history. Wouldn't it be more accurate to say that history, like philosophy, is nothing more than a library with a single book repeated *ad infinitum*? Or better *ad nauseam*?

Istoriai, history and at times History, is only a book called history, with an author, title on the cover and publisher's imprint. Its colophon is sometimes nothing more than a bad reading. All history has a spine to make it a volume. The name of it is, in the last extreme, only a Greek accident. No more nor less than the word metaphysics.

(March 1991)

CASTROENTERITIS

Portrait of an Ageing Tyro

Foreword to Family Portrait with Fidel *by Carlos Franqui*
(Random House, 1984)

There are actually two portraits – or, rather, two versions of the same picture on the jacket of *Family Portrait with Fidel*.[1] Taken at the end of Batista's reign or just after the fall of that Cuban Humpty-Dumpty (he thought the Americans would pick him up again but not all his soldiers or all his policemen could keep him up there for ever), the photo shows Carlos Franqui wearing a black, unkempt beard that instead of evoking the image of the Cuban *guerrillero* recalls what Robinson Crusoe must have looked like on his solitary island just after his rescue. But remember that if Robinson 'was past running any more hazards', Crusoe 'had a great mind to be upon the wing again'.

In the second, *revised* print the photo has become a curious document: Fidel Castro is still, as usual, in the foreground with the same, still anonymous man Friday with a mike facing him. But between the two men there is a strange void, a blank space that is really the black hole of the totalitarian time: the eternal writing and rewriting the cloth of history on which a revisionist Penelope weaves the image of her constant (by night), inconstant (by day) Ulysses the crafty. But instead of taking the mick out of the group, they achieved just the opposite: the empty space in the photograph is Franqui who has disappeared from the picture but has left his shadow behind. By an unkind stroke he has been rubbed out from the history of revolutionary Cuba, from the Revolution, from the future itself. Banished, one might say, from Marxist eternity. There's the rub. Such sleights of hand are not only possible but necessary in today's Cuban historiography. In other totalitarian countries in the past there were doctored photographs

---

1 The original photograph showed Fidel Castro with Carlos Franqui and another man; Castro later had it doctored to eliminate Franqui. The book jacket juxtaposes these two versions with a third – to show Castro alone.

in which Trotsky appeared briefly alongside Lenin – from which Stalin had him banished forever, to Prinkipo and after. Goebbels had Ernst Röhm graphically purged from all photos with the Führer: had Hitler won the war he would have been standing (photographically) alone today like a solitary eagle where Röhm used to roam.

The first version of this curiously historic Cuban photograph (which would have been banal and therefore forgettable if it hadn't been turned into a true palimpsest: rubbed off for further use) was published in the too independent newspaper *Revolución*, more a mouthpiece for rebels than a megaphone for the revolutionary Government. It happened in 1962, when Carlos Franqui was editor-in-chief. The second, apparently definitive version, appeared in the official sheet *Granma*, a granny with big teeth under the shawl. It was 1973. In eleven years Franqui had gone from being a key man in the Revolution, a leader who made and unmade ministers and one of the most widely known figures on the Cuban scene at home and abroad, to being a non-person, a cipher, an invisible man in Castroite hagiography. Unquiet Franqui, a Peter made up to look like a small Judas, could not coexist with Fidel Castro, Maximum Messiah. Not even in an old photo. He was punished by erasure, not by firing squad, much in the way in science-fiction movies the hero's lieutenant (never, of course, Captain Quirt himself) is zapped into nothingness and beyond by a raygun. Whaam! *Sic transit rebellis*.

The same technique *Playboy* once used on excessively public pubic hair and too tender buttons, an airbrush with invisible ink, was used here. But why would anyone go to so much trouble to eliminate Franqui, quite frankly, when he just stays in the background taking nothing away from Castro's image? The English historian Hugh Thomas got to know Franqui personally rather well after he had shaved off his beard early in 1959 in Havana. Now in London, Thomas stared at the cover of this book for a good three minutes – and then asked me who the man was who had disappeared from the picture! I had to explain that it was Carlos Franqui with a beard. He had pulled a disappearing act that even the Great Houdini himself would have envied – and tried to copy. Lord Thomas did a historical doubletake. Both Fidel Castro and Franqui contributed to this successful revival (total in Cuba, partial abroad, like an eclipse) of *A Revolutionary Vanishes*. Franqui's book describes just how the *truco* was pulled off. As in many magic tricks, the explanation is better than the trick itself. (Ah, that's how it's done! Clever. I thought you always used mirrors.) If Fidel Castro is a Marxist Mandrake the Magician, Franqui is merely the man who lost his shadow in a picture. From an untouched

Lothar, Mandrake's sidekick, he became for the love of Circe, the witch and bitch Revolution, a retouched Schlemihl, whose shadow was stolen by the red devil. But this invisible man, erased by totalitarian hands with a touch of the airbrush, has now produced a very visible book, a credible *wündersame Geschichte*. Like Chamisso, Franqui has been banished from his country. Unlike Chamisso, he is no aristocrat but a man of the humblest extraction.

Carlos Franqui is one of those rare cases of a revolutionary who decides (or is forced by political pressure) to become a writer. Franqui, a cunning man who was slow (or cautious) even about answering letters when he was in power, is now an author in his own write. The most eminent example of this metamorphosis of revolutionary into writer is, of course, Trotsky. The comparison, if we set aside time, distance and Franqui's still untouched head, is not a bad one. But unlike Trotsky, Franqui joined the Cuban Communist Party without second thoughts when he was still very young. He was so young, in fact, that he must have been placed in the rank and file of the Communist Youth. He was so enthusiastic and eager and therefore useful to the cause that he was soon promoted to being a *cadre*. Poor from birth, a peasant who didn't even have the benefit of a nearby city or town, Franqui was what is called in Cuba a *guajiro macho*: a hick from the sticks. But as luck would have it, he was discovered when he was a mere boy by an extraordinary teacher, Melania Cobo, a well-educated black woman. With just one single stroke Franqui began his education and was spared the stupid prejudices that white peasants have against blacks in Cuba. Melania Cobo, who loved painting and music, stimulated Franqui's interest in the arts early in his life, nourishing alongside it his keen sense of social justice and his dabbling in politics. He was thus already highly developed politically when Fidel Castro was still an apprentice Jesuit in the most expensive religious schools in Santiago de Cuba and in Havana.

But if Franqui lived to become a Communist – or lived at all – it was because of his father's heroic tenacity. As a child Franqui almost died from a *cólico miserere*, as a ruptured appendix was called then. He survived only because his father, whom Franqui adored, carried him on horseback all the way to the nearest town and hospital – miles away from the family ranch. From that time on, with the same silent heroism as his father's, Franqui has continued to save his own spiritual self. He has put his life on the line time and time again because of his courage and his convictions. If he were to write about how he overcame all the obstacles he has had to face, in politics as in life, in and out of history, he would need yet another book – one his modesty forbids. In *Family Portrait with Fidel* he limits himself to his relationship with Castro, personal and political. But he never describes his last dangerous days on the island, his mind already made up to leave Cuba for ever: how he managed to abandon ship with wife and family, closely watched by the sinister servicemen of the State Security, how he duped Raúl Castro and Ramiro Valdés, the Cuban Beria, and even Redbeard Piñeiro, head of Counter-Intelligence. Franqui says nothing of his ruses and his fear of never actually outwitting Castro or of his dramatic flight to Europe and his peripatetic exile in Italy, hounded by the same men he had named diplomats in France and England.

As a matter of fact, Franqui doesn't even begin at the beginning: how he started out in Havana as a proofreader for the Communist newspaper *Hoy*, how he was soon promoted to copy editor and then elevated to the proofreader's heaven – the editorial board. But happiness is a word frequently misspelt. One day he had to stand in for a friend, a proofreader who was both a fanatical Communist and a movie fan. His former colleague wanted to attend a one-night stand of his favourite film. The time it takes to see a movie, those few precious hours of fun and fantasy colliding with ideological dogmatism, became a clash of symbols that changed Franqui's life. A crucial typographical error appeared in an editorial which today is dogmatic nonsense prose but then seemed to state something borrowed, something true: the unthinkable such as 'The triumph of Communism will never take place' – tautology in the place of ideology. The typo is the thing that will catch the tyrant with his political pants down. The truly funny item is that this theological (or teleological) mistake was a clerical error: the fault of an elderly editor and not of an ill-intentioned or lazy proofreader.

Franqui not only took the rap but he committed the crime of refusing to attend a self-criticism meeting; some sort of jam session by the Party where they always promise jam not today but tomorrow. The fan who was a fanatic was fired from the newspaper but kept in the Party. As luck would have it, Franqui was fired from the paper and expelled from the party and bitterly denounced everywhere for his contumacy or contumely or whatever. I happen to know all about it not only because I did know Franqui well then but also because my father wrote for the same newspaper. (He, too, was an old Cuban Communist.) Franqui was hunted then as he was to be later when he left Cuba in the late sixties. Aníbal Escalante (see under old Communists), the editor-in-chief of *Hoy* newspaper, told my father that Franqui, an enemy of the Party or of the people (whichever comes first), should not, I repeat, should not be given sanctuary in a Communist house. My mother, who could be a formidable fury, retorted:

'Go and tell Aníbal to come and tell *me*!' Aníbal, who was no Hannibal, never dared cross my mother's Alps – or for short, cross her.

Left out in the ideological cold of the tropics and nowhere to live, Franqui sought refuge working on a magazine run by another journalist who had been expelled from *Hoy* and the Party. He was a man wounded in the Spanish Civil War (where he was sent by the Party when he was not yet eighteen) and now become a rabid anti-Communist. Franqui quickly realized that this Rolando Masferrer (who would be blown to bits in Miami years later, dying just as he lived – dangerously) had devolved, almost without knowing it, from sworn anti-Communist to gangster to hired assassin: from Stalin to Prío to Batista. A double-play and a double-cross. Under Batista, Masferrer organized a gang of thugs called *tigres*, whose evil eyes burned holes in the body political day and night.

Franqui judiciously abandoned that precarious shelter and returned to indigence. Then he found work in another newspaper: a proofreader again, a galley slave. Soon thereafter, in the summer of 1947, he embarked on his first military venture – or was it adventure? He joined an action group whose purpose was to bring down General Trujillo, the dictator of the neighbouring Dominican Republic. Two sworn enemies also participated in that military mission: Masferrer and Fidel Castro. At the time Castro was a prominent member of another Havana gang of daring shootists, the UIR, rivals of the MSR, run by Masferrer – all under cover of the word 'revolution': that's what the twin Rs stood for. This wouldn't be the only time Franqui and Fidel Castro would be together in an anti-tyrant battle. But it would be the last time Masferrer would accompany them. Soon Franqui and Castro would be in another group, the 26th of July Movement, attacking yet another dictator who seemed to be forever in power in Cuba. Fulgencio Batista was back on his throne of blood again. Masferrer would eventually become one of Batista's cruellest *shirri*. Once more, Cuba, the Pearl of the West Indies, was in for a dip in the deep gulf of extremes.

The only reason Franqui did not take part in the 26 July 1953 assault on the Moncada barracks in Santiago, led by Fidel Castro, was that he had no idea it was to take place. He didn't know because he was then a militant in a different anti-Batista group and they all operated like watertight compartments. However, on reading Castro's speech to his judges during his trial (*History Will Absolve Me*, a *samizdat* document we now know to have been written by somebody else: Castro's university professor Dr Jorge Manach, then an undercover anti-*Batistiano*), Franqui realized that his political die had been tossed, although the cast of the die would not abolish the tyrant's fortune or men's ideas. Franqui and Fidel Castro frequently wrote to each other during the two years Castro was in gaol. When Castro was paroled in 1955 there was Franqui waiting for him, apparently a journalist sent by the magazine *Carteles*, but in fact a supporter of Fidel, as Franqui always called him. During Castro's imprisonment, Franqui was appointed national head of propaganda for the 26th of July Movement and was founder of the underground newspaper *Revolución*. Suddenly he was arrested by Batista's political police, tortured, threatened with murder and finally gaoled. But his head wouldn't roll. Like Castro, he was freed very soon. Batista turned out to be only a part-time tyrant – the rest of the time he was too busy being a thief and playing canasta.

Franqui went directly into exile, first in Mexico, then to New York. Later he flew on to the Sierra Maestra, where Fidel Castro was learning how to be a guerrilla chief. In the Sierra (a geographic term that became then an almost theological definition: the Sierra was where the good guys went, the heaven of marksmen and Marxists) Franqui built Radio Rebelde from scratch. During the guerrilla war against Batista, Radio Rebelde had the same function as the BBC had during the war against Hitler: it broadcast not only the partisan truth but instructions for direct political action, such as sabotage and terrorism. Franqui allowed the voice of Fidel Castro to be heard for the first time all over Cuba. Castro sounded truthful, modest and hopeful – not at all the herald of Armageddon he later became.

When Batista fled in the still of the morning on 1 January 1959 and his fearful followers scattered out of the country, Franqui returned to Havana for the first time since his imprisonment in 1957 – just ahead of Castro's chaotic stampede on the capital. Franqui immediately started publishing *Revolución* above ground and it soon became a leviathan, both in Jonah's and Hobbes's sense. This was Franqui's heyday. Soon afterwards his fortunes began slowly to decline: from those of a politician in Castro's grace to those of a man who fell from grace with God into a sea of troubles. Like all good ships, *Revolución* the newspaper sank with him.

Franqui, we must remember, is a journalist first and foremost. So his book is interspersed with scoops – some quite sensational. The most scandalous was picked up by the international press agencies and printed by *Time* magazine. But it's worth repeating. It goes like this. During the October crisis Fidel Castro, on a visit to a supposedly secret, Russian-manned missile base on the western end of the island, innocently asks a bilingual technician (all Russians speak with forked tongue) to show him the button that fires the rockets. The Russian complies. The Russian also shows Comrade Castro a radar screen which at that very moment is tracking an American reconnaissance plane on a routine flight over Cuba. 'Is that an American spy plane?' asks Castro. *Da da!* Suddenly the Prime Minister presses the button. Swoosh! He didn't even have to aim: that was handled by computer. In any case, Castro has always had more faith in the trigger than in the bullet. The Russians, aghast, can only watch as their missile rises on the green, ghostly oscilloscope of the radar to collide with the moving spook. One second later the two shadows disappear from the screen.

American planes had been flying these Cuban routes with schedules as regular as those of commercial airlines since 1961 – and not even the Russians were paying them any attention. But Fidel Castro, wanting war, courting conflagration and wishing apocalypse now or never, dared to shoot down an unarmed U-2. All this was very shocking to the Russians, veterans of the Cold War and old hands at escalation and de-escalation games. The result was that the only casualty of the undeclared missile war of 1962, that poker game for world powers, was caused by a Head of State posing as trigger-happy gunner. (More than a Marxian war was a Cuban Buzz Sawyer introducing his sidekick Roscoe Sweeney!) But to accomplish his feat Fidel Castro had to use the sophisticated weaponry of the Soviet Union. For years Russian politicians (Brezhnev more seriously than Khrushchev) had considered this exotic and picturesque Third World leader a potentially dangerous man. Now they knew he was an actively dangerous man. That tardy conclusion cost Khrushchev his insolent office and his delightful dacha. Brezhnev inherited the hot air.

But more significant for the historians who know Cuba well is to find out in Franqui's book that the real strategist for the Cuban troops at the Bay of Pigs was not Fidel Castro, the commander-in-chief, as he was always called in Cuba and elsewhere, but an enigmatic General Ciutat. Like Lietenant Kije, he was an invisible Russian soldier. Now we know that F. Ciutat was a true general in the Red Army, even though he was a Spaniard and a veteran of the Spanish Civil War as the last Loyalist commander in the Basque country. A tough military man, he ended up in Stalin's Russia, where he fought the Germans. General Ciutat was a confirmed Stalinist and loyal to the Russians even from his days as a general with the Spanish Republic. The Russian High Command chose him to plot the strategy to defend Castro against the CIA landing. General Ciutat came secretly to Cuba under the alias of Angel Martínez – but he was no angel. The war plans were top secret, of course, but the KGB was in possession of the American landing maps months before the CIA invasion took place. It was a doublecross for the doubly credulous.

The Cuban commander-in-chief, even before he had declared himself a socialist for life, was already just another pawn in the Soviet global strategy – a charade more than a chess game. From a literary point of view (the only view of things that interests me) it's like learning that Tolstoy's hero General Kutuzov never commanded the Russian army at Borodino. In fact, an unknown English marshal under a Muscovite pseudonym secretly gave all the orders! The historians – even Hugh Thomas, the European who knows most about Cuba – had to revise their thinking and correct their textbooks. The truth is that Fidel Castro's real genius lies in the arts of deception and while the world plays bridge by the book, he plays poker, bluffing and holding his cards close to his olive-green chest. He has practised and mastered the dealer's art from the beginning, actually even before the beginning. His true master is Machiavelli, in that he sees history as the manipulator who uses it as an instrument to control men and politics as a way of masking truth and reaching power. Machiavelli was a playwright, Castro is an actor playing Macbeth every night. But he is Macbeth with a vengeance: he strives for a bigger kingdom – and the world is his stage. As a grand deceiver he is really extraordinary. But even more astonishing is the capacity of all concerned, both yesterday and today, close to him, as Franqui was, never really close, as I was, to let themselves be fooled willingly and cry out 'Long live Fidel!' – at least part of the way.

In his book Franqui commits a sin all of us who worked on *Revolución* committed at the time. Whenever we learned of a new arbitrary decree or of another injustice in the name of justice or some other political crime (and even murder) committed by the regime, we would always say 'Fidel probably doesn't even *know* about it,' or 'This is Raúl's doing,' or 'That's one of Che's Argentine tricks,' or 'It's Ramiro Valdés's fault – he is the Minister of the Interior, isn't he?' (Did any of us dare to think that Ramiro Valdés had been named head of the political police by Fidel Castro himself?) These were variations on a theme by Koestler entitled 'Refusal to Believe in Atrocities'. Or our own unwillingness to think of our saints as sinners. Albert Speer repeats the pattern often in speaking about Hitler, and the same applies to Stalin's tales of horrors as told by Khrushchev. The guilty parties are always different but the innocent is always one: Hitler, Stalin, Castro. Wolves in wool pulled over all eyes.

Franqui still finds himself in the same old ideological trap and almost shouts out now: 'It cannot be possible that Fidel was like that!' He doesn't excuse that tyrant or put the blame only on his agents. Mephistopheles isn't the devil, Lucifer is. Satan, says the Book of Revelations, is the deceiver of the whole world. The devil's disciple is just one more damned soul: Raúl and the others are either stooges or stoolies. Franqui in the last analysis is a humanist: he believes in humanity. He refuses to reckon that others, Sartre's hell, are evil and that human beings, given the chance, will behave atrociously: people are intrinsically bad. This is of course heresy for both Communists and Christians. It is not that power corrupts historically and that absolute power corrupts absolutely, as Lord Acton decently warned us. It is that man is already corrupt the minute he is born, for all his associations are power relationships: in sex, the family and society. Moreover, man is, in genetic rather than racial or social terms, a sick animal who knows he is going to die today, tomorrow, eventually anyway. He is avaricious, vain, and lusting for power always, everywhere. After such knowledge, what forfeiting? All that inner, innate perversity creates his thirst for posterity (and its instant form, success), for immortality and, in political terms, his hunger for history. Man is the only animal on the vast desert of eternity who believes that political mirages are for real, that history is an oasis, that true hell can somehow become imaginary heaven.

With this book Franqui sails in the stream of personal confessions as negotiated by Rousseau more than swum across by St Augustine. I'm thinking of the political vessels of Trotsky, Milovan Djilas, the early Koestler. But politics and journalism tend to fade: that's their fate. Despite Dante's feuds, poetry is what remains: Gobelins are more pertinent today than glib Ghibelins and Guelphs are just a joke. History, too, is unimportant. Here it doesn't even count, because Franqui offers the opposite of a history book – which perforce describes change. The book is titled a *Portrait* and a portrait is the most obvious form of stasis. Nothing moves in a portrait, be it a photo or a painting: it doesn't even have a *discorso proprio*, as Leonardo saw five hundred years ago. '*Eppur si muove*,' said the man who recanted: it is a written portrait and writing moves precisely because language *is* movement. Leonardo and Galileo are pertinent here because Franqui is an exile in Italy.

Lezama Lima in his Dantesque paradise would approve of Franqui's change of heart. 'Cuba is frustrated in its political essence,' was one of Lezama's favourite sentences and one that Franqui repeats again and again in his book: 'Cuba is frustrated in what's politically essential.' Or perhaps 'Cuba is frustrated in what's essentially political.' What Lezama implied in any case was that the poet's sole realm was that of poetry. The usurpers (usurper is one of the possible translations for tyrant) were the others, those political leaders who were (and are) merely bad jugglers whose oranges always end up on the floor. But Cuba is also frustrated in its historical essence, as Franqui lucidly dares to point out. Nevertheless, I think that Cuba has managed to express itself in a distinctive prose (as opposed to that of Spanish or South American writings) even *before* being a nation. Martí, Lezama, Virgilio Piñera, Lydia Cabrera, Carpentier (*et tu*, Alejo), Lino Novás Calvo, Severo Sarduy, Reinaldo Arenas, and now Franqui invent our literature with each new book from the nineteenth century to today. That Cuban invention tries to be a poetic perpetual motion of the first kind in prose. Finally, *Family Portrait with Fidel* is not a testimony: it is the testy matrimony of tender time and horrible history.

This necessary book will be attacked (it already has been in Spanish) with clamour or with silence: such are the forms of fanatical fury. It will be assaulted in concentric Cuban circles and in that central circle that is the Miami of all exiles: remember that Franqui is a revolutionary of the first water who never lets up. A brushing aside in writing can work as well as the retoucher's airbrush. Some people will try to dismiss Franqui because he writes as a poet and not as your run-of-the-mill political agent, or the embittered journalist, or a professional *exiliado* – but as a joyful peasant poet. One of those foreseeable attacks, one I have already heard, is directed against Franqui's style: against that form of writing of his which is an idiosyncratic way of speaking about whose originality I cannot say enough. It has been claimed, and not by a buffoon but by Buffon, that the style is the man. I could even go further to say that style in Franqui is history. History, as we all know, is nothing but a book called *History*. Historic justice, as in this book, should be called, then, poetic justice.

The Tyrant and the Poet

Sebastian Venable, the poet as pervert in *Suddenly Last Summer*, claimed as new and personal an old and decadent dictum now rephrased to suit the stage: 'The life of the poet is the work of the poet and the work of the poet is the life of the poet.' This is, naturally, Oscar Wilde as rewritten by Tennessee Williams. The author of this gruesome playlet must have had in mind the notorious Algerian meeting, nearing the *fin de siècle*, in which Wilde, holding Bosie's hand, boasted to a timid André Gide of having put all his genius into his life (looking at Bosie) but only his talent (looking at Gide) in his writing – and in the same bad breath told Gide, a prim and puritan pederast, that there was an Arab boy he shouldn't miss *à poil* for all the mint tea in Araby! Williams made his pervert as a poet die cannibalized on a Mediterranean beach. Not far from fashionable Morocco in any case.

Here, in Tangiers, Williams's friends William Burroughs and Paul Bowles (both decadent and pervert but no poets, who practised literary cannibalism only) used to dwell so swell. They passed the time rehashing hash and cultivating their poppy fields – and like candid Candides they told all. A motion picture of the same summery title and along similar lines (though the star was a Venus flytrap), was shot in Mexico, the nearest nirvana, and exhibited in the late fifties but now screened only in the late late shows. Unnaturally the Mediterranean bugger boys become riotous hungry children – of Sánchez perhaps? – eager to devour the pederast poet. As with so much propaganda posing as art made by American libbers with lots of reactionary American money (see *Reds* – or rather, don't) the spectator never knows if he is watching a battle of attrition in the Third World in two dimensions or an act of contrition for (not against) Plutocracy. But Pluto is a monster of such frightful mien that only Dickens could look it in the face and not vomit sweet and sour curses like (check list) imperialists, exploiters and, last but not less, anthropophagi – a word that only Lord Olivier can pronounce in black face and get away with it.

This frantic fable is merely a Grand Guignol with delusions of a

Grander Guignol and is apposite now only because you cannot understand
Herberto Padilla's poems unless you know about Padilla's hard times in
Cuba. With him, as Sebastian Venable pretended, the life of the poet is
really the work of the poet and Padilla has spent half his life (and most of
his *oeuvre*) hostage to a tyrant. Therefore to know Padilla's life and work
you must first know the tyrant – at least what's left of him. What's left and
what's right too. This tyrant, as you might have guessed by now (what with
Padilla being a Cuban poet in exile), is called Fidel Castro. Or as *The
Times* insists on calling him, *Dr* Castro.

If they ever erect a statue to Fidel Castro in Britain (why not? after all he
rules in the name of Marx and this German machine of hatred has his
statue here: neither Nietzsche nor D'Annunzio has one) this will be a
monument to the unknown tyrant. In fact the British know less about
Cuba now than they did about Argentina before the Falklands fiasco.
Then all they knew was that that country, where the gaucho roams free on
the pampas, invented the tango and was ruled by a fake blonde actress
called Evita. She sang 'Don't cry for me, Argentina' at every crisis, political or personal, or on curtain calls – whichever came first. (Usually the
curtain call came first.)

Of course, it's easier to know about an inept military dictatorship than to
find out about a successful totalitarian tyranny. This can be clearly seen in
opaque Spain under Franco as opposed to Ceausescu's shadow fiefdom in
Romania or Enver Hoxha's total blackout over Albania – of which all one
knows for sure is that its capital is aptly named Tirana.

I've already told readers of the *London Review of Books* (in the 4–17 June
1981 issue in fact) all about those brave encounters with Fidel Castro
(hereinafter called the Tyrant) that Heberto Padilla (from now on being
called the Poet) has had in the past. We left the Tyrant saying goodbye in
his fashion to the Poet from the door of one of his many dens in Havana.
The Tyrant (a.k.a. the Beast on his island) has no fixed abode: the whole
of Cuba is his maze and he is central to it, but his hell is a spiral with no
centre. When the Poet, with a desire called *Deseo* in Spanish, left the
labyrinth, it was with the help of an unlikely Ariadne, whose name on the
ballot for President of the USA in 1980 was Senator Edward Kennedy.
When Kennedy came to welcome blandly the Poet at the airport in Naxos
or Nassau all he said was 'Hello! Goodbye! I must be going!' – and
disappeared gently as a blond good knight. The Poet was now on his own
and with the dangerous knowledge that he had not really killed the
monster but, what was worse, had only wounded his pride, thick as his
hide. Once more he had to live by his wits.

In his new country the Poet heard threats from the Tyrant's henchmen but never from the Beast himself, a proud monster. His pursuers were worried (agents are a worrying lot) about the Poet's singing. Not that they feared he would compose lyrics for songs and sing them but, in the underworld's parlance, that he could *spell* the beans. That is, the possibility that he might write about the maze that some visitors, in uttered amazement, had called a magnificent building. (Some knew that it was a *spydrome* but kept a Byronian profile nevertheless.) He wrote poems, gave lectures and even published a novel he had cunningly smuggled out of the island. This book showed that nightmares are only the dream History is made of. Just like Goya, only worse. Just like Shakespeare in *Macbeth*, though not happening in Scotland in the remote past, but now, today, in the murky waters of present-day politics where the ceremony of innocence – a baptism in fetid fonts – is drowned in obscene shouts: *'Heil Hitler!'* *'Evviva Il Duce!'* *'Viva Fidel!'* The Beast is full of passionate intensity – while the best not only lack the right convictions but sometimes also entertain the wrong ideals. Above all when the best are the guests, like King Duncan, of the Beast!

Two English writers went to Cuba – hee hi hee hi ho! (This must be sung to the tune of 'Old Macbeth Had a Farm'.) One went after Fidel Castro became lord and master of the island or rather archipelago. The other went before and after that unholy second coming. This is what they said they saw there. It happened some time ago but it was all so memorable that I'll remember it all till the day I die. (To make myself sure that I wouldn't forget I took notes.)

Edna O'Brien, poor girl, visited Cuba the way Alice travelled to the other side of the looking glass – darkly but gladly. England can be so boring on a wet afternoon! Besides she had never tasted looking-glass milk. That's what they call a daiquiri in Havana. So there she went. She was given a guided tour of the island (left side only), talked to some minor leaders who quickly assured her that they were major leaders and her photographer took colour pictures everywhere it was allowed: weather permitting. (You know, the rain in the tropics – that sort of thing.) She brought back, like a trophy from the world the other side lives in, a pitiful portrait of a shirtless and shoeless peasant with his wife (they looked like the Arnolfini Couple in the mirror) whose misery, like everything that's written in Cuba today, was made in the USA – *before* the Revolution. She had got what she took for the lot – plus the cover of *The Sunday Times Magazine* and a vast spread inside. Unfortunately for the British (and for us Cubans) down the Havana way she had been had. She behaved impeccably (from the official point of view) but committed one peccadillo too many for those English readers who had never heard of Cuba before and what was going on there after the evil Yanks finally went home.

That was O'Brien's acquired sin by contagion. Her original sin was not to speak Spanish. In any country a native who knows a foreign language tends to become a liar: he speaks with a forked tongue, you see. That's the aboriginal sin. In Cuba any national who comes in close contact with a foreigner (especially if he is a journalist or a writer: totalitarian regimes value the word: they know that's the main ingredient in propaganda) belongs to State Security or G2 or he must obtain Security clearance to entertain any alien visitors. (Otherwise he is bound to be in trouble.) Foreign Affairs officials, functionaries from the Tourist Commission and the junior executive of the Writers' Union who bid you welcome at the airport and bid you goodbye as well – all wear crocodile smiles. But so do guides, interpreters and even that nice old gentleman you meet everywhere you go. Yes, that one who sports the kind smile of a crocodile with dentures: he works for G2 too. In Cuba not only Big Brother is watching you. So is his little brother, Raúl Castro.

They all took Edna in, sent her up and flew her back to Britain, younger and seemingly wiser too. (The things we see behind the mirror image, dear – and the things we *hear*!) Let me illustrate for you. Ms O'Brien talked in her article about the *infamos* (her italics), that looked to her – how should she put it? Well, *weird*. You know, different. Those infamos, however, compared with any passerby strolling along the King's Road, Chelsea, at the time must have looked like late hippies to any pink punk of today. But beatniks, hippies and even dull punks are all equally forbidden in Cuba, according to a law against 'extravagant and anti-social behaviour'. Such behaviour includes the social crimes of wearing jeans and/or sneakers, failing to cut your hair short and even sporting a beard – unless your name is Fidel Castro or you are one of the happy few oldtime *comandantes* from the guerrillas. (By the way, these *comandantes* have all been promoted from modest majors to brigadier-generals and they must dress accordingly – which is according to the rules of the Frunze Military Academy in Moscow.) What Edna O'Brien misheard was the word '*enfermos*' (literally the sick ones, socially sick) and that's how those poor purple people were known before they were labelled '*escoria*' (scum) and expelled from Cuba to the United States as undesirables via the port of Mariel in 1980. Those who were lucky enough to qualify as pederasts, lesbians and bums left Mariel as *escoria* to become '*gusanos*' (worms) on landing in Miami. All these labels were concocted by Dr Castro, a linguist as imaginative as Dr Goebbels. They think alike, like all great minds. They even look alike. Dr Goebbels is the swarthy little man with the swastika armband on the right. Dr Castro is the tall dark fellow with a beard smoking a cigar with a band.

The other English writer of note to visit Cuba and to write about it is Graham Greene – the man who calls Philby his friend. He was in Havana before but not after Edna O'Brien – I believe. Though he used to see Castro on his way to visit General Torrijos, the late Panamanian strong-man. In any case he has been in Cuba several times all told. Some time during the Batista regime, most of the time after Castro seized power. Greene chose to be inimical to Batista and amicable with Castro for religious reasons. He sees himself as Castro's paraclete when he is only the devil's advocate. Be that as it may, Cuba under Batista proved perhaps not too congenial but it was certainly more fruitful to him than under Castro. He hasn't yet written *Our Man in Havana* (Part Two) and he had censorship problems when shooting the movie in Havana early in 1959. *I know* – I arranged Greene's final meeting with Castro in Cathedral Square to iron out the difficulties encountered with the censors then by Carol Reed.

However Greene wrote many articles about it and gave interviews on the subject and published at least one long story on Castro and his Revolu-tion. The most important article is the least useful to an understanding by the British of Communist Cuba and what's going on there. This piece is actually a paean to Castro called 'The Marxist Heretic' – something of course Castro is not and never has been. Witness to this is Castro's servile support of the Soviet Union in Czechoslovakia (1968), Afghanistan (1979) and Poland (1982). The man is obviously a red puppet in olive-green fatigues.

Greene tries at least to establish a comparison between Castro and Batista that is grossly biased. 'Cuba is a country now,' he states flatly, 'and not merely a pleasure-capital as it was in Batista's day.' Apart from not disclosing how less discerning men than he can tell when a country is not a country (what divining rod did Greene use – Aaron's rod?) he chides Cuba (he probably meant only Havana) for being a pleasure-capital when Batista ruled the island. I wish it had been just that then! Believe me: I *lived* there and I saw suffering enough to make not a phrase but to fill a volume. And what's wrong with being a pleasure-capital? Perhaps it is to masochists wearing hairshirts in the tropics but not to me. Is a pleasure-capital worse than a *Das Kapital* capital? If only Batista, a cruel crook, had proved to be a Kubla Khan and built a pleasure dome in Cuba and named it Xanadu!

Greene probably meant to say (I haven't decided yet if he is a confusing writer or just a confused man) that there were gaming houses in Havana under Batista – and of course long before him for surely Batista didn't invent roulette or create the croupier. There were casinos then and cabarets and brothels and even a peep show featuring a black man with an oversized penis who called himself Superman without the benefit of having read Nietzsche. The display fascinated foreign visitors including Ava Gardner, and by osmosis Francis Ford Coppola, who fantasized about Superman decades later in *The Godfather* (Part Two).

But if he meant only gaming houses, Greene gambled in those pleasure palaces of green felt and red chips. He had the time and the money and he visited Havana several times before Batista folded shop and presented Castro with a whole island to play poker with with the Americans across the Gulf Stream. As before Hitler had done with Chamberlain across the Channel, Castro won by merely shuffling his cards to bluff. For Greene's baize information, today there are more casinos and gaming clubs in London than there ever were in Cuba before 1959 – and that doesn't make London a pleasure palace.

If the choice had been between a country and a pleasure-capital surely one and a half million Cubans would not have fled at their own risk and by whatever means from an island surrounded by barbed-wire and infested with policemen. Compared to Cuba, East Germany with its Berlin Wall was a playground with a high fence: an invitation to escape following Baudelaire plans for a trip. The rest of the article is Graham Greene chasing after Fidel Castro all over Cuba the way his Holly Martins pursued Harry Lime all over Vienna in *The Third Man*: the haunted on the hunt of the old haunt. He doesn't know yet that his hero is actually the Godless villain of the piece but he will love him to the bitter end and after. He also has his Cuban version of Anna Schmidt – but more later. Greene even compares (how long can you strain a comparison?) Castro with the Scarlet Pimpernel! Why not Bloody Red Pimpernel? He begins his write-up with a ditty that, though translated by him from the Cuban, nevertheless sounds like a Baroness D'Orczy deliciously delirious in her inverted coma.

Talking of heroines instead of heroes, Graham Greene wrote about Celia Sánchez, a feminine factotum to Castro, and Haydée Santamaría, a professional *prócer* (notable) of the Revolution. Both women are now deceased. Srta. Sánchez died of cancer and was buried with full honours. But Heroine Haydée (whom Greene thought everybody in Cuba called Haydée when she was in fact known as Yeyé, her notorious nickname) blew her brains out recently. Now Greene makes the mistake of the man who thinks he knows by making you think *he* knows. (This has more to do with double wishful thinking than with ESP.) Greene dreamt in his article what would have happened if Haydée Santamaría had been killed in the assault on the Moncada barracks in Santiago de Cuba in 1953 led by Fidel Castro. (Santamaría was one of two women who went with the attackers as nurses.) Had she died then, speculates Greene, 'she would have been buried in the heroes' pantheon and her funeral would have been a rendez-vous that they [the Cubans] could be certain Fidel would keep.'

Oh history, you naughty girl! Your true name's Irony and you never said it. As it happened, before killing herself (on 26 July 1980, the anniversary of the Moncada assault) Yeyé, as her testament, sent a goodbye letter to Fidel Castro. Of course this last letter from a disillusioned revolutionary leader who committed suicide was never made public. (Yeyé was being naïve to the last – but so was Greene.) Haydée Santamaría was neither buried in the Heroes' Pantheon nor had a public display of mourning from a grieving Castro. (She had instead a private wake at a second-rate funeral parlour in Havana.) This was one predicted historic rendezvous Fidel Castro devoutly failed to keep. As a matter of fact Castro never came to Yeyé's wake. He did not even attend her burial.

This is an error of judgement Graham Greene couldn't have foreseen at that time, but some other statements of his are not mere bad judgements. Curiously they have the same ring of wilful wrongness that another Anglo-Saxon writer, Ezra Pound, did broadcast, in every sense, about another Latin tyrant, Mussolini. Greene claims about Fidel Castro that even his name is an object of veneration: Fidel 'whom no Cuban except an enemy calls by the name of Castro'. What does he mean? Is this hagiography or just journalism? Let's see. What if one called Mussolini Benito? Would that have changed the colour of his shirt? Had German Jews called Hitler by the name of Adolf, would he have been a less demented tyrant? What about a Polish officer calling Stalin Joe in Katyn Forest? One of the most hideous tyrants in America ever, the Mexican Porfirio Díaz, was always called respectfully by Mexicans Don Porfirio and only his enemies called him Porfirio. (Or Díaz as in *dias contados*.) It's all too laughable really. But the laughs are not on Graham Greene or Edna O'Brien but on us Cubans – in and out of Cuba. The laugh is also on you, British reader. Like Humphrey Bogart in *Casablanca*, who came to a desert town for the waters, you too have been misinformed.

Cuba is a Communist country – no matter what anybody thinks or says.

That's a political fact, just like Britain is a parliamentary democracy and a kingdom. Or the United States a republic and a democracy. A Communist country is a world of deception and deceit. Here, as never before in history, as Orwell discovered all by himself to the discomfort of English (and of course American) liberals and the hatred of all Marxists united, the charlatan's doubletalk can be transformed into the intellectual's doublethink instantly – and nobody notices it.

Heberto Padilla's poems were written, most of them, in the capital of Cuba, Havana. Cuba, in spite of the charm of the tropics, the Gulf Stream flowing free nearby and the lure of music in the moonlight *is* a Communist country. This is the Caribbean island where Fidel Castro, its President for Life (and he certainly has been more than a *lifer* to us for nearly a quarter of a century), a first generation Cuban whose father was born in Galicia, Spain, who was educated by Spanish Jesuits, could shout in a mass rally and through the PA system: 'We're *not* Latin! We're *more* than Latin! We are *Afro* Latin Americans!' (Castro, like Hitler, like Mussolini, like all verbal volcanoes, always delivers his message with exclamation marks all over the speech: more than speaking he erupts!) Of course nobody bothered to ask him if this was genetically possible. Nobody asked if Galicia now had a border with Namibia. Nobody questioned his *ars combinatoria*. Why not Latin-Afro American or Afro-American Latin or – what the hell! Nobody asked anything: nobody ever does in Cuba and lives to tell it. But what he meant was that *his* Cuba (with a pressure-capital) had the racial right to intervene militarily in Africa. If this is not as racist a right as the one Hitler claimed for his annexation of Austria, you tell me. Wait! Don't tell me, I'll tell *you*.

Fidel Castro, who as a university student was known by his classmates as *el Gallego* (the Galician), was actually a Spaniard in the works. Or rather, he must be included as part of the Spanish heritage in America. From the country that gave you Cortés, Pizarro, and Aguirre and the conquistador now comes – the *caudillo*! I give you the Latin American *Caudillo*! That's what Francisco Franco wanted to be called in his Spain: *El Caudillo, Por la Gracia de Dios*. By the Grace of God goes *El Caudillo*. No buts. Perhaps but – the birthmark to know a born *caudillo* is very simple. If he can be played by Charlton Heston in a Hollywood epic, he is a *caudillo*. Such was El Cid, big as a legend. Franco, barely five foot four, was no *caudillo*. He was a military midget. But if he wanted to be a *caudillo*, then Ronnie Corbett could play him in the smallest screen.

Castro is merely an updated avatar of the Spanish *Caudillo*. There have been other avatars, equally modern then, obsolete now. There was Rosas in Argentina whose hands didn't smell of roses exactly. There was Francia in Paraguay, who called himself 'I, the Supreme'. (The perfect title for Diana Ross's autobiography.) There was Gómez in Venezuela, who ordered his political enemies to be buggered in prison. There was Somoza as a dynasty in Nicaragua. There was Trujillo in the Dominican Republic who plucked his eyebrows and pencilled his moustache first thing in the morning and renamed the capital Ciudad Trujillo. There was Pérez Jiménez, also in Venezuela, greedy for palace pleasures – wearing only spectacles the better to chase naked chorus girls from a motorscooter on his private beach. There was Don Porfirio, of course, and the Peróns, Juan and Eva, and Batista, who always dressed in white and bathed too often to get rid of his tar. And there was – oh my God, it's quite a list to be a coincidence, you know.

But when the latest avatar dies in Cuba (he looks more and more like his own waxwork), instead of paying homage at Castro's Mausoleum in Revolution Square, Havana, English writers and journalists won't have to go in there on foot under the fierce Cuban sun. To pay homage to the Spanish-American *caudillo* you just go to Southampton and visit the old cemetery by the bay. There you'll find the tomb of Rosas, who died in that foggy city in 1877. The gaucho general, whom Borges describes in a poem like an Argentine Macbeth ('and more than one thrust of the dagger invoked Juan Manuel Rosas'), became an exile in England and died here. When Perón came back from the dead to snatch the presidency legally a Marxist Argentine journalist came to visit me. 'I'm here on an official mission,' he confided. 'I came to take Rosas back with me to Argentina.' He didn't say he was taking with him some dust or perhaps a bunch of brittle bones. I knew he came to take the ghost of Rosas back from the dead *caudillos* to present-day chaos. He wanted me to go with him to Southampton. I proposed that we first go sightseeing in London. 'Ah,' he said. 'You want me to visit the tomb of *Carlos* Marx!' 'No,' I told him. 'I want you to see Mosley's house.' He didn't understand. 'Mosley who?' How could I explain? A throwback, an ancillary avatar, a freak of history – Oswald Mosley, an English *Caudillo*, of course.

Everything began to turn sour for us Cuban writers and terribly wrong for the Poet when the notorious 'Meetings with Fidel Castro' took place at the national Library in June 1961. But for the Poet wrongness began earlier. In 1959, to be exact, when he became chief correspondent in Europe for Prensa Latina (the Cuban official news agency founded by two Peronist exiles from Argentina who were appointed to their job by Che Guevara:

totalitarians always come in threes). He came to London – and made the wrong choice. As headquarters for Prensa Latina he chose a building in Fleet Street where the American news agencies AP and UPI already had their offices. When this spatial coincidence was known in Cuba, the Poet was accused of selling (secrets? news?) or just selling out to Yankee Imperialism and was immediately recalled to Havana. Later came the conversations turned monologue with Fidel Castro which ended with the banning of the literary magazine I edited since it was founded by Carlos Franqui in 1959 and to which the Poet had been a frequent contributor. That was the beginning of the end – though nothing ever begins exactly then.

I can only add now, as a postscript to that scenario, that the Poet was arrested and made to confess newly minted crimes (still unmentioned today) under an extreme duress that you would call torture. His interrogators in fact used a Communist version of the medieval *Ad extirpanda* – invented by the Inquisition in the fourteenth century. It has been perfected into an *Ars extirpanda* in Cuba today: the hunt for heretics in the arts and literature had begun in earnest. It was April, always a cruel month for poets. The year was 1971 – exactly ten years after the 'Meetings at the Library', when Fidel Castro concluded his speech (and the meetings) with a dictum all ad liberals everywhere found felicity itself but we heard as ominous. Said the Maximum Leader and waited for the applause (and it came: from all of us): 'Within the Revolution, everything. Against the Revolution, nothing!' Of course, he kept everything to himself and left us nothing.

At long last *Legacies*! This is a selection more than a collection of Padilla's poems. Here the ordinary reader will find many masterful poems but the *enterado* will miss a poem or two that turned evidence for the prosecution in what was known as the 'Padilla Case' – and sounds more like something only an Hercule Poirot would crack. It's understandable that those poems are missing: such is the will of the Poet. (Or at least his desire.) He himself collaborated on the rehabilitation of these poems so they could stand up on their own and put their best iambic foot forward. This is tantamount to seeing Oscar Wilde reject the foul curiosity gathering around 'The Ballad of Reading Gaol', like a morbid mob, simply because the poem brought the author painful old memories no longer private. Or, less permissible, because he still believed in art for art's sake and this particular poem sounded more like a cry for justice than a moving ballad. Both poets (the Irish idol, the candid Cuban) are right – and so could I be. Indeed the life of the poet is the work of the poet as much as the work was, is and will be the life of the poet. Even if, as in the case of Padilla, his poems were once in Cuba the life of the Party.

'The Travelling Companion' is History (Padilla's own capital) as seen from a train: steam, wind and speed creating the illusion of a *perpetuum mobile*. The Poet knows better; 'But I only see/road and barbed wire/and beasts'. The ending of this short poem has been masterfully translated, with the Poet seeing the fellow-traveller as a girl 'with eyes/beautiful but beyond salvation'. In 'Calm' the lyric lines are transformed into a totalitarian warning by the insurgence of the carefree spy who eats his breakfast not with strong Cuban coffee but with watery tea in a glass. (It was Chesterton, that connoisseur, who said that tea, like everything that comes from the Orient, becomes poisonous if made strong.) In the poem a cherished daydream turns into a nightmare: Morpheus is now amorphous.

In 'The Lovers of the Izmailovo Forest' the poet's only haven in Moscow is to read Blok and Esenin – until he finds them to be just books 'with new wormholes'. The Poet never says that in the Soviet capital he shared the print shop with Anibal Escalante, a defeated Cuban Hannibal banished to Moscow after a puny Punic War with Fidel Castro. Escalante, once the most powerful Communist leader in America, unlike the original Hannibal chose exile instead of poison. He was now a galley slave sitting on the bench next to the migratory Poet's – reading proofs. After the Russian winter of the malcontents, 'the last Spring arrives in Moscow' and both the Poet and the politician are able to return to Cuba. The Tyrant, you see, forgives though he never forgets. The Politician came back to try once more to snatch Communist power from Castro's jaws – and to end reading in gaol. The Poet tried to tame the Beast with poems that were Marxist Carols for a Santa Claws – who had already abolished Christmas anyway. Now we have a red Navidad in July but are still dreaming of the white Christmas we never had.

Padilla had to be set free in Cuba sooner or later – and he was. Now he is also Scot-free working with Alistair Reid, formerly from the East Neuk of Fife. Padilla is from Pinar del Río, the pinewood by the river, in western Cuba: tobacco country by the tobacco roads. In *Legacies* the kilt matches the Havana wrapper perfectly. Here are some samples. Ladies first.

'Advice to a Lady' is a poem in which Padilla, like a Cuban Sextus Propertius, or rather like a pubic Ovid, gives her cue to a lady from the Cuban *haute bourgeoisie*, reluctant to vanish, on how to behave improperly – according to the new times and Marx's mores. That *dama* must even bed a young *becado* (a grantee of the Revolution) and let her 'thighs enact the struggle of the contraries'. Reid has an elegant phrase to sum up this battle of the sexes that begins and ends in a clash of classes: 'Take a scholar to bed.' Turning the *becado* into a scholar is giving the English reader the benefit of choice. But *becado* has a very particular Cuban connotation. Especially since 1960 when the Revolution began giving grants to students from the provinces to come to Havana to study. The winners were mostly ignorant peasants, uncouth town-dwellers and ungracious provincials – and all very, very young. Padilla, who hates plays on words (so does Castro: he prefers to play on swords), probably never noticed that *becado* comes comically close to *bocado* – a bite and a dish. *Bocado* also has all the sexual connotations of the typical male innuendo feminists despise so much. But now the gourmet is the female of the spices.

Padilla owes a lot to a few English poets: he is an admirer and a translator (one can be both, you know) of Coleridge and Keats and Byron, but he seems to be particularly fond of William Blake, a poet I find crude and clumsy. Poetically Blake is as naïve as he is primitive as a draughts-man: an illustrator of biblical themes who entertains metaphysical preten-sions above his station of the cross. 'Tyger, Tyger burning bright . . .' This is to me worse than Stevenson's 'Windy Night'. Rhymes for children who are fond of things that go oompah-oompah in the night!

In 'A Prayer for the End of the Century' the Poet claims that 'the error exists today/that someone will have to condemn tomorrow'. In an ironic error in historic calculations the Tyrant let the Poet get away. This is the blunder of yesterday that he has regretted ever since: these poems are memoranda as a gadfly. Poems never killed a tyrant – the opposite is truer. Tyrants have been heard to have killed poets because of a sonnet or two sung off-beat. But they are still, in totalitarian regimes, like the furuncles of Marx: an irritant that might become one day the written spur of political turmoil – and even the cause of strife and revolt. Otherwise, why make ecce Esenin kill himself or kill mild Mandelstam or enforce poet's block on Blok?

Padilla is however far from being a political poet by most Marxist standards. Communist poetry, at its best, is cynical and callous, as in Brecht. At its worst it's maudlin and as meaningless as a raised fist. To bite your thumb at a rival or an angry pedestrian who gives you the finger is a much more effective gesture. At least it can become the beginning of a tragedy by Shakespeare. Or, by turning the hand around, be converted into the Churchillian V sign. Sometimes – and this is the case of Mayakov-sky – it's impossible to tell poetry from propaganda, though we know that they are inimical to each other: propaganda always provokes in the reader an immune reaction. Even publicity can be a pop-protein but propaganda is a killer disease of the creative spirit. All Dr Faustus did in fact was to sell his soul to *Propaganda Fidei*.

The Poet calls Cuba 'Marx's Dream' (actually Marx's pet project in Spanish) but the dream turned out to be one of St John's most sinister revelations. Apocalypse not now, as the movie-maker pretended – but apocalypse then and later and always. Communism is Vico's vicious nightmare: constant Armageddon. The reflection is mine now but it has been mutual, like the displeasure of some new acquaintance. For the Poet and me Cuba is a midnight dream that turned sour the morning after. We even shared the same experiences separately. The Poet is approached in the poem by a Russian teenager who had been stalking him 'in a huge square'. All he wanted was to buy the Poet's nylon windbreaker, a cheap garment made in the West. Years before I was crossing Moscow's Red Square on a windy autumn morning with Carlos Franqui (the only real revolutionary who did something for culture in Cuba without using it for personal or political gain – which cost him his job and his country and almost cost him his life too!) when Franqui, with his vast clandestine experience, noticed that we were being cautiously followed. Spy or cop we let our follower approach to confront him and ask him in Pidgin Esperanto what the hell he wanted. But all the stalking prey did was to point to Franqui's raincoat, a cheap nylon affair made in the West. It was obvious that he wanted to buy it badly. The stranger was risking gaol for this antisocial activity of his in front of distinguished foreign visitors. Recognizing one of the 'poor people of this earth', singled out in 'L'Internationale' to be better off in Communism, Franqui took off his raincoat and gave it to this Lenin child who was actually re-enacting Gogol's 'Overcoat' – one hundred years later. Now Padilla, to a Russian still craving the fundamental freedom to buy a raincoat, gave him his poem – twenty years after the event.

'Techniques of pursuit', published in America while the Poet was still an inmate on Devil's Island, is a poem on the techniques of pursuit as a cure to paranoia. (There's no paranoid delusion where you are really persecuted: to the hunted fox the ghostly hounds running after him in the morning mist look terribly real.) The Poet's pursuers are now two lovely young things and they are shapely real: in Cuba young girls make the best agents. (You see, they can perform cover and uncover jobs.) These two young spies are members of an exclusive club: the Cuban KGB, familiarly known by an American code-name taken from Batista's army: G2 (part two). If you belong to G2 and you are young and female and beautiful you can become a delectable detector of enemies of the party, the people and the fatherland. Take your pick, *compañerita*.

In 'Via Condotti' one must praise Catholically the translator of Padilla's Cuban simile ('*y desnudo/como un Cristo veloz*' – naked like a speeding Jesus) for a 'streaking Christ'. This is certainly *very* close to the irreverent parody of Jarry's 'The Passion Considered as a Bike Race in France', which begins simply '*Jésus démarra*'. In another poem Padilla addresses the legendary second king of Rome as 'my old Numa Pompilius' – perhaps because he always called Dr Castro by a familiar Fidel. But I recognize that quaint familiarity with the Ancients that enabled Cavafy to admire Antony and ogle Octavius – or vice verses. Such familiarity, like any other, breathes contempt. Then the poet chafes at ideological icons like Marcuse and Adorno. Marcuse should be read here as Marxcuses and Adorno means only adornment in Spanish anyway. To end the paragraph I must point to the turning of '*una formulación rabiosa de la vida*', so rabid, into a perfect threefold alliteration: 'furious formulation of life'. That's what I like about English – Cubans can see poetry clearer through a glass of Scotch amber.

To my chastising chagrin one of the best poems in the book is the long ode to 'The Childhood of William Blake', a poem so splendid that I felt the temptation to quote it entirely. But the writer as critic must be wilder than Wilde and resist every temptation, including quotations. In the end I had to give in and reveal to you the end:

> Night, you somehow know him
> For a few hours now,
> let poor Blake sleep at last.
> Sing to him, tell him a happy story;
> let him rest on your waters,
> to wake far away,
> serene, Mother, in your sanctuary of cold.

There it is! (Even the semi-colon is there and God knows I hate semi-colons more than I hate inverted commas.) It is indeed beautiful in English and in Spanish too. But let me tell you something: it's not at all in the Spanish grain. Not even in the most recent tradition, that of Lezama Lima, obscure and splendid as he is in his unnatural coupling of Góngora and Mallarmé: sodomy and miscegenation. This is the English tradition in Spanish, of which Borges is both disciple and master. It's in the next poem, however, 'Wellington in His Garden Contemplating a Portrait of Byron', that Padilla takes a step further Cavafy's way with the historic past that is transformed into a historic present. But Cavafy, a Greek among Greeks in a Greek city, didn't have to conceal that he was slightly different – not bent in bed and breakfast but a poet. Padilla had to hide that he was, in fact, a heretic among believers. Such men are dangerous – and I mean of course, believers, even if they are faking. Especially when they are faking.

Towards the end (of the book, of his sojourn in goal) Padilla shows a metaphysical turn, probably after committing the bourgeoisism of translating his English peers and master for Cuban gaolers and brother inmates. It would have been more profitable, of course, to translate Russian past poets and even better, to invite his Soviet contemporaries to voyage abroad – to the tropics. But these are no masters. More like slaves I should say. Not a task for the Poet then. He had to weave his verses in the dark and walk by night those meaningful streets of Havana like a sleepwalking artist on his high-wire act. In a Communist country (and Cuba really is one of those) every footstep tonight could be an incriminating footprint tomorrow: a giant hound is always after you.

'Legacies', the poem that gave the volume its title, is a haunting poem: a five finger exercise on a Horacian theme. Death conquers everything, even conquerors, and our love for the dead is only love for death. Death moves in stealth like the knight. But in the next poem nostalgia is the unseen conqueror now. Memory, beware: the invisible tiger of oblivion is at the gates and waiting. Somehow even nature, like the night, has its claws too and is ready for the kill. In 'Just by Opening Your Eyes' the Poet discovered that 'a terrible beauty exists even in the landscape'.

Arguably the best poem in the book, 'Portrait of the Artist As a Young Wizard' (there's a catch in the Spanish title: *duende* means perhaps a magician, as in De Falla's *brujo*, and surely also an elf, but I'd rather have imp here and make the connection between Poe and Poet), is free of history, free of politics (corrupted and corrupting), free of Cavafy, free of Kant and Marx's cant – and the rest of the gang. The Poet is, like the Djinny in *The Thief of Baghdad*, free. Free at last! This poem should have been written on the green campus of Princeton, where Padilla now roams, with his dark lady who writes sonnets, his young son and their mad English dog who barks at all the trees – right or wrong.

'Note' ('For Those on the Trail of the Marvellous') is the best translated of the poems. The marvel trackers are the followers of Alejo Carpentier – deceased, therefore Castro's favourite Cuban writer. These camp-followers believe that the fiddler on the roof is the emblem of a new aesthetic credo and not a *faux-naïf* painting by Chagall, good enough to title a Broadway musical where only the fiddler feels as fit as his fiddle. In some South American novels people take off at will to fly up and away. This is supposed to be the most marvellous feat of all. Why, that's what the novice did all the time in *The Flying Nun* TV series! No wonder such writers believe that magic realism was invented in South America by a French author born in Cuba who spoke Spanish with gargling Gallic Rs. (If you can believe that you can believe that not only nuns but nannies can fly.)

A strange bond of poetry unites Borges and Lezama to Padilla (though there was no love lost between the two Cubans). This bond is called Quevedo, the baroque Spanish wordsman and swordsman. But Padilla would rather be shot at dawn than be called baroque point-blank. There it is, though, his 'Monologue of Quevedo' and, going for baroque, this is followed by 'The Apparition of Góngora', the man who invented the brand of bubbling champagne called *El Barroco*, a heady wine of a style which, according to Borges, carries its own parody in its bottle. But Padilla never parodies anyone's style, much less his own.

In 'Relief', where

> Every time a generation
> comes in or goes out, slamming doors,
> the old poet tightens his belt
> and tunes up his cornet like a little rooster.

We hear the challenge of the once cocky young poet as he snarls at this bantamweight opponent: 'Come on, punk – sing!' But immediately after, in 'Occasional Wicked Thoughts', the Poet speaks about a very personal problem that concerns, or should concern, every Communist or would-be Communist poet – and of course every poet. Yet one cannot help wondering. Was this man, a literary not a political animal – was he really ever a Communist? The only possible answer is in 'According to the Old Board' – which should be the final poem of the book, regarding as it does poets and the Poet:

> Don't you forget it, poet.
> In whatever place or time
> you make, or suffer, History,
> some dangerous poem is always stalking you.

A few more poems follow this time-capsule of politics. There's even one where, briefly, Heberto Padilla sums up his *caso*:

> The Right praises me

(in no time they will defame me)
The Left have given me a name
(have they not begun to have doubts?)

But the anthology has ended by then and one feels that this is more an afterthought than a confession. However, Heberto Padilla has been forced before to make more than one confession under duress. The Defence rests.

The last episode of the continuing story of the Poet and the Tyrant (the pecking order is now a Peking order) took place in Barcelona this summer. Padilla came to Spain with wife and son for a holiday in the sun and the language and to see his Spanish publishers. He planned to show them how far he had got in his memoirs and instead of going to a hotel he went to stay with his friend Mauricio Wacquez, an exiled Chilean writer. (This is the morning of the Age of Exile not of Aquarius.) One afternoon they all went for a walk in the Ramblas and to have lunch at an *al fresco fonda*. When they came back they found the door of Wacquez's apartment ajar: it had been pried open. Inside, everything seemed to be in order. Only minor household appliances were missing and apparently the thieves had failed to steal even Wacquez's new electric typewriter. But something else was missing: the manuscript of Padilla's memoirs.

Padilla phoned me after the robbery and told me that the purloined manuscript was only a copy. 'Do you think that I was going to leave my original script lying around just like that?' He chortled. '*Mi amigo*, I've lived in Castro's Cuba long enough to know that a careless mind can become a stiff body in a jiffy!' He laughed now. 'They knew I must have had a copy or kept the original somewhere else. You see, they know I'm all but dumb.' He became more serious now: 'This is simply a warning, like the alarm that rings before the burglary. They wanted me to know they can reach me anywhere whenever they need to. This is just a signal in their Morse code.' I interrupted: 'A Marx code then? I'm sorry, old boy. I couldn't help it. Do go on.' Padilla was deadly serious: 'Castro doesn't want me to disclose all I know about Fidel. He must know by now that I'm not telling all. I am a poet and I know that poetic justice has nothing to do with poetry.'

It has even less to do with poets, not even with dead poets. Some people in Spain refused to believe that the burglary ever took place and countered over the counter that it was all a clumsy scenario for a cheap publicity stunt. It is actually a moot point whether the thievery really happened or not. What's pertinent is that if it didn't happen, it could have. How many people of good will would have said, *before* the fact, that a Bulgarian writer in exile in England could have been killed in broad daylight, near the Strand, using a common English apparel, concealing the most uncommon weapon, loaded with the deadliest poison known to man? And what about the recent episode of the Romanian writer marked to be killed at a party in Paris! Bizarre murders don't necessarily have bizarre motives.

For the friends of the plausible (who are sometimes also friends of progressive causes) the latest development in Heberto Padilla's open case is not the arm of the Tyrant trying to test how long his reach is, but just another turn of a shrewd poet who is a good PR man for himself. Perhaps. But then when was Pound really true? When he broadcast garrulously on Mussolini's behalf or when he was put in a cage by his American captors and chose silence for ever? On the other hand, the left one, was Lorca really shot by the Fascists or was it all some publicity stunt that backfired at dawn?

Footnote. This essay was originally published in the *London Review of Books*, 1 December 1982. A rebuff from Graham Greene shot back. I cannot print his letter, but I can do better: see my letter reprinted in this book on page 246. He was, I must say, totally rebuked.

Castro's Convertible

Fidel Castro was born a bastard. I'm not being offensive or facetious. When he was born, in the Twenties, being illegitimate in Cuba meant being a social outcast for life, without any hope for reprieve. Usually people born out of wedlock were branded in the Civil Register as 'SOA'. (It meant '*sin otro apellido*': no other name.) Contrary to Spanish usage, such a person had not the right to have two surnames.

Being a bastard in Cuba was tough luck. Consider then the implications in Castro's case. His mother and the legitimate mother of his brothers and sisters lived in the same house. The situation becomes psychologically complex when your mother, the fierce Lina Ruz, is your stepmother's maid. This made the whole mesh into a mess. The household was coming apart at the seams when Castro was a boy called Fidel after some local merchant.

I remember one night in the editor's office at *Revolución* newspaper, which was Castro's mouthpiece, when he came in fuming (he smoked cigars then) and hollered from the door: 'Franqui, I want your front page to call that brother of mine a bastard!' Ramón Castro had voiced very bold opinions about how unjust the Agrarian Reform was. (Ramón, being the eldest, had inherited his father's farm.) His statement had made the front pages of an evening newspaper that was anathema to Castro. When he called his brother a bastard we all looked at each other utterly baffled. If Fidel called his older brother a bastard, what did he think he was? Raúl, being a younger brother, is not a bastard. But the Castro brothers became a dynasty eventually. Ramón, obviously pardoned by Fidel, runs the agriculture in a bigger farm called Cuba. Raúl's wife is some sort of smiling Lady Macbeth. Raúl himself has always been forced to play Mr Hyde to Dr Castro's Jekyll. Now that he is terminally ill with cirrhosis of the liver, Castro is auditioning healthier candidates for the part.

Robert E. Quirk's biography[1] begins with the author impersonating a

1 *Fidel Castro* (W. W. Norton, 1993).

very young, hapless Fidelito. To start with, Castro was never called Fidelito. Quirk does not make such a mistake but he seems as if about to fall
into the unknown territory of subjective third person narration. Fortunately just one paragraph is all we get of a psychological portrait of the
Maximum Leader as a peasant boy. Or as Huck would have it. With Huck
out of hock and into prehistory, Quirk is soon on the right tracks. But for a
moment, for just a moment, I thought of Roald Dahl and his story of how
the Führer was born, with the fateful embryo in Frau Hitler's womb
struggling to get out.

The Führer connection is apt because like Alan Bullock's *Hitler*,
Quirk's *Fidel Castro* is a study in tyranny. This is a political biography and
Fidel Castro is seen in his exact historical context. His throne of blood (in
Cuba they call him the Beast from Birán, the town where he was born) was
firmly, now wobbly set in Cuba but the book does not apportion all the
blame to the Cubans and calls a political spade an *espada*. The Russians
were not only coming, they were there – they still are. The enormous radar
station is eagerly listening at the continental USA from a place in Cuba
called, like the French sanctuary, Lourdes. Though this Lourdes cannot
work miracles for Castro anymore. Quirk also states that the Americans,
from Eisenhower and the history beyond, are responsible for Batista
becoming once more *El Hombre* and their son of a bitch – and for Fidel
Castro's longer tenure as our Maximum Leader. The US are also to
blame since Kennedy's Bay of Pigs fiasco for trying to get rid of Castro
with comic book accuracy by offering him exploding cigars, sending out
marksmen disguised as Marxmen and romancing him with latter-day versions of Mata Hari to make his coitus more interruptus than it usually is.

Quirk has read everything about Castro's Cuba but, unlike the smart set
that have gone to the island and come back to tell it like it wasn't, he tells
all. Furthermore his conclusions are all truthful. His heart is not with the
high brass telling tall tales but with ordinary Cubans, and he never praises
the five-year plans but their thirty-five years plight. Castro once said,
'History will absolve me.' History might but not this biography of a man
who ruined his country to rule over the ruins. The book is implacable too
with the bookmakers of history, but it has the polite tones of the political
biography initiated by Plutarch in his *Lives*.

Angel Castro, Fidel's father, had left Spain penniless to become in
Cuba a rich landowner. Lina Ruz saw her husband die and her son
become head of state through violence and demagoguery, traits that were
also present in her husband's character. From his mother Castro received
a combination of will and whim. So often dangerous in a public figure, it

becomes lethal in a dictator. Like Hitler, a non-German, and Stalin, a non-Russian, Fidel Castro is barely Cuban. Unlike Stalin, who revered Moscow, Castro is doing to Havana what Hitler did to Berlin. Defame first, then destroy. Havana, like Berlin, was not a city but a living metaphor.

As a boy Castro loved to hunt things smaller than himself. His father, who ruled over his cane cutters (mostly Haitians and Jamaicans), wanted to rule over the unruly boy. To do just that he sent Fidel to Santiago, the big city on the Caribbean, to be disciplined more than educated by the Jesuits, who ran a famed school called Colegio Dolores – literally the school of pains. Like Loyola, the founder of the order, he was nourished on miracles and steaks. Like Saint Ignatius, Castro left primary school a believer – in himself. Later his education as a Jesuit was completed at a secondary school in Havana, Colegio de Belén. Much more prestigious than the Dolores institution, Belén was for even richer young men. It was engaged mainly in forming the character of its charges in some sort of privileged high school. A Catholic version of Eton College, those graduating from Belén went straight to university to become mostly lawyers and physicians and hence to the better jobs in their professions. One can safely say that Castro won his best battles in the playing fields of Belén: baseball, basketball, boxing under the (modified) motto of the *Societa Jesu:* 'Ad Majorem *Mea* Gloriam'.

The cannon-ball that struck down Ignatius was for Fidel Castro the ball of fire of university politics. He realized, like the first Jesuit, that 'education and companions were required to execute' his plans for his greater glory. He even declared openly at the University that his greatest ambition was 'to have a line about me in Cuban history'. In the quotations above, where St Ignatius said God, read History.

The university was not his first school but it was his first political education – and his first failure. A public fiasco in fact. It should have been a lesson to him but Castro was too proud to learn from his *fracaso* – in Cuba an extreme form of failure. He would never learn that all pride will have a fall. He tried to cover it up with ambition but the cruel boy became a crueller man and armed himself with a gun to try to snatch ballots with bullets. But he not only failed to be elected president of the students' federation, he wasn't elected even as the leader of his college. Another kind of Jesuit, the Communist candidate, defeated him. This queer fellow would become, when Castro seized power in 1959, his minister for propaganda, a Cuban Goebbels. Small, cunning and a sedulous ape for those in power, he is called Alfredo Guevara. After defeating Castro he tried many times to win him for the Communist cause. He was attracted to the big, uncouth peasant and tried to be his political Pygmalion. You see, Castro didn't know his ABC of politics then. But, tired of the Communist entreaties, he rebuffed Guevara: 'Listen, Alfredo,' he said, 'I'll be a Communist the day I could be Stalin.'

Law School had been his university but the young Castro refused to chew the cud and joined an association called UIR, the Union for Insurrectionist Revolutionaries, that was in fact a wild bunch of political gangsters. Quirk maintains that Castro was always a solitary but the opposite is closer to the truth. He always tried to belong but on his own terms. What Castro wanted most was to become a member of a *grupo* and, once accepted, to try to dominate. All he wanted was to be the captain of the ship, any ship – a dinghy would do. But failure haunted him. Together with a black student leader, Justo Fuentes, he managed to hire an hour from a local radio station. Soon he got in trouble for denouncing real or imagined racketeers. Sometime later the station was stormed and Fuentes was shot dead. Because of illness Castro did not come to broadcast that fateful day. It was the first but not the last of his narrow escapes: out of harm's way and into failure.

In 1947 a motley political group of Cubans and Dominicans (not the friars but exiles from Trujillo's Dominican Republic) set out to liberate Trujillo's fiefdom. Considering the frightful mien of the liberators, I should have used inverted commas. The most relevant leader of them was Rolando Masferrer – a former Communist become anti-Communist, later a defender of democracy for President Prío, much later a henchman for General Batista who employed his *Tigres*, a Cuban version of the Haitian Ton-ton Macoutes. At the time he was the head of MSR (Social Revolutionary Movement) and mortal enemy of the UIR to which Castro still belonged. As a matter of fact Castro would be involved in the killing of Manolo Castro (no kin but a former full-back with the varsity team and later depicted by Hemingway as a hero, virtually penniless when he was shot), and everybody thought at the time that the other Castro did it. Be that as it may, there was no love lost between Masferrer and Castro and they were both heavily armed. A showdown was imminent and it had to be to the death for all the liberators were cramming a beach on a minuscule islet aptly called Key Confetti. The duel never came to a head and the duellists decided to decamp and then camp on either side of the key.

But as fate would have it, the expedition never reached Ciudad Trujillo, now Santo Domingo. President Grau, pressed by Trujillo, decided to intervene and the invasion of just one crowded small tramp steamer was aborted. The engines were stopped not far from the coast near Angel Castro's farm. Castro Junior, always a strong swimmer, jumped ship and sought asylum with his mother. Nor was this the only enterprise in which Fidel Castro embarked to land on failure. There was the time when he went to Bogotá to some student shindig with another student called Rafael del Pino from the students' federation. The trip was paid, surprise!, by Juan Domingo Perón. Bogotá was as quiet as an Indian but no sooner had Castro landed than there was an awful magnicide: the famous Colombian politician Jorge Eliecer Gaitán was assassinated. A riot ensued that made Bogotá into a nightmare city and Fidel Castro was creating havoc with a borrowed rifle. Nevertheless the mutiny never led into a feared *coup d'etat* and del Pino and Castro had to seek asylum in the Cuban embassy. Lo and behold, President Prío sent out a plane to retrieve the pair. Years later del Pino shot himself (it is not healthy to be that close to Castro) and Masferrer, a brilliant albeit an erratic journalist, left Cuba as Castro seized power. He lived in exile in Miami, where he was blown up with his car. His was the loudest exit.

The other important character in Quirk's biography of Castro and Cuba is not a Cuban. He came on the invader's boat with the queer name, *Granma*, that headed for trouble in the general direction of the island – and missed. This invader was not a soldier but a doctor. His name was Ernesto Guevara but he was called Che, which in Italian means What? He was with Castro since that fateful shipwreck but died alone in the wilds of Bolivia. It was no picnic. But in the Sierra Maestra it *was* a picnic. Castro ate the biggest Loyolan steak this side of Texas and Guevara imported maté herb from Argentina. They both smoked the best Havanas from Havana. Though an asthmatic Che caught the vice from Castro, as he learnt many traits from him: he dressed like him, walked with a martial gait like him and became a guerrilla leader like him. But Guevara was a shrewd man and was wary of Castro's monumental vanity. The late *comandante* Duque used to tell a story of a shooting match in Sierra Maestra that he witnessed. Castro and Guevara were engaged in a war against general tedium and were doing target practice against some dangerous empty beer bottles. Castro was hitting all the bottles but Guevara hit none. Later Duque asked Guevara, who was a sharpshooter famous all over the sierras. 'Why Che, you could do better than that!' Guevara answered with a sneer and a true confession: 'You want me to make our leader lose face? You should know better than *that!*'

Quirk writes that Castro later missed the quiet afternoons in the sierras. Those were the days! Idle days of rum and cigars. There was so much leisure that Fidel Castro was photographed lying in a hammock (the swinging bed the Cuban Indians gave the British navy and the world), wearing glasses to better read a book by Thornton Wilder, *The Ides of March*. He was not looking for style or historical accuracy in fiction but was on his perennial quest for anything relevant to the life of Julius Caesar or Alexander the Great, whose name was his *nom de guerre* in those palmy days.

Guevara was never really liked in Cuba, in power or when he left the island apparently chased by boredom or Fidel Castro, whichever came first. A born loser, his importance grew only when he lost. First he lost his job as a minister for the National Treasury, after being dismissed from La Cabaña fortress because he was no longer necessary: Castro yielding to international pressure, had stopped the executions of *batistianos*. There is a story on how Guevara became a minister. At one of the first meetings of his cabinet Castro asked who among them was an economist. Guevara raised his hand and Castro swore him in as the treasurer of the Republic. When the meeting was over, a surprised Castro came to ask Guevara: 'Che, I didn't know you were an economist.' 'That,' said Guevara, 'I'm not.' 'Then,' Fidel wondered, 'why did you raise your hand when I was looking for an economist?' 'An *economist?*' said Guevara. 'I thought you were looking for a Communist.'

Like most Argentines, Guevara was a petulant man playing the role of a dour delegate of Castro. He wanted to be taken for an avenging Engels but the only Cubans he knew were the men in his escort plus the Castro brothers. Once, at the very beginning, he went on television to be interviewed by Germán Pinelli, the best-loved compere on Havana's television. 'Good, Che—' started Pinelli and Guevara stopped him for good: 'I'm Che to my men and friends. To you I am *Comandante* Guevara.' This was not suffered gladly by the Cubans, who already considered him trigger-happy when he was at La Cabaña. On top of that as Treasurer he issued a new series of bank notes – and he signed his name 'Che'. This was considered disrespectful by the public. As elsewhere, the bank notes bore the venerated images of Cuban patriots and the one-peso bill had none other than José Martí, also known as *El Apóstol*. It was meant to be funny but it was not.

But Guevara had read more books than Fidel and Raúl put together – which was not an exploit. The Raúl Castro I met early in 1959 was recently married to Vilma Espín, a Vassar girl who came from an incredibly wealthy family related to Bacardi, the rum-makers. There were no books in their apartment and Raúl's only claim to fame was that he could take apart a Walther pistol and put it back again in record time – blindfolded.

Years later when he was in search of his South American destiny, Guevara produced a bitter version of his fate. Meeting Carlos Franqui, the former editor-in-chief of *Revolución* newspaper, in Algiers, the last leg of his political wanderings, he confessed that his ties to Castro had been like a failed marriage you cannot dissolve. 'It's as difficult,' he avowed, 'to live with Fidel as to run away from him.' It was a marriage of inconvenience.

Guevara was severely critical of Castro's policies but very conscious of his many failures. He was however very different from Castro. Not a man of cant but of Marx and just the opposite of an opportunist. In a way Guevara was Trotsky to Castro's Stalin. He left behind a philosophy of sorts embodied by a vision of the revolutionary as a New Man. Castro disowned Guevara's socialist dream but when he died he adopted the policy of the New Man as a creation of his. The New Man of course won't be found anywhere in Cuba today. Instead Cuban youth has an obsession called also New Man – not an ideology but a pair of jeans.

Guevara never suffered, like Raúl, Vilma *et al.*, from Castroenteritis. For instance, he was a gourmet who had French wines with his meals. He left his first Argentine wife and took another, a Cuban beauty. He adopted all the Cubans as his for a while, but he never paid any attention to his own children.

Che, like Trotsky, advocated permanent revolution. But loving humanity, an abstract idea, he forgot all about people. He believed in the New Man but not in human beings, new or old. His cherished dream was a Third World nightmare. 'How bright and wonderful,' he mused, 'the history of the peoples would be if two, three, many Vietnams appeared on the face of the earth.' But he did not stop there: 'with their daily quota of death, tragedy and heroism.' One man's myth is another man's prison. Guevara was a cruel man – with himself as with others. That, of course, is called sado-masochism.

Che Guevara's expedition to Bolivia was a complete disaster that ended with his life, the liberator killed by the Indians he came to liberate. What happened? What went wrong? Who failed who? Guevara did what any other movie star would have done. He wrote his press releases in the form of a book, *Guerrilla War*, about a puny guerrilla in a war that never was – it was only a series of skirmishes with an army, Batista's, that never really fought back.

When he died in that Bolivian ambush Guevara, *Comandante* Ernesto Guevara, became El Che. The dead body, not unlike Lenin's, was embalmed into a modern myth: he made it to the popular posters that culminated in a movie filmed by the hated United States. Or at least in Hollywood, with Omar Sharif, an Egyptian, still with a gap between his front teeth, who quarrelled constantly with Jack Palance, a Polish Fidel Castro. The epitaph came in neon and Che Guevara was the name of a *boutique* in Swinging London. *Sic transit* the man who was called Che only by his friends.

Enter the third man, General Fulgencio Batista y Zaldívar. But before he does one must admit that Cubans live in sunny geography and darkest history. Batista, unlike Castro, was born in direst poverty. His grandmother was a slave, his mother very black. But he wanted to be called *Jefe Indio*, the Indian Chief, and sometimes *El Hombre*. He was produced in Banes, a backward zone of Oriente province not very far from Birán, the Castros' cradle. Legend has it that Batista was a cane cutter in Angel Castro's farm. From cane cutting he went to become a professional soldier of the lowest rank. When he learnt speedwriting all by himself he was promoted to sergeant. As a stenographer he came to be present at the trials of the military brass Dictator Machado left behind after he flew to the USA. Batista learnt all about his former superiors and in the confusion of a god who abandons his believers Batista was able to stage his first *coup d'état* in 1933. Fidel Castro was only seven at the time and one can dream of Sergeant Batista, a friend of Angel's now, sitting the boy Fidelito on his lap, the boy prone to dream all our nightmares! The rest is a mixture of history and infamy that Borges never wrote into his *Historia Universal de la Infamia*.

But there is a but. Batista, the opposite of Castro, played a game of success when he, unlike Machado, came back to power with another coup in March 1952. It was a bloodless affair, a walk on the safe side as it were. He walked his way into the Columbia Military Camp, made invisible, he claimed, by an Indian magical mystery mist called the 'Light of Yara', some sort of Cuban aurora borealis, and the general came back at dawn. You see, Batista believed that he was under the protection of pre-Columbian Indian deities. Instead of being killed when the Presidential Palace was stormed in 1957 he escaped by the skin of his strong teeth. Finally, when he left the Palace, the presidency and the country for good, he did it in an orderly fashion, under the cloak of the longest night of the year: 31 December 1958. Most of his henchmen (and not a few hangmen) and his closest minions escaped with him heading south by southeast, flying over Oriente. The operation was so smooth that the populace didn't hear of the news of the night before until late next morning. Operation Goodbye was carried out in secrecy and stealth and Batista and his *entourage* flew to the Dominican Republic – to become a hostage of yet another Caribbean dictator, Rafael Leonidas Trujillo. He subjected Batista to ransom for a million dollars each day he was his golden guest. It was an *exile doré* – for Trujillo. As to Batista he dressed as usual in a one hundred per cent linen suit made to measure and he wore his Panama hat even indoors and had plenty of handkerchiefs to wipe his hands, his palms greased by so many years of graft and foreign grief.

Batista came to power to commit grand larceny protected by the law of the land. He was a crook and like a burglar caught in the act he killed because he had to. He was not averse to bribing the police, silencing witnesses and killing the opposition, but he let his minions spill the enemy blood. He was an extremely successful thief. When he died in exile the poor cane cutter from Banes was among the world's wealthiest men. Death came to him in a Cuban way but in sunny Spain, where the rich live when they become lizards. But it was as hot as any other part of the peninsula that day. Batista lunched on his favourite meal: black beans and rice and roasted pork with a side dish of fried plantain. He always had a big appetite and that day he had a second helping. Then he retired to his room for a nap but forgot to tell his butler to wake him up at five in the afternoon. He never woke up. The general died with his socks on.

Fidel Castro did not win the war because, simply, there never was a war. Batista's army did not surrender or collapse. (It was in fact not Batista's but Dad's Army.) Castro's men at their best were no more than 1,000 badly armed guerrillas. The regular army was some 30,000 troops. The guerrillas, being guerrillas, never engaged in anything you could call a battle. The débâcle affected only one man, the President who was the Chief of the Armed Forces, the so-called Indian Chief: Batista ran away leaving the army and its General Staff to fend for themselves.

Paradoxically without Batista there would never be any Fidel Castro. But Batista in power was despised and not always for political reasons. He had ensnared some big names in Cuban society to his military bandwagon, but, another paradox, for a name in the Havana Debrett to be associated with him was not the done thing. Batista was blackballed because he was, well, black. Orestes Ferrara, a viper and a wit, then Batista's ambassador in Rome, was questioned by Count Ciano, Mussolini's son-in-law and Foreign Minister. He asked Ferrara, who was Italian too: 'They tell me that Batista looks black.' Ferrara feigned surprise. 'On the contrary,' he said. 'He looks white.'

Almost fifty years later a Hollywood director had an Italian film producer, Valerio Riva, over for dinner. Talking about that disaster of a movie called *Havana*, Riva wanted to know why the picture had depicted Batista as blond as Robert Redford. 'Of course you know Batista was black.' His host almost choked. 'Bah-Bah, Batista – *black?*' 'Not only that. He was not your average nincompoop. He had written three books.' The director went from surprise directly to chagrin: 'Why is it that people tell me these things only when it's too late?' By then the movie, like dinner, was over. Otherwise he could have quoted a dirty ditty heard in real Havana circa 1958:

> Long live Cuba!
> Long live Fidel!
> Who will come down from his tower
> to kill the nigger in power!

The bitter truth is that Batista's army consisted almost entirely of blacks. Especially the rookies conscripted to fight Castro's guerrillas in 1958. Because they were so young they were called *casquitos* – toy helmets.

The vacuum of power created with the sudden departure of Batista was such that Camilo Cienfuegos, one of the guerrilla leaders, left his home base in Las Villas province and seized Camp Columbia virtually all by himself. He arrived with some seventy-five men in Cuba's main military concentration. Inside the camp there were at least 20,000 troops. The confusion at the General Staff was such that I went to Camp Columbia with Carlos Franqui, virtually unknown at the time. Coming directly from Sierra Maestra he was bearded and wearing green-olive fatigues, and all the brass, made of *batistiano* colonels and lieutenant colonels, called him *comandante*. Though I was wearing a sports shirt and trousers, and despite the fact that I was small, thin and wore thick eyeglasses and was far from being impressive, they called me *comandante* too and saluted. They were not trying to be funny. They were ludicrously fearful of any young visitor.

In a few sentences Quirk conveys the mood of Havana that early morning of 1 January 1959. There were no crowds leaving the ballrooms at midnight to bask in the neon lights and drinking champagne from tulip glasses to celebrate the tumbling of a tyrant. As a matter of historical fact the 26th of July Movement had asked the population to boycott *las fiestas*, meaning Christmas Eve, Christmas and New Year's Eve. There were no crowds in the street, no riots, no mobs running amok – only the eerie silence first and then the disbelief that it was all over. Coppola in *Godfather 2* and Pollack in *Havana* spent reels of film and thousands, perhaps millions, of dollars in a reconstruction that was glittery, thunderous – and untrue. It was also bad fiction. Reared on the role of the masses in Soviet films, they couldn't believe that there was nobody that morning engaged in history in the making. The historical truth is that the People had nothing to do with Batista's downfall. It was all preordained by the gods. Or their nearest versions who inhabit the White House and the State Department. The wheels of history might run silent but never deep. Batista was the Cuban puppet and the puppeteer lived in Washington.

Failures were disguised as hopes that could lead only to fiascos: Castro has been leading the Cubans as the Pied Piper led his charge. The original Piper rid Hamelin of all the rats he could. When the bill he sent to the elders for doing his job was not met he led all the youths in town into destruction.

There have been more biographies of Fidel Castro than of any other Cuban leader, including José Martí, often invoked as a saint and a martyr. Not a lesser god but a lay prophet. This is not particular in Cuba. There have been more biographies of Hitler than of Bach, Beethoven, Goethe, Hegel and Nietzsche put together. But the similarities between Castro and Hitler are uncanny. Both were in fact bohemians. Castro even declared once, 'I must admit that I'm somewhat of a bohemian and disorderly by nature.' Both were dirty. Hitler vowed at the beginning of the war not to take off his uniform until the war ended. Castro has been all his life unwashed, dirty and smelly. In his university days he was called Grimeball. Both Hitler and Castro adopted a distinctive disguise to appear publicly.

Both the Führer and the Maximum Leader always wore military uniforms without having had a military career. Both were great actors who made respectively the PA systems and the television the tools of their rise to power. There are of course obvious differences. Hitler had an artistic temperament, Castro was merely a gypsy who couldn't sing, couldn't dance but he could talk. He has become an *hablanero*, the chatterbox of Havana. But he is not the child of the mountains, *montes parturient*, just the product of Cuban politics as originated in 1902 with independence from Spain and come to a head in 1952 with Batista's last *coup d'etat*. Batista was a direct descendant from the military leaders who came from the wars against Spain to become true warlords and govern the republic since its inception. Like Castro, he was not a true military leader and when they don their uniforms they look as if wearing a costume, ready for a masquerade or a mass meeting.

Bullock uses for Hitler a quotation from Aristotle that would fit Fidel Castro to a T for tyranny. 'Men do not become tyrants,' says Aristotle, 'in order to keep out the cold.' Or to keep out the heat. (We must remember that we are dealing with a tropical Führer.) Under Castro as under Hitler, 'the will of one man and one man alone is decisive.' Castro too is an extremely unreal person. After many meetings in which he will talk *at* you endlessly, your sole reaction is that he is not to be believed. You suffer an uncanny strangeness.

Of all Castro's schemes to get hold of power by violent means, there was one that seems like a cock-and-bull story but it rings true. Castro had no notion of what power was at the time but he knew where it resided and how to get it. He was a child prodigy of unlawful politics, the Mozart of *coups d'état*. Not yet twenty he conceived a plan to oust President Grau San Martín by staging some students' riots and going to the Presidential Palace to ask for a private audience. Then he would show the President the mob underneath the presidential balcony, give Dr Grau a shove and transform the push into a *putsch:* a neat copy of the legendary defenestrations in Prague! It was of course a tropical *praguerie*. The President, an insanely brave man, came onto the balcony – and nothing happened. The alleged magnicide suffered from vertigo.

The coup he attempted next was a bloody mess. Fidel Castro led a group of students without any military training to storm a well-known army barracks in Santiago de Cuba on July 1953. Most of the attackers got lost in a city they had never visited before. The result was a massacre by the frightened soldiers in which most of the assaulters died or were killed later in cold blood. The Castro brothers fled to the outskirts, where they were apprehended two days later. They saved their skin thanks to the archbishop of Santiago, a friend of Castro's father. As with President Grau, Castro always knew people in high places.

But not in Mexico. After serving only two years of his sentence of twenty-two, thanks to a pardon given him and his assaulters by Batista, they all fled to Mexico. Castro foolishly announced in Mexico City that he would invade Cuba within the year – that is 1956. Not even Hitler in jail in Munich was as reckless as that. The future invaders chose Mexican parks to ape drills and tell droll stories. The police took the invaders seriously and after discovering and seizing their arsenal, they all went to jail – including Castro of course. A Mexican soothsayer told Castro, 'November is here and the year is almost gone.' Released from jail Castro made haste with his troops and with a greater speed bought a yacht, then embarked all his men in a boat that barely loaded twenty. 'To Cuba!' he yelled to the skipper, who had never made the crossing. With heavy seas soon all the soldiers now sailors were seasick.

The storming of the Moncada barracks on 26 July 1953 was really the bungling that started at dawn. The landing of the *Granma*, as Che

Guevara would call it, was actually a shipwreck. Instead of the intended bay of Santiago, a swamp south of Sierra Maestra was what they hit. Soon the castaways were discovered by Batista's fighter planes and fighting soldiers. Soon Castro's force was either killed or wounded. Most of them, including the leaders, ran for their lives. Desperate straits not sylvan impulses led Castro to seek shelter in the mountains. But these high sierras were the last refuge of outlaws. Of the expeditionary force only fourteen were left (the magic of numbers made the historians reduce the survivors to twelve) but as soon as they were together Castro standing erect addressed them: 'The days of the dictator are numbered!' Later Guevara said that he thought they were being led by a madman.

But their refuge in the jungle-cum-brush was so deep-seated that everybody in Cuba, including Castro's followers in the cities and even Batista himself, though they had all been exterminated. Only an American journalist from the *New York Times*, the late Herbert Matthews, came with the newspaper's equivalent of the 'Message to García', delivered by an American scout to the Cuban general leading the *mambí* guerrillas circa 1898, to find in 1957 a talkative and duplicitous Castro who tricked him into believing that his scant and badly armed wild-looking bunch were in fact a regular army. Matthews found this guerrilla chief in search of an army intelligent, forceful and *simpatico*. If he found faults with Castro he didn't say and thus became the leader of all the American journalists who came in contact with this Potemkin in the jungle and later, much later, Cuba's variation of the strongman. It is only with the publishing of Quirk's book that the crooked record has been set straight.

At the time, writes Quirk, 'Castro's men suffered more from insect bites than from the harrassments of Batista's army'. More than a sanctuary the sierras were a sanatorium for the urban guerrillas suffering from tortoiseshell shock in their eyeglasses, but there was nothing wrong with their political sight. There were also visitors from the American outer space. They all came mostly from New York – asking the guerrillas to take them to their leader. One of them was Robert Taber, who, turned partisan, was later wounded during the Bay of Pigs mock-invasion. 'Taber like Matthews,' writes Quirk, 'believed what Castro wanted him to believe.' Quirk is always ironic about life in the sierras around the man who was then becoming the Maximum Leader, with capitals if you please. Castro in Sierra Maestra, not any small sierra for him, became a Captain Ahab crossed with Father Mapple in his pulpit. 'We are breaking our skulls here,' he wrote – and it is uncanny how many letters he could write in the bush and always find a punctual postman. In one letter to Celia Sánchez, who later became his secretary, jill for all purposes and even his mistress, he wrote about 'how to take care of such a large family'. During his invasion of Angola he claimed that he not only followed the lot of his men in Africa but gave battle orders by mail and even found a way to send sweets to the soldiers. But sweets were bad for him in the sierra and like Hitler he suffered from bad teeth. 'When are you going to send me a dentist?' he cried to Celia. But he was unmoved when about that time Frank País, his second in command left behind in Santiago, was ambushed and killed by the police. Obviously Castro's teeth caused more intimate pain than País' body in the morgue. He is a creature of such monstrous egoism that he makes other world leaders look like versions of Mother Teresa.

Quirk appears to have read everything that was printed in Cuba in the daily press and the magazines from the Batista era and later. Once he was in power, the same press that he would later suppress celebrated Castro as some sort of tropical Messiah. *Bohemia*, a magazine rabidly opposed to Batista, now printed without blushing things like, 'Fidel Castro, the invincible captain' or 'The man whose very name is a banner'. Its owner Miguel Angel Quevedo (who ended up as an exile and a suicide in Caracas) published a portrait of Castro in which he was a Jesus look-alike wearing a halo! Quevedo was not a sycophant but a fan. Meanwhile the press, radio and television applauded all, even the horror show-trials.

In one of them, set in Havana's main sports stadium, a Batista army colonel was tried in front of a packed audience. Even the defendant, who came from the sticks where he ruled like a local tyrant, claimed that it was like a Roman circus. It was not like a circus, it *was* a circus. Revolutionary justice also made mockery of the double jeopardy principle when forty pilots of Batista's army were tried, and found not guilty only for Castro himself to order that they be tried again – and found guilty. It is significant that President Urrutia, Fidel Castro and Dorticós, his second president when he deposed Urrutia, were all lawyers. Dorticós was a practicing professional and Urrutia was formerly a judge. When he was tried, after the murderous assault of the Moncada barracks, revolutionary justice, says Quirk, 'showed none of the leniency accorded to Fidel Castro.' Now in that same Santiago, Raúl Castro executed more than five hundred men without a trial. Thus Raúl began to play quite soon his infamous role, being Mr Hyde to his brother.

Castro, now a prime minister without a fixed abode, took personal charge of each new venture – and the old ones to boot. 'No matter was too small, no site too remote,' writes Quirk. He even found time to be prosecutor in the case of the army against *comandante* Huber Matos, one of the regional chiefs now accused of rebellion. When Castro indicted Matos he claimed not to be a man of 'rancor or base passions'. Immediately afterward he addressed the judges selected by him: 'If this court fails to find the defendant guilty, history will condemn you.' History or her nearest agent.

Then, all of a sudden the Russians were coming. When they came they found that Cuba was not what they thought. Said Anastas Mikoyan, the first Russian to come: 'If this is an underdeveloped country' – and then being cautious Canastas, as they christened him in Havana, said no more. The rest of the Russian contingent found that 'Havana was far more modern and with more conveniences than Moscow,' says Quirk. It was difficult for the Russians to see Cuba as a backward country – and they proceeded to buy all the McGregor shirts, chino pants, tailored jackets and first-class shoes they could find. Like the soldier ants Charlton Heston fought with water and fire, the invaders stripped the city clean. 'Castro had exchanged,' writes Quirk, 'one kind of dependency for another.' Cubans claimed at the time: 'He swapped a cow for a goat.' Castro, 'whose whims passed for administration', governed without a constitution and without laws. It was a government of outlaws who appointed all the judges and lawyers – actually hanging judges. On a continental and even international stage, as the UN, Castro not only supported or applauded the Russians, he even 'leaped to his feet,' said Quirk, 'like a cheerleader'. He had progressed from major to majorette of the Russian team.

In the meantime he had 'made himself an expert on everything', a real Zelig travelling in history as in time with the greatest of ease. There is a story from the early days in which Castro sent people to sample the opinion of the marginalized in Cuban society. They were gathered in an enormous room facing a TV set as the *Comandante en jefe* started to talk in Havana. He talked, literally, about everything. From the United States to the United Nations and then about pastures, milk cows and potent bulls, from stallions to charcoal as national fuel bravely made by the heroic charcoal burners of the swamps, etc., etc. When Castro's speech was over – many hours later – the samplers tried to find out what the audience thought of the speech. Everybody agreed that it was outstanding. Finally they talked to a charcoal burner from the swamps. He agreed with the rest of the audience. 'Fidel knows about everything,' said the swamp dweller. 'He's a genius! Of course he doesn't know a word about charcoal.'

That's how he came to be known as the costliest student of agronomy in the world. He never graduated but in his day as a bogus expert Castro had more than one encounter with the real McCoy. One was a French specialist on grass who was a crank like most agronomists, starting with Trofim Lysenko, Stalin's favourite crank. His name was André Voisin. Castro invited him to Cuba and treated him like a *bon voisin*, a good neighbour – but he became too much for Castro. The very first night of his arrival, Castro invited the old agronomist, who was only a Frenchman with a jet lag, to a Cuban dinner. After dinner, the atmosphere leaden with speeches and spirits, the Maximum Leader invited the frail Frenchman to have some cheese as he produced what looked like Camembert. Then ensued a scene out of Chaplin's *The Great Dictator*. 'What do you think of it?' asked Castro eagerly. 'Of what?' asked Voisin somewhat dizzy. 'Why, the cheese!' 'Not bad', said Voisin. 'Not bad!' cried Castro. 'Try some more.' 'I will,' said Voisin, conciliatory, and he did. 'Not too bad.' 'That's *Cuban* Camembert!' 'Yes,' said Voisin, 'it's Cuban Camembert but in the French style.' Castro was outraged. 'You must agree that mine is better.' The Frenchman did something that made a Socratic sage of him. He dared to take a cigar from Castro's breast pocket and said: 'Is there a better cigar in the world than this?' Some of the guests laughed but not Castro. 'My cheese,' said Voisin finally, 'and your cigar have centuries of experience behind them.' End of the Great Cuban Camembert Contest. Two weeks after eating Castro's own Camembert André Voisin died in Havana.

Castro soon forgot all about that fateful dinner with the killing Camembert and he invited yet another French agronomist, René Dumont. To whom he announced his grandest (and craziest) agricultural plan ever: to desiccate the Ciénaga de Zapata, the landing site of the Bay of Pigs invasion. 'It is the biggest swamp in the Caribbean,' claimed Castro. Dumont was not impressed. Why this dehydration project? Cuba is not Holland. 'To have more arable land of course!' said Castro the enthusiast. 'You don't need more land than you have now.' Dumont fell from grace instantly and some time later Castro called him an agent of the CIA.

It was about this time that Castro gave *his* version of the New Man according to Guevara. He 'would be an engineer, an agronomist, a manure expert': a superman of the soul and soil. To try to attain this goal Castro invited to Cuba two English agricultural scientists. No more meddling French gardeners! They were Thomas R. Preston and Malcolm B. Willis. They came, they saw, they suffered the outrageous schemes of an obvious madman – and they left. Willis reached a conclusion on which many Cubans agreed. 'He suggested,' says Quirk, 'that the only hope for Cuba was the assassination of Castro.'

Nevertheless Fidel Castro went on swamping the land with slogans concocted by this Maximum Publicist. See some samples: 'Join the War Against All Weeds', 'Land or Death!' To bigger billboards urging all Cubans to the joys of 'Artificial Insemination – Not One Cow Left Barren!' It was a campaign that lasted two generations of Cubans. Not two years ago he exhorted all good men and true to do battle for the potato. 'This is a battle we must win,' he said on the May Day parade. 'We will win the battle for the potato.' It was more Groucho than Karl: 'Potatoes of the country, unite! You have nothing to lose but your roots!' Potatory.

Castro, still the best vet, owned 'the most excellent cows in the world'. He also owned the best bulls. One bull he called almost Blue Velvet he claimed could inseminate, in a year, '15,000 cows'. Another bull 'was even more potent'. This Minotaur, the bull not of King Minos but of King Midas, 'produced 22,000 doses in a twelve-month period'. But he died prematurely – worn out by too many masturbations. Castro had in Cuba the world's largest private farm. But like his prize bull too many ejaculations brought him disrespect. This never happened before. In his heyday his voice, though thin, was the word of God. This was, no doubt about it, the beginning of the end.

The idea of history has in fact proven more harmful than the practice of religion. For Fidel Castro history became a surrogate of religion. Educated by the Jesuits he went to university with a sense of mission and he tried to rape his alma mater in a missionary position. He failed. He was never elected to president of the student federation. He tried to do the same with the Republic and unfortunately he succeeded – without being elected. Though he had a little help from his enemies. That includes many Cubans but also many Americans, especially President Kennedy, who gave the green light to an old Eisenhower war plan. Both were trying to live again their days of glory at war. Instead they gave Castro his only lasting victory.

For the first and not the last time the Russians came to his rescue. The invaders, almost all amateur soldiers, were less than 1,500 troops. The moment Castro knew that the invasion was reduced to one single spot (an absurd reduction made no doubt by misfortune: Kennedy or his men chose that fateful swamp Ciénaga de Zapata to stage a parody of the D-Day landing) Castro sent over his best professional soldier. Not Che Guevara but a man who had served Batista well: he was capable of sudden and opposite loyalties. Castro had an expert tactician on his side and the invaders were stranded in a swamp. Castro won, we know that. He had not only won but kept the victor's glory all for himself.

After the battle there was an exchange between Castro and his faithful camp follower, she who killed herself many years later out of too many lost illusions. She was Haydée Santamaría and she often told this story of her talking to the Maximum Leader about the Bay of Pigs victory or fiasco, according to who won and who lost:

YEYE: What would you've done, Fidel, if the Soviet Union did not exist?

FIDEL (he always uses the majestical plural): We would have played ball with our bourgeoisie. For ten years if needed.

YEYE (with starry eyes): You're a genius, Fidel, you know that?

The answer belongs to Bullock writing about Hitler: 'His mastery of the irrational factors in politics, his insight into the weaknesses of his opponents, his gift for simplification, his sense of timing, his willingness to take risks. An opportunist entirely without principles, he showed considerable persistency and an astonishing power of will in pursuing his aims. Cynical and calculating in the exploitation of his histrionic gifts, he retained an unshaken belief in his historic role and himself as a creature of destiny.'

Castro has not promised like Hitler the Millennium but he came near enough: *pangola* fields forever. Cuba will produce more milk than Holland, *zebu* bulls will be crossbred with Dutch cows, Havana will make more cars than Detroit, there will be new trains all air-conditioned to crisscross the island, a large merchant and fishing fleet, eggs will be free. You name it, he will dream it and the dreams will be real real soon. He even dreamt the nightmare of crossing German shepherd dogs with wolves! The populace calls him not *comandante* but *El Delirante*, the delirious madman. Fidel's fever went from afflatus to flatulence. Suffering from aerophagia he is constantly swallowing air. To relieve himself he now burps and belches in public.

In *White Heat* James Cagney, playing a mad gangster at the end of his tether, has climbed on top of a butane balloon armed with a gun. He dares the lawman to take him alive for he is ready to blow himself up and his world, the exploding tank. Edmond O'Brien, a lawman, pumps lead into Cagney with his rifle. But Cagney is still alive, still defiant. Asks O'Brien, 'What's holding him up?'

After ruining his country, making life a misery for his countrymen, failing in all his enterprises from holy-milk cows to invading Africa with 300,000 men and bringing some of them back home (the rest just died for an unknown cause), forcing a million and a half Cubans to go into exile, thousands to drown while trying to escape – and much, much more mischief – why is he in power? I think I can tell you.

Besides the national police and the DTI (Technical Department for

Investigations), the Intelligence and Counter Intelligence Services, the State Security, trained by the East German Stasi, and the paramilitary police *Brigadas de Acción Rápida* (Rapid Action Brigades), a true fascist faction, Castro has the *Comités para la Defensa de la Revolución* (Committees for the Defence of the Revolution), a Cuban copycat of a totalitarian concept. 'Their principal function,' writes Quirk, 'is to serve as agents of surveillance . . . under the direct supervision of the Ministry of the Interior, the Intelligence and Counter Intelligence Services.' The CDR 'deals with suspected and *potential* enemies' of the regime. This evil apparatus, like the guillotine, was created by the Jacobins during the Terror. It has survived in France to this day as that Parisian snooper, the *concierge*. Hitler adopted (and readapted) it as the *Blockwart*, the Nazi Party's political watchdog. Next to the Gestapo they were the most feared and loathed police corps in Germany. That this is a political cancer was proven by its Cuban counterpart. When *Fidel Castro* was being written there were 2,200 members of the CDRs. Last month its Overseer General (of all names) Batista announced proudly, 'We are now 7,602,000 strong.' A man for exact figures the Overseer General produced his pocket calculator (batteries included) to add: 'That's 89.8 percent of the population.'

Just after being decorated as a national hero General Arnaldo Ochoa saw what Cuba had become during his African years. He went to a dinner party innocent enough. As the house was bugged, probably by the CDR, General Ochoa expressed one single opinion that became a *faux pas*. 'Things are going bad,' he said. 'We must do something about it.' Fidel and Raúl Castro, already worried by Ochoa's popularity in the army ranks, apprehended Ochoa. They accused him of smuggling cocaine from Colombia (remember that Ochoa was in Africa most of the time), an accusation that the FBI has previously made against Raúl Castro. Fidel Castro ordered the trials to be taped, edited and then shown on television. With Raúl as an emcee who quipped, drunk as usual: 'Who says you cannot speak freely in Cuba? I'm here and I'm talking freely, am I not?' There was a prosecutor who could read the cruel scenario without moving his lips and an obviously drugged Ochoa first appeared in the dock in his army general uniform and later was demoted to wearing a ridiculous sports outfit that did not fit. Ochoa, like Bukharin far away and long ago, confessed to all crimes – after the prosecutor voiced them. It was a tropical version of the Moscow Trials of the Thirties, but for Ochoa the Cuban version was real enough. The verdict, as usual, came before the arrest. Ochoa was shot not by a firing squad but with a bullet behind his head. In true Stalinist fashion he was buried in an unmarked grave.

Fidel Castro had the first and last word about the trials: 'All criticism is opposition, all opposition is counterrevolutionary.' In that same speech he said something that could be his famous last phrase: 'Long live rigidity.' But he is just the opposite of a rigid man. He is a crude opportunist and has always been and this biography proves it. One must not forget that the dreams of liberty can create monsters too. Fidel Castro 'has become a caricature of himself', writes Robert Quirk. What is worse, 'he has become irrelevant: he has stayed too long'. History hasn't absolved him, history has left him behind. He has become, in fact, prehistorical.

This book could very well become the Maximum Leader's tombstone. If so his epitaph would be Hamlet's valediction. Because of his obsessive lust for power the inscription will read: this man 'shall in the general censure take corruption/from that particular fault: the dram of evil'.

The cover though portrays a much younger man. Gone as if vanished by a flattering brush are the actual grey beard, the bushy eyebrows, the snowed-on temples, the receding hairline and the mien of a demented prophet. He looks in this photograph like an actor – and that is what he is. Perhaps the world's greatest actor trying to play King Lear but playing instead the demented usurper Macbeth. But 'there is no denying the distressing fact that millions loved him and venerated him as a demi-god'. Naive Herbert Matthews writing about Castro? No, knowing Arthur Koestler talking of Hitler. But Fidel Castro is not a demi-god but a demagogue playing the liberator. In Cuba dreams are the only private property. On the other hand nightmares are all nationalized.

(November 1993)

PARALLAX LIVES

All biography constantly aspires towards the
condition of history.

Two Wrote Together

There are no lives more unlike (and yet more alike) than those of José Lezama Lima and Virgilio Piñera. They were born not far apart in time (Lezama in 1910, Piñera in 1912) and almost in the same space (one in Havana and the other in Cárdenas, sixty miles from Havana) and the two died in Havana – Lezama in 1976, Piñera in 1979. Virgilio was born in Matanzas Province but after a disturbed childhood and an ambulant adolescence (he hated it to be called peripatetic), he came to set himself up in Havana, our ancient Rome, while Lezama had fixed (perhaps the verb that best suited him: all is a fixed idea in Lezama) on the capital from the moment of his birth on. The two were technicians' sons. Lezama's father was an army colonel and a military engineer, Virgilio's a land surveyor. But while Lezama, an only son, lost his father as a child, Virgilio, one of several children, saw his father become a very old man who, no wonder, suffered from ambulatory mania. Lezama never recovered from his father's death, Virgilio saw death as a liberator of his father, blind and senile. The two were precocious writers. But Lezama graduated as a lawyer, while Virgilio never completed his education (Philosophy and Letters probably) and between the two there were always interposed the aloofness that Lezama maintained almost until his death and the accessibility of Virgilio, not to mention his modesty (which hid an enormous intimate immodesty), his scorn for respect and his defiance of social conventions.

Very few people (perhaps only his mother and his sisters, who called him Joseíto) called Lezama by a name other than Lezama, if they knew him, or Lezama Lima from afar – but there were some who called him Maestro without Lezama's disowning this form of address. While Virgilio Piñera was Virgilio to all his friends and even to mere acquaintances and was Piñera only to his enemies. Virgilio would have dispatched with one of his solid sallies anyone who addressed him as maestro – even in lower case. Physically they could never be confused. Lezama was enormous: a tall fat man like Chesterton, Catholic like Chesterton, authors of allegories both. Virgilio was rather short, always thin and sometimes, at the beginning and the end of his life, flirted with cachexia. He was an agnostic as well. To accentuate the opposite he wrote a play, *The Thin Man and the Fat Man*, in which the Fat Man is a voracious glutton who makes references in passing to a Master, a gourmet: the two gluttonous faces of Lezama, who gorged himself on foods that he classed as exquisite. The Thin Man, like Virgilio, is a galling, gaunt, famished man locked up with the Fat Man in an isolated enclosure. He ends up, premonitorily, killing the Fat Man, devouring him whole (intellectual cannibalism?) and wearing his clothes – which make him into what he always wanted to be, the Fat Man. Inside every thin man there's a fat man fighting to get out.

The two, Virgilio and Lezama, were profoundly Cuban, from Havana rather, and both had connections with the most *criollo* of Cuban cities, Camagüey: where Virgilio had lived as a child, where Lezama's father was from. Their early first books (both poetry collections) were both dedicated to Greek themes: Lezama, *The Death of Narcissus* (1937), Virgilio, *The Furies* (1941), with a noticeably different approach in each case. Lezama was already baroque and obscure, while Virgilio showed himself to be colloquial, almost streetwise. But although Virgilio's poetry is notable (above all his third book, *Up Goes the Island*, 1943), there is in it not a single line with the imperishable beauty of 'Thus the mirror found out quietly, thus wingless Narcissus at rip tide took off in flight' and much less some of the strange perfection of the poems in *Enemy Hearsay*, which Lezama published back in 1941. In *Up Goes the Island* Virgilio showed himself to be a poet of a considerable Cuban voice, although some accused him, futilely, of copying Aimé Cesaire. But around that time, before that time, Lezama composed poems that are among the most beautiful written in Spanish this century. Nevertheless there is a line by Virgilio, 'You had a big foot and a crooked heel', memorable for its humour at once cruel and melancholic, when you know that shoe, heel and foot belong to a Cuban character, a humble Havana lady called Bow-legged Chencha.

It was inevitable that Lezama and Virgilio would meet in sharing, it was also predictable that they would separate in violence. Virgilio was quarrelsome, Lezama solid – but the two were vulnerable in more than one sense. Both homosexual, their sexual interests were markedly different: this was visible even in their respective outfits. Lezama invariably wore a jacket and tie and if he didn't have a waistcoat on he seemed to carry one, visible in its constant invisibility. (A facetious greeting of Lezama was often: 'Look at me now in my Mozartean waistcoat over my Wagnerian belly.'). Virgilio always wore cheap trousers and short-sleeved sports shirts (perhaps out of necessity, surely by choice) and if he ever had a suit, he never used it. (I don't even remember him wearing a suit in Paris, in the hostile spring of 1965, although he was surely dressed in a coat and a raincoat against the weather and against habit.) Lezama was addicted to livid languid literary ephebes: he was a lover of forms. Virgilio preferred rough, rude, rentmen of the plebe (bus drivers, doormen, night watchmen, assorted bums and maybe a soldier on leave), all of whom he paid their stipend religiously – in spite of his poverty. There were no loves lost for Virgilio. Only sexual action, sudden sodomy: appetizing young love for sale – and what it cost. At times Virgilio withheld or pretended to withhold the ritual payment after the intercourse. He confessed that nothing gave him more pleasure than the *frisson nouveau* produced by the anger of the rentboy who was still unpaid – 'None of that lover boy stuff, kid,' revealed Virgilio. 'Really a mean bugger' – and seeing himself on the verge of getting a beating for pretending that he wouldn't let loose the rusty coins in his lusty hands.

Two incidents reveal the sexual divergencies of the two poets. But first I must say that Virgilio detested the idea of having commerce – the word was never more adequate – of a carnal kind with anyone even slightly in contact with culture. One day, when an imminent lover confessed to him *in passim* that he liked books, Virgilio angrily abandoned the room, still half-dressed, and disappeared to the amazement of his lover-to-be. 'Real men don't read books,' he explained. 'Literature is faggotry and for a faggot, me, myself and I.'

On one extra-literary occasion Virgilio picked up a formidable black in Parque Central. Together they went to a foul *posada* on Calle Amargura (no symbols here though it means Bitter Street) and stepped into the building and the room. Virgilio was going through one of his many money crises and was eating badly and little and was thinner than usual – almost a metaphysical poet. Behind closed doors he took his clothes off as discreetly as possible in bed. He lowered the sheet to cover his naked bones as quick as he could. The taxi lover ('A turgid Turk'), suspecting that something was afoot with that disrobing more prudent than prurient, came to the bed still dressed and with a flick of his powerful wrist pulled the sheet off Virgilio – to uncover the campy concentration camp body of the eponymous writer.

The bugger by contract discharged words of filth ('He covered my naked body with curses,' recounted Virgilio, master of roguish matters), insults, and improprieties: 'A skeleton! A skeleton fag! A shitty skeleton!' – outrageously uttered by the not-yet lover before the naked vision, more a

Buchenwald survivor than a Botticelli Venus. Right away the taxi turned truck, offended for having been presented with bare bones when he was expecting propitious buttocks, an agreeable ass, glutei maximi, took off his belt and attacked Virgilio with bestial, savage lashings – the slave now a master. Finally, before leaving, a black Nemesis, he searched in the pockets of the uselessly discarded pants and left Virgilio punished and without a penny – but happy in his coitus without a penis.

These heroic erotic adventures were not for Lezama, who would consider them sordid and even vulgar. The opposite of Virgilio, Lezama was an active homosexual, an absurd distinction for what another Cuban writer, Calvert Casey, called the 'modern school', which meant another route of deviations for what can be considered the 'old school'. Both Virgilio and Lezama abhorred mutual fellatio and the 'cross of swords'. But the same militancy marked differences of appearance and of public conduct. Virgilio was very effeminate and shy. A valiant virility made Lezama what the comic opera character Sopeira, a gallant Galician, used to call a 'Spanish gentleman'. Lezama was a Cuban gentleman. Even an identical vice separated them. The two of them smoked a lot, but while Virgilio, he of a Dantesque profile, would light one cigarette after another and would inhale them with a languid abandon that would seem strange to Marlene Dietrich, Lezama, he of the rough face, would bite a cigar like a bullet. That along with his rotund humanity made him a dark version of Sydney Greenstreet, the actor who in the forties was the incarnation of menacing girth, a villainous bon vivant, in contrast to the sinister although equally obese evil of Laird Cregar. Often Cregar and Greenstreet seemed passive pederasts. Lezama never looked that way. Like in the joke of the Havana wag who called Lezama's literary review *No One Seemed to Be* – 'and all of them were'.

Among Lezama's 'adventures in stealth' is his encounter with the beau as a scribe whom the years would transform into an apprentice cultural commissar and whom a brief spell of fame, the ephebe as ephemera, as a revolutionary novelist (according to certain Cuban critics) granted a renown that he did not deserve. I am not going to name him but I am going to tell one of his first sullied sallies. This novelist as a young man (already at that time he was ambitious and ambiguous) adulatingly approached Lezama, who fell captive of his beauty. It's true that he was false but he was beautiful. Tall, slender, fair, with amazingly blue eyes, and Lezama, the reverse of Virgilio, always allowed himself to be admired by good-looking youths – perhaps looking at them as possible lovers or as future disciples. One day Lezama brought his literary find to a get-together on the fruit farm of a literary Maecenas, then a powerful journalist, energetic and aggressive and rich and not the poor peaceful exile that he is today. He was a former contributor to *Orígenes* and a sponsor of Lezama. It would appear that the proud poet did not need, in Cuba, a sugar daddy. But he was always at their whim and had countless ones.

In the reunion the writer, the ephebe or whatever he was then, sat at Lezama's feet, attentive to the robust rumour of the poet. When they were alone, leaning against the friendly knees of Lezama, the boy said to him: 'What pretty hands you have, Maestro!' Lezama, who never had anything pretty, understood that the praise of his thick black pudding fingers was meant as an advance – and decided to invite his fawning friend to take a walk through the airy orchard. In a recondite nook Lezama tried (as the writer recounted) to give him a kiss on the lips. The boy felt a sudden irresistible revulsion. (It is possible that it happened like this but it was an intimate occurrence anyway.)

After that this ephemeral ephebe set himself up to publish a short-lived libel where he printed a story called 'The Fat Man'. He related the incident, adding to his physical revulsion quite a bit of literary nausea (existentialism was all the rage then) and although he didn't name names the description of Lezama was letter perfect. (Not content with the publication the libellist made sure to slip a copy under Lezama's door.) Maybe Lezama felt wounded but his cries were as always literary. Knowing that the infamous ephebe was living now in the home of a painter as Chinese as he was black and as talented as he was deviant, he published in *Orígenes* the first instalment of a novel in code, a true *roman à Klee*, where he described how a blond pubescent creature was living with a Malay painter. By night from the underbelly of the Asiatic painter there hung out a worm that groped on the almost albino body of the host – to insert itself obscenely.

Maybe both stories are apocryphal but what remains today is the bad writing of 'The Fat Man' contrasted with the powerful prose of the tale of the Malay painter, his burrowing worm and the nestling ephebe turned nubile by night. From that particular inferno *Paradiso* rose to the public.

The only time the pederast ways of Lezama and Virgilio met was on the corner, at once pious and perverse, of the Callejón del Chorro. There, on one side is the baroque Cathedral and on the other stood at that time a plush male bordello notorious though supposed secret. Nobody knows what Virgilio was doing in those parts. As always, he didn't have a cent and he wasn't interested in pretty boys but rather in mature, dominant men, the more lower-class the better. He was escorted by the composer Natalio

Galán, rich in rhythms but poor as a brothel's butter. (It was he who told, much better than I, this story.)

Galán was then doing research for a novelist turned musicologist, whose future fame would cover up how cheap he was. Natalio Galán was making a pittance for unearthing old scores – discoveries that would be attributed to the author and not to the investigator. In the noontime sun and standing on that corner at once saintly and *non sancta* (Virgilio was possibly holding up his hunger against the pious phallic pillar that marked the entrance to the alley), they saw Lezama leaving the men's brothel. He was coming along placidly, with a recently lit Havana in his mouth, on his face an air of satisfaction that was perhaps produced by the cigar – or by thinking up a poem. Lezama noticed the two artists (who looked more like two young toughs because of their poor bearing and their smirks), but he didn't flinch and out loud, with his asthmatic accent, he said: 'What, Virgilio, you too are looking for the unicorn hidden in the thicket?' To which Virgil answered, strangely, since although he could be ingenious he was never precious: 'No, Lezama, but we hunt in the same game preserve.' Natalio later told me precisely: 'It was the only way that Virgilio could say at that moment to Lezama: "We cover the waterfront." '

Lezama lived seemingly for ever in the same house on Trocadero Street. But Virgilio had to live in many towns and in many houses, among them, significantly, on Panchito Gómez, a Havana street if there ever was one. He also lived alone in many lonely rooms, always on the move, chased by the rent collector and hungry buggers – hungry for money and sex. Virgilio inhabited, among other poet's hells, the infamous *azotea* of Malecón and Paseo del Prado, where all the renters were poor but pederast. It was there that Virgilio learned that his neighbour, another famous Cuban poet, Emilio Ballagas, was abandoning his homosexual quarters and lifestyle, was converting to a practising Catholic and was abjuring his vices against nature to be married by the Church. Not a week had passed since this demure departure, since such an oath and since said vow when Ballagas returned in a hurry to beg and borrow the use of his room from Virgilio. Ballagas had forgotten, in his sexual haste and heat, the horror that Virgilio felt if someone was occupying his bed who wasn't his occasional lover – or better, his momentary bugger. Virgilio said no resoundingly and then, thinking better of it, added: 'But you can use the bathroom,' referring him to the common *escusado*. 'Thanks,' said Ballagas gratefully. 'Thanks a lot! Virgilio, you won't regret it. You'll see, he's the cutest sailor, *une trouvaille!*' Ballagas disappeared down the stairs to return in a jiffy but out of breath, almost dragging along a sailor indeed – whom

Virgilio recognized instantly as the elect ephebe over whom there had once been a dispute, in a row of rhymes, between Lorca and the Colombian poet Porfirio Barba Jacob, of many pseudonyms and few teeth. 'But the Jacobean or Lorcan beautiful boy was now a wreck,' Virgilio recounted. 'A ghost sailor who was still living to captivate, like the Flying Dutchman, pederast poets.'

In another house even older than that notorious rooftop Virgilio rounded up a room. It was a house virtually falling down that should have been cleared out a long time before but was still inhabited and there Virgilio took refuge – a ruin among ruins. One day he went to make use of the sanitary facilities whose sanitation was only nominal. He was seated as if meditating on the bowl (thinking perhaps of what Swift said about man being the gravest when he is at stool), when suddenly the floor gave way under his weight, which was never much, and Virgilio, the force of necessity against that of gravity, still sitting on the bowl, still in Rodin's *Thinker*'s position, went crashing down to the lower depths – on top of an unheard of ironing table, right in the middle of some Chinamen. He had fallen into a Chinese laundry! The whole Confucian tribe took offence at his obscene presence: *alea dejecta est*. 'But,' as Virgilio told it, 'in spite of what must have been Cantonese curses at first, later they were the sweetest things and even helped me to get out of the bowl and of my embarrassment.' Miraculously Virgilio didn't get even a scratch on him. Peripatetic poets all die in bed.

Lezama lived surrounded by books, by papers, by galley proofs (he was always, from 1937, involved in editorial enterprises: journals, books, publications) and his asthma fed on the dust that printed paper gathers. Virgilio never had one single book and he made a big deal of that absence that wasn't a lack. 'They're all here in my head,' he used to say. 'Why would I pile them up in my living room?' In the two houses I saw him live in I never found a book. I don't believe he even saved copies of his uncollected works.

Lezama and Virgilio met not only on the corner of the doubly sinful brothel on Callejón del Chorro. They were also together on more respectable tasks. *Orígenes* got them together but the association didn't last long. Soon there were literary differences between them, that at once became a grudge, then a soured relationship and later a row. Finally they collided on another corner, that of the venerable grounds of the Lyceum and Lawn Tennis Club. Despite its English name and its apparent dedication to tennis, the Lyceum was a cultural society with a performance *salle* (for lectures, plays and chamber music), an exhibition hall and the first circulating library in Cuba. All its areas were public.

I never found out if Virgilio and Lezama met in the library or in the exhibition hall – it happened in the afternoon. What I do know is that they both went out to the street to settle their fight in the macho Cuban way ('Come outside and we'll settle this' – I simply can't see either Virgilio, so pugnacious, or Lezama, so stable, voicing such a challenge) or the way of the laconic cowboys from old Westerns. But ritually or silently they went out to the street and no sooner had they uttered two words or a sudden silence, then Virgilio jumped over the short hedge to enter the gardens. He didn't pay attention to the sign ('Don't walk on the grass') and poking around the giant flamboyant tree he looked for something. A buried treasure? A murder weapon? Lezama didn't hit upon guessing what Virgilio's quest was (the philosopher's stone, perhaps) until he saw that it wasn't a stone but pebbles. When Virgilio figured he had enough garden pebbles he started to throw them at Lezama, aiming at the powerful legs, at the flat feet of his once literary friend now mortal enemy. Every time Lezama saw a small stone coming he took a leap, (Or rather a little hop: what his girth would allow him.) Virgilio was laughing diabolically or amused. As a response Lezama was aiming verbal threats at Virgilio, a Havana still in his mouth, fuming, warning: 'Virgilio, I'm going to chastise you.' But this smoking Goliath wasn't doing anything to reach his opponent, stone-throwing David.

Soon there was a mob of street urchins who were gleefully witnessing the skirmish – the strife of stones against speech. At the end the urchins included themselves in the combat as a chorus: 'Make the fat man jump! Make the fat man jump!' Which didn't get any points with Lezama who never tolerated being called fat – not even affectionately. Finally the stoning stopped because Virgilio ran out of ammunition and the boys began to vituperate Virgilio. With the irregular duel over, each opponent went back to his literary corner – but they didn't speak to each other again for thirty years.

Virgilio left the country in some sort of literary exile. He chose Argentina as a destination and there he lived for sixteen years, working at the consulate as a mere civil servant, living in Buenos Aires a life as precarious as in Havana – a poor *payador*. Lezama kept putting out *Orígenes* and publishing poetry collections and books of essays, roaming obsessively up and down the same street in Old Havana that not by chance was the street of the bookshops. He travelled once to Mexico, invited by his journalist protector. The never forgotten death of his father in the United States had convinced the whole family that being abroad kills you and Lezama was not away one week. The trip produced an extraordinary poem, 'Arriving at Montego Bay', with one line that though food for parody is no less beautiful and personal: 'Permission for a slightly sudden shock'.

Lezama's local fame became greater all the time, in spite of his increasing obscurity that the tropics don't allow. On one occasion an intellectual who saw through Ortega y Gasset's eyes, Jorge Manach, the mouthpiece of the generation of 1927, undertook in the popular journal *Bohemia* a stoning more painful than Virgilio's: he tried to lapidate Lezama and to put up a stone fence around him for ever. Lezama responded with his accustomed impenetrable prose. He lost the polemic but poetry won. His followers were turned into disciples and they considered Lezama a true master, a gifted prophet, with not always genuine adulation or faithful devotion – as time would show.

Virgilio, for his part, attained a certain continental fame but no one recognized his true importance. After all he was a pioneer of absurdist literature and in his plays (Virgilio was able to express his genuine sense of drama in a theatre that was Cuban and at the same time universal, with wit and parody and paradox), especially in *False Alarm* written in 1948, two years before Ionesco premièred his *Bald Prima Donna*. He was one of the first to discover (theatrical) form as a metaphysics of the absurd.

A literary disagreement (in truth a personal and literary feud) made José Rodríguez Feo, the patron thanks to whom the journal *Orígenes* was published, and Lezama break bitterly. Rodríguez Feo published his own version of *Orígenes*, while Lezama tried in vain to continue his old one with his poor means. Lezama had to give up and Rodríguez Feo published then, with the original *Orígenes* dead, a literary journal called *Ciclón* (nicknamed Stormy Weather) that he funded and founded. This almost religious schism would appear to be the cause that brought Virgilio back to Cuba, upwardly mobile on the island. But his definitive return did not come about until two years later, in 1958. No one could conceive of Virgilio as a civil servant and he would later confess that he devoted part of his time in Buenos Aires, as in Havana, to being a more or less literary *pícaro* to be able to survive. Faced with his brand-new consular post (actually an uncivil servant) he had had to turn himself into a translator of languages he didn't know and even a proofreader by night.

If his book *Cold Tales* had appeared under the prestigious label of Editorial Losada (bestowing a South American seal of approval on a collection of Cuban stories) it was because Rodríguez Feo paid for the edition. Rodríguez Feo, even before breaking with Lezama, was already protecting his challenger. But there were not only literary links uniting Virgilio and Rodríguez Feo – without forgetting the defeat inflicted on Lezama under the flamboyant tree. There was the old closeness of the days that saw the birth of the original *Orígenes* and that 'mystic bond of brotherhood' (Virgilio would probably insist that it was 'of sisterhood') which formed an unstable sinful triangle with Lezama: homosexuality. At the same time that it separated them from Lezama, one thing united both ambiguously, a particular fault: faggotry. Lezama always tended towards respectability and his very pederasty could be taken as an intimate form of his maestro mode. Virgilio, as we have already seen, was anything but respectable. As far as Rodríguez Feo went, he cultivated the image of a pervert playboy.

Spectacularly rich, he lived in the penthouse of a modern apartment building he owned in El Vedado and used to go out to roam Havana – to score, really cruising in his enormous convertible – in search of trade, almost always young men, almost always athletic, almost always half-naked. In the mid-fifties Feo busied himself with tending his bar on Playa Guanabo, where the employees seemed, rather than barmen, Cuban versions of Charles Atlas on the beach. From turning himself for ever into a dark Mae West, there came to save Rodríguez Feo the *Orígenes* feud and the return of Virgilio. All three (Lezama, Virgilio, and Rodríguez Feo) were caught in their diverse functions by the triumph of the Revolution. None of them had the least idea of what politics was about. For Virgilio the revolt was always literary and Lezama understood it as an act of aesthetic pilgrimage. No one seemed prepared for the shame of things to come. The future warnings of an internal Armageddon would be, most probably, a false alarm.

I've already told how I saved Lezama Lima from a fate worse than death: the ignominy of looking like a civil servant for Batista and how Lezama celebrated the Revolution, quite early, calling it a 'dawning occurrence' – we were all that credulous. Virgilio (who had resigned or been fired by the Cuban Consulate in Buenos Aires) was able to insert himself easily into our version of the Revolution. I brought him to the newspaper *Revolución*, on the express invitation of Carlos Franqui, its editor, and he later went on to make up part of the team of contributors on *Lunes de Revolución*. Rodríguez Feo who, in spite of his show barmen and his money, was the only one of the trio who had political consciousness, carried his adherence to the Revolution so far that he voluntarily gave up his skyscraper to the Urban Reform (which would have confiscated the building from him in any case), including his penthouse (which he would certainly have been able to keep) and divested himself of the diversion of his public bar and private brothel. Virgilio got a bad reception at first on the newspaper (his reputation as a fag had reached the leadership of the 26th of July Movement, which was, like the whole Revolution, ostentatiously *machista*: you only had to see Fidel Castro or Che Guevara walk – Virgilio on the other hand had the look of a pederast that all the willpower of a willow did not manage to erase. But soon his industriousness and his literary value, besides his impeccable conduct (helped by the evident fact that there were no tempting derelicts on the editorial board of the newspaper and because I asked him not to go nosing around the newsvendors' entrance and he promised me that he would never graze in those blue pampas – an Argentinism no doubt – a promise he kept), earned him the respect of everyone, even of the many machos.

I don't remember if Virgilio was among those who encouraged Heberto Padilla to write the savage attack against Lezama that I published in the magazine. That was almost an official condemnation not only of Lezama's person but of his poetic art. (When I saw it in print I had the impression of having set a pack of pit bulls on a tied-up man.) In any case Virgilio got on very well with Padilla – also back from a brief American exile. (Like Virgilio an economic and cultural not a political exile and a man of dangerous tongue and bifid pen.) Virgilio and Padilla also had in common their antipathy against another contributor to the magazine, the poet José Baragaño, who came back from a complicated exile (poetic – political – paternal) spent in Paris and whom I invited to be a contributor – our Surrealist on salary.

Baragaño, who profoundly hated Lezama, a hate that went beyond aesthetic differences, was pleased by the attack made by his *paisano* Padilla, now a partisan poet, and they renewed their provisional, provincial friendship: they both came from Pinar del Río Province. Virgilio, as if on an aesthetic tightrope, wrote a column in which he attacked Baragaño's person (he called him a bum and a sponger and, I even believe, politically opportunistic) but he praised him extravagantly as a poet. Baragaño chose to ignore the personal attacks and read only the poetic praise.

With these divergent literary forces in unstable equilibrium, I could after a little while (with the help of Pablo Armando Fernández, another poet in economic exile in New York, returned to work on *Lunes* as assistant editor, a born diplomat) secure a special contribution from Lezama to be published (with the natural and supernatural opposition of Virgilio, Padilla, and Baragaño) in a special issue of the magazine subtitled 'To Cuba with Love'. I gave Lezama – what else? – the assignment of writing about a family food. The insult forgotten, probably because of the food, the obscure poet wrote a clear and erudite essay about the origin, at times exotic, of all Cuban fruits – the most lasting contribution of the issue.

Lezama was ascending little by little on the official ladder until he became one of the literary advisers of the National Printing Press. In those travails we met again, as I hadn't seen him since the days when I briefly directed the Cultural Directorate (that would later become the National Council of Culture, controlled by the Communists), a painful, pathetic encounter. Lezama was now feeling more secure not as a poet but politically and he suggested some titles – *The Trial* by Kafka – that Alejo Carpentier found 'hardly fitting to our reality'. Virgilio for his part was becoming the leading Cuban playwright, opening new pieces of the absurd or restaging his old pagan plays. Like *Electra Garrigó*, a national tragedy that was a parody of its Greek model and at the same time a staging of Cuban popular forms, like 'Guantanamera'. In fact he was the first to rescue from the red record (criminal, not Communist) the radio rhythm, a ransom that served as a basis for the present-day version of that old peasant tune – now converted by the unaware into a kind of revolutionary hymn thanks to the savvy singer Pete Seeger and to a renegade from the Revolution. As a contribution to historical irony I must say that the author of the melody 'La Guantanamera', a man fallen from artistic grace then, sang the Cuban chorus in a restaging of *Electra Garrigó*, during which Virgilio sat between Simone de Beauvoir and Jean-Paul Sartre – who applauded enthusiastically although they didn't understand a word. For Virgilio it was a form of literary *gloire*.

But Virgilio always mistrusted the ephemeral posterity of success. He was right. Not long ago Joseíto Fernández died. The obituary of the singer rescued by Virgilio, the author of a single song, that now official 'Guantanamera', appeared in the *Guardian* and the *Herald Tribune* – and I have the right to suppose also in the *New York Times*, besides innumerable Latin American dailies, subscribers all. When Virgilio died not one obituary, not even a notice appeared in any of those newspapers – with the exception of *El País* of Madrid. The irony is also political: the obituary of Joseíto Fernández was carried by the Cuban agency Prensa Latina. Virgilio Piñera was not in the pantheon of illustrious Cubans – so he died anonymous.

Lezama always aspired to the condition of absolute master. His massive presence, his orotund oratorical style when speaking were as paradigmatic as they were charismatic and asthmatic. His studied, sage pose, always reposed, served his purpose – and he had disciples and even apostles and among them (how could he not?) a propitious Judas. But Virgilio, despite his horror of masters (in *Electra Garrigó* a character of burlesque is the Greek grotesque Pedagogue), his absence of magisterial tone and his inability to pontificate (although he made himself heard when he wanted to) also had his followers. Many too close, to their harm – not Virgilio's.

The opposite of Lezama's, Virgilio's disciples were from the younger generation. I can cite two names because both have a place in the history of Cuban theatre. The strictly literary disciples, among short-story writers and novelists, don't deserve to be mentioned and Virgilio himself repudiated them. 'They don't know,' he would say, 'that literature is not style but breathing' – with which he came closer to Lezama than he would have admitted. They are the playwrights Antón Arrufat, who was also on the committee of contributors to *Lunes* and José Triana, who published one of his best plays in our magazine. Both homosexual, both suffered abuse for their sexual preferences and in one case (Arrufat) for his work. Even in hot pursuit the reluctant master preceded the determined disciples.

In 1961 Virgilio asked me for leave from the magazine to take a trip to Europe, invited to Belgium by an old friend, a sporadic writer and now the secretary of the Cuban Embassy in Brussels as before he had been a civil servant in Buenos Aires. On his return Virgilio, dramatically, absurdly, had no sooner got off the plane than he felt an irresistible impulse to kiss Cuban soil – without realizing that he was really kissing the asphalt of the landing strip. This flaw Virgilio must have seen, since he knew Greek tragedy well, as a form of hubris. Nevertheless he seemed very happy to have come back to Cuba. After a few days he found himself dangerously involved in a historic event.

In between there was the Bay of Pigs fiasco and Virgilio celebrated victory with the same praises with which we all did it in the magazine and everywhere. But this isn't the historical event to which I'm referring. It happened that a few weeks after the victory on the Bay of Pigs my brother Sabá and the photographer Orlando Jiménez-Leal premièred on the programme *Lunes de Revolución on Television* a short shot late at the end of the last year that celebrated Havana and the night and the music. The camera and the microphone captured their varied vitality in bars all over downtown and on the docks and in the town of Regla across the bay: they also covered the waterfront. When the two film-makers sent the film in for a licence from the Comisión Revisora (actually an office of censorship inherited from former governments), this body showed itself to be the instrument of censorship it really was – and sequestered the copy.

Since 1959 there had been constantly aggravating rivalry between the

Film Institute and *Lunes* and *Revolución* because of opposite interpretations about the nature of culture in Communist Cuba. The Film Institute became more and more Stalinist every day but its measure was really the pits of the polemic. It was the first time a film had been censored in Cuba – not for political reasons but on account of its subject. Of course, *P.M.*'s content was its form, but it turned out to be considered not only negative art but adverse to the historical moment too. Totalitarianism, constantly aspiring to the condition of history, takes care of its eternity as the body cares for its skin.

The magazine contested the seizure with a letter signed by almost two hundred writers and artists. In those days the first Writers' and Artists' Congress was gestating. An event conceived by the Communists as a culmination of sorts, supported not only by all the Communist intellectuals and leaders, but backed personally by President Dorticós himself – a mere marionette, a stately stooge. Coincidentally Fidel Castro had declared Cuba a socialist country only a few weeks before. Faced with the fact that our open letter denouncing the sequestering of *P.M.* was about to become public, it was officially decided to postpone the Congress. In its place there were held three meetings, one each consecutive Friday, with writers and artists, in the National Library auditorium. The event was as secret and damning as a coven, with the participation of more than five hundred delegates (who had to identify themselves dutifully at the door: *Ego sum scriptor*) and presided over by Fidel Castro and President Dorticós plus the official cultural apparat. The importance of the meetings seemed decisive. As the editor of the magazine and producer of the television programme I found myself an outsider at that presidential table.

After the first session was officially declared open, President Dorticós in voiceover requested everyone to say frankly what he or she had to say, not only with respect to the movie (which was shown earlier to all the participants), but also to its seizure. He didn't call it prohibition but interdiction, as if it weren't the same, but this ignorant lawyer in the course of his discourse mispronounced quite a few words – a mighty Mr Malaprop. After this awesome opening a vacuum and void fell as a form of silence that grew embarrassingly. Dorticós was already about to say: 'Speak now or forever hold your peace,' when suddenly the most improbable person, all shy and shrunken, got up from his seat. It seemed as if he was going to take flight but he went up to the microphone and declared: 'I only want to say that I'm very frightened. I don't know why I'm so frightened but that is all I have to say.' It was of course Virgilio Piñera who had expressed what many in the room felt and did not have the courage to say publicly. That is before that imposing panel, in front of Fidel – frightful and fraught with a gun.

The result of those meetings is only too well known. But it is well to remember how the movie was not only banned but condemned, how the disappearance of *Lunes* was decreed and how the Stalinists made off not only with cultural power but with total power in Cuba. Fidel Castro, revealed as the leading Stalinist, delivered his long diatribe against free culture, ending with his version of a totalitarian credo: 'Within the Revolution everything. Against the Revolution, nothing.' His Supreme Power would determine where the *con* ended and the *contra* began. Obviously *P.M.* fell into a suicidal no man's land: the little night movie was visibly a-revolutionary.

In those meetings there were several speeches from the floor, many showing to what point *Lunes* was hated and feared. A fear produced by its literary critiques tinged with political shading and at the same time delivering final judgements backed up by the authority of *Revolución* and its moral force. But the newspaper was not now the official organ of the 26th of July Movement that it had been in 1959 and 1960. Apart from the speech by Virgilio two more dissimilar ones stood out. One was virulent, purely concentrated hate, made by an exiled Spanish journalist, a social not socialist writer, a mediocre novelist, a pretentious person and rancorous rival, a dentist for the wealthy and now an aspiring diplomat. He took advantage of the occasion to organize a speech that was at the same time a settling of accounts in which he avenged a negative critique that Antón Arrufat had made of him, denouncing his malpractice as a novelist (way back in 1959!) and a fit of breast-beating – which got him named Ambassador to the Vatican. No such opportunist could be a bad diplomat and besides he was a converted Catholic.

The other speech, characteristically, was Lezama's – an old Catholic attacked atrociously in *Lunes*. If anyone had reason to feel aversion to the magazine it was Lezama and that was the moment to air his grievances and climb on the bandwagon. But Lezama limited himself to speaking of literature, of the eternity of art and the permanence of culture. If he made a reference to *Lunes* it was to say that it was proper to youth to commit excesses: literary youth committed literary excesses. Lezama was the personification of generosity, in literature and in life: wordy, worthy.

Now that *Lunes* was theoretically banned (in practice the ban wouldn't take place until October: there was no reason to give a Russian appearance of crime and punishment) all of us contributors to it avoided continuing the gatherings that coincided with its closure so as not to create difficulties for *Revolución*. (The newspaper was the true target, *Lunes* was a mere decoy.) The literary meetings took place now in my apartment on La Rampa and sometimes in Pablo Armando Fernández's mansion in Miramar. But principally they took place in Virgilio's house on the beach. It was more like a bungalow than a house by its beachfront look, although it stood far back from the waterfront. There was in it, as in any of Virgilio's places, not a single book and neither could one see signs that anyone wrote in the premises – except for an old Remington in a cosy corner. We met outside, forced by the small cramped house on to the patio, under a spreading avocado tree, made memorable by its avocados ripe on the table when we ate Virgilio's delicious *Pasta Pignera* – they were Saturdays of verbal spell and spaghetti. To these gatherings went with us foreign writers, always badly looked upon elsewhere in Havana, always welcome in Virgilio's bungalow. Everyone except the American writer guest who said to Virgilio, thinking he was paying him a beatnick compliment: 'Virgil, you are a beautiful queen!' Virgilio never forgave him for calling him queen, even as a courtesy – especially as a courtesy. Those get-togethers, like the love of that Swedish girl in the movie, only lasted one summer.

Not long afterwards Virgilio was trapped in the infamous Night of the Three Ps. This was a moral-Marxist dragnet, aimed at all Havana prostitutes, pimps and pederasts. One would think that it would take place in the centre of the city, within a radius of a few blocks around the Colón scarlet streets (where, curious thing, Lezama always lived), that was the Red-Light District. (It was done largely in secret, suddenly.) But how, if Virgilio lived on Guanabo beach, fifteen miles from the Colón district, did he end up being detained? Was he in Havana near the whorehouses? Was he visiting his father perhaps, although he lived in Ayestarán, on the other side of the city? Not at all. Virgilio had stayed in his beach house the whole time. It turned out that he had been pointed out by his neighbours as a pederast who staged orgies. Apparently they were Roman feasts with spaghetti!

V's sexual bent had always been well known, under constitutional governments and under dictatorships, with Grau and with Batista and with the Revolution. But now he was a perilous pederast. Virgilio, to top it all off, was not even arrested during the notorious night. It happened in the early morning the next day. As he always did he headed at daybreak to drink his morning coffee at the nearby coffee corner. As usual he was dressed in shorts, sports shirt and sandals – a get-up that the Revolution considered decadent. In the coffee shop he was accosted by a stranger who asked him his name and for a moment, after he said Virgilio Piñera, he thought he had in sight an early morning pick-up. But the stout stranger simply told him: 'You're under arrest.'

Virgilio didn't want to believe it or thought it was a joke. But it was not a joke. The stranger identified himself with a badge as a policeman and said: 'Come with me.' Like K, V felt instantly guilty although he did not know his crime. Virgilio asked if he could go home and change: it was ridiculous to go to prison in that outfit. He was allowed to return to the bungalow. Along the way he mustered up enough courage to ask his guard, escort or keeper: 'What am I accused of?' The policeman told him: 'Of assault on revolutionary morality.'

But it was the same bourgeois morality that used to condemn Virgilio before, except that he had never been arrested, only shunted aside, an alienation that Virgilio himself seemed to seek at the time. To complicate matters now the policeman told him in the doorway that he wanted to search his house. Chance would have it that Virgilio had as a guest in his other room a theatre friend who was accompanied by a young man – his lover. The agent took all three down to the police station. It was from there that Virgilio called me. He hadn't reached me at home because I was serving my voluntary but compulsory militia dawn guard duty on the newspaper *Revolución*. The call puzzled me not only because of Virgilio's neutral tone (he was always very effeminate in voice and gesture) but because of what he told me. 'I'm under arrest,' he just whispered. Once I had recovered from my puzzlement that had become astonishment and I was able to ask him why, he added: '*Por* Paderewski,' and he popped his p's. 'For what?' I asked him and he insisted with as many p's as possible: '*Por* Paderewski. *Pederastki*. Get it?' At the end of his pianissimo I got it. I asked myself not what the police would decipher from his pederastkey but what Paderewski would say about his name being used as a sexual mask.

Virgilio sounded really anxious. I told him not to worry, that everything would be all right. Although I knew the nature of his crime I did not know its history. But that morning it was already known about the round-up and about the Night of the Three Ps in the newspaper – and at the UPI and AP offices. I immediately called Franqui at his home. He sounded very worried (he knew about the raid too) but he said to me: 'Call *la* Buchaca,' admitting his own impotence. I called Edith García Buchaca, who was at the peak of her cultural power before falling into her political disgrace, still inexplicable – from the rim to the bottom of a well. She showed herself to be at first puzzled and then as worried as Franqui but much more decisive. She told me that she was going to call Carlos Rafael Rodríguez, who was then not as powerful as now but still had quite a bit of political pull. Before hanging up *la* Buchaca assured me that everything would be all right.

I had no other news that morning except a visit by Franqui who rarely came by the newspaper so early. He spoke with me confidentially (we were already afraid that there were agents not precisely press agents within) and he tried to spring Virgilio with two or three phone calls as ineffective now as they would have been effective in the past. When my guard duty was over I went home. It was there that I learned that the well-known theatre guest of Virgilio and his lover were also arrested with the playwright. There were other calls – among them those from Arrufat and Triana. They were worried not only about Virgilio's hide but about their own. That kind of panic is common among the disciples when they arrest the teacher. I imagine the same thing happened in Athens and in Jerusalem in different ages. Although Virgilio was a secret Socrates, I couldn't picture him drinking hemlock. Besides, the Revolution, that had its Marxist martyrs, was not going to crucify the author of *Jesús*. Unsettled, I nevertheless waited patiently for the decision of the powers that were.

At five in the afternoon Edith García Buchaca called to tell me the verdict without a trial. They were going to release Virgilio, imprisoned then in El Príncipe castle. I headed there to wait for his release from prison, actually an exit. I could see Virgilio, going down the stairs with some of the care he would use to go down the Pyramid of Gizeh, still trembling from head to foot not because of the steep steps, which were not many, but because of the fear of the prisoner that is being freed. I have known it: there is always the concern that they may put you in prison again. He was escorted in his descent by the *régisseur* and his lover. I took all three with me to the two-bedroom apartment on the twenty-third floor of a building on La Rampa that was my home.

Soon the flat was filled with people welcoming Virgilio (underground rumours usually run faster than official news) as if he had just returned from accompanying Dante on his stroll through hell – and who's to say it wasn't a season in Hades that Virgilio had just spent? (Mantua is after all close to Cárdenas.) Part of his ordeal, according to what he told me later, was finding himself among counter-revolutionary prisoners who upon learning that he was not merely a pederast poet prisoner but a contributor to *Revolución*, treated him like a collaborator and beat him and threatened to crop his head Paris-style – after the Liberation.

That afternoon of a fag there came with the gift of their adherence pseudo-disciples and true admirers and colleagues – some of them heterosexual. Virgilio was not interested in homages to an author who wanted to be considered anonymous now. That night Virgilio didn't dare to leave my refuge and stayed to sleep over with us. His prison pals, the theatre person and his constant companion, didn't want to go out either to breathe the aromatic air of the tropical night – which was for them the summer of their discontent. Both slept in the living room, on the granite floor. We gave up our best bed to Virgilio. Or rather not all the bed. Instead we ceded him the box-spring and we laid out the mattress on the studio floor and there Miriam Gómez and I slept, all of us with our clothes on: more cautious than chaste. The next day the theatre producer (who lived absurdly hardly three blocks away) and his fast friend left, blending with the more or less normal people who crowded La Rampa day and night, in transit, strolling or looking to score. A few days later Virgilio summoned up the nerve to go back to his beach house.

That afternoon I was coming from Channel 2 (*Lunes* had not yet been suppressed nor its television programme cancelled) with Pablo Armando Fernández. Both of us were walking with that patient pace of the day due East for dusk in the tropics, passing next to the La Rampa theatre, once such a perfect place for premières, going on along the pavement of the one-time Edén Rock, a restaurant now called Volga, beside the Marakas, a coffee shop adjacent to the Fox and the Crow, a night-club. It was there and then, I don't know why, that I looked towards my building, I ran my eyes over its red and black façade – and there on the twenty-third floor balcony could be seen the figure, svelte but shortened by the height, of Miriam Gómez who was waving, raising her arm rather. I raised my arm too to greet her but I saw that she was waving both arms now, that her waves were moving from mere greetings (shifting from red to black) into frenetic signals for help – calling me urgently.

To the astonishment of Pablo Armando and his protests I took off running toward the building, up to the elevators (which as usual were on another floor) to wait impatiently for them to come down, Pablo Armando joining me while I was trying to guess what could be happening, imagining the most terrible accidents involving my daughters, my mother, my whole family – a catastrophe. I was about to take off up the stairs – to the twenty-third floor – but an elevator opened. When we got to my floor the door was open. Inside I saw Miriam Gómez in anguish, not knowing what to do or able to speak, pointing at a white cane chair – where there lay stretched out, apparently unconscious, paler than the cane, Virgilio Piñera. I asked what had happened and Miriam Gómez answered me, recovered, with a Havana phrase which meant that Virgilio had had a sudden seizure. She had already called the doctor.

It happened, according to what Virgilio was barely able to get across before passing out, that he went, as he had planned, to the beach, back to his house – to find it sealed 'by a warrant from the proper authority'. Virgilio was being treated now like a fugitive, an enemy of the State, a political prisoner – after having been persecuted as a sex criminal. I can imagine the shock that it must have been for Virgilio to encounter the only house he had in his life (although rented it was his and it was a house not the rooms, if not dumps, where he had lived in the past) and to learn suddenly that he was, worse than hopeless, legally excluded, excommunicated – which was the same as being free but incommunicado.

Now Virgilio was lying stretched out on the chair, white as its white seat, having regained consciousness somewhat while the doctor was going over him painstakingly. 'This man has suffered a collapse,' was his diagnosis, which in Cuban medical terminology could mean anything from a cardiac arrest to a stroke or a nervous breakdown. I inclined towards the latter option as an opinion. The doctor produced a syringe from his black bag and prepared to give Virgilio a shot. His horror of injections made him regain his lost consciousness. 'It's nothing,' said the doctor, while he was injecting him. 'Now he needs to rest, to spend a while on the beach.' A medical irony no doubt.

For three days and three nights Virgilio rested in my place – sleeping now on the whole bed. Resurrected on the third day, he insisted that I go with him to Guanabo, to take possession of his house. It was, evidently, more than repossession an obsession: go back to the beach, go back to his house. But there was some reason in his unreason. Both of us went to Guanabo in my car. Just like Ugarte he was carrying a letter of transit for Virgilio to reach his house, signed by Edith García Buchaca.

The whole trip Virgilio did nothing more than ask why they hadn't searched his house before sealing it, over and over again in a litany for the inviolability of his domicile. It was incomprehensible to me, Virgilio's preoccupation with his house – a virgo intacta inviting violators. Its interior contained nothing more than some paltry poor pieces of furniture, a decrepit typewriter, and, perhaps, many manuscripts. Could these be the source of his concern? For a moment I thought that Virgilio was perhaps writing a story or a novel or a counter-revolutionary comedy. Suddenly I heard myself saying to myself that if a movie as innocent as *P.M.* could be considered threatening to revolutionary stability, then anything could be counter-revolutionary, even Virgilio's plays, so absurd – perhaps because they were absurd. I do not believe because it is absurd, *Comandante*. It was not the moment not to believe or to be absurd.

But Virgilio stopped asking about the inside of his house to tell me, 'It's all the fault of that damned man.' I thought he was cursing and blaming Fidel Castro, but I asked him what man and what blame. He mentioned the name of a notorious homosexual who had already left the country – an active pederast. 'He left me those filthy things. Me. He could still have left them with Pepe Rodríguez Feo, who enjoys them – but me! They don't even interest me. They've never interested me. I'm a homosexual, yes, but not libertine.' Which I knew but I asked him about the photos I didn't know. 'Photos, what else?' he said as if my question were interrupting his train of thought. 'Postcards. Of little boys naked from behind, of nude weightlifters, of enormous penises. Filth. Pornographic postcards. I don't know why I accepted them but he begged me. He told me he didn't have anywhere to leave them, that he'd send for them with a messenger. A mess he should have said.'

Virgilio was a curiously moral homosexual, almost a Victorian moralist, a prude pederast and the furthest thing there was from a libertine, as he said. I told him not to worry, that nothing was going to happen, that it all had been an everyday mix-up and mistakes are rarely repeated. (Of course I thought just the opposite: errors, like errata, multiply alarmingly.)

We arrived at the Guanabo police headquarters, a nondescript house, which calmed me but not Virgilio: he had already been there once. After a good deal of waiting, I had a lot to explain and about as much to hide to succeed in convincing those armed men (with a different uniform but the same police suspiciousness as always) that Virgilio *was* in the country, that he was a citizen (of course I didn't use this word: they had already begun to make a moral and, especially, a political distinction between the Cubans that deserved the friendly treatment of 'comrade' or of 'citizen', which meant quite the opposite of what it meant, for example, for Robespierre), a beach resident who had absented himself only for a few days (I didn't specify why and the police still had a short memory: it became evident to me that they didn't want to remember Virgilio) and on his return he had found his house sealed by the authorities, evidently an error without malice, since the revolutionary police may make a mistake but always corrects it. The defence rests. There was much coming and going, some paper shuffling, more waiting. But in the end Virgilio obtained the authorization (I requested it in writing) to go back to his house, guaranteed by *la* Buchaca and the state apparat, now his protector.

When we arrived at his bungalow the so feared seal on the door was a coarse curse: a mimeographed piece of paper that I tore up with pleasure. Once inside the house that before had been so charming, so beach-like and so tropical and was now dark and empty, Virgilio headed quickly to the kitchen and from a pigeonhole in the sideboard, that must have held the silverware, he took a profusion of photos. He didn't even let me see them and that disappointed me. I have always felt curiosity about the image of sex, any sex and even a photo of an elephant trying to mount a rhinoceros intrigued me because of its bestial, blind sexuality. Virgilio rapidly threw the photos into a paper bag that was an anachronic remainder from a famous department store before the Revolution which disappeared consumed by counter-revolutionary flames. (As it was not called the Phoenix it was never rebuilt.) Virgilio took me out of my sumptuous memory and incendiary reflections. 'We have to get rid of this garbage immediately,' he told me putting a stress of repulsion and fear on the word garbage. It became an obscene entry. I agreed. We ran out of the house and got in the car, going up the highway, leaving Guanabo behind headed for Matanzas, looking for an adequate dump for Virgilio to get rid of the pouch full of poached pornography. It was for him, by the way he was holding his load in his hand, an unstable explosive. Amused by that excursion and incited by the constant 'Say whens' from Virgilio, every time he got ready to throw far from the car and beyond the highway his erotic burden, I lied to him warning him that he couldn't do it then because I saw in the rearview mirror an enemy car – perhaps a spy driving high.

Finally feeling sorry for Virgilio's anguish I told him that now he could throw overboard his negative (or positive, since they were photos) booty – and Virgilio hurled the bag as far as he could. A little further on I turned around and we confirmed that the package had fallen off the edge of the highway. But then we saw that it had opened when it struck the hard ditch and its pornocopia was scattered over the nearby countryside, a true fragmentation grenade of dirty trash. Virgilio was both relieved and anguished. His anxiety increased when I told him: 'Wouldn't it be a pederast irony if those photos fell into the hands of a curious hick kid to awaken in him a violent homosexual passion that had been previously latent?' It cost me a lot of lip to convince Virgilio that it was just a joke, that such a possibility was remote (indeed, improbable), that nobody was going to accuse him of perverting the peasantry – a homosexual agrarian reform.

Virgilio recovered from his ordeal and tried to adapt to the speed with which the Revolution was heading into the savage jungle of Stalinism – or of its Caribbean version. But he was never really accepted. In the first Writers' and Artists' Congress, where the Writers' Union was made (even more) official and it was decreed that *Lunes* would stop being published 'due to lack of paper' and at the same time would be replaced by two publications, the *Gaceta de Cuba* (which could well have been called the *Gaceta Oficial*) and the *Revista Unión*, where some of his articles appeared, in that arbitrary election, unlike Lezama or indeed me, he was not named to any post on the UNEAC – which had a surfeit of vice-presidents. He left his house in Guanabo (where there were no more literary gatherings or intimate or literary visits) and came to live in the same apartment building as Rodríguez Feo – next door to his old friend and protector. But while Rodríguez Feo, always living dangerously, didn't allow anything to spoil his taste for anal adventures and installed in his house and his bed socialist versions of his old facsimiles of Charles Atlas, now with more clothes on, Virgilio recounted horrified what he considered a frightful boldness, incapable of understanding for himself how Pepe could run such risks, daring polity and the police – for a penis.

Both Virgilio and Lezama led lives of complete sexual austerity, each one dedicated to cultivating his literary garden. But the Revolution made them die by (word of) mouth. Lezama was always a prodigious glutton capable of gobbling up a suckling pig or a sucking lamb, both roasted, in one sitting, despite his eternal lack of money. Before the Revolution he was invited by his assorted cronies: successful painter friends, sculptors with commissions in parks or churches and well-paid journalists. Virgilio was a vegetarian and it was not difficult to find him in 1959 or 1960, his salad years, in one of the vegetarian restaurants of Havana – that ceased to exist at the end of 1961, due to the strange scarcity of garden greens or vegetables, which were always cultivated in the countryside and of olive oil, which was sometimes imported. (This disappearance caused Virgilio great mortification.) Now he was thinner than ever, although he kept his natural elegance that an Argentine writer, when Virgilio visited him in Buenos Aires in 1956, had confused with dandyism, after Virgilio showed up with a splendid winter outfit – lent him by Rodríguez Feo. But Virgilio, with his scanty clothes from Havana, was really a natural dandy. Which could not be said of Lezama who, although always wearing a tie, displayed an untidiness to which the ashes thrown off by his perennial cigar, an overt volcano, contributed.

Contemporary photographs show Lezama with the torpor of the fat, tall but top-heavy from his obesity, justifying the nickname that the criminal classes had given him in his days as a probation officer, Lead Tank. Virgilio for his part had a noble ugliness: he was svelte, wide-eyed, long-necked and with a face that could have belonged to some enlightened Florentine of the Renaissance. Both, nevertheless, although they showed close Spanish kinship, were very Cuban. Lezama used to proclaim his Basque ancestors though and now someone had proposed that a Bilbao street be named after him – which is much more than they'll ever do in Havana. No one has proposed in any city anywhere that a cul-de-sac be called Virgilio Piñera.

The respective families of our heroes have diverse ties with their writer sons. Lezama was practically an only child through his relationship with his mother widowed when her son was a little boy. There are two sisters but one of them, Eloísa, is all devotion towards her brother and an enormous literary admiration become idolatry. When this sister got married, Lezama stayed alone with his mother in the old house on Trocadero Street and the day that Eloísa Lezama started on the road to exile, which was forbidden to her brother, Lezama's loneliness intensified and so too grew the dependency of his mother, who was now an old lady more needy of care than able to offer it.

For Virgilio, one among several children, the separation from one brother who was an eminent figure as a serious intellectual (the opposite of Lezama, there was nothing that Virgilio detested more than being considered an intellectual), a university professor and then a political exile, had no consequences. I do not believe that Virgilio remotely regretted his brother's exile as Lezama suffered his sisters' flight. There are their heart-rending letters to show this. Virgilio was also close to his sister – who maintained that Virgilio was her artistic debtor. 'Dear boy, I was the one who put the first volume of Proust in his hands,' she used to say. 'He didn't even know his name then.' (She would fail to consider that her brother was the last writer in Spanish who would owe anything to Proust.) If Luisa Piñera had talked like that about Kafka perhaps she would have managed to convince us. Although Virgilio wrote his first Kafkaesque short stories long before Kafka was translated into Spanish – and he didn't have any German. Luisa, the reverse of Eloísa Lezama with her brother, was affectionately irreverent with Virgilio but they shared more than one taste – and not only literary ones. She had married a city bus driver, whom she cheerfully called 'my *guagüero*', a man who felt curiously comfortable in the literary discussions between his wife and his brother-in-law and though Virgilio disdained cultured conversations, they were none the less on a level superior to the possible understanding of the busman. But Virgilio felt a real affection for his brother-in-law – which isn't strange when one remembers that Virgilio used to pick his lovers from among the humblest. That rough driver husband of his sister was perhaps very far above Virgilio's bedmates. A sally by Luisa perhaps better illustrates the family relationship. Virgilio came up leading his blind father by the hand, returning to his house, and when she saw them Luisa said, referring as much to her father's blindness as to her brother's effeminacy: 'There comes Oedipus holding Antigone's hand.'

When *Lunes* ceased to exist in a hara-kiri ordered by the Emperor, I yielded to Virgilio the position of editor of *Ediciones R*, a house that we built as a publishing branch of the magazine. Virgilio was head of publishing (he enjoyed an editor's job for the first time in his life and apparently felt fine being something more than a literary figure) until the newspaper *Revolución* itself disappeared under the buffetings of a Stalinism now masquerading as Fidelism. In Brussels in some sort of official exile I learned that Virgilio had suffered one more attack from *machismo* as a political manifestation. On a visit to the Cuban Embassy in Algiers, Che Guevara browsing found in the meagre Algerian library Virgilio's *Complete Plays*, published by *Ediciones R*. He took it out as if to leaf through it but what he did was to address himself to the ambassador, a minor *comandante*, with a sharp statement: 'How come you have this fag's book in the embassy!' And without another word he threw the volume to the other end of the room, crashing it against the wall like a bad egg: purulent, virulent. The ambassador excused himself for his lapse as he tossed the book into the wastepaper basket.

Almost at the same time I knew secretly that there would be a meeting in Paris with Carlos Franqui, who was enduring some sort of semi-exile, and Heberto Padilla and Pablo Armando Fernández, both with unstable and precarious official posts in Europe. There as well, with all honours, was Nicolás Guillén, Poet Laureate, who would be offered an ostentatious cocktail party in the Cuban Embassy in France to which I, as chargé d'affaires in Belgium, was invited. Of course there would never be a similar homage to Virgilio, an anonymous author.

We also met Virgilio in Paris and although it was April the old resident of Buenos Aires, who stood up against the cold of the south, was shivering that spring and was not wearing an elegant greatcoat. Miriam Gómez also noticed that Virgilio seemed as helpless as in the days of his imprisonment: he even had to be helped to cross the least travelled streets, fearful not only of the cars but of the pedestrians. In the hotel room we met Franqui in secret. At one point in the conversation he advised Virgilio not to go back to Cuba, but to invent some pretext, valid or not, to stay in Europe, in Paris, in Madrid, or in Rome – wherever he most wanted. Money would be no problem: Padilla, Pablo Armando and I could pay his way for a while. In any event the winter in Europe would be agreeable compared with the hell that was being set up in Cuba. Franqui knew that in Havana they were preparing a persecution campaign against all homosexuals so thorough that it would convert the Night of the Three Ps into a dragnet with notes. Now, five years later, total power was organized to exterminate in the name of the future the perversions of the past, bourgeois decadence – and even the love that did not dare to say its name would now confess itself to be the evil against Marx. Then Franqui told the tale of Che Guevara and Virgilio's book being repudiated physically and morally.

Suddenly Virgilio started to cry, which he had not done when he was arrested as a pederast on the beach. Miriam Gómez and I were afraid that his collapse in the apartment in La Rampa would be repeated – worsened now by fear, the Paris weather, the shabby room in the hotel. All so distant from the tropical sun, from the comfort of pre-revolutionary Cuba that still endured in my elegant apartment. Here in Paris were some of his friends, it's true, but Virgilio must have seen a new exile, this time for ever, as a murky landscape. He insisted that he wanted to go back to Cuba, that it didn't matter to him what could happen to him, that he could stand confinement, prison, the concentration camp – but not being far away from Havana. I understood his attachment to this city that was once like a spell. Besides there was the quotable answer from his story in which a man condemned to hell is offered the opportunity of salvation, of abandoning his infernal cell for the promised heaven but he answers negatively and then explains: 'who gives up a cherished habit?'

In 1965 on my return to Havana (curious and curiouser, I never thought of it as a return to Cuba and in fact I never left Havana then) for my mother's funeral, I met Virgilio at the wake. Later we saw each other often, at gatherings in my father's house similar to those held before in my apartment. Now we chatted about all sorts of topics to keep from talking about what was an imminent hunt for homosexuals (it had been confirmed for me by a beautiful lady friend: once a fashion model, now a secret agent of the Ministry of the Interior) and this prospect was becoming for many of them the shape of destiny. I only saw Virgilio nervous twice. Once when in one of my first open-door reunions an uninvited guest whom I didn't know but everyone feared showed up. He was, apparently, a *Seguridad*, a secret policeman. Another time there suddenly visited me (it was a petty meeting in the afternoon, with Virgilio, Antón Arrufat and Oscar Hurtado) a former political activist who had been particularly courageous, almost rash during the Batista dictatorship and was now urging all of us to offer an active resistance to the Revolution, for which she had been ambassador until not long before. She even told poor confused Hurtado to stop eating ice cream every evening at El Carmelo and not to talk any more about Martians who will invade in the near future. 'The Martians are already among us and they have the rank of *comandante*. Fight them even if it's only with words.' When the impromptu visitor left as quickly as she arrived, Arrufat asked: 'But who is this woman?' Virgilio offered his version: 'She has to be an *agente provocateuse*.'

Afterwards, in the nightly gatherings at El Carmelo, in which Hurtado again talked of invading Martians, Virgilio spoke only of literature. (But I remember that he never talked about his literature, a secret passion.) Around that time Lezama (who had recovered from the atrocious blow of his mother's death and had got married – to the surprise of those who did not know that that marriage was his mother's last wish) showed his degree of intellectual courage not only in a defence, before an expulsion committee of the Writers' Union, of the black intellectual Walterio Carbonell, a former contributor on *Lunes* to whom he was not related by any personal, literary or political tie (Carbonell was an old Communist, expelled from the Party for being too Marxist) but by writing in silence the frantically homosexual chapters of *Paradiso*, a novel he would publish the following year, with the massive persecution of passive pederasts in full swing. Everyone knows the later success of this book abroad but little has been said of how it was almost not published, how after being published and faced with the comments about its homosexuality, it was on the verge of being impounded and how the intervention of Fidel Castro (Big Brother is reading you) decided to allow that first printing of the book – but prohibited any other in the foreseeable future.

Virgilio hid in his house and immersed himself in another cherished custom: playing canasta with several retired old ladies. It was in one of these sessions of the game that also absorbed Batista that he authorized by phone the signing of the infamous collective document of the Writers' Union against Neruda – without even asking what the manifesto was about. So tame had become the former rebel.

In 1968 an Argentine journalist who had been in Havana to talk to Lezama, then at the peak of his South American fame, came to visit me in London for an interview. But this journalist told me that when he was visiting Rodríguez Feo's apartment, chatting with the old playboy, now impoverished, the door opened and a kind of disjointed rather than dematerialized ghost entered. He apologized for interrupting and said that he was only coming by for some sugar, Pepe. This apparition withdrew silently with his sugar and Rodríguez Feo explained: 'That was Virgilio Piñera' – which for a non-writer was a choice of words worthy of Flaubert.

The interviewer said that he wanted to interview Virgilio Piñera, who was known in Argentina too. (The Argentines, literary elephants, never forget an author, from the interviewer to Che Guevara.) But Pepe Feo said that it was useless even to try.

In 1971 at the time of Padilla's 'spontaneous confession' in prison, which implicated Lezama among other writers, sinners all, there was a notable absence in the lecture hall of the Writers' Union. With his strange stubborn courage Lezama did not attend this masquerade that was a poor copy of a Moscow trial. Not for nothing has Lezama celebrated the sure step of the mule above the abyss in one of his poems as enigmas that we now know were an *emblema*. The international fame of *Paradiso* had finally caused Lezama to be used by the propaganda machinery of the Fidelist faith and so his complete poems (as obscure as codes for the bureaucrats) were published and he was interviewed in the principal Cuban publications – the few that remain.

But after 1971 and Padilla's recantation a double dome of silence fell on the poet and on *Paradiso* and when he won a prize in Italy and he was invited to Rome he was denied an exit visa. They also prevented him from travelling to Mexico, although he wouldn't have got to Montego Bay with his auroral exultation of love. His life became more difficult than it had ever been and after writing steadily more pathetic letters in which he asked his sister for medicines and communication with the same rhythm, not hesychastic but indeed asthmatic, he died of a pulmonary oedema in a nondescript hospital, in an anonymous room, without being recognized as the greatest poet Cuba has produced – as far as death from his cherished house on Trocadero, this obsessed witness of the ruins of Old Havana. It is evident that *Paradiso* does not hark back to Dante as has been believed but to Milton and *Paradise Lost*. That paradise is the Cuba that went away. Or rather from which the paradise was expelled by a new god, cruel, usurping – the maximum heretic.

Virgilio was hiding in his job as translator for the National Printing Press, but after the resolutions of the First Congress of Culture and Education in 1971, which expressly prohibited contact between homosexual intellectuals and artists (a strange, almost clinical story of a government's obsession) and the means of cultural diffusion and propaganda, the media, his activities were restricted and Virgilio became again what he had been in other difficult times: an invisible man. (Concerning the word 'contact' used above it must be said that its use is not metaphorical: after the promulgation of the resolutions of the Congress Antón Arrufat, the last disciple of Virgilio, who had ended up as a librarian in a small library, was exiled inside the library, among the books, prevented from having *contact* with the readers: pederasty is contagious – a sexual syphilis, a disease of love.) I don't believe that Virgilio wrote many letters, which could be used against him. I don't recall his having written me one single letter at the many stations of my exile. So a letter from Virgilio is not only a rare message but a communication from beyond that reached me from Cuba by way of the USA. It was written to his friend Carlos X, who was living in a city that was common to them, Cárdenas. Here is the short letter from Virgilio, one of the last he must have written:

> Charlot,
>
> I'm dictating these words to you since I cannot do it myself because of the limp state in which I find myself – and still more than that – indolence, because of my age or because of . . . ? Here you have me at 66, which means that at any moment I can make an exit and final curtain . . . I get up, as usual, at 5 a.m., I write until 7, afterwards I go to SuperCake (!), where there are cakes and other filthy things. I stop by the office (?) a moment, I take route 2 and return home, but first I stop by 'milk point', where I get yoghurt. From there to see if there's food or if the milk has come. I have lunch at 11 a.m., I take a nap until 3, I get up and browse around the house – there's a little laundry to do, the phone to answer, an untimely visit, a little reading of any kind. – If I don't have canasta, then I have a snack – meal at 7, then a visit or simply walking around those streets of God. That is my day. No more and no less. I imagine that you're in good health, enjoying the company of your dear nephews and grandchildren. Maybe I'll visit you in the winter. *Un abrazo.*
>
> Virgilio

The letter could not be a more absurd message. In it Virgilio even gets to the point of speaking of winter – in Cuba! Did he mean *infierno* instead of *invierno*?

I don't think that Virgilio was at Lezama's wake or funeral. At this wake very few turned up and when the priest arrived (Father Gaztelu, the old poet from *Orígenes*, Lezama's confessor) for the last rites – those who were and called themselves friends left the chapel as if the Devil had come in and not a vicar of God. Now Virgilio's death (the definitive one: Virgilio had become one of the undead), which given Virgilio Piñera's taste for classical parody would have to be called *Der Tod des Vergil* – his durable death reunites him with Lezama. The two, Virgilio and Lezama, had again become friends in life. One of Lezama's last poems is a celebration of Virgilio and is entitled 'Virgilio Piñera Celebrates His Sixtieth'. The only possible celebration by the poet for the parallax writer would be a poem that could say, in mangled Mallarmé: in themselves eternity unites them but the literary life reunites them.

(April 1980)

Two Died Together

At the end of the thirties there were two *emigré* Cuban women and as the French *mot* indicates both lived in Paris. One came from a musical family, the other was the daughter of a lawyer successful since the last century. Those women were Anaïs Nin and Lydia Cabrera. Anaïs became French in Paris and later American in New York. Lydia went back to Cuba to fulfil her Cuban destiny.

Lydia became the greatest Cuban woman writer of the century. She invented what I have called anthropoetry, a mixture of anthropology and poetry, with which she recovered the legends become religion brought from Africa with slavery to Cuba. Sister-in-law of the scholarly ethnologist Fernando Ortiz (who coined the term Afro-Cuban, from which come all the Afros, including the hairstyle that made Angela Davis so popular – but then again, who's Angela Davis?), Lydia came from a patrician family and went to Paris to study art as was the Cuban custom. It was as a student in Paris that she met the blue bird: there she heard Negro art talked about for the first time. Thus she changed her life when she wrote a book, published in France in 1936, called *Contes nègres de Cuba*, translated by Francis de Miomandre, translator of Cervantes and Quevedo. Lydia went back to Havana to find that her old black nurse still remembered everything about the blacks from Africa in Cuba. The blue bird was in fact a black bird.

The *tata*, called sometimes *chacha* like the girl that she was, transported her to Africa and Lydia never looked back. She later published numerous books about the Bantu and Yoruba gods that coexisted in Cuba with the Catholic religion and the Spanish saints. So Changó was syncretized with St Barbara: both carried a sword, her name meant a depository for explosives in Spanish, he was the god of war, one remembers her when it thunders, the other was the keeper of lightning. Besides, consider the literary facts: to make fun of his enemies Changó, like Achilles, disguised himself as a woman (St Barbara) but he was given away, like Achilles, by his sword: his virility. Thus was born *santería*, the most powerful syncretic union of the African mythologies with Catholicism. It was not extinguished by atheist persecution but left Cuba as an exile and was spread through the Caribbean basin and to the north in Manhattan and New Jersey and, north by northwest, got as far as the land of dreams in Hollywood.

At first her family and her friends were alarmed at Lydia's interest. She was too friendly with the *santeros* (witch doctors) and, what is even worse, with the *abakuás*, the secret society known – and feared – as *ñáñigos*. But Lydia was received by the sect members as one of them. Perhaps it may have helped that she was from high society, but if they thought she was only slumming they were wrong. Or perhaps it was all due to her personal charm, that charm with which she won over the gypsy friends of Lorca in Spain. Lorca himself had dedicated his best poem, 'The Unfaithful Bride' to Lydia – and Lorca added with a wink 'and to her little black girl'. It was Lydia who put Lorca in touch with actress Margarita Xirgu, with the result we all know: she became Lorca's best tragedian. But also Lydia brought Lorca to an *ekbó*, a *santería* ceremony, and the poet, always delicate, fainted (or faked fainting) in the arms of Lydia – who was a fragile-looking but strong woman.

Her enormous charm was still visible when she was over ninety. Charm once meant sorcery and perhaps Lydia put the wizards of the secret tribe under a spell to master the black magic – in which she never believed. It was because of this that they allowed her to enter the *fambá* room (she was the first woman ever to get in), which was the *sancta sanctorum* of the *ñáñigos*. She was, in her dealings with men and women, of a rare charm, *encantadora*.

But she was also a serious investigator of the African cultures in Cuba, survivors all of the great racial shipwreck that was slavery. Black folklore survived all the disasters and had a more potent resurgence than in black Africa, left behind but transformed into a nostalgia with drums. This is the principal reason why they survived in Cuba, in Haiti, and in Brazil: the slaves kept their drum as a source of magic and of music. In Anglo-Saxon America they took the drum away from them and fixed their colour for ever: there are no mulattos in the United States. All the Negroes are black.

Lydia always reminded me of Karen Blixen, an apparently fragile woman who was tough, hard and who loved the Africans more than anything in the world. But Blixen stayed out of Africa, as her masterpiece claims, while Lydia, constant, constantly in all her books always goes back to Africa. Lydia wrote her epitaph in an interview (she was the most interviewed Cuban woman this century) that she once granted: 'If there had been no blacks in Cuba, I would never have lived there.'

She died in Miami, where she lived for more than a quarter of a century with her constant companion, Titina de Rojas, a society beauty whom Lydia converted into an important archaeologist. Titina was the owner of the fabulous Quinta San José, where Lydia also lived. When both were exiled in 1960 the Mayor of Marianao ordered the villa and the palm trees that surrounded it to be razed. Ironically Fidel Castro sent commissars as emissaries to tell her that his Government would give her a pension. He even tempted her with other mansions in Havana when Lydia was living in a minimal flat in a Miami suburb. Lydia Cabrera stood firm – magnificently stubborn in exile till the end.

A legend runs through exiledom that goes like this:

A *tasca* in old Madrid on a November afternoon in 1976. Two middle-aged men are talking seated at a table. One of them is an imposing black who could easily play Othello, the other is white, short, with protruding eyes that seem to see everything. He could be played by Peter Lorre in *Casablanca*. Both are Cuban, both exiles and they have been talking louder than the Madrileños around them – and that's saying a lot. One of the two Cubans was a powerful journalist, a managing editor but actually the editor-in-chief of the conservative *Diario de la Marina*, one of the oldest newspapers on the American continent. The other man is a writer, a professional survivor and a traveller without a compass.

They are, from right to left, Gastón Baquero and Enrique Labrador Ruiz. They are talking their way downhill. When there is a clearing in their conversation, one hears an unusual thunder: the whole *tasca* applauds. They are still applauding the two Cubans who talked. They heard them as one hears the rain at first, then they listened attentively, then they applauded deafeningly. The Madrileños, who know about *tasca* talk, recognized the two foreigners for what they were: masters of conversation. The two writers were talking cheerfully although they were reminiscing about their youth out loud. Baquero is the leading poet of Cuba, Labrador, as everyone called him to invoke the sun of his conversation shining, was a novelist famous all over South America. The two Cubans now allowed themselves to venture into what Dante called the 'greatest grief' and remembered happy times in the midst of sorrow. The two friends in the *tasca* were both exiles and the only thing left to them in life was their art. In which figured, prominently, conversation.

Labrador was a pioneer in Spanish America of what was later called, with more noise than accuracy, the Boom. He was also a rebel within a Revolution. He paid dearly for both feats. In 1933 Labrador published a novel (*El laberinto de sí mismo*) that he called *gaseiforme* (of a gaseous form), and one must wait for Lezama Lima, whose *Paradiso* was published in 1966, to find a similar approach to the art of narration in the tropics. Then he displayed several subjects of experiences that were objects of experiment, like *Cresival* (1936) and *Anteo* (1940), whose very titles were novel in the extreme. Later in his life he became preoccupied with certain formless forms that he called '*novelines neblinosos*', because they were something more and something less than novels: they were enveloped in a mist of prose that was to be dissipated with reading. In 1940 he published a book whose content was almost a prescience of that Madrid afternoon thirty-five years later. It was called *Paper for Smoking – Ashes of Conversation*. Unlike their audience, neither of the two men smoked.

Labrador was a voracious voyager who devoured leagues – major and minor. He was also a prolific writer who published a lot and got to know everyone who was anyone in America – and elsewhere. His last book, published in Miami in 1990 (when he was already locked up in the labyrinth of senility), is called with a chosen play on words, *Cartas à la carte* – in which *cartas* means letters. In Spanish, a Spaniard said, writers are descended from one-armed Cervantes or from Quevedo skilled in duels. Labrador comes from Quevedo. But, the opposite of Quevedo, so pugnacious, Labrador was a friendly, gregarious man, who could be a friend at the same time of tame Asturias and of the literary lion who was Neruda. A drinker after the Irish manner (shades of Flann O'Brien), Labrador boasted about having banished Neruda (as good a drinker as he was) to sleep under the table in each duel of drinks.

But the opposite of Neruda, Labrador was a democrat all his life who never boasted of getting the Stalin Prize and tried to leave Castro's Cuba like a boat that sank before its anchor. He didn't succeed until 1976. The price he had to pay was to leave behind not only Havana but also the sixty thousand volumes of his library (I saw it, I saw them), many of which were autographed by their authors. Labrador was prouder of his books than of his meetings with his 'friend Johnny, last name Walker'. As in an Irish wake (so similar to the old Cuban *velorios*), one must drink Labrador's health singing a song that goes: '*Sobre una tumba una rumba.*' On his grave never be grave.

Vital dates: Enrique Labrador Ruiz, writer and *causeur*, was born in Sagua la Grande, Las Villas, 11 May 1900, married to Cheché, died 10 November 1991. Lydia Cabrera, anthropoet, was born in Havana, 20 May 1900 and died in Miami, 19 September 1991.

(November 1991)

Montenegro, Prisoner of Sex

It takes some effort to believe, I know, that the newspaper *Hoy* in the forties was a university. So it was at least in the first five years of the decade. The Communist Party, of which it was the organ, was on the upswing then. The Party was legal. To boot, Batista had given them the Cuban Confederation of Workers, the powerful CTC, and two of the Party's most distinguished members were made by him ministers without portfolio. With Batista the Party had quite a lot of money at home in the form of anonymous sinecures and abroad Stalin was 'Uncle Joe' for the frivolous Roosevelt and also (why not say it?) for the astute Churchill. Recently the three had sat down at the same table to carve up the map of Europe – and of the world.

Then the American Communist leader Earl Browder, in agreement with Moscow, had created a whole revisionist theory in which Communism and capitalism were the same thing but with gulags – about which nobody in Cuba knew or wanted to know. (Neither about gulags nor about purges.) The Americans without much difficulty got the Communist leader, aliased by himself as Blas Roca, to emulate (a favourite verb with Communists) Browder and to declare that in Cuba the Communist Party, having become the inoffensive Popular Socialist Party, was now converting to Browderism as some sort of Marxist Platt Amendment. To top it all off, the so-called workers' party, in less than four years of sharing power with Batista, a mulatto like Roca, would support for the next President of Cuba Batista's candidate, Carlos Saladrigas – a haughty member of the white Havana upper class. You have to see it to believe in Marx.

I knew nothing of this, of course, when I went with my father for the first time to the newspaper *Hoy* on 27 July 1941. The date is marked with ink in my memory because there I saw and heard for the first time collective typewriters tapping in unison, to create that *sui generis* sound of city offices that has disappeared today with the plague of the word processor – the mute machine that types green letters. Another thrilling discovery was seeing the linotype, a bird invented by man, hunting letters like insects to cook them in a soup of molten lead. The largest, noisiest and happiest invention was the rotary press, seen in the cinema always producing sensational extras, to read all about it, but now deafening the floor, and making an impression on me as on the endless roll of newsprint. Like an emanation, the odour of the ink went from weak, in the typewriters, to heavier in the printing press. Everything became an unforgettable spectacle that was started with an electric bell announcing that the show was about to begin – just like in the theatre in my home town.

With time the gathering of so much talent under one roof would turn out most unforgettable. It would be list-making to mention only the names of the men and women who at that moment worked on *Hoy*. Present is, first because he was the one with the most talent, Lino Novás Calvo. Then came Carlos Montenegro, of whom I will be talking very soon. And Rolando Masferrer, who had been, like Lino and Montenegro, in Spain during the Civil War. But Masferrer had gone as a combatant. Now he was lame from a wound that he suffered on the Madrid front. Masferrer had been an urban fighter in Havana as well, at the University and in other parts of the city, sent as a gunman by the Party. Now he looked more peaceful as a chief of cables, translating from some rolls that came out of another marvellous machine, the teletype, a typewriter that wrote by itself – but only messages in English. Masferrer later became a gangster and then a *sbirro* of Batista and would die blown up by a bomb in Miami – after finishing a sentence in Sing-Sing. He showed himself to be one of the best journalists that Cuba has ever produced, writing a dynamic and audacious prose that he borrowed from the Spanish anarchists, as did Hemingway: powerful paragraphs loaded with *cojones* and *carajos* that he handled freely, without a censor. Who dared correct the incorrigible leader of the Masferrer Tigers? (Not a ball club but a paramilitary gang capable of terrorizing anyone who lived in Cuba from 1952 to 1959.) Masferrer's last name was fear. Once, before the coup by Batista, the police caught him in the act of burying alive a member of the opposition – who surely deserved it.

Among the women on *Hoy* were Emma Pérez, who had married Montenegro in prison, and Mirta Aguirre, an obvious lesbian, who wasn't married to anyone. Emma Pérez, a professor of pedagogy at Havana University, went, together with Montenegro and Masferrer, to set up a faction around a newspaper, *Tiempo en Cuba*, and then the magazine *Gente* – which she edited with an iron fist. She produced, as later in her column in *Bohemia*, a refined journalism not at all restricted but a show-off instead: she handled high and pop culture with the greatest of ease. Mirta Aguirre was a film critic with a partisan yardstick, but with a sure and sagacious grasp of the cinema. She also did music and stage criticism with the same snobbish authority. Aguirre was a woman of a rare courage, even physically, and when I met her as an adult (we were both professors at the School of Journalism) I could appreciate her mordant wit capable of being a gag for others. A Socratesa, she was accused by her own Party of perverting her female students and there and then ended her days (and her nights) under Castro.

There were other writers on *Hoy* who would be out of place anywhere, like Carlos Franqui and Agustín Tamargo. Both would go off to join Masferrer but Franqui did so only for a short time.

The editor-in-chief of the newspaper at the time was Aníbal Escalante, later famous for his double bout with Fidel Castro, which showed that Escalante was not only a very intelligent politician but a man of extraordinary courage. (Many, for doing less, were shot by Castro.) Aníbal, as everyone called him, *almost* made off with power with the Russians' blessing. Be that as it may that era is known as the time when Castro ruled under the pseudonym of Aníbal. Aníbal – not many know this because he hid himself, *larvatus prodeo* – was a man of considerable culture and his library, which he allowed few to see, was vast. But, he was, he always was, a rabid Stalinist. That was how he could face that other Stalin. But there can't be more than one Stalin at a time. Aníbal found out only too late. Like Khrushchev he died in obscurity.

The dominant literary lion on the newspaper (besides Nicolás Guillén, also called the Mane, poet in residence) was Carlos Montenegro, he of the memorable name, formidable in figure. Montenegro was the managing editor, which meant that he concerned himself with literature. It was the most important editorship after the information editor, a more journalistic post. Montenegro was then a tall, hirsute man: an ugly face with thick glasses gave him a mole-like look. He was stooped, rumpled and flatfooted and one wonders how he was once sexually irresistible. The answer is prison: where he had spent fifteen years of a life not too long then.

Like Novás Calvo, Montenegro had worked, as a young man, in assorted jobs. 'Cabin boy, banana loader in Central America,' enumerates Enrique Pujals on the cover of his best book. Born in Galicia, Montenegro emigrated at seven to Cuba. At thirteen he sailed on a coaster tramp, lived for a year in Argentina, was a miner and worked in an arms factory in the United States. Pujals states that he was beaten up and put in prison in Tampico – which may be a false fable. Another fable, this time more true to life, is that at eighteen he was sexually assaulted by a sailor on the Havana waterfront – whom he killed. He was tried, sentenced to life and served fifteen years in El Príncipe gaol in Havana. It was in prison that he began to write and won a story competition sponsored by *Carteles*, then the most important magazine in Cuba.

His life, a parallax to Lino Novás Calvo's, changed when he won this prize and all of cultural Havana learned that the author of the story ('The Sprout', influenced, of course, by Maxim Gorky, a social realist with an unbearable sentimental baggage – then in vogue) was in prison for what the morality at the time considered the defence of a man's honour. First a pressure group was organized, then a protest and finally a petition for pardon. Montenegro was released – not without first getting married in prison. A curious way of getting out of one sentence to start another.

In freedom Montenegro, the golden boy of the liberal Left, followed the way of all political flesh: he became a Communist and his fame grew under the spreading social tree of the Party. He published, inevitably, a book entitled *The Sprout and Other Stories* (1929), next *Two Ships* (1934), another collection of stories, and then he went off to Spain as a foreign correspondent during the Civil War. From there he returned with a book of war reportages and a partisan prose poem, 'Planes Over the People'. Not long before going to Spain he published his masterpiece, the novel *Men without Woman*, which is totally different from the Gorkian story that he wrote in prison. Hard, or rather implacable, as the title barely indicates, and full of sex from beginning to end – of the *only* kind of sex possible in prison. An autobiography on the surface, *Men without Woman* is a book in which pederasty and that form of sodomy to which Cubans are particularly partial, buggery (the active possession of one man by another, who will take then the place of the woman) form the only possible relationship. The book was considered in its time, in Cuba and elsewhere, to be a masterpiece – and it is.

In Spanish one will have to wait until the publication in 1976 of *Kiss of the Spider Woman*, by Manuel Puig, which is a work of fiction created by the imagination of its author, to find a book that resembles it. *Men* is a cruel autobiography: the destiny that its author avoided with the death of his assaulter is fulfilled in prison, with its protagonist finally yielding to the same sexual requirements but through the will of desire. Montenegro says in his note to the reader, 'I consider it a duty . . . to describe in all its crudeness what I lived through.' The novel is a forerunner of Genet. Better than Genet because it does not have the burden of pseudo-Romantic literature with which Genet idealizes crime. Besides, Montenegro was never a thief. He was free therefore from publishing a poem to thieving maids.

Men without Woman is not only a great Cuban novel but a solitary work in the Spanish language. But the lunatic cry of the prisoner, desperate to have a woman, who howls: 'I want to eat white hen meat!' recalls strangely the moment in *Amarcord* when the giant madman perched in the tree (of life) cries in the wind: *'Voglio una donna!'* Fortunately, not for the author who is dead but for his readers, the book is not totally forgotten and there have recently been two successive printings in Mexico and in Spain. The enthusing young men of Málaga didn't waste their enthusiasm when, to launch their publishing house, they chose this book, so locally Cuban. (Moreover belonging to Havana, even more pertaining to El Príncipe prison, shut up in it like a prisoner.) They congratulated themselves on their choice, when declaring themselves fortunate at revealing to the Spanish reader a memorable forerunner – a masterpiece in no way ordinary.

The Montenegro who commanded the literary office of *Hoy* not as an exalted gaolbird but as an author laureate (he had just published his third volume of stories in 1941, *The Heroes*, and would win the prestigious Hernández Catá Prize in 1944) never attached much importance either to his prizes or to literature itself. (It is the same existential error committed by Lino Novás that never even passed through the heads of Virgilio Piñera or of Lezama.) Now, shuffling along rather than pacing around the editorial office, Montenegro was like a benevolent bear and if Hollywood had made the movie of his life they would have given the part to Walter Matthau.

One day when I was darting into the editorial office from the wire room, where the results of the World Series were coming in, baseball a *pasión* then rather than an *afición*, Montenegro caught me in mid-flight.

'Come here,' he called out to me.

It was of course an order. He told me that he saw me so much around the city desk that he believed I wanted to be a newspaperman when I grew up. I thought, but I never told him, that at twelve years old I only wanted to be a ballplayer, to play if not in the major leagues at least in the Cuban winter league. Infantile fantasies. But Montenegro continued: 'Can you type?'

I told him no. He told me then that he was going to teach me and he gave an expert half-turn to his typewriter, which was on top of a satellite – a word that still amazes me. (Was every newspaperman a planet then?) He put it in front of me.

'Type.'

I tried but badly, of course.

'To be a newspaperman,' he instructed me, 'you first have to know how to type. Understand?' I told him yes. I tried again. 'No, no,' he told me. 'Never type with all your fingers. Newspapermen type with only two fingers. If you type with all your fingers you'll never be a newspaperman – you'll be a typist.'

This lesson, the only one that I learned to learn to write, I have never forgotten. Every time someone, seeing me type with my right middle and left index fingers, tries to get me to type with all my fingers I know that he is reducing me to a typist.

When Montenegro, Emma Pérez, Lino Novás Calvo and Masferrer and his people left the newspaper I did not see them again. As a group. Yes, I saw Lino Novás many times but never after he left Cuba as he left *Hoy*. I saw Montenegro too in his Miami exile. He was shut up in his apartment as if it were his voluntary cell. White-haired, he had taken on as an old man a noble aura. Now he didn't look like a mole: he looked like the birdman of Alcatraz in the movie! (There was even a certain resemblance between Montenegro and Burt Lancaster.) To accentuate the similarity Montenegro's apartment was full of cages with birds: canaries, mockingbirds, bluejays and, I believe, even passerines from Pinar, that bird that is so Cuban.

I spoke with Montenegro and he remembered *Hoy* but he remembered it badly. He assured me that he had left it in 1938 – when it had not yet been founded. I told him that on that date he was co-editor of the journal *Mediodía*. He did not remember. Nor did he remember having given me a typing lesson. Some old people remember the more remote past, but others, from a particular flaw of the memory, don't remember anything. In the case of a writer one must search not for his recollections but for his books. It surprised me though that Carlos Montenegro, before dying, already didn't remember anything about his life – not even his books. Lino Novás Calvo, more badly treated by age than Montenegro, at least remembered the exactness of an article that replaced a pronoun. That is not grammar, which is the typing of writing. That is, no more and no less, literature. Montenegro died in Miami out of gaol but in solitary confinement.

(January 1992)

The Ninth Moon of Lino Novás

Lino Novás Calvo has just died in New York after ten years of ignored agony. The author of *Pedro Blanco, the Slave Trader* had suffered a series of strokes in the 1970s that had left him half-paralysed first and then completely paralysed and finally converted into that living vegetable that at times seems to be the way of all flesh. We will never know for certain how much Lino suffered lying in state still alive, but we do know what his widow Herminia del Portal suffered from his death in life. Miriam Gómez and I went with her to a hospital where just visiting him was a violent vision of the hell of senility. Old man's dementia, paralysis agitans and senile stupor were the décor there and the only possible landscape. Among these offenders whom Jonathan Swift with irreverent irony called the Immortals (sentenced to life, prisoners of their survival in the prison of longevity), there Lino gave a last demonstration of his creative energy.

I have on my shelf of Cuban books a cheap but for me a precious first edition. It is *The Ninth Moon*, a remote title, published in Buenos Aires in 1942: that is, more than forty years ago. This volume of stories is a masterpiece of the genre and when one day the definitive history of the short story in America is written it will be seen that Lino Novás is among the masters: Horacio Quiroga, Borges, Felisberto Hernández, Juan Rulfo, Virgilio Piñera, Adolfo Bioy Casares to cite them in chronological order. Lino Novás was the first who learned to adapt the American narrative techniques (Hemingway but above all Faulkner) to a writing that was truly Cuban – and what is more, of Havana. In his stories one hears Havana speaking with very little distortion for the first time. Above all the Havana of the outskirts, the one that conversed on Diezmero and Mantilla and Jacomino and Luyanó and even Lawton Batista: in the back yards.

All that urban, suburban subworld was orally new. When another Cuban writer born in Spain, Antonio Ortega (from Gijón, Asturias) acquainted me with the stories of Lino (from then on no longer Novás Calvo) it was as if with this book he had opened a little door to a wide world – but one's own – contained under the strange title of *The Ninth Moon*. I remember having taken along the little volume on the ritual return for Christmas to my own town, reading it all to become worn out in my second-class compartment, the train transformed into my particular Trans-Siberian, the trip long in time lost in space: an Orient Express through the looking glass.

The train had left the old Egido Terminal at ten in the evening, with Chelo's livid arm waving goodbye from the receding platform and at daybreak we were still in Las Villas Province, going straight down the immense prairie (Cuba, like Africa, is nothing but an extended savanna) that was the landscape from Placetas to Cacocún – the Holguín junction – and the rest of the crossing made in the narrow-gauge gascar to Gibara: hills, a tunnel, the sea finally. That whole journey in the last days of 1947 (the end of an era and the beginning of literature) I had spent reading and rereading the rare writing of Novás Calvo. Rare not because remote but because close: those people with exotic names like Acerina Canadio, Silvia Silva, Nazario Niela did not live in *The Ninth Moon*, in the outskirts as in the story, but among us in Zulueta 408. 'He laughed his rattling death laughter,' barely giving a pause to a vertiginous image: 'and his eyes were *estriados*' ('striated'). Believe me, one didn't read like that in Spanish before 'In the Suburbs' was published. One didn't again write like that afterwards.

I remember having read then his story 'Angusola and the Knives' with a strange feeling that was the stirring art of the words that carried it all: the names, the men and the women (ah, Sofonsiba Angusola!) and the startling sex in a dark vital violence. Despite my respect for Carlos Montenegro (another dead writer forgotten in exile), Lino Novás Calvo became my favourite Cuban writer and, until the arrival of William Faulkner and of Borges, my favourite writer of all. I would have done (indeed, I *did*) cartwheels to read a new story by Novás Calvo. They were truly becoming scarce.

I remember Lino, the person, at the door of *Carteles* waiting, a driver getting on in years, for Herminia del Portal, his wife, then the editor of *Vanidades* and the journalist who had single-handedly revolutionized the Cuban woman's press as she would do later with the continental woman's magazine. Lino waiting would greet me as I passed by him with the faked falsetto he always used to refer to my television programme saying: '*You'll see, you're going to become an actor*' – perhaps wanting to warn me against the image, personal and virtual on television. Around that time Lino had stopped writing stories and was doing rapid reportages for

Bohemia (of which he was now literary editor), some so admirable that they seemed to qualify reluctantly as literature. He used to utter unusual sayings, like 'One must not write stories. Literature is finished. What one must do now is reporting. Movies and television have annihilated literature. Nothing is left but journalism.' An attitude that astonished and bothered me, believing, as I believed, that the only reason to do journalism, then and now, is to do daily or weekly literature: the newspaper as a literary pretext.

When Lino chose exile we were at opposite poles. That did not stop me from leaping on a solitary (and no doubt only) copy of *The Ninth Moon*, cinnamon and lemon, old and yellowed, unusual, in an old bookshop in Old Havana at the end of 1961 – the end of another era. How I took that book out of Cuba, and I still have it, a rare copy, is a story in itself – another story. The one for now is about Lino and literature.

In 1967 I published a book entitled *Tres tristes tigres* that contained a series of literary homages, in the form of parodies of several Cuban writers, from Martí to Virgilio Piñera. There was, there had to be, a parody of Lino: of his style, of his names, of his prose. Lino had gone back to literature in his exile, which instead of destroying him had strengthened his old vocation: he had written stories, published books and was then teaching Spanish at Syracuse University, in the state of New York – where his ashes have now returned. From there he wrote me a letter that showed that he had taken as an attack what I had intended as honouring him. He was really hurt and he called me Guillermito. But his tone was surely not one of affection. Please! If I had even paid homage to Alejo Carpentier, a truly unpleasant person, how was I going to attack Lino! What Lino believed to be jeering was not even burlesque: it was praise. I didn't answer his letter because I thought that it would only exacerbate his bitterness.

In the summer of 1980 I lived for three months in Manhattan and I decided that it was time to visit Lino and chat. I knew that he was confined to an old people's hospital and after insisting with Herminia del Portal, she consented to the visit on which she would accompany Miriam Gómez and me. I didn't know it then but we were going to see the living remains of Lino Novás Calvo. It was, however, a memorable occasion.

The hospital where Lino was shut up smelled of what old dotards smell of – acrid sweat, urine, dribble – and Lino came up in a wheelchair. He had suffered more than one change. The thin, neat, natty citizen of Havana had been converted, by the magic of the biological return, into a strong Galician. He didn't look clean but he wasn't a complete invalid and he could paint, although he coordinated his hands better than his ideas.

We talked, with Herminia as a sympathetic, pathetic interpreter, getting across our questions to Lino by the method of repeating in echo and raising her voice. In an uncanny moment I found myself talking with Lino directly and I told him the story of my first encounter with *The Ninth Moon* under the Cuban sun. He didn't seem to have any idea of what Cuba was and of course he knew nothing of moons. I mentioned to him in passing one of his lost masterpieces, the story 'Angusola and His Knives'. Lino corrected me right away, 'And *the* Knives. *The*.' Everyone was surprised at that sudden awakening of his mind in hibernation. Or not everyone. I had seen in this correction a surge of the nature, second or first but always verbal, in the writer from among the labyrinth of his wandering mind. Lino had shown that up to now, in his seventy long years, in spite of the strokes and the cerebral embolisms, despite the methodical, almost malevolent destruction of his mind by his body, his writer's memory was intact: a word had been enough to activate it. But for a writer a word is always more than a word. For him it was now the past creator Novás Calvo breaking into the present limbo of Lino.

I left with more hope than when I came that Lino would come back and recover. I told Herminia, converted into a sudden analyst, that Lino's mind needed exercise as much as his body: some frequent literary conversations would heal him. That was my therapy: literary conversations! As at other times, I was very much mistaken. The strong Galician peasant to whom Lino had reverted sustained his body but not his mind. Lino had two more strokes and finally became totally invalid, almost quadriplegic: except for one arm that jerked in spasms he could not move his body – not even the hand with which he wrote *The Ninth Moon*. He lived more than a year and a half more. Now he has just died, the man who was born in Galicia in 1905 and at the age of seven had been sent, alone, to Cuba to live with a distant uncle and perhaps to 'do the Indies' and become a rich *Indiano*. Without knowing it his mother had sent him to be a great Cuban writer.

I would have liked Lino to have lived for ever so that he could write things as Cuban, as of Havana, as the beginning of 'A Bad Man' and transform them anew into universal things. 'Well,' began the narrator who perhaps was Lino himself, 'I was a cab driver, like him, but I had started earlier, being younger, with a borrowed title and a little rented car with three pedals, perched high up there, on the front seat, and hearing them shout, "bad driver!" No matter.' Swift, who died a victim of senile dementia, wrote in his years of literary lucidity about the Immortals in *Gulliver*: 'That the question therefore was not whether a man would choose to be always in the prime of youth, attended with prosperity and health, but how he would pass a perpetual life under all the usual disadvantages which old age brings along with it.' What is the question then? Swift chose another immortality as his answer. Not that of the spirit, in which it is obvious that he did not believe although he was a cleric, but that of letters. He wrote, among other things, that *Gulliver* that I can now cite a little more than two hundred years later as if Swift were still alive and were not just dust of madness and desire.

Lino Novás Calvo, on being sent to America, also chose that destiny, even though he may seem to have renounced it during a moment of despair faced with inattention and inertia. Now he lives for ever in his books – and he will live as long as he is read. *The Ninth Moon* is his eternal moon: always new, always full, always shining over the dark horizon. So wrote Lino, so he began a story with the phrase 'This Captain Amiana!' to say then: 'The island was not at all alive in itself. An apparition, like a dead man having appeared. One felt that below it there fluttered something that did not flutter, that did not have a dead life, that saw things with different eyes.' It was that story of his that I parodied in part. Its title is, not by accident, 'The Dead Came Out That Night'. They come out with every reading.

(July 1983)

A Poet of a Popular Parnassus

Why did Neruda in his memoirs give Nicolás Guillén the nickname of 'Guillén the bad'? It wasn't so much an evaluation of *Jorge* Guillén as a devaluation of *Nicolás* Guillén. Neruda and Guillén were active in the same Communist Party, they were Stalinists together and the two enjoyed the same privileges as Louis Aragon, who went on from being a Surrealist to become a Stalinist (there is not a single convertible poet from the thirties who has not sung the praises of Stalin), to travel through Paris in a chauffeured Mercedes as I saw him on the rue Bonaparte in the autumn of my discontent in 1965 – collecting old letters and young boys to the double horror of André Breton who only murmured, '*C'est dégueulasse!*'

Neither Nicolás nor Neruda was a pederast or a collector (wait, Neruda had a collection of shells) but they were rivals. Each one aspired to be the Great Poet of America and, as we know today, neither was. But Neruda defeated Nicolás in the sweaty race to Sweden: it was Neruda who won the Nobel Prize. Nicolás, it must be said, never became the great poet that he constantly aspired to be. But when he started out, equipped as few were, it seemed that he would go far.

The thirties, a hard decade in Cuba, began under the best auspices for Guillén. In 1930 he published his *Motivos de son* based on the *son*: song and rhythm and popular poetry were already in his first poems. In that year he met Lorca, who became more than an influence, a master of the art of popular poetry presented as a sophisticated song. Not long afterwards, Guillén stopped being censor for the dictator Machado and wrote his best poems. He travelled to Spain at the beginning of the Civil War and the assassination of Lorca became one of his obsessions. To exorcize them he joined the Communist Party, where they elevated him to the rank of a grand master. A wag declared then: 'The *son* also rises.'

But if one reads a Guillén poem from after his conversion one sees how his art turns into crass craft and his poetry becomes Party propaganda broadcast. At times he sounds like a hack at ten cents the line, as with his poem to Stalin (written during the great purges), in which he employs *santería* (about which he knew nothing) and invokes the Afro-Cuban gods as if they were dubious deities:

> Stalin, may Changó protect you
> and may Yemayá care for you!

The curious thing is that Nicolás Guillén was not a Stalinist. He never was a *bon mourant* but a *bon vivant* and an insecure artist whom Communism offered a nice niche in the night. I met him when twelve – that is, I was twelve and Nicolás was forty – at the newspaper *Hoy*, where my father was a journalist and Guillén the poet in residence. The editorial board of *Hoy* was then some sort of Academe, where writers like Lino Novás Calvo and Carlos Montenegro had desks.

Lino Novás and Montenegro left the newspaper and the Party. But Guillén stayed loyal to those diverse allies of the Communists that go from Batista to Castro, while he composed a soulful soft sonnet to each. The Revolution made him a Poet Laureate and he was happy for a while. In Madrid, in 1965, sitting in a café watching all the Spanish girls pass by, he felt as in the garden of delights, when he exclaimed: 'This is the right country to seek asylum!' There is no need, I believe, to recall that Spain then was governed by the same Franco who assassinated Lorca and killed Miguel Hernández – and sent into exile what Augustín Lara sang as 'the cream of intellectualdom'.

After *Hoy*, that today which is now yesterday, we ran into each other in the most familiar places. One of them was at the Nuestro Tiempo Society, a cultural club that became a front organization of the Communist Party and stopped being a comfortable place. I left. It was there that he announced to me one day, 'I've already told your father that every day you resemble Gorky more.' Guillén could not know that Gorky, author of *The Mother*, was one of my brown beasts to browbeat. But I always suspected that Nicolás had read not even one line by the author who invented social realism. Guillén was only interested in poetry – in *his* poetry.

At the end of 1960 *Lunes*, the literary supplement of the newspaper *Revolución*, which I edited, invited Pablo Neruda to Cuba. Immediately Nicolás Guillén wrote a piece in *Hoy* in which he said that it wasn't a bad idea to invite Neruda 'but we must also invite other progressive [read Communist] poets' like Rafael Alberti, Nazim Hikmet and the Chinese poet Kuo Mo-ho. The note did not dare declare that what Guillén wanted was for Neruda *not* to be invited at all. I retaliated with an anonymous answer in *Lunes* where I said that those poets and some others[1] would be invited and I festively ended the note: 'As for Kuo Mo-ho: *¡cómo no!*' This was a catchy little rustic refrain that Guillén used a lot in his poems in lines like: '*Sí señor, ¡cómo no!*' That Monday afternoon Carlos Rafael Rodríguez (then the editor-in-chief of *Hoy*) was on the phone asking me: 'But why do you do these things, Guillermito? You know how sensitive Nicolás is. He's just spent an hour on the phone complaining about your parody.' Guillén really was like that.

With Neruda in Havana an episode took place that ended up comic – although it wasn't comfortable for Neruda. He gave readings in his plaintive voice and got together with the *Lunes* staff and still in his plaintive voice answered a question about the Revolution and the arts with a 'One must also sing to the moon', which was a brave statement in front of the then rampant social realists. But one noon when it had been planned to extend his triumphal stay in an extended tour and perhaps, like Lorca, to go to Santiago with Matilde's dark head of hair, I brought him back to the Riviera Hotel, where he was staying, from a trip to Old Havana. When he got out of the car he looked at the Malecón and asked me: 'What's that?' It was a barricade and I said: 'It's a barricade.' 'But, why are all the cannons pointing at the sea?' 'They're expecting an invasion.' 'Here?' 'Everywhere.' Neruda, who had an impassive face that went very well with his monotone voice, could not help turning pale to his teeth. He didn't say anything else and went up to his room. But in the afternoon he asked that his Cuban stay be cut short 'since he had urgent matters pending in Mexico'. Coincidence? Perhaps. But Guillén, four months later, wrote a heart-rending poem about the death of a militiaman, while Neruda, safe and sound, composed his *Canción de gesta*, exalting Fidel Castro in the Sierra – which is one of his worst poems. In a certain way Guillén 'the bad' was vindicated.

In 1961 at the closing party of the First Congress of Writers and Artists, of which Nicolás Guillén had been elected president (I was, a joke of a job, one of the seven vice-presidents who surrounded Nicolás like a Cuban version of Snow White), I introduced him to an American publisher and she exclaimed in ecstasy: 'Ah, the great black poet!' To be cut off immedi-

---

1 Some day one will have to wonder why American poets of this century like Eliot and Pound and even an Irishman like Yeats were Fascists, while *converso* Spanish American poets like Neruda, Vallejo and Guillén and one contemporary Spaniard or another chose to be Stalinists. That is, just as totalitarian.

ately by Guillén: 'Not black, mulatto.' The American lady stood corrected, rooted to the spot.

It may be splitting kinky hairs (the hair of blacks according to the Real Academia dictionary) but the difference between blacks and mulattos was established by Spaniards and Portuguese very early in the history of America, where a slave girl made pregnant by a white man (sex is colour blind) became free at the moment of birth. In the nineteenth century there were many distinguished mulattos in Cuba (and in Brazil: one has only to name Machado de Assis), although the country was governed by Spaniards and Cuban whites (those who called themselves *criollos*: sons of whites) rested their leisure and their business on black slaves. In the twentieth century Nicolás Guillén was one of the two best-known mulattos on the island. The other mulatto was Fulgencio Batista. One famous, the other infamous.

Guillén lived in Paris from 1952 to 1959, because so they say, Batista (curiously Nicolás was named Guillén Batista) did not allow him to return to Cuba. But during that time he was very popular on Cuban radio and television. Eliseo Grenet, author of 'Mamá Inés', had set more than one of his poems to music, Bola de Nieve sang songs with words by Guillén and even a popular poem player, Luis Carbonell ('The watercolourist of Caribbean poetry'), recited his verse (and his obverse) on the stage, radio and television. Never, at street level, had Guillén been more broadcast.

From his Paris period Guillén told me an anecdote that Neruda, for example, would never have told. Nicolás was sitting on the terrace of the Deux Magots Café when he overheard a conversation (his French was perfect) that concerned him. Two women's voices were apparently talking about him. He turned half around and saw two girls who looked pretty and intelligent – in a word perfect. They stopped discreetly: there was now no doubt what they were talking about. They went on glossing on his abundant (poet's) locks, his profile, his whole leonine head. Guillén got up to establish a beachhead. But before he started his move a phrase from one of the women chilled his ardour: 'But he's a dwarf!' Guillén allowed himself these revelations but he never would have allowed them to come from another person.

When Guillén came back to Cuba in 1959 (he was coming from abroad while Fidel Castro was coming down from the high Sierras) he was not as popular as John Lennon when he declared himself more popular than Christ, but he *was* more popular than Che Guevara. But, of course, only one man is free in Cuba and when they named Guillén president of the recently created Writers' Union he soon fell foul of Fidel Castro. When the Student Premier appeared at the university, in one of his impromptu speeches as students' leader, he became ever so garrulous, a critic of arts and letters. He praised Alejo Carpentier for his novel *Explosion in a Cathedral*, showing by the way that he had not read it since there are few books more precisely counter-revolutionary – although Carpentier's target was long ago and far away: the French Revolution. Castro now said that there was no writer more hardworking, more prestigious. When one of the students asked him about Guillén, the Maximum Leader maximized: 'He's a good-for-nothing bum who only writes *one* poem a year! He's probably the best-paid poet in the world, too expensive for us.' Then he praised a poetaster, who called himself Naborí the Indian, who wrote a poem every day for *Granma*, the official newspaper. Naborí was neither a poet nor an Indian and he wasn't even called Naborí, but Castro liked his Russian rhymes about hammers and sick capitalism. Naborí was almost named official poet: the Poetaster Laureate.

Suddenly, as in a poetic lynching, a political mob sprang up in the heat of the afternoon. Some students painted polemic placards and led by one Rebellón (not a rebel but a former student leader and now an official buffoon who sat at Castro's feet), they organized a chant for a choir in Guillén's style:

> Nicolás, don't work no mo'!
> Nicolás, you ain't a poe!
> No mo', no mo', no mo'!

The demonstration went down University Hill to the street where Guillén lived (not far but quite high: on a seventeenth floor) chanting and shouting. One could think that it was a student prank – but the presence of Rebellón gave the mock mob an *official* character. Guillén took it all to heart naturally. It was punishment without a crime. He was a poet not a rhymester of poems by the foot in a boot.

In June 1965 I came back to Havana from my diplomatic post in Brussels for my mother's funeral. Days after the funeral I went to the Writers' Union to say hello to Guillén. We had been Cuban together in Paris barely a month before, besides Guillén always struck me all right: he was very Cuban, very human. The Writers' Union was in a colonial mansion, almost a palace, left behind by a plantation owner on the lam who didn't even bother to close the door behind him. Guillén was in his office talking to a splendid blonde: Nicolás always preferred blondes. Right away he excused himself for not having been at the funeral with me but, a fatal coincidence, his mother had also died in Camagüey (his birthplace) and he had to be there. Guillén loved his mother as much as I did mine.

Then in a whisper that I thought formed part of his condolences he asked me to go out with him to the back yard. There, under an enormous mango tree, he asked me, still in a whisper, if I knew what had happened. Another whisper like a sigh. (In Cuba even blondes have ears and who knows if microphones grow on trees.) I said to him, embarrassed, that I knew nothing. Nicolás was on the verge of tears when he told me what I have already told you.

'The son of a bitch sent a mob after me! To my house!'

He didn't say who the son of a bitch was but it was understood: there's only one son of a bitch ruling Cuba.

'I wasn't there but they shouted at my wife, so frail, that I was a bum who doesn't write any more. That son of a bitch who hasn't worked a day in his life, a papa's boy first and then a professional gangster – dared to call me a bum! You know something? One day's he's going to send that mob to your house and they're going to lynch you because you're younger than I am. He's worse than Stalin, I'm telling you! Because Stalin died years ago but this gangster is going to outlive us. You and me.'

The old poet was right – partially. Guillén died last week and Fidel Castro buried him with honours.

But Guillén, even under the spreading mango tree, furious but dying from fear, was a poet. Able to fuse medieval metres with a modern and colloquial subject, he knew classical poetry like no one in America, except perhaps Rubén Darío, the Indian with white rhyme. But the opposite of the black poets of the Caribbean, Guillén never got to where he should have got, although he was in his day a better poet than Derek Walcott from Santa Lucía and Aimé Cesaire from Martinique. Like Louis Aragon, Guillén became a Communist when he was at his peak. After that, after *Motivos de son*, *Sóngoro cosongo* and *El son entero*, he went downhill. Although he was famous in the Spanish-speaking world and even in Paris and New York and was nominated twice for the Nobel Prize – after so many honours on the summit, he fell from grace with the muse. The tragic thing is that Guillén, at the end of his long life, knew it.

Obsessed by posterity and the lady on the road in his poem:

> I was going along a road
> when I met up with death,

his bedside book was a horror called *The Encyclopedia of Death*. He read to me, on a date as early as 1962, a passage that dealt with what happens after the death of the body, worms and all. 'Read,' he advised me, 'what it says there about rigor mortis and the onset of putrefaction.' He was not the poet Pope but perhaps Poe. 'But,' he summed up, thinking perhaps of M. Valdemar, 'the opposite of man, poetry never takes corruption.' The words are his, the ambiguity mine.

Nicolás Guillén has now had a Marxist (or martial) funeral, with four soldiers in mourning carrying on their shoulders the dead body of the poet who wrote:

> I don't know why you think,
> soldier that I hate you.

His remains were laid out in the Pantheon of the Heroes and Martyrs of the Fatherland, as befitting the funeral honours of the National Poet. Moreover two days of national mourning were officially declared. But I am sure that the day when Fidel Castro called him a good-for-nothing bum (in public) still smarts his memory. Nicolás Guillén was what Faulkner called in *Intruder in the Dust*, concerning Lucas Beauchamp, 'a proud Negro'. Although Nicolás will find fault with me from the beyond and will say in his grave voice: 'Proud yes but not black. I am still a mulatto.'

(July 1989)

Alejo Carpentier, a Shotgun Cuban

It was the late Ithiel León, musician, publicist and, in his next-to-last incarnation, acting editor of the newspaper *Revolución*, who referred for the first time to Alejo Carpentier's French accent as an added value price. 'Alejo must impress the Venezuelans a lot,' said Ithiel, 'with those r's of his.' This happened at the beginning of the fifties when Carpentier came on a visit to his native Havana from his adopted Caracas. (Or was it the other way around?)

At the time Carpentier must have also adopted not only the capital but the country as well in a citizenship as he was living, working and writing in Caracas. Even his American publisher had him, on one of his covers, as a Venezuelan. This is not strange because he was the co-owner of a thriving advertising firm in Venezuela, besides being a cultural boss – something he had never been able to achieve in Cuba. His activities extended even to organizing artistic events for the dictator Pigpig Pérez. He was not as important again until he became a minion of Fidel Castro in the sixties, first as a cultural adviser, then as head of the National Printing Press ('the tsar of the book', a journalist on the run nicknamed him) and finally he was an official envoy to France until he died in Paris, the city of his dreams – and his nightmares.

It was during one of his nightmares (hunger's fault more than man-made) that Lydia Cabrera met Carpentier in Paris in 1932. One day I asked Lydia if Alejo already talked like that, with his rolling Rs full frontal. Lydia assured me that he always did. Wasn't it true then, what Rogelio París, the film director, had heard? He was the producer of a television show sponsored by the Council for Culture, which Alejo supervised. París, whom Carpentier always called Pagrís, told me that during a rehearsal for the programme an expensive cyclorama fell down and split in two. A shocked Alejo, to the amazement of everyone, let loose a quite audible swear word. París finished up: 'The guy, *mon vieux*, didn't say *cagrajo* but very clearly *car*-ajo! He lost his French R when he lost face.' Lydia, who detested Carpentier, though not as much as Lezama did, always called him *Alexis*. (More, later.)

I met Carpentier, who right away became Alejo, in 1958. He came to *Carteles* introduced by his best promoters, Luis Gómez Wangüemert, who in spite of his surname was as Havanan as the sea of columns that fascinated Alejo. He was the city editor of *Carteles*. Celebrity hunter Sara Hernández Catá, Wangüemert's lover, was a literary Amazon, who having lost a lung to cancer still smoked cigarette after cigarette, all neatly stuffed into the longest holder ever. She assured me it managed, by alchemy, to eliminate the tar and leave the smoke as clean as the morning mist.

Carpentier came to publicize the sale of his recent novel, *The Lost Steps*, to the movies – specifically to Tyrone Power. He was carrying like an ID a photo of the author with the actor to prove it. (The only thing surprising about that dubious duo was that Carpentier was much taller than Power.) Alejo, a solid-looking man with his snub nose and his bug eyes, reminded one of Donald McBride, a character actor of the thirties. But if one wanted him to resemble someone prominent then the resemblance was to J. Edgar Hoover, full frontal and profile, like in a mug shot. When he came back to Cuba a year later the first thing that Alejo did was to reclaim the snapshot that he gave me to publish.

I remember that we went to the café on the corner (run by my friend Pastorita) with Prof. Sergio Rigol, who was the librarian for *Carteles*, a magazine that allowed itself such luxuries, and Rine Leal, a stage critic reduced at that time to a modest version of a star reporter. I still have a snapshot taken by Raúl Corrales, also called Raoul, in which we appear all young, all smiling, and Alejo looks pleased by our reception of one of his racy anecdotes. Carpentier, who was up to date on everything published in Paris, talked to us about the most amusing new novel that he had read in a long, long time – *Zazie dans le Métro* by Raymond Queneau. (All the French *mots* rolled perfectly out of his mouth.) When he had told all about the adventures of Zazie, aged eight, and the misadventures of her uncle Gabriel, a transvestite, he quoted the first line to us. 'Doukipudonktan,' said Alejo and when he saw the three of us with our three mouths open, he explained then translated: 'It's Paris argot. It means why do the French stink so much?' Ah! aha! ahahaha! I told him it reminded me of an American novel called *Lolita*. 'Who's it by?' The author is a Russian exile called Nabokov. 'I am not familiar with him.' It's very entertaining. It came out in Paris in English. I bought it at the Casa Belga, where they sold it to me as pure pornography. Ah Alejo. He seemed uncomfortable. 'Actually,' he told us, 'of *Zazie* I've read the fragments that the *Nouvelle Revue Française* published. Very amusing, very amusing.' It was weird because Carpentier was the furthest possible reader (and writer) from Raymond Queneau. It must have been because it was a French book. That or *Lolita* disturbed him.

He kept telling tales of the adventures of Cuban politicians on *terra firma*. Although a journalist always pretends not to have to work and besides *Carteles* was a weekly, we all had to go. Carpentier said goodbye. Alejo, *aléjate*. I did not see him again until he returned to Cuba, to set himself up when Fidel Castro, not the Revolution, looked firm. It seemed, in fact, eternal.

Carpentier was apparently born in Havana in 1904, but even his most fervent exegetes admit that the only (incomplete) biography of Alejo is the one he wrote himself. Carpentier according to Carpentier is the son of a Frenchman and a Russian woman who emigrated to Havana, Cuba, in 1902. But Carpentier himself says: 'I must explain that I was raised in the Cuban countryside,' (that is, not in Havana) 'in contact with black country people and their songs.' The narrative account by Heberto Padilla that describes Carpentier as a milkman in Alquízar is therefore not so hard to believe. But it appears rather that Carpentier grew up in Oriente Province, perhaps in the heights of Alto Songo, where there abound, in contrast with Havana Province, black farm workers galore.

Not in vain does one of his biographers note that 'there is really very little information about Carpentier's life' – to point out one truly significant fact: 'most of it has been supplied by Carpentier himself'. Accordingly Alejo 'spent more than twenty years of his adult life in France', while he studied 'from 1912 to around 1921' in a French *lycée*. 'In 1939,' continues his biographer, 'Carpentier returned to Havana after having spent eleven years in Paris.' He was 'thirty-five'. The chronology stretches and shrinks like a rubber band. More still: when he arrived in Caracas from Havana in 1945, Carpentier was interviewed by a journalist and the biographer notes that Alejo spoke to the interviewer 'as if Carpentier had just returned from Europe, skipping the six years' that he had just spent in his native country. Cuba not France.

A relevant accident in Carpentier's life (his four months in prison for opposing the dictator Machado: some say that it was forty days, others that it was only four, but nobody says what the anti-Machado action was that Carpentier dared to carry out), ended with his exile in France – a country from which he had returned only six years before. Carpentier himself tells how he tricked Machado's police by exchanging passports with the French poet Robert Desnos, visiting Havana then. But nobody tells with what document the generous Desnos travelled back to France. Did he use Carpentier's incriminating passport? Or did he have a new French passport made for himself in Havana, to the confusion on board of two different passengers with the same passport? Or did Desnos, always adventurous, travel incognito? He was prone to using pseudonyms until he died in a concentration camp.

Carpentier, always in flight, returned to Cuba fleeing from the Nazis in 1939. The same year his protector Desnos embarked on his last adventure – in which his false papers did not save him from certain death. Here it is necessary to make it clear that Carpentier went back to Cuba under the Government of the still dictator Batista. He lived in Havana during the period when Batista, varnished with legality, governed with the help of the Cuban Communists – to leave for Venezuela as soon as there was democratic Government in Cuba (from 1944 to 1952, presided over by Dr Ramón Grau San Martín, champion of *laissez-faire* and the corrupt but no less democratic Carlos Prío). The decade would not end without Carpentier's serving another dictator – Piglet Pérez, in Venezuela. Carpentier's connection with culture under a dictatorship had started when he went to Haiti in 1943 as a cultural attaché of the Cuban Government. Carpentier recounts, without blushing, this title and this expedition – to emphasize that he travelled with the French actor Louis Jouvet. But he forgets to mention that in the group, or in the *troupe*, travelled a minor Surrealist called Pierre Mabile, a man more decisive in Carpentier's life than the actor Jouvet.

Fools and knaves always coincide in disinformation. Thus it is repeated everywhere now that Carpentier 'created magic realism'. They do not know (or they forget) that this tag was fabricated by a German named Franz Roh in 1924 when Carpentier had just left college in Havana or a French *lycée* and wanted to be an architect because he knew that architecture is congealed music or brown brick letters – whatever one wants to believe. Roh, curiously, bestowed his rubric on minor and mediocre artists who ended up being cultivators of National-Socialist realism – Nazis for short. What Carpentier created (with a little help from his friend Mabile) was another tag, 'the marvellous in the real', that served him only for a short novel, *The Kingdom of this World*. Later he forgot the *pot-au-feu* as he eliminated the recipe from the now invisible prologues to his French and American editions. No longer does magic realism or even the marvellous in the real belong to Carpentier. They are not his inventions but Roh's and Mabile's. Carpentier was always a good adapter from his days on French radio until CMZ, broadcasting for the Ministry of Education in Havana in the early forties. Curiously the CMZ had its headquarters inside the Columbia military camp.

One of the reasons that Carpentier was not appreciated in Cuba is that he was a bore, without a sense of humour. All his conversation was supported by seemingly comic anecdotes and stories that his way of telling them made boring. But me, personally, I liked Alejo. He was a man cautious to the point of cowardice and distrustful to the point of loneliness. But I liked him really. Once, in a cocktail party at the Barra Arrechabala, a handsome colonial building across from the Cathedral, we were alone for a moment. It happened in 1960 and he was already installed in Cuba for ever. It was then that it occurred to me to ask him about the Venezuelan Miguel Otero Silva as a writer. Carpentier looked over one shoulder, then over the other – as if he were expecting furious fans of Otero to jump him. He finally told me, his voice quite low: 'He's very bad.' Otero Silva, owner of the Caracas daily *El nacional*, a millionaire several times over, might have been a very powerful man in Caracas, but in Havana Lisandro Otero, then a young apprentice commissar, was more important. Was Alejo referring perhaps, with so much caution, to the other Otero?

Carpentier had come from Caracas to Havana in mid-1959, carrying a curious tropical variant of a capitalist publishing house on his literary shoulders: a portable book fair. In the company of Manuel Scorza, a Peruvian writer, he was publisher and seller. Carpentier, who feared above all criticism by *Lunes*, was elated when Calvert Casey wrote a paean not a panning of one of the novels that he had published, *The Impure* by Miguel de Carrión. I don't know if he was also amazed at the good reception that Carlos Franqui gave him in the newspaper *Revolución*, at the beginning. But I do remember that it was opportune and necessary for him.

Like Alicia Alonso, Carpentier did not come very well recommended by the mission of the 26th of July Movement in Venezuela. Both had distanced themselves violently and voluntarily from the Cuban exiles and Madame Alonso, who had enjoyed a subvention from the Batista Government, permitted herself to say in Caracas that she was a dancer – and never got involved in politics. The displeasure with Carpentier did not have the public character of the rejection of *la* Alonso (called then, because of her Communist affinities, La Alonsova), who was the target of a repudiation that is still going on. But it ended officially when she danced on tiptoe and in tutu to 'The Internationale', barely two years later. I do remember how Carpentier, as the official pressures against *Revolución* mounted, was getting further away from the newspaper until that shameful moment when he declared, like Fidel Castro, in unison with Fidel Castro, that he had always been a Communist. He was given prizes in Cuba several times, but he never got the Nobel Prize he was so anxious for: the real cause of his return from a democratic Caracas: they never forgave him for his alliance with another cosy *caudillo*.

When I went back to Havana in 1965 I went to visit Carpentier at his brand-new office at his headquarters of the National Printing Press. The office was refrigerated as few were then and it was pleasant. Alejo always had a taste for interior decoration and for his women's exterior. The last, Lilia, was still in her middle age a brunette beauty. Daughter of a black aristocrat and a white woman, the old Cubans said that they never let her enter society. This, they say, was the cause not only of the exit become a flight of both of them to Venezuela, but of their hatred of the Havana upper classes and their allegiance to the destroyers of what should have been their peers. I only saw Lilia one time, the last time, at the entrance of a theatre near my father's house and she looked really radiant in the Havana evening.

Carpentier, now in his role as a publisher, overwhelmed me with a long list of publications and a large quantity of editions, with a fastidiousness that betrayed the writer hidden behind not his desk but his bureau. I didn't want to throw a Baragaño blow, and ask him why they weren't publishing any of the canonical texts of Surrealism as they should. He ended up showing me, with the pride of place an artist would, an engraving that he had on the wall to his right. It showed a romantic scene *d'après* Géricault. One could see a raft adrift in which desperate shipwreck victims battled against a school of sharks who were ferociously circling the fragile craft. Carpentier, pleased, bragged: 'Of course you sugarly have grealized what there is in the background.'

I looked closely and saw – the Morro Castle! The shipwreck took place in Havana waters. Amazed I said: 'You can almost see the Malecón!'

'Almost. It's a gromantic engraving and it takes place in front of the Malecón. Not in time but yes, in space.'

Carpentier was euphoric at his discovery. I said goodbye. When I saw him a few days later going into the Riviera Theatre he didn't look so cheerful. He spoke to me about the absurd story of a suitcase, never recovered, that he had left in Madrid in my brother's care.

'It doesn't have anything more than some used shirts. Of no importance,' he explained.

Nevertheless it seemed to be a serious matter to him. I never understood why Carpentier, the man who confided to a Cuban friend that he had strong savings from his Venezuelan days in a numbered account in a Swiss bank, was getting so worked up. Why was a simple suitcase with old clothes so valuable to him? The shirts would never have been any good to my brother, since Alejo was a big man.

'Not big, no,' Lydia Cabrera corrected me when years later in Miami I told her the story of the lost suitcase that was as urgent as if it were full of dollars at the end of *The Killing*. 'Alexis is not big, he's only tall.'

I mentioned Baragaño a moment ago as his public nemesis. But there was another nemesis on *Lunes* around 1960: Heberto Padilla. The Surrealist poet José Baragaño never forgave Alejo for his prologue to *The Kingdom of this World*. Carpentier manhandled Baragaño's tutelary gods, Comte de Lautréamont and André Breton, and, crime of crimes, Surrealism. Padilla, who was never a Surrealist, wrote after Carpentier's death a version of Alejo's life that was debunking in a constant mirth. In the biography, brief but poignant, Padilla described Alejo as born and raised in Alquízar, in the Havana countryside. After the desertion of his French father (which really happened), Alejo, according to Padilla, mounted on a burro, delivered door to door the cow's milk that his Russian mother milked. (Padilla did not again publish that life of a Cuban literary hero in his memoirs.)

When Baragaño died in 1962 his widow took pains to give the atheist poet a *missa brevis* in the Colón Cemetery. Half of *Lunes* was in the small-sized chapel, despite the fact that Baragaño had betrayed us during the *P.M.* case. Carpentier came too. Late but he came. He went directly up to the bier and muttered not a requiem but a rush of relief: 'One less!' was what he said. But when he saw Padilla come into the chapel too he exclaimed: 'There's still one left!'

Along the way through the baroque cemetery to the open grave, Padilla took revenge. Walking next to Alejo to the slow step of the cortège, 'Alejo,' Padilla said he wanted to know, 'what's happening with your little novel? Are we going to read it in Cuba? It will turn out to be the last place you publish it.' Carpentier didn't answer but Padilla kept on as if nothing were wrong. 'That little novel, Alejo, is going to sink you when Fidel reads it.'

But Padilla was mistaken. The little novel was a big novel, *Explosion in a Cathedral*, and it was exalted by Fidel Castro and Raúl Castro – who declared it mandatory reading for army officers. 'Neither of the two read it,' declared Franqui. 'If they had they would have realized that the novel was profoundly counter-revolutionary.' The debate is still open although I cannot offer an opinion: I have never read *Explosion in a Cathedral*. The same exhaustive enumeration that led me to parody it repelled me. I know, though, that my parody threw Alejo and he found himself shipwrecked on his literary raft – haunted by a single shark far from El Morro.

After the encounter at the movie entrance (and his gripe about the lost suitcase, which seemed to be a story by Gogol) I didn't see Alejo again. But I learned of him by a third party: the writer Juan Arcocha, who was press attaché at the Cuban Embassy in Paris. He had as Ambassador one Doctor Carrillo, a physician who had never practised medicine but was a specialist in political opportunism. How he had got to be Ambassador in France is a chapter of the Cuban revolutionary roguery. Raúl's own roguery.

But the Cuban Embassy in Paris had what in Cuba is called *ñeque*, in Venezuela *pava* and in Spain *gafe*: a jinx. The first Castroist Ambassador, the absent-minded Professor Gran, an eminent professor but a naïve politician, found himself involved in the attempt at treason by Roberto Retamar, then his cultural attaché. Gran refused to report him to his ministry, the decent physicist the contrary of the bogus physician and he was recalled to Havana. Gran was succeeded by the musician Harold Gramatges, an old friend, and for years a closet Party member. Harold, as we all called him, then the president of the cultural society Nuestro Tiempo, had come out of his Communist closet in January 1959, when he invited Che Guevara to give a regrettable talk on social realism – the Argentine mistaken then as in so many things in Cuba later. Thanks to Che, Gramatges made friends with Raúl Castro, always fascinated by Marxism, who named him Ambassador to France. I was a guest of Harold in Paris when he was not yet an ambassador and later.

On one occasion I noticed the embassy had changed receptionists and, instead of the handsome Havana girl of before, a dry and disagreeable old woman opened the door. When I asked Harold about her, he said: 'You don't know who she is?' I didn't know. 'Caridad Mercader' he said and he didn't have to tell me that she was the mother of Ramón Mercader, Trotsky's assassin – whom all the historians gave as the only truly import-ant influence on her son. Harold, who was homosexually discreet, was a maliciously indiscreet gossip. Amused he told me how German Trotsky-ites came to look for their Cuban visa and no one even suspected that the woman who opened the door was the intellectual author of the assassin-ation of Trotsky. 'Cachita,' as Harold called her, 'was more Stalinist than Stalin.' Now perhaps she is resting in the hell of Colón Cemetery next to her son, who lived and was buried in Cuba. Both magnicides were in fact Cubans by birth. 'Cachita', as her name indicates, was from Santiago de

Cuba – where Harold Gramatges is also from – in that Oriente Province where Batista and Fidel Castro were born too.

In Europe Carpentier had been quite different (and deferential) from the almost comic figure that he turned out to be in Cuba. I had seen him in Paris in the winter of 1962, when my *Dans la paix comme dans la guerre* came out in France. Gallimard (or rather Roger Caillois, the legendary editor of the collection La Croix du Sud) threw a cocktail party for me in the publisher's *salons*. Alejo Carpentier and Miguel Angel Asturias were guests of honour and with their respective massive frames they looked almost like my South American bodyguards.

I saw Carpentier again in Brussels. He was passing through on his way to Paris after giving some talks in Stockholm in 1963. Euphoric from the reception that he got in Sweden, Carpentier confessed to me that they had assured him *over there* that the next Nobel Prize was his. When I visited Roger Caillois in his office at Unesco some time later, I told him that Carpentier thought the prize was surely his that year – or the next. With quiet insistence Caillois told me: 'They will never give it to him. *Never*. The worst thing that Alejo did was to go to Sweden. In Stockholm they consider these visits by candidates intolerable canvassing.' From that interview I remember that Caillois spoke Spanish with a French accent – very much like Alejo's.

One of the most ridiculous manifestations of Alejo's accent happened when he became all French in Havana. Carpentier, like any *salonnier* of the provinces, gave get-togethers in his house every Saturday – where only French was spoken. I never went to them but Sergio Rigol, who did go, remarked to me that it was not forbidden to speak Spanish – but it was not well looked upon either. I forgot to ask him (and now it's too late) about Lilia's French. Rigol told me that in one of the last gatherings he attended, Carpentier celebrated, I suppose with *Champagne grand cru*, the fall of *Lunes* and of all the Icaruses who tried to fly higher than their fastened feathers allowed. We were without knowing it, according to Alejo, *d'appellation controlée*.

But there were important people who did not believe that Carpentier was funny. On the contrary they took him very seriously. One was Juan Marinello, the highest intellectual figure of the old guard. Another, Carlos Rafael Rodríguez, had now become very powerful indeed. Late at night on 2 October 1965 I went with *Comandante* Alberto Mora to visit Carlos Rafael in his office at the old *Diario de la Marina*. Thanks to Alberto and, especially, to Carlos Rafael I would be able to leave Cuba the next day.

The two, I think, knew it was for ever or until Castro fell – whichever came first.

Carlos Rafael greeted me with his affection of always. He was one of the old Communists I met on the newspaper *Hoy* when I was a boy. They still called me Guillermito, the son of the veteran *Hoy* journalist Guillermo Cabrera. We talked about what I had always talked about with Carlos Rafael, even when he was finally editor of *Hoy* years before – literature. The conversation came around to Carpentier all by itself.

'Have you seen the latest instalment of Alejo's novel?'

'*Year 59*? I saw it in *Bohemia* but I didn't read it.'

'It's the second instalment,' Carlos Rafael said, 'but it's worse than the first.'

I let him talk – not only deferential but curious too.

'Alejo is an interesting writer but I would like him to be less baroque. He is, of course, an asset but he doesn't understand the Revolution. Imagine him calling the *barbudos* the *barbados*!'

'You are, of course, one of them.'

Carlos Rafael had let his beard and moustache grow since he went up to the Sierra in 1958. But his beard was a goatee that, without his knowing it, made him closer to Trotsky than to Stalin – to whom he had been and was devoted.

'Imagine! But speaking seriously, Alejo worries me. I don't know where he's going to end up with his novel, but I don't want it to become more a political than a literary problem. The last thing we want,' and he seemed to include not only the authorities but Alberto and me, 'is another Pasternak case.'

It surprised me then and now that Carlos Rafael could think that Alejo, so timorous, would become a dissenter. But perhaps he knew that Pasternak too was a timid man. Then I thought that Carlos Rafael, with subtlety, was talking not about Alejo but about me. I believed that, when we said goodbye to each other, instead of see you he had said to me: 'Save yourself.' But I know that if the night has a thousand eyes and a thousand ears it also has a thousand lips and says things that the morning disavows. In any case the conversation was memorable and in order not to forget it I noted it down on a leaf of a book that finally stayed in Cuba.

Before leaving Cuba in 1945 Carpentier completed in Havana a really notable book: the best and most complete study of music in Cuba. (It is called with tautology *Music in Cuba*.) Carpentier completes a circle of music from the dawn of the nation until 1945, helped by Natalio Galán, the musician who copied all the scores and to whom Carpentier owes more than one discovery. Here he develops a theme that is irrefutable. Cuba, poor in arts, mediocre in architecture and babbling in theatre, becomes a realized people in its music. Regrettably Carpentier limits himself to serious (which would later be serial) music and covers popular music – the truly great Cuban creation – only in a suppurated appendix. Although Alejo brings off true *trouvailles* (a word that he would like) when describing Havana's musical life of the nineteenth century, truly brilliantly, he errs in the simplest notes of popular music. He even gets to the point of confusing a manner of dancing (the *bote* meaning boating, which was, fortunately, ephemeral) with a new rhythm – never new because it was unborn. In his farewell from Cuba he was nevertheless much more fortunate than in his arrival in Caracas, with the service that he lent right away to a tyrant in a minor key.

Carpentier collaborated with a major tyrant, Fidel Castro, in a game of simulations: Carpentier was not nor had he ever been a revolutionary, Castro was not nor had he ever been a Communist. Alejo was obedient and even submissive on the National Council of Culture, in the Writers' Union (of which he was vice-president for life), at the National Printing Press and, last to the last, in the Cuban Embassy in Paris. Earlier he was a courier for the tsar. Or some sort of failed Strogoff.

It happened in 1967 when Mario Vargas Llosa won the Venezuelan Rómulo Gallegos novel prize. Mario allowed himself to be blackmailed by another fugitive, Edmundo Desnoes, opportunely visiting London. Desnoes persuaded Mario to put together a cable, transmitted by the Cuban news agency Prensa Latina, but intended to bother the Venezuelan rulers, entangled in a bloody war against the guerrillas of Cuban origin. (He thus pleased Haydée Santamaría, the papess of the Casa de las Américas.) When Mario, who lived quite close, told me what he had done, I quoted to him a Cuban popular proverb that was a wealth of wisdom: '*Cuando te tocan el culo una vez y lo admites, te lo tocarán tres.*' ('Give them an inch and they'll take a mile' – in a coarser vein.)

Enter Carpentier from France unsmiling. Alejo called Mario and told him that he wanted to see him personally. He would come to London and would call him. He came and called. He wanted them to get together in a Knightsbridge restaurant. (Patricia Llosa showed it to me one day: 'On that terrace Mario had his interview with Alejo.') Alejo was a man with a mission. (Remember that this is the haughty writer, an elitist aspirant to the Nobel Prize for literature.) Alejo's mission was that of messenger with the trimmings of a spy. In the empty restaurant after lunch, Alejo told Mario that he was carrying a verbal message from Haydée Santamaría – who greeted him as a true revolutionary. The last thing a writer wants is to be confused with something he is not, but Alejo was talking now writer to writer. Haydée *wanted* Mario to donate, publicly, his prize (some 30,000 *bolívars*: Alejo, trained in Venezuelan arithmetic, calculated that this was about 25,000 dollars) to the guerrilla war. The Casa de las Américas (that is, the Government of Castro, who always paid his diplomats through the Russian Narodny Bank), would return to Mario that same quantity at the rate of a thousand dollars per month – which Alejo would bring him in person. (Alejo completed the numbers asking the nearest waiter for a brandy, in French s.v.p.) The proposal fell, the opposite of the words in the Zohar that Carpentier admired so much, into a vacuum. Mario might have been a political naïf but he was not a fool. Accepting the offer he could refuse meant becoming, in fact, a Cuban agent, paid by the Castro Government from Paris through the Narodny Bank. Mario said no – and right there began his difficulties with the Cuban Government. They culminated in 1971 when Haydée Santamaría accused Mario of refusing to help in the struggle of the Venezuelan people (read the Castroist guerrillas), buying himself instead a house in a rich part of Lima.

This and other messages (to the press, to the people of France) Alejo Carpentier had to accept delivering. He was, besides a messenger for Castro, a distributor of Havana cigars throughout Paris: almost the Alquízar milkman again. Once he personally brought a box of Havanas to Sartre and the smoking philosopher refused to receive him: he was beginning to fall into as much disgrace as the regime that he represented. On another occasion Sartre and his carnal Simone ran into him on the rue Bonaparte and Alejo had to turn halfway around, in a hurry. He even ran in the direction of the church at St Germain pursued by the delicious duo shouting in unison: '*Voyou! Vieux con! Dégueulasse!*'

But Alejo had other worries up Paris and, especially, down Paris.

Fausto Canel, the Cuban film director who was living in Paris at the time and keeping ties with the Castroist diplomats, tells that he was going one day down the rue de la Paix towards the Cuban Embassy when he saw Alejo get out of a taxi. Immediately he headed for the entrance to the Métro and was lost in it. Canel was going to tell him, as if Alejo did not know, that he didn't have to catch the Métro, that the embassy was around the corner, when he saw him emerge agitated through the other entrance, walk a few steps – and head resolutely to his embassy! It was obvious that Alejo had gone into the Métro and Carpentier, the functionary, had left it. Why these *petites manoeuvres*? Strategies of a socialist diplomat who didn't want his colleagues to know that he came to his embassy in a taxi and that, a humble

Castroite, he travelled in the Métro like them. Fakeries of a man who all his life was a faker.

But it was in that embassy, not when it was on the rue de la Paix, so chic, almost facing the Opéra, so chichi, but on the elegant avenue Foch, in an apartment full of Victorian nostalgias, that Alejo showed signs of a saving political realism. Carpentier had come to France to lecture. He started in Bayonne and must have headed for Bordeaux, a destination he never reached. Three days later, Ambassador Carrillo was nervous, then very nervous and on the fourth day he decided to give up Carpentier for lost – never *sperduto nel buio* but lost to the cause. He composed a cable that the G2 agent on duty immediately offered to transmit in code. Juan Arcocha, who was the press attaché then, no friend of Carpentier – in fact he couldn't stand him – but who had his head on straight and was not an opportunist like the ambassador nor a cop with a code like the local G2, said that they must at least wait one more day to see if Alejo appeared.

And on the fourth day Carpentier resurrected: battered but faithful, with his basset hound face sadder than ever. The ambassador hinted to everyone: nothing's happened here, gentlemen. But as a cultural attaché he had Juan David, an excellent cartoonist, a mediocre functionary and a good friend of Alejo's. On the way to the airport going back to Havana he told Carpentier the short story of the long wait and the cable in code. According to David, Carpentier turned into a political Goliath to exclaim, deafening the taxi driver: '*Come mierdas!* As if I didn't know from a long way back that the wgriter disowned by the Left is lost' – and he put the emphasis on lost. Actually Carpentier had met up with a lovely lady listener and had invested the lost weekend in won labours of love: he left Bayonne to enter Bordeaux. Paris was well worth the black mass officiated by an ambassador who had no idea of how compromising a committed writer can be.

Pardon a parenthesis. Not long ago *The Chase* was published again in England and the book editor of the newspaper the *Independent* asked me for a review. There I said that the brief book 'was one of the most perfect novellas in Spanish, a language in which perfect novellas had been written since the Renaissance'. Later I pointed out that Carpentier had uselessly spirited away the period of the action, that it could not have happened under General Machado – *Machado about Nothing* – but that it seemed to belong to the era of the avenging gun that started with the Grau and Prío Governments (1944–8). The coverleaf mentioned the 'background of the violent Batista tyranny', making the reader see as the ignorant see that the deadly game happened elsewhere. I saved Carpentier the writer from drowning among the SS by denying that he had anything to do with magic realism – grey shades of the Nazi Roh! The Cuban author was far from those authors who write with a tutti-frutti pen. (It was an allusion to the falsely exotic Carmen Miranda, once called 'the lady with the tutti-frutti hat'.)

It was a review no less praising than the one I had written on *The Lost Steps*, a masterpiece that converts lost time into recovered space and in which real time is a voyage to the aboriginal origins. But I never pointed out to the reader the singular resemblance between *Steps* and *La Voie royale*, written by André Malraux in 1929: the adventures of an archaeologist in Indochina, tropical inferno and topical paradise. Antón Arrufat and I amused ourselves by pointing out with arrows daubed with literary curare the many coincidences. But always, *always*, we ended up concluding that the copy was much better than the original and if Alejo had stolen from the Frenchmen Mabile and Malraux it was to create dissimilar facsimiles. The Cuban was more of an artist – but was Carpentier really Cuban?

In his brief biography Heberto Padilla complains, precisely, of how sketchy it is, to add: 'It is almost a fake,' and goes on to quote Alejo himself: 'My grandmother was an excellent pianist, a student of César Franck. My mother was a pianist too and quite a good one. My father, who wanted to be a musician rather than an architect, began to work on the cello with Pablo Casals. I learned music at the age of eleven. At 12 I was playing pieces by Bach, by Chopin, with a certain authority.' After this quote Padilla tears the official autobiography to shreds. 'But no one,' says Padilla, 'in Cuba had news of his grandmother or of his mother as "quite a good" pianist. Not to mention whether his father "worked on" the cello with Casals.' (I can add that Natalio Galán assured me that Carpentier read music with difficulty.) Padilla continues: 'His infancy had no harmony,' an apt musical term, 'to rule his statements. He lived until his adolescence in the country, in the outskirts of Alquízar, a quite poor town several miles south of Havana.' Now Padilla makes more indiscreet revelations and, as before, full of a corrosive humour: 'His father disappeared from the country when Alejo was almost a boy, running off after a *mestiza* Cuban and was lost for ever in the Panama Canal.' (Not in the jungle.)

Padilla draws an erotic parallel when he reveals Lilia Carpentier's father in a scene taken almost from *The Kingdom of this World*: in 'the house next to the Almendares River there was seen to appear one afternoon, suddenly, a great oil painting located between two doors of the dining room that looked out on the garden. It was a black man, dressed after the fashion of the Haitians described by Carpentier, filling out all the space of the canvas. We found out that it was Lilia's father, the only black Marquis in Cuba.'

Thus Padilla tears to shreds the annotations of another biographer about French lyceums and European education.

I never saw Carpentier again, but I learned of him with the aid of the technology of the electron, to which Alejo was addicted since, as he told it, he had written ballets for the experimental composer Edgar Varèse in his grave grey days in Paris.

The first piece of news was brought taped on a cassette by Alex Zisman, a South American Literature student at Cambridge. Zisman, a Peruvian, is, as the *Limeños* say, a *plato* – a gift of Mario Vargas Llosa, about whom Alex was writing a never-ending master's thesis. Carpentier came to Cambridge in 1971 for a talk with questions from the audience.

The first question was from Zisman, who asked the most, in Spanish and about the Cuban people's difficulties after the cruel rationing imposed by Fidel Castro. 'It's not true!' answered Alejo, agile but with rolling Rs. 'Everyone in Cuba eats well.' How well? Alex asked Alejo. Lilia, from the audience but audible on the tape, affirmed: 'They eat as well as we do.' Is it necessary to remind you that both Carpentiers, Lilia and Alejo, were diplomats and lived in Paris?

Alex (what a curious play on names and nouns) abandoned the topic, What Do Cubans Eat When They Do, to enter into literature and ask about a book of mine. Carpentier lost his composure but not his accent: 'I have not read that book.' But, continued Alex, there is in it a parody of your style and even of your titles. (The parodic version is entitled 'Lot's Steps', which is a parody of *The Lost Steps*.) Carpentier insisted: 'I grepeat that I have not gread that book.' But do you know – Alex wanted to find out – its author, who is Cuban as well? Alejo coming out of some steep steps exclaimed: 'That man is *not* Cuban!'

Zisman changed authors but not topics. Heberto Padilla who is in prison in Havana for his poetry is not Cuban either? 'That gentleman,' said Carpentier and even on the recording one can hear his hatred still moving, 'is not in prison for writing some poems here and there. He is in prison for graver greasons that will soon be grevealed.' End of the recording but not of my commentary. 'That gentleman', that is, Heberto Padilla, the night of that same day, would make his mandatory confession in the conference room of the Writers' Union in Havana. It is evident that Carpentier was already informed about 'what will happen' – or he enjoyed an astonishing gift of prescience. A foresight saga.

More astonishing than prescience is technology. Never will my amazement die out before the videotape, which makes possible one of my dreams:

the cinémathèque for one alone. More amazing is the fax, that telephone that transmits not one's voice, after all an everyday happening, but instant messages, with as much safety as a certified letter – and with almost the same privacy. But the fax, like the telephone, sometimes produces crossed messages and the machine receives an alien or anonymous fax. I have received a lost letter from Major Ferguson, father of the Duchess of York, assuring me that he will certainly come to a tea party – that I will not give. A lady editor with *Vogue* recommends to me a model (who may be stupendous or stupid) for an occasion of *haute couture* – with little attendance. (At least the lady to whom the fax was addressed never received her invitation.) Also a well-known butcher sent me a list of choice meats on sale that neither I nor the true addressee will eat – vegetarians both. These mistakes, owing to the telephone that writes messages, make me ask myself in turn where my fax that doesn't hit the target will end up? Perhaps with Princess Diana – otherwise as inaccessible for me as for Charles.

But a fax, an anonymous artefact, destined to become notorious, came from Paris without return to sender. It was a true facsimile: the copy of a birth certificate issued in Switzerland – an *acte de naissance*. It said, succinctly, that on 26 December 1904 was born in Lausanne, Switzerland, Carpentier, Alexis, son of Georges Julien, of French nationality (Marseille, Bouches-du-Rhone), domiciled in Saint-Gilles-les-Bruxelles (Belgium), and of Catherine *née* Blagooblasof. The document was issued in Lausanne, 17 September 1991: just issued in Switzerland and sent from Paris from where it reached me, a facsimile on my fax.

The news was extraordinary but explainable. The document uncovered the multiple and successive inventions of Carpentier to be Alejo, why Lydia Cabrera, knowingly, always called him Alexis, why Alejo displayed that lasting rancour against Padilla (the man who knew too much) in Cambridge and why Carpentier had always, like the English, taken Havana for a port of call and, still more terrible, why he had behaved so badly with Cuba all his life: how he had lent himself to every dirty trick to serve two masters, Communism and Castro, whom he must have seen as a usurper but was his ambassador extraordinary many times using his fame for an infamy. This birth certificate, apparently innocent, explained more than one evil.[1]

---

1 Truth is more fact than verba: a stubborn creature. Many years ago back in Havana Alejo's Russian mother exclaimed: 'My, how it snowed the day Alejo was born!' She was talking to Carpentier's former wife Eva Frejaville. She was French and discreet but couldn't help thinking how odd it was that it snowed in Havana! She didn't say anything then but with Cartesian logic she pursued the truth behind a mother's reverie. It was she, Eva expelled from paradise, who, after being snowed, discovered in Switzerland the lost but not forgotten birth certificate. It happened after Alejo died – believing that he had fooled all.

But chance can abolish foresight. By sheer chance along for tea came Valenti Puig, a Catalonian writer who is the correspondent for the ABC of Madrid in London. I showed him the fax like a kind of Cuban curio. When Puig read Carpentier's birth inscription and saw that it was genuine, he asked my permission to pass it on to his paper. Half-amused, half-bemused, I gave it to him. Puig transmitted, by fax, the copy of the document and ABC published a slight and hardly relevant note. But before that, from the editor's office they called Lilia Carpentier in Havana. She reacted with vertiginous virulence: 'That is an infamy invented in Miami!' (Poor Miami, so far from Cuba and so near Havana.) The *acte de naissance* from the canton of Veaud, cannot be any further from Miami and nearer the truth, because it is a Swiss document and therefore neutral, as antiseptic as the Red Cross. It originated, in fact, with a functionary who if he had ever heard mention of Alexis Carpentier would have confused him with Georges Carpentier, not the fleeing father of Alejo, but the Orchid of the Ring, French champion of the heavyweights, famous for his physical courage and his elegance, close to a Parisian dandy – but quite far from Alejo.

Antonio Ortega Returns
to Asturias – Dead

It happened almost forty years ago in Havana and I remember it as if it had happened last year in Bath. I had met Antonio Ortega a month or two before when I brought to his office at the magazine *Bohemia*, where he was fiction editor, a story of mine – the first one I wrote. It was some sort of serious parody of a writer who later came to win the Nobel Prize – but whom I never considered even second to Ortega. For the fiction editor of the leading weekly in Cuba, Ortega was incredibly accessible. (He always was.) That easy access allowed me to reach him timidly when I was only seventeen and I had the perfect look of being a nobody. (Not a difficult trick to perform because I was a nobody, you see.) I didn't even aspire to literature yet and writing was another adolescent game. (Like chess but easier.) Ortega not only read my story but published it and even became my mentor.

Now I visited him assiduously in his house on Amistad Street and he chatted with me while he taught me – once I knew how to cut through his thick Asturian accent. Ortega, a former lecturer, professor of natural sciences, was that rare thing: a born teacher. Of course he also lent me books – by some authors whom I had not even heard of before, like Kafka or Silverio Lanza, strange and exotic. I walked every Saturday afternoon from our family room in the *solar* (read Havana tenement) at Zulueta 408 to his house on the corner of Amistad and Trocadero. Ortega, who was one of the few really aristocratic persons I have known (and later I would come to know even English lords, with a genealogical tree planted *before* the Norman conquest, who are vast boors), was also humble in the extreme. His cramped apartment, which he shared with his wife Asunción, also Asturian, was then almost in the navel of the Havanan red-light district – the notorious Colón borough in which, as always in Havana, decency cohabited with prostitution, good and evil paving hell and heaven.

Curiously, at the beginning of that Trocadero Street were the editorial offices and print shops of *Bohemia*, a popular review. But, amazement, at the end of the street, a few blocks further down, lived until his death José Lezama Lima, the rarest and most hermetic poet of Cuba and editor of *Orígenes*, an exquisite literary review not at all read by the hoi polloi. Those whores – whom neither Ortega nor Lezama ever frequented, for opposite reasons – had the opportunity to be *hetairas*. (That is, prostitutes enlightened almost by contagion.) On more than one occasion I could get a glimpse of some half-dressed pupils in the darkness of a *bayú* (cheap brothel) and once, coming one Saturday afternoon out of Ortega's house, I saw a young whore with white and wholesome flesh who was streaking to make the street into an Olympic track: a nymph in the nude.

Lezama was visited by Spanish euphuistic Catholic poets and even Juan Ramón Jiménez, exiled in Havana then, negotiated the impudent whorehouses more than once to reach Lezama Lima's house like a Montego Bay beyond. Among those indolent or insolent whores the poet was known as Brother Black Beard – he who sauntered as if he was passing a nunnery. According to Lezama, to insult the colony, Juan Ramón used to say that Colón reminded him of Huelva in summer. (I didn't get the point of this Andalusian barb until becoming acquainted years later with Huelva, where Jiménez was born.) There is no doubt that the poet was a cool customer.

Ortega was visited by Dr Gustavo Pittaluga, one of the most illustrious Spanish scientists from before the Civil War, the philosopher María Zambrano, Lino Novás Calvo and many eminent exiled Spanish writers. One evening I met there the poet Luis Cernuda, dressed after the English fashion, all pipe and tweeds. Neither the dubious morality of the neighbourhood nor the certain humility of his apartment was ever important to Ortega. He followed without knowing it that English proverb that recommends stoically: never complain, never explain. In a city menaced by rather than crowded with automobiles, Ortega did not have his own car until the editor of *Bohemia*, Miguel Quevedo, gave him his sister's old Studebaker. Ortega always called it affectionately his jalopy. An incurable democrat, Ortega represented the best that the Republic gave Spain and Franco displaced into a several times miserable exile. Ortega was more fortunate than most – but only for a while. I met him at the end of 1947 and by the beginning of 1960 he was already a political exile from his second country. As his stories testify, Ortega had two fatherlands, Gijón and Havana.

One December day in 1947, a year so often mentioned by me as memorable (almost everything began then), Ortega contributed to making it extraordinary by handing me a hardcover folder with the manuscript of a book called, exotically strange, *Coconut Hearts*. It was typed in an impeccable hand – which could not be Ortega's. Like other Spaniards of his generation (for example the Galician poet Angel Lázaro, still a living testimonial to this time, in Madrid), who worked in newspapers and magazines and lived in the midst of the printed word and the typewriters, Ortega scorned the typewriter. I always suspected that rather than scoffing at the typewriter they all feared failure with a new technology. Though that technology was then almost a century old (the first typewriter was created around 1865: curiously this invention by a man has done more to open doors for women than all the feminist movements: this has nothing to do with Ortega's stories except that they were all meticulously typed), this did not make the typewriter more respectable if one compares it with the scores of centuries in which all writers used vertical pen and horizontal paper on top of a table.

But the manuscript had numerous annotations by hand, made by Ortega in his regular, minuscule script and at the same time eminently legible. It always was for me, who scratches and scribbles more than writes, a perfect calligraphy. At the end the book was signed in pen: *Antonio Ortega*, naturally. But neither of the t's was crossed nor the i dotted and the A was missing the crossbar. When I asked Ortega the reason for this naked signature he confided to me that during the Civil War, as the political commissar from the Asturias region, he had to sign so many documents, edicts and proclamations that in order to simplify this process and make possible the largest number of signatures in the least time, he had eliminated every superfluous stroke. I think now that those i's without dots and those t's without crosses contributed to Ortega's exile, to his pains as a double exile (from Spain, from Cuba) and finally to his miserable death in Maracaibo.

When I went back home that afternoon and my mother saw that *Coconut Hearts* was not yet in book form but was already a book, she was paralysed by reverence – or at the privilege conferred on her eldest son. 'You take good care of that book,' she advised me. 'Writers *never* give people their work in progress to read.' For her, poor, as a Communist who believed in Christ, every book was a possible version of the Bible or of *Das Kapital* – that other Bible no less sacred because impenetrable. Of course I took care of *Coconut Hearts* although it was not a true manuscript but a typewritten copy. I was supposed to read it in a week and return it to Ortega the next Saturday – I read it in one night.

I knew Ortega as a novelist, the author of one novel, *Ready*, that I couldn't appraise because it was the life (in barks that talk) of a mongrel that roamed Havana in a canine picaresque novel of which Ortega was more a Guzmán than a Quevedo: not cruel at all. I couldn't praise that book when I read it because my love for dogs prevented me then. Now I remember that *Ready* was like an amiable version of *White Fang* or of *Call of the Wild*. The ferocious fauna that Jack London set in the inhumane Yukon or in the impossible American tundra, were transformed by Ortega into a delicious playful pack among streets and alleys of a city, Havana, that was, if anything, sweet and sour. The precise prose of Ortega contrasted with the warm and bland climate of the tropics. But this book, curious thing, was a bigger bestseller in Cuba than the much-praised novel by the future Nobel Prize winner and present forgotten Indian. (To parody the title of one of Ortega's most brilliant stories, 'The Forgotten Chink', which closes this exceptional volume.)

Coconut Hearts, more than in any of his books, more even than in an unpublished novel (untitled, unfinished, uneven but from which I remember having read some memorable chapters in his El Vedado house, at the end of the fifties: this time the manuscript was really a manuscript), which culminated in an indiscriminate killing of hundreds of crabs run over on the highway when they were going blind on the way to the sea, shows (a preoccupation proper to the naturalist) that Ortega was truly a natural storyteller. Much more genuine than other writers of his Spanish generation and later, who wrote fiction as they did journalism or advertising – or that putrid political publicity that is propaganda.

I don't know which writers could have influenced Ortega, who shared many of the literary superstitions of his time and country. I could never really understand how this cultivated and cultured man could consider national mediocrities as possible Nobel Prize winners. Perhaps the explanation is not in literary kindness, but in his genuine generosity. Ortega protected, for example, in *Bohemia* first and in *Carteles* later, a compatriot of his whom he hated as a writer and as a person – Luis Amado Blanco, the Dantesque dentist. He was detestably jealous of Ortega, whom he survived to die not amidst the blood and the horror in Maracaibo, Venezuela, but with the scorn of all the Spanish exiles although in official exaltation by Castro. Ortega also welcomed books and authors whom he must have known to be mediocre and more deserving of contempt than of appreciation, even appraisal.

If Ortega was exceptional as a person he was also extraordinary as a writer. Better still: he was an original. An originality found from the beginning, natural, never worked over. On the contrary, if he had paid more attention to the modes (and the fashions) of his time, I would not be writing these pages, trying to rescue his writing from oblivion: they would be superfluous. But his time was implacable. If to all of us come bad times to live through, if it is true, to Ortega there came times of impossible survival – and he escaped by a miracle. Only for a while. If he had not been exiled to Cuba they would have shot him in Spain under Franco. But if he had not always been a democrat and a Republican (always an anti-fascist) or had been able to dissimulate and swallow the bait and spit out the hook, if he had not been exiled again and left Communist Cuba for democratic Venezuela, he would now be celebrated everywhere: in Cuba and in Spain and, sordid irony, also in Venezuela, where only the few recognized his worth. But he preferred individual honesty to collective opportunism. The man was lost because of his decency, which is a tragic but honourable destiny. We can meet the writer now.

A new reading of *Coconut Hearts* almost forty years later shows Ortega as fresh as he was that Saturday evening in 1947 when I had the privilege and joy to read his book of stories – and to let myself be influenced by his style, a contagion that Ortega diagnosed immediately. Now the book appears to be unpublished still in his native Asturias, a land that Ortega made mythical for me. Such was his power of evocation that I came to yearn for the *bable* tongue and the *orvallo* rain as of a country that I believed also to be mine. When I visited Gijón for the first time in the summer of 1981 I did not find, of course, either of the two. Everyone was speaking Spanish and the sun came out three days running – which for a Londoner is not Asturias but the Riviera. It rained one day but it was such a short shower that it seemed like a squalid squall. Asturias is a myth that Ortega invented.

But when one reads these stories Ortega comes back and with him return also the time of the *orvallo* and the noise of the *bable* that is not spoken in his stories. Still there is an exotic touch that I have later learned to recognize as close to home. When I read the book in Havana I met characters who 'caught cold' – and died! From Cuba this illness seemed to me as impossible or at least as remote as sleeping sickness and the tsetse fly. Now after years of exile in London I find the favourite illness of Ortega's characters is not only possible but is the favourite of many Englishmen, who can catch a chill and die – like the antagonist in 'Seven Letters to a Man'.

'Coconut Hearts', the story, is a tale that Ortega could have made into a novel, just as he could have fallen more than once into sentimentality. He successfully avoided both temptations. I have nothing against the novel, much less against sentimentality. On the contrary, many of my best friends are sentimental. By friends I'm referring to boleros and tangos and those old films with a happy ending. Also to much mellow music. Chaplin, for example, is shamelessly sentimental. John Ford is a dry, restrained sentimentalist. Ortega is a sentimentalist who wants to be hard at times or rather to declare that he is above all else a scientist. But this scientist, the son and brother of scientists, came one day to his doctor brother's laboratory and found a curious little guinea pig: a puppy with the number 3 hung around his neck for experiments *in anima viles* and vivisections and final dissection. Our hard core scientist was so moved that he rescued the mutt from a fate worse than death. He brought the dog home and named it Three. (In Havana in the fifties Ortega still had a dog named Three.)

I confess that I am really moved by the story of Palmira who used to eat coconut hearts. But neither the story nor the plot moves me. I am moved by the prose of Ortega, who knows like Chekhov how to be emotive and at the same time to make an almost medical diagnosis of his characters. With a single phrase Ortega establishes a relationship between the reader and the rigorous ordering of the elements of his prose. So when he writes 'The soft and fresh breeze of February shook blandly the tall and dark casuarina', the reader knows that he is confronted with true literature – barely signalled with a substantive as tenuous as the name of the casuarina tree. Or this other better beginning: 'It rose unexpectedly from a mountain of memories: behind a suffocating odour of tuberoses.' The casuarinas and the tuberoses make of the memory not an impressionist odour but are rather exact nouns. Ortega knew that the written page doesn't smell but speaks to our eyes, silent and at the same time incredibly garrulous – like some women described by him. Or like his the letters from his characters.

'The Escapee' is a story in which, as in 'The Flight', there is a political relationship inferred or inherent to the story. 'The Escapee' appears to be a reluctant compromise, while in 'The Flight' Ortega admits that the only way of speaking about politics in fiction is to do it with the language of the press – like a reportage but avoiding the opinion page, the editorial and the impotence of the insult. There are other stories in the book, like 'Seven Letters to a Man', in which the device so often used (because of its communicating hermeticism) of epistolary literature is justified: a letter is always a deaf monologue not a valid interlocutor. Letters talk but they never hear: to answer them is to make an incursion into *my* monologue. This story is sometimes painful reading and I believe it got a prize in Spain before the Civil War.

In Cuba an even more painful story, 'The Forgotten Chink', won an even more celebrated prize: it was important and even decisive then – and Ortega was famous for a while. Later, little by little, he was swallowed up by journalism: he was literary editor and right-hand man of *Bohemia*'s editor and later he was himself editor-in-chief of *Carteles*. The reverse of the hero of *The Vortex*, he didn't get lost suddenly when entering fully that savage jungle. But I don't believe that Ortega wrote anything again – not even an editorial. Not in Cuba in any case: Ortega, who was reserved in the extreme in his private life, had no literary secrets for me. When I published 'The Flight' (a story of frank anti-Francoism and of effective Republican call to arms in which even the word of peace *bous*, a boat, sounds like an anagram of *obús* or howitzer) in *Lunes de Revolución*, which was the most important literary supplement ever published in Cuba, he seemed pleased. But his abrupt exile to New York not long after showed that his satisfaction was, as always, personal: a courtesy, another elegant refinement of a Spanish gentleman. Ortega never told me, as I found out later, that he did not want to associate his writing with the strident partisan literature anthologized in *Lunes*.

These collected short stories are rare examples in a literature, like the Spanish, not at all adept in the cultivation of the short story. They show besides a characteristic that reveals the good writer and that relates Ortega to Lino Novás Calvo. That distinction is in naming names and sonorous surnames. Curiously Ortega and Novás Calvo often use almost the same Cantabrian last name: Novás Calvo calls one of his heroes Fenollosa, Ortega names another Felechosa. For me they are only suggestive sounds, for them perhaps they have a literary value. In any case it is impossible to know now – and a writer only proposes models of readings.

Finally I want to say that this is an occasional presentation, not the careful literary analysis that Ortega deserves and that I, who owe him so much, cannot do because there that trait that he appreciated above all others, loyalty, would always interfere. That loyalty is personal but also literary. Like the characters of Antonio Ortega, I cannot write him even a few lines without their being converted into a split private message, at once joyful and painful: letters to a dead man.

Now you have the stories of Antonio Ortega, an author whom exile tried thrice to make anonymous. Read them and learn to appreciate them knowing that it is a pity that their author is no longer among those who were his preferred readers: those who still hear the *bable* and the *orvallo*. I was about to say that it does not matter that he is not here because his literature is here. But the terrible thing is that it does matter: nothing so kills a writer as being forgotten. Still, reading, that verbal memory, can never restore life to a dead author. Literature, like this introduction, is after all only an extended epitaph.

(August 1982)

Goodbye to the Friend with the Camera

The automatic answering machine is no such thing. It is an artefact to reveal one's soul – or at least one's character. The answer is repeated but is never automatic: the author finds himself facing the hidden microphone with the need to say something and be brief. He has to write his script and be an author doubling as an actor. Some answers are truly witty and even entertaining. John Kobal, for example, who was an actor, often changed his answer, always with background music, to inform us, almost in secret but never in a whisper, where he was and what he was doing and when he would be back. Paquito D'Rivera, who is a musician, plays the clarinet and answers in duet with his wife Brenda, who is a singer, to the samba sound of his latest record, *Tico Tico*.

Néstor Almendros was different. He never changed. That is, he was the same. His answer was always the same: a little dry (like his Castilian father), a little Catalan (like his mother) and, in English, he had a slight Cuban accent. He was direct, informative and deferential too, and he distanced every word so that there would be no doubt of what he was saying. If every message can begin as a mess, now the hard thing is that there will not be another message from Néstor. A double message then as when he used to hide behind his machine and say as he recognized a friend, 'Ah it's you.' There will be no more of a friend, alas, who was a friend for almost half a century.

Néstor Almendros arrived in Havana in 1948 to be reunited with his father, an educator and Spanish exile he had not seen since his flight in 1938. Néstor was then seventeen. I met him in the summer course on film that the University of Havana had that year. The cinema united us. I believe – I am sure – that Néstor is my oldest friend. Painfully where I said *is* I now have to say *was*. But, through Néstor, I met friends who were friends of the cinema and others who showed they were friends more of power than of the cinema – or friends of power through the cinema.

For Néstor, as for me, Havana was a revelation. But if I came from a poor town, Néstor came from Barcelona and his surprise was always a greater amazement. He was astonished at the multitude of cinemas (and a surprise that was never mine: all the movies were in the original version), he was amazed at the many newspapers and the profuse magazines dedicated especially to the movies. He was amazed and astonished at how many blond people there were in Havana. 'It's your people's fault,' I told him. 'Haven't you seen how many Catalan names there are in Cuba?' Even a president was called Barnet, another was Bru. It made him happy that the first martyr of the independence of Cuba in the nineteenth century was a Catalan. Néstor, who had a Castilian father and in Cuba became cosmopolitan, was a Catalan and in that strange tongue he communicated with his mother, the kind María Cuyás, who survives him, and with his brother and sister María Rosa and Sergio. His sun-drenched apartment in El Vedado was a Catalan house.

We always knew that we were going to make movies. Néstor chose the most difficult part or art, photography. Joyce declared once that he was an original by his own will – although he was less gifted than anyone for such decision. Néstor became a photographer by an iron vein in his character that amazed those who didn't know him. He began with an ordinary box camera and became a first-rate photographer. But when he made his first photographs of me and took two hours shooting, at the end of the session he discovered that he had left the cover on the lens! Since he was a boy he had been very absent-minded and now as a professional photographer he had assistants to make sure that he wouldn't forget anything. He used to run into every object in his way – and even into some that weren't. Néstor, who appears in his last photographs with his eyes naked (he was of course wearing contact lenses), had on thick bottle-glass eyeglasses when I met him. I don't remember having met anyone more near-sighted. But he already had the movie eye.

When Néstor discovered Havana he discovered himself: discovered his sexuality. It changed his life. But he was always the soul of discretion: in dress, in speech and one thinks that Constantine Cavafy must have been very like him. Havana was his Alexandria. But, among friends, he could joke in a fashion that was surprisingly Cuban and at the same time very much his own. Néstor, so serious, used to be devastatingly funny in close company with his nicknames for friends and enemies. He even christened as La Dahlia for ever a well-known Cuban commissar.

Néstor left Cuba during the Batista dictatorship and returned with the seizure of power by Fidel Castro. (By chance he had met Castro when he photographed him in prison during his Mexican exile.) He was soon disillusioned when he discovered that Fidelismo was the poor man's Fascism. He had, he told me, his past experience from Franco's Spain: 'Fidel is the same as Franco, only taller – and younger.' We had both founded, together with Germán Puig, the Cinemateca de Cuba that foundered on politics. We were both founders of the Film Institute. We both later discovered that it was only a propaganda machine run by tropical Stalinists. At the time of the ICAIC's (Film Institute's) banning of *P.M.* a modest exercise in free cinema, made by my brother Sabá and Orlando Jiménez, Néstor, who had become film critic for *Bohemia*, wrote a praising review. He was kicked off the magazine immediately. This expulsion was his salvation. Soon afterwards he left Cuba for the last time.

Néstor became a famous photographer in Europe. This is a reduction of reality. Néstor endured odd jobs, needs and even hunger (as his friend Juan Goytisolo can attest) in Paris. He did not become the favourite photographer of Truffaut and of Rohmer from the tropical night to the French morning. I saw him often then and learned that he got to the point of sleeping on the floor of a filthy hotel room that a friend was renting. Néstor was always indifferent to food, but what he had to eat in *la Cité Universitaire* was not exactly *nouvelle cuisine*. To pursue his vocation he went so far as to reject an offer from a wealthy American girls' school (where he had already taught in his second exile) to continue unhelped in his persuasion in France – where he supported himself by making documentaries for educational television. Years passed before they invited him to photograph a short for a film with stories. It was thus, with work, through his work, that he became the photographer he was.

I have to talk, though briefly, of his job that was a profession that was an art that was a wisdom. Néstor was not the chosen one of Truffaut, of Rohmer, of Barbet Schroeder, of Jack Nicholson, of Terry Malick and finally of Robert Benton because of his pretty face – that he never had in spite of his flirting with contact lenses and slouch hats. ('I have,' he used to say, 'a fish face.') All those directors (and others that I forget) used Néstor time and again because Néstor not only photographed his movies but worked out problems of sets, of makeup, of costume with his considerable culture. He even rewrote the scripts – as he did with the failed next-to-last film by Benton. He worked with the director before and after the shooting, straightening out gaffes, that were frequent. He also resolved acting problems during the shooting – and even earlier.

Not long ago an award-winning American screenwriter asked him to read his screenplay about the life and deeds of Cortés. Néstor made his always wise comments. He even prevented the writer from committing a Herculean howler when Cortés was made to study his Mexican campaign plan – on a globe! Néstor, more courteous than Cortés, told the screenwriter that this was an anachronism – as when Shakespeare in *Julius Caesar* makes twenty-one cannons roar to announce Caesar's entrance into Rome. The comparison with Shakespeare was not only charitable but flattering. Néstor Almendros was like that.

If Néstor had a discreet sex life, he had a wide open political life. Few foreigners (although Néstor was an honorary Cuban: most of his friends and many of his enemies are Cuban) have done so much, but no one more, for the cause of Cuba. It was Néstor who alerted the world, graphically, to what the sexual witch-hunt was like in Castro's Cuba. In his *Improper Conduct* the UMAP concentration camps for homosexuals that Castro built were revealed and almost seen through its protagonists. Many could have said that he had a vested interest in it. But Néstor produced another documentary, even more revealing, in *Nobody Listened*, about the abuses against human rights in Cuba. This documentary was essential for the Castro regime to be condemned everywhere and especially in the United Nations now. As with *Improper Conduct*, Néstor had come to these projects by a vision that was a conviction: he transmitted his anti-Fascist horror – born in Franco's Spain but rediscovered in the Cuba of Castro. Right now, already mortally wounded, he was working (jointly with Orlando Jiménez-Leal, his collaborator on *Improper Conduct*) on a documentary on the life, trial and death of General Ochoa – Castro's scapegoat.

It's hard that Néstor died. For me, for his friends, for his fans who swore that he was one of the great cinematographers in film history. For me, as a spectator who believes that photography is the single essential part in the art of film, he has, perhaps, only one current rival in Gordon Willis, who was the favourite photographer of Woody Allen and of Coppola. The advantage of Néstor is his classical modernity, visible as much in *Wild Child* as in *Claire's Knee*. Or his romantic aura in *Days of Heaven* (which won him the Oscar in 1979). Or his *art deco* elegance in *Billy Bathgate*, his last film – the one that contributed so much to his death.

From a constant that chance will not abolish, I called Néstor for the last time two Sundays ago. I knew (like all his friends) that Néstor had disappeared, I learned that the so-called disappearance was into a hospital in search of a desperate treatment. Although Néstor had not told anyone what his illness was, many of us suspected that it was the Disease. I listened to his discreet recorded announcement again, but when I was getting ready to leave my message, Néstor came on saying: 'Ah it's you.'

Although Néstor was desperately hoarse and his very message seemed to come from beyond the grave, he told me, for no reason, about the day of his arrival in Havana in 1948. How he was kept in quarantine on the ship and how his father came to rescue him with a friend who was a friend of an immigration inspector. 'In Cuba,' remembered Néstor, 'there was always a friend who knew another friend who was coming to save you.' Later we said goodbye – this time for ever. The next day, Monday, Néstor would go into a coma – never to come out of it again.

Once Billy Wilder ran into William Wyler at Ernst Lubitsch's funeral. 'How sad!' said Wyler. 'No more Lubitsch.' Wilder answered him: 'The sad thing is that there will be no more movies by Lubitsch.' How sad that there will be no more films by Néstor Almendros! How much sadder that there will be no more Néstor Almendros!

(March 1992)

Reinaldo Arenas,
or Destruction by Sex

Three passions ruled the life and death of Reinaldo Arenas: literature not as a game but as a flame that consumes, passive sex and active politics. Of the three, the dominant passion was sex. Not only in his life, but in his work. He was the chronicler of a country ruled not by Fidel Castro, already impotent, but by sex.

A recent diatribe in the weekly *Juventud Rebelde* (this *Rebel Youth* ought to be called *Obedient Dotage*) warns, with the prose of a parochial circular, against what it calls 'excessive fornication'. Indulged in by the city-dwellers, libertines never at liberty, forced to work in the country as volunteers according to Orwell. The editor accuses those sudden urban farmers of making not only a collective exhibition of the most crude coitus, but of staging nocturnal emulations between both sexes. In other words, a neverending orgy – perennial like the tropical foliage.

The call to order before the disorder of sex is not new in Cuba. A royal decree issued as early as 1516 (a few years after the Discovery) condemned the sexual practices of the natives and the Crown knitted its brow when accusing them, besides, of bathing too much. 'We are informed,' ended the royal admonition, 'that all of it does them much harm.' Something has been gained since Charles V: now the Cubans, due to the lack of running water and the scarce soap, bathe much less than their ancestors. The practices *contra natura* though reach bothering heights.

If homosexual writers like Lezama Lima and Virgilio Piñera, deceased, and the late pederast poet Emilio Ballagas, left behind a homoerotic vision of the world, they always expressed it by evasion and subterfuge, by more or less veiled insinuations, and, in the case of Ballagas, by coy epicene verse. Even Lezama (the eighth chapter of his novel *Paradiso* caused a sensation, in 1966, among Cuban readers repressed by the regime and the author himself suddenly suffered an odious ostracism) operated in his poems by obscure similes, by metaphor and by stealth, as in his notorious mysterious declaration: 'I feel like the possessed one penetrated by a soft axe.'

Our town also produced notable but anonymous mottoes. One was: 'I fuck your ass comfortably at home. Bring in a horse and I go out to the country.' Another was an effective test to prove madness: 'Put your balls on an anvil and hit them hard with a hammer.' Another was to exclaim: 'He let out a metaphor!' To express a wild action, a lack of restraint. The declaration itself was a metaphor. Never as in *Paradiso* was this folk phrase converted into a poetic system. But his Havana readers wanted to read a crude, rude realism that Lezama disdained as direct. That is, gross. Not even Virgilio Piñera, who saw himself as the epitome of the literary fag (which cost him prison in 1961 and the damning scorn of Che Guevara at the Cuban Embassy in Algiers, witnessed by Juan Goytisolo – and ultimate oblivion), never had the oral frankness (in all its senses) of his disciple Reinaldo Arenas.

His memoirs, *Antes que anochezca* (*Before Night Falls*), published in Barcelona, are written on raw flesh and read somewhere between indecent and innocent. (Like his life.) Borges says that there is no obscene act – only its telling is obscene. In the book by Arenas not only is the telling obscene, all its acts are obscene. This narrative, nevertheless, has nothing to do either with Piñera or with Lezama, his master mentors, but is rather hitched directly to another extraordinary Cuban book dominated by sexuality in general and in particular by pederasty and its Cuban all brand: the passive homosexual is an extreme woman, the active homosexual is a supermacho – because, they reason, he fornicates machos only. It is not strange that Arenas now renders homage to Carlos Montenegro.

Reinaldo Arenas goes beyond Montenegro and speaks of sex in prison, on the outside, in the city, in the country, in his childhood, in his adult life. His kind of sex is man infested: with children, with boys, with adolescents, with beasts from the barnyard and of burden, in the yard, with trees, with their trunks and their fruits, edible or not, with water, with rain, with rivers and – with the sea itself! (And even with the earth.) His pansexuality is, always, homosexual. Which makes him a country Cuban version of a Walt Whitman of prose and, at times, of a poetic prose that is on occasions a brown man's burden.

Reinaldo was a peasant born and reared in the country and educated by the Revolution in Havana, who thought himself a writer and succeeded. I have often asked myself why the Castroite regime that made him tried so hard to destroy him. A possible answer is that Arenas was not a revolutionary but a rebel, who showed with his life and with his death ('*Sicut vitae, finis ita,*' the Romans used to say) that he was a courageous man. With an unpolished talent, which in this posthumous book almost attains genius. If his life is like its ending, from the beginning it was a never-ending coitus. At times solitary, almost always in the company of other men. But if it is true, as Cyril Connolly points out, in a book whose title seems a fitting epitaph for Arenas, *The Unquiet Grave*, that a man who does not know in his life even one woman dies incomplete, Reinaldo, after having had such an active homosexual life, never seemed incomplete. He had, yes, a sexual relation with a girl cousin (those country girl cousins – always ahead of their boy cousins), but it happened long ago and far away. The two were not yet six years old and their extreme pleasure together was eating dirt until the gastric not erotic paroxysm.

Arenas, who seemed more like an ancient Roman than a *guajiro*, a peasant in Havana, was not a delicate Roman. More a gladiator than a court poet, he was rough, rude and resilient and he never knew fear. Although, like all truly courageous men, the first feeling that he confesses to in his book is cowardice. I wonder if this confession, among so many bold confessions, is nothing more than a show of vanity. But his life was a hazardous trek in a penetrable forest of penises, leaving behind the sign of his semen and of his writing. (He was a Hansel who always craved to be Gretel in the legend.) In the land of political myth he was a Sir Roger Casement of the tropics, with his outrageous confessions but always a patriot of the islands.

The *caso Arenas* is a much less well-known case than the *caso Padilla*. But of the two the one who suffered most at the hands of State Security was Reinaldo Arenas. Born in Aguas Claras, more than a village a jumble of derelict houses between Gibara and Holguin, on the extreme east of the island, rather than poor he was destitute from the cradle. A bastard and a fantasist, in his confusion of adolescent readings he joined a confused Castroite guerrilla gang that was fighting a confused little war against an invisible enemy – and rather than looking for a fight they were always looking for food. On the seizure of power by Fidel Castro he came to the capital like thousands of country boys, seeking Havana as the farm boys of Latium sought Rome. Still an adolescent, he won a prize with his first novel *Celestino antes del alba (Celestino Before Dawn)*, whose title echoes that of his last book. *Celestino* is a demented narrative located not far from Faulkner territory, but very contemporary in its paranoid description of a forest all of axes and a grandfather who fells every tree on which his grandson writes a poem. Allegory all?

His second novel, *El mundo alucinante (Hallucinations)*, is a masterpiece.

But he won with it a second award in a local competition, when he should have won first place all over Spanish America. As a disconsolate prize the novel was never published in Cuba. Arenas, anxious like any young tyro to see himself in print, sent the manuscript abroad – and committed a crime. There began what the good and bad consciences of the island called 'his problem'. His problem became grave and then acute when he was sentenced for pederasty, a crime that actually seemed one of *lèse* authority. Reinaldo became furtive all over the island and in the end, like the hunted protagonist of *I am a Fugitive from a Chain Gang*, he could mutter from the darkness: 'Now . . . I steal.'

But in real life there was an ending after the ending and Arenas found himself, like Edmond Dantès, worse than Dantès in the Castle of Château d'If, a prisoner among killers without a name and, once more, among homosexuals who were not gays and fags, but dangerous desperados. He would have had to spend the rest of his life in the other bigger prison that is the island (in a camp for homosexuals, in homosexual Havana), until in his next-to-last flight he slipped out between the fugitives from the Mariel exodus – and managed to escape to Miami using a subterfuge as refuge.

Then came his new-found freedom in New York, other books, other lovers and in a true ending to his love life he was caught by AIDS and died by his own hand to escape from a fate worse than death. In a last photo one sees Arenas as what he always was: not a Roman but a Cuban Indian – with the sad face of a brave in a reservation called life.

Before Night Falls is a novel which is a memory, a fusion of fiction and a life that painfully imitated fiction: that atrophied reality that is his last flight. There is nightly entertainment too – namely sex and Arenas who confesses to having gone to bed with more than five thousand men in his life and nobody claps. (They cheered Georges Simenon when he confessed to having gone to bed with more than ten thousand women – was it because of the number or because of the sex?)

Before, reading or not being able to read the free books of Arenas, I believed that he should have stayed in Cuba and repeated the successes of *Celestino* and *El mundo alucinante*. As at other times, I was wrong: Arenas would have ended up being a professional fugitive not a writer. For the writer who planned pentalogies and other projects, *Antes que anochezca* is a book difficult to read in parts not because of the style but of the stiletto. Written in a race against death, a downpour often not even badly written but barely written: dictated, spoken, shouted, this book is his second masterpiece. He could never have written it in Cuba, either as a functionary or as an outlaw.

Some have compared him with Genet, delicate delinquent, or with Céline, professional of bitterness: the two are writers without the slightest humour. It is because of this that one must look for its true peer in the picaresque novel, because its protagonist is a sexual *pícaro* – without doubt a *buscón*: he who mixes and mashes. But it often brings to memory that primeval novel, a masterpiece of the erotic picaresque – *The Satyricon*. Although in the book by Petronius, where the pederasts are heroes and the sodomites heroines, there are heterosexual relations. Even depraved or tenuous or fleeting but there are. In the novel of the life of Reinaldo Arenas there are only penises and pain.

But if these memories prove anything at all it is that the harsher the persecution against homosexuals in Cuba became, the more enjoyment (that is the word) it gave homosexuals, in private and in public. The island, as it regressed economically and politically, was regressing to the empire of a single sense. The lay-offs, the harassment, the prison and the concentration camps for homosexuals only seemed to be, if one believes Arenas, more of a spur than fame. Now, with all the sick homosexuals behind the bars of the infamous AIDS sanatoriums, called *sidatorios*, Castro reveals that homosexuality is a dominant obsession. Only the electric fences and the iron grilles are good for those behind bars who are never called comrades but citizens. Or, more familiarly, *enfermitos* – the morally and physically ill.

Be that as it may, contradictions of Communism, Havana is again a paradise only for tourists. Among the forbidden fruits that are offered, as much to Adam as to Eve, are the most delicious damsels (visibly not in distress in *Havana* by Jana Bokova) and the most desired male prostitutes, called *jineteros*, whorsemen – in search of whom many travel to the island now. Both objects of pleasure do it not for the money, which can buy nothing, but for a meal, for the price of admission to a cabaret, to spend the night from the night-club to the bed of a hotel only for foreigners. It is the sole way of cheating Castro's *apartheid*. Unless, of course, he or she is an informant of the Havana variant of State Security – and so able to pass from ecstasy to the Stasi.

(1992)

LIVE LIVES

Capa Son of Caissa
A Life in Chess Moves

'Where are you going in such a hurry?'
'To the Café Flore. Céline and Henry Miller are
    playing a game.'
'Bah! Minor writers!'
'But they're playing Capablanca.'
'What are we waiting for?'

The first time I saw Capablanca was the last. My mother
took me to see him. She, I must say, had no idea what chess was about but
she did know who Capablanca was. One late afternoon, or early evening
rather, she dragged my brother and me to see Capablanca. We left after
eating and arrived at our destination, the Capitolio Nacional, when it was
almost dark. The enormous white building was lit up for a party – to which
we were going. We climbed the tall, broad granite staircase to the Hall of
the Lost Steps (good name, too bad it was borrowed) and there in the
middle was Capablanca in his role of an eminent chess-player who had
suffered a checkmate. When we approached, reverently, I could see all
that could be seen of Capablanca: just his torso. He was terribly pale, grey
rather, and on his nose and in his ears he had thick cotton plugs. Capablanca looked immobile and ageless: he was dead – although he was an
immortal.

The catafalque (said my mother: a new word) lay right on top of the
diamond in the centre of the enormous hall where our steps were now
being lost. In the middle of the middle, central, was the diamond. It was
protected by a thick glass pane that assured its possession and at the same
time increased its size and its value. The diamond, like many women, was
at once attractive and inaccessible. It seemed in fact a Cuban version of the
colossal Koh-i-noor that Raffles (his silky hands never alighting on the still
stone) stole in his night dreams. The diamond, besides, was not only a
precious stone but a milestone: it marked mile zero of the central highway,
by order of General Gerardo Machado, dictator on duty. Now, gem on

gem, the coffin in which Capablanca was resting, his case, was posed heavy, with its precious bier a burden on top of the popular diamond. The embarrassment of riches was almost unendurable for a boy who was trying to understand what so much veneration meant. My mother, mad about culture, said with some finality: 'He is a glory of Cuba.' She did not say was but *is*. Capablanca is.

Capablanca's life starts where chess begins. His game is his life. Caissa was his mother.

Chess-players, to your corners! Women beware!

José Raúl Capablanca y Graupera was born in Havana on 18 November 1888, the son of a Spanish soldier and a Catalan lady. As the great Golombek said, 'Everything about Capablanca was legendary, except that of course we know he was born.' Legend has it that when he was only four Capa (his favourite nickname) made fun of his father when he was playing chess because he made illegal use of a horse. Capita was referring not to a 'soliped animal that is easily tamed and is useful to man' (and sometimes to woman), but to the chesspiece called knight in English and leaper (*Springer*) in German. No one ever gave chess lessons to the precocious player.

Capablanca's version:

> I wasn't yet five years old when, by accident, I went into my father's office and found him playing chess with another person. I had never seen a chess game: the pieces interested me and the next day I returned to watch them play. The third day, while I was watching, my father, very poor at openings, moved a knight from a white square to another of the same colour. Apparently his opponent, who was no better, didn't notice. My father won and I told him he was a cheat and I laughed at him. After a scolding he almost took me out of the room, but I was able to show him what he had done. My father asked me what I knew about chess. I answered, enough to defeat him: he told me that it was impossible, since I didn't even know how to place the pieces. We tried with our endgames and I won. That's how I got started.

Capablanca senior, among others, became mum in amazement and then clamoured with enthusiasm. Pepito (as his mother called him) defeated his father, first, his father's friends next and though he wasn't allowed to play in public, at the age of eleven he defeated the future champion of Cuba, Juan Corzo, who in a turn as return appears in all the histories of chess without having won but lost. 'Capa beats Corzo' is, in fact, one of the most memorable games completed by a child prodigy and both, like Napoleon and Wellington, made history together by winning and by being defeated.

Capablanca was a survivor from boyhood: another brother died very young. The Freudian theory that claims that chess has an Oedipal motivation (junior kills the king) makes a slip here: it was the dead older brother who should have challenged the father. Capablanca becomes Oedipus two. Freud, when he explains chess in terms of the Oedipus complex (the tragedy is after all only a Greek play that flopped on its first night) has always seemed to me freudulent. Nevertheless it is true that Capablanca learned to play chess by himself only to beat his father – and did manage it. Capablanca senior has been obliterated, played out into oblivion. When one says Capablanca we all think of the player who was known as 'the chess-playing machine'.

Four months after defeating Corzo, who was now national champion, Capablanca participates in his first Cuban championship and ends up in fourth place. Corzo encourages the young Capa to become a professional player – but Papa says no. The Cuban champion nevertheless lives long enough to see Capablanca crowned international champion and dies only four years before Capablanca. A Cuban industrialist (now in Republican Cuba) offers to finance the young chess master's education. Capablanca enrols in the University of Columbia, which is, fortunately for him, in New York – where the Manhattan Chess Club is. There he spends the time that the New York girls leave him free:

> I'm a Latin from Manhattan
> and I call myself Dolores.

In the Chess Club the prodigy who was an amateur in New York became a professional: *Capablanca from Havana*. (Now Capablanca was called Capa almost everywhere.) In the Chess Club he played hundreds of games with the leading players of New York. It was here that he also played against Lasker, Mr Emanuel, the German world champion of Jewish origin, to whom many point as the best player of all time – a little below Capablanca. The trio of terror in chess is made up in fact of Capablanca, Lasker and Paul Morphy (1837–84), the Southerner who was so afraid of having black blood to live an American tragedy. Fischer could have completed the triad, but his brilliant triumph over Boris Spassky in Reykjavik in 1972 was erased by a juvenile dementia he never got over. Fischer, a fanatical anti-Communist, curiously, did not suffer from the odious Oedipus: he played, literally, against his mother – called the red queen.

In the Manhattan Chess Club the Cuban grew close to one of the greatest American players, Frank Marshall, whom he would defeat decisively in 1909. Capablanca was twenty-one years old, Marshall thirty-three. A very bored Capablanca playing against Marshall nodded off more than once. With a sense of humour often absent from across the chessboard, Marshall tells: 'I made the worst move of the game. I woke up Capablanca.' Capa proceeded to execute a reveille checkmate.

Capablanca became a master of the *Zugzwang* – which is better than a Zen master. The *Zugzwang* fixes in German the position where a player obtains a worse result if it is his turn to move than if it is not. (*Pace* Marshall.) The good-looking, elegant, urbane Capa smiled observing his opponent's face when he produced what looked like a zigzag and was a *Zugzwang*.

There was a Polish player named Johann Hermann Zukertort who got furious when they translated his name. Everyone called him Sugar Cake. Capa smiled when in corny college capers they called him White Cloak. It was, of course, the wolf's disguise when he visits Little Red Riding Hood in winter. But when the mute motor of his grey cells began to work, they compared him with the silent efficiency of a running Rolls-Royce.

As a student (not of chess: he was born knowing how to play – because of this they called him the 'Mozart of chess') Capablanca would play more than once with Lasker. Neither of the two knew then that Capablanca would seize from Lasker the queen and the crown. In chess one doesn't intuit, one knows (as in an exact science) what is going to happen many moves later. Chess is an autistic game. The spectators sitting in front of the invisible double wall know it. The players walled up in the defence and offence know it. Concentric circles of mental exercise made into play, often the game ends in the check of madness. The game of Bobby Fischer, the only candidate for the cursed crown of Capablanca, has been called 'lunatic manoeuvres'. Fischer was never crazy, not even now when he has become the Greta Garbo of the game. But there are cases of genuine madness.

Like the pathetic paranoia of Paul Morphy, the first modern champion, whose solitary and sombre strolls of the streets in the old New Orleans that saw him born were the stuff nightmares are made of. Morphy was a leper in England and a celebrity in France. In Paris he defeated the Duke of Brunswick, playing together with Count Vauvenargues, in the duke's opera box – during the intermission of *The Barber of Seville*. Figaro here, Figaro there.

That was quick thinking (and playing) by the man called Morpheus. But Capablanca played with such speed that in the famous tournament for the championship, held in Havana, Lasker, his opponent, complained that Capablanca's timer had been fixed by the Cubans – so that it would run more slowly! But during the tournament Capablanca lost eighteen pounds.

Capablanca commented: 'There was a moment in my life when I was very close to believing that I couldn't lose a game.' When Capablanca entered the New York tournament of 1924, Lasker, always generous, declared: 'Capablanca could rest on a record that no one had ever had before nor will anyone equal later. In ten years he had played ninety-nine tournaments and – lost only one game!'

Like the Apaches according to Miguel Inclán, Capablanca was a proud man. When he was on the brink of losing a game against Marshall in Havana in 1913, a game of no importance, he got the mayor (of the city where he was born) to empty the game room before admitting defeat. But when he lost so strangely (and surprisingly) to Alekhine in Buenos Aires in 1927, the night before the deciding game he was dancing tango after tango with a local beauty. You see, like Borges, Capablanca liked Argentine women. Says Alexander Coburn, an English commentator, 'One of the most interesting aspects of Capablanca's personality is that, like no master before, he was very interested in women.'

It's true. Capa, son of Caissa (Caissa is the goddess of chess and an amusing muse), was more interested, always, in cavorting with women than in playing chess. In a tournament held in London, before losing the championship, he was invited with Alekhine, who then was posing as his best friend, to the music hall with the famous Bluebell Girls (all tall, all blonde, all legs) and the whole time that the show lasted, Alekhine did not stop consulting his pocket chess game, while Capablanca was all eyes for the blondes on stage. Careful with the queen! It's the most perilous piece in the game.

When asked about sex Bobby Fischer answered: 'I prefer to play chess.' Alekhine, for his part, was only interested in studying Capablanca – his playing considered as a foreplay. He spent, according to his own confession, *thirteen* years studying the champion up close. That night in London he was studying him still and he noted cryptically in his diary: 'It takes two to tango.'

Capa stayed in the United States during the First World War, playing, and wrote about chess (what else?) to the champion Lasker, a German citizen and patriotic Jew to boot. One day in 1918 two grey gentlemen from Washington came to visit him. They were from the Counter-Intelligence Service investigating his foreign correspondence, full of strange symbols: 10Bxe7 Qxe7 11 0–0 Nxc3 12Rxc3 e5. 'What code is this?' Very seriously Capablanca answered: 'They are signs for a liberation manoeuvre.' 'What?' said the two agents in unison. Capa chuckled: 'These are chess signs, an international convention.' After explanations and examples with the aid of a board and several pieces, the agents understood. 'Ah, like checkers.' 'Right,' said Capa, 'but with chessmen.' Capablanca realized that counter-intelligence is the contrary of intelligence. Nevertheless, they were right, those visitors. Emanuel Lasker had already invented a war tank for the enemy when it was still a friend.

Before entering the first circle of the spiral of madness (a labyrinth without a Daedalus) Morphy, a Morpheus who could not sleep, was in Havana in 1864 – 'which was now a chess centre' – to perform several simultaneous displays, with his eyes blindfolded. The rest was the deafening silence of the player's mind in a game without end. Capablanca, who could never imagine the social pressure on his mental health that Morphy endured, always conducted himself above his peers who believed him to be a Spanish aristocrat. In London they thought him a cold man when he was merely calm: cool not cold.[1]

According to Gerald Abrahams in *The Chess Mind*, Capablanca 'possessed a judgment calculated to prevent him from ever risking the loss of control'. George Steiner in his essay *Fields of Force: Fischer and Spassky at Reykjavik*, says 'More than any other master, [Capablanca] saw the armature of pure logic.' He seemed to have, he adds, 'the taut directness . . . which chess-playing computers have been programmed for'. Capablanca, still according to Steiner, 'has the monotony of perfection'. Capablanca, Steiner *dixit*, won a famous game against the famous Lasker 'with impeccable rigour' and in fifty-one quiet movements he worked it out to have 'a pawn advancing to the eighth row to be queened' – in the most dangerous sea change of the game. For the pawn dies after being crowned.

Capablanca, now, seemed for a moment to regret that his old friend Lasker was losing a game that he had already won and he did not move from his seat – not even when the applause thundered. His attitude during the game, after the game, was quite different from Bobby Fischer's. This is how the *International Herald Tribune* describes Fischer playing for the world championship in Reykjavik, Iceland in July 1972: 'Fischer is almost never still and continually swings around in his special $470 swivel chair while Spassky is deep in thought over his next move. Fischer bites his fingernails, pokes his nose and cleans his ears between moves.'

Fischer, who with his height, his eccentricities and his addiction to comics was the Howard Hughes of the royal game (rather than the royal of

---

1 On one occasion the champion, *nonchalant*, turned up to renew an interrupted game – dressed to play tennis and with a racquet in his hand! It turned out that he had made a date with a socialite, also a fan.

the game), did not play chess but practised continuous exercises of annulment of his opponent. Capablanca played with gentility, sureness and the absolute conviction that the game was his: chess had been invented for reds. Caissa did it. Still rather than with that indecision of Morphy (on his face could be seen the shadow of a doubt when he shaved: demented, delirious), Capablanca is often compared to Fischer. It must have been the case of twins joined by a board – but, like the pieces, one was white, the other black.

As a final analogy of opposites, people have imagined a single set to resolve (a key word in the game) the last problem in chess. *Could Fischer have defeated Capablanca?* Fischer sought always to demolish his opponent, physically and mentally. The only way that Fischer would have been able to finish off Capablanca would have been to take advantage when Capa pressed the button of his timer to have, behind Fischer's back, a parade of chorus-girls, models and stripteasers to distract the naked eye of the Cuban. Capablanca could, in revenge, have reminded Fischer of his mother: the black beast who was, for her son, red as the square with the tall towers of the Kremlin.

Capablanca was accused many times of being too easy because the game was as easy for him as music was for Mozart. It was kind of – well – like breathing. They also called him lazy at other times, as happened to Rossini. The Young Gioacchino always composed in bed from fear of the cold. (Like Capablanca, Rossini suffered from everlasting cold.) Therefore he got up late – or didn't get up at all. One day he saw one of the pages from his *Barber* fall off the bed. He didn't bother to get out of bed to get it but wrote it all over again. This is the best part of the score. Capablanca, by his art, didn't study an opening in his life.

They said that Capa was an incurable womanizer as if he suffered from a venereal disease. 'Just like a Cuban' said Alekhine, who had been married four times, beat his women and drank so much he turned up drunk to play in important tournaments. Vodka cost him the world championship in 1935. He was anti-Semitic to the point of writing articles defaming the Jews in chess, published in the Nazi press during the occupation of France. He suffered from acute attacks of violence, as when, after losing an easy game, he destroyed the furniture in his hotel room in Pskov.

But Alekhine was the first great Russian chess-player before Stalin's dirty tricks. Today he has a tournament in his name in the Soviet Union and the Russian authorities have tried several times to take away to Moscow his remains that rest (if they can) in the Père Lachaise cemetery in Paris. On his tomb there is an idealized bust of the player and below it there is a chessboard. In the middle glares a bronze inscription that exalts the memory of a great player who was not son of Caissa but son of the Bitch.

Alekhine was Capablanca's Salieri. After the unexpected defeat of the Cuban at the hands of the white Russian in Buenos Aires in 1927, Alekhine refused systematically to grant Capablanca a rematch for the world championship (at the time the rules of the game were different) and though he promised to do it many times – he never did. As irony would have it, Alekhine lost the world championship at the hands of the dull and grave Max Euwe. In 1937, nevertheless, Euwe, the non-flying Dutchman, gave Alekhine a lesson in sportsmanship (at any rate useless) and granted him a match and rematch. The tournament did nothing good for Euwe except that he was defeated for good. As Richard Eales says of Alekhine in *Chess: The History of a Game*, 'the contrast with his own treatment of Capablanca was only too obvious'.

Relations between Capablanca and Alekhine got to be so bad that Capablanca refused to participate in international tournaments – if he had to play with Alekhine. Capa had his name *blanca* among the whites, but Alekhine decided to play with the blacks until the bitter end. In 1940, living in occupied France, Alekhine (whom my mother used to call 'a vile villain') requested permission to emigrate to Cuba. He promised that if they let him into the island he would play Capablanca for the world championship. Batista, a great friend of the Soviet Union at the time, was the President of Cuba. He refused. Ironies of the board, not long after Alekhine's death, Stalin decided to consider him as a Russian glory.

Capablanca's letter of resignation to Alekhine is one of the most eloquent, elegant documents in the history of chess. '*Cher* Monsieur Alekhine,' wrote Capablanca in French and there is an erasure where there must have been an *e* that changed the *cher* into *chere*: Alekhine was a woman. Either Capa had little practice in resigning or too much skill in conquering women. The letter continues: '*J'abandone la partie*' and for a moment I read '*la patrie*'. Capa renounces his right to continue to play and loses the game and the world championship. Still he has salutations '*pour Madame*'. The letter is dated 29 November 1927 and the place where it was written is Buenos Aires, Argentina. It was the last of a champion and the end of an era in modern chess. At that age Mozart had composed his *Requiem*.

Alekhine, who never felt guilty about not having given the rematch to Capablanca and kept the title until his death, used to tell a story, at the end of his life but not of his tether. Just like Casanova but without the generosity with women that Casa had in his memoirs. Infirm but firm he tells what happened to him when he was playing Capablanca in Petersburg in 1914. One night, at the height of a tournament, like in 'The Queen of Spades' by Pushkin, someone knocked on his door. Alekhine opened it and came face to face with an old Russian peasant in rags who asked him if he could come in. He said he had found a secret of the highest import for chess. The man was insistent and Alekhine let him come in but did not invite him to sit down. 'I have found the way for the whites to get checkmate in *twelve* moves!' he claimed. Alekhine realized that he had a madman in his room and tried to throw him out. But the old visitor insisted. 'I'll show you,' he kept saying.

To get rid of the infuriating intruder Alekhine got the board and pieces ready. Twelve moves later the Russian champion and future king of world chess deposed his wooden king. Pale as plaster Alekhine almost begged: 'Do it again – please.' The old man repeated his performance and defeated Alekhine again and once again – and again. Alekhine grabbed the old man by one arm, went out into the hall and entered Capablanca's room without knocking. As usual the Cuban was in bed but not sleeping. He was playing the balalaika so that a gorgeous gypsy girl could dance a salmonella – or whatever that Russian rough and rude dance is called. With great effort Alekhine got Capablanca to stop making music (or whatever he was doing) to attend to the old peasant. Who proceeded to defeat the uncrowned champion of chess once and again and again – always in twelve moves. 'Twelve fateful chess moves!'

Here Alekhine seemed to end the story.

'But,' his impatient interlocutor wanted to know, 'what happened?'

'What happened?' Alekhine asked rhetorically. 'Capablanca and I killed the old man. Right there in his room and then we dumped him through the ice and into the Neva. That was what happened! If we hadn't done it neither Capablanca nor I would have been chess champions of the world. Of the world! I still am,' Alekhine affirmed in his bed in the middle of the white room, struggling one more time to take off like a Russian Houdini his white straitjacket, at the same time as he watched his analyst with eyes where a chessboard – the whites play – was reflected.

This incomplete story appeared in *The Complete Chess Addict* by Mike Fox and Richard James, and I reproduce it here because it reveals the character of the chess-player and the personality of Alekhine – a man capable of resorting to murder to win a game. Or the championship of the world. Whichever came first.

Dr Félix Martí Ibáñez, another analyst, affirms: 'To checkmate the opponent's King in chess is equivalent to castrating and devouring him, becoming one with him in a ritual of symbolic homosexualism and canni-balistic communion, thus responding to the remnants of the infantile Oedipus complex.' Written in 1960, this string of Freudian pearls is no less fantastic than the story of Alekhine and the checkmate in twelve moves. The whites play and win. The fable may have been cooked up in relish by Lord Dunsany, a master of the fantastic. Dr Ibáñez may well be related to Blasco Ibáñez, the man who wrote *Blood and Sand*. Capa, for his part, played to a draw with Lord Dunsany once. He was an amateur to reckon with.

Later in St Petersburg, the white nights of a black pawn. In 1925 the Soviet director Vsevolod Pudovkin made a minor movie called *The Chess Player* and his protagonist was none other than Capablanca. There he plays with his name and with the white cape of snow. The film started out as a documentary about the Moscow Tournament in 1925, when Capablanca was still champion of the world. Capa, in the middle of a symphony for boards and a toccata of pieces, seems involved in a romantic affair with a Russian beauty – the booty. Everyone appears to be suffering from chess fever (which is the alternate title) but a question stops the traffic: 'Is love more powerful than chess?' Capablanca goes even further by saying, 'When I see a beautiful woman, I also make haste to hate chess.' But he carries off the heroine – down to the tournament. At the end, with his Russian girlfriend returned to her Russian boyfriend, Capa in a cape and on the snow appears to say goodbye. At that moment a black pawn falls on the white pavement. *Koniesh filma*.

Capa always felt a vague antipathy toward those who don't play chess. 'It's as sad,' he affirmed, 'as a man who has never had relations with a woman other than his mother.' In a word, he didn't understand the con-firmed bachelor or the ignorant man who doesn't know what to do with a pawn. (The piece that strangely resembles a clitoris which moves inexor-ably towards the opposing queen.) Capablanca proposed once that the board be expanded by adding two extra pawns on each side and two new pieces. Capa thought, you see, that the possibilities of the game had already been exhausted. Some say that our man in the queen conceived this variant of the game (if not of the game's space: that meant in turn an alteration of the rules of the game) because he was fed up with the number of games that ended in ties. Others, more to the point, say that Capablanca found the game so easy that he got bored. The new pieces and the new space of the game would be like putting another woman in his bed.

Capablanca, who was a great cook and regarded himself as a gourmet, rarely got up before lunch and desserts and coffee (Capa, whose name means wrapper and is essential to the cigar, did not smoke or drink) and went off to play always bored and impatient to end the game, muttering, 'To supper, I suppose' – making a play on words by preferring, like Brillat-Savarin, the table to the board. The classical Capablanca was accused of being the first player affected with narcissism, which is a Romantic ill.

Capablanca was defeated, on the board, by a woman once. She was Mary Bain and vanquished him in simultaneous games. Miss Bain has the record as the simultaneous player who defeated Capablanca the fastest. Mary was not only young but pretty and the suspicion exists among the old chess-players that Capa let her win. The defeat, the concession, whatever it was, took only eleven moves. 'Chess,' said Sir Richard Burton, chess-player and translator of the *Kama Sutra*, the Hindu code of love conceived by the true inventors of chess, 'is an erotic game: everything consists of putting the queen in a horizontal position.' For those who believe in the importance of being honest, Capablanca put forward a theory: 'Chess is a science that looks like a game.'

An Alekhine anecdote reveals a compassionate, almost sentimental Capablanca. He was playing with Lasker in Moscow in 1914 and Capablanca noted how the then champion Lasker turned pale, ashen almost. He had realized that he had committed an error so grave that it might cost him the game. (Lasker's hands were trembling so much that he could hardly hold on to the piece that he wanted to move.) Capablanca knew at that precise moment that very soon he would be the world champion. But, he declared, he could not suppress a feeling of great pity when he saw the paralysing effect that the imminent defeat was having on Lasker. 'He had wielded the sceptre of chess for twenty years,' writes Capablanca, 'and in that instant he knew that his end had come up.' The irony of the moment is that the end had not arrived for Lasker just yet. The champion managed to get a tie and win the tournament. Capablanca called Capa was what Alekhine, for example, or Bobby Fischer, was not: a placable player.

Capablanca, nevertheless, rarely pardoned a woman: he was a Don Juan capable of inviting the dead Comendador to a stone tournament and in between moves going to bed with Inés, with *dõna* Ana and with the belle Isabel. For him a *ménage à trois* was not *une partie étrange*. Or an endgame. Capa was, besides, an expert athlete: the basketball boards were as familiar to him as those of chess, he practised fencing with the idea that chess was just another duel and he had browsed through more books about cooking than about chess. He never ever played chess except in tournaments and competitions. He had a secure social position (which the envious called a sinecure) converted into a propagandist for Cuba on salary from the

Cuban Government. Not very different from the position of all Soviet players, amateurs in name only. Lasker left it written down that Capablanca was, above all else, a modest man: 'He had the fundamental modesty that is the mark of true intelligence.' He wanted, yes, always to win in everything. But he did not have that killer instinct either against his opponents or with his lovers that Lord Byron or Hemingway had. Like Mozart, he was a classic who became a romantic in his performance.

Was all that what was in the luxurious coffin – in the tumulus – in the middle of the Lost Steps Room?

In 1913 Capablanca was named Cultural Ambassador for Cuba. The Governments of the island, in spite of the sun, were never very luminous. But now they understood that Capablanca had a publicity value (propaganda had not yet become established in Havana) and that his name was worth as much as any cigar brand. (Let's say La Corona, Partagas or Por Larrañaga.) Capablanca was like a non-smoking Montecristo. His colleagues, in Cuba and in the chess world, objected to what they called a sinecure *sine die*. Only Lasker, always short of cash, understood that Capablanca was a man with the luck to have his country behind him. The Russians, when they became Soviets, would understand too.

Capablanca became such a masterful player that he won a reputation as invincible and earned the moniker of 'the chess-playing machine'. (With all its fantastic implications: Maelzel's automaton, the inventions of Poe, the wiles of Dr Mabuse called *Der Spieler*, the gambler.) A new challenge from the young master to the old trickster only got Lasker to resign his title in favour of Capablanca. But as Procol Harum says, 'the crowd cried out for more'. It cried for, in fact, a tournament in wood in which the spears would be spared and became pawns, the maces bishops in a maze, knights on jumping horses and castling in those distant towers that are El Morro Castle and La Punta at the entrance to Havana Bay. The purse was enough to tempt a cloistered monk: 25,000 pesos when the Cuban peso was worth more than the dollar – it was the era of the fat cows. Playing like the master that he was, Capablanca won the most decisive victory ever achieved by a challenger to the world championship. He was so ecstatic that he committed the first error of his life with women: he got married. His bride in white, to top it all off, was named Gloria.

Capablanca went up his stairway to far a dais. Of the 158 games and tournament matches since 1914 he had lost only four games. Known by crowds who did not know how to spell chess but were somehow under his spell, Capablanca became the brightest star of the game. Perhaps he is – despite Alekhine, despite Fischer – as Ali said, the greatest. Capablanca was not only the world champion but the simultaneous game champion of his time. Because of what Petronius would have called *elegantiae*, Capablanca always refused to play blindfolded. Now he tilted his head backwards once more, tossed away that last cigarette he never quite lit and said defiantly to the lieutenant from the Spanish army of occupation who resembled his father so much: 'I don't want the blindfold!'

With the exception of Lasker, Capablanca was not very appreciated by the chess-players of his time. They found him a distant tremor when he was an earthquake: a natural destructive force that shook the board and knocked over the pieces, especially the king and queen. But, a fate worse than hate, there was a player who flattered him, who praised him always – Alexander Alekhine. 'The wicked, wretched man!' as my mother taught me when I was ten – making me a prodigy Capaist. (I think that I was the last person to see Capablanca dead.) My mother called him Alekineh. For her, Alekineh was the worst: a White Russian. Alekhine, the devil closest at hand, tempted Capablanca as if he were a mean Mephisto: *Vade retro Capanegra!* But Capablanca accepted the challenge and Alekhine, wonder of wonders, defeated Capablanca for ever. Alekhine declared with false modesty what was nevertheless a fact: 'I do not believe that I was superior to Capablanca. Perhaps the reason that I won was that he overestimated himself and did not estimate me enough.' These were the Devil's reasons: 'God never loved me, Mephisto.' Metaphysics aside, the true truth is that Alekhine became champion of the world and made off with the championship by crook and by hook. Until he died. God only knows what he told the Devil.

After his unexpected defeat, Capablanca began to behave like a tower of snow: the white ones castle and lose, the black ones checkmate and go away. His marriage became a divorce, but he continued playing: he won some and he lost some. In 1987 his widow, Olga Capablanca de Clark, sold the unpublished manuscript of a Capablanca–Tartakower game for $10,000. He was still deified in the chess world and in the world: Capablanca became a beer brand, a chocolate and vanilla ice cream, a rum cocktail with whipped cream on top. In Russia, which was now called the Soviet Union, he was more popular than he ever was under the tsars: chess was king and Capablanca his prince consort. Capablanca married a Russian woman – from France – whom he met in 1934. The wedding took place in 1938 in Paris but it had its bridal wave in Havana. His first wife's family managed something more devious than Alekhine: Capablanca stopped being ambassador at large. They demoted him to a mere attaché. But Capablanca did not stop playing and winning: Caissa begat him.

Mozart could, with his back turned to the piano, say the number and name of the notes of a chord that another person had just played: preferably a woman's fingers. Capablanca, by only casting a glance at the board, saw all the pieces and their position and disposition and knew exactly which were the possibilities of that particular game. Disdainful of openings (never, according to him, did he study them) he always showed a striking skill at endgames. Perhaps it influenced him in this that he learned to play when the pieces were already on the board and the game had begun. His adversary of always, an extraordinary Luzbel, Alekhine said that he had not seen another player with his 'speed of comprehension' – that was his apprehension. A classmate, a strong player, declared that Capablanca 'never learned how to learn'. For Capa chess was a game and not for nothing was he declared the playboy of Western chess. In opposition to the emerging Russian school headed by Alekhine, which was all study, effort and bad faith.

The word 'playboy' suggests a Porfirio Rubirosa, a chocolate officer who made his way on Trujillo's island and in the world by blows of penis. Rubirosa was a reformed knave, Capablanca was exactly the opposite. It is still believed that Capablanca belonged to *criollo* high society. Nothing is farther from the truth. Capablanca senior was only a lieutenant in the Spanish army on the always loyal island. His mother was a housewife. The two had nothing more than their memorable names and a prodigy for a son. Even the Cuban patron who paid for his studies in the United States concluded that Capablanca spent more time playing (chess but also baseball and basketball) than studying and withdrew his stupendous stipend. It was then that Caissa came to rescue Capa from ignominy: Frank Marshall agreed to play against him calculating that it would be child's play. But Capablanca beat him decisively. An unprecedented deed: a mere amateur defeated a canny champion. Marshall, impressed by his defeat (that is by Capablanca's victory), got him invited to San Sebastián in 1911. Capablanca, an unprecedented feat, won a great tournament than in his first attempt. The rest is history: chess history, precisely.

One evening in 1942 (it was March, it was snowing) Capablanca as he did so many times, went into the Manhattan Chess Club. It had been his favourite hangout as a young student and later as an aspirant to any tournament and even much later as a grand master and finally world champion. Capa, chilled but not damp, headed quickly for the game room without even taking off his overcoat. In spite of his years spent in New York and in Europe (in spite of the Russian snow) Capa was always cold. Except, of course, when he was playing – with some woman in the snow.

The doorman, the hat-check girl and even the club members were used to seeing Capablanca tucked in a black overcoat down to his ankles, moving from board to board, in silent simultaneous display: hovering, watching and taking in with a single glance the state of the set and the ensemble of pieces scattered in disorder all over the board. (For him it was all an all – the game.) Now he noticed that there was not a single player of his age. They were all very young or old: these were times of war not of the game but of the game of war.

At another board, above a young player, he saw at a glance that the other, an old man, had the game lost. The young player tried to start a killing move without thinking about it, thought better of it and went no further. But he had touched his queen and according to the rules of the game when one grazes one of his own pieces he must move it forward. The other player, the old man, wrapped up in defeat, had not noticed the slight movement by the other and the young player pretended that nothing had happened.

Perhaps Capablanca remembered the first time that he noticed, more than a half-century before, a move to register foul play. Now he said nothing, of course: he was still a gentleman. But he lifted his arms in a strange way, brought his gloved hands to his throat and begged almost with a shout: 'Help me with my cape!' in Spanish. That was his final phrase: '¡Ayúdenme con mi capa!' He said no more and fell to the floor, dead. He had suffered, according to the autopsy, a massive brain haemorrhage. The pathologist said that nothing looked out of the ordinary in Capablanca's brain, which was particularly normal. It is obvious that the chess moves and the many women cannot be seen in one's brain. Was that all there was in his embalmed head?

(November 1988)

Actors and Sinners

Once I wrote an essay disguised as an article called 'The actor as politician, the politician as actor'. No one, I think, read it. In that article I spoke of what was transparent in a certain uncertain actor of the American cinema convertible into a President without precedent. But, an opaque object, it was not apparent that I was going to speak of the actor and the politician – and of someone else. Now that I am trying to give mouth-to-ear resuscitation to that essay that almost became an *articulum mortis*, I must repeat what I said though not exactly as I said it – never verbatim. In spite of galloping technology I still believe that it is *verba* and not fax that motivates a writer. So I will try to bring off a faithful rendition of what was, actually, a secret communiqué.

During the American election campaign in 1980 and afterwards it was repeated until one was fed up that Reagan was a bad B-movie actor – a double political sin apparently. To attenuate the remark (which was an accusation or an unasked-for explanation) Reagan himself was presented saying: 'I was the Errol Flynn of the B-movies.' As will be seen very soon none of it was true. (Not always in any case.) At the end of the thirties, at the beginning of his career, Reagan shared the billing of *Dark Victory* with Bette Davis and Humphrey Bogart. There is nothing to object to in his company, greater actors. At the beginning of the forties Reagan was in *Santa Fe Trail*, which, like *Dark Victory*, was anything but a B-movie. (Unless the B of Warner doesn't mean 'brothers'.) Reagan, not by accident for sure, had as a cowboy companion none other than Errol Flynn. Directed by the ace director at Warner, Michael Curtiz (*Casablanca et al.*), its leading lady was the apple of the eye of the studio, Olivia de Havilland – if Olivia de Havilland could ever have been an apple.

Later Reagan was in *King's Row*. *King's Row* was one of the major productions by Warner in the forties and was intended by Jack and bros to compete with Metro in formal elegance and technical perfection: double dominion of MGM. It is in this movie that Reagan loses both legs in an unnecessary amputation. (It is actually a matter of a criminal revenge by the old surgeon who only wants to teach a lesson to the loser from the other side of the tracks – so that he will stay in his place.) When he wakes up from the anaesthesia and discovers that half his body is missing, Reagan exclaims half-surprised and half-terrified: 'Where's the rest of me?' one of the most painful exclamations in Hollywood history. For years this line became a poisonous quip on the lips of a few fans of film noir and sick jokes. Reagan, in a gesture of typical self-deprecation (as shown by those jokes that were his own medical releases when he was shot), called his autobiography *Where's the Rest of Me?*

Later Reagan made important movies, like *The Voice of the Turtle*, where he had the pleasant task of making love to the truly beautiful Eleanor Parker. Here he proved to be a considerable comedian. Surprise, surprise Reagan acted in *Storm Warning*, in which he shared billing with stars like Ginger Rogers and Doris Day, the old and the new blondes of the studio. But the unusual thing is not the company he kept but that this movie was an effective plea against the Ku Klux Klan. For another thing Ronald Reagan had around that time married Jane Wyman, who was an Oscar winner in 1948. One already knows that in the strict Hollywood heirarchy a star in her apogee never marries an aspirant to failure – not even in film fiction as in *A Star Is Born*. (Greta Garbo never married her discoverer Mauritz Stiller, but Ingrid Bergman did marry Roberto Rossellini in the climax of *Stromboli*.) Reagan's last film was indeed a B-movie, *The Killers*, based not on the Hemingway story but on an earlier version of the story made in 1946. Playing against Lee Marvin's noble because naïve gangster, Reagan enacts a canny capitalist who secretly finances a hideous heist while plotting a doublecross on his own gang. *The Killers* is from 1964 and it is surprising to know that never has a parallel been drawn between its fiction and political life. All the negative emphasis was always on Ronald Reagan's being an actor – and worse still, an actor in B-movies. As if acting yesterday in a cheap movie cheapened his future performance as President.

It must be pointed out that B-movies are sometimes much better than superproductions: imagination winning out over money. If one reproaches them for their low cost, why then curse Hollywood in the same breath for spending fortunes on a single movie – its cost larger than the budget of poor countries? Like hell, the cinema is paved with costly good intentions and so one of the films that has lavished the most money in Hollywood history is *Apocalypse Now!* – praised by the critical Left for its anti-war stance.

I saw and heard Ronald Reagan in his debate with President Carter, an appearance that cost the Democrats the presidency. In this confrontation Carter came across as nervous, vacillating, indecisive. (In a word, he was histrionically ineffective.) Carter is, we already know, a lousy actor because he is insecure. So with his presidential image already established he decided to change the way his hair was parted – taking his head for his brain. At the same time he tried to free himself from his accent as a Georgia cracker to resemble a Southern politician who can read without moving his lips. The result was a ridiculous appearance and one of the most atrocious deliveries that the American scene remembers. Carter now made unusual pauses that did not match the grammatical or logical order of the English language and he was always seen as forced as he was false. 'Here he goes again,' summed up Reagan, who projected calm, sureness, benevolence and (a very important quality in an American President) showed authority without authoritarianism. He was, it's curious, very close to the John Kennedy who defeated Richard Nixon in a similar debate in 1960. Although Carter's aides shouted at the end out loud, 'We won! We've won tonight!' it was obvious, for the spectators and the polls, that Reagan had won not only the debate but the election. He owed his triumph to his quality as an actor.

There was another important election around that time which a different actor won. It is not an election of international relevance nor is it even a national election – but perhaps it turned out as decisive in the long run for Europe as it was for England. I am referring to the election within the British Labour Party to choose its chief – or political leader. The election was held among the Labour Members of Parliament only. No one else had a right to vote. There can be no election more restricted in the United Kingdom, if one excepts, of course, the admission as a member of a gentleman's club in London. (That is perhaps more democratic than the old election of the Dalai Lama between three Tibetan monks in communion with the occult.) The election of the Labour leader was won by Michael Foot, a facile failure. His only opponent was Denis Healey, the favourite of the best betters and pure politicos.

In the last Labour Cabinet Healey had been Chancellor of the Exchequer, the English equivalent of the Minister of the Treasury in less esoteric countries. But it is actually the most important public post after the Prime Minister in 10 Downing Street: the Chancellor controls lives and property. Healey is a good old-fashioned character actor and in a John Ford movie, for example, he would have been played by Thomas Mitchell: the good doctor, sober or inebriated according to whether he was drinking whisky or coffee, in *Stagecoach*. Healey, affable, optimistic, capable of radiating unlimited confidence in the midst of the English chaos, combing eyebrows so bushy that they look false and with such a good easy smile, was the natural father of Labourism. Hiding his rare erudition (or his erudition of the rare: he is one of the English readers who knows the most about the mystery novel in England, which is saying a lot in these islands where exists not the crime of passion but rather the passion for crime) behind a jocund bonhomie. Healey should have won but did not. Hazards of politics? No, tricks of the trade. He was defeated by Foot's anaemic party oratory, a strange mixture of a certain tone, mellifluous without being unctuous, in distant discord, which exerts at the same time a peremptory power, so incantatory – with registers appropriate to a bass singer who knows the bravura repertoire of Lenin. His gestures are as incisive as his words, in a combination of menace as inevitable as history and a fatal free will derived from singing *The Passion According to Marx* once too often. As a political columnist, who knows him by hearsay, defined him, he is a man who knows how to ennoble resentment, a disguise necessary for the costume ball in a country of castes which dance to the tune of a genteel waltz – while the orchestra of the times plays a frenetic rock rhythm.

Healey, dancing a calm waltz, played the role of kind father, Santa Claus mistakenly perched above his station. Foot was an acid grandfather now, pure punk, but a possibly benign man ('Save me the waltz, please'), the one who knows more because he is an old politician than because he is an intellectual. That prickly personality was well hidden by Foot for a time, but he let it be seen often through his venerable white hairs and his glasses of a near-sighted granny facing the steppe wolf. Foot presented himself in fact as an audacious alternative to the extreme Left of the Party – but he remained well within the orthodox Left to which he has always belonged. His position was well into the eccentric centre. And there is nothing that the English like more (even those Englishmen, internationalists in theory, who are the Labourites) than an eccentric in the family. Michael Foot was, besides, the predictable eccentric. His scale would always incline to the platter that the goddess Justice carries to her left on top of the Old Bailey – without the conventional blindfold over his eyes without glasses.

No sooner had Foot won – than he broke an ankle. As in an anatomical metaphor it was his right foot that he stuck in the wrong place. It is not necessary to take this rightist fracture as a sign to predict on which foot Foot limps. He leans to the Left wing of the Party, where he is active, and still further, where the Labourites can barely be distinguished from the infiltrating Communists. That tenuous political frontier is for the Labourite nation a mirage and a menace on an electoral desert.

In this election, which is rather a selection, not the best man but the better orator won. Michael Foot, with quicksilver hair and a volatile character in appearance, is like every politician, like every actor, a histrionic chameleon whose mask – thick glasses, mugging in a mobile metamorphosis – hides what no politician can show, intelligence. (Trotsky was an extreme example of this brain drain.) Denis Healey, more frank than Foot, showed his *vera effigies* of an eminent Oxfordian underneath his village doctor eyebrows – and lost. He had to lose, you see. 'Labour' does not mean elite but work and although it also means childbirth, Healey was no Thomas Mitchell in *Stagecoach*, the doctor on board, but an aspiring parliamentary leader. Healey lost from not knowing how to hide his histrionic intelligence. Actors must never look more intelligent than their role. Or their audience.

The American electoral columnists made, before the elections, a rough rude racket remembering Ronald Reagan's résumé and pointed out how many actors are now politicians – but they never revealed that all politicians are actors. It is the unusual actors making it as politicians who are the greatest actors. Like Zhou En-lai, with his doubtful double past as actor and actress. Zhou was apparently so pretty as a youth that he played leading ladies in the traditional Chinese theatre. Even as the extraordinary Prime Minister, second only to Mao, Zhou was a statesman with a handsome face, who knew the value of his inscrutable features and the price of the circumflex accent his dusky eyebrows fixed on his conversation.

Eva Duarte was an Argentine actress so mediocre that there was no other way, to attain fame, than to use her notoriety as a scarlet starlet to make herself into Eva Perón. In a leap further forward she became Evita, lover of the shirtless, implacable politician, heroine of that interchangeable political – or is it poetic? – myth, that goes from the extreme Right in the fifties to the current extreme Left: a queen twice after dying. Eva Duarte de Perón had been made into books, exalted to the pop musical tragicomedy and finally returned from the stuff of which dreams and the movies are made: incarnated this time by Faye Dunaway, the out-of-luck outlaw of *Bonnie and Clyde*. She is an eminent example of an actress, a lover, a public figure turned political goddess and in a grotesque destiny that nobody could ever have predicted (though perhaps the first Eve might have dreamed it) converted into the mummy of a saint of the century. There is no other political personality in the *soi-disante* Latin America that can equal her. Not even that of her desperate compatriot Che Guevara, the guerrilla who *looked like* an actor.

It is at the other extreme of the globe, in China, almost on an exact parallel, that one can find Evita's only rival. She was called Jiang Qing. She was also an actress in cheap films, as ambitious and audacious as the Dragon Lady and almost as terrible: it is that woman we all know now as the alliterative Madame Mao. The failed actress was soon transformed into a political partisan, a groupie of the eminent leader from Hunan, a camp-follower next to the promoter of the Long March, the lover and finally wife of Mao himself. Don't they seem like parallel lives for Plutarch, one Chinese, the other Argentine? Jiang Qing had more success than Evita but at the same time her failure was greater. She climbed higher perhaps but she fell more noisily. After Mao's death this actress, who loved the movies as a passive spectator as much as she craved active power, almost became the most powerful woman in Chinese history – singularly almost like Ci-Xi, the legendary and cruel dowager empress who reigned implacably in Beijing barely a hundred years ago. But Madame Mao, alive in prison today, is not a myth but its opposite, the dead myth.

The fact that Che Guevara did not know how to act (he was a man condemned by his virtue, frankness) disqualified him as a political leader in Cuba and forced him into suicidal exile. If only he had been able to get rid of his Argentine accent! If he had not followed to the letter his own instructions for a guerrilla war! If there had been two, ten Vietnams! Never has a hero so magnificent (for the naïve Left) had so few real followers. Only when he became a martyr did proselytes rise up to the occasion. But they were only cosmetic facsimiles that copied his outfit become a fashion, his erratic beard and his attitudes of a *partisan terrible*.

His fellow-traveller Fidel Castro is not only a considerable orator, as effective in moving multitudes to the point of making them mobile masses as Adolf Hitler, but also a consummate actor and his political platform is the stage of endless Marxist monologues. (Even on television, a minimal stage, he obtains that capacity of persuasion without subtlety that only great actors master – without the stage freight of ridicule.) If all politicians perform, tyrants are not necessarily the worst actors. (Who is a better Arab, Omar Sharif or Saddam Hussein?) Hitler and Stalin, for example, could give lessons to the players of the Berliner Ensemble or of the Moscow Art Theatre. One has only to watch old Nazi newsreels to come face to face with a voluntarily Wagnerian actor, an apocalyptic Aryan, who offers the miraculous millennium or the twilight of the German gods by only moving his vociferous mouth under an always Chaplinesque but never comic moustache. Stalin, in his conversations with H. G. Wells and later in meetings with Roosevelt and Churchill, appears as a humanitarian man or a reasonable statesman and at times he is even a timid totalitarian.

(This is the sly tyrant type, in a low tone if one compares him with the exalted Hitler.) Still we all know what Stalin was like – and whoever does not know, let him browse through any one of the three volumes of the *Gulag Archipelago*, the prologue of his *opera magna*.

Fidel Castro is perhaps the best television actor in the world, with a mastery of the medium and an absolute control not only of his voice and his gestures but of his temper. I remember having seen him one day in the waiting room of a television studio about to go on the air. Meanwhile, he killed time joking, strolling around calmly as he slowly smoked his habitual Havana, talking about cows and green pasturage and milk production, smiling satisfied: the agreeable agronomist. But no sooner had they introduced him to the well-lit studio and the camera had focused on him, than he came on the air transformed into a true Zeus thundering terrible traumas against an invisible opposition. He was not the elder Marx but the young Jupiter.

Eva Perón was a professional but Perón learned on his own an Argentine histrionics that owed as much to Mussolini (what a grand operatic actor Italy lost! I can see him on the Milanese billboard of La Scala: 'Questa Sera – Mussolini in *La forza del destino* – Benvenuto, Benito!' Ah the opera, ah Il Duce!) as to Carlos Gardel, the martyr of the tango. Perón knew it, of course. His is the famous dictum: 'The Argentine who can laugh at the people from the platform like Gardel on the screen, will have Argentina in a fist.' The metaphor is a bad mixture but the political feeling was precise, direct.

There is, as always, one exception to the rule. Only Franco among modern dictators was a poor player: on top of his El Pardo balcony he only looked like a spectator of history seen as a distant tragedy. Franco was a little dictator. When I saw him first and last he looked diminutive and remote, incapable of mastering the stage. When he spoke his voice was not the braying of the dwarf in the inn who threatens terribly from his high window, but a monotone falsetto and, for me, on a short visit, quite disappointing as a political performer. But one doubt remains – perhaps Francisco Franco was an excellent actor playing the role of a bad actor.

Charles de Gaulle is perhaps the greatest actor that France has had since Molière. At least he is the most grandiose. Like Molière, de Gaulle wrote his monologues and composed his lines. De Gaulle was a Molière who believed he was Louis XIV and could almost say, with a greater resonance, 'Before me the deluge', a Noah of the Liberation. But after de Gaulle has come, for France, the carnival of the political animals.

Richard Nixon was the opposite of a dictator: tyrants never resign.

Either they promote a constant *coup d'état* or they shoot themselves in the right temple. But Richard Nixon shares with Ronald Reagan not only the same party but a common and distant past of an aspiring young actor. Nixon tried (he is still trying) to tread the boards and the only ones he has trodden, not very firmly, were those of the party platform.

Winston Churchill, for his part, was a politician with total success but a failed actor. Laurence Olivier tells how difficult it was to do Hamlet when Churchill was in the audience – which was every time they staged *Hamlet* in London. Churchill would sit invariably in the first row and would not only repeat out loud each speech by the doubting Dane, but do it with his voice slurred by whisky, declaiming every monologue: 'Tho be or noth tho be, that ish the queshtion.' Churchill and Nixon were horrible hams. But there is a slight difference between both atrocious actors. Churchill was a great ham and he knew it. In the middle of the war he offered the English only blood, sweat and tears on the radio. He did it in the best English stoic tradition of a Nelson at Trafalgar ('England expects') but at the same time as heroic as a false Falstaff on the stage. The falseness was cancelled out by the art of absolute deceit. It was not Churchill who improvised the historic speech but rather the text was read by an actor who imitated the actor who played the part – of the Prime Minister!

Nixon, poor ham, would never have come up with such a trick of the perfect double because he is a triple. On the contrary. In his last days in the White House, when television showed his sweating face, his furtive eyes and his need to project veracity at all cost from coast to coast ('Friends,' he promised, 'let me be perfectly clear'), one saw on the screen the worst actor in the world playing an absolutely bankrupt politician who refused to recognize it – and it showed.

Ted Kennedy lost the primaries to Carter because he has become a young ham. Behind his liberal speech one hears now the cunning politician, the false apostle and the demagogue. He looked capable of saying no matter what lie – for example, hiding the obscure Chappaquiddick episode until making it murky – to be President. But his hollow words can never stop up with their resonance his own Watergate. His brother John Kennedy was totally opposite: an excellent actor who was born with the halo stars have. Bobby Kennedy, for his part, was the actor as a born loser. The reverse of Jack, whose death was an almost grandiose scenic spectacle, Bobby died with a kitchen sink in the background. Lincoln, great character actor that he was, fell in the theatre, at the same time a spectator and an actor – like the great tragedians.

Ronald Reagan comes from another dramatic tradition, American naturalism, begun in the movies by Gary Cooper, which consists of following a golden rule: the actor acts so little that one cannot see the acting, only the character barely covered by the transparent mask of the player. In his historic debate with Jimmy Carter, Reagan was seen to be simple, sincere and amiable. Contrasting favourably with the tension, the vacillation and the poor mastery of the Carter character – nothing less than the President of the most powerful nation on earth. That contrast made us lose sight of the fact that Reagan was acting with effective skill not to master his medium – television after all is only the cinema by radio – but to make us forget that we had on the small screen not a consummate actor but the only possible President of the United States. This has been the best performance in the career of a politician classified by his enemies as a bad actor in cheap movies, while his followers wanted precisely to make us forget that he had ever acted. Ronald Reagan was only a sincere All-American, a patriot, the father (but never the grandfather) of every American and the saviour of whatever remains of what was the American Century. Reagan deserved the Oscar for his brilliant performance that memorable night – and, you already see, they only gave him, as a consolation prize, the Presidency of the United States for life.

Almost all the incidents that happened around Reagan, protagonist or not, now installed in the White House, reveal rather than they announce the born actor. He inaugurated, for example, Oscar Night by remote control, was the victim of a failed attempt on his life filmed with the means of a B-movie and the visual effectiveness of a big production in the latest hand-held camera style. His frustrated assassin appeared motivated by seeing on the screen the more virtual than virtuous image of a prostitute Lolita, larger than reality, and the actual contract written with the juvenile star who plays her as human bondage. Still in hospital, gravely wounded with a handgun wound, Ronald Reagan has no last message for humanity (or, more ambitious, for the nation) and does nothing else but imitate a movie comedian – Bob Hope full of hope. (Or that grave iconoclast who was W. C. Fields, his epitaph precisely: 'On the whole,' was the first and almost the last thing Reagan said, 'I'd rather be in Philadelphia.')

It has been claimed that Reagan was a political cowboy but the real cowboy – one has only to hear his Texan drawl – is President Bush. But Bush is a poor actor or, if one wishes, a ham roasted on mesquite. One who *is* a consummate actor is his associate or *sosias* in the Kremlin. Mikhail Gorbachev is a good actor with a bad script, written, alas, not by Groucho Marx but by Karl. It is, besides, an interpretation that is a translation. 'Capital, capital,' the music-hall comics from Marx's era always used to say and they were not referring to capitalism. In fact the word meant something brilliant and successful – which is the opposite of Capital.[1]

There is a ritual phrase that is always intoned when the campaign to elect the American President starts which seems like an exhortation to an obstacle course: 'May the best man win.' 'May the best man win,' says that starting phrase but it should say: 'May the best actor win.' So when he knew that he was shot and believing that he was dying, Ronald Reagan could have breathed an appropriate but foreign final phrase – addressed to the ubiquitous microphone and camera: *'Qualis histrio pereo!'*

In savage symmetry Margaret Thatcher lost the party elections (like Denis Healey), and the leadership of the Conservatives (like Edward Heath) and did not lose her head because this civil war did not take place in Cromwell's times. But perhaps *la* Thatcher (strictly for show business) imitated something more than the image of Barbara Stanwyck, whom she copied even in her weird hairdos that were, like a Chinese box, all lacquer. Barbara Stanwyck, called Bad Babs for her many villainies in the movies, was a great actress. Margaret Thatcher turned out finally to be a bad actress because she showed herself to be a false facsimile.

In *The Bitter Tea (of General Yen) la* Stanwyck was very young and like the young Thatcher was modest and modish. Her encounter with General Yen was something less than promising, as happened when Margaret Thatcher met Edward Heath, the powerful Prime Minister. General Yen had run over *la* Stanwyck's rickshaw-boy and when she came to protest to the slightly wounded general, the latter gave her a lesson in Oriental wisdom: 'Has he died, madam? Then you must thank me for it. Life, even in its moments of greatest exaltation, is barely endurable.' Haughty and arrogant like Heath, the general fell before the angry Chinese Boxers, while Heath was dethroned by the coal mob and the angry miners. In an intra-parliamentary election, *la* Thatcher defeated Heath and was promptly elected leader of the Conservative Party. The general drank at dawn the Chinese equivalent of hemlock (possibly something with soy sauce) and Barbara then sailed down the river of sanity on her way both to the West and oblivion.

---

1 To show that he is an *alias inter pares*, during the first Gorbachev–Reagan summit, when the two Presidents were alone (the magazine the *New Yorker* tells it), the Russian asked the American immediately about his Hollywood days. 'The two,' says the magazine, 'talked about similar experiences.' When he gets to the experiences the historian puts similar in quotes. Less modestly I can add that surely the experiences were in fact identical. Or, at least as Plutarch has it, parallel.

That story is told only to present the protagonists. There is another Barbara Stanwyck movie which is an atrocious analogy. It is called *The Strange Love of Martha Ivers* and this is its box-within-a-box story. Martha Ivers inherits a considerable fortune and for the next twenty years she controls an enormous factory in a small town in America. But she runs into (more or less accidentally) a childhood friend who returns to rekindle an old flame (apparently it all started when they were children) but he only revives that old guilt complex: there is a dead man in their past. (Perhaps the same general feeling called *Yen*.)

This dark synopsis omits the point of view (the revelation) when Martha looks through the window that opens into the past and sees how passion (or its object) is leaving the mansion, the town and her life without even looking back. But one sees her as through a glass darkly that is only the curtains creating a last veil effect. All the English spectators, who love television more than crime, could see Martha Thatcher, hidden in the house of the winning Chancellor John Major, which is 10 Downing Street, cast her last defeated glance from the first-floor window and behind the curtains as through a vain veil – Salome when she glances. Babs saw the ghost of power escaping from her behind the ubiquitous curtain of the camera lens. It was the extreme love of Margaret Ivers for power that was vanishing like the ghost of Hamlet that adviseth, 'Leave her to Heaven.'

This essay has a history. I wrote it in 1982, when Ronald Reagan had just been elected, and sent it to several Spanish publications, where it met different treatment but the same destiny: it was rejected, it was lost or it disappeared without trace. There was a single reason for it all: Reagan was *persona non grata* then in certain concentric circles. The only publication that accepted it, as other times, was the review *Vuelta* in Mexico. Ten years later it was published by *Claves* of Madrid. I decided to update it then and that is how my pages are now peopled by other political ghosts (Mrs Thatcher, Gorbachev) who are also ancient history.

DISCOVERIES

An Encounter with the Intelligence of Franco

Address to the International Congress of Intellectuals and Artists, Valencia, 1987

I remember the day I found my mother crying. There had been no domestic reason (that day) and I asked why as a boy of eight asks why. My mother explained to me: 'Santander fell.' I supposed that Santander was an intimate friend or a close relative and his fall had been surely deadly – and a deadly fall it was for my mother and for my father. Santander had surrendered to Franco. My mother and my father, Communists both, had suffered prison under Batista for being so. Barely a year later they would be campaigning for Batista for President – following the dictates of the Party. Those were early political lessons that I never forgot. I was already, at eight, a veteran.

Thirty years later and in exile I had come to live (not to die) in Madrid. I found it, from darkest Havana at noon, luminous, in spite of the fact that in the zone of shadow the city was the back yard of a convent, with nuns asleep in a siesta that God could make eternal. I was busy rewriting my novel *Tres tristes tigres*, that had earlier had the illusory title of *Vista del amanecer en el trópico*, and I discovered that it is easier to rewrite fiction (or that other fiction, history), than one's own life.

I had lived for nine months in Spain and had decided to settle there. I now needed to apply for a resident's visa (the current one was for somebody I have never been, a tourist) and the answer to my application appeared in the form of an appointment in the Ministry (I almost write Mystery) of *Gobernación*, i.e. of the Interior, that I thought routine: every tourist, even a reluctant one, must be innocent.

Upon arriving at the Puerta del Sol and entering the penumbra of the edifice its shade blinded me until I stumbled into the reception desk. I said the name of the functionary named in my summons and the receptionist told me to go up to the third floor – door 304. I went up in an elevator that creaked obsoletely. When I arrived at said door I saw on the frosted glass a sign: 'Arab Affairs'.

I assumed it was an error at the reception desk and I went down to the lobby, to its shadow, to have the mistake cleared up for me. The receptionist, fine and firm, told me that *that* was the door. As I was not an Arab or even a Muslim I supposed that it was a Spanish version of the fable of Kafka before the doors of the law. I did what I was ordered to by the receptionist – who was the law. I went up again, opened the door of Arab Affairs, now without inverted commas, and someone within pointed at a narrow door. I opened it too. There, in an office of an imposed but imposing order, was a functionary with the look of a civil master because of his impeccable suit and his pressed hair, thirties' style. He was seated before an empty desk and directly underneath an enormous map – of Cuba. For a moment I thought that the Caribbean Sea was the Persian Gulf – or better still, the Red Sea. Politics, as we know, alters perception.

The civil servant (or policeman: in totalitarian countries they are indistinguishable) made me sit at his desk but at the other end. He started talking to me about his job, always onerous but which the times made necessary. After his self-portrait he passed on to do my literary and political biography. He showed me what he knew about that zone of penumbra where literature and politics touch and then are confused. In my case the shade and shame was a magazine, literary but nevertheless the supplement to *Revolución*, called *Lunes*. He numbered for me almost like a newsvendor the issues of *Lunes* devoted to the Republic, to the Civil War, to the Spanish literature of exile: what was called with pathetic fallacy 'the Spain that suffers'. I founded and directed that magazine, he knew, from 1959 until it was suppressed with a violence in no way literary in 1961. The last issue, a double issue, was dedicated to Picasso. Aside from the drawings, paintings and engravings, his pamphlet 'Fear and Lie of Franco' was included. My interrogator, who was an index, showed me that the police of Franco might not have a long arm but certainly the longest memory, a postmodern Proust. Then he passed on to solicit my collaboration.

He would like, he said to me almost in anguish, for me to speak to him about what was happening in Cuba. I explained that it had been nine months since I had left Havana and a newspaper from Madrid could give him more and better information. For example, the daily *Pueblo*, whose correspondents travelled to Cuba with the frequency of stewardesses. It was at that moment, on the word information or perhaps stewardesses, that I noticed that there was on the naked desk a block in white that stood out against the black of the table. I asked myself why I hadn't seen it before but I didn't have time to answer myself once I noticed how the well-made hand of the policeman (its fingernails had white moons) was resting on a pen as if by chance, perchance to be. It was a Parker, a pen that I never liked. I could explain to you why but I don't believe that it's pertinent. In any case, in the question-and-answer session I can talk to you about pens, pain and policeman – in that order.

Suddenly the civil servant revealed his true nature and asked me directly: 'Do you know Blas Roca?'

The question was so grotesque that it looked laughable. But I didn't laugh. Blas Roca (real name Francisco Calderio, who had adopted and adapted the rock as Stalin did with steel) was the former Secretary-General of the Cuban Communist Party, now reduced by Fidel Castro to a mere wax figure, which is the end of any Communist rock. Lenin, who was harder, also ended up waxy.

'I don't know him,' I said. 'What's more, I've never seen him in my life.'

The policeman did not believe me. That is what the police are all about: not believing. It is what sets apart a policeman from a priest or a psychiatrist: not believing confessions.

My policeman now decided to show that he was understanding: 'We know that your father lives in Cuba.' How did they know so many things? Someone, me I believe, had underestimated Franco's police. 'Believe me, everything you tell us' – and here appeared at last the plural of majesty: the man was not a policeman, he was *the* police – 'we will keep in the strictest confidence.'

For a moment I thought that he meant he wouldn't tell my father. But I thought better: the policeman was telling me that the police of Franco would not say anything to the police of Fidel Castro. These exchanges between totalitarian police forces were known to all. Of course I didn't believe him: does Sherlock Holmes ever believe Inspector Lestrade?

Then a doublebind began. My interlocutor was trying to follow me, faithful as a police dog – and I in turn was following him comfortably. My education in posses was given to me by Westerns. John Wayne was my teacher. Tired, Don Lestrade made a gesture of despair with his eyebrows and with his voice he explained cuttingly: 'Since you travel so much—'

Which was not true: in nine months I had made a trip to Paris in the winter and another to London now in the summer, looking for work: Unesco, the movies, the Reuters agency.

'You travel so much,' he said again, displacing the pronoun: they work better at the beginning of a sentence even without a trial – 'we are going to give your resident's visa to a Cuban who needs it more than you. Have a good afternoon.'

End of the interview. End of my stay in Madrid. Santander had fallen again. That's how I lost Spain and gained England. Good bye, Madrid! Hello, London?

These two lessons of practical political pure reason are what have brought me here today. Maybe you don't see the connection. The connection, of course, is me.

Spanish is Not a Dead Language

I read, not without amazement, about the funeral eulogy for the Marquise Du Chatelet, that Voltaire, her lover, wrote not long after her death: 'From the tenderest age she had nourished her mind reading the great authors in more than one language. She began to translate *The Aeneid* . . . She learned English, Italian . . .' Here I, not Voltaire, make a pause before the ultimate surprise: 'If she made little progress in Spanish it was because they told her that there was only one famous book in that language and it was a frivolous book.' Voltaire annotates this scorn but he neither qualifies nor justifies it. Apparently for Voltaire, who was not a frivolous man, this so frivolous declaration is acceptable. What is more, it was very common in its time in France. Also in England and in what today we call Italy. Only in Germany did they concern themselves seriously with Spanish literature, as the works of Schiller and the readings of Goethe attest. But Lichtenberg said that Spanish was the poor man's Latin.

This lack of interest is not strange in the European countries where another language is spoken. But it has been equally intense in zones of the planet where the vernacular is, basically, Spanish. I am referring of course to Mexico, to Central America, to South America. A writer like Borges, whose native tongue was Spanish and not English (his ideal language) permitted himself an elegant scorn of Spanish and, at times, a magnificent contempt. Says Borges: 'I pass on to comment on a distinct equivocation, the one that postulates the perfection of our tongue and the impious uselessness of remaking it.' The Argentine declares this in no less than his essay 'The Language of the Argentines'. He continues thus in his useless impunity: 'Its greatest and only argument rests on the sixty thousand words that our dictionary, the Spaniards', records.' Here there are a crass error (the one about the sixty thousand words that reduce Spanish to a mere despairing Esperanto) and a pernicious paradox: the one that declares Spanish ours, that is, also his, Borges' – and at the same time imputes the dictionary to the Spaniards, like an alien blame. The language always rings twice.

Borborygmi by Borges: 'Perfect synonymy is what they want, the *sermo hispanicus.*' Later, blaming the Argentines for vulgarity for trying to derive a *sermo vulgaris, Lunfardo*, from another vulgar tongue and its argots, he postulates that 'there is not a "great thought or a feeling" ', that is, a philosophy, in Spanish, although it has been said often that in Spain philosophy has not been the task of philosophers but of writers. Borges errs when he concludes that there is not 'a great poetic literature' in Spanish. But then he corrects himself: 'I confess – not unwillingly and even with alacrity and joy in my spirit – that some example of the Spanish genius is worth entire literatures: don Francisco de Quevedo, Miguel de Cervantes.' Only to bite at once his tongue from the Plate in a malicious question, 'Who else?' His corollary is that: 'The Spanish mediocrity of our language is diffuse and not at all golden.' There is, though, in that phrase a contradiction in terms that is eloquently voluntary. But he goes even further when he speaks of the language: 'A charm which no reality ever supports.'

In another place, in another book Borges speaks, not without reason, about how a synonym is only the intent to change ideas merely by a change of sound. He ascribes it to Spanish and the Spaniards, but that pretence, I well know, occurs in other languages. (Or at least in the three languages that I can read without moving my lips.)

Borges, to his later embarrassment, tries to defend a dialect, the Argentine, at the expense of a language, Spanish. I must confess that not only Borges has committed that crime of America. I myself, in an editorial note to *Tres tristes tigres*, take on that greater task. Why insult a language to praise a dialect? That happened twenty years ago and today I see it as presumptuous and vain. I did not want to write in a dialect but in an exclusive universal language. I wanted for myself the possibility of Esperanto in the reality of Spanish. But – why write in Cuban, a language dead for me? It was like Lichtenberg's Latin without its metaphysical fitness. I decided then to look in English for what I had not found in Spanish.

But now I repudiate Borges' aggressions. If I cite them above it is because I know that he is a not at all grey eminence of the language: his Spanish is already classic. Since the death of Calderón in 1681 there has been no other writer in Spanish with the universal appeal of Borges. Not to admit it or to deny it is an act of mere pride – or of literary envy. Borges, besides, is the only writer who has written in Spanish in the twentieth century who will surely be read in the twenty-first century. His influence outside the area of the language has become greater with the passing of time. When I arrived in England hardly anyone knew him and his translations were published in small select booklets sold under the counter: the booksellers handled them as pure pornography. Twenty years later not a day passes when he is not quoted in the English press from *The Times* to the *Standard* and critics who barely know how to pronounce his name (they all make him into a Scandinavian: Borg) invoke him on the radio and the television. Like Coca-Cola, Borges is it!

I chose to quote Borges because it was not possible to carry his complaints like burnished lances against a language that was, that is, not only an instrument of work for many writers, a means of communication for everyone from the Pyrenees to the other side of the Andes and a pleasure for those of us who know that, as a language, it may have its faults, inconveniences and strange manias (why is the Ch *another* letter?) but as an *alba* mater, that language from the dawn of consciousness, that mother tongue that limits us but also defines us, that nourishes us and leaves us out of breath, that sets up obstacles for us to leap over in a verbal steeplechase to a rhetoric eternity.

Perhaps Somerset Maugham was right. He said, joining *facta* and *verba*, the contrary to Voltaire: 'Spanish is the greatest literary creation of the Spaniards.' He was reducing, it is true, all Spanish writers to a single book, the dictionary – but it sounds true. I once wrote, in a book that nobody remembers, a provocative phrase. Nobody paid the slightest attention, but the statement turned scandalous when I repeated it on television years later: 'Spanish is too important to be left to the Spaniards.' There was too polemical an emphasis here but it was what I believed. I still believe it but in a different way. Do I make myself clear? Perhaps not. Let's see if I have better luck in the next paragraph.

Spain was not really interested in her empire in America. At least not in the nineteenth century when the empire was springing leaks. Hostility mixed with mirth can give you Pepe the Bottle to nickname Napoleon's inebriate brother José, Regent of Spain. But the most serious Napoleonic Wars and the restoration of the Bourbons converted the short republic into a risky hymn of easy humming. No one, in spite of the South American wars, was really interested in South America and the 'Always Faithful Island of Cuba' was only a motto for credulous Cubans and a consolation for imperialists. Not a single Spaniard, in spite of the occupation troops, fought a single battle for the Spanish language, left in the hands (or in the mouths) of Indians, *Indianos* down on their luck, mulattos and a lineage of pseudo-patricians who called themselves, strangely, *criollos*. *Creole* comes originally from the French and in the English of the Deep South it was a mixture of black and white who, if they were women, usually had a special grace for dancing the rigadoon, a dance in duple time that graces the MGM comedies – with Ingrid Bergman as a typical Creole. In Cuba, Venezuela, Colombia, Peru and Argentina a *criollo* was a Spaniard's son who was white but more American than the natives. Spain, the mother country, always considered her sons in America as wayward – or in the worst of cases, as rebels. That is, contrary, opposed.

The Spanish language of America, when it was not contaminated by Chibchas or Cholos, was a mixture of Africa and its worst legacy, the slaves. As we know they were guilty of slavery (without slaves there is no trade) and everything it brought with it: bad colour, bad odour, bad speech. In Cuba the slavers (that is, the whole white population of the island) thought that the next person had of *carabalí*, tar, what it did not have of *congo* soot. For another thing the common people (slaves or children or grandchildren of slaves) suffered strange Spanish aspirations and used to exclaim during the siesta: 'Ah, how I would like to be white – even if I had to be a Catalan!' The language, naturally or unnaturally, aspired too to be white. Although, perhaps frightened by a Pompeu Fabra engraving that illustrated its grammar, it did not aspire to be Catalan. So in Cuba, the island that I know, the language is not exactly *mestizo*. It could be defined for you with the dilemma of the zebra. Are they black stripes on a white background or white stripes on a black background?

In Spain there are people who are amazed (it has happened to me not only in Imperial Madrid but in Moorish Seville and in Celtic Santiago, but it has never happened to me in Barcelona) that I speak more or less intelligible Spanish. (I know that there are people who still wonder that I write it.) But there is in any case something in the language of the Cubans that is not exactly Spanish. The same thing happens in Mexico, in Colombia, in Peru. The language is white but with black stripes. Or is it the reverse, as in Bolivia and in Paraguay, bilingual natives all? The only country where there is no idiomatic interbreeding in America is – who would've guessed it? – Argentina. There the dialect is that atrocious jargon, *Lunfardo*, mixed with *Vesre*, which Borges classifies as collegiate – and lyrics from literary and trite tangos. It is this *olla podrida* that Borges attacked by the strange method of discrediting Spanish. It is like beating the mother to make the crying child shut up. Now I also want to denounce the argots, even the one that was mine – especially that one of mine. Spanish, it seems to me, is a language too important to be left in the holes of the most dialled dialects.

(January 1987)

Columbus Route One

Address to a symposium on 'Latin America: its artistic expression',
Leeds Castle, 1 May 1989

There are certain intimate moments in the early history of America that belong more in the history of literature than in mere history.

After landing on Cuba in a village called Gibara (where I was born, by the way) a scout named Rodrigo de Jerez came back from an outing with good news for the Admiral. 'A rare and precious sight, sir,' he claimed. 'We've seen men who smoke like chimneys. Please come with us, sir, and see.' Columbus, still seasick, agreed. He went to meet the *cacique* (new word), an Indian chief who sat under a *simaruba* tree. (Nobody knows where the *cacique* really sat and a *simaruba* is a wild guess: it is here because it sounds good. The *simaruba* is of the family of the ailanthus (or tree of heaven), the seringa and the quassia, which sound even better.) The chief was smoking an ur-cigar, though for him it was the real thing. De Jerez was delighted, as was his boon companion Luis de Torres, who came to America because he could speak Aramaic. On hiring him Columbus thought that a traveller never knows when a man speaking Aramaic might be handy and besides that was the language spoken by Our Saviour. De Torres was, like Columbus, a *converso* who could converse in six languages.

Columbus came, saw and was conquered by his obsession. He asked the *cacique* between the thick and thin of smoke: 'Do you know the land where gold grows?' The chief, after many a sign and some Aramaic, understood: 'Ah yes, of course,' he said. 'You mean Cubanacán.' We all know (or should know) that Cubanacán means in Taino the centre of Cuba – but Columbus understood what he wanted to hear. 'Ah, Cuba na Khan,' he exclaimed. 'The kingdom of the Mighty Khan!' (He almost said King Khan.)

There is also the life and death of a man not obsessed with gold but with eternal youth. As most people concerned with youth he was no longer young. Youth conquers all, he thought, except of course time. Ponce de León wanted like Dorian Gray to be young for ever. Not by having his picture painted but by finding the Fountain of Youth hidden somewhere in America. An early version of Faust, he heard Mephistopheles whispering in his ear that the magical source was located in what is *Miami Vice* today. 'Go west, old man,' said the devil. West he went to discover some swamps infested with snakes and saurians he called Florida. As a retribution he was killed by an Indian marksman who transformed his dream into a vulgar nightmare: death by an arrow. Which sounds very much like death by an error.

Ponce's last words are very contemporary. He said, 'I want to see Havana before I die.' Today he would have said something slightly different: 'I want to see Havana after *he* dies.' Exit Ponce pursued by a lion.

What Florida had been to Ponce de León, the Mississippi was to Hernando de Soto. Like his namesake Hernán Cortés, he had sailed from Cuba to conquer the continent – or bust. (It was bust.) He first went to Cuzco as a lieutenant to Pizarro, the man who fucked up Peru when he found it. After helping to achieve that, De Soto came back to Havana, where he would be Governor of Cuba and *adelantado* of Florida. He left for the continent again, sailing north by northwest, an unlikely bearing. He left behind his wife Isabel de Bobadilla, about to become the first professional widow of America to publish her inconsolable memories. De Soto discovered the Mississippi, was killed by yet another Indian sharpshooter and was buried in muddy waters late at night – so that the Indians believed he was still alive: Hernando hides away. This is an old Spanish trick. They used it with El Cid for the first time. The last time they played this trick was with Franco, who died a thousand times before being buried. Still some claim that he was buried alive. In the twentieth century the legend that was De Soto became an eight-cylinder car. Raymond Chandler uses the name a lot, as in the Philip Marlowe phrase, 'A De Soto was tailing me.' So much for legends.

In Peru once and to alleviate the captive Indian's boredom De Soto taught Atahualpa to play chess – after convincing the prisoner that the kings and queens of the game were for real. Somehow Atahualpa came to believe that if he won against the opposing monarchs, he would be free. Of course if Atahualpa could believe that he would believe anything. But he became such a keen player that he won all his games with De Soto, including the last one in the tournament. Atahualpa was right. Immediately after the last game he was freed. Pizarro liberated him with extreme prejudice. Atahualpa was strangled in a checkmate. He never knew that the phrase *jaque mate* meant death to the king. (Chess has always been a dangerous game.)

So is life in America. Since the beginning our daily bread has been fear and loathing everywhere. Bread and terror for breakfast, terror and bread for lunch. Dinner is always eaten under curfew and even in bed pillows have ears and tongues. Anybody can be awakened after midnight, taken away and be considered guilty until proven dead. Life is lived from here to obscenity. Obscenity is still here, for obscenity outlives man and some-times woman. In Hispaniola, the island most loved by Columbus, obscenity has been the staple food for ages, some sort of poisonous cassava for the soul you cannot call soul food.

In Cuba, which Columbus called the most beautiful land human eyes have ever seen, the obscenity is still there. Obscenity is loose upon the world, especially in the New World. Take a look at Panama – any newsreel would do. This was the Panama that Lope de Vega sang to in the seven-teenth century: '*Me voy a Panamá*' was his favourite refrain. Panama existed for him only as an exotic name. But what about the present? What about Lope, would he go there as he wanted? Would he dare? What about us? Do we dare? Do I dare?

Lorca, three centuries later, proclaimed:

> *Iré a Santiago de Cuba,*
> *Iré a Santiago*
> *Con la rubia cabeza de Fonseca.*

Do I have to tell you that Fonseca doesn't live there any more?

But from such mighty porn seeds might come. They came from the very beginning, even before the beginning. *Ab ovo* to use a seed on which Columbus proved right because he made an egg stand on end. (Here the egg is the Western world.) Columbus wrote in his diary, actually a log, in a Spanish contaminated by Portuguese. The two literary languages of South America were already present in the Grand Admiral's prose. He showed in his diary that he was our contemporary. The diary was lost and what we have is a facsimile done by Father Bartolomé de Las Casas, the priest who, according to Borges, took 'great pity on the Indians who were languishing in the hellish workpits of Antillean gold mines and suggested to Charles V a scheme of importing blacks, so that they might languish in the hellish workpits of Antillean gold mines'. Father Las Casas was also the first fax machine to work in America. What Las Casas copied is an invaluable document and a literary masterpiece in which Columbus, the writer, is seen in the third person singular – to become a character in his own narrative. The first truly American great notion was entered on 9 October, exactly three days before the Discovery. The final entry on the log before the Discovery is one of the most mysterious, glorious and beautiful phrases in the history of literature. It says: 'All night long they heard birds passing.' It is even better in Spanish: '*Toda la noche oyeron pasar pájaros.*'

Pasar pájaros is to welcome the New World with an alliteration. Those birds could have been night birds. But many centuries later, another Jewish writer, a Columbus of prose, Gertrude Stein, wrote, 'Pigeons in the grass alas.' She knew Spanish, so that the alas should be read as *alas*. Wings and the pigeons are flying Columbus – the man with a pigeon in his name. One single dove came back to Noah's ark with an olive leaf in her mouth to announce that the flood (that is the ocean) was at an end. Christopher means the bearer of Christ and with Columbus Christ came to America on the first trip.

But Columbus was a greedy man. A harbinger of Christ who could cavort with the moneylenders. He thought that gold came second only to God. Money makes the world go round but with Columbus money made the man go around the world. Exit Columbus pursued by a dream that is sometimes a nightmare.

The shy poet Louise Bogan wrote about the 'Ornamental structures, continents apart, separated by seas', in a poem aptly named 'Baroque Comment'. The literature of my America, even that of Brazil, even the drum songs of Haiti, speaks not a simple, single language but the signs of dour dialects that form a baroque commentary. It all startled with Columbus but also with Hernán Cortés.

Cortés, who was tall, well-built and red-bearded, was able to seduce a Mexican princess from Tabasco named Malintzin. She was christened La Malinche by the Spaniards. Cortés called her *mi lengua*, meaning my tongue, for she became his translator: the key to the Aztec kingdom. Later Cortés had a son with her. This *mestizo* was, in fact, the Spanish language of America. But the travesty claims '*Lo Cortés no quita lo Pizarro*', meaning that the play on tongues does not abolish cruelty, greed and malice.

Though written in English and read in Pidgin, these words of mine would never have taken place without Columbus or Cortés. La Malinche (listen to the evil in the name) has often been described as a mixture of the Enchantress and she who spoke with a forked tongue. If that is true then Cortés, of all people, became our Adam. Columbus, who has Christ in his name, has to be our God: he who created a world by discovering it. He didn't give us everything – but who can count the gifts of God?

All those soldiers, adventurers and men of action were also extra-ordinary writers. There was plunder but there was also wonder.

Neither Hernando de Soto nor Pizarro and much less Aguirre, who lived days and nights of wrath, could write and they were dead before they could learn. But other *conquistadores*, like Bernal Díaz del Castillo, who wrote his memories at eighty, or Alvar Núñez Cabeza de Vaca, who wrote like a fallen angel (he is in fact a natural movie writer) about his shipwrecks and captivity among the hostile Indians of the Gulf: their chronicles made you believe that these men were not at all ordinary. Until the reader remembers that these Spaniards in the word were kin to those Spanish writers who invented the picaresque novel, the greatest avatar of the novel since Petronius – who wrote of sex *pícaros* about Rome. At the end of the era (which coincided roughly with the end of the century) along came that enormous picaresque novel that created, as in passim, the modern novel. I'm talking of course about *Don Quijote*, a book which, if only the bureau-crats who took over from the *adelantados* had granted one Miguel de Cervantes y Saavedra permission to emigrate to America, would have been written in the New World. (What about *Don Quijote de las Indias*? Or Sancho Pampa?)

All these men, starting with Columbus, became writers in America, where the Spanish language clashed with lives bigger than life. The clash of the language with the account of adventures and dangers impossible to imagine in Spain made these writers into authors of chivalry novels come true. These men became writers because they faced, all of a sudden, a world so new that it was measureless to man – except in writing. It started with Columbus and we are still at it. The measurements, it appears, won't ever be completed – but we can only try.

Back to Columbus then. For in the beginning there is also the end. Columbus met the Indian chief under the *simaruba*. As a present the *cacique* gave the Discoverer a cigar, remember? It was a live cigar not a dead stub: the *cacique* was not an Indian giver. Columbus took the cigar to take a look at it – by the wrong end. He sniffed at it and was repelled by the live ember. Columbus bowed at his host and begged, his *gesta* reduced now to a gesture that has become an antifad: 'Do you mind if I don't smoke?'

Scenes of a World without Columbus

A hypothesis is hype with the consistency of a dream – or of a nightmare – and it has almost as much reality. But *really* – can you imagine a world without Christopher Columbus? Or maybe that Columbus had never come to the New World? That nobody, *nobody*, had discovered America? As an aid more to imagination than to navigation, I make lists.

Let us imagine, the reader and I, that the mutiny attempt on board the *Santa María* 3 October 1492, spirited out of his ship's log later by the Grand Admiral himself, had really taken effect the night of the sixth – only *six* days before the Discovery. Instead of backing his admiral, Martín Alonso Pinzón comes to the flagship to add himself to the so-called 'rising of the Biscayans'. Columbus, in the midst of the confusing betrayal, upbraids the mutineers and confronts them with their outrageous villainy: they are not respecting their oath of loyalty made when they left the port of Palos. Now Columbus invokes the Capitulations of Santa Fe and the confidence placed in him by Their Catholic Majesties. Besides the grace of his sovereigns to which he alludes, the Grand Admiral of the Ocean Sea addresses sailors and officers and cabin boys: the whole crew and stowaways. Then he makes a last plea that they desist: 'If you don't do it for the King – do it for the Queen.'

Fatum O'Nihil, the only Irish sailor on board, inquires: 'Isabella? What about Queen Isabella?' But Columbus cannot answer him. Not because he doesn't know English but because at that moment he is carried on the crew's shoulders, like bullfighters in triumph, barely bearing his bearing. Columbus is thrown, without the ceremony that would accompany a dead body entrusted to the depths, headfirst into the sea. (Which just at that moment has ceased to be an ocean: no more Atlantic, quasi Caribbean.) He does not last long among the waves: he is not the floating Admiral. Columbus, ladies and gentlemen, didn't know how to swim! (As will be seen right away.) What is still visible of his body – flapping arms, a face of *horror vacui* (or rather *aquae*), fair hair that the black night makes dark –

sinks in 'the frozen waters of egoist calculations' (see *Communist Manifesto*), as another Jew said on another occasion. Moments after sinking a third time, which is the last, Christovoro Colombo, born in Genoa, Italy, of doubtful age and discoverer by profession, disappears for ever from the face of the earth.

The captain's flagship, now without a captain, after this drowning that recalls the fall of Icarus according to Brueghel, changes its heading and followed always by the *Pinta* and the *Niña*, heads the helm back to the Canary Islands and finally to Spain.

Centuries later a recorded *guaracha* records the extreme wantonness of the act:

> About the Discoverer:
> All the Pinzón brothers
> were fags & mothers.
> Friends of the Lady Bobadilla
> they liked to eat tortilla.
> That's all we uncovered.

Since Columbus did not discover America, there would be no America. That Italian usurper Amerigo Vespucci, who has as much of Marco Polo as of Machiavelli, would never come to America and would not write what an obscure German geographer would not call his *Quattuor Americi Navigationes* – or insist that the Southern hemisphere be called '*ab Amerigo*'. Vespucci himself would not write his letters from America because there would not be a Casa de Contratación de Indias to hire him nor would he defect, because he would have no motive or rancour, to Portugal – to not discover Rio de Janeiro. The whole immense Brazil would not end up in Portuguese hands.

Meanwhile Father Bartolomé de Las Casas (whom a writer, who would never be called Borges, would not have injured with the epithet of 'a curious variation of the philanthropist') would not have copied Columbus's *Diary*, which one Pinzón (or the other) would have destroyed because it was evidence of the mutiny and of the murder. So the good Father would not have described the forests of Cuba, 'on top of them and from branch to branch a squirrel could traverse the island from one extreme to the other' – among other things because in Cuba there were no squirrels. Besides the island itself would not exist by not being on the maps.

The Aztecs would persist in their splendour of Metshiko, feeding themselves, literally, on other tribes. From time to time they would celebrate their rites, in which the *pièce de résistance* would be to take the beating heart out of Toltec virgins with a stone knife. The Mayas, already in their dour decline, would have left behind (uselessly) their magnificent pyramids that Japanese tourists would never be able to photograph. But the equivalent of the Greek goddess of victory, Niké, would be called Nikon. Even though the invention of the hand camera would still be delayed because there never was an inventor named Edison to not invent film nor did another man named Eastman create the Kodak camera.

Since the Viking sailors did not write ships' logs North America would not take place. Without the USA the German defeat in the First World War (that did happen) would be converted into a victory, to which England would have to make adjustments and France would be saved the humiliation of the Occupation and the opportune collaborators of later on. Hitler of course would have had to continue his career as a house-painter (from house to house) and Mussolini would perhaps have debuted in La Scala – as a *partichino*. Neither would there be *partigiani* to fight his wrong notes with imported Bronx cheers and rotten tomatoes.

Lenin would not have travelled (in the historic first-class coach of a sealed German train) to the Finland Station because the Germans, having no reason to do so, would not have offered him a ticket to ride. Kerensky, conveniently embalmed, would occupy today Lenin's place in the St Petersburg mausoleum, because, among so many things that would not happen, Moscow would not become capital of Russia again. Marx, on the other hand, would exist, but as an amateur economist whose capital work, *Das Kapital*, would be his revenge for too many boils. Nobody would read this book, or translate it into any other languages. So it would never become the Bible of state capitalism. Karl yes, damn it, but no Groucho, alas.

If Martín Alonso Pinzón had carried out what he intended once (or twice) and the rabble on board, who wanted to get back home in time for their gazpacho more than to reach America, had mutinied and murdered the obstinate mad mariner or had forced him to take a nautical U-turn, there would have been neither Communism in Russia nor its consequences, Nazism and Fascism. Franco, of course, would have retired with the pension of a general who never won a battle. His lieutenant, Manuel Fraga, would not now put on the airs of a flying statesman, nor have had to inaugurate a museum in his parent's house in Cuba, because there would have been no Galician emigration to a land that never existed.

In Stockholm they would not have ignored the great Darío, who as a pure Indian and not a *mestizo* would not have written a single line of verse in Spanish. (They still would have given the prize to Juan Ramón Jiménez, who would not have been a follower of Darío but perhaps an original poet.) As with Borges, they would have given the Nobel neither to Neruda nor to Miss Mistral, because they would not have existed. But perhaps Asturias would have received a consolation prize for being Indian. Although the Indians, without a Columbus to come to the Indies to name them, would not be Indians either.

In Spain no one could go partying (such sweet sorrow) to a *guateque* or smoke *puros* (but *porros* yes) or cigarettes made of tobacco and they wouldn't call their politicians *caciques*. A third of the *Dictionary of the Royal Academy*, which would continue to be royal, would remain blank from an absence of Americanisms. In the non-*guateques* nobody would dance rumbas or *sones* (which would never be called salsa) or mambos, although the chachacha, because of what it has of a Madrid schottische, would perhaps have been created by a Jorrín de Jérez. But, think about it, there would be no Antonio Machín to sing boleros. Worse still, there would be no Olga Guillot or Celia Cruz or Beny Moré – or Pérez Prado to put the pain of Spain in the mambo. Nor would there be *habanera* competitions in Tarraza nor would anyone dance tangos like Valentino in *Apocalypse* then. Nor would there be jazz or blues or rock or rap because there wouldn't be blacks in an America that never existed. As there was no slavery, the whole continent would end up as an infinite Indian boredom and the only entertainment, to the sound of fifes and flutes, would be the *tamborito* in the south – while in the north there would be the tribal wars to perform, in which the Cheyennes would try to exterminate the Sioux, and the redskins would finish off the darker Apaches without even using the horse or the repeating rifle. But worse than no horses, no Westerns or John Ford – and, what is worse still, there would be no Westerns by John Ford.

Nobody, of course, would eat potatoes, neither French fried nor as Spanish straw. But there would not be the great famine in Ireland in the last century because of the failure of the potato harvest and no Irishman would have emigrated to some United States that never existed. (Perhaps thus the world would have been freed of the Kennedy blight for ever.) There would have been bananas but Africa grown and there would be neither avocado nor tomato to make a mixed salad. There would be coffee but there would be no chocolate and the Godiva lady would end up being naked for ever. There would be no Panama and so, no Panama hats. And though there would be opium and morphine and heroin, there would be no cocaine, that stimulant so dear to the movie world.

But there would be no movies because the Lumière Brothers only adopted and adapted an invention by Edison, who as we have already seen was an inventor who never invented. There would be no Hollywood therefore and though sooner or later the Germans would have invented the *Kino*, nobody would call Berlin the Mecca of the Kino. There would be photography thanks to Daguerre and to Niepce but never *le cinéma* in France. There would be no Marilyn Monroe alive or dead. Nor would there be Ginger Rogers's gorgeous bare back or Kim Novak's true sacred cow beauty or Cyd Charisse's legs too. And though there would have been a Rita Hayworth, called Margarita Cansino in Seville, she wouldn't be the same – believe me. Greta Garbo would have stayed in Sweden, still named Gustafson. There would be no Fred Astaire, although there would be a gypsy dancer in Cádiz named Alfredo del Aire. And, think about it, there would never have been a round world to go around.

If Columbus had not invoked the Catholic Kings, Christ and God himself, who had created the pole star to guide the flagship. If Martín Alonso Pinzón had not rowed from his caravel to the *Santa María* and backed up the Grand Admiral in his vision of an Asia for the Europeans. If Columbus had not praised himself as a saint before King and Queen on his return (yes, from America) declaring that he was guided more by Isaiah's prophecy than by the celestial bodies, which governed only his compass and his astrolabe but not his luck. If the hallucinating Admiral, God's secret agent, had not seen the American dawn, none of the afore-mentioned would exist – not even as a negation. And I have left out more, much more. (Or rather, less, much less.)

Without Columbus there would have been no America, but no Latin America either and the natives of the centre and of the south, pure Indians all, would not be called Latins, a tag they do not understand in a language they do not speak and would be Aztecs or Mayas or Chibchas or Incas or Araucanians or Quechuas or Guaranís who bear a Latinity as the baptism of a lay religion. Or a mockery.

If Christopher Columbus had not discovered America, I would never have written this vertiginous list that you will read perhaps with equal vertigo. But neither would Fidel Castro have existed nor the totalitarian horror that he implanted.

If the price of leaving nothingness for a moment only to enter nothing-ness again, which is being, were not being, I would pay with content the other nothingness. So with the pleasure of knowledge I would see the mutineers of the 9 October 1492 converted into exterminating angels of history – to throwing the hated Genoese once and for all into the sea.

(February 1992)

Spain Stays Mainly in the Plain

*Read in Spanish at the Sánchez-Ruipérez Foundation
in Madrid in October 1990*

The title is inevitably ambiguous. But if ambiguity can lead to wit or to deceit, Empson has it that it is 'any verbal nuance, however slight, which gives room for alternative reactions to the same piece of language'. To enunciate that 'any prose statement could be called ambiguous', does not include military or political pronouncements. Aldous Huxley, our cult contemporary, decreed that there are three kinds of intelligence: human, animal and military. It is known that poets speak in verse – and politicians in perverse. (This ambiguous purge is known in England as Empson Salt.) Empedocles, older but less ambiguous than Empson, proposes that the visible world is composed of air, fire, earth and water. All these elements (according to the philosopher who helped to fell a tyranny and later rejected the crown they offered him) are governed by concord and discord. These two opposed states of mind will unite my talk – with the help of a third agglutinant, saliva.

I live in England amidst books and a mist of dust and movies. I come from America – never from *Latin* America. I left Cuba exiled for ever or for eternity – whichever lasts least. I tried to live in Madrid but the unforgettably Francoist political police prevented me, with a courteous gesture that does not eliminate the bizarre, from residing in Spain or any Spanish territories. I could not even live in Ceuta or Melilla, North Africa. What about Andorra? I asked. Severe frown on a severed head that denies like a pendulum. 'You travel.' I who had so little money that I couldn't travel on the Madrid metro to Finisterre! Index finger that points. 'Yield your visa to your compatriots who don't travel.' Since then, impelled by that finger, I have been around my world several times over. (Womb, I have travelled.)

I spoke of America and I have to speak, once and for all, of the Grand Admiral, so demeaned these days. I am speaking of Christopher Columbus, whom the poet Paul Claudel, playing with his name, called 'the dove who carried Christ'. I truly believe that Columbus is the most decisive historical character since the death of Jesus. Christ changed history, Columbus changed, at the same time, history and geography, which is more important than history because it contains it and is another name for eternity. (The two, Columbus and Christ, distant twins, were Jewish.) America is announced as the new world with a phrase that seems to belong to Genesis: 'All night long they heard birds passing.' It is Noah, no?

There is now an ambiguous attitude in Spain towards the Discovery that is nothing more than just a concession to historical blackmail. Soon only the Italians will claim Columbus, who will be called, like a television hero, Colombo. With no excuse I can celebrate him before his official celebration because, simply, without the erred Navigator I would not be among you now. (Which after all would be a relief for some.) But, please, consider this: if I weren't here I wouldn't be anywhere. With more Indian than Spanish blood (although my paternal grandfather was born in the Canaries and my maternal great-grandfather was born in Almería, which, come to think of it, is not being too Spanish either) I could claim the land where I was born without feeling shaken by any tremors of remorse for a remote conquest.

It is the professional Latin Americans who while they deny Columbus in Spanish establish themselves in the nations of America where Spanish is (barely) spoken. Or in the *mestizo* medley of America like Mexico that in its visible world owes more to Cortés than to Moctezuma. It is in Peru that the Indian population is decisive even in elections. While (casual or causal?) in Argentina the extermination of the Indians was not foreign but domestic. As a witness of another genocide one only has to ask the parrot of the Atures. (More later.)

Columbus left medieval Spain and with one single voyage he entered the modern world on landing in America – in a true historical time warp all humanity travelled with him on those three caravels. *I* know the possible risks of this apologia. An old cartoon from *Punch* illustrates it. One sees an Anglo-Saxon farmer who is resting against his plough. Beside him appears a villein from the village seen in the background. (There is also a haughty castle.) Both, farmer and villein, are dressed like characters from Chaucer. The villein is bringing the farmer the morning news: 'Did you hear? Today end the Middle Ages.'

Spanish is of course the name of our language. Castilian is the language of Castile not of America. Political reasons (which are always the most irrational) insist that the language both of Spain and of America be called

Castilian. It is as if the mother of all Parliaments were to decree that from now on English be called Anglo-Saxon. But in Britain there are political reasons (which are the most opportunistic) called Scotland and Wales – although Scotland did not insist on the Gaelic, holding both breath and bag for the bagpipe.

If Castilian is the language of the Reconquest, by extending itself to America in the Conquest it became Spanish. The American contribution to the language has been enormous. Just a little island like Cuba spices up the language like pepper with endless entries and the idiom of the Indians endures in the word books like the parrot of the Atures. But the first literary work of America was written in a Castilian plagued with Italianisms. This Spanish book became American when Father Las Casas (a strange character who was a saint for the Indians and a devil's advocate for the blacks) transcribed it – that is, translated it – to preserve it. The result then is not historic but a literary upheaval. By copying Columbus Las Casas produces a work of fiction – an adventure novel. Fearful that they might accuse him of altering the sacred original, the good father proceeds to alter it for ever by reproducing Columbus's every phrase and every word. But by changing the grammatical person where Columbus imposed his I, Las Casas proposed an absolutely singular third person. Through a zeal for fidelity the *Diario* is thus transformed into the first novel of America.

But America is not a novel, it is a comedy of errors. Columbus discovers it by error when he is on the way to the Indies and calls the island that he believes a continent by this name – in an atrocious geographic anachronism. Then he christens its inhabitants Indians, when they were all as far from India as from Cipango or Cathay. The continent later takes its name not from Columbus but from an obscure Italian navigator in the service of Spain: he knew how to draw maps and wore the sonorous name of Amerigo. The errors multiply and grow. The centre of Cuba, called by the Indians Cuba*nacán*, is taken by Columbus for the *siège* of the Great Khan. Looking for gold the admiral on land meets and then disdains tobacco as a verdant Green. When the Cuban *cacique*, as a burnt offering, hands him a Havana, Columbus turns his back on the green gold. Later his errant comrades in error insist on calling the banana plaintain, the *ananás* pineapple and they hear dogs that don't bark. They believe too that the manatees are sirens and now in a vertigo of name-calling they christened what was ostensibly another world, New Spain. As the noble Scot Macduff says, 'Confusion now hath made his masterpiece!'

For some time now I have organized skirmishes against the entrenched

habit of calling that continent-and-a-half by the name of Latin America
as if one were dealing with a single country. The tag was printed in
France in the last century and later pinned on us with cement glue by
the United States, a nation ruled even then by a collective guilt complex.
In 1880 they felt so guilty about having appropriated the name America
for their exclusive use that they anointed us as *Latine* – that came from
Paris like a rare perfume from a Christian Dieu. Who is Latin in Central
America? What delicate Roman gallops eternally over the *pagos* of the
pampa? Where is the Latium in South America? I fear that that land lies,
like Utopia, in no place at all. Utopias tend to end up as Ethiopia, but
Latin America is only that notion of geopolitics which declares it easier
to conquer a country than a continent – as Bolívar discovered more than
a century ago. The Liberator has at least stayed around as a cigar called
Bolívar.

More harmonious, I believe that it is a slim service that is lent Cuban
music now by calling it Latin, as is done in the press. It is to erase with
one beat (of the drum) the majority of Cuban musicians, who are, as in
jazz, almost all black – unless one wishes to grant them Roman citizenship
and noses. The Cuban music in exile, which many call *salsa* when that is
just gravy, could be sung like this:

> She's a Latin from Manhattan
> and she calls herself Dolores.
> (Which rhymes with dollars.)

Am I a Latin in London or in Londonderry? I would say rather that I am a
piercing bore by insisting on the late Latinness of America as a tinhorn
Spanish Seneca. If I qualify to be among you it is not by being Latin but
because I can speak Spanish with a Havana accent. I am now in Madrid
and a question assaults me like an armed *chorizo* – is Spain Latin too?

Speaking of assaults, not long ago I suffered rather than tolerated in
London a confused interview. I have always preferred my interviews to be
written. Especially if I write the answers myself – if not the questions.
(They are rather more faithful like that.) In this recent interview the
interviewer, who was beautiful like the beauties in films noirs, came with
her tape recorder in tow. (Which seems to me more dangerous than
brandishing pencil and notebook.) I have never believed that high fidelity
helps the state of the arts, but rather of noise. The interviewer published,
in effect, a mirror image. I opposed to the French proverb 'Africa begins at
the Pyrenees' an English saying that says: 'Blacks begin at Calais.' The
opposition came out printed on the other side of the fastidious fax like a

cloudy cliché. What I said, precisely, is that America *must* have begun in the Pyrenees. A European Spain is for me like an England in Europe. Both nations are too different, too original to sit well beside Belgium or Holland. Who can imagine a European Spain raising fighting bulls?

I foresee a future press release: 'Yesterday on the Plaza de Ventas the skilled Dutch matador Van Gogh cut off an ear.'

The other false American notion pertains to literature. The recent novel in Spanish that came from America has been read in Spain as a coherent corpus. That vision is a Spanish mirage. A summary examination would show that Cortázar is from Argentina, Donoso from Chile, Roa Bastos from Paraguay, Vargas Llosa from Peru, García Márquez from Colombia, Onetti from Uruguay, Juan Rulfo from Mexico and Lezama Lima and Carpentier from Havana. But all are perceived here as if they were regional not national writers. Some time ago those countries ceased to be provinces of Spain and each one of them, like those writers, has its own characteristics. To believe anything else is to look at Canadian literature as if it came from the United States. It is Spanish, that we all speak with a different accent, that confuses or deludes. (Or both.) Latin American literature does not exist. There exist, yes, some writers from America who seem to write in the same language sometimes.

Personally I can say that in Spain they have been extremely generous with me – literally speaking. Here my first novel was given a prize, here all my books (except three) have been published first, here the critics have treated me as if I were at home. Under Franco's censorship I was banned at first but later publication was authorized of two of my books that were subversive enough never to have been published in my country. I could not get to my father while he was alive and through my Spanish publishers even one copy of those that they sent to his name in Havana. (In Cuba the postman also wears two uniforms.) I don't regret it. If I have lost a country I have gained new readers. Among the most faithful in my country are the State Security agents who over the years have learned to read without moving their lips. For another thing I have contributed not a little to the Cuban black market.

According to an English writer who visited Havana last year my books were the object of a strange cult among the ruins. Smuggled into the country, they were sold under the counter for the price of – ten tins of condensed milk! *La Habana Para un Infante Difunto* was then on the list of the best milked books. In the first slot, uncomfortably placed, was a book about perestroika (which in Havana is pronounced '*la espera estoica*' – the stoic wait), its author called, he is still called, Mikhail Gorbachev. It was the first time that in Communist Cuba a Soviet author collected his officially tax-exempt royalties not in pesos but in barter.

I feel truly honoured to be a friend and admirer of those who have shared this literary week with me. But also to have announced five years ago now that the next wave of the novel in Spanish would come not from the Atlantic or from the Pacific but from the Mediterranean – although I have my doubts about the Cantabrian. I thank many of those who have been here for their constant literary appreciation. (The cinema is for me storytelling by better means.) Also for an affection that goes beyond the years (mine) and the distance (the one there is between Madrid and London) that has allowed me to be able to gauge their talent at close range. They too have made possible this new Spain.

I want to end, as the Infante Don Juan Manuel used to do, with an example.

There were so many parrots, lories and macaws in the New World that America was known on the maps of the sixteenth century as *Terra Psittacorum*, the land of the free parrot. The psittacologists repeat that the Spanish navigators used the first captive parrots as symbols of the lure of the islands. Columbus himself came looking for spices but he acquired some specimens of a species called the great red parrot of Cuba – considered then a very magnificent bird. (It is now on the road to extinction.)

The intrepid German explorer Alexander von Humboldt (of whom it is said that he was the second discoverer of Cuba) sailed from the Caribbean to the continent and went into the interior of Venezuela. Humboldt tells that he found in the Orinoco jungles a very, very old parrot that grew up among the Ature Indians. The Ature tribe, as was the custom among the Arawaks, proved more extinguished than distinguished and disappeared from the face of the earth without leaving a trace. The parrot nevertheless lived to tell all about it. Humboldt wrote in wonder: 'The bird was the last living thing in this world capable of speaking Ature.' Will the Spanish of America be one day all Ature and we American writers only printed parrots?

Letter to Marta Pessarrodona

London, 12 March 1992

Dear Marta – This is a letter, of course, for your records. But you can make it public if you wish.

I cannot be with you, as in other years, because my presence in Barcelona would mean putting a seal on another presence undesirable to me: the Spanish Government has decided to fête Fidel Castro during the Quincentennial celebrations. That he is coming as Head of State is all right, but that they are deciding to celebrate the Day of America in Seville on – the *26th of July*! – seems an enormity to me and a slap in the face to all Cubans – on the island or in exile. As you know 26 July was when Castro and his terrorist group attacked a barracks of Batista's army in Santiago de Cuba. It happened in 1953 and since then it has been a date marked in the Castroist calendar. Even the terrorist group that brought him to power was called the 26th of July Movement. These are not secret facts and the Spanish Government as well as its Foreign Affairs Ministry know them. (If they don't know them then they are of an abysmal political ignorance.) But Fidel Castro has it quite well in mind and will be in Seville on the twenty-sixth precisely to give a talk open to the public. This occasion will be for him, who knows it, and for those who don't know it or who wish to ignore it, a Castroist fiesta – and a disgrace for Spain and democracy. It does not escape me that if a minor tyrant (his retirement proves it) like Augusto Pinochet were still the Chilean Head of State either he would not be invited by the Spanish Government or the public protests would be in full swing by now. It is for this reason that I make my protest public, using José Martí's famous phrase: 'Of the tyrant say all – say more!'

Forgive me that I cannot be with you. But to paraphrase Martí, if the Castroist flag is flying in Spain I cannot enter. This peninsula is not big enough for the both of us, the tyrant and me, even for only a little while. The words were Gary Cooper's in *The Virginian* but now the message is mine.

To Be or Not to Be Brief

Address to the Congress of Catalan Culture,
Barcelona, 1992

All orators since Demosthenes (who was a stutterer, and therefore knew how to dwell on a single word) have begun to speak with the same phrase: 'I will be brief.' I wonder why. (Especially when only Pepin admitted that adjective as a name.) No orator should have the intention of being brief but rather that of being effective. But to declare one's intention to be brief when everyone knows that nobody else will be is an incantatory phrase, a magic formula, a ritual and a dogma without magic. Every one of you, that is of us, will say, we will say, that we will be brief and that phrase will be the only brief thing there is or will be.

So we will see the anchor man pass around successive slips (of paper) asking, begging, ordering that I be brief, that I hurry the end. No one will imitate Demosthenes, who, faced with a similar threatening order, as Lemprière says, drank from a little flask that he always carried with him and drained the hemlock so dear to his master. (Plato *dixit*.) Brevity is an art that one must learn in silence at one's own peril for it is the art of silence.

In an old but immortal cartoon from the *New Yorker*, one of those after-dinner speakers so abundant in the Anglo-Saxon social calendar got on his feet after the desserts and the coffee (they also passed around cigars: those were the days, my smoking friend) to declare, 'I will be brief.' At that moment an enormous chandelier that was hanging exactly above him fell and flattened not flattered the speaker to make him brief for ever.

This afternoon there will not be an artefact like a guillotine over my head. To reassure myself that it is so someone will read what I have written and my posterity will depend on the safety of strangers. The connection between my words and ears as attentive as Van Gogh's (also known as Vincent Van, a vehicle), is me.

Culture is made, like every human collection, from memory. There is no culture, primitive or sophisticated, without memory. One of the most apparently backward peoples on the globe, the Aborigines of Australia, are among the most sophisticated plastic artists in the history of painting from Altamira to Picasso, that fake primitive. The exquisite art of the Aborigines is a manifestation of the race's memory. Its religion, one of the most moving that I know, is all made of memory.

The Aborigine (that is, the true, real Australian) idolizes an Australia that does not lie on the map but is made of the memory of his dreams. They call it, because it is not in space, *dreamtime*, the *alcheringa* where they once lived their metaphysical golden age and where they go to live every night – when time and space mix and flow. Heraclitus's river then becomes the enormous desert to which they return: it folds around them. During the day they wander without rest in search of their lost era, helped by the whisky – to the veneration of which the whites initiated them not long ago. I have seen them in Alice Springs, a town of the West that they transform into a real ghost town, while they parade under the desert sun with their blinded eyes, coming from prehistory without ever arriving at history. For an Australian Aborigine there is only memory and emptiness. They fill that abyss with the dreams of the tribe. There is no other nation exiled in its land that lives so much from the memory that peoples its dreams every night. The only exception possible is the Jews who engendered the Wandering Jew: from among them rose *Jewlysses*.

The times are *dreamtime* for all: time is memory's space now. Time makes us roam the space of memory. Culture has become memory. The great literary monuments of our era are *tours de force* of memory and even a scientific theory, Freud's, is based on a mechanism of memory – dreams. Without memory there is nothing. This line that I now write would have no meaning, would not even be possible – without memory. At the end of the line, now, the previous words would have been erased for ever. There are servitude and use in memory. The phrases 'If memory serves me well' and 'If my memory doesn't fail me' make memory seem like a careless servant. Nevertheless there is no stickier company: we carry our memory everywhere. Memory is a vade-mecum: she goes with me. She is also morality's mother: our conscience is made of memory. Guilt is the memory of a crime.

In our time memory seems to have been born in exile. Joyce in Trieste remembers all of Dublin, Proust in his cork exile remembers his whole life. One of the great memory memories in the second half of the century happens when Nabokov remembers in exile the passing and passage of his memory. The book is called *Speak, Memory*. Mnemosyne is our goddess: she is the mother of the muses and of memory.

In fiction there are two memorable characters made of pure memory: without it they would not exist. I am referring to Ireneo Funes in Borges' 'Funes the Memorious' and to Mr Memory from *The Thirty-Nine Steps*. Funes, an invalid, lives to remember and Mr Memory, valid, lives by remembering. The two are killed by memory. Mr Memory, who is memory seen as a show, remembers it all and shows to what extent to remember is to trivialize or to live again: life is filled with memory, death is a rest in oblivion. On his last night as a spectacle, Mr Memory is asked from the audience: 'What are the thirty-nine steps?' and the memory machine cannot avoid spelling out the beans: it is an organization dedicated to evil. His memory condemns him and from a box they shoot him. Memory, we now see, is life and death. But memory is outside time.

There is a phrase of Horace that I know by heart. It says: 'Ruins would find me unmoved.' When I went back to Havana in 1965 and saw her ruins, I did not find myself unmoved but very moved. Are these my mother's remains? I was held there by the police for four months that I do not want to remember and still I do not forget. When I returned to Europe, to Madrid to be precise, I found that the only task that was of any consequence for me was to reconstruct Havana by memory and to relive her lost splendour in a book. Certainly, for me to relive Havana was to resuscitate her and for me to live again. That labour began more than a quarter of a century ago. I am still at it.

Memory is the first and the last time-machine. There is only time and memory. Nostalgia is the memory of the soul. But there is also oblivion. A Chilean philosopher sang once: 'They say that distance is forgetting.' To add later his negation of time: 'I do not conceive such a reason.' But our problem, mine and yours, now, is what Bergson called duration. Will I or will I not – wouldn't I be brief?

AN EXILEDOM BY THE THAMES

A Vindication of Exile

In a barely remembered movie called *Forbidden* the hero (in name only) Adolphe Menjou is an elegant (Hollywood version) American politician who is travelling on a steamship headed for Havana. There he meets a spinster librarian (the great Barbara Stanwyck) who is taking the first vacation of her life. The encounter happened because the politician, drunk, thought that he was rightly going into stateroom 99 when he had slipped into cabin 66 – which is a 99 turned around by the *tedium vitae* on board. But it's where she sleeps. The two passengers (the name was never more fitting) chat, converse in verse, fall in love and she makes plans to stay in Havana for ever and live off what is most abundant. 'We will be,' she proposes to him, 'worms.'

The rest of the love story is devoted to the crassest democracy (it's Capra crap), the politician goes back to the United States, runs for office and ends up as governor of the state. As far as she is concerned, only death does them part. But the two, when they meet, dream about Havana and about the trembling leaves in the palm trees late at night.

Hearing (Distant) Voices

Several Cuban voices come close in haste but without hate to ask me: 'Is writing worth it?' and the rest of the phrase can be: 'in Miami' or 'in Manhattan' and even 'in Kansas City, Kansas'. Even a pretty poetess from Johannesburg whispers: 'And here in South Africa?' All the questions wanted to express a single, timid question: 'Is it worth it to write in exile?' My invariable dreaded answer was: 'Is life worth living?' For me living and writing are one and the same thing. To those questioners who were young but not too young (no one is ever *too* young) I could say: Is life worth it? To some who wanted to keep writing I could have asked: Is it worth living beyond life – and I could still answer them yes! Life, even continuing tediously in itself, is worth it. All the options in life are valid, from love to dying of love – and even suicide.

Of course nothing so kills a writer as to stop writing. Even not to publish does not mean that the writer is dead. The writer dies at the same moment that his words die. When this death is voluntary the writer is a suicide who has pushed up his appointment in Samarra with silence. Nothing is deader than something that has not lived. I mean that the only pleasure (you will never hear me speaking of duty) for the writer is writing – even if he knows that he will not have readers. Nobody writes to be read. One writes to have written and after one has finished this gratuitous act it is possible to publish and so the writer makes a gift to the reader of his prose – or of his verse. (Others of his obverse.) I do not believe that there is a writer, not even the most deformed professional, who writes for his readers. The reader always stays on the other side of the horizon on the border of the page that is not its margin. The writer travels in his ark of words to meet the reader beyond the flood, where the page is peopled with words chosen by a Noah who has heard the order of a literary God to sail across seas of madness. The writer, by the intervention of stevedores, wholesalers and customs agents (read publishers and booksellers), delivers to the reader his payload of words. But by then the voyage has ended. The writer does not feel regret because his pleasure was always in the journey.

I even believe that my metaphor of the voyage that culminates in disillusion was true for Ulysses, for Marco Polo and even for the greatest of voyagers, the floating admiral Christopher Columbus. In some way America must have been an anticlimax for Columbus. The excitement was always caused by the voyage towards the unknown: the mock ship's log, the mutiny, the threat of impending shipwreck. The adventure was the true trip. The little island, the profuse palm trees and the few confused Indians constituted, I am sure, a disappointment. It was this frustration that made the Grand Admiral undertake other voyages – to find other islands and other Indians that were not Indians. From the sentence of living for ever in that disappointing nature there came to save us that equivocal friar named Bartolomé de Las Casas. Like Columbus, Las Casas was a *converso* and with the demented and vehement eye of the *converso* he saw the noble savage suffer and proposed that to help the Indian (we will never know the intent of an adjective) other men had to come to give them a hand (and even an arm): blacks from Africa – apparently not as ignoble savages.

Without knowing it Las Casas, ignorant as a friar, was establishing the future foundation of Cuba, which could now be something more than an island, some palm trees and a few Indians: it could become a nation. Are nations necessary? I don't know. But the certain fact is that they are there, like the islands. Nations are historical islands in a political sea. Islands are all geography, nations are notions. It is perhaps because of that that we all have (or have had) the secret dream of going off to live on a desert island. Some nevertheless wish to leave our secret island to go to live in other nations – which are sometimes real islands. That forced flight is called exile and the dreamed island is the real island left behind in a perversion of the myth of the blue bird on the back yard.

I do not believe that it is exaggerated to call Columbus the father of the island: Cuba is more like our mother even though they call her a fatherland. A mother made of dirt like Adam, but of blood as intimate as Eve. Not our own mother, true, but evidently more lasting, eternal – if by eternity we understand what has been before and will be after and is unalterable. To that eternity we owe not only our existence, we owe it our essence. To be Cuban is to be born in Cuba. To be Cuban is to go with Cuba everywhere. To be Cuban is to carry Cuba in a persistent memory. We all carry Cuba within like an unheard music, like a rare vision that we know by heart. Cuba is a paradise from which we flee by trying to return.

I do not have, nevertheless, illusions about going back. I never pray like the old dispersed Jews who yearn to go back to Jerusalem – 'Next year in

Havana.' I do not have illusions about going back to Cuba and that past which is always present only becomes future in literature and in dreams – which are for me another form of literature. But I don't want to talk of myself, I want to speak about the Cubans in exile. Not all of them, of course. I am not moved by the crowd, only by a few individuals. I will talk of those Cubans who were exiled from the island as mediocre poets, budding writers, frustrated novelists, precarious prose writers, unknown short-story writers and in general poor writers.

Abroad, far from the island, in exile and for unknown reasons, they became known and were transformed not only into eminent writers, but, in one or two cases, into writers of genius. To many of them we owe not only Cuban literature but that they are our tradition: its realization is our possibility. They are Cuba: much more than an inhabited island, than a geography and a history. They, in their posterity, can talk of voyages with Homer, dine with Petronius, weep in exile with Ovid, remember the happy time in disgrace with Dante, drink with Rabelais, shake hands with Shakespeare, take Cervantes by an arm, satirize with Swift, create suns of digressions with Sterne, gossip with Jane Austen, listen to Dickens dramatizing himself, discuss a *mot juste* lightly with Flaubert, recommend a remedy for syphilis to Nietzsche, make the eulogy of madness to Maupassant, hurt with the molars of Huysmans and with the teeth of Oscar Wilde, lament the pyromania of Gogol or the filthiness of Tolstoy or the tuberculosis of Chekhov, praise the extreme cleanliness of Baudelaire, fan themselves with a poem by Mallarmé, tell Melville what the atrocious colour of a white shark is, appreciate a good Havana with Mark Twain, not understand anything of what Conrad, who speaks Polish in English, says; try to guess the subject of a piece of gossip with Henry James, want to guess a single word by another James, Joyce, all (except one) lament that Cavafy pays so much attention to boys, not always Greek, and with Proust that he is wasting away in bed, tell Kafka that the Statue of Liberty does not have a sword in her hand but a torch; comment with Gertrude Stein on how insular the literary life in London is, tell Hemingway that he never truly lived in Cuba but in the Gulf Stream of the old man, and lament before Faulkner that his syntax is more obscure than his dynasties and, finally, because they are Cubans and, like me, arbitrary, stop their voyage to Parnassus by reproaching Nabokov for so many dead butterflies.

Those exile writers have all disappeared but they still talk to us. They are not ghosts. Their voices come from their books. They inhabit that country where all voices are a single voice. They are, finally, literature.

(July 1991)

The Invisible Exile

Address to the Wheatland Conference, Vienna, 1987

Now I live in an exiledom by the sea. Here I work and play and I even watch other people work and play from a cosy vantage point: my bay windows by the bay. It was here that I read a romance that is the story of my life. (A historian is only a writer with hindsight.) In a cosy chair by the fire while outside squalls made the street squalid I began to read. 'It's horrible,' he said. 'But what devilry must happen to make a man invisible?' Another voice said: 'It's no devilry. It's a process.'[1]

That's what it is: a process and it began some years ago. Now I am invisible too. Not invincible but just the opposite: being invisible means to be as vulnerable as the unseen. You are less a person than a non-person. You are pure spirit and you can be blown out like a candle in the wind – and who's going to remember what kind of flame you were before the candle was blown out? This is a metaphysical problem but being invisible is a very physical thing with me. This happens, like it happened to that man Griffith, every time I take off my jacket, my tweed jacket, my pullover which is 100 per cent wool, my trousers of twill, my usual suede shoes – I must wear warmer clothes in my exiledom by the sea than in the tropics, where I was born, where I choose exile rather than being a pawn in a monstrous game of chess in which only one man can play the king.

Now I get rid of my underwear and I look at myself in the full-length mirror. I look at myself in the mirror not once but twice – and I see a void. Nothing! Not a thing! Am I like the stranger who came into an inn on a winter night in England? Could I really be *invisible*? I am fully dressed but everybody thinks I must wear a disguise, though I'm perfectly naked when I undress. If I get rid of my English garments nobody sees anything or everybody sees nothing, whichever comes off first. I am the opposite of that king who plays murderous chess with his subjects. I am (and even the

1 The quotations are from *The Invisible Man* by H. G. Wells.

proverbial five-year-old can tell it) a Cuban exile. But with me exile comes closer to *exit*. My clothes make an Englishman of me but my nakedness erases me. I cannot find refuge even in a nudist camp: the invisible nudist is an obscene peeping Tom. (I cannot even be a sight for sore eyes.) I am myself if I wear my clothes. Just like the invisible man in book and movie. Sometimes I think that I too am an invention of H. G. Wells. But even Wells went to Russia and couldn't see the invisible Russians, those who saluted Stalin because they were about to become invisible for ever. Their chess king, bishops and commissars and all the knights and red pawns were the only visible Russians to Wells. It's a dirty trick but it has happened so many times in this century of voiceless invisible men that nobody cares any longer.

The Romans not the Greeks had a word for them and the Romans invented the perfectly invisible man. His name was Ovid and after the Romans saw him once or twice they never saw him again. He was too busy making himself the perfectly invisible poet. He was the perfect exile in any case. Or rather the perfectly visible courtier in Rome who became invisible in exile. The Russian Empire has a few of those. The most visible invisible man in Russia was of course Osip Mandelstam. Stalin made him invisible with the deadly accuracy of a tragic wand.

As for myself, who am not a poet, the word that could define my status is not invisible. Even that Latin word is different when it applies to a Cuban. It is as if you said the perfectly visible invisible man abroad. In Cuba before (and this always means BC, before Castro) the Republican refugees from the Spanish Civil War (even Pablo Casals and Juan Ramón Jiménez were there, briefly) were called *exilados*. Now all the exiles who speak Spanish are called *exiliados*. Perhaps you don't mind that extra I but I do. All Cubans do. We must remind the world of those stubborn Jews who in another diaspora were fleeing from Hitler. But the Jews were not exiles. They were not even Jewish because that word implied that they were slightly Jew. Remember the ordeal of Walter Benjamin before the gates of Spain? He was not a German and yet not a Jew.

We are not *marranos* but we are *gusanos*, worms, and lately those Cubans exiled from Cuba via Mariel, 120,000 of them in barely one month in 1980, those men, women and children were called *escoria*, scum. Goebbels used to call all Jews *Ungeziefer*, vermin, which is not by chance what Gregor Samsa is called in 'The Metamorphosis'. It is easier to eliminate a man when he is not a man but scum from the slums, a worm, an *Ungeziefer*. But there always are, I'm afraid, bloodstains, a mess to clean up. It is cleaner, therefore desirable, to make an invisible man out of him – and 'out of him' is the operative phrase.

My invisibility is more visible in Spain, in the Spanish-speaking countries and among Hispanics in the USA. There is in Spain a great authority in rendering almost anything invisible. It is a Big Brother (or rather Big Mother) of the language and it's called the Royal Academy of the Spanish Language. The Academia, as she is called for she is an old and respectable lady, is a shredding machine very busy eliminating the undesirable. *The Dictionary of the Real Academia* is Big Mama's troubleshooter. Troubleshooters, as we all know, can become accurate hit men. Each word in the language is a contract to be shot off if the Academia doesn't love it – or even like it. The Academia particularly dislikes foreign words or words to that effect, like most Americanisms. Those words are sitting ducks and the word that is not in the dictionary is a dead duck. Or should be pronounced dead as in a dead tongue. All words are suspect or guilty until proven innocent. Let's consider now the word exile. Exile is not a Spanish word. Never heard of it, said the Academia. I don't know what it means.

In Spanish there are words for exile, of course: *exilio*, which is the condition of exile, as in the case of the Roman poet – or what Ovid saw. An *exiliado* is an exile or what Stalin did to Mandelstam for a poem he wrote. An offshoot of the *Dictionary* is the *Manual*, which is very much like the Concise Oxford Dictionary but made palatable with illustrations and diagrams. This dictionary is close to the spirit of comic strips. This is not, I must say, a Spanish invention but it has a Spanish antecedent. Alphabet charts in Cuban schools always began with a big cross and the young student, reading the primer aloud, had to say Christ, ABC etc. Christ came before letters – that is before words. That too was an invention of the Academia. (Little did the Old Prude know that Christ could be a swear word!) On page 711, column A, the dictionary performs a grand jeté and jumps from *exiguo* to *eximio*. In between those graciously bandied legs the dictionary inserts a suppository called *eximente*. That is from eminent to excuse oneself. Hey presto! Exile has disappeared and all exiles are sent to Siberia on Iberia. Legerdemain or *leger des humains*?

My edition of the *Diccionario* is by Espasa-Calpe, printed in 1950 when Franco was king. For Franco there was no exile. Exiles simply didn't exist. They were only enemies rapidly running for cover. As the other grotesque dwarf King Ubu used to say, 'If there is no Poland, there won't be any Poles.' I think Jaruzelski should meditate on this axiom. If there are no Poles there won't be a Polish problem. Solidarity would melt and then solve into a dew. Heard on the BBC: 'Today Poland went to the polls.'

For those who believe that tomorrow is a better world (it is not even a better *word*), in 1956 the big *Diccionario de la Real Academia* admitted exile finally – but not exiles. This dictionary that moves ahead in reverse gear is still revered by many writers in the Spanish-speaking world. One of those admirers was a very well-known literary critic from Uruguay, Angel Rama who died in a plane accident. Before dying he wrote the longest article ever on political exiles in Latin America and he named only one exile from Cuba. His name was José Martí – who died in Cuba in 1895! Later a laureate writer from Colombia made a speech before another academy, not on literature but on exiles. He chose Chile as the country which bans most people from its territory in America. He quoted figures: one million Chileans left Pinochet to rule alone over the condor, the Chilean vulture. He cried out loud 'It's a decimation!' – devoutly to be wished. He finished his speech with not one single mention of Cuba. There are no exiles from Cuba. As we know, this is a model country when it comes (and goes) to dissidents and malcontents. Fidel Castro is a very exquisite tyrant. If you don't believe it, see how he treats his opponents. He has a motto, 'Semper Fidelis', which most Cubans read as, 'Sic semper Fidelis'.

But truth is always buoyant and it surfaces in the murkiest water. There are about a million and a half Cubans living in exile since 1959, which includes, as a tropical Kerensky, the first revolutionary President the island had. It is only now that Cuba has more than ten million inhabitants. It is therefore more than a decimation. (Or a decimation and a half.) But all this is the unmentionable. You cannot call Cuba a tyranny because it is a Third World tyranny. In the Third World tyrannies are always called developing countries and the crimes the tyrant commits are mere *accidents de parcour*, as the French so elegantly put it. An Argentine writer living in Paris most of his adult life was asked by a French newspaper about Cuban writers in exile and he answered with a French accent 'There are no exiled writers from Cuba. There are only worms abroad.' A worm in Spanish is also a caterpillar and the risk of exiling caterpillars is that they can become butterflies. This Argentine writer, now deceased, was close to Marx but very far from Linnaeus.

A group of political refugees gathering in Madrid recently had what you can call a worm's eye view. They were from every Spanish-speaking country – from all of them, that is, except Cuba. Nobody at the party missed the Cubans, who had been in exile longer than all of them put together. Curiouser and curiouser! said a logical Alice. The meeting was an occasion for Party-goers and they were all having a political fling. They even called exile an acquired taste, just like caviar. Here, have some: caviar from the General. (Who could be Pinochet or Stroessner.) Some canapés? It's for the sake of the Party, the political party. Some vol-au-vents? They keep the exile spirit flying.

Hmmm! It's delicious! It's delightful! It's delovely! It all seemed like inverted nostalgia for Franco. Ah, those were the days, my friend! See here, have some oysters and you won't feel ostracized. This elixir of exile was Spanish but it is in the collective mind as well. Cuba cannot be as dreadful as all that. You simply leave your island paradise because you want to live abroad: you must miss the wine and all those tall blonde girls. Get back, get back to where you once belonged. Cubans go home. The Cuban Minister of Culture should have been called, like a tropical Goebbels, Minister of Enlightenment and Propaganda. I know he exists because I've seen his photo in the newspapers. He was wearing a dark pinstripe three-piece suit and he looked, I swear, like someone out of *The Godfather Part Two*. He had a waspish lisp and his name could be Mr Malaprop. He once said on Cuban television that Fidel Castro was not ill, simply tired with a *pneumatic* in his lungs. (He meant of course walking pneumonia!) On another occasion when I introduced him to a particularly beautiful girl, he exclaimed: 'She has a very perfect facial ovulation.' He also says *hiralious* instead of hilarious and he believes that it was Beethoven and not Van Gogh who lost an ear and very fittingly when he wants to be intimate he just intimidates. This is Cuba's Minister of Culture. As you can see Fidel Castro is a tyrant with a sense of humour. His name is Armando Hart and this Hart belongs to Daddy.

Dr Hart – the tyrant and his minions really love to be called doctor – declared to *El País*, the Spanish newspaper, that no writer of 'high stature' (his very words) had left Cuba after the Revolution. He names a few names: Fernando Ortiz, Alejo Carpentier and Lezama Lima – and he manages to pronounce them all without a wisp of a lisp. But he forgot to say that all the aforementioned were writers who remained in Cuba simply because now they all live underground. You see, they all died many years ago. I can add to those egregious names the name of Virgilio Piñera, Cuba's greatest playwright, who stayed behind to die like most internal exiles, of fear and neglect.

All those writers cannot move unless they are carried on the shoulders of 'politic worms', as Hamlet calls us. Otherwise, I don't see how they can leave the island. Unless, of course, they swim across the seas to become in turn invisible corpses in exile.

Then Dr Hart, the Minister of Propaganda, exalted the memory of Lezama Lima, perhaps the greatest poet who wrote in Spanish this century. Dr Hart mentioned *Paradiso*, a novel he couldn't read without moving his lisp, *lips*, but he never said that only five thousand copies of this novel were printed in Lezama's lifetime. I know why. Lezama praises homosexuality in his book and this wouldn't do in a country where they build concentration camps for homosexuals. This *bête noire* with two backs was condemned publicly by Fidel Castro himself in 1971, in a famous/infamous speech. After that the bulky Lezama became an invisible man.

An internal exile, not even a letter by him was published after his Faustian condemnation by Mefistofidel. But invisible Lezama wrote letters with invisible ink. He was still writing when he died. Most of those letters were written to his sister in exile in Puerto Rico and she made them into a book. This epistolar legacy from the nether world shows Lezama preoccupied not only with food and medicines but also with the quality of life under socialism: 'It is not the same,' he wrote, 'to be out of Cuba as to observe the conduct one must be obliged to lead here inside the oven. There are Cubans who suffer outside and those who suffer equally here, even more so, being within the burning hole and the horrible disquiet of an uncertain fate.'

There are, as you might have noticed, repeated words like *burning, oven*, etc. Don't they proclaim that the hermetic poet is speaking not of paradise but of hell and the burning poet, himself, as some sort of condemned Faust? It was Lezama who created a phrase to define the creator, the poet, a 'possessed person penetrated by a soft axe.' But what about the possessed poet who is denied all except the killing axe? Essence and existence and even the solid body that contains his conscience are owned by the state. Lezama and Piñera are here with me, invisible men all. We are like the man who arrived at the Coach and Horses in a remote part of England almost a century ago. This is how arrival and welcome are described by a man who knew about such things:

> 'You don't understand . . . who I am or what I am. I'll show you.' . . . He put his open palm over his face and withdrew it. The centre of his face became a black cavity . . . The nose – it was the stranger's nose – rolled on the floor with a sound of hollow cardboard. Then he removed his spectacles and everyone gasped. He took off his hat and with a violent gesture tore at his bandages . . . A flash of horrible anticipation passed through the hall . . . It was worse than anything. The stranger was an invisible man.

The Bird of Paradise Lost

My first encounter with William Henry Hudson took place in Havana twenty years ago. He was called Guillermo Enrique then, almost a namesake, and it was Borges who called my attention to his work. Borges, bilingual, talked about *The Purple Land* in Spanish and about *Far Away and Long Ago* with Argentine tenderness in English. As if by magic I had just now negotiated Belascoain Street with the favourable green light and crossed through a colonnade to head for one of those secondhand bookshops in Old Havana back then that should have been called *old-hand bookshops* because of their totally *ancien régime* clientele. That luminous afternoon, a time for a holiday and not for a book, *l'après-midi d'un* fan or a siesta for two I had left Miriam Gómez with the didactic exercises of a dubious dramatist (the word *dramaturgo*, originally German, was pronounced gutturally in Spanish to be able to hear Bertolt Brecht behind it) who was an Argentine from East Berlin. Since Antón Arrufat, a friend and a Conrad lover, had told me that this bookshoppe, dark and little frequented before, was in liquidation, I entered decisively. A man not yet thirty with a dry mouth, I came looking for Hudson, any Hudson, and I didn't know if I would ever find him. I observed immediately that there barely were books in that bookstore now in its death throes.

I looked without hope at an almost empty shelf behind me and among the present dust the clear mark left behind by the absence of a book, a fleeting ghost, I saw a volume and a spine materializing and then the name *Nostromo*. Get Conrad! But beside him there was another book and another little title and another name: *Far Away and Long Ago*. Coincidence? Perhaps. But I think that it was instead the call of the purple plain, the lure of the open spaces, the spell of the pampas. I had run into the Hudson Stream! I grabbed the book as the shipwrecked man seizes a raft.

It was at the beginning of 1962 and books were starting to get as scarce as the food. By books I mean free books, literature, those that offer you adventures in reading. But if one means propaganda one could find a lot of it everywhere in that city that was once only a farm and a yarn and a bar for

Hemingway, a male brothel for Somerset Maugham and a brothel and a casino for the man that was Greene. I didn't want a client faster than my eye to reach for the book first and to beat me out in getting hold of that curious old English writer, born in Argentina to American parents, who lived and endured hunger and poverty and died in London, far away and long ago.

That book (illustrated with a naïve, native craft) barely in Spanish, translated in Argentina from Hudson's brand of English (an unfathomable language for the translator no doubt), was the first work by Hudson that I read and it was all quite an experience from the chance of a *trouvaille* to the planned reading. I was charmed, delighted, bewitched, despite the language of the Argentines that Hudson shared but not I. Not I. Hudson wrote of a time remote for me, truly long ago and far away, but I made his time mine and together we roamed the pampa on the pale mare of memory.

Then came exile. Mine, Miriam Gómez's, my daughters'. It was not sudden or dramatic but slow and furtive – though not because of that, any less painful. What does it matter how they cut your cord? The navel always remains. Almost without knowing it I found myself lost in the literary mist of London, from Chelsea to Kensington, in that Wild West End swinging between the hostile and the hospitable. Nostalgic among amnesiacs I never forgot Havana. Hudson and I now shared the same past, the same pasture, identical grey grazing lands that were once green. His pampa of dreams, forever quiet, was my Gulf Stream of consciousness, my exterior monologue, ever flowing, conscious, unconscious and both the pampa and the sea were infinite because memory has no shores.

Hudson flowed like the river without banks of memory (Thames, Mnemosyne) and I read as many of his books as I had at hand. I was very poor then, poorer than Hudson in London perhaps – but I managed. There are many lending libraries in London, floating shelves, perambulating bookstores and in each one you could explore his vast territory: Hudson found, Hudson sound. The search was deliberate and without that tremor of chance at the bookshop in Old Havana. I made American discoveries in each book of his, which an exile from America like him and an exile from Europe or Africa or Asia, exiles from everywhere towards everywhere, *any* exile can truly appreciate. His books are, all, the book of exodus.

I remember a moment, only an inkling, a fleeting instant in one of his books whose name I cannot remember – not now, maybe later. (The title is not important, only the book's duration in time that was eternal.) The writer, Hudson himself or myself, hears a bird singing while he is going down a London street. I don't remember the bird. I only remember (and what a memory it is!) the writer going down the unevenly paved street that the democratic asphalt had not yet reached, in Chelsea, yes. But it does not seem as if that green door on Sloane Avenue or on Bywater Street will open. While the bird keeps singing to the summer or to whatever birds sing in the summer. When finally the door opens, the exile asks the woman who came to answer it if that bird (his arm raised, his hand stretched out, his index finger pointing at the sound) is singing on her patio. The woman nods. 'Is it by chance a bird from Argentina?' asks Hudson. The woman says yes. She brought it herself from Buenos Aires where she lived for a time. Hudson, so tall, so thin, so fragile, with his long white beard and his snowy hair floating in the English summer breeze, an albino in Albion, stands there and does not move or say anything, standing there listening. Just listening. Not to the woman, who does not talk either, but to the bird that is singing. Then he also nods.

Hudson has realized that the bird that is singing, for it is still singing, did not come from Argentina. It comes from his childhood and from his dreams: out of the past. That bird arrives, now I remember it, from yearning and it is called nostalgia. This bird (from his pampa: from my savanna and my Havana: from the prairies: from the plains: from the steppes) any exile can hear singing everywhere, always. It is the emperor's nightingale returning.

Index